A HISTORY OF
SECULAR LATIN POETRY

A HISTORY OF
SECULAR LATIN POETRY
IN THE
MIDDLE AGES

BY

F. J. E. RABY

VOLUME I

OXFORD
AT THE CLARENDON PRESS

Oxford University Press, Great Clarendon Street, Oxford OX2 6DP

Oxford New York

Athens Auckland Bangkok Bogota Bombay
Buenos Aires Calcutta Cape Town Dar es Salaam
Delhi Florence Hong Kong Istanbul Karachi
Kuala Lumpur Madras Madrid Melbourne
Mexico City Nairobi Paris Singapore
Taipei Tokyo Toronto Warsaw

and associated companies in
Berlin Ibadan

Oxford is a trade mark of Oxford University Press

Published in the United States by
Oxford University Press Inc., New York

ISBN 0–19–814325–7

1 3 5 7 9 10 8 6 4 2

Printed in Great Britain
on acid-free paper by
Bookcraft (Bath) Ltd.,
Midsomer Norton

PREFACE

THE present sketch of the history of the Secular Latin poetry of the Middle Ages is in some measure complementary to my *History of Christian-Latin Poetry*, which was published by the Clarendon Press in 1927. Its material is not entirely different from that of its predecessor, and it might well be argued that one comprehensive history of medieval Latin poetry would have possessed obvious advantages over a division into two separate treatises. But the total bulk of the material is immense, and if the method which I have adopted has not prevented a certain amount of overlapping, it will be found, I think, that the story of Secular Latin verse presents enough unity to justify its separate treatment.

In the first place, there is the theme of the continuity of the rhetorical tradition, from the classical age of Latin poetry right down to the age of the fully developed literary vernacular. I have only hinted at the manner in which this school-rhetoric contributed to the vernacular poetry of the modern world. The details of the process are beyond my province and beyond my competence. I have traced the stream of rhetoric from its apparent beginnings, and have abandoned it somewhere in the thirteenth century, leaving it to others to say how far it owed its continuance in the vernacular to the persistence of classical studies and how far to its establishment in the national literatures from the time when they began directly to employ the rhetoric of the schools, which was so obvious and so useful a resource.

One advantage, at any rate, can be claimed by the adoption of the theme of the continuity of rhetoric. It has made it necessary to begin with the history of classical Latin and even of Greek poetry, and so it has been possible to demonstrate with unmistakable clearness the continuity between the literary history of antiquity and that of the Middle Ages. This is a fact which our English histories of Latin literature have not been wont to emphasize, though in Germany it has long been recognized, so that the great histories of Schanz and of Manitius form a stately succession.

Secondly, I have given an account of the secular lyrical poetry, and have made an attempt at a discussion of its 'origins'.[1]

---

[1] For convenience I have grouped under the heading of 'the Latin Lyric' a large mass of poetry which can be vaguely described as 'Goliardic' or

I have emphasized its general dependence on the vernacular, a dependence which seems to me to be clearly demonstrated in the case of the Latin *pastourelles*, and to be equally certain for the Latin love- and nature-poetry generally. At any rate, I do not see how this lyrical poetry can have issued out of the tradition of the schools, when this other tradition was inescapably present and accessible.

Historical, epical, philosophical, satirical, and grammatical poetry fill out much of the remainder of the history, and there is also an account of that characteristically medieval *genre*, the versified tale or *comoedia*.

I am conscious that my treatment of a very wide subject is far from adequate, but I hope that it may be of some use to students of the general history of the Middle Ages, and also, perhaps, to students of medieval vernacular literature. Many problems remain unsolved, and it is not the least among the services of a general literary history that it is able, if only from its very deficiencies, to suggest new lines of research.[1]

It will be clear that I owe a large debt to my predecessors. In the earlier part I have learned much from that great and lamented scholar, Ulrich von Wilamowitz-Moellendorff, from Eduard Norden, and from Professor J. W. Duff, whose *Literary History of Rome in the Silver Age* I have always consulted with profit. My debt to Max Manitius, whose unwearied labours in the cause of medieval literary history have culminated in the third massive volume of the *Geschichte der lateinischen Literatur des Mittelalters*, is obvious on most of the pages of my book. I cannot adequately express what I owe to the pioneer work of Karl Strecker in almost every period from the Carolingian to the twelfth century. And it will be clear that my section on the *Streitgedicht* could not have been written without the aid of Hans Walther's remarkable book. Dr. Otto Schumann has most kindly answered questions about *Carmina Burana*.

I am grateful to Mr. Stephen Gaselee and to Dom André Wilmart for their kindness in reading the proofs of my book and in making valuable suggestions.

satirical. Properly, the term 'lyric' should cover only those pieces composed primarily to be sung, which are the main subject of my last section but one —on 'the Origins of the Latin Lyric'.

[1] I have inadvertently omitted to mention Stephen of Rouen (twelfth century) whose *Draco Normannicus* is an epic dealing mainly with the deeds of the Norman princes. This and other poems of his are dealt with by Manitius in vol. iii, 690 sqq. of his *Geschichte der lateinischen Literatur des Mittelalters*. I must refer also to J. S. P. Tatlock's study, 'Geoffrey and King Arthur in *Normannicus Draco*', *Modern Philology*, xxxi (1933), pp. 1 sqq., 113 sqq.

It is difficult to give a just estimate of the extent to which the London Library helped me during the years when this book was being written. Through the constant kindness of the Librarian and other officers of the Library my access to its resources was made easy, and many books were specially procured at my request. Most of the texts and many important periodicals relating to medieval Latin literature are available there, and in this great institution the scholar who has but little leisure finds exactly what he needs.

Lastly, I must thank the Delegates of the Clarendon Press for their great generosity in consenting to publish this lengthy book. The skill and competence of the staff of the Press need no testimony from me.

F. J. E. R.

CONTENTS

VOLUME I

LIST OF ABBREVIATIONS

Abh. d. bayer. Akad. = Abhandlungen der kgl. bayerischen Akademie der Wissenschaften, Philos.-philol. Klasse.

Anal. Hymn. = Analecta Hymnica Medii Aevi.

Anzeiger für deutsch. Alt. = Anzeiger für deutsches Altertum und deutsche Literatur.

Archiv für lat. Lex. = Archiv für lateinische Lexikographie und Grammatik.

Arch. Lat. Med. Aevi = Archivum Latinitatis Medii Aevi (Bulletin Ducange).

Berlin. Sitzungsber. = Sitzungsberichte der kgl. preussischen Akademie der Wissenschaften, Philos.-hist. Klasse.

Byzant. Zeitschr. = Byzantinische Zeitschrift.

Christian-Latin Poetry = Raby, F. J. E., A History of Christian-Latin Poetry.

C.S.E.L. = Corpus scriptorum ecclesiasticorum latinorum. Vienna.

D.N.B. = Dictionary of National Biography.

E.H.R. = English Historical Review.

Gött. Nachr. = Nachrichten der kgl. Gesellschaft der Wissenschaften zu Göttingen, Philol.-hist. Klasse.

Hauréau, Notices et extraits de quelques mss. = Hauréau, B., Notices et extraits de quelques manuscrits latins de la Bibliothèque Nationale.

Hist. Jahrb. = Historisches Jahrbuch.

Hist. Litt. = Histoire littéraire de la France.

J.T.S. = Journal of Theological Studies.

Leipzig. Sitzungsber. = Berichte über die Verhandlungen der kgl. sächs. Gesellschaft der Wissenschaften, Philol.-hist. Klasse.

Manitius, Gesch. = Manitius, M., Geschichte der lateinischen Literatur des Mittelalters.

Manitius, Christl. lat. Poesie = Manitius, M., Geschichte der christlich-lateinischen Poesie bis zur Mitte des 8. Jahrhunderts.

Meyer, Rythmik. = Meyer, W., Gesammelte Abhandlungen zur mittellateinischen Rythmik.

M.G.H. Auct. Antiq. = Monumenta Germaniae Historica, Auctores Antiquissimi.

M.G.H. SS. = Monumenta Germaniae Historica, Scriptores.

Migne = Migne, J. P., Patrologia Latina.

Neues Archiv = Neues Archiv der Gesellschaft für ältere deutsche Geschichtskunde.

Neue Jahrb. f. d. klass. Alt. = Neue Jahrbücher für das klassische Altertum.

Norden = Norden, E., Die antike Kunstprosa.

Notices et extraits des mss. = Notices et extraits des manuscrits de la Bibliothèque Nationale.

Poet. Lat. Aevi Car. = Monumenta Germaniae Historica, Poetae Latinae Aevi Carolini.

Rev. Bénéd. = Revue Bénédictine.

Rhein. Mus. = Rheinisches Museum für Philologie.

Rolls Series = Rerum Britannicarum medii aevi Scriptores (Chronicles and Memorials of Great Britain and Ireland during the Middle Ages).

Schanz = Schanz, M., Geschichte der römischen Literatur.

Wiener Sitzungsber. = Sitzungsberichte der kaiserl. Akademie der Wissenschaften in Wien, Philos.-hist. Klasse.

Zeitschr. für deutsches Alt. = Zeitschrift für deutsches Altertum und deutsche Literatur.

I

THE INHERITANCE OF THE MIDDLE AGES

§ 1. *The Creation of the Medieval Outlook.*

THE problem of what has been called, somewhat unfortunately, 'the fall of the Roman Empire' is assuming an
increased importance for the historian of the Middle Ages, who
is now in no danger of forgetting the doctrine of the continuity
of history, that simple doctrine which has been so lately and
so painfully discovered. The so-called Middle Age is now seen
to be the true child of late Antiquity, and the problem of late
Antiquity itself is now merged into the problem of the origin
of medieval civilization.

While it is, doubtless, ultimately necessary, for the consideration of one of the main elements in the problem, to go back to
what has been called the 'new spiritual enlightenment', which
'came to all the civilized peoples of the earth in the millennium
before the Christian era',[1] it is possible to begin at the later
stage of development represented by the Hellenistic age, for
then the various forces and influences are seen in action with
greater clearness and apparent vigour.

It is now generally recognized that if a conception is required
to make intelligible the change from the ancient to the medieval
world, it can be found in the progressive orientalization of that
Graeco-Roman culture which is the basis of our modern
western civilization. A study of the course of Hellenism from
the death of Alexander to the age of Justinian and beyond can
hardly, at the present time, fail to suggest the conclusion that,
'if we are really to grasp in its fullness the most difficult of all
problems, that of the "decline of the ancient world", we must
choose our point of vantage not in the west but in the east of
the Mediterranean area, and must also take into the scope of
our consideration the early Islamic world. The way to the
understanding of the Middle Ages lies through the East.'[2] In
other words, we are to watch from the Oriental fringe of the
Roman Empire, from Asia, Syria, Egypt, and also from Mesopotamia, Armenia, and Persia, the slow transformation of the

---

[1] W. R. Inge, *The Platonic Tradition in English Religious Thought*, London 1926, p. 7; C. Dawson, *Progress and Religion*, London 1929, p. 119.

[2] E. Kornemann, 'Die römische Kaiserzeit', in *Einleitung in die Altertumswissenschaft*, Leipzig 1912, iii. 296.

B

West under the manifold influences that flowed from the Oriental and Oriental-Hellenistic world.

The conquests of Alexander opened up the East to Greek travellers and settlers, and to Greek civilization. Greek cities with Greek institutions and language sprang up as far as the borders of India, but the process of hellenization was practically confined to the civic centres, and powerful national reactions set in as soon as the political strength of the succession kingdoms began to wane. The emergence of Parthia created a barrier between India and the West; Bactria, Iran, Mesopotamia, and Armenia resumed their independence. The old Persian religion regathered its strength both in the homeland and in Cappadocia, where Persian influences were becoming stronger than the Hellenistic, in spite of the continued use of Greek for business and other purposes. Similar reactions are observed elsewhere; in the new kingdom of Pontus, whose rulers claimed Persian descent, though they preserved a veneer of Greek culture; in Judaea, where the Jews rebelled successfully against Antiochus; and finally in Egypt, where there was a significant revival of the national culture. At Alexandria, the Greek aristocracy soon began to lose its supremacy, Egyptian names in the second century B.C. tended to predominate in the records, and the native Egyptian religion not only maintained itself, but spread, especially in the form of the worship of Isis, first to the limits of the Ptolemaic influence in the Aegean and finally over the Western Roman world.

The Hellenistic kingdoms were deprived of the strength which only a vivid national consciousness is capable of providing. Beside the Greek κοινή, the language of business and of international intercourse, the vernacular languages persisted and, above all, the native religions lost none of their old vigour, though in the cities the process of syncretism had clothed them in a Greek dress. If Heracles was worshipped at Tarsus,[1] he remained essentially the oriental Sandan, and Zeus as Baal-Tersios equally retained his Syrian characteristics.

From these populations of superficially hellenized Orientals, vast numbers came as slaves, adventurers, or merchants to the Roman West. In the late Republic there had been at first a flow of settlers from Italy in the wake of the Roman conquests in the East. The massacre of Mithradates and the consequent sense of insecurity extinguished or checked this

[1] On Tarsus in this age, see H. *Augusteischen Zeitalter*, Göttingen 1913. Böhlig, *Die Geisteskultur von Tarsos im*

movement,[1] and Italian colonists were henceforth employed, along with the military colonists, in the more important task of latinizing Gaul, Spain, and Africa, including Numidia.[2] The most enduring monument of this intensive colonization was the establishment of the Latin language as the medium of ordinary intercourse, especially in the urban centres, and it was not long before the schools were producing orators and men of letters in all these western provinces.

But in the train of the Italians came the Orientals. To Rome and Italy at large incredible numbers of slaves were imported from the eastern provinces; manumission and the granting of practical freedom went on at a great rate as ever fresh supplies of slaves came pouring in. In a few generations the already declining Italian and Roman stock was almost completely over-whelmed by a population descended from Hellenistic-Oriental slaves, or, to a smaller extent, from free settlers who had come in search of a fortune. Lucan had spoken of Rome as

nulloque frequentem
cive suo Romam, sed mundi faece repletam,[3]

and Juvenal, voicing his hatred of a 'Greek city', said

iam pridem Syrus in Tiberim defluxit Orontes;[4]

but not until the inscriptions were examined did the full significance of such testimonies become clear. From a study of many thousand inscriptions, Prof. Tenney Frank has arrived at the conclusion that 'nearly 90 per cent. of the population permanently resident at Rome in the Empire bore the taint of foreign extraction', being descended from 'that part of the slave-producing world in which Greek was the language of commerce, that is Asia Minor and Syria'.[5] The great cities of Italy show a 'strikingly large proportion of non-Italian names in their cemeteries', and 'the very core of central Italy whence the hardiest soldiers were once drawn seems to have become largely foreign; a careful reading of the inscriptions of the Marsi and Vestini will allay the most obstinate doubts on this

[1] Tenney Frank, *Economic History of Rome*, London 1927, p. 150 sq., points out that these settlers were mainly Greek and Oscan (Southern) Italians, and not Roman citizens; cf. M. Rostovtzeff, *Social and Economic History of the Roman Empire*, Oxford 1926, p. 35.

[2] Rostovtzeff, loc. cit.

[3] *De bello civili*, vii. 404–5.

[4] *Sat.* iii. 62; Tenney Frank, op. cit.,

p. 202, quotes the remark of Cicero's brother in 64 B.C. (*De Petitione Cons.* 14. 54), 'Roma est civitas ex nationum conventu constituta'.

[5] Tenney Frank, op. cit., p. 213; also by the same author, 'Race Mixture in the Roman Empire', *American Historical Review*, xxi (1915–16), p. 690; see also A. M. Duff, *Freedmen in the Early Roman Empire*, Oxford 1928, p. 199 sq.

point. In a word, the whole of Italy as well as the Romanized portions of Gaul and Spain were during the Empire dominated in blood by the East.'[1] How persistent was the Oriental influence in Gaul is shown by the numerous references in the writings of Gregory of Tours in the sixth century to the presence of Syrians, mainly engaged in trade.[2] Such traders appeared in all the Roman provinces in the West, and they are a witness to the continuity of the movement from East to West.

The preponderance of the Oriental element in the population must obviously be taken into account in the study of the movements which transformed the whole religious outlook of the Graeco-Roman world. These movements are best presented in relation to the mystery-religions as we observe them already working in the Roman Empire. The aim of all these 'mysteries' is one which was foreign to the indigenous cults of the West— the union of the initiate with the god who is his saviour or deliverer. As the Hermetic tract, *Poimandres*, puts it: τοῦτό ἐστι τὸ ἀγαθὸν τέλος τοῖς γνῶσιν ἐσχήκοσι θεωθῆναι. The mystes is to become God. This is the way to immortality, and it is guaranteed by initiations and sacraments. The salvation assumes various forms; it was a redemption for the Orphic-Pythagorean sects from the circle of births; for the followers of Mithras from the 'bitter and inexorable necessity'[3] imposed by the stars or by destiny; but every religion promised a blessed existence in the world beyond death. These religions were all religions of revelation and the one essential was the possession of the divinely revealed γνῶσις or knowledge, the key to salvation. The idea of γνῶσις, it has been said, is a central idea round which the mystery-religions resolve in concentric circles. It does not imply knowledge in the intellectual sense, it is the secret and magical knowledge imparted by revelation and through a personal relationship with the godhead.

[1] Tenney Frank, op. cit., pp. 215–16.
[2] Dill, *Roman Society in Gaul in the Merovingian Age*, London 1926, p. 244. The references to Gregory of Tours are given in the excellent monograph of J. Ebersolt, *Orient et Occident (Recherches sur les influences byzantines et orientales en France avant les Croisades)*, Paris 1928. Ebersolt shows how constant was the intercourse between Gaul and the East, as the pilgrim literature proves, as well as the history of Gallic monasticism. E. Buonaiuti, *Il Cristianesimo nell' Africa romana*, Bari 1928, p. 165, points out that the confessors in the persecution at Lyons in A.D. 177 were mainly of Anatolian origin. The names given in the letter in which the account of their martyrdom is set forth (Eusebius, *H.E.* v. 1) are sufficient evidence of this. Cf. also F. Wieland, *Altar und Altargrab der christlichen Kirchen im 4. Jahrhundert*, Leipzig 1912, p. 46; Bury, *Later Roman Empire*, ii. 316.
[3] See the so-called Mithras-liturgy, in A. Dieterich, *Eine Mithrasliturgie*, Leipzig 1910, p. 4.

The mysteries of Isis, of Attis-Cybele, of Mithras, came into a world which was ready to welcome them, for in the multitude of gods the chances of salvation appeared to be more secure.[1] Polytheism is tolerant, and the process of syncretism can work wonders in making strange and even repellent deities respectable. Thus the old pantheon could be retained along with the new; but, while the greater gods retained their position in the public cults, the real savour had gone out of the Olympian religion, and the new religious needs could be met only by cults which promised all or more than all that men could hope or desire. The height of spiritual and moral fervour to which the mysteries could lead their votaries is manifested in Apuleius's account of the initiation ceremonies of Isis, and in that precious Hermetic tract which goes under the name of *Poimandres*.[2] In the Hermetic literature and in the remains of Gnosticism are seen what Bousset has called 'Those mixed constructions in which philosophy and orientalized beliefs and mystery ideas are blended'. The true initiate is possessed by a power from above, and becomes a new creature, ὁ ἔννους ἄνθρωπος, or a πνευματικός who is already on the way to deification. The saviour is generally a suffering or dying god, whose myth is based originally on some primitive vegetation ritual, like those of the Babylonian Tammuz, the Syrian Adonis, or the Egyptian Osiris, but the myths are now interpreted in a religious and more or less ethical sense. One of the most significant figures is that of the Anthropos, a primitive god-man, who sinks down into matter and frees himself by rising again. This divine process is repeated in the individual experience of the worshipper, which is paralleled in the cult by a sacramental union with the god, whose death and resurrection are mystically shared by the cult-community. A liturgical fragment from the Attis ritual which enshrines this idea has been preserved by Firmicus Maternus.[3]

θαρρεῖτε μύσται, τοῦ θεοῦ σεσωσμένου.
ἔσται γὰρ ἡμῖν ἐκ πόνου σωτηρία.

In this unparalleled theocrasia, it might well be difficult to choose one's saviour god. The problem was solved by many by successive initiations into several different mysteries. Beside the more private mystery-cult, except in the case of Mithraism,

---

[1] J. Geffcken, *Der Ausgang des griechisch-römischen Heidentums*, Heidelberg 1920, p. 228.
[2] R. Reitzenstein, *Poimandres*, Leipzig 1904; W. Scott, *Hermetica*, i, Oxford 1924.
[3] *De errore profanarum religionum*, xviii.

stood the ordinary public cult to which the multitude resorted, but the full power and real religious spirit, in the new sense of the word, resided only in the mystery.

Turning from religion to philosophy and following the progress of the latter from Plato to the close of the ancient order, we see how deeply the shadow of the East was cast over the whole world of speculative thought. The practical Socratic interest in man had given the impulse to new ethical systems which were demanded by the altered conditions of the Greek world. The age which saw the decline of the city-state and the setting up of great country-states was an age of immense dislocation, of changing political and individual fortunes. Amid this insecurity, only the strong man who was aided by the new goddess, Tychê or Fortune,[1] could hope to find his way successfully. Philosophy turned aside to meet these practical needs. Cynic and Stoic and Epicurean produced their ideal of the wise man, whose self-sufficiency and autonomy are his armour against the attacks of fortune. Philosophy was striving to give the educated classes a substitute for the traditional morality which had lost its application in a changed world. The ethical interest is, therefore, dominant, and the Platonic quest for knowledge is replaced by a dogmatic construction of the universe, borrowed by the Stoics from Heraclitus and by the Epicureans from Democritus.

But the matter did not rest there. Stoicism, for instance, could not remain outside the religious tendencies of the age, especially when it found a permanent welcome on Roman soil. Here its practical side was appreciated and it became for the finer spirits of the Roman aristocracy not only a rule of life but a religion. Posidonius[2] (*circ.* 135–51 B.C.), a Syrian from Apamea, brought God and the warmth of religious feeling into a system too cold and rational for the times, and so created the Stoicism of the Empire, which sustained and comforted the aristocratic martyrs in the days of tyranny. From Posidonius a stream of religion flowed into the whole of the later philosophy of the ancient world. A man of great learning and of varied gifts, he is without a rival until we reach Plotinus and Porphyry. He broke loose from the narrowness imposed by tradition and

---

[1] On the cult of Tychê, see Kaerst, *Das Wesen des Hellenismus* (vol. ii of *Geschichte des hellenistischen Zeitalters*, Leipzig 1909), pp. 202 sqq.; Rohde, *Der griechische Roman*, 2nd edit., Leipzig 1900, pp. 296 sqq.

[2] See E. Schwartz, *Charakterköpfe aus der antiken Literatur*, Leipzig 1912, i. 72 sqq. There is a considerable modern literature (mostly German) about Posidonius.

embraced in the scope of his vast system the science of the Alexandrines, Neopythagorean and Oriental piety, and all that appeared to be of value in the popular religions. Like a true Oriental he was more of a theologian than a philosopher. If he investigated the relation of the moon to the tides, it was to demonstrate the 'sympathy' which unites the cosmos, and his theological bias led him not merely to rehabilitate the gods, but to take a more questionable interest in astrology, divination, magic, and dreams. His philosophy culminates in a religious mysticism based on the unity of the rational soul with its divine source, the celestial fire; but in its lower stages it finds room for many of the superstitions gathered round the popular demonology and polytheism. The Posidonian eschatology is well reflected in the Sixth Aeneid and in the *Somnium Scipionis*. The pages of Seneca in the warmth of their religious feeling often betray the source of their inspiration. Eclecticism and religious fervour are now the notes of philosophy. Plutarch (*circ.* A.D. 46–120) embodies those tendencies which were to govern the future in their weakness and in their strength, in their puerile speculation, in their dependence on the mystery spirit, as well as in their moral insistence and their spiritual longings. In Apollonius of Tyana, resurrected in the tedious romance of Philostratus, Neopythagoreanism raised its head, presenting a revelation of what the third century demanded of a religious teacher. The sage is a man without a system, but with pedantic scruples and an irrational piety; a worker of miracles who possesses a knowledge beyond that of the sciences; in other words, he is the complete pietist and charlatan. To such a depth had philosophy sunk when the Egyptian Plotinus[1] (A.D. 204–70), the last great thinker of the ancient world, appeared. He stands above his contemporaries in his realization of the value of exact studies, his superiority to a passive acceptance of dogma, and his use of the dialectical method. In his passion for dialectic, he is father of Scholasticism, for he exalted it as the philosophic method *par excellence*. It is not without significance that it was his pupil Porphyry's introduction to Aristotle's *Categories* which set for the Middle Ages the problem of *genera* and *species*, with which the classic age of Scholasticism began. In Plotinus science and mysticism were reconciled. He saw the highest point of experience and of knowledge in the ecstatic union with the divine, but retained an ineradicable polytheism combined with the current

---

[1] Geffcken, pp. 38 sqq.

demonology. His asceticism shows a larger spirit than that of his followers; for the history of Neoplatonism is one of the gradual degradation and 'medievalization' of the last great speculative system of the ancient world. The decline began at once with Porphyry[1] (A.D. 233–*circ*. 301), whose Tyrian birth was a guarantee of his Oriental preoccupation with religion. Demonology was a study which absorbed his interest. For him, as for the Christians, the demons were the cause of evil both moral and material, and an elaborate theurgy was the means of dealing with their machinations. He firmly believed in oracles, but took the Pythagorean view that the true gods required only the sacrifice of the heart and that the demons alone longed for the smoke of blood. While there was much in polytheism which Plotinus had ignored, Porphyry openly criticized the offensive practices of certain cults. On the whole, his criticism served to weaken the cause of heathendom, but his error was soon remedied by his successor Iamblichus, with whom philosophy descends still lower into the dusk of superstition and credulity. Pure learning was now reaching the level of the medieval theory which subordinated it to the religious end. The allegorical method was used to explain everything which otherwise would admit of no explanation. Of pure literature in the third century there is hardly a trace. Oriental romanticism and Neopythagorean reminiscences fill the Ethiopian story of Heliodorus the Phoenician, which is as crowded with allegory, demonology, and asceticism as a medieval tale.

The political and economic troubles of the third century doubtless contributed much to the decay of learning, but they also disturbed the security of the official cults, which depended on the State for their sustenance. Christianity was, all this time, a growing force, and was now attracting the notice of the Government, whose efforts to stem the tide of religious and political disintegration were seconded by the Neoplatonic movement. For Neoplatonism, having gathered into itself all that remained of permanent strength and value in the religion of the Empire, consciously took up the spiritual struggle against Christianity. It was Iamblichus[2] (*circ*. A.D. 280–335), again a Syrian, who continued the work of Porphyry and carried still further the reconciliation of religions and philosophies among themselves, and of religion itself with philosophy. His attempt to demonstrate the ultimate agreement of Plato and Aristotle, Heraclitus and Democritus, Jews and Egyptians, Gnostics and

[1] Geffcken, pp. 56 sqq.   [2] Geffcken, pp. 103 sqq.

Pythagoreans, produced an heterogeneous whole in which there was room for every system, every cult, and every superstition. Criticism is thrown to the winds, the conception of a natural order is abandoned, the approach to the gods is through the symbolical and magical practices of the common cults, by divination, dreams, and oracles, which reveal a higher truth than that of natural knowledge. Iamblichus sketched the first outline of a Catholic Church of heathendom, that impossible ideal which made such an appeal to Julian when he attempted his religious reformation. Iamblichus looked to Egypt for an organized priestly system in which the ecclesiastical hierarchy reflected the majestic hierarchy of the gods. Julian caught the infection of his fanaticism as well as what remained of spiritual and moral power in this strange representative of the Platonic tradition. The last heathen Emperor, who proudly regarded himself as the heir of Greek and Roman glory, was groping in the dusk of the Oriental twilight which preluded the sunset of the ancient world. The measure of his intelligence can be estimated by his slavish admiration of the impudent charlatan Maximus, and his feeble grasp of realities is seen in his attempt to make the heathen priest the counterpart of the Christian saint.

After his death in the East, the battle of Christianity was won, though the cause of heathendom was defended with dignity by a remnant of the Roman aristocracy, and Neoplatonism found a belated exponent in yet another Oriental, Proclus of Lycia (A.D. 410–85),[1] who followed in the footsteps of Iamblichus. Thrice a day he prayed to Helios, and, if time had allowed, he would have prayed to the whole family of gods, Oriental, Roman, and Greek. His writings show how the atmosphere of medievalism was being prepared, while it was yet the common property of every religion. As Venantius Fortunatus was healed by S. Martin, so Proclus was cured by Asklepios, who became thereafter an object of his devotion. Like some medieval solitaries he has a torturing consciousness of sin, and cried to Helios, like an Egyptian hermit, against the demons that assault the soul. Like some of the Christian Fathers in an extreme mood, he has no use for any learning that does not make for edification. Books lead to error and perplexity. Proclus would willingly put them all out of reach, except the Chaldaean oracles, and the *Timaeus*. As tediously as some Christian writers he dissects and comments and allegorizes on

---

[1] Geffcken, pp. 202 sqq.; also Introd.   ed. E. R. Dodds, Oxford 1933.
to Proclus, *The Elements of Theology*,

the basis of sacred texts whose truth he will not call in question. He catalogues gods, demons, and heroes, and classifies prayers according to their magical effects. The characters of Plato's dialogues change under his hands to figures of allegory. He takes the myth of Er and tries to demonstrate its probability by arguments which remind us of Augustine in his less happy moments. Oppressed by the sense of sin, living in a disordered world of demonology and magic, he represents to the full that orientalization of western thought out of which the outlook of the succeeding centuries was largely made.

In 529, with the closure of the schools of philosophy at Athens, the professional philosophy of the ancient world was ended. In its final stage it had become not merely the handmaid of religion but the slave of the popular phantasies and superstitions. This mixture of the highest and lowest, this rejection of the sciences for the secret wisdom of the religious East, this substitution of dogma for investigation, of revelation for reason, was the end of an inevitable process, a process which is reflected at the same time in the unfolding of Christian thought.

Christianity became a universal religion when it spread into the Hellenistic world. What has been called Pauline Christianity had some points of purely superficial contact with the mystery-religions. It is not necessary to point out the external signs which suggest analogies with these other cults. For the resemblance is almost wholly external, and, although, even at this distance of time, we are able to guess how men of serious and deeply religious nature found their spiritual longings satisfied in the new life of their initiation into one or more of the mystery-cults, yet we are much more impressed by the original power of the new religion as we see it embodied in its literature, from the epistles of Paul to the apologists of the succeeding centuries. And this difference it was which remained all through the course of history and dominated—even if we cannot see precisely in what manner—the thought of the Middle Ages. Christianity and the mystery-cults never came really close together, in spite of the priest of Cybele who said to Augustine 'et ipse pileatus christianus est'.[1] The educated Christian felt that he was nearer to the Neoplatonists, who had the knowledge of the true God, as Augustine testifies in his *Confessions*. But how clearly Augustine perceived what Christianity had

[1] 'And Attis himself is a Christian', *In Joh. evang. tract.* vii. 1, 6; see Cumont, *The Oriental Religions in Roman* *Paganism*, Chicago 1911, p. 71; H. Hepding, *Attis, seine Mythen und sein Kult*, Giessen 1903, p. 219.

given over and above this, that which neither the philosopher nor the mysteries had dreamed of! In the 'books of the Platonists' he found '"in the beginning was the Word", but that "the Word was made flesh and dwelt among us", this I found not there'.[1] It was the 'et homo factus est' which was unique in Christianity and left its profound mark on the whole of human life in the following centuries. And it was round Christianity that the new order was to grow. It was to provide the strength and sustenance of the new civilization. It was equal to its task, for, in spite of inevitable compromise, it preserved through everything the essentials with which it began, and took from its surroundings whatever seemed wholesome and necessary.

It was from Asia and Syria that Christianity, in the post-apostolic age, spread westwards to conquer the world. The first Christian school was at Alexandria, and the great Fathers of the fourth century came from Cappadocia.[2] The links which bound Christianity to the Hellenistic-Oriental world were strong, and, after the Western Church had begun to set off on its own separate way in the fifth century, the centre of gravity of Greek Christianity was in the eastern provinces.

The last enemy of the Church was Neoplatonism, which had in the fourth century gathered together the forces of paganism for a final battle on behalf of the old gods. It failed, but it bequeathed to the Church the best of its thought, which survived at the centre of the mystical theology of the Middle Ages. It was mainly through the writings of the Pseudo-Dionysius that Neoplatonism made its contribution to medieval mystical theory and practice. The Pseudo-Dionysius is steeped in the popular as well as the higher religious speculation of orientalized Hellenism. Fortunately he knew his Plotinus well;[3] so amongst the dross the pure gold shines, and under the guarantee of the name of Dionysius this fifth- or sixth-century author imposed his revelation on the succeeding centuries.

Along with this mysticism in which the religion of the ancient world found its culmination went a conception of the universe which the East had likewise imposed on the West, a conception that held its own until Copernicus, and still survives in the popular religion. This is the system which was worked out on

---

[1] *Conf.* vii. 9.
[2] Basil, Gregory Nazianzen, and Gregory of Nyssa.

[3] H. F. Müller, *Dionysios, Proklos, Plotinos*, Münster 1918; cf. also H. Ball, *Byzantinisches Christenthum*, Munich 1923.

the basis of Chaldaean astrology, a mixture of scientific knowledge and theological speculation, which exalted the heavenly
bodies as eternal and visible gods and made them (especially
the planets) the arbiters of human destiny. From Babylon
astrology passed to Syria and Egypt, and thence to the West,
where it made a permanent conquest. Its alliance with Stoicism, seen in Posidonius, assured its future as a constituent of
all later religious systems. It permeated the mystery-religions,
and under the guidance of oriental priests it retained in the
West its sacerdotal character, developing towards a kind of
solar pantheism,[1] in which the Sun, 'invictus aeternus', is the
central point of the cosmic order, the highest God, the source
of life, and the seed of souls. But this system was gradually
refined and purged of its more material elements. A 'Juppiter
summus exsuperantissimus', a supreme God, was enthroned
above the Sun,[2] who mediates between God and His world.
Below are the planets, through which the soul descends and
acquires its qualities, and through which it ultimately ascends
after purifications in the sublunary world of the four elements.
It has then become, in the words of Dante, 'pure and ready to
mount to the stars'. The eternal home of the initiates and of
the purified is now fixed in the heavens; purgatory is inter-
mediate between heaven and earth, and the gloom of Hades is
the abode of evil spirits.[3] This is the world-structure, in all essentials, of medieval Catholicism, for the Church, naturally, accepted
it as the dominant semi-scientific system of antiquity, a system
bequeathed by the East and developed in detail in the West.

Into Christian keeping passed too, by an inevitable process,
the treasures of legend and wonder enshrined in stories which
prolonged their life by a ready adaptation and change from one
generation to another. These products of Oriental phantasy,
such as the legend of the Seven Sleepers, stories of letters from
heaven, of talking beasts, of miraculous cures, were adapted to
Christian uses.[4] In fact the greater part of the early medieval
literature of edification must descend from that Hellenistic
Kleinlitteratur over which the shadows of Oriental superstition
had gathered.[5] It is only necessary to read the *Dialogues* of

---

[1] Cumont, *The Oriental Religions in Roman Paganism*, p. 134.

[2] Cumont, *Astrology and Religion among the Greeks and Romans*, London 1912, p. 135; and the whole chapter on Theology, pp. 101 sqq.

[3] On punishments in the lower world, see Cumont, *After-Life in Roman Paganism*, London 1922, p. 174.

[4] See R. Reitzenstein, *Hellenistische Wundererzählungen*, Leipzig 1906; E. Bevan, *Sibyls and Seers*, London 1928.

[5] P. Wendland, 'Christenthum und

Gregory the Great or to open the medieval *Physiologus* to realize that the East has conquered. As in the Oriental civilizations, the scholars are now the priests. Western civilization is approximating to the oriental pattern.

The very appearance of the great western cities was changing. It was from the eastern provinces that the later Empire derived its grandiose and elaborate architecture.[1] From Apollodorus of Damascus, the architect of Trajan's Forum, to Isidore of Miletus and Anthemius of Tralles, the builders of S. Sophia, the East was dominant in the fine arts. From the eastern provinces and perhaps beyond came the elements which made up the characteristic constructions of the Byzantine and Romanesque architecture of the Christian centuries. The new decorative and symbolic art came indubitably from the East, and it lies 'at the root of that whole which we call medieval art'.[2]

The picture is not yet complete. The East impressed itself profoundly on the political institutions of the Roman Empire, bequeathing to Europe, Western and 'Byzantine', the secrets of government applied to great territorial states. The Empire, as Augustus found it, was virtually without a constitution. Egypt[3] and, in a lesser degree, the other Oriental kingdoms supplied the only models of a centralized bureaucratic state, and following these examples the Principate and Empire steadily progressed towards a despotism, with the omnipotent Emperor at the head, an organized hierarchy of officials, an elaborate system of taxation, a standing army, and a peasantry which was slowly sinking to a condition of feudal dependence and serfdom. In other words, the conscious imitation of the East, apparent in the constitutional reorganizations of Augustus, Hadrian, Diocletian, and Justinian, aided by the operation of special economic and political causes, created something entirely new to the West, 'an absolute monarchy, theocratic and bureaucratic at the same time; the form of government of Egypt, Syria, and even Asia Minor during the

Hellenismus in ihren litterarischen Beziehungen', *Neue Jahrbücher für das klass. Alt.* v (1902), pp. 1 sqq.; Geffcken, p. 237 sq.; R. Reitzenstein, *Des Athanasius Werk über das Leben Antonius; ein philologischer Beitrag zur Geschichte des Mönchtums,* Heidelberg 1914.

[1] On the material superiority of the Hellenistic civilization, see Kaerst, pp. 168 sqq.; E. Meyer, *Kleine Schriften,*

pp. 135 sqq.; von Bissing, *Das Griechenthum und seine Weltmission,* Leipzig 1921, p. 62.

[2] J. Strzygowski, *Origin of Christian Church Art,* Oxford 1923, p. 162 sq.

[3] Kornemann, 'Aegyptische Einflüsse im römischen Kaiserreich', *Neue Jahrbücher für das klass. Alt.* ii (1899), pp. 118 sqq.

Alexandrine period was the ideal on which the deified Caesars gradually fashioned the Roman Empire'.[1] This system was transmitted to the Byzantine State of the Middle Ages, which remained for centuries the only example of culture and organization presented for the imitation of the semi-barbarous West. It is true that the advent of the North and the peculiar development of feudal monarchy influenced on special lines the growth of the national kingdoms of the West, but the mark of the East, impressed on Rome and Byzantium, reappears, if more faintly, in the Empire of Charles and the Ottos, and, we may perhaps add, in the Norman kingdoms of England and Sicily and in the Latin kingdoms of the Levant.

The aim of this survey is not so much to demonstrate a thesis as to show what different and complicated factors have to be taken into account before we can make a beginning of a right understanding of the Middle Ages. The picture given is obviously far from complete, but it is sufficient to suggest to the reader the immense and impressive forces whose operation was necessary for the transforming of a vast civilization. It also indicates, with less of precision than of suggestion, what new conditions, racial, political, intellectual, and spiritual, were to influence the literature of the succeeding centuries. It is idle to attempt a precise estimate of the contribution of any single factor to the new literature. It is enough to have described the conflict at the heart of the old civilization and the manner in which it was finally to be resolved.

§ 2. *Greek and Roman Rhetoric from Gorgias to Apuleius.*

This conflict, this contrast, this blending of East and West are present, too, in the whole history of classical literature from its Greek beginnings; they persist throughout the period of Roman maturity and decline, and they find a new expression in the literature of the medieval world. This is one reason why it is proper to look back not merely to the nearer Roman past but beyond it to the Hellenistic, the Attic, and the Ionian age before attempting to depict as a living thing a literature, or a part of it, which otherwise appears a chance and freakish birth.

That brilliant Ionian civilization, a civilization of cities in fertile valleys, had, as its background, older Oriental cultures which provided part at least of the material for its precocious

[1] Cumont, *The Oriental Religions in Roman Paganism*, p. 5.

advance. Indeed, it must have contained from the first a permanent Oriental element, which was reinforced from time to time from the lands beyond its borders. This mixed civilization was a permanent factor in the intellectual and spiritual life of Greece. The Homeric epic was shaped on Ionian soil. The beginnings of Greek science and philosophy are associated with Thales, Anaximander, and Anaximenes, all of Miletus, and with Heraclitus of Ephesus. Pythagoras was born at Samos, Xenophanes at Colophon, Anaxagoras at Clazomenae. The works of these men hardly belonged to literature,[1] but in the fifth century there were tales and histories in prose, full of that richness of colour and material which only the East could afford.[2] To this circle belongs Aesop, the Phrygian, whose beast-fables come out of the dim Oriental past.

When the Attic age began, Athenians and Ionians joined in a common effort, though the tragic drama remained the triumph of Athens alone. The new thing that came from Asia was Rhetoric, the art of the Sophist. The Sophist was the man who came to meet the needs of the new civilization, to give to those who could pay for it the knowledge and assurance necessary for success in life. Part of the necessary equipment was the ability to speak well and persuasively, and this could be achieved by studying the system set out orally and in treatises by these masters of all knowledge.

What is of primary importance to us is the influence of this movement on literary style. In the third Book of his *Rhetoric*[3] Aristotle says 'The first improvement in style was naturally made by the poets; for words are instruments of imitation, and the voice is the most imitative of all our organs. Thus the arts of recitation, the art of acting, and more besides, were formed. And, as the poets seemed to have won their present reputation, even when their thoughts were poor, by force of their style, the first prose style was led to become poetical, like that of Gorgias.'

Now, Gorgias, the most famous of the Sophists, and a man whom even Plato would appear to have respected,[4] was an Ionian, although his home was Sicilian Leontini. He is the real

---

[1] Wilamowitz-Moellendorff, *Die griechische Lit. des Altertums*, p. 55 (in *Die Kultur der Gegenwart*, i. viii, Leipzig-Berlin 1912, 3rd edit.).

[2] Wilamowitz-Moellendorff, p. 56, 'Denn nur Ionien besass im 6. Jahrhundert die Fähigkeit eine Novelle zu erzählen, weil es die Menschen menschlich anzusehen gelernt hatte. Dazu

wird der Orient nicht nur Stoff, sondern auch Vorbilder geliefert haben: an ihn denken wir ja immer, wenn wir von Erzählern und von Novellen reden.'

[3] III. i. 8–9, Jebb's translation, Cambridge 1909.

[4] In the dialogue Plato deals more harshly with Polus, the 'young colt', than with his master Gorgias.

founder of that 'artistic prose' (*Kunstprosa*) which exercised such a fateful influence over the whole course of the later literature of Greece and Rome. The marks of this new style, besides the use of fine words taken from poetry,[1] and a tasteless and excessive use of metaphor,[2] consisted of elaborate antitheses, playings on words, and balanced and rhythmic clauses, with end-assonances or rimes.

The emergence of this style, with its marks of exuberance and excess, set up an inner conflict at the heart of ancient literature which was appeased only by the complete success of the new over the old. The triumph of rhetoric is the triumph of the 'Asiatic' or 'Asianic' style, as it came to be called, because it grew and flourished among the Asiatic Greeks, from whom it passed to fresh victories in the Roman schools. For it was the Ionians who took the new art and set it free from all restraint ;[3] they divorced it from the study of the arts and from philosophy, and made it an instrument of pompous and empty phrases, of effeminate rhythms, foolish metaphors, and circumlocutions. So at any rate the style appears in comparison with Attic gravity and restraint, and so Quintilian puts the difference with sober sureness:

> Et antiqua quidem illa divisio inter Atticos atque Asianos fuit, cum hi pressi et integri: contra inflati illi et inanes haberentur; in his nihil superflueret: illis iudicium maxime et modus deesset ... Attici limati quidam et emuncti nihil inane aut redundans ferebant, Asiana gens tumidior alioqui atque iactantior vaniore etiam dicendi gloria inflata est.[4]

In spite of moderating influences, in spite of the examples of great and original orators and writers, the Asiatic style survived and struck new roots and spread fresh branches until it overshadowed the literature of the West. In Greece, Thucydides and Plato, in Rome Cicero and Tacitus knew how to

[1] Cf. Philostratus, *Lives of the Sophists*, 492 (p. 30, Loeb edition), περιεβάλλετο δὲ καὶ ποιητικὰ ὀνόματα ὑπὲρ κόσμου καὶ σεμνότητος.

[2] Aristotle, *Rhetoric*, III. iii. 4, p. 154 (Jebb).

[3] Norden, *Die antike Kunstprosa*, p. 131.

[4] Quintilian, *Inst. Orat.* xii. 10, 16–17; cf. also Cicero, *Brutus*, xiii (51): 'Nam ut semel e Piraeeo eloquentia evecta est, omnes peragravit insulas atque ita peregrinata tota Asia est, ut se externis oblineret moribus, omnemque illam salubritatem Atticae dictionis et quasi sanitatem perderet ac loqui paene dedisceret. Hinc Asiatici oratores non contemnendi quidem nec celeritate nec copia, sed parum pressi et nimis redundantes; Rhodii saniores et Atticorum similiores'; and Petronius, *Satyricon*, 2: 'Nuper ventosa istaec et enormis loquacitas Athenas ex Asia commigravit animosque iuvenum ad magna surgentes veluti pestilenti quodam sidere afflavit, semelque corrupta regula eloquentia stetit et obmutuit. ... Ac ne carmen quidem sani coloris enituit, sed omnia quasi eodem cibo pasta non potuerunt usque ad senectutem canescere. Pictura quoque non alium exitum fecit, postquam Aegyptiorum audacia tam magnae artis compendiarium invenit.'

use what they chose of rhetorical fashions: their genius was their own. But with the Hellenistic age in Greece and the age of literary maturity in Rome there was a growing divorce between the language of literature and that of everyday use, and the age of the schools had begun. Not only oratory, but written prose and poetry are *eloquentia*, and come under the control of the teacher. It is for the modern critic to try to distinguish between 'pure poetry' and the rhetorical product of the school.

That Hellenistic poetry, much of which still retains something of the old Greek freshness, was not written in any spoken dialect.[1] The poets composed after old patterns: in the epic they imitated Homer; in elegies they used an artificial Ionian, and their 'dialect' poems were as sophisticated as those of modern poets. Great talent, of course, was not lacking, but when poetry becomes an affair of the schools the breath of its life is gone. The way is open for perversions and ingenuities such as were loved in a later time of scholastic poetry—the early Middle Ages. A lack of artistic seriousness induced the practice of τεχνοπαίγνια, *tours de force*, like the verses which Theocritus composed to adorn a pan-pipe, and which when copied out reproduced the shape of the musical instrument.[2] Such 'picture-poems' had great popularity in later days, when they flourished along with such other perversions as acrostics and centos. Here they are only noted as symptoms of declining taste, and it is significant that they belong to an age which demanded short-cuts to knowledge such as were provided by *compendia* and extracts, dictionaries, anthologies, and commentaries. There was a multiplication of literary genres. The philosophic dialogue broadened into the diatribe, an ancestor of the Christian sermon. Moral precepts were provided in great quantity, to be used by a succession of moralizing philosophers, rhetoricians, and poets. Menippus of Gadara, a Cynic, made a new and fruitful literary creation by mixing prose and verse. We shall trace this mixed form through Martianus Capella and Boëthius to Bernard Silvestris and Alan of Lille.

Poetry was employed to teach astronomy. The *Phaenomena*

---

[1] Cf. Wilamowitz-Moellendorff, p.150.

[2] Theocritus, however, did not invent this fashion. Simias of Rhodes before him had made picture-poems representing the wings of Eros, an axe, and an egg. We hear also of a circle and a chair as subjects or objects of such poems. An altar was also a favourite subject.

See C. Haeberlin, *Carmina Figurata Graeca*, Hanover 1887. Dosiadas and Theocritus enlivened their technopaegnia with riddles. Some deny that Theocritus composed the 'Syrinx'; see A. Gow, 'The ΣΥΡΙΓΞ technopaegnium', *Journal of Philology*, xxxiii (1914), pp. 128 sqq.

of Aratus (*circ.* 280 B.C.) was read by generations of astrono-
mers; it was accompanied by learned commentaries, and, translated into Latin, helped to instruct the Middle Ages. Nicander
(*circ.* 250 B.C.) set forth in verse, though with studied obscurity,
the making of antidotes to poisons,[1] but it was not until several
centuries later that a doctor wrote prescriptions in distichs or
a mathematician composed or collected arithmetical problems
in epigrams. History was still written, but it might easily lose
its gravity and become romance; for what did the rhetorician
care for truth? Cleitarchus (*circ.* 300 B.C.), an Ionian, clothed
the story of Alexander in the hues of wonder and of Oriental
fancy, and began the Alexander-legend which endured through
the Middle Ages. Historical novels are associated with the
name of Phylarchus, an Athenian; and a rhetorician of Priene,
named Myron, invented the first Messenian war, which has
found its way into our histories. Myron made use of the love-
motive, which now appears in a whole group of novels. For in the
Hellenistic-Oriental world the position of women was not what
it had been in classic times on the Greek mainland. There the
love-romance could not have come to birth, nor the love-poem
of the anthologists. But at Alexandria or in Antioch it was
a different world, and beneath the outer appearance of Greek
civilization there lay the eternal phantasy of the East. The love-
romance, which the Orientals had known for centuries, became
easily popular in the mixed civilization of the Hellenistic
monarchies with their social order and varieties of custom so
different from those of Periclean Athens. Below the level of
literature we must imagine, too, in the great cities and in the
market towns, the endless train of story-tellers, who recited
half-obscene, half-sacred tales, stories of the deeds of a god
(*aretalogies*); producers of rude mimes, or singers of songs;
and all the other hangers-on of festival or of fair. Among them
were wandering preachers, and more respectable itinerant
missionaries of virtue.

The large cities were naturally the homes of learning and of
letters. The centre of gravity of the Greek world had shifted
to Egypt, to Syria, and to Asia. The literary language had to
be learned in the schools by Greeks and barbarians alike,
because it was now no longer closely related to the language
of ordinary intercourse. Hence the schools became more and
more important, as without their aid it was impossible to enter
into the select company of men of taste and education.

[1] Wilamowitz-Moellendorff, p. 213.

Callimachus, a Dorian from Cyrene, had to learn laboriously his Attic and his Ionic. It was not by accident that he and others like him cultivated the epigram, the small thing that could be polished to a semblance, at any rate, of brilliance.

When the intensive influence of the Greek world was brought to bear upon Rome it was this modern poetry and this modern rhetoric that Roman talent chose to imitate. The Romans learned from their Greek masters to make their prose poetical and their poetry rhetorical. Cicero says of poets that they are closely related to the orators,[1] and Ovid writing to a rhetorician goes even farther when he declares:

> distat opus nostrum, sed fontibus exit ab isdem,
> artis et ingenuae cultor uterque sumus.[2]

For the rhetoricians claimed poetry as their own, and they were to retain it for centuries. Here, as in prose, only genius could rise above the example of the schools. Poetry like prose was written to be read aloud. This is a fact that must not be lost sight of if we are to appreciate the effects which a poem was intended to produce, not on readers but on an audience which wished to recognize unmistakably and applaud the skilful points or respond to the demand of a not over-refined pathos. The dominance of the spoken word is expressed by the use of the term *eloquentia* to describe both prose and verse. In his *Dialogus de Oratoribus* Tacitus makes Maternus call poetry 'sanctiorem illam et augustiorem eloquentiam'.[3]

In those days tragedies were written to be declaimed, not acted. Indeed it may be said that under the Empire declamations, public and private, provided the best means by which poets and rhetoricians could 'publish' their works and make themselves known. In spite of the encouragement which these gatherings gave to artificiality and emptiness, and the opportunity which they afforded to the composers of endless elegies, epics, and tragedies—

> impune ergo mihi recitaverit ille togatas,
> hic elegos? impune diem consumpserit ingens
> Telephus, aut summi plena iam margine libri
> scriptus et in tergo necdum finitus Orestes?[4]

—they met a real need and made criticism and the exchange of ideas possible in an age which had neither newspapers nor

---

[1] *De Orat.* iii. 7, 27, 'Atque id primum in poetis cerni licet, quibus est proxima cognatio cum oratoribus.'

[2] *Epist.* II. v. 65–6.
[3] Cap. 4.
[4] Juvenal, i. 3–6.

reviews.[1] How systematized the study of rhetoric had become is shown by the admirably arranged treatise *Ad Herennium*, which was once ascribed to Cicero, and how tiresome its application could be made in an essay on a set theme—a *suasoria* or a *controversia*—is illustrated in the examples given by the elder Seneca.[2]

From the first the Roman orators had fallen under the spell of the 'Asiatic' rhetoricians. Even the elder Cato, speaking, appropriately, for the Rhodians, could talk like this:

> Scio solere plerisque hominibus in rebus secundis atque prolixis atque prosperis animum excellere, atque superbiam atque ferociam augescere atque crescere.[3]

The Gracchi went to school with Asiatic teachers, and Crassus likewise. Cicero studied in Asia and at Rhodes, and although he was not opposed in principle to 'Asianism',[4] and never abandoned the use of the rhetorical figures of antithesis, isokolon and homoioteleuton, he freed himself from a youthful tendency to follow the fashion and learned by degrees the necessity of that discipline and restraint which made him the master and not the slave of a method.[5] But with the Empire there was a change. With the eclipse of liberty the public exercise of oratory virtually ceased. The orator left the forum for the lecture room,[6] and although the debate of ancient and modern, Attic and Asianic, went on in the schools, it became clear that the victory lay with the latter, and, as Norden has pointed out, the victory was inevitable, for the new style was closer to the needs of modern men who 'could not write and speak like Plato and Demosthenes, because they no longer thought as *they* did'.[7] Quintilian strove against the extreme

---

[1] See art. 'Recitationes', in Pauly-Wissowa.

[2] On Seneca the Elder, see the introduction to *The Suasoriae of Seneca the Elder*, by W. A. Edward, Cambridge 1928. 'The suasoria is a fictitious deliberative speech in which the speaker gives advice to an historical or semi-historical character regarding his future conduct; whereas the controversia is a fictitious speech in an assumed civil or criminal suit' (p. xxxi). Suetonius, *De clar. rhet.* i, gives an example of a subject for a controversia. 'Aestivo tempore adolescentes urbani quum Ostiam venissent, litus ingressi, piscatores trahentes rete adiere et pepigere bolum

quanti emerent: nummos solvere: diu expectaverunt, dum retia extraherentur: aliquando extractis, piscis nullus infuit, sed sporta auri obsuta. Tum emptores bolum suum aiunt, piscatores suum.' A stock theme for a suasoria was 'Deliberat Alexander an Oceanum naviget', or 'Deliberat Cicero an scripta sua conburat promittente Antonio incolumitatem si fecisset'. These two are in Seneca's book of suasoriae.

[3] Aulus Gellius, v. iii.

[4] Norden, p. 225.

[5] Cf. his own remarks, *De Orat.* iii. xxv.

[6] Norden, p. 248.

[7] Norden, p. 276.

party, and Tacitus in his dialogue speaks his mind in the same sense through Messalla.[1] But in vain; a rhetorician called Votienus Montanus, quoted by the elder Seneca, laid down the aim of rhetoric quite clearly:

Qui declamationem parat, scribit non ut vincat sed ut placeat. omnia itaque lenocinia conquirit; argumentationes, quia molestae sunt et minimum habent floris, relinquit: sententiis, explicationibus audientis delenire contentus est. cupit enim se approbare, non causam.[2]

Hence that emphasis on form which, as it was thought, could be separated from content; so that audiences could listen without boredom to the discussion of imaginary situations and moral commonplaces, admiring the prologue, the *captatio benevolentiae*, listening carefully to the rhythmic periods, murmuring approval of each pointed sentence, and rewarding the peroration with clamorous applause. To avoid tedium, the rhetorician would introduce picturesque digressions, a description of a storm, or of some natural scene. Or he would describe the beauty of a woman in poetical language, the detail of a picture, or the appearance of a famous city.

It is in the *Golden Ass* of Apuleius (second half of the second century) that we can most conveniently discern all the resources of the later rhetoric gathered together and employed successfully with the aim of carrying on a long and complicated story to the continual entertainment and delight of the reader. Apuleius belonged to an age when Greek literature had risen again, after a long eclipse, to take its place beside the literature of the Latin West. The period of the Antonines was one in which East and West were again closely united, not only because the Emperors spoke and wrote in Greek and followed the Philhellenism of Hadrian, but because conditions were once more favourable for letters and the literary superiority of the Greeks made itself easily manifest. It is only necessary to mention the names of Plutarch (*circ*. 40–120), Aristides (d. *circ*. 190), Dio Chrysostom (d. *circ*. 112), Appian (d. *circ*. 160), and Lucian (d. *circ*. 180), to show the reality of the re-emergence of Greek, but if Plutarch was a true homeland Greek, Aristides came from Mysia, Dio from Prusa, Appian from Alexandria, and Lucian from Samosata. These authors represent, for the

---

[1] Tacitus, *Dial. de Orat*. 28. Unfortunately Messalla's speech has not been preserved in full.

[2] Seneca, *Controv*. ix, praef. 1; cf. Tacitus, *Dial. de Orat*. 20. On the introduction of poetical ornament he says: 'Exigitur enim iam ab oratore etiam poeticus decor, non Accii aut Pacuvii veterno inquinatus, sed ex Horatii et Vergilii et Lucani sacrario prolatus.'

most part, a reaction from Asianism to an Attic simplicity which had to be learned by close study of the classical writers.

It was a feature of the age that Greeks took the trouble to acquire Latin, and that writers who ordinarily wrote in Latin took pride or pleasure in writing equally well in Greek. Hadrian and Marcus Aurelius, Aulus Gellius, Fronto, Apuleius, and the Christian Tertullian wrote Greek with perfect ease.[1] But if in writing Greek they followed the Attic fashion, in Latin they might easily adopt all the excesses of Asiatic rhetoric. Although Fronto was a pedantic Atticist, in Latin he exercised his pedantry by despising Cicero because he did not consult old authors for unexpected and out-of-the-way words, and by collecting for his own use an archaic vocabulary to adorn his laboured style. We shall see how this fashion was handed on to the Middle Ages through Martianus Capella and the compilers of glossaries, so that Irish and Carolingian scholars might parade this mysterious knowledge to increase their reputation.

Fronto, Apuleius, and Tertullian were from the Roman province of Africa. The birth-place of Gellius is unknown. The similarity of their style, together with their excessive display of rhetorical devices and of long-disused words, led to the theory of a special 'African Latin' which had its origins in the early Roman colonization and had also undergone Semitic influences making for excess and swollen pomposity.

This legend is now exploded. If these Africans derived their archaistic colour from the early colonists of the province, why was a similar phenomenon not recognizable in the case of the men of letters of the Spanish group? Further, it is obvious that the African writers were composing with a thorough knowledge of what they were doing, and in accordance with strict rules. The pomposity is merely derived from Asiatic rhetoric, and the difficult constructions, such as Tertullian so often presents, become simple when they are seen to be derived from the Greek, which had at that time an influence more penetrating, as regards syntax and vocabulary, than ever before.[2]

Tertullian takes his place properly in the history of ecclesiastical Latin, and in him we have to reckon also with borrowings directly, or through the old Latin versions of the Bible, from the vulgar Latin. Besides this, he was a man of original genius

[1] Norden, p. 362 sq.

[2] F. Skutsch, *Die lat. Sprache*, p. 547 (in *Kultur der Gegenwart*, i. viii), 'Wie manches Stück ihrer Schriften kaum viel mehr als Übersetzung aus dem Griechischen ist, so ist auch nie die lateinische Syntax und das lateinische Lexikon so von Gräzismen durchsetzt gewesen wie jetzt.'

and he could coin new words to meet an occasional need.
Apuleius is of greater significance for the present purpose, for
his example was to bear fruit in distant ages. The *Metamorphoses* professes to be no more than a Milesian tale, written to
beguile and please. 'Fabulam Graecanicam incipimus: lector
intende; laetaberis.' It is written in a style which leads
Norden to exclaim in the words of Persius: 'haec fierent, si
testiculi vena ulla paterni viveret in vobis?'[1] For Apuleius
knows nothing of moderation; he gives everything in excess—
'antithesis, isokolon with homoioteleuton, play upon words,
the complete transfusion of prosaic and poetical expression, the
frivolous method of using language as the subject of an experiment in the coinage of new words with an occasional mixture
of archaisms'.[2] This is Norden's just catalogue of his vices,
which appear for the most part in the *Metamorphoses* and the
Florida. For Apuleius, like a true sophist, and for that matter
like most ancient writers, suited his style to his matter. In his
Apology, for instance, he writes mostly in simple and unaffected
Latin. But in the *Metamorphoses* he is a conscious follower of
the developed Asianism of his age. And how else should he
tell the wonderful tale that he had to tell? How else could he
sustain those long descriptions, with their detail that must not
grow tedious, which were part and parcel of the rhetorical
stock-in-trade, and, although he did not know it, involved
possibilities important for the future?

It is true that he commits enormities like *saeva, scaeva,
virosa, ebriosa, pervicax, pertinax*,[3] but there is the suggestion
of a new music in lines like those containing the litany to Isis:[4]

Tu quidem sancta et humani generis sospitatrix perpetua,
semper fovendis mortalibus munifica,
dulcem matris affectionem miserorum casibus tribuis.
nec dies nec quies ulla ac ne momentum quidem tenue
    tuis transcurrit beneficiis otiosum,
quin mari terraque protegas homines et depulsis
    vitae procellis salutarem porrigas dexteram,
qua fatorum etiam inextricabiliter contorta
    retractas licia,
et fortunae tempestates mitigas,
et stellarum noxios meatus cohibes.

        Te superi colunt,
        observant inferi,
        tu rotas orbem,
        luminas solem,

regis mundum,
calcas tartarum.

Tibi respondent sidera,
redeunt tempora,
gaudent numina,
serviunt elementa:
tuo nutu spirant flamina,
nutriunt nubila,
germinant semina,
crescunt germina.

Tuam maiestatem perhorrescunt aves caelo meantes,
ferae montibus errantes,
serpentes solo latentes,
beluae ponto natantes.

At ego referendis laudibus tuis exilis ingenio
et adhibendis sacrificiis tenuis patrimonio:
nec mihi vocis ubertas ad dicenda quae de tua maiestate
    sentio sufficit,
nec ora mille linguaeque totidem vel indefessi sermonis
    aeterna series.
ergo quod solum potest, religiosus quidem sed pauper
    alioquin, efficere curabo:
divinos tuos vultus numenque sanctissimum intra
    pectoris mei secreta conditum perpetuo custodiens imaginabor.

This is a rhythmical poem, anticipating or foreshadowing the
poetry of the future, which was to spring from the manifold
suggestions conveyed by those who wielded this rhetorical
prose more boldly than others.

The language of this novel of Apuleius stands on the border-
line between prose and poetry. It was the precept of the schools
that prose must borrow from poetry the ornaments that poetry
had always possessed. And it was now to give back to poetry
the more questionable gift of those borrowings added to and
transmuted in the course of centuries.

But it is necessary here to make a distinction. In the Roman
period rhetoric and poetry lived side by side; or rather the
school of the rhetorician sheltered both orator and poet. While
the poet did not adopt to any great extent a device like homoioteleuton or any rhetorical devices which would interfere with
the traditional form of his verse, he freely accepted and applied
the rest of the apparatus of rhetoric—the construction of
speeches, whether pithy and compressed, or long and pompous;
the use of apostrophe, of rhetorical questions, and of digressions; the manipulation of descriptions, whether of natural
scenery or of the human form; the picturing of love scenes and

lovers' trials and adventures,[1] and a hundred other things now indispensable for the maker of verses or the writer of a romance.

So from Virgil and Ovid onwards the poet became more than ever the pupil of the rhetorician. The so-called Silver Age is the age of rhetorical poetry, and this poetry lasted as long as the schools of rhetoric and their successors existed in the West, that is, until the end of the Middle Ages. The history of quantitative poetry in the Middle Ages is, formally considered, a continuation of the history of the rhetorical poetry of late antiquity. But the new music and the new feeling which, as early as Apuleius, had found a vehicle in rhetorical prose, had also a future—in religious and romantic poetry. For the Asianic rhetoric made its contribution to the new verse-forms which were developed in the medieval and modern world, and, joined with all that the Christian Church had gathered together to be the religious inheritance of the West, helped to create a new poetry which was to diverge slowly from the poetry of the old tradition and fade into the vernacular poetry of the European nations.

§ 3. *Poetry and Rhetoric in the Ancient World.*

In discussing the relation of poetry to rhetoric[2] it is necessary to guard against the danger of seeing merely rhetorical figures in the natural devices of poetry.[3] For rhetoric borrowed from poetry in its beginnings, and many passages of high solemnity in Greek tragedy might well appear to be tinged with rhetoric but for their lovely refinement and tempered pathos, which rise above the sententiousness and pretence associated with rhetoric in the narrow sense of the word.

The famous speech in the *Oedipus Coloneus* (607 ff.) is perhaps as good an example as can be chosen.

> ὦ φίλτατ' Αἰγέως παῖ, μόνοις οὐ γίγνεται
> θεοῖσι γῆρας οὐδὲ κατθανεῖν ποτε,
> τὰ δ' ἄλλα συγχεῖ πάνθ' ὁ παγκρατὴς χρόνος.
> φθίνει μὲν ἰσχὺς γῆς, φθίνει δὲ σώματος,

[1] Norden, p. 434: 'Die erotischen Romane sind, wie nach Rohdes Ausführungen jeder weiss, von Rhetoren verfasst und nur in engem Zusammenhang mit der rhetorisch-sophistischen Bewegung zu verstehen. Senecas Kontroversen lassen sich durch die griechischen Erotiker, diese durch jene kommentieren.'

[2] On the subject of this section, see J. F. D'Alton, *Roman Literary Theory and Criticism*, London 1931, and especially the excellent chapter 'The Supremacy of Rhetoric', pp. 438 sqq.

[3] Cf. D'Alton, p. 440: 'Poetry may be said to have a "rhetoric" of its own if the expression be used with due safeguards.'

θνήσκει Δὲ πίστις, βλαστάνει Δ'ἀπιστία,
καὶ πνεῦμα ταυτὸν οὔποτ' οὔτ' ἐν ἀνΔράσιν
φίλοις βέβηκεν οὔτε πρὸς πόλιν πόλει.
τοῖς μὲν γὰρ ἤΔη, τοῖς Δ' ἐν ὑστέρῳ χρόνῳ
τὰ τερπνὰ πικρὰ γίγνεται καῦθις φίλα.

Here, at any rate, are antitheses, and much material which could easily pass over into rhetorical prose. But for all that, it is pure poetry, serene and perfect, shining by its own light.

It is true that Euripides, who as a pupil of the Sophists knew all the tricks of their trade, sometimes used rime to heighten the effect of his verses exactly as it was used in rhetorical prose.[1] But rhetoric never dominated Greek poetry, though, according to Norden, it did worse—it destroyed it. However this may be, it is true, as Norden points out, that after Theocritus no authentic poetry arose until the new religious needs of Hellenistic-Oriental cults and of Christianity demanded it.[2]

In Latin literature the conditions were different. Rhetoric became the vehicle of Roman education. The poets went to school with the rhetoricians, and the worst among them had no better ideal than to be considered proficient manipulators of the arts they had learned in the schools; while some of the greatest never escaped the influence of *suasoriae* and imaginary cases debated under the eye of the rhetor.

Classical Latin poetry begins and ends in dependence on rhetoric. The homoioteleuta of Ennius are well known.[3] Norden gives examples of his love of antithesis and points out how he uses that fatal *bon mot* of Gorgias, the absurd γῦπες ἔμψυχοι τάφοι which found so many delighted imitators:[4]

> volturus in spinis miserum mandebat homonem.
> heu quam crudeli condebat membra sepulchro.

Even Lucretius could use it, in

> viva videns vivo sepeliri viscera busto,[5]

and Ovid, of course, could not reject the opportunity of applying it to the case of Tereus who had eaten his son Itys:[6]

> flet modo seque vocat bustum miserabile nati.

Lucretius and Catullus stand apart among the great poets.

[1] Norden, p. 832 sq., gives examples.
[2] ib., p. 888.
[3] Cicero, *Tusc.* i. 69 and 85.
[4] Norden, pp. 889 and 384 sq.
[5] v. 991.
[6] *Met.* vi. 665; cf. also Seneca, *Agamemnon*, 26–7, where Thyestes speaks of himself as
> 'liberis plenus tribus
> in me sepultis'.

It is useless to collect evidence of their knowledge and use of rhetorical devices, though the former uses occasional rime and alliteration, and in one poem at least, the *Peleus and Thetis*, Catullus composed speeches which might well have found imitators in the schools. Virgil was regarded in antiquity as a master of oratory. The scholars who met at the house of Macrobius during the Saturnalia 'omnes inter se consono murmure Vergilium non minus oratorem quam poetam habendum pronuntiabant, in quo et tanta orandi disciplina et tam diligens observatio rhetoricae artis ostenderetur'.[1]

It was after listening to the multiplication of examples by Eusebius, in order to show that Virgil used a host of rhetorical figures, that the company arrived at this conclusion: that Virgil was to be reckoned no less an orator than a poet. Proofs were brought forward, in addition, to show that the would-be orator could learn more from Virgil than from Cicero. For Virgil exhibits perfectly every oratorical style, Cicero but one.[2]

The truth is that the *Aeneid* made a great appeal to rhetoricians, for it was the rhetorical element which they perceived there that attracted their interest and admiration. Servius tells us that the rhetoricians Titianus and Calvus chose all their themes for declamation from Virgil,[3] and Servius himself, following the grammarian Donatus, specially noted *loci rhetorici* in Virgil.[4]

We may perhaps say that Virgil used his knowledge of rhetoric, as Cicero used his, with a perfect sense of what he wished to do and with perfect success. But his very success encouraged his imitators and set the seal on the process by which poetry became identified with rhetoric. Horace was too great and too various to find imitators, and he owed little or nothing to the rhetoricians. What he found he made his own, and he has no rival. Besides, he took too serious a view of poetry, and urged the intolerable truth: 'poeta nascitur, non

[1] *Saturnalia*, v. 1.

[2] D'Alton, p. 447, says justly: 'Now, all this study of the art of the poet, especially if directed by teachers who were insensible to his inner spirit, would inevitably tend to draw poetry more and more within the ambit of formal rhetoric. It would tend, also, to engender the idea that many of the ornaments of verse were merely applied ornament, to be used or discarded at will. That was especially true of the Figures, which many were inclined to consider as different colours to be laid on according to a writer's caprice.'

[3] Norden, p. 887; Servius on *Aeneid*, x. 18.

[4] See J. L. Moore, 'Servius on the Tropes and Figures of Vergil', *American Journal of Philology*, xii (1891), pp. 157 sqq.

fit.' Only Persius read him, in later days, with understanding, though it was not, of course, the *Odes* that most attracted him.

The Roman adaptation of the Greek elegy afforded the rhetorician his best opportunity. The Greek elegists had attracted Catullus, who used the metre, as the Greeks had used it, not in a succession of epigrammatic couplets, but as the medium of a progressive and continuously unfolding theme. The sense is not broken at the end of each pentameter, and there are no antitheses and studied points.[1] Those admirable poems, the *Copa* and *Moretum*, follow the same method. Tibullus and Propertius show the beginnings of the invasion of rhetoric; the hexameter and pentameter tend to form a closed couplet, and the pentameter does not always serve to advance the sense of the hexameter. Instead, it repeats or embroiders on the idea already expressed or provides an antithesis. A few verses from Propertius will make this clear:

> Sunt aliquid manes; letum non omnia finit,
>   luridaque evictos effugit umbra rogos.
> Cynthia namque meo visa est incumbere fulcro,
>   marmor ad extremae nuper humata viae;
> cum mihi ab exequiis somnus penderet amarus,
>   et quererer lecti frigida regna mei.[2]

It was Ovid who saw the possibilities of such a treatment of the elegiac measure which was suggested by the short parallel or antithetic members of the rhetorical prose. It seemed obvious that poetry would gain by imitating the much-admired features of the Asiatic style. Ovid had won great fame in the schools as a declaimer, and he studied under the professors of the new style.[3] Latin poets generally avoided homoioteleuton as an ornament proper only to prose, and Ovid does not exceed in this respect. But once, at any rate, he did not refrain from a leonine verse, which is precisely of the kind that must have delighted many a reader in the Middle Ages. And it is hard to doubt that it pleased the poet himself when it came into his head to write

> quot caelum stellas, tot habet tua Roma puellas,[4]

as the climax of a number of comparisons.

But this was a chance embellishment of his verse. What

---

[1] The *Coma Berenices* is a good example.

[2] iv. 7, 1–6.

[3] Arellius Fuscus, one of his masters,

belonged to the Asiatic school; Norden, pp. 266–7.

[4] *Ars amatoria*, i. 59.

Ovid relied on was graceful expression confined within the limit
of the couplet. The length of the period is thus artificially
determined as in the couplets of Pope. And it is with Pope
that Ovid can most properly be compared. Both possessed a
'prodigious talent'[1] which was denied to their imitators. At
their best they triumphed over the difficulties inherent in their
metre, and achieved great success in avoiding monotony; what
they accomplished seemed so simple and the method so obvious
that they had a host of imitators who aimed at reproducing
the superficial qualities of their art, the tricks of composition,
without the genius or the talent to use them. Ovid's example
is important because he served as the poet's model *par excellence* throughout the whole of the Middle Ages, and, as long as
the couplet was used, the scope of expression was limited as
much by what the couplet would allow as by the poet's own
ability.

The elder Seneca tells a delightful story of Ovid, which
illustrates that perversity for which his admirers have always
been ready to forgive him. 'It was only in his poems', he says,
'that he was guilty of verbal extravagance, and here he was
not ignorant of his faults, but actually loved them. For he was
once asked by his friends that they might choose three lines
to be erased from his poems; he demanded, on his part, that
he also should be allowed to choose three which he could not
endure to have sacrificed. So it was agreed. The friends wrote
down in secret the lines which they would remove; the poet
wrote those which he would save. On each tablet the same list
appeared, and according to Pedo Albinovanus, who was one of
the judges, the first line was

> semibovemque virum semivirumque bovem,

and the second,

> et gelidum Borean egelidumque Notum.

It is clear from this that this man of great talent lacked, not
judgement, but will to curb the extravagance of his poems: for
he used to say that sometimes a face was more pleasing in which
there were a few blemishes.'[2]

Ovid was incurably frivolous, but he was to be one of the
most admired teachers of the Middle Ages, for to the medieval
reader he was not only an incomparable master of verse, but

---

[1] Matthew Arnold on Pope, in his   [2] Seneca, *Controv.* ii. 2.
lectures *On Translating Homer*, i.

the dispenser of learning and of a shrewd wisdom.[1] As he himself said of poets as a class:

> at sacri vates et divum cura vocamur;
> sunt etiam qui nos numen habere putent.[2]

Manilius, the mysterious author of the *Astronomica*, belongs by right of survival to the Augustan age. He is a Stoic of the new type, composing a laboured reply to Lucretius. An impressive witness, as regards his material, to the orientalization of thought, he had made a thorough study of Ovid and was versed in the modern rhetoric.

With this rhetoric Phaedrus, the Thracian slave, who began to publish under Tiberius, would have nothing to do.[3] His fables conquered the medieval and modern worlds, and his influence will be apparent when we have to consider the fabulists of the Middle Ages.

In the same reign, Pedo Albinovanus, a friend of Ovid, wrote a poem on the naval expedition of Germanicus. The elder Seneca has preserved from it a description of a storm in which, he says, the poet surpasses the efforts of the Latin declaimers at this well-worn subject. A few verses will give an idea of the fitness of the passage for declamation and show how the way was being prepared for Lucan and Statius:

> iamque vident post terga diem solemque relictum
> iam pridem notis extorres finibus orbis
> per non concessas audaces ire tenebras
> ad rerum metas extremaque litora mundi;
> nunc illum pigris immania monstra sub undis
> qui ferat Oceanum, qui saevas undique pristis
> aequoreosque canes, ratibus consurgere prensis.
> accumulat fragor ipse metus.[4]

The reigns of Claudius and Nero saw the triumph of rhetorical poetry in the younger Seneca and in Lucan. Two poets have such rare quality that they stand apart—Petronius and Persius. Petronius himself is pictured for ever by Tacitus.[5] His amazing novel, of which only a fragment remains, is based as regards form on the Menippean satire which Varro had introduced into Roman literature. This mixture of prose and

---

[1] See E. K. Rand, *Ovid and his Influence*, p. 111.
[2] *Amores*, III. ix. 17–18.
[3] Phaedrus, iv. 7.
[4] Seneca, *Suasoriae*, i. 15, p. 6 (Edward); cf. vi. 26 (p. 31) for a lament for Cicero by Cornelius Severus in his epic on the war with Sextus Pompeius. On it Seneca says, 'nemo tamen ex tot disertissimis viris melius Ciceronis mortem deploravit quam Severus Cornelius'. He quotes him, of course, for his rhetorical qualities.
[5] *Annales*, xvi. 18–19.

verse was later made to serve for more serious themes, but the *Satyricon* itself was read with delight as late as Sidonius Apollinaris. Then the length of the work and the passion for summaries and condensations, as well as its lack of appeal to medieval readers, led to the loss of the greater part. But in the ninth century Heiric of Auxerre included extracts in his collection from classical authors,[1] and Auxerre and Fleury seem to have been the chief centres in which it was known in later Carolingian times.[2] It is not certain whether Eugenius Vulgarius (d. 928) quotes directly from Petronius or from the grammarian Flavius Caper;[3] but John of Salisbury in the twelfth century seems even to have known the fragment containing the *Cena Trimalchionis*, which is preserved only in one manuscript at the present day. For he says: 'Cenam Trimalchionis, si potes, ingredere, et porcum sic gravidari posse miraberis, nisi forte admirationem multiplex, ignota et inaudita luxuria tollat.'[4] John knew Petronius well and often referred to him.[5] Both in his prose and in his poetry Petronius is exempt from rhetorical exaggeration. He had his own opinion of Lucan, as we may gather from his picture of the poet Eumolpus reciting from two to three hundred verses on the civil war. 'Some people seem to think', says the poet, 'that it is easier to write a poem than a *controversia* adorned with glittering epigrams.'[6] There is a little group of poems associated with Petronius, apart from those contained in the *Satyricon*.[7] Even if they show the influence of the Greek epigrammatists, they convey the impression of great originality and of a pure poetic feeling such as was hardly to be known again until the rebirth of 'pure poetry' in the Middle Ages. Sometimes, indeed, it may be that even in a brief poem one or two verses only contain

---

[1] Manitius, *Gesch.* i. 502; A. Collignon, *Pétrone en France*, Paris 1905, p. 7.

[2] See E. T. Sage, 'The Text-Tradition of Petronius', in *American Journal of Philology*, L. i (1929), pp. 27 sqq. There are Petronian reminiscences in Heiric's writings.

[3] Manitius, *Gesch.* i. 434; Collignon, p. 9. Winterfeld, *Hermes*, xxxiii (1898), p. 506 sq., thinks that Eugenius made his quotation from Caper.

[4] *Policraticus*, viii. 7.

[5] Collignon, p. 10 sq.

[6] *Satyricon*, cxviii. It is amusing to notice that scholars have quarrelled fiercely over these verses of Eumolpus,

being unable to agree whether they are a parody of Lucan, or an attempt to show how the poet should handle the epic, not in Lucan's manner (he was accused of writing like a historian), but in the old manner with full mythological apparatus. I am afraid that the latter is the true conclusion; but the verses have some very clever touches. On this question, see Schanz, *Gesch. d. röm. Litt.*, ii. 2, p. 114 (3rd edit.).

[7] On the question of the authorship of this group of epigrams, see Schanz, p. 131, and H. E. Butler, in the Loeb edition of Petronius, p. 340 sq.

this suggestion of wonder, as the first and the last in these lines on autumn:

> Iam nunc algentes autumnus fecerat umbras
> atque hiemem tepidis spectabat Phoebus habenis,
> iam platanus iactare comas, iam coeperat uvas
> adnumerare suas defecto palmite vitis:
> ante oculos stabat, quidquid promiserat annus.[1]

Or again it is the well-known

> primus in orbe deos fecit timor . . .

or

> O litus vita mihi dulcius, o mare! felix
>   cui licet ad terras ire subinde tuas!
> . . . pervixi; neque enim fortuna malignior umquam
>   eripiet nobis, quod prior aura dedit.[2]

Lastly, the fourteen verses, irresistibly tempting a sonnet-translation:

> Lecto compositus vix prima silentia noctis
>   carpebam et somno lumina victa dabam:
> cum me saevus amor prensat sursumque capillis
>   excitat et lacerum pervigilare iubet.
> 'tu famulus meus', inquit, 'ames cum mille puellas,
>   solus, io, solus, dure, iacere potes?'
> exsilio et pedibus nudis tunicaque soluta
>   omne iter incipio, nullum iter expedio.
> nunc propero, nunc ire piget, rursumque redire
>   poenitet et pudor est stare via media.
> ecce tacent voces hominum strepitusque viarum
>   et volucrum cantus turbaque fida canum:
> solus ego ex cunctis paveo somnumque torumque
>   et sequor imperium, magne cupido, tuum.[3]

This curiosity for the expression of things that had not been expressed before, and the refusal to follow the fashion,[4] are shown in the other poems, and especially in two or three extreme examples by which he has been best known.[5] It is this experimental curiosity which gives a modern feeling to his poetry, as well as that absence of the fashionable rhetoric which he despised.[6]

---

[1] Bährens, *Poet. Lat. Min.*, iv. 74.

[2] ib., p. 92; but perhaps we should read 'hora' in the last verse.

[3] Bährens, *Poet. Lat. Min.* iv. p. 98.

[4] Professor J. W. Duff points out (*A Literary History of Rome in the Silver Age*, p. 195, note 2) that these 'elegiacs show Petronius's departure from the rigorous Ovidian disyllabic ending in the pentameter'.

[5] e.g. nos. 100, 101, and 114 in Bährens, *Poet. Lat. Min.* iv; but we cannot be sure that they are really the work of Petronius.

[6] The *Satyricon* begins with an attack on the schools, where the young men hear of nothing but 'piratas cum catenis in litore stantes, sed tyrannos edicta

Like Petronius, Persius stands alone, but with a great difference. For Persius Stoicism had provided the religion which he needed, and he expounded it with a schoolboy's ardour and a grave dignity. He had hated rhetorical exercises, and he loved the Augustan writers, Horace above all. At school he would rub his eyes with olive oil to make himself appear ill, so that he need not declaim the last words of Cato before the foolish applause of his master, with his father and a crowd of admiring friends in a stifling room.[1]

Persius was loved in the Middle Ages because he was a moralist, and a moralist of the right kind, serious and high, who could appeal to men in such lines as these:

> O curvae in terras animae et caelestium inanes!
> quid iuvat hoc, templis nostros immittere mores,
> et bona dis ex hac scelerata ducere pulpa?[2]

Persius used well his garnerings of Stoic book-lore, and his *Satires* are diatribes or sermons, obscurely written, but charming as the work of youth. Isidore of Seville knew the satires well, and so did the mysterious Gildas in remote Britain. Heiric of Auxerre, of course, read him, and the unknown author of *Ecbasis captivi* knew him.[3] Onwards, from Froumond of Tegernsee, who transcribed him, he is read or referred to by a host of authors.[4] So the Stoic commonplaces extended their influence over the centuries.

But Stoicism had greater things to offer, and the Christian Church perceived the truth of this in Seneca, who, besides uttering moral commonplaces, spoke of God and His 'everlasting power and divinity'. Had he not said, 'Prope est a te Deus, tecum est, intus est. . . . Bonus vir sine Deo nemo est. . . . Ille dat consilia magnifica et erecta'?[5] For in spite of all that has been said of Seneca's inconsistency and weakness, he found in philosophy the truth and loved it.[6] His style is disconcerting, and it has been said of his prose that 'it produces an effect analogous to that of his nephew Lucan's hectic verse'.[7]

At S. Gall about the end of the tenth century or early in the

scribentes, quibus imperent filiis ut patrum suorum capita praecidant, sed responsa in pestilentiam data, ut virgines tres aut plures immolentur, sed mellitos verborum globulos et omnia dicta factaque quasi papavere et sesamo sparsa'.

[1] *Satires*, iii. 44–7.
[2] ii. 61–3.

[3] Manitius, *Gesch.* i. 753, Index s.v. Persius.
[4] ib., ii. 859, 518.
[5] *Epist.* IV. xii.
[6] Mr. J. W. Duff in his chapter on Seneca refuses to follow the scoffers and does full justice to Seneca the Philosopher, while admitting his lack of 'true moral bravery' (p. 204).
[7] J. W. Duff, p. 230.

eleventh, they transcribed the Ἀποκολοκύντωσις, the 'pumpkini-
fication' of Claudius, that clever and unpleasant satire in the
Menippean manner of mixed prose and verse.[1] The Tragedies
were known to the Anglo-Saxon Aldhelm, and in the eleventh
century or earlier they were in the library of Montecassino.[2]
They did not seriously influence the poetry of the Middle Ages.
Prudentius had, indeed, closely studied these productions of
his fellow countryman,[3] but they could not be of great interest
to later generations who had no conception of the conditions
under which they were produced and had definitely lost contact
with the dramatic tradition of the ancient world; for that
tradition had died with antiquity. It is enough, therefore, here
to say that the dramas were written, not to be acted, but to
be declaimed. This is, perhaps, sufficient excuse for their
rhetoric and the crowded *sententiae*, and explains the parade
of mythological learning and the tedious length of the speeches,
for which the test of production could not provide a corrective.
Yet the verse shows a decided and firm competence, even if
the general effect of his iambics is a 'polished monotony'.[4]

Seneca's nephew, Lucan, followed the family tradition in
philosophy and rhetoric. Cornutus made him a Stoic, and the
masters of the new style taught him rhetoric. He astonished
his professors by his brilliant declamations, and first won the
friendship and then incurred the jealousy of Nero. His *De Bello
Civili* is a presentation of the history of the extinction of
liberty, much as the Stoic 'opposition' under the Empire had
accustomed themselves to picture it;[5] but it is also a series of
declamations strung together to make an epic.

Petronius blamed Lucan because he discarded the mythological and supernatural apparatus which Virgil had taken over
from Homer. But how could a Stoic do otherwise with such
frivolities? It is to Quintilian that we must turn for a juster
criticism. 'Lucanus ardens et concitatus et sententiis clarissimus, et, ut dicam quod sentio, magis oratoribus quam poetis

---

[1] Schanz, p. 72. Paschasius Radber-
tus knew it in the ninth century.
[2] Manitius, *Gesch.* i. 436.
[3] *Christian-Latin Poetry*, p. 70.
[4] J. W. Duff, p. 269.
[5] G. Boissier in *L'Opposition sous les
Césars*, pp. 272 sqq., shows how the
anti-Caesarian feeling grows in the later
books, reflecting the quarrel with Nero,
whom he grossly flatters in the opening
lines of the poem. For Lucan, the ex-

tinction of liberty dates from Pharsalia:

redituraque numquam
libertas ultra Tigrim Rhenumque re-
cessit
ac, totiens nobis iugulo quaesita, vaga-
tur,
Germanum Scythicumque bonum, nec
respicit ultra
Ausoniam—vellem populis incognita
nostris.   (vii. 432–6.)

imitandus.'[1] The rhetorician could find in him more material for study than the poet. This is not to deny his ability—but how little this avails a poet! Everything can be traced back to the school—the *sententiae*, the innumerable speeches, the soliloquies, the apostrophes—and over them all is the bright hardness of the monotonous verse.

'Nothing in moderation' would seem to be Lucan's motto. Is he describing an army tortured by thirst? He must tell how deep they dig for water, deeper than the 'pale searcher after Asturian gold', how their entrails are burned as with fire, their lips are dry, their tongues harsh and scaly, their lungs—but this is enough.[2] The soldiers surrender to Caesar and drink from the river. They do not drink wisely and the windpipes of many are choked. In the end strength returns to the weary soldiers—'et vires rediere viris'. This is the time for a reproduction of Cynic or Stoic commonplaces on the simple life—it is pure water and not

> nobilis ignoto diffusus consule Bacchus

that has enabled them to regain their strength. Luxury is apostrophied as 'prodiga rerum', never content with what costs little:

> satis est populis fluviusque Ceresque.[3]

When Sextus visits the Thessalian witch to learn his fate the episode is told in more than four hundred verses, in the course of which the question is asked: Why do the gods obey the spells? Are they willing or unwilling servants? Then the horrors of witchcraft are set forth in the descriptive manner taught in the schools, and the speech of Sextus in which he consults the hag is another school exercise. Her horrible brews, and the raising to life of the corpse that is to reveal the secret known in hell, are described in full. The corpse, too, speaks the language of the schools in delivering his oracle.

The final episode, the murder of Pompey, is treated in the same way. Pompey is making for Egypt. There the boy Ptolemy has decided that he must die. Action is suspended while the poet bursts into a long apostrophe addressed to Heaven, which permits a Roman, and such a Roman, to fall by the hand of a foreigner. No, after all, it is 'civil war' that is being addressed. 'Thus far, O civil war, at least keep faith; provide at least hands of fellow countrymen to do the deed,

---

[1] Quintilian, *Inst. Orat.* x. i. 90.   [2] iv. 292–336.   [3] ib., 381.

and avert the prodigy of such foreign disgrace.'[1] But in the
next lines it is Ptolemy himself who is apostrophized, and the
reader grows weary. The murder is described with a ruthless
accumulation of detail. That nothing may be lacking Lucan
gives the speech which Pompey was composing at the moment
when the sword pierced his side. It is the speech which Lucan
would have made in the schools for the applause of his friends
—'the thoughts which Pompey the Great revolved in his mind
when the sword of Achillas pierced him'. Well, as Lucan himself says, he hoped that what the fame of Pompey and the
others might lack in making them immortal might be contributed by his own verse, and that, in reading his poem, future
generations would take the side of Pompey.[2]

And yet it is impossible to dismiss Lucan with scorn. He
was read by the generations following, and he can still hold us
even against our will. We must not forget that his verses were
written for recitation—Suetonius says, 'poemata eius etiam
praelegi memini'[3]—and that they lose much of their point and
impressiveness when they are read in cold blood. He was a
poet who made a popular appeal, as the inscriptions testify;[4]
he found many commentators and, although he did not win
much attention from grammarians, Priscian quotes him frequently. Throughout the whole of the Middle Ages he was read
and valued. Walafrid Strabo studied him diligently at Fulda
in the ninth century, and in earlier times Isidore of Seville,
Aldhelm, and Bede quote him. Fortunatus, of course, knew
the *Civil War* well, and Alcuin and the other Carolingian
scholars did not neglect a poet who could be read for matter
as well as for style.[5] In the eleventh century Wipo[6] gives
Lucan a place in the catalogue of the great poets of antiquity
much as Dante did some centuries later.[7] Gerbert read Lucan
with his pupils at the school of Reims, and quotes him in a
poetical epitaph.[8] Walther of Speier mentions him also as one
of the usual school poets.[9]

[1] viii. 547–9.
[2] vii. 205–13; cf. ix. 985–6:
Pharsalia nostra
vivet, et a nullo tenebris damnabitur
aevo.
It was this passage which led to the
wrong title *Pharsalia* being affixed to
Lucan's epic. As Professor Housman
has shown, the passage, which is part
of an address to Caesar, means 'Our
Pharsalia' (i.e. fought by you and told
by me) 'shall live', &c.

[3] *Vita Lucani.*
[4] Schanz, p. 112.
[5] See Manitius, *Gesch.* i. 748, s.v. Lucanus. Among his admirers in later
days were Shelley and Macaulay.
[6] *Tetralogus*, p. 27.
[7] *Inferno*, iv. 90.
[8] *Letters* (ed. Havet), no. 77, line 3
(p. 71): Lucan, i. 70 sq.
[9] *Vita et Passio S. Christophori*; see
below, i, p. 392.

To the minor poetry of the Neronian age belong the *Eclogues*
of Calpurnius Siculus, the anonymous *Aetna*, and the Latin
Iliad. It now seems established from internal evidence that
the author of these *Eclogues* lived under Nero. He is mentioned
here not for his merits, though the poems, conventional as
they are, are pleasant enough, but because he made an appeal
to the court poets of Charles the Great. Extracts were then
made for use and imitation in the schools;[1] Paul the Deacon,
the unknown author of the eclogue called the *Contention of
Winter and Spring*,[2] Raban Maur, and Modoin of Autun were
all acquainted with the *Eclogues*,[3] and we may be sure that
Theodulf of Orleans knew them.

The poem on Etna, half-scientific, half-moral, is generally
accounted dull, and the Latin *Iliad* is not an Iliad at all, as it
consists of just over a thousand verses giving a mere summary
of Homer's story. But how precious it was to the Middle Ages![4]
Columbanus the Irishman knew it well, and Raban Maur, and the
author of the *Gesta Berengarii*. It was designed presumably as a
school book, and a school book it remained for many centuries.[5]

It is pleasant to end this survey of the age of Nero with
Lucius Junius Moderatus Columella, and his *De Re Rustica*,
that honest and conservative treatise on agriculture and all
the practical business of farming. The tenth book deals with
gardens,[6] not quite as the 'purest of human pleasures', but as
Walafrid Strabo deals with the subject in his monastery at
Reichenau, mostly from a practical and utilitarian point of
view.[7] Walafrid knew and loved the work of Columella; both
had simplicity and gentleness, admirable qualities not rare in
those who tend gardens, and both could turn from useful herbs
and delicious vegetables to rose and lily, hyacinth and narcissus
—'terrestria sidera', as the older poet calls them.[8] Walafrid
seems to have read these verses of Columella in his boyhood at
Fulda, and he had, we may suppose, a transcript of the Fulda
manuscript at Reichenau.[9]

[1] Manitius, *Gesch.* i. 255, note 1.
[2] Usually ascribed to Alcuin; see
Christian-Latin Poetry, pp. 160–1.
[3] Manitius, *Gesch.* i. 731, s.v. Calpurnius; also p. 248.
[4] ib., p. 744, s.v. Ilias latina.
[5] Duff, p. 342.
[6] It begins (ed. Postgate, *Corp. Poet.
Lat.* ii. 206):

Hortorum quoque te cultus, Silvine,
    docebo

atque ea, quae quondam spatiis exclu-
    sus iniquis,
cum caneret laetas segetes et munera
    Bacchi
et te, magna Pales, nec non caelestia
    mella,
Vergilius nobis post se memoranda
    reliquit.

[7] Cf. Duff, p. 166.
[8] x. 96.
[9] Manitius, *Gesch.* i. 309 sq.

The age of the Flavian Emperors extends from A.D. 69 to 96. Among the poets there are only four names of importance —Valerius Flaccus, Silius Italicus, Statius, and Martial. Rhetoric still dominated education, and did its best to strangle poetry. In his *Argonauticon*—an epic on the tale of Jason— Valerius mixes old words and words newly coined in a way that his readers at S. Gall about the ninth century would have loved.[1] Those who have read him refuse to call him really dull, and they reserve that epithet for Silius Italicus and Statius. Silius wrote seventeen books on the second Punic War; Professor Duff compares his industry with that of Southey, and it is perhaps unnecessary to say more.[2] It seems that he was read at S. Gall and then forgotten until the Renaissance.[3]

Statius had a better fortune. Famous in his lifetime, he was read and loved in the Christian centuries. Dante revered him and placed him in 'the milder shades of Purgatory', because he was a poet and, the legend said, had been secretly baptized.[4] Statius was born at Naples, the son of a schoolmaster and a poet. He owed much to his father's example, and carried all before him in the schools and in poetical competitions. All his work bears the impress of rhetorical precept. The *Thebaid* is an epic on the story of the Seven; it bears upon it the evidence of a study of Virgil and of Lucan. The *Achilleid* remained a fragment. Virgil made of the *Aeneid* a national and religious epic, such as the times demanded. Statius chose his subject because one story was as good as another, and would win equal applause with another in a public declamation. Juvenal tells how popular these recitations of Statius were, and how melodious the voice of the poet:[5]

> curritur ad vocem iucundam et carmen amicae
> Thebaidos, laetam fecit quum Statius urbem
> promisitque diem. tanta dulcedine captos
> afficit ille animos tantaque libidine vulgi
> auditur.

The epics of Statius display all that wealth of mythological learning which the school imparted, all the careful description with its refusal to mitigate horror and its absence of pathos, all the heaping of episode on episode which was the only method of construction possible for a poet who had to publish

---

[1] On Valerius Flaccus in the Middle Ages, see Manitius, *Philologus*, xlviii (1889), p. 254
[2] Duff, p. 462; p. 463 on his rhetoric and his love of descriptions, which he overdoes in the manner of Lucan; p. 465 on his *sententiae*.
[3] Schanz, pp. 149–50.
[4] *Purg.* xxi–xxii.
[5] Juv., *Sat.* vii. 82 sqq.

his poem by reciting it piecemeal. But each episode is elaborated with enormous care, and if the verse is monotonous it
is far from being slipshod and incompetent.

The same care is lavished on the collection of small poems
called by the title of *Silvae*.[1] Looked at from one point of view,
it is a collection of rhetorical exercises, fashioned according
to rule, abounding in mythological allusion and in detailed
description—whether it is a villa or a bath that is being described; the Emperor's favourite or a statuette of Hercules;
the construction of a new road or a spectacle given by Domitian
at the Saturnalia. The compass is small and the reader can
seize more easily on the rhetorical touches. If Statius wishes
to say that Vopiscus's villa at Tibur is cool, he says that on
the visitor 'Sirius has not barked, and the offspring of leafy
Nemea (i.e. the constellation Leo) has not looked fiercely on
him'.[2] Epicurus is concealed under the title of 'senior Garget-
tius',[3] and it is impossible to proceed far without a commentary. The poet must be allowed some latitude, but this is
the first step towards learned obscurity.

Yet the *Silvae* have their own special attraction, for they
deal, for the most part, with just those passing events or things
in fashion for which a graceful description was a sufficient
memorial. It is this attraction—a closer relation to real things
—which makes so much of the work of his later imitators, such
as Claudian, Ausonius, or Sidonius, tolerable. The *Silvae*, as
much as some of the epigrams of Martial, set the fashion for
what has been called the genre poem, and, as long as the schools
of rhetoric and their influence lasted, it was better that poets
should compose these 'occasional' verses than attempt ambitious epics or tragedies. The influence of the *Silvae* stretches
right down to the Carolingian age, but beyond that time they
appear to have been little known.[4] But the *Thebaid* and
Achilleid were much read for their story, which supplemented
the *Aeneid* and what was known of Homer. Joseph of Exeter,
as we shall see, made Statius one of his models in his *De Bello
Troiano*. In modern times Statius has been best loved for his
little invocation *To Sleep*, which begins:

> Crimine. quo merui, iuvenis placidissime divum,
> quove errore miser, donis ut solus egerem,

---

[1] For an excellent account and criti-
cism of the work of Statius, see the
Introd. to the Loeb edition (1928) by
J. H. Mozley.

[2] I. iii. 5–6.
[3] ib., 94.
[4] Schanz, p. 176.

somne, tuis? tacet omne pecus volucresque feraeque
et simulant fessos curvata cacumina somnos,
nec trucibus fluviis idem sonus; occidit horror
aequoris, et terris maria adclinata quiescunt.

The last four verses are, of course, the usual rhetorical catalogue of things, but somehow the catalogue rises above the
precepts that regulated it, and becomes poetry. This, as we
shall see, is the promise that is contained in ancient rhetoric,
and is one justification for the long survival of its influence.
For it is a constituent element of the language of modern
poetry.

Martial is by far the ablest of the group of Flavian poets;
like all the greater men he saw exactly what rhetoric was
worth, and how and when to use it. He knew that the long
turgid tragedies were talked about, but that his own epigrams
were read and re-read. Writing or declaiming about 'the banquet of the cruel Tereus or of Thyestes, who had indigestion
afterwards' was trifling, but the trifles about which he himself
wrote were of enduring importance.[1] This was not conceit, for
he knew that some of the epigrams were poor, and others only
moderately good.

sunt bona, sunt quaedam mediocria, sunt mala plura
quae legis hic: aliter non fit, Avite, liber.[2]

His aim, he says, is not to emulate the grave old men who
compose laboriously by the midnight lamp. The Muse Thalia
has given him this advice:

at tu Romanos lepido sale tingue libellos:
adgnoscat mores vita legatque suos.[3]

Whatever Martial owed to his predecessors—and he names
Catullus, Pedo Albinovanus, and others—he is no imitator. He
was an observer of life, whereas his later imitators wrote, like
the rhetoricians, on set themes which they had picked up in
the schools. It is hard to think that many of the subjects of
the later epigrams were taken from life. Martial's manner
seemed so easy that he found many followers. He took the

---

[1] *Epig.* iv. 49; cf. ix, *Preface*:
ille ego sum nulli nugarum laude secundus,
quem non miraris sed puto, lector,
amas.
maiores maiora sonent: mihi parva lo-
cuto
sufficit in vestras saepe redire manus.
Also iii. 50, about the poet who invited

you to dinner and declaimed a book of
his epic at each course.   [2] i. 16.
[3] viii. 3; cf. x. 4:
hoc lege, quod possit dicere vita 'meum
est'.
non hic Centauros, non Gorgonas Har-
pyiasque
invenies: hominem pagina nostra
sapit.

epigram at a stage of its development from the Greek prototype—that lovely and delicate thing, fashioned for epitaph or
inscription or to immortalize a moment's experience—and with
the aid of the very refinement of rhetoric made it the instrument of comment, abuse, and wit.[1]

Martial has never been without readers from his own day to
this. The grammarians quote him constantly, and the Latin
fathers found much apt illustration in his records of life. Gildas
knew him, and the Carolingian and post-Carolingian scholars—
among them Theodulf, Raban, and Servatus Lupus; in the
twelfth century John of Salisbury quotes him under the
curious name of Coquus, which somehow or other was then
attached to him.[2]   The spasmodic occurrence of epigrams
throughout the Middle Ages is directly related to the study of
Martial in the schools, especially in the eleventh and twelfth
centuries.

Martial found it safe to publish in the days of Domitian. He
flattered the tyrant and was careful to give no offence to the
powerful. His friend Juvenal waited for quieter times before
publishing his tremendous denunciation of a whole society.
We must believe Juvenal when he says that he wrote from
indignation: 'difficile est satiram non scribere'.[3]   And why
should he not write? He has been through the schools,

> et nos ergo manum ferulae subduximus et nos
> consilium dedimus Sullae privatus ut altum
> dormiret.[4]

And when he writes it is rhetoric, but rhetoric in its proper
place, subdued to the grave and serious temper of the man who
had no use for trifling and would not be satisfied by cheap
applause. Like Martial, he says that his business is with life;
it is in her school that he has learned his wisdom.

> magna quidem, sacris quae dat praecepta libellis,
> victrix fortunae sapientia: ducimus autem
> hos quoque felices qui ferre incommoda vitae
> nec iactare iugum vita didicere magistra.[5]

The influence of Juvenal throughout the remainder of antiquity and during the whole of the Middle Ages was immense.
If he was somewhat neglected by the archaizing writers of the

[1] See the admirable remarks of Duff,
pp. 511 sqq. Some of the epigrams are
descriptive after the manner of Statius,
e.g. iii. 58, which describes Faustinus's
villa at Baiae. The farm is delightfully
pictured with all its activities, and animals. Here are no useless spaces laid
out as ornamental gardens; cf. also xii.
18 on his own estate at Bilbilis in Spain.
[2] See the references in Schaarschmidt,
Johannes Saresberiensis, p. 100, n. 3.
[3] i. 30.   [4] ib., 15–17.   [5] xiii. 19–22.

second century he came into his own in the third century.
Lactantius had read him, and the grammarians often refer to
the *Satires*. The influence of Juvenal is evident in Ausonius,
and he was the model for Claudian in his satirical invectives.
In the Middle Ages he was best appreciated in the eleventh
and twelfth centuries, when society had reached a sufficient
complexity to make satire possible or necessary. But he was
studied assiduously by the Carolingian scholars. Heiric of
Auxerre in the ninth century gave much attention to him
among other classical authors. The *Satires* were read in the
schools and used as models of prosody. It is for this reason as
well as for the moral value of his work that he is so often cited
by medieval writers. In Gerbert's time he was taken, indeed,
as a model of rhetoric, and, as Schanz points out,[1] a poet who
was read regularly in the schools must have exercised considerable influence over poetical production. The satirists of
the twelfth century knew him well, and the monk of Cluny in
his *De contemptu mundi* mentions him by name as one of the
great Roman satirists.[2] Giraldus Cambrensis,[3] Walter Map,[4]
John of Salisbury,[5] and all the humanists of that age found in
him a storehouse of maxims.

Juvenal lived long enough to discover new hopes for literature in the accession of Hadrian—'et spes et ratio studiorum
in Caesare tantum'. But, so far as Latin poetry is concerned,
it was a barren age. Greek was assiduously cultivated by the
dilettanti, a numerous class, and there was an Attic revival
which influenced contemporary Roman archaists. Poetry was
still a 'subject' in the schools,[6] but a new breath was necessary
to bring it again to life.

§ 4. *The Third and Fourth Centuries*

Superficially considered, the third and fourth centuries appear to belong to an age of decline, and, indeed, so far as poetry
is concerned, they present little of intrinsic interest. The truth
is that the provinces—Spain, Africa, and Gaul—were now
becoming more important than Italy, which was steadily losing
its intellectual supremacy. But, at the same time, it was only
in the new Christian Latin literature that the pulse of a new
life was beating; the prose and poetry of the old civilization,

[1] pp. 212–13.
[2] See *Christian-Latin Poetry*, p. 316.
[3] ib., p. 339.
[4] *De nugis curialium*, i. 15.
[5] Schaarschmidt, p. 100. John refers to Juvenal very frequently.
[6] Statius calls it 'studia nostra', *Silvae* I, *Praef.*

with few exceptions, had lost their hold on what was real in the world around them. Poetry was more than ever an exercise of ingenuity, and the poets of these centuries set many bad examples which the versifiers of later times were only too eager to copy. There was talk of *poetae neoterici* at the beginning of the third century;[1] they were poets who attracted attention by composing 'reciprocal verses', i.e. verses which read the same backwards as forwards:

> Nereides freta sic verrentes caerula tranant,
> flamine confidens ut Notus Icarium.
> Icarium Notus ut confidens flamine, tranant
> caerula verrentes sic freta Nereides.

These poets also turned, like some of the Alexandrines whose work was well known to them, to the versification of unusual themes. Terentianus, who belonged to Mauretania,[2] put into verse for school use a treatise on 'letters, syllables, and metres'. Quintus Serenus (who was not a physician but took his matter from books) laboriously versified a series of medical remedies—'prurigini, papulis ac scabiei arcendis' and the like. He had learned his art in the schools of rhetoric and knew that his readers, if he had any, would not trouble much about his subject-matter. M. Aurelius Olympius Nemesianus, a Carthaginian, is a figure of more importance, because he continued the tradition of the Eclogue and although, for the most part, he is a close imitator of Calpurnius, yet now and again we almost forget that we are reading a poetical exercise and hear the murmur of the river and the voices of Lycidas and Mopsus, the shepherds, singing in the shadows:

> hac age pampinea mecum requiesce sub umbra;
> hic tibi lene fluens fons murmurat, hic et ab ulmis
> purpureae fetis dependent vitibus uvae.
> cantet, amat quod quisque: levant et carmina curas.[3]

Besides his *Eclogues*, Nemesianus wrote a poem on hunting—the *Cynegetica*. His verses were well known to the Carolingian poets.[4] Paul the Deacon may have introduced them along with

---

[1] Schanz, VIII. iii. 21.
[2] Terentiani Mauri *de Litteris de syllabis de metris libri tres*, ed. H. Keil, *Grammatici Latini*, Leipzig 1874, vi. pp. 313 sqq.; on this treatise, see the interesting remarks of Paul Monceaux, *Les Africains*, Paris 1894, pp. 387 sqq. Terentianus' work is worth reading, for it is the work of a man of intelligence, in spite of its curious construction with its changes of metre, &c. He

wrote in verse, he says (p. 334), 'sane modorum quo sonora levitas addita stili levaret siccioris taedium'. A book like this would of course appeal to medieval readers. Isidore of Seville knew it, also Bede, and the Irishman Clement. (See Manitius, *Gesch.* i. 760, s.v. Terentianus.)
[3] *Eclogue*, iv. 46–9 (Bährens, iii. 189).
[4] Manitius, *Gesch.* i. 248.

Calpurnius's into the circle of court poets,[1] some of whom composed poetical dialogues under this influence.[2] In Hincmar's time the *Cynegetica* were read in the schools.[3]

Hardly to be called poetry, yet immensely treasured in the Middle Ages for moral precept and usefulness in the school, the *Disticha Catonis* must here receive mention. The wisdom of these uninspired couplets is commonplace and is certainly not Christian; but the Middle Ages managed to find some food there. The African Christian Commodian, in the middle of the third century, found them to his mind, and later they were regarded as the work of the elder Cato.[4] Every scholar who passed through the medieval schools knew them—probably by heart—and they were translated into the vernacular in many countries.

Two poets, Pentadius and Hosidius Geta, both Africans, wasted their time on trifles. Pentadius, besides writing epigrams, composed longer pieces in epanaleptic verse, i.e. elegiac verses in which the latter half of the pentameter repeats the first part of the preceding hexameter. Here is the beginning of a poem *de adventu veris*:

> Sentio, fugit hiems: Zephyrisque animantibus orbem
>   iam tepet Eurus aquis. sentio, fugit hiems.
> parturit omnis ager, persentit terra calores
>   germinibusque novis parturit omnis ager.
> laeta vireta tument, foliis sese induit arbor,
>   vallibus apricis laeta vireta tument.[5]

And so on. It is to be assumed that this fashion and that of the cento had their home in the schools.[6] In any case, they struck a firm root, and the medieval poets took them very seriously. Hosidius Geta's tragedy, the *Medea*, which is made up entirely of Virgilian quotations, has the honour of being mentioned by Tertullian.[7] Christian poets, among them a lady named Proba, adopted the cento, and Ausonius essayed it as well; but after a time poets lacked the courage or the skill to pursue this difficult accomplishment farther.[8] The centos con-

[1] ib. i. 270, note 5.
[2] ib. i. 550, note 4, on Modoin's knowledge of Nemesianus.
[3] Bährens, iii. 174–5.
[4] For a note on the immense influence of the *disticha*, see Schanz, VIII. iii. pp. 38 sqq. For John of Salisbury's references to the *disticha*, see Schaarschmidt, p. 100.
[5] Riese, *Anth. Lat.*, no. 235 (p. 163).

[6] See my note in the *Athenaeum*, Nov. 7, 1919, p. 1154.
[7] *De prescript. haeret.*, 39; text of the *Medea* in Riese, no. 17 (p. 49); Bährens, iv. 219.
[8] See Manitius, *Christl. Lat. Poesie*, pp. 124 sqq.; *Christian-Latin Poetry*, p. 16. For texts of non-Christian centos, see Riese, nos. 7–18 (pp. 22 sqq.); Bährens, iv, 191 sqq.

tinued, however, to be admired and read. Isidore of Seville[1] knew all about them, and the Carolingians can hardly have overlooked them.

To complete this account of the poetry of the third century it is only necessary to mention Vespa's *Contest of Cook and Baker*, a school piece which gives the opportunity for a rhetorical setting forth of the merits of each trade, with proper mythological allusions, and Reposianus' equally scholastic piece, in the descriptive manner, *De concubitu Martis et Veneris*.

This is the tale of the third century, and that of the fourth is not dissimilar. The corruption of triviality had eaten deeply into poetry, as is seen with startling clearness in the verses of Publius Optatianus Porfirius,[2] who appears to have been the City Prefect of the years 329 and 333 and was addressed as 'frater carissime' by Constantine the Great. His letter to the Emperor about his ridiculous verses, and the Emperor's reply, are extant. The poems themselves give some welcome but incomplete biographical details about their author, who had suffered exile for some reason or other, but had now recovered the Emperor's favour. But what interests us is the 'architectonic' nature of his verse.[3] For most of his poems are *carmina quadrata*, i.e. they contain as many lines as each verse contains letters—and in addition there are acrostics, telestichs, and figures embedded in the square. One poem gives us the figure of a palm tree, another an organ, and yet another a pan-pipe like that devised by Theocritus. There are also an altar, a ship, and a ☧ monogram. But the fifteenth poem is the triumph of the poet's futility. The first four verses consist respectively of words of two, three, four, and five syllables; the fifth verse begins with a word of one syllable and continues progressively until it ends with a word of five syllables; then verse seven gives all the parts of speech; and the poem ends with a series of verses which if read backwards form an intelligible poem in a different metre.

In composing these incredible poems Porfirius handed on the Alexandrine example to the Middle Ages. Not that he was seriously imitated after the time of Ennodius and Fortunatus, although acrostics and alphabetical poems were still manufactured, and a writer like Bede could speak of Porfirius as though he were one of the classics.[4] The Carolingians certainly

[1] *Etym.* i. 38.
[2] Ed. E. Kluge, Leipzig 1926.
[3] The expression is Schanz's, VIII. iv. i, p. 12.
[4] *De arte metr.* (Gramm. Lat. vii. 258, 20).

took him seriously, and Theodulf of Orleans attempted a picture-poem after his manner.[1] The *scholia* necessary for the understanding of the scheme of the picture-poems seem to date from the Carolingian age. Raban Maur and Walafrid were familiar with these poems, as also was Hincmar of Reims, who himself composed a kind of figure-poem.[2] In the early tenth century Eugenius Vulgarius wrote verses in the form of a pyramid and of an organ,[3] and later in the same century Abbo of Fleury sent Archbishop Dunstan two poems in which he imitated Porfirius.[4]

Rufius Festus Avienus, an Etrurian, made a version of Aratus' astronomical poem, with additions which he derived mostly from Greek *scholia*; he likewise versified from the Greek a *descriptio orbis*, also with additions, and a description of coasts—*ora maritima*—in iambic *senarii*, after the model of his Greek original, and without troubling to bring the geography up to date. He was, indeed, a mere versifier, and did not care whether his reader were misled or no. But the medieval scribes found it worth while to copy him as an authority on the heavens and the earth.

A certain Tiberianus is the reputed author of four short poems[5] which rise somewhat above the ordinary school production of the age. The first is a pleasing description of a river, in trochaic tetrameters, beginning:

> Amnis ibat inter arva valle fusus frigida,
> luce ridens calculorum, flore pictus herbido.
> caerulas superne laurus et virecta myrtea
> leniter motabat aura blandiente sibilo.
> subter autem molle gramen flore adulto creverat:
> tum croco solum rubebat et lucebat liliis
> et nemus fragrabat omne violarum de spiritu.

It is tempting to place somewhere round about the same date the *Pervigilium Veneris*,[6] and to call it the last lovely flower of ancient verse and the first romantic poem of the new world. But wherever it is to be placed, it remained without successor, the work of some clever and precocious poet with the melancholy of his youth not yet put away:

> illa cantat: nos tacemus. quando ver venit meum?

---

[1] *M.G.H. Poet. Car.* i. 482; *Christian-Latin Poetry*, p. 176, note 2. Raban Maur also attempted such a poem.
[2] Manitius, *Gesch.* i. 353.
[3] *M.G.H. Poet. Car.* iv. 412 sqq.

[4] Stubbs, Memorials of S. Dunstan *Rolls Series*, 1874, pp. 410 sqq.
[5] Bährens, iii. pp. 264 sqq.
[6] Riese, no. 200 (p. 144).

quando faciam uti chelidon, ut tacere desinam?
perdidi Musam tacendo, nec me Phoebus respicit.[1]

The second piece ascribed to Tiberianus is a rhetorical exercise
—on the evil nature of gold; the third is equally a school piece,
with a moral, and the last is a massively-rhetorical address to
the omnipotent Ruler of all things, a Neoplatonic prayer.

To the fourth century belongs that fine poem on the Phoenix,
which, if it is the work of Lactantius, was written before his
conversion, since it is thoroughly pagan in feeling, with no hint
of Christian meanings.[2] It is rhetoric flowering into poetry.
The descriptive method, learned in the school, is here turned
to profitable account, and this, as we shall see in the course of
our study, is a step of great significance.

This same flowering of rhetoric is, perhaps, perceptible in
another poem of the same century, which has been ascribed,
without due warrant, to Ausonius.[3] It is a description of a
rose-garden on a spring morning. It is very rhetorical, very
precise in its detail, and commonplace in its sententious close.
But there is a hint, a promise of something new, of something
better than the usual school exercise. There is a promise also
in the title—*De rosis nascentibus*.[4] But, as the poet says,

quam longa una dies, aetas tam longa rosarum.

[1] Yet the historical allusion in the
next verse comes from the poet's rhetorical training,
sic Amyclas cum tacerent perdidit
    silentium.
[2] See Pichon, *Lactance*, Paris 1901,
p. 464 sq.
[3] See Schanz, IV. i, p. 39.
[4] *Idyll*. xiv. The first few verses run:
Ver erat et blando mordenti a frigore
    sensu
  spirabat croceo mane revecta dies.
strictior eoos praecesserat aura iugales
  aestiferum suadens anticipare diem.
errabam riguis per quadrua compita in
    hortis
  maturo cupiens me vegetare die.

vidi concretas per gramina flexa pruinas
  pendere aut holerum stare cacumini-
  bus,
caulibus et teretes patulis conludere
  guttas.
.   .   .   .   .   .
vidi Paestano gaudere rosaria cultu
  exoriente novo roscida lucifero.
rara pruinosis canebat gemma frutectis
  ad primi radios interitura die.
ambigeres, raperetne rosis Aurora ru-
  borem
  an daret et flores tingueret orta dies.
ros unus, color unus et unum mane
  duorum;
  sideris et floris nam domina una
  Venus.

POETRY OF THE RHETORICAL TRADITION FROM THE FOURTH TO THE END OF THE FIFTH CENTURY

§ I. *Latin Christianity: the Old and the New.*

WITH the establishment of the Christian Empire under Constantine and his successors, Christian literature now openly appeared, and it was not long before it won a dominating position. That literature was not a new thing, for, from the second century onwards, Christianity had drawn to itself men of outstanding ability and original power. To speak only of the West—Tertullian, Minucius Felix, Cyprian, Arnobius, and Lactantius were all steeped in the rhetorical tradition of the schools, and wrote for an educated public. They were the bitter adversaries of heathendom, but they recognized that if Christianity was to succeed in capturing the Roman world it must take hold of the best education of the day, and, purging it so far as was possible of its dangerous associations, adapt it to its own uses. To the question put by Tertullian—'Quomodo repudiamus saecularia studia, sine quibus divina non possunt?'[1] —there could be only one reasonable answer. But with the peace of the Church the problem took on a wider aspect. The Church became a vast organization with great basilicas in all the big towns, and large congregations of recent converts also required instruction and admonition by the Bishops, whose task it was to fulfil their apostolic duty of regular preaching and exhortation. The age of the preachers had begun. Basil, Gregory Nazianzen, and John Chrysostom had studied under celebrated teachers.[2] The great Libanius had said, when dying, that Chrysostom would have been his natural successor, 'if the Christians had not stolen him'. The sermons were delivered in church much in the way in which the discourses of the profane rhetoricians were given forth in the lecture rooms. 'The preacher sat in his official chair: it was an exceptional thing for him to ascend the reader's *ambo*, the modern "pulpit": the audience crowded in front of him, and frequently interrupted him with shouts of acclamation. The greater preachers tried to stem the tide of applause which surged round them:

---

[1] *De Spect. XVIII*; cf. *Christian-Latin Poetry*, p. 6.

[2] Hatch, *The Influence of Greek Ideas and Usages upon the Christian Church*, London 1888, p. 109 sqq.

again and again Chrysostom begs his hearers to be silent.'[1] It is the same in the Latin West. Augustine had to say to his applauding audience: 'periculum autem meum est, si adtendam quomodo laudatis et dissimulem quomodo vivatis.'[2] Ambrose also spoke to audiences that listened eagerly to a homily as to a rhetorical exercise. The passion for the spoken word was in their very blood, and they waited in tense excitement for the pointed epigram or for the rimed periods which were worthy of their applause. And the preachers knew that they must be given what they demanded, although they themselves recognized a truer eloquence in the simplicity and grandeur of holy Scripture, in the prophets, in the Psalms, in the Gospels, and in the Epistles.[3] Yet Augustine in his sermons could pile rime upon rime in an array of parallel phrases,[4] and use all the resources of rhetoric in tasteless profusion.[5] These sermons were intended for the more or less educated dwellers in towns, and it was for the same congregations, whose ears were thoroughly accustomed to assonance and rime, that Augustine composed his celebrated rimed and rhythmical *Psalm*.[6] The rime is, indeed, rudimentary, for it consists merely of the device of ending each verse on the letter *e* or *ae*. Precisely the same rime in *e* had been used by Commodian (in the middle of the third century) in one of his acrostics,[7] and in the sixth century it was used by the author of the poem *Ad Flavium Felicem de resurrectione mortuorum*.[8] There are traces of rime in the numerous verse-inscriptions, but it is comparatively rare. The following epitaph on a mare belongs to the early second century. It is in rimed iambic dimeters:

> Gaetula harena prosata,
> Gaetulo equino consita,
> cursando flabris compara,
> aetate abacta virgini
> Speudeusa Lethen incolis.[9]

[1] Hatch, p. 110; in note 2 he observes how 'Augustine makes a fine point of the analogy between the Church and the lecture-room (*schola*): "tanquam vobis pastores sumus, sed sub illo Pastore vobiscum oves sumus. tanquam vobis ex hoc loco doctores sumus, sed sub illo Magistro in hac schola vobiscum condiscipuli sumus." *Enarrat. in Psalm. cxxvi.*'

[2] Augustine, *Sermo* 339, c. i (Migne xxxviii, 1480).

[3] Cf. Augustine, *De Doctr. Christ.*, iv. 6.

[4] Cf. K. Polheim, *Die lateinische Reimprosa*, Berlin 1928, p. 243.

[5] Cf. Norden, p. 623, for examples.

[6] It is true that in his *Retractationes* he says of this *Psalm* that he wished it to come 'ad ipsius humillimi vulgi et omnino imperitorum atque idiotarum notitiam', but this would quite well describe the congregations which listened to his sermons.

[7] *Christian-Latin Poetry*, p. 14.

[8] *C.S.E.L.* iii; *Christian-Latin Poetry* p. 24.

[9] Buecheler, *Carmina Latina Epigraphica* (*Anth. Lat.* ii), Leipzig 1897,

A later example of rime is the couplet,

> Hunc Placentia habet, patria quem Roma creavit,
> marmoreo positum solio, aramque sacravit.[1]

Acrostics and telestichs[2] are very numerous in these inscriptions, but there is no sign of any popular versification not based on quantity.

Many of the acrostics are in Christian inscriptions, but the acrostical form was used equally by profane writers, and was part of the stock-in-trade of versifiers like Porfirius. It is reasonable to assume the same of the alphabetical poem, for Augustine, speaking of his *Psalm*, says, 'Tales autem *abecedarios* appellant', as though it were a familiar form.[3] Hilary of Poitiers, like Augustine, adopted the alphabetical device in two of his hymns, probably for the same reason—that it afforded an aid to the memory of the congregation. Sedulius followed this example, and Bede, who was learned in the history of Christian poetry, thought it worth imitation.[4] So these devices, which were a kind of by-product of the schools of rhetoric, found their way into Christian hymns, and, as we have seen, Christian poets composed Virgilian centos.

Hilary and Ambrose are the real beginners of Latin hymnody in the West. But Hilary made his hymns severely theological and almost obscure, so that they soon ceased to be used in church. Ambrose rejected metrical complication, chose the easy iambic dimeter, and wrote with an engaging simplicity, dignity, and fervour. There are, indeed, touches of rhetoric which might have been extracted from a sermon:

> egressus eius a patre,
> regressus eius ad patrem,
> excursus usque ad inferos,
> recursus ad sedem dei.[5]

or

> hamum profundo merserat,
> piscatus est verbum dei,
> iactavit undis retia,
> vitam levavit omnium.[6]

But here again the Christian idea was making rhetoric its material for the creation of something new and beautiful.

---

no. 218, p. 103; for other examples of rime, see nos. 11, 193, 220, 225, 237, 670, 798, 849.

[1] Buecheler, no. 478, p. 227. Buecheler's note is 'Romae in macello ad arcum Gallieni rep. cippus marmoreus'. It seems to be of the third century.

[2] Cf. in Buecheler nos. 220, 271, 273,

301, 437, 438, 511, 512, 513, 514, 515, 516, 669, 704, 712, 726, 727, 747, 748, 749, 1550.

[3] *Retractationes*, i. 19.

[4] *Christian-Latin Poetry*, p. 148.

[5] *Anal. Hymn.* l, p. 14.

[6] ib.

What an impression of unexpected music breaks in lines like
these:

> Splendor paternae gloriae,
> de luce lucem proferens,
> lux lucis et fons luminis,
> diem dies illuminans;[1]

or in:

> Deus, creator omnium
> polique rector, vestiens
> diem decoro lumine,
> noctem soporis gratia.[2]

These hymns were sung and loved throughout succeeding centuries, and the choice of the iambic dimeter was fortunate, for
the example of Ambrose secured its survival and later adaptation as a rhythmical scheme adorned with rimes. In Prudentius, too, the old and the new are blended. This great Spanish
poet had read his predecessor and fellow-countryman Juvencus,[3] whose versification of the Gospels was an attempt to
provide a Christian epic in Virgilian style. But his own aim
was different; he had something of his own to give in spite of
his profound knowledge of the classical poets and his special
fondness for Seneca and Lucan. It is to his lyrical poetry that
we must look for what is new in power and feeling, derived
from the illumination of Christian thought and emotion. Perhaps we recognize it most easily in the poem set to the measure
of the trochaic tetrameter, that of the popular marching song,
of which Hilary could make nothing, but which Prudentius
handed on, for new and splendid adaptations in the future:

> Corde natus ex parentis ante mundi exordium,
> Alpha et Ω cognominatus, ipse fons et clausula
> omnium quae sunt, fuerunt, quaeque post futura sunt.[4]

New music was to be made out of this rhythm in the days to
come. In Carolingian times they used it for the hymn for the
blessing of the oils, with this refrain,[5]

> o redemptor sume carmen tecum concinentium,

and then in the eleventh century they doubled the first half
of the verse and made rimed couplets,

> Me receptet Sion illa
> Sion David urbs tranquilla;[6]

---

[1] *Anal. Hymn.* l, p. 11.
[2] ib., p. 13.
[3] Manitius, *Christl. Lat. Poesie*, p. 64.

[4] *Cath.* ix. 10 sqq.
[5] *Anal. Hymn.* li, p. 80.
[6] ib. l, p. 411.

or completed the whole scheme while retaining the couplet:

> Salve, mater pietatis
> et totius trinitatis
> nobile triclinium.[1]

Peter Damiani in the eleventh century used the trochaic
tetrameter as the model for his rhythm on the glories of
Paradise:

> Ad perennis vitae fontem mens sitivit arida,
> claustra carnis praesto frangi clausa quaerit anima:
> gliscit, ambit, eluctatur exsul frui patria.[2]

This is the process by which the new arose out of the old in
order to meet the needs of Christian poetry and hymnody;
for the Christian poets demanded and found a greater freedom
in the rhythmical measures which, while they never entirely
drove out the learned metrical verse, were felt alone to be
adequate to convey the profounder emotion—lyrical and, later,
intensely personal—of Catholic Christianity.[3]

The Greek hymn writers seem to have realized this at an
early date, and this is why so much of the liturgical verse
possesses the freedom, the amplitude, and the solemnity of a
choric ode. Is there, too, something oriental, not merely
borrowed from the Psalms, in these vast rhythms with their
magnificent schemes, their endless elaborations, and their
sensuous appeal?[4] The great master of these odes is Romanos,
a Syrian from Emesa, once the city of the sun-god, Elagabalus.
He has been accused of diffuseness,[5] but his inspiration came
in floods and, like an oriental, he saw no virtue in concentration. A quotation, not from Romanos, but from the great
Akathistos Hymn of the Patriarch Sergius,[6] will illustrate the

---

[1] *Anal. Hymn.* liv, p. 383.

[2] ib., xlviii, p. 66.

[3] See *Christian-Latin Poetry*, pp. 27–8.

[4] Cf. now, 'The paper that Romanos swallowed,' *Speculum*, vii (1932), pp. 3 sqq.; on the 'crossing of Greek and Syrian influence' in the Christmas *Kontakion* of Romanos, which begins, 'Η Παρθένος σήμερον τὸν ὑπερούσιον τίκτει. (Text, ed. P. Maas, *Byz. Zeitschr.* xxiv (1923), pp. 1 sqq.)

[5] J. Tixeront, *Précis de Patrologie*, Paris 1918, p. 410. For texts of hymns of Romanos, see J. B. Pitra, *Analecta Sacra Spicilegio Solesmensi parata*, Paris 1876, i, pp. 1 sqq.

[6] Text, Pitra, i, p. 250 sqq.; W. Christ and M. Paranikas, *Anthologia Graeca Carminum Christianorum*, Leipzig 1871, pp. 140 sqq. This hymn was written by Sergius in 626, it would seem, to commemorate the deliverance of the city from the Avars. The suburbs of Constantinople were burnt, but the Church of the Theotokos, the saviour of the city, remained un-harmed. On the hymn, see K. Krumbacher, *Geschichte der Byzantinischen Literatur*, 2nd edit., Munich 1897, pp. 671 sqq.

The use of the rhetorical rime was thoroughly familiar to the Byzantine

sumptuous rhetoric of Byzantine hymnody and offer a striking
contrast to the creations of the contemporary West. The following are the first two stanzas of this ὕμνος τῆς θεοτόκου.

Ἄγγελος πρωτοστάτης οὐρανόθεν ἐπέμφθη
  εἰπεῖν τῇ θεοτόκῳ τό · Χαῖρε!
καὶ σὺν τῇ ἀσωμάτῳ φωνῇ
  σωματούμενόν σε θεωρῶν, Κύριε,
ἐξίστατο καὶ ἵστατο, κραυγάζων πρὸς αὐτὴν τοιαῦτα·
χαῖρε, Δι' ἧς ἡ χαρὰ ἐκλάμψει·
  χαῖρε, Δι' ἧς ἡ ἀρὰ ἐκλείψει·
χαῖρε, τοῦ πεσόντος Ἀδὰμ ἡ ἀνάκλησις·
  χαῖρε, τῶν Δακρύων τῆς Εὔας ἡ λύτρωσις·
χαῖρε, ὕψος Δυσανάβατον   ἀνθρωπίνοις λογισμοῖς·
  χαῖρε, βάθος Δυσθεώρητον   καὶ ἀγγέλων ὀφθαλμοῖς·
χαῖρε, ὅτι ὑπάρχεις   βασιλέως καθέδρα·
  χαῖρε, ὅτι βαστάζεις   τὸν βαστάζοντα πάντα·
χαῖρε, ἀστὴρ ἐμφαίνων τὸν ἥλιον·
  χαῖρε γαστὴρ ἐνθέου σαρκώσεως·
χαῖρε, Δι' ἧς βρεφουργεῖται ὁ κτίστης·
  χαῖρε, νύμφη ἀνύμφευτε.

Βλέπουσα ἡ ἁγία   ἑαυτὴν ἐν ἁγνείᾳ
  φησὶ τῷ Γαβριὴλ θαρσαλέως·
τὸ παράδοξόν σου τῆς φωνῆς
  Δυσπαραδεκτόν μου τῇ ψυχῇ φαίνεται·
ἀσπόρου γὰρ συλλήψεως   τὴν κύησίν πως λέγεις κράζων·
  Ἀλληλούϊα!

It is not without significance that Nicetas, Bishop of Remesi-
ana in Dacia, a province where Greek and Latin were spoken
side by side, did not select a Latin model for his great hymn,
although it was Latin that he used always in his various
writings. He composed his grand *Te Deum* in rhythmical prose,
and so endowed it with a majesty and freedom that no other
hymn of the Latin Church possessed. It is a marvellous
example of an inspiration that does not so much triumph over
the rhetorical temptation which lay so very near as soar
beyond it for ever:

> Tibi omnes angeli, tibi caeli et universae potestates,
>   tibi Cherubin et Seraphin incessabili voce proclamant . . .
>
>   .   .   .   .   .   .
>
> te gloriosus apostolorum chorus,
>   te prophetarum laudabilis numerus,

poets; cf. these verses from the *Akathistos Hymn*,

  χαῖρε, βλαστοῦ ἀμαράντου κλῆμα·
  χαῖρε, καρποῦ ἀκηράτου κτῆμα.

The alphabetical and acrostical constructions were also frequently employed.

te martyrum candidatus laudat exercitus,
te per orbem terrarum sancta confitetur ecclesia . . .

.   .   .   .   .   .

te ergo quaesumus tuis famulis subveni,
quos pretioso sanguine redemisti . . .

But this was an isolated voice, and the schools of rhetoric
persisted, going their old way under the Christian much as
under the heathen Emperors, though there were signs from
time to time that all was not entirely as it had been.

§ 2. *Poets in Gaul.*

(1) *Ausonius and Paulinus of Nola; Rutilius Namatianus.*

From the end of the fourth century onwards the Empire was
unmistakably Christian, and the foundations of the Catholic
order were being laid. Gratian (375–83) was the first 'most
Christian Emperor';[1] Theodosius the Great was taught by
Ambrose the limitations and the responsibilities of his power;
the career of Damasus shadowed forth the possibilities hidden
in the position of the Roman bishop; Jerome provided the
final form of the Latin Bible, and Augustine gave the first
sketch of the idea of the medieval Church. It was a great age
when measured in the terms of men and of forces, and we have
seen how profound was the Christian impress on the new
literature in spite of the survival in undiminished activity of
the old schools of grammar and of rhetoric.

In the two succeeding centuries—the fifth and the sixth—
the old and the new existed side by side. Of this the external
appearance of the city of Rome stands out as a symbol and
a sign. For there the temples, the forums, and the basilicas,
the triumphal arches, the memorial columns, and the theatres
stood as in the days of heathen glory, hardly touched as yet
by the dilapidation which slowly accumulated under the stress
of neglect and poverty. The aqueducts still supplied abundant
water, and the baths were frequented until the Gothic sieges
in the sixth century. The dress of the people was hardly
changed. Each year a consul wore the toga with its purple
border, as did his colleague in the East, and the government
continued in the name of the Senate and the Roman people.

But although Virgil was still declaimed in the forum of
Trajan, the altars of the gods had no incense. The venerable
statue of Victory, the last hope of the great families which still
regretted the old religion, disappeared for ever from the Senate

[1] G. Costa, *Religione e politica nell' impero romano*, Turin 1923, p. 176.

house, and the tombs of apostles and martyrs were the goal of the crowds of strangers filling the streets as of old.

But the breath of antiquity still lingered, and we feel it in the pages of the men who wrote in the service of the new order until the beginning of the seventh century. It is this dying contact with antiquity that we have to trace in the poets who wrote in Gaul, in Africa, and in Italy before the twilight of the seventh century settled on the continental West.

The social and intellectual conditions of Gaul in the later fourth century are mirrored in the pages of Ausonius. The frontier was still secure, although from Trier southwards the towns were surrounded with massive walls. But the Moselle flowed past peaceful and luxurious villas, and the slopes were covered with vineyards that cast their reflection on the river. In spite of earlier economic distress, a measure of the old-time prosperity appeared to have returned. The Gallic aristocracy as never before seemed to be as devoted to letters as to sport or to politics. The famous schools of Gaul not only attracted students from the rest of the Latin-speaking world, but sent professors to Rome and to Constantinople.[1] It was in the schools of Bordeaux that Ausonius was educated, although for a time he studied at Toulouse under his uncle Arborius. About the year 334 he began to teach as a humble grammarian, and he married and prospered. He became a professor of rhetoric, accepted the new Christian order without undue enthusiasm, and won a reputation as a teacher. The death of his wife affected him profoundly, and he did not marry again. His pride in his family, a good Gallic stock unmixed with foreign blood, is shown in his *Parentalia* in which, as he says, he celebrates

nomina carorum iam condita funere iusto,

the names of his dear ones buried decently, and remembered with that 'maesta religio'—his own phrase—that religious sadness, which belonged, as he recognized himself, to the heathen past; for of the *Parentalia* he says: 'antiquae appellationis hic dies et iam inde ab Numa cognatorum inferiis institutus: nec quiquam sanctius habet reverentia superstitum, quam ut amissos venerabiliter recordetur.'

The verses dedicated to these relatives, near or remote, are a charming gallery of portraits or miniatures. 'They enable

[1] For a picture of the social life in Gaul in these days, see Sir S. Dill, *Roman Society in the Last Century of the* *Western Empire*, London 1905, pp. 167 sqq.

us', as Dill has said, 'to imagine how quiet people were living in the last years of Theodosius.'[1] Virtuous and dutiful, these excellent men and admirable women represent the sound and unadventurous element which was the strength of provincial society. It was this society that Ausonius had to leave (*circ.* 364) when Valentinian called him to Trier to become tutor to his son Gratian, the young Augustus. He now became involved in the life of the court. Honours were not long in coming; he was made *comes* and *quaestor sacri palatii*, and Gratian later gave him the prefecture of Gaul, Libya, and Italy (378). His crowning glory was the consulship of 379, but the hard work of the prefecture was perhaps done by his able son Hesperius, who was associated with him in that office. The murder of Gratian in 383 ended these days of dazzling success, but Ausonius went back gladly enough to Bordeaux and his estates by the Garonne. He had friends—among them the great Symmachus —and money enough, and more than enough leisure to compose or revise his verses, those trifles of which he was so vain. For it was on trifles that he exercised his art, and he good-humouredly recognized that he was not concerned with anything higher. At any rate, he was, at least, half serious when, in his dedication of his *Eclogues* to his son Drepanius, he said:

> at nos inlepidum, rudem libellum,
> burras, quisquilias ineptiasque,
> credemus gremio cui fovendum?
> inveni, trepidae silete nugae,
> nec doctum minus et magis benignum,
> quam quem Gallia praebuit Catullo.[2]

And when Symmachus gave him more than handsome praise for his poetry he probably knew the truth. But he was not exempt from vanity and he returned the flattery of Symmachus with such compliments as only a rhetorician could compass without shame.

Ausonius had, of course, a thorough knowledge of most of the Latin poets. As M. Pichon has said,[3] 'Son style, bourré de citations, de plagiats et de pastiches, est bien celui d'un vieux professeur qui a la tête meublée d'expressions consacrées, et qui croit rendre aux auteurs qu'il a si longtemps expliqués un suprême hommage en pensant et en parlant sans cesse d'après eux.' For Ausonius was always the professor of rhetoric, and

---

[1] Dill, p. 170.
[2] xxiii (p. 120); cf. *Epist.* viii. 14 (p. 166). I use Schenkl's ed., *M.G.H.*,

Auct. Antiq. v, ii.
[3] R. Pichon, *Les derniers écrivains profanes*, Paris 1906, p. 155 sq.

intellectually he never looked beyond the school. So he catalogued in verse the professors of Bordeaux whom he had known
either personally or by report. He can be forgiven for this,
since, in spite of tedious rhetoric, we can piece together a great
deal that is of value about the schools and the society of
provincial towns. Christianity had, as yet, made no profound
impression on these hard-working and somewhat pedantic
lovers of ancient mythology, who, like Ausonius, went willingly each year to the services of the Easter festival,[1] and
would have nothing to do with Arianism, but looked askance
at asceticism. In these poems on grammarians and rhetors
Ausonius adopts the conventional pagan attitude of doubt as
to the survival of anything 'when the funeral pyre was out
and the last valediction over':

> et nunc, sive aliquid post fata extrema superfit,
>   vivis adhuc aevi, quod periit, meminens:
> sive nihil superest nec habent longa otia sensus,
>   tu tibi vixisti: nos tua fama iuvat.[2]

In the *Ephemeris*, an account of the doings of a typical day
in town, Ausonius shows us this mixture of pagan and of formal
Christian feeling. He begins in sapphics with the break of day
and an address to his lazy servant, Parmeno, who sleeps like
Endymion, endlessly; not under Luna's incantation, or like
dormice that sleep and take no food, but because he eats and
drinks too much. Perhaps, he reflects, the sapphics are too
soothing; will the quick iambic wake him? In iambic dimeters
he calls for shoes and clothes and water to wash his hands and
face. The oratory is to be opened so that he may say his
morning prayer, not with incense or cake of honey, but with
pure words to God and the Son of God Most High and the
Holy Spirit. A long dogmatic prayer in hexameters follows;
it is little more than a school exercise with an assortment of
scholastic commonplaces on the virtuous life. So,

> satis precum datum deo,

and it is time to go out and say good-day to his friends. But
Sosias the cook must have his orders for luncheon, as guests
are expected. Then the shorthand writer is called in, a clever

---

[1] Cf. *Epist.* viii. 9–10 (p. 166):
instantis revocant quia nos sollemnia
    Paschae
libera nec nobis est mora desidiae.
But on this see P. de Labriolle, *La*
*correspondance d'Ausone et de Paulin
de Nole*, Paris 1910, p. 58.
[2] *Prof. Burdigal.* ii. 39–42 (p. 56);
cf. xxiii. 22 (p. 70); xxiv. 13 (p. 70);
xxvii. 7–8 (p. 71).

boy, who anticipates his thoughts and has them fixed in wax almost before he utters them in words. This idea pleased Ausonius and he proceeded to expand it with futile elaboration:

> quis, quaeso, quis me prodidit?
> quis ista iam dixit tibi,
> quae cogitabam dicere?
> quae furta corde in intimo
> exercet ales dextera?
> quis ordo rerum tam novus,
> veniat in aures ut tuas
> quod lingua nondum absolverit?
> doctrina non hoc praestitit
> nec ulla tam velox manus
> celeripedis compendii:
> natura munus hoc tibi
> deusque donum tradidit,
> quae loquerer ut scires prius,
> idemque velles quod volo.[1]

Mere school exercises are the tetrastichs on the Caesars—with a mnemotechnic poem containing the names and order of the first twelve. Then follow similar epigrams on the Caesars after the time of Suetonius, from Nerva to Elagabalus. These exercises are as useless as the epitaphs on the heroes of the Trojan war, which Ausonius translated from the Greek, but he may have thought that the information conveyed was sufficient justification of his labours. The fashion of setting all kinds of themes to verse with such an end in view was taken by the Middle Ages from the practice of the school poets of late antiquity. The *Idylls* and *Eclogues* of Ausonius provide good examples of this kind. Thus he writes on the 'Yes' and 'No' of Pythagoras, on the ages of man and other living things (from Hesiod), on the pound (or balance), on childbirth, on the names of the days of the week, on the months, and other lore of the calendar, on the games of ancient Greece, on the Roman festivals, on the labours of Hercules.

Those who have patience to study Ausonius' *Technopaegnion* will discover that it is an exercise in verses ending with monosyllables. The piece is dedicated to Pacatus, the proconsul, whose virtue will make them something more than monosyllables. 'Tu facies', he says, 'ut sint aliquid: nam sine te monosyllaba erunt vel si quid minus.' Although the production may look like play, it has meant much labour; if it looks too much

---

[1] *Epigr.* cxiv (p. 226); but this piece is not always regarded as belonging to this series.

like hard work, it is really play. The smallest section of this poem (which deals with such subjects as the parts of the body, the gods, foods, legends; monosyllables in Greek and Latin) gives quite a sufficient idea of the whole. The subject is early spring:

> annus ab exortu cum floriparum reserat ver,
> cuncta vigent: nemus omne viret, nitet auricomum rus
> et fusura umbras radicitus exigitur stirps.
> non denso ad terram lapsu glomerata fluit nix.
> florum spirat odor, Libani ceu montis honor tus.

The *Cento nuptialis*, made up from tags of Virgil pieced together with incredible ingenuity, reflects no credit on the author, who, although he excuses himself by the plea that the Emperor Valentinian of sacred memory had commanded it, and by that other plea,

> lasciva est nobis pagina, vita proba,

yet complacently dedicates it to Paulus, years after it has been written and laid aside among other scraps of verse.

Like most school poets, Ausonius composed numerous epigrams, and following a tradition, which he helped to hand on to the Middle Ages, he gave them a sprinkling of obscenity. This was not so much perverseness as the blind imitation enjoined by the schools. We shall meet with it again in men who were more closely touched by religion than Ausonius ever claimed to be.

His most considerable poem is the long description of the Moselle. It is composed according to the precepts of the schools, and doubtless the poet had examples to follow, as the description of natural scenery in verse or in prose was an obvious theme for composition. An analysis of the poem will show its thoroughly artificial structure; it is not a progressive and coherent unity, but is, like most rhetorical compositions, a collection of parts or episodes. The exordium sets forth the poet's journey to the Moselle; his sight of the river and of the landscape that reminded him of his own country. Then the river itself is addressed in an apostrophe which is also a fairly complete description of the Moselle, including the means and methods of navigation. 'Thou must oft-times wonder at thine own windings and think that thy stream flows too slowly.' Then there is a long list of the fishes to be caught, with a precise description of each. The Naiad dwelling in the stream is asked to tell the catalogue, and the fishes are addressed in turn—the barbel, the salmon, the perch, the eel-pout, and

the sheat-fish!'[1] A rhetorical transition follows, which is medi-
ated in a too obvious manner:

> iam liquidas spectasse vias et lubrica pisces
> agmina multiplicesque satis numerasse catervas.
> inducant aliam spectacula vitea pompam . . .[2]

The tale is now of the gifts of Bacchus, that is of the vineyards
on the terraced slopes. Now is the opportunity for learned
allusions and mythological excursions. Yet, for a moment,
Ausonius remembers his own loved Garonne, and the way the
vineyards are reflected in the yellow waters:

> sic mea flaventem pingunt vineta Garumnam.

Then he pictures the banks covered with vines; the husband-
men working with happy shouts, while the passer-by on
the bank below and the boatman floating along exchange
their coarse pleasantries with the men above, late at their
work.

Next there is an elaborate and ingenious description of the
reflection of the landscape in the water. The hills float on the
river, vines and grapes are seen in the water, so that the boatman is deceived and counts the green vines as he floats past:

> tota natant crispis iuga motibus et tremit absens
> pampinus et vitreis vindemia turget in undis.
> adnumerat virides derisus navita vites—
> navita caudiceo fluitans super aequora lembo,
> per medium, qua sese amni confundit imago
> collis et umbrarum confinia conserit amnis.[3]

After a description of mimic combats on the river, Ausonius
goes back to the fishes, and tells how they are caught by net
and rod. Then he talks of the estates and villas that crown the
banks. The architecture is worthy of the 'winged man of
Gortyn' ('Gortynius aliger') or of 'Cecropian Philo' or of
Archimedes, or of several others who are mentioned by name,
with learned allusions. After much description Ausonius gives
a list of the tributaries of the Moselle, and it is long before he
cries to his muse to lay aside the lyre. But, even after this,
nearly a hundred verses follow—his peroration, his final praise
of 'corniger Mosella'!

The *Moselle* must have delighted his contemporaries, and

---

[1] I take the names from Mr. H. G.
Evelyn White's translation in the Loeb
Library.

[2] *Mosella*, 150–2 (p. 87).

[3] *Mosella*, 194–9 (p. 88); as Mr. Evelyn White points out, Pope imitated this
passage in *Windsor Forest*.

it has had a good deal of praise in our own day. But it is essentially a collection of episodes, strung together after the fashion of the schools. Ausonius had an incurable frivolity which clung to all his work, and he could not see beyond that little world in which the trivial was enthroned in the place meant, as it seemed to some of his contemporaries, for the eternal. This is why he could not understand his dear friend and pupil, Paulinus, who forsook everything that made up life as Ausonius knew it, and deserted Apollo for Christ. Pontius Meropius Anicius Paulinus[1] was, like Ausonius, a native of Bordeaux, and he belonged to a rich and noble family. Ausonius taught him all he knew and trained him, successfully as he believed, to spend his time in the versification of trifles. His affectionate pupil once sent him a long poem called *De regibus*, a versification of a book by Suetonius on the lives of kings.[2] Ausonius was delighted; the poem must be answered by a poem, but it is a poem which breaks into prose in praise of the genius of one who could write lines like these:

> Europamque Asiamque duo vel maxima terrae
> membra, quibus Libyam dubie Sallustius addit
> Europae adiunctam, possit cum tertia dici,
> regnatas multis, quos fama oblitterat et quos
> barbara Romanae non tradunt nomina linguae—
> Illibanum Numidamque Avelim Parthumque Vononem
> et Caranum, Pellaea dedit qui nomina regum,
> quique magos docuit mysteria vana Nechepsos
> et qui regnavit sine nomine moxque Sesostris . . .[3]

'Haec tu quam perite et concinne,' says Ausonius, 'quam modulate et dulciter, ita iuxta naturam Romanorum accentuum enuntiasti, ut tamen veris et primigenis vocibus sua fastigia non perirent. iam quid de eloquentia dicam? liquido adiurare possum nullum tibi ad poeticam facundiam Romanae iuventutis aequari: certe ita mihi videris.'

He speaks, he says, with the feelings natural to a father. Paulinus is his favourite son.

Ausonius had proudly watched his career—first his brilliance in the schools, next the consulship, and the governorship of Campania. But Paulinus married a rich and pious lady, Therasia, in whom Ausonius saw the cause of the silence and estrangement which ensued when husband and wife retired to their estates in Spain. 'Tanaquil tua' Ausonius called her, in the first letter

---

[1] The best biographical sketch is by A. Baudrillart, *S. Paulin, évêque de Nole*, Paris 1914 (3rd edit.).

[2] *Epist.* xix (p. 179).

[3] There are two other poems of Paulinus written before his conversion. They accompany a gift of birds and of oysters; *Paulani Nolani Carmina*, ii. 1–2 (*C.S.E.L.* xxx).

that has survived of the strange poetical correspondence between the old rhetor and his 'son'.[1] In the next letter[2] Ausonius tries to coax his friend by employing those devices which he had learned to use so skilfully in the schools. 'Why have you not answered? Even enemies say *salve* to each other in battle. Rocks and caves are not so rude as to refuse to echo the human voice. The cliffs by the sea make a sound, the rivers murmur', and so on. *Nil mutum natura dedit.* 'Cymbals, the stage beneath the dancers' feet, the stretched skins of a drum, the sistra and other religious instruments all make a noise.' After this Ausonius resorts to mythological and historical allusion, ending with an appeal to the 'Boeotia numina, Musae', to bring back the poet.

Could he resist the appeal of these familiar things? Well, Paulinus did not answer him in cold prose, but none the less he replied in a manner that left no room for doubt:

> Quid abdicatas in meam curam, pater,
>   redire Musas praecipis?
> negant Camenis nec patent Apollini
>   dicata Christo pectora.

Once he and Ausonius had agreed together to summon the deaf Apollo from his Delphic cave, but now a greater God claims him, who demands again from man the gift He gave, 'that we may live unto the Father of life'. God forbids us to spend our lives on fables; His will is that we shall obey His laws and see His light, which is only darkened by sophistry and rhetoric and the vain inventions of poets. This is Paulinus' answer to the blandishments of Ausonius, who did not know that he had now to deal with a saint. What did Ausonius think, we may wonder, of the hymn to Christ that follows—Christ as the revelation of God?

> Hic veritatis lumen est, vitae via,
>   vis, mens, manus, virtus patris,
> sol aequitatis, fons bonorum, flos dei,
>   natus deo, mundi sator,
> mortalitatis vita nostrae et mors necis.
>   magister hic virtutium,

---

[1] *Epist.* xxxiii (p. 186); I follow here the chronology set forth conveniently by Labriolle, *La correspondance d'Ausone et de Paulin de Nola*, Paris 1910, p. 52. Schenkl, Schanz, and others agree in adopting it. According to this scheme Ausonius wrote first a letter which failed to reach Paulinus; then a second letter which reached Paulinus at the same time as letters xxviii and xxix. In xxix Ausonius tells us that it is his *fourth* letter. Paulinus replies in *Carmen* x. Ausonius answers with *Epist.* xxvii. Paulinus finally replies in *Carmen* xi.

[2] *Epist.* xxiv (p. 187), the fourth letter.

deusque nobis atque pro nobis homo
    nos induendus induit,
aeterna iungens homines inter et deum
    in utrumque se commercia.

Paulinus is given up to Christ, but he is not, therefore, guilty of impiety towards his 'father' Ausonius. How can a Christian lack 'pietas'? and how can he fail in love to one to whom he owes everything—'disciplinas, dignitatem, litteras'? If he lives in retirement it is because he pleases to do so.

But still Ausonius could not understand. He only sees the end of a friendship in which each had borne an equal yoke, while Concord held the reins. Their own fathers had been friends—but Ausonius cannot speak long without falling back into the tricks of the school, and he drags out his complaint with all the mythological examples he can muster—Peirithous and Theseus, Euryalus and Nisus, Pylades and Orestes, Damon and Pithias, and even Scipio and Laelius. Then he remembers, and calls on the Father and Son to restore his dear Paulinus, who has forgotten his old friends and has forsaken them for strangers. Perhaps one day he will hear some one say: 'Paulinus is coming. He has left Spain, his boat is in sight, he has landed, he has passed his own house and now knocks at your door.'

credimus? an, qui amant, ipsi sibi somnia fingunt?

The reply of Paulinus is the last letter of this correspondence that has survived. It was the year 393; Ausonius was now in extreme old age, and it was doubtless his death soon after that closed the exchange of letters for ever. Paulinus was profoundly affected by the accusation that he had failed as a friend, and he felt that Ausonius laid a large share of the blame to the charge of his wife. He will have no veiled accusations against Therasia—

formidatamque iugalem
obicis et durum iacis in mea viscera versum.

This said, he is all tenderness again, and he reminds Ausonius that a father's words should not be steeped in bitterness—like wormwood mixed with honey. For Ausonius is still revered as a father; not by Paulinus only, but by his household, which is joined together in this as it is in the worship of Christ. Ausonius has been led by lying reports to vent his bitterness on Therasia, and to accuse Paulinus of what amounts to ingratitude. Then—sincerely—he says that the complaint that he had refused to bear the yoke of learned studies with which

he had been joined with Ausonius is beside the point. He
never bore that yoke, because he was never the equal of his
master; descending to rhetoric, he proceeds in the way Ausonius loved, to elaborate the theme—do you compare a calf
with a bull, a horse with a wild ass, moorhens with swans,
nightingales with owls, hazels with chestnuts, bushes with
cypresses? The only yoke he will recognize is the yoke of
love, for there the lowly and the great can join. Then Paulinus
leaves the hexameter and in grave iambics, simple and won-
derfully touching, he tells Ausonius of his unchanging and
unchangeable affection:

> Ego te per omne quod datum mortalibus
>   et destinatum saeculum est,
> claudente donec continebor corpore,
>   discernar orbe quamlibet,
> nec orbe longe nec remotum lumine
>   tenebo fibris insitum:
> videbo corde, mente complectar pia
>   ubique praesentem mihi.
> et cum solutus corporali carcere
>   terraque provolavero,
> quo me locavit axe communis pater,
>   illic quoque animo te geram;
> neque finis idem qui meo me corpore
>   et amore laxabit tuo.
> mens quippe, lapsis quae superstes artubus
>   de stirpe durat caeliti,
> sensus necesse est simul et adfectus suos
>   teneat aeque ut vitam suam,
> et ut mori, sic oblivisci non capit,
>   perenne vivax et memor.

It is as if Paulinus were paying Ausonius in the purest coin of
the old world that was now passing. He says nothing more
than any Neoplatonist of a generation before might have said—
'solutus corporali carcere', 'communis pater', 'de stirpe durat
caeliti'—all this is shared with the enlightened beliefs of
heathendom, and is devised thus tenderly by Paulinus to soften
what he has to say.

Not long afterwards Paulinus and Therasia left Spain, and
gave themselves entirely to the life of religon at Nola in Campania. The death of their only child had broken the last tie
that kept them in the world. Under the protection of their
saint, Felix, to whom Paulinus had been dedicated in his
youth,[1] they lived a life of devotion and of good works. In

409 the people made Paulinus their Bishop. When he died in 431 the Jews and the heathen mourned him as their father.

This episode of Ausonius and Paulinus is instructive as a sign of the change that was falling across the Western world. The old civilization was still in being, but the finer spirits knew that they could find no satisfaction in the old paths. In spite of the troubles that descended on Gaul, culminating in the setting up of a Visigothic kingdom, the Gallic aristocracy were able to pursue a life of leisure and of literary trifling. But nearly all the poets whose works have survived followed the spirit of Paulinus' example and devoted themselves to the Church. Claudius Rutilius Namatianus may perhaps be accounted an exception; but, although he wrote his poem *De reditu suo* in 416, he belongs to the old order. This able and intelligent man was *magister officiorum* and had been *praefectus urbi*. He travelled back from Rome to his native Gaul by sea, and when he reached his estates he employed his leisure in describing his journey in a long elegiac poem. The first book and part of the second have alone survived. The poem is well known for its expression of that deep feeling for Rome which filled the hearts of men throughout the provinces of the West. It is, in addition, a good example of an interesting literary *genre*, the description of a journey, of which the author had examples before him in Horace and in Ovid. It is worthy of note that Rutilius expresses his hatred of the Jews as well as of the monks who were now forming settlements on the islands, in search of solitary places:

> processu pelagi iam se Capraria tollit;
>   squalet lucifugis insula plena viris.
> ipsi se monachos Graio cognomine dicunt,
>   quod soli nullo vivere teste volunt.
> munera fortunae metuunt, dum damna verentur:
>   quisquam sponte miser, ne miser esse queat?
> quaenam perversi rabies tam stulta cerebri,
>   dum mala formides, nec bona posse pati?[1]

But Rutilius cried against the new order in vain. At Nola Paulinus showed how the arts learned in the schools could be turned to other uses. He heads the long line of Christian rhetoricians who proceeded from the schools of Gaul. His hexameter poem on John the Baptist[2] is an excellent example of traditional rhetoric adapted to Christian uses. It is a narrative in epic form, a succession of episodes adorned with numerous rhetorical speeches. This is the old receipt for the

---

[1] *Poet. Lat. Min.* v. 20.   [2] *Paulini Opera*, ii. 7.

epic, employed ever since Lucan by generations of versifiers. The speeches are just such as the students might have been called upon to compose in the schools, in spite of the fact that the Gospels provided the material. In order to realize how compelling was the impulse to rhetorical treatment, even where the subject-matter and the fine simplicity of the Gospel narrative might have suggested a reverent restraint, one should study the whole of the speech of the angel of the Annunciation to Mary:

> ille ait: o toto quem solis circulus ambit,
> quaeque fuere prius, quae sunt, quae deinde sequentur,
> virginibus cunctis felicior orbe puella,
> magno lecta deo, mater dicaris ut eius,
> cuius et ille pater! felix age concipe pondus,
> inpolluta viro coituque inmunis ab omni,
> verbo feta dei; corpus tua viscera praestent
> illi, qui caelum terras mare sidera fecit,
> qui semper fuit et nunc est et tempore in omni
> semper erit mundi dominus lucisque creator.
> et lux ipse poli per te mortalia membra
> induet atque oculos hominum coetusque subibit.
> inperturbatos tantarum in praemia laudum
> tolle animos; dabit ille tibi viresque fidemque,
> qui voluit (nam cuncta regit nutuque gubernat)
> filius esse tuus, domini cum filius esset.[1]

The fifth century in Gaul was the great age of Christian poets. They were all accomplished rhetoricians who used their gifts with the practical aim of edification and exhortation. But we are not here concerned with their work, except in so far as they illustrate the continued existence of the rhetorical tradition, or themselves wandered into secular or semi-secular verse.

§3. Poets in Gaul.

(2) Fifth-century Christian Rhetoricians.

During the political troubles of the fifth century the public schools disappeared,[2] but in spite of danger and disorder education had to be provided for: and here and there a few professors kept schools for those who were willing and able to attend. So we hear of Sapandus lecturing at Vienne, where Avitus, the future Bishop, was one of his pupils,[3] and there

---

[1] *Paulini Opera*, ii. 11; p. 12 for Elizabeth's greeting to Mary.

[2] Roger, *L'enseignement des lettres classiques d'Ausone à Alcuin*, Paris 1905, pp. 56, 82.

[3] For references see Goelzer and Mey, *Le Latin de S. Avit*, Paris 1909, p. 4. Apollinaris Sidonius (*Epist.* v. 10, p. 85) expresses much admiration for Sapandus, to whom he writes: 'tua vero tam clara, tam spectabilis dictio est', etc. On the schools at Périgueux

were others who helped to keep alive the tradition of letters. But the ravages of Vandals and Huns were soon repaired, and the settlements of Visigoths and Burgundians did not seriously interefere with the habits of the cultivated Gallic aristocracy.[1] Yet the insecurity, the economic distress of the masses, and the deeds of violence that followed these invasions made a profound impression on the writers of this age. Paulinus (perhaps the Paulinus who was Bishop of Béziers about the year 400) wrote a poetical dialogue (*circ.* 408) between two monks, a 'father' and his visitor, a young man, Salmon.[2] The older man asks how Salmon fares in his own monastery. He answers that the barbarian has overrun the land, its fields, and villas, but worse than Sarmatians, Vandals, and Alans is the inward evil (*interior pestis*) of sin. He proceeds then to a bitter satirical attack on individuals disguised under the names of Pedius, Polio, and Albus:

> moechus erat Pedius: moechatur, durat in isdem
> leprae dum furiis; livebat Polio: livet;
> Albus, cunctorum quondam captator honorum,
> orbis in excidio minus ambitione laborat?[3]

This is the first voice of serious indignation that a poet had raised for many generations, although, if Paulinus had been a student of sermons, he might have found material to hand. He next attacks women, although he admits that men abet them in their vices. Instead of reading Paul and Solomon, they love to hear about Virgil's Dido or Ovid's Corinna, and they fill the theatres where the mimes of Marullus are played.[4]

The 'father' remarks that there are still many good people in the world, and Salmo willingly admits it. This is, he says, his only consolation. Then, as he asks the 'father' to tell his own story, the poem breaks off with a promise that this shall be done next day.

Not long after Paulinus, another Gallic poet[5] wrote a religious poem, *De providentia divina*,[6] in which he revolved the problems raised by the terrible ravages of the barbarians, who had

see E. Labroue, *L'école de Périgueux au Ve siècle*, in *Atti del congresso internazionale di scienze storiche*, ii, Rome 1905, pp. 161 sqq.

[1] Dill, *Roman Society in the Last Century of the Western Empire*, p. 190, points out that 'the similarity between the world of Ausonius and that of Sidonius is very remarkable'.

[2] *S. Paulini Epigramma*, ed. Schenkl,

C.S.E.L. xvi, pp. 503 sqq.

[3] *Paulini Epigramma*, 35–8.

[4] Marullus, a writer of mimes, lived in the second century. He was, evidently, still popular centuries after.

[5] It has been conjectured that the author was Prosper of Aquitaine; see Manitius, *Christl. Lat. Poesie*, p. 171. The date is about 416.

[6] Migne, li, cols. 617 sqq.

spared neither old nor young, and made no distinction between priests or bishops and common folk. In simple elegiacs he proceeds with his catalogue of wrong, and shows how even in time of peace the same problem of evil is presented. We need not follow the details of this remarkable poem, but we must note that it begins in good Ovidian elegiacs, and then, when the time comes for the reply—the justification of the ways of God— the poet changes his metre and adopts the hexameter, which does not delay the full sweep of the argument:

> at ne sermo moram patiatur ab impare versu,
> herois numeris porrige, pentametrum.

Orientius, another Gallic poet, who wrote a didactic *Commonitorium*,[1] chose the elegiac for his series of moral exhortations. He knew the *De providentia divina*, and, in the stress of invasions, had similar problems to solve. Neither poet wasted time on rhetorical trifling, and both of them can be read with pleasure at the present day.[2]

Claudius Marius Victor, a rhetor of Marseilles, composed a poem called *Alethia*, in which he deals with events in the Book of Genesis until the death of Abraham. It is almost to be described as a philosophical poem; the action is not of first importance, the implications and the exposition are everything. If it is rhetorical, it does not descend to the level of Ausonius. It is always well conceived, and the author consciously made a demand on his readers' intelligence. The speeches are elaborately constructed, though without affectation, but occasionally the poet attempts a more daring point. God is pronouncing sentence on the fallen angels—the sentence and the creation of Hell are one,

> dumque reos punit sententia, Tartara fecit.[3]

Or Marius Victor is describing the world outside the gates of Paradise; Adam and Eve look on the rough jungle that meets them, and 'ah! with what eyes, with what feelings do they look on this sight, in whose hearts paradise still lives!'

> heu quibus haec spectant oculis, quo pectore cernunt,
> quorum animis paradisus inest! neque causa doloris
> una subest, quod cunctorum iam plena malorum
> se pandit facies, sed, quod meminere bonorum.
> nunc honor ille sacri nemoris maiore sereno

---

[1] Ed. Robinson Ellis, *C.S.E.L.* xvi, pp. 205 sqq.

[2] Orientius shows borrowings from Virgil and Ovid; also Horace, Martial, Lucan, Juvenal, and the *Disticha*

Catonis; see Manitius, *Christl. Lat. Poesie*, p. 199 sq.

[3] *Cl. Marii Victoris Alethias Lib.* i. 474 (*C.S.E.L.* xvi, p. 381).

> inradiat, nunc divitias cumulatior edit
> silva beata suas, nunc pomis dulcior usus
> nectareusque sapor, vivis nunc floribus halat
> tellus et absenti tristes perstringit odore.[1]

This is thoroughly rhetorical, with its rime and its periods leading up to the final *sententia*,

> et absenti tristes perstringit odore,

which in a public declamation would draw the expected applause. But who will say that it is not a just and eloquent elaboration, an excellent substitute for poetry itself?

Hilary, Bishop of Arles in 429, who composed an ingenious epigram on the 'burning fountain' of S. Bartholomew near Grenoble—

> si vere exurunt ignes, cur vivitis, undae?
> si vere extinguunt undae, cur vivitis, ignes?[2]—

also wrote and dedicated to Pope Leo a poem on the Creation,[3] which is conceived in the spirit of Lucretius and does not follow the narrative of Genesis very closely. The rhetorician peeps out in many passages. The following is a curious example, addressed to the Creator:[4]

> tunc 'faciamus', ais, 'hominem'. dic, optime, cum quo
> conloqueris? clarum est: iam tum tibi filius alto
> adsidet in solio et terras spectat amicas.

The *Heptateuchos* of Cyprian is merely a plain versification of the Old Testament from Genesis to Judges. The narrative proper is in hexameters, but the poet had the happy idea of rendering the songs, such as the canticle of Moses, in hendecasyllabics.

Although his years of literary activity fell towards the end of the fifth and the beginning of the sixth century, Saint Avitus belongs to this group of 'epic' poets, who illustrate so well the passing over of the old rhetoric into Christian uses.

Alcimus Ecdicius Avitus, who succeeded his father as Bishop of Vienne in 470, belonged to the Gallic aristocracy, and if in prose he was an exponent of the worst excesses of an age of declining taste, he kept to the older tradition in his verse.[5] His hexameter poem in five books (on the Creation, on Original Sin, on the Sentence of God, on the Deluge, and on the Crossing of the Red Sea) is a collection of episodes accompanied by speeches and digressions in the best rhetorical manner. But Avitus is

---

[1] ib. ii. 15–23 (pp. 384–5).
[2] Riese, *Anth. Lat.*, no. 487.
[3] *Hilarii Genesis, C.S.E.L.* xxiii, pp. 231 sqq.

[4] ib. 116–18 (p. 235).
[5] Cf. Manitius, *Christl. Lat. Poesie*, p. 242; and *Christian-Latin Poetry*, p. 109.

master of his material, and has something to tell us. He composed his verses with great sureness and good taste, and his rhetorical devices are quite legitimate. Most remarkable, in this connexion, are the numerous speeches with which the narrative is broken. When Satan sees the newly created man and woman in Paradise he breaks into a long soliloquy—an exercise in an imaginary situation, which Avitus handles as he had often handled such themes in the schools. The beginning of the speech is enough to raise the familiar echo of the old declamations:[1]

> pro dolor! hoc nobis subitum consurgere plasma
> invisumque genus nostra crevisse ruina!
> me celsum virtus habuit, nunc ecce reiectus
> pellor et angelico limus succedit honori.
> caelum terra tenet, vili conpage levata
> regnat humus nobisque perit translata potestas.
> non tamen in totum periit: pars magna retentat
> vim propriam summaque cluit virtute nocendi.

Similarly the speeches made by God to Eve, Adam, and the Serpent after the fall are developed in this rhetorical manner.[2] Thoroughly scholastic too is the long digression in the second book on the subject of magic, astrology, and serpent-charming.[3] There is also a description of the Nile, one of the rivers of Paradise, which is so elaborate that it probably owes something to an earlier poem on the subject. The description of rivers, as we have seen,[4] was a favourite subject in later Latin poetry, and it must have been practised in the schools.

A close study of the language and expresssion of the poem shows how the mind of the author moved in the circle of rhetoric. This is his description of the flooding of the Nile:

> caeloque vacante
> terrestrem pluviam diffusus porrigit amnis.[5]

Or again it is the Tower of Babel,

> cum fureret mortale genus cassoque labore
> inrita transcensis caementa inferret in altum
> nubibus et refugum sequeretur machina caelum.[6]

Or (in the poem to his sister) Avitus is describing the earthquake and darkness at the crucifixion:

> nam sol obductus vultumque retortus ab orbe
> cesserat iniustas nocturnis luctibus horas

[1] *Alcimi Ecdicii Aviti Opera*, ed. Peiper, *M.G.H., Auct. Antiq.* vi. 2, p. 214.

[2] iii. 81 sqq. (pp. 226 sqq.).

[3] ii. 277 sqq. (p. 219 sq.).

[4] See above, p. 59.

[5] i. 268–9 (p. 210).

[6] iv. 118–20 (p. 239).

atque peregrinis aditum dabat ipse tenebris.
temporibus magno mutatis ordine rerum
nox erat in superis lucemque inferna videbant.[1]

Viventiolus, a rhetor of Lyons, once spread a report that, in his sermon at the dedication of the new basilica in that city, Avitus had committed a false quantity, saying *potītur* for *potĭtur*. He ought, according to Viventiolus, to have followed Virgil's example in his *vi potĭtur* (*Aen.* iii. 56). Avitus answers seriously and learnedly in a studied letter, meant for the admiration of his friends and of posterity. He points out that Virgil often, 'poematis necessitate', alters the natural quantity of a syllable and he gives examples. But as in *potiris* the middle syllable is long, so it is in *potitur*. If you say *potĭtur*, you must also say *potĭris*, which is repugnant to all example and practice—'quod utique ab omni exemplo atque usu integritas Latinitatis excludit'. After a little further argument, he asks the rhetorician, in the most friendly manner possible, to be good enough to answer him.[2]

The other Christian poets of the century need not detain us long, for we have already sufficiently illustrated the manner in which the rhetorical practice was maintained in the fifth century. Prosper of Aquitaine (b. *circ.* 400) is more of a theologian than a poet; his one aim was to attack the Pelagian heresy. His *De Ingratis* is a long attack on Semipelagians. The book of epigrams is interesting because it is a versification of *sententiae* from Augustine;[3] it was just the kind of thing that the medieval schoolmaster delighted in, and had a great success as a school book in the Middle Ages.[4] It is of course a Christian successor of the ingenious exercises of Ausonius or of the young Paulinus of Nola, which have already been described,[5] and so carries on the tradition of the schools.

Paulinus of Pella (b. *circ.* 376) was a grandson of Ausonius. He was born at Pella while his father was Prefect of Macedonia;

---

[1] vi. 231–5 (p. 281 sq.). It is interesting to note that in this poem to his sister (*De Virginitate*), who had entered the religious life, Avitus exhorts her to read (among other things) the Christian poets:

nec, si quid sacrum nostri cecinere
    poetae,
te latet (vi. 409–10, p. 287).

But the only Christian poet to whom he refers and the one he seems to have known best is Prudentius:

discribens mentis varias cum corpore
    pugnas

prudenti quondam cecinit Prudentius arte (vi. 371–2, p. 285);
though he knew as well Sedulius and Juvencus and the poem *De ave Phoenice:* see Goelzer and Mey, *Le Latin de S. Avit*, Paris 1909, p. 7.

[2] *Epist.* lvii (pp. 85–6).

[3] Migne, li, cols. 499 sqq.

[4] Manitius, *Christl. Lat. Poesie*, p. 202.

[5] See above, pp. 58 and 61, for Ausonius's verses on the Caesars and Paulinus's poem based on the *de Regibus* of Suetonius.

his mother was a Greek lady of good birth. As a boy he came to his grandfather's house at Bordeaux, and in the schools of that city he painfully learned the language of Virgil. He already knew Greek, which he had picked up easily from the Macedonian servants of his childhood:

> nec sero exacto primi mox tempore lustri
> dogmata Socratus et bellica plasmata Homeri
> erroresque legens cognoscere cogor Ulixis.
> protinus et libros etiam transire Maronis
> vix bene conperto iubeor sermone Latino.

So he describes his studies in his *Eucharisticus*,[1] a poem written in his eighty-fourth year, when he looked back, in thanksgiving and gratitude to God, on a life of many changes, misfortunes, and spiritual blessings. The poem is a 'confession'—a thanksgiving in the form of an autobiography, like the *Confessions* of Augustine, and it has, therefore, a reality that compels attention. Whether the choice of verse was happy may well be doubted, but the temptation was great, and if Paulinus had not written in verse his 'little meditation, which he dedicated to Almighty God',[2] and which contains so much useful historical material, it might not have attracted enough interest to secure its preservation to our own time. Paulinus is modest about his literary attainments; he thinks that he did make some progress in his studies under the instruction of Greek and Latin professors,

> Argolico pariter Latioque instante magistro,

but a severe attack of fever about his fifteenth year set him back, and he was not allowed to work hard again. Instead he took to outdoor sports, to the hunting in which his father delighted, to racing, and to tennis. His marriage put an end to more questionable pastime, and he settled down to the quiet and sometimes strenuous life of a country estate. But the death of his father and the inroads of the barbarians were the beginning of evil days. He lost his property at the hands of Goths, went through dangerous adventures at the siege of Bazas, and was long in learning that it was for his own good that he was deprived of things that were perishable:

> sero quidem, sed nil unquam, deus, est tibi serum.

So he turned his heart to God, and determined to live according

---

[1] *Paulini Pellaei Eucharistichos*, C.S.E.L. xvi, pp. 289 sqq.; also in Loeb Library, vol. ii of Ausonius, pp. 304 sqq., with useful translation.   [2] *C.S.E.L.* xvi, p. 290, *Praefatio*.

to a strict rule. But he fell into some kind of heresy, and did long penance before he could at Easter approach the altar again. Family troubles continued all this time, and his mother and his wife died, two of his children also. In poverty Paulinus came to Marseilles and settled on a tiny plot, 'non sine vite quidem vel pomis', with a vineyard and an orchard. The venture did not prosper, but finally a Goth bought the little farm for a good price, and Paulinus now had leisure to remember the school exercises of his youth, and enough inclination to record his gratitude in uninspired hexameters which contain much that is precious to the modern historian.

His namesake, Paulinus of Périgueux, was a second-rate rhetorician, who put the life and miracles of S. Martin of Tours into hexameters.[1] It is hardly necessary to give examples of his tedious and insipid rhetoric, but the opening of the second book will give some idea of the worst poetry of the fifth century:

> Panditur ecce novum pelagus flatusque benigni
> rimosam in medios fluctus traxere carinam,
> ac dum placati rapiunt me gaudia ponti,
> inrupit vastum temeraria cumba profundum
> vix vel vicinis bene radens litora terris.
> nunc quid ago et dubiam trepidus quo dirigo proram?
> flamina sollicitant cursum, formido regressum.
> pergamus, quia terra procul, quo traxerit unda:
> tantum ut placatam Martini spiritus auram
> diffundat flatumque levem sic praestet eunti,
> ut putre sustineat felicia flamina velum.
> hactenus, ut mores monachi vel gesta referrem,
> ripa fuit: nunc pontus erit doctrina cathedrae.
> clara sacerdotis magni nunc gesta retexam.[2]

So with the sail of his verse Paulinus sets out on the great deep.

Two Gallic poets of the fifth century remain—Sidonius Apollinaris, who carried on the secular tradition, and Auspicius of Toul, who adopted the new rhythmical verse in the single poem of his that has survived.

§ 4. *Poets in Gaul.*

(3) *Sidonius Apollinaris and Auspicius of Toul.*

C. Sollius Modestus Sidonius Apollinaris was born at Lyons about the year 430, and died in 479.[3] He belonged to a

---

[1] *C.S.E.L.* xvi, pp. 1 sqq.
[2] ii. 1–14 (pp. 34–5).
[3] *Gai Sollii Apollinaris Sidonii Epistulae et Carmina*, ed. C. Luetjohann,

M.G.H., Auct. Antiq. viii. 1887. In quoting the letters I have freely used Mr. Dalton's translation, *The Letters of Sidonius*, 2 vols., Oxford 1915.

distinguished family, and professed, like Ausonius, a twofold patriotism, Gallic and Roman. Like Ausonius, too, he could never lay aside the belief that the pursuit of letters, according to the precepts of the schools, was perhaps the highest human activity. In his youth he composed poetry; in his maturer years he hoped to win immortality by following the example of Pliny in publishing nine books of carefully composed epistles. The poems belong, for the most part, to the days when he was advancing along the path of political honour which was still open to men of birth and fortune. The letters fall within the time when the direction of his career was changed, and he was called upon by the Church to rule the diocese of Auvergne and be the protector of his people in days of stress and anxiety. If Sidonius professed to have renounced poetry after he had entered upon his sacred office,[1] he did not renounce the equal vanity of rhetoric employed for trivial ends. For his letters are composed in a style which was the admiration of his contemporaries and is often the despair of his modern readers.[2] In these letters he follows Pliny's rule that each must have one subject only,[3] and this is fortunate, as it led Sidonius on several occasions to produce long descriptions of persons, of places, and of events in accordance with the accepted rules. So he describes, for the benefit of his friend Herenius, his journey to Rome in 467. He begins,[4] 'Your letter finds me at Rome. You are solicitous to know whether the affairs which have brought me so far go forward as we hoped, what route I took, and how I fared on it, what rivers celebrated in song I saw, what towns famed for their fair sites, what mountains reputed as the haunt of gods, what glorious battlefields, for it is your delight to check the descriptions you have read by the more accurate relation of the eyewitness.' Letters as well as poems[5] must be adorned or eked out with an imposing number of historical, literary, and mythological allusions,[6] and in this

---

[1] *Epist.* ix. 12: 'Primum ab exordio religiosae professionis huic principaliter exercitio renuntiavi.'

[2] Mr. Dalton (op. cit. i. cxliii) does tell us, however, that one of Sidonius's friends, Ruricius of Limoges, found him somewhat obscure.

[3] To his friend Constantius he says (*Epist.* vii. 18), 'If you ever allow yourself a rest from your unending studies in religious literature, these trivialities should afford you innocent distraction.

There is here no interminable theme to weary you; each subject ends with its containing letter; you can see where you are at a glance, and have done before the inclination to read has died within you.'

[4] *Epist.* i. 5 (Dalton, i. 9).

[5] Cf. the poem to Felix mentioned below, p. 81.

[6] See the inappropriate mythological allusions in *Epist.* vi. 12, addressed to Bishop Patiens of Lyons.

respect Sidonius does not spare his readers. But the letter devoted to a description of Theodoric, the Visigothic king,[1] is an example of rhetoric usefully applied, and the historian is equally grateful for the elaborate pictures of villas and of life on large estates which the Bishop loved to paint.

The Letters illustrate as well the attitude to literature and especially to poetry of the cultured Gallic aristocracy. Writing in 478 to his friend John, a grammarian who continued to teach in spite of the occupation of Aquitaine by the Visigoths, Sidonius says, 'Since old grades of rank are now abolished which once distinguished the high from the low, in future culture ("litteras nosse") must afford the sole criterion of nobility.'[2] To Hesperius he writes: 'What I most love in you is your love of letters. . . . The numbers of the indifferent grow at such a rate that unless your little band can save the purity of the Latin tongue from the rust of sorry barbarisms we shall soon have to mourn its abolition and decease. All the fine flowers of diction will lose their splendour through the apathy of our people' ('sic omnes nobilium sermonum purpurae per incuriam vulgi decolorabuntur').[3] In a similar strain, he laments to Sapandus, the eminent rhetor of Vienne, that 'there are now, alas! so few who have any respect for polite studies', and he complains that 'it is a defect rooted and fixed in human nature, to think little of the artist when you know nothing of the art'.[4] But these defenders of a dying cause could at least keep up the appearance of success by mutual praise and admiration. There is Placidus, who preferred Sidonius's 'trifles in prose or verse to all the other volumes on his shelves',[5] and Petronius, who devoted patient hours to the perusal of his Letters.[6] But it is difficult to believe that his friends surpassed Sidonius himself in the art of flattering literary vanity. To Claudianus Mamertus, who had composed a hymn, he writes at length: 'And now for my opinion on your hymn. I find it admirable at once in brevity and richness of content, at once tender and exalted, in poetic charm and truth to history superior to any lyrics or dithyrambs that I know. It is your peculiar merit that you observe each foot in the metre, each syllable in the foot, and each emphasis in the syllable; and in a restricted measure none too rich in opportunity, you contrive to include great opulence of words; the compressed, terse

---

[1] *Epist.* i. 2.
[2] ib. viii. 1.
[3] ib. ii. 10.

[4] ib. v. 10.
[5] ib. iii. 14.
[6] ib. v. 1.

metre does not exclude long-drawn beauty of ornate diction. It seems mere play to you, with your tiny trochees and tinier pyrrhics, to surpass in effect not merely the molossian and anapaestic ternary, but even the quaternary, the epitrite, and paeonian rhythms.'[1] There is more to the same effect, ending with this pronouncement: 'I will assert that neither Athens was ever so Attic, nor the Muses so musical as Claudianus, if indeed a long period of inaction has not robbed me even of my critical capacity.' But Claudianus was not the only great genius in Gaul. There was Polemius, the Prefect, a Platonist, and a descendant of Tacitus. 'If I compare you with your ancestors', says Sidonius to him, 'I must consider you more than the equal of Tacitus in eloquence, and in poetry above Ausonius.'[2] Then there was Sapandus, with whom 'only Quintilian in his force and his intensity, or Palladius with his splendid manner can be fairly compared; and even that comparison I should not urge—I should merely yield it acquiescence'.[3] These judgements illustrate the incurable frivolity of a man who represented, for his own and the next generation or two, the highest achievement in literary culture. This frivolity it is which is the one constant feature of his poetry, though he once pretended that he was subject to the poet's moods—'nosti enim probe laetitiam poetarum, quorum sic ingenia maeroribus ut pisciculi retibus amiciuntur; et si quid asperum aut triste, non statim sese poetica teneritudo (his sensitive soul) a vinculo incussi angoris elaqueat'.[4] It now remains to examine the verses about which Sidonius has so much to say, although he has really renounced such trifles since he became a Bishop. His collected poems number twenty-four; of these eight fall under the heading of panegyrics, while the remainder are mostly shorter poems. We begin with the three long panegyrics and their prefaces. How they came to be composed on three successive emperors is a not entirely edifying story which need not here be retold in detail.[5] The three emperors are Avitus, Majorian, and Anthemius. The first was the poet's father-in-law, who rewarded him with a statue in Trajan's Forum. But Avitus was deposed by Ricimer, who made Majorian Emperor. With him Sidonius had to make his peace, and the price was a long panegyric. When Ricimer murdered Majorian, he put Severus in his place. In 465 Severus died,

---

[1] *Epist.* iv. 3.
[2] ib. iv. 14.
[3] ib. v. 10.   [4] ib. viii. 9.

[5] Hodgkin, *Italy and her Invaders*, ii. 374 sqq., and Dalton, I. xviii sqq., have told it fully.

poisoned, so it is said, by his barbarian master. Anthemius succeeded in 467 as the nominee of Leo, 'Emperor of the Eastern Romans'. Sidonius travelled to Rome and seized his chance on New Year's Day 468. His panegyric drew the applause of the Romans and won him the City Prefecture. But before long he retired to Gaul, to find the true work of his life as Bishop of the people of Auvergne.

The panegyrics follow the traditional manner and owe much to a study of Claudian. If they are the despair of the historian who tries to extract from them some solid grains of fact, they are repulsive to an ordinary reader who seeks in vain some glimmer of reasonableness, some promise of sense. A brief analysis of each will illustrate how the poet employed the usual mythological apparatus in order to give substance to his impossible theme; but it will hardly be necessary to quote any of the verses in the original, if the preface to the panegyric on Anthemius[1] is here given in full. Although it is in elegiacs and the panegyrics are in hexameters, it will give an idea of Sidonius's manner, and of the futile ingenuity which was the admiration no less of himself than of his contemporaries. 'When the young Jupiter entered heaven, the gods hailed him each in his own manner. Even Chiron neighed a welcome. So perhaps Sidonius, humblest of all, can dare to praise Caesar.' But it is the detail more than the general idea that is ridiculous:

> Cum iuvenem super astra Iovem natura locaret
>   susciperetque novus regna vetusta deus,
> certavere suum venerari numina numen
>   disparibusque modis par cecinere sophos.[2]
> Mars clangente tuba patris praeconia dixit
>   laudavitque sono fulmina fulmineo;
> Arcas et Arcitenens fidibus strepuere sonoris,
>   doctior hic citharae pulsibus, ille lyrae;
> Castalidumque chorus vario modulamine plausit,
>   carminibus, cannis, pollice, voce, pede.
> sed post caelicolas etiam mediocria fertur
>   cantica semideum sustinuisse deus.
> tunc Faunis Dryades Satyrisque Mimallones aptae
>   fuderunt lepidum, rustica turba, melos.
> alta cicuticines liquerunt Maenala Panes
>   postque chelyn placuit fistula rauca Iovi.
> hos inter Chiron, ad plectra sonantia saltans,
>   flexit inepta sui membra facetus equi;
> semivir audiri meruit meruitque placere,
>   quamvis hinnitum, dum canit, ille daret.

---

[1] *Carmen* i (op. cit., p. 173). [2] i.e. σοφῶς, the exclamation used in applause, 'bravo'.

ergo sacrum dives et pauper lingua litabat
    summaque tunc voti victima cantus erat.
sic nos, o Caesar, nostri spes maxima saecli,
    post magnos proceres parvula tura damus,
audacter docto coram Victore[1] canentes,
    aut Phoebi aut vestro qui solet ore loqui;
qui licet aeterna sit vobis quaestor in aula,
    aeternum nobis ille magister erit.
ergo colat variae te, princeps, hostia linguae;
    nam nova templa tibi pectora nostra facis.

The verse of Sidonius does not often rise above this level.

When the panegyrics were published their historical sequence was reversed, but it is better to consider them in order of composition. On January 1, 456, Avitus assumed the Consulship, and Sidonius, who was then about twenty-six years of age, recited a poem of over six hundred verses in honour of his father-in-law. The Senate and the people were Christian, and Leo the Great was Bishop of the city. But Sidonius could offer nothing better than a dull imitation of Claudian without a trace of his strength and spirit. He begins with an assembly in heaven; all the gods come at Jove's bidding. They are catalogued with absurd epithets.[2] Then Rome appears, slow of step and dishevelled; she complains of her sad estate, and goes over a great deal of Roman history.[3] What she needs is an Emperor, a second Trajan. Can Gaul provide him? Jove replies that he is bound by fate, which rules him and all things; but, nevertheless, Rome shall have her request, and salvation shall come from Auvergne. Jove then proposes to give a *brief* survey of the early life and deeds of Avitus, but his enthusiasm carries him on for 460 weary lines of exaggeration and servile flattery. He closes with a prophecy that Avitus will conquer Africa, and the gods duteously applaud his speech:

finem pater ore
vix dederat: plausere dei fremitusque cucurrit
concilio.

[1] Victor was Anthemius' *quaestor sacri palatii*.
[2] See e.g. l. 32 (p. 204),
Saturnus profugus, vaga Cynthia, Phoebus ephebus.
There are river gods as well, including the Nile,
ignotum plus notus, Nile, per ortum.
[3] The absurd verses 79–82 (p. 205), which form part of her complaint, deserve quotation, as they illustrate a trick which medieval poets like Mat-

thew of Vendôme imitated (see *Christian-Latin Poetry*, p. 304 and note 7; also below, chapter X, § 3.
vae mihi! qualis eram, cum per mea iussa iuberent
Sulla, Asiagenes, Curius, Paulus, Pompeius
Tigrani, Antiocho, Pyrrho, Perseo, Mithridati
pacem, regna, fugam, vectigal, vincla, venenum.

The second panegyric is addressed to Majorian. It was delivered in 458 at Lyons, after that city had been captured by
the new Emperor. It begins with a short dedicatory poem
addressed to Peter, the Emperor's secretary, who is depicted
as the poet's Maecenas. In the preface to the panegyric
Sidonius follows up this suggestion by saying that like Virgil
and Horace he has been in opposition to his Augustus, but like
them he has received his pardon. The panegyric begins with
the picture of Rome, the warrior-goddess, enthroned; her
armour and her shield are carefully described, and there is
a catalogue of all the nations that bring her tribute.[1] Africa
comes in weeping and asking for aid. She goes rapidly through
a series of examples from Roman history which seem pertinent
to her argument, and finally mentions Majorian's name. Here
is a warlike Emperor at last. Africa then says that she will
give, in brief, the reasons why she desires that Majorian shall
come to her coasts. This is the occasion for a long description
of Majorian's career,[2] all his brave deeds, and his virtues that
recall the golden age. Then the horrible vices of the Vandal
king are set forth in imitation of Claudian's manner. What can
Rome do but promise that Majorian shall be the avenger?
But first he must visit Gaul. Next Sidonius takes up the tale
and relates the further exploits of Majorian, among them a
crossing of the Alps in winter with all the appropriate rhetorical
embellishment of anecdote and description. Finally, after
more compliments to Peter, the poet appeals on behalf of the
distressed city of Lyons, exhausted by war—yet since it
suffered at the Emperor's hand, its very ruin is not without
a kind of sweetness:

> fuimus vestri quia causa triumphi
> ipsa ruina placet.

What comment could be adequate to this?

Majorian went as Avitus had gone, Severus too, and Anthemius

---

[1] It is nothing better than a catalogue (verses 42 sqq., p. 189):

> fert Indus ebur, Chaldaeus
>   amomum,
> Assyrius gemmas, Ser vellera, tura
>   Sabaeus,
> Atthis mel, Phoenix palmas, Lace-
>   daemon olivum,
> Arcas equos, Epirus equas, pecuaria
>   Gallus,
> arma Chalybs, frumenta Libys, Cam-
>   panus Iacchum,
> aurum Lydus, Arabs guttam, Pan-

> chaïa myrrham,
> Pontus castorea, blattam Tyrus, aera
>   Corinthus;
> Sardinia argentum, naves Hispania
>   defert,
> fulminis et lapidem.

[2] The worst piece of rhetoric, perhaps, is in the speech of Aetius, when
he rejects the suggestion that he shall
murder Majorian. It contains the usual
geographical and mythological catalogues (verses 279 sqq., p. 194).

sat on the throne of the West. Sidonius journeyed to Rome,[1]
and, after careful inquiry and much thought, attached himself
to Basilius, an influential senator, who became his patron.[2] It
was through Basilius that he was able to use the occasion of the
Emperor's consulship to recite a panegyric which won him the
office of *praefectus urbi*. The poem begins with the subject of
the New Year. Janus must not fear the light that breaks, for
like the sun it comes from the East. Leo has sent Anthemius
from Constantinople. He who can create Emperors is something
more than an Emperor. The eastern capital is now praised,

> salve, sceptrorum columen, regina Orientis,
> orbis Roma tui, rerum mihi principe misso
> iam non Eoo solum veneranda Quiriti,
> imperii sedes, sed plus pretiosa quod exstas
> imperii genetrix.

Sidonius soon has the occasion for introducing the biographical disquisition which is the main constituent of his panegyrics.
He relates the portents at Anthemius's birth, his prowess in
hunting while still a boy—Paean himself could not surpass him,
even in the battle with the Python;[3] his careful education, which
is proved by a long catalogue of authors, the best authors of
course, both Greek and Latin;[4] his marriage with Leo's
daughter; his marvellous exploits in battle. Then the poet
draws breath and summons Phoebus to come with his lyre.
It is not now time to sing of the slaughtered Python, nor of
the 'twice seven wounds of the Tantalids'. The Castalian
Muses are also needed to tell, in brief, how Anthemius came to
assume the purple. This is the way in which Sidonius con-
trives to introduce the inevitable mythological episode.

Severus had joined the gods. Oenotria (Italy) saw his exit,
as she was journeying to Rome from the heights of aëry Appen-
nine. Wherever she goes, plenty follows; she is making for the
dwelling of Father Tiber. The old god is afraid when he sees
her, and in his fright he drops his urn and oar. She says that
she has come to ask him to persuade Rome to turn her eyes
to the East and demand thence a new ruler. Western rulers
have fortune against them; this is why the Vandals assail the
Italian coasts, and only Ricimer holds them at bay. The king-
maker is then praised respectfully, though the poet explains
that one man cannot do everything. An 'armed princeps' is

---

[1] His journey is described, *Epist.*
i. 5 (see p. 74 above).
[2] *Epist.* i. 9.
[3] ib., 152 sqq.

[4] This absurd list extends from
verse 156 to 192. It begins with
Thales and ends with Tacitus.

needed, and all will be well. Father Tiber 'heard and agreed'.
He goes to the city at once, sees and adores the goddess,[1] and
tells her his request. Rome departs at once for the East to
seek Aurora,

> nascentis petiit tepidos Hyperionis ortus.

Here the poet digresses to describe the Eastern paradise and
performs once more the hackneyed school exercise on the subject of the marvellous Phoenix. It is a miserable performance
with its tedious botanical catalogue,

> violam, cytisum, serpylla, ligustrum,
> lilia, narcissos, casiam, colocasia, caltas,
> costum, malobathrum, myrrhas, opobalsoma, tura
> parturiunt campi.[2]

At length the Eastern goddess appears, seated on her throne.
Rome has to explain hastily that she has not come in search
of Eastern conquests,

> totum hunc tibi cessimus axem,

but she goes briefly over the story of her former Eastern cam-
paigns, the results of which, she points out, are kept by the
Eastern half of the Empire. All will be forgiven and forgotten,
she says, if the East will but give Anthemius to the West.
Ricimer will marry his daughter; what a wedding this will
be! There is no pair to equal these if you go over all the
marriages of antiquity. This, unfortunately, the poet proceeds
to do. But at last the speech is ended, and the 'Tithonia
coniunx' answers, giving her assent. So the West has won
Anthemius.

The remaining poems of the collection are introduced by
a piece in three hundred and forty-six hendecasyllabics,
addressed to Felix, in which he gives countless examples drawn
from mythology, literature, and history of what the reader
will *not* find in his poems. There are two epithalamia in which
the same tasteless mythological apparatus is introduced as in
the panegyrics. The first is for the wedding of Ruricius and
Hiberia. The scene opens with a long description of a marvellous cave by the sea. There Venus dwells, and Love comes
to tell her that he has wounded the haughty Ruricius with
his dart:

[1] The goddess (Rome) is, of course,
carefully described, and the subjects on
her shield are catalogued; verse 396:

> illius orbem
> Martigenae, lupa, Thybris, Amor,
> Mars, Ilia complent.

[2] Verses 413–16.

> esset si praesens aetas, impenderet illi
> Lemnias imperium, Cressa stamen labyrinthi,
> Alceste vitam, Circe herbas, poma Calypso,
> Scylla comas, Atalanta pedes, Medea furores,
> Hippodame ceras, cygno Iove nata coronam:
> huic Dido in ferrum, simul in suspendia Phyllis,
> Euadne in flammas et Sestias isset in undas.[1]

Then Venus praises the bride at greater length and with the same mythological display. After this Venus and Amor, with the Graces, Fortuna, Flora, and others, come to the place of the wedding and the goddess bestows her blessing.

The second epithalamium is in honour of the philosopher Polemius and Araneola. It begins with a description of Pallas and of two temples, one of which is dedicated to the philosophers and the other to the domestic labours of the loom. The classical philosophers are dealt with at tedious length, and then we come to the tapestries, the subjects of which are catalogued in the usual manner:

> sus, leo, cerva, gigas, taurus, iuga, Cerberus, hydra,
> hospes, Nessus, Eryx, volucres, Thrax, Cacus, Amazon,
> grex, fluvius, Libs, poma, Lycus, virgo, polus, Oete.[2]

In the very presence of Pallas, Araneola (it will be observed that the occupation is suited to her name) herself weaves, and the subject is the story of Diogenes and Lais. Pallas smiles and pronounces a gentle rebuke; then she unites the pair under her blessing.

Another long hexameter poem has for its subject Burgus, the castle or villa of Sidonius's friend Pontius Leontius.[3] The picture is full of interest, but before we see it we have to watch the construction of the mythological framework in which, to satisfy the poet, it is to rest. So the poem begins with Bacchus and his train returning from India. The conqueror was making his way to Thebes when he met Apollo, who, guessing that he was on the way to Thebes, or perhaps Crete, asked him to stay his steps. Apollo can tell him of a better place to visit—the site of Leontius's villa in the years to come. Prophetically the god describes that villa with a wealth of detail, welcome to the historian, but with an insistence that would have wearied his listeners whether gods or men.

The next poem, addressed to Consentius, is in praise of

[1] *Carmen* xi. 65 sqq.   [3] *Carmen* xxii (p. 244).
[2] Verses 141-3.

Narbo and of its two famous citizens, the Consentii, father and son. Its only value is in its picture of an active intellectual and social life in one of the great towns of Gaul.[1] Its vices are those which mar the other poems. The collection ends with a *Propempticon ad libellum*, also in hendecasyllabics.[2]

Besides these collected poems there are poems scattered about the letters. They are mainly short pieces—epitaphs, epigrams, inscriptions, and the like. A copy of verses by Sidonius was greatly prized by his contemporaries, and he could not refuse a correspondent who asked for something to recite at table. Thus he writes to his friend Gelasius:[3] 'In so far as no letter in this collection bears your name, I have indeed offended. But you write that you will regard the fault as venial, provided I send you something for recital at table, like the letter in prose and verse which I sent not long ago to my friend Tonantius for a similar purpose.' Gelasius had complained that Sidonius wrote nothing but hendecasyllabics, and asked for senarii. So the Bishop gives him over fifty iambic verses, and talks playfully about his own incompetence to comply worthily with the request. He is a common poet,

> gregarius
> poeta, ut ipse cernis esse Sollium;
> mihi pecten errat nec per ora concava
> vaga lingua flexum competenter explicat
> epos.

But the verses were doubtless loudly applauded when Gelasius read them after supper; as were the verses sent to Tonantius referred to in the same letter.[4] These latter are called by the poet 'Asclepiads forged on the Horatian anvil', *quibus inter bibendum pronuntiandis exerceare*. To Tonantius he sent with these verses a copy of a poem which he produced *ex tempore* at a banquet in the reign of Majorian. Sidonius and three friends were to compete, and the subject was a book by Peter, Majorian's secretary. But each was to write in a different metre, so that there should be less jealousy when one of them was proclaimed the victor. The poem which Sidonius composed is of little account; it begins,

> Age, convocata pubes,
> locus hora mensa causa
> iubet ut volumen istud,
> quod et aure et ore discis,
> studiis in astra tollas.

---

[1] *Carmen* xxiii (p. 250).   [3] *Epist.* ix. 14.
[2] *Carmen* xxiv (p. 262).   [4] These are in *Epist.* ix. 13.

What is interesting is the suggestion which the poem and its occasion give of the way in which aristocratic society amused itself in the fifth century. Sidonius treasured this piece and found it, so he says, years afterwards at the bottom of a drawer, and rescued it from the mice.

On another occasion he had to produce impromptu verses at short notice.[1] He dined at Arles with the Emperor Majorian at a time when a satire was in circulation attacking people in high places. In the conversation, the word 'satire' was mentioned. Majorian turned to Sidonius. 'It is news to me, Count Sidonius, that you are a writer of satires.' 'Sire, it is news to me too,' was the reply. 'Anyhow,' said the Emperor laughing, 'I beg you to be merciful to me.' So the conversation went on, until Sidonius said, 'Whoever my accuser be, let him come out into the open. If I am proved guilty, let me abide the penalty. But if, as will probably be the case, I rebut the charge, I ask of your clemency permission to write anything I choose about my assailant, provided I observe the law.' The accuser Paeonius, who was present, agreed to the conditions, if Sidonius would produce the verse on the spot. Almost instantly the epigram came:

> Scribere me satiram qui culpat, maxime princeps,
> hanc rogo decernas aut probet aut timeat.

When the applause had died away the Emperor told Sidonius that in future he might write what he pleased. So the malicious tongues were silenced.

We have another impromptu epigram of Sidonius composed on a happier occasion.[2] The occasion was the annual festival at the tomb of S. Just at Lyons. The nocturnal office was over, and the crowds poured out of the great church of Bishop Patiens.[3] The sultry night was yielding to a cooler dawn of early autumn. A group of friends rested at the monument of Syagrius, close to the church, whither they were to repair again for Tierce, when Mass was to be sung. After they had grown weary of jest and pleasantry, some played at dice, others at ball. Sidonius led the ball-players—'you know that book and ball are my twin companions'. The 'illustrious Filimatius', too old for the game, tried to recapture the skill of his younger days, but, after several falls, collapsed from exhaustion. He called for water. It was produced, with a ragged towel, which

[1] *Epist.* i. 11.
[2] *Epist.* v. 17.
[3] See *Epist.* ii. 10, for Sidonius's metrical inscription for this church; also *Christian-Latin Poetry*, pp. 80 sqq.

had just been washed, but it served its turn so well that Filimatius called on Sidonius to 'dictate a pair of couplets in its honour'.

Sidonius tells the rest of the story as follows:

'"Very well," I replied. "But you must get my name in," he rejoined. I said that there would be no difficulty in that. "Dictate away, then." I smiled; "I would have you know," I said, "that the Muses are upset if I frequent their company before witnesses." At this he burst out in his explosive but delightful way (you know his ardent nature, and what an inexhaustible flow of wit he has): "Beware, my lord Sollius! Apollo may be still more upset if you tempt his pupils to secret interviews all alone." You can imagine the applause aroused by a retort as neat as it was instantaneous. I wasted no more time, but called up his secretary, who was at hand with his tablets, and dictated the following epigram:

> Mane novo seu cum ferventia balnea poscunt
>   seu cum venatu frons calefacta madet,
> hoc foveat pulcher faciem Filimatius udam,
>   migret ut in bibulum vellus ab ore liquor.

Our good friend Epiphanius the secretary had hardly taken down the lines, when they came to tell us that our time was up, and that the bishop was leaving his retreat; we therefore rose to go. You must not be too critical of verses written thus to order. It is another matter with the longer poem which some time ago you two asked me to write in a hyperbolical and figured style on the man who bore good fortune ill. I shall send it off to-morrow for your private revision. If you both approve of it, you can then publish it under your auspices; if you condemn, you can tear it up and forgive me as best you can. Farewell.'

It was not, of course, torn up, but it has not survived. Sometimes Sidonius wrote to young men who were following, afar off, in his steps and were striving to become wielders of rhetoric and fashioners of curious verses. Burgundio, a rich young man of Clermont, sends a messenger who is to bring back an example of a 'recurrent verse', along with a definition of it.[1] It is, replies Sidonius, 'one which reads the same backwards as forwards without changing the position of a single letter, or making any alteration in the metre. Here is the classical example:

> Roma tibi subito motibus ibit amor.

[1] *Epist.* ix. 14.

Here is another:

> Sole medere pedes, ede perede melos.'

But, proceeds Sidonius, there is another kind of recurrent verse, in which the words and not the letters are read backwards. He himself has composed such a distich; it is about a stream which had overflowed after a storm:

> Praecipiti modo quod decurrit tramite flumen
> tempore consumptum iam cito deficiet.

Reversed it reads, without alteration of metre or of sense:

> Deficiet cito iam consumptum tempore flumen,
> tramite decurrit quod modo praecipiti.

The pupils of the rhetoricians were taught to accept these trifles as a part of serious literature, but Sidonius seems more solemn about them than a Bishop should have been.[1] Yet he felt, at times, that he was not quite like the other Bishops, men of sanctity and exempt from the desire for fame. There was Lupus of Troyes, for instance, to whom he wrote: 'Suffering deep need of your salutary converse, yet standing in great awe, I am driven by the memory of my guilty life to cry to you, as once that great colleague of yours cried to the Lord: "Depart from me; for I am a sinful man, O Lord." '[2] All these Bishops were rhetoricians and used rhetoric in the service of the Church. For most of them it was a means and not an end, and they had a sense of reality to restrain them.[3] Now it was precisely this deeper sense of reality that Sidonius lacked. Yet his vanity was confined to his dealings with letters. As a bishop and a member of a noble house he showed true courage in days of stress, and, dying in his own church, was remembered as a saint.[4]

A friend of Sidonius practised verse of a different kind. This was Auspicius, Bishop of Toul, who about the year 460 addressed a poem in rhythmical iambic dimeters to Arbogast the Frankish Comes in Trier.[5] It is a poem of greeting, of

[1] There is nothing to show that this letter is earlier than many others which belong to the years after Sidonius became Bishop.

[2] *Epist.* vi. 1.

[3] I have borrowed here from a remark on the abuses of rhetoric in sermons about this time, made by Dom Wilmart, 'Un prétendu Sermon Pascal de Saint Augustin', *Rev. Bénéd.*, 1929 (xli), pp. 202–3. 'Augustine lui-même dut résister sans cesse, soutenu par un sens profond des réalités, aux mauvaises tendances qui l'entraînaient de ce côté.'

[4] Gregory of Tours, *Hist. Franc.* ii. 23, relates his end.

[5] Ed. W. Meyer, 'Die rythmischen Jamben des Auspicius,' *Gött. Nachr.* 1906, pp. 194 sqq.

praise, and of admonition. The content, however, is of little importance. The interest centres in the rhythmical scheme:

Praecelso et spectabili	magnas caelesti domino
his Arbogasti comiti	rependo corde gratias,
Auspicius, qui diligo,	quod te Tullensi proxime
salutem dico plurimam.	magnum in urbe vidimus.

multis me tuis actibus
laetificabas antea;
sed nunc fecisti maximo
me exultare gaudio ...

As in the Ambrosian hymns, there is a strophic arrangement, and there is a more or less distinct sense-pause at the end of each pair of verses. There is a good deal of hiatus and a general avoidance of elision. Rime is occasional and apparently accidental. But did Auspicius attempt to build up rhythmical iambic dimeters on the principle of the substitution of verse-accent for word-accent? This was strenuously denied by Wilhelm Meyer, who was perhaps concerned to combat any idea that exceptions might exist to his own theory of a development from merely isosyllabic lines.[1] But it is possible to accept Meyer's general theory, and yet admit that Auspicius in modelling his verse on the iambic dimeter came naturally and without much thought to write his rhythms as he did, with a rough correspondence of word and verse-accent.

However this may be, Auspicius stands in isolation as a maker of rhythmical iambic dimeters, though others must have been making somewhat similar experiments at the same time. The fact is that the materials do not exist for the construction of a complete theory of the origins of rhythmical verse. Much of this verse was produced obscurely and perished almost as soon as it was born. The poem of Auspicius, therefore, stands as a reminder of our ignorance, a production preserved by chance, but with no ready explanation attached to it.

§ 5. *Poets in Italy: Claudian and others.*

During the reign of Theodosius the Great (382–95) the Empire appeared gradually to recover its strength as the Emperor disposed successively of various perils that threatened it, and when in 395 he left it to his sons, Arcadius and Honorius, no one could have foreseen that its very life was at stake. There were, of course, numerous settlements of barbarians within the Roman borders, and Goths and Vandals held high

---

[1] ib., p. 211; see *Christian-Latin Poetry*, p. 82.

office at the Eastern and the Western courts. They were mostly Christians, although many of them followed the Arian heresy. Their leaders were often men of ability who made themselves at home in the cultivated society with which they were brought into close contact.

This society was still only partly reconciled with the Christian order. Many members of the old families clung to the ancient religion, to which they joined some version of Neoplatonic philosophy. Symmachus and Macrobius and their circle affected, so far as they could, to ignore the dominant religion. Symmachus could not ignore it altogether, for he was the spokesman of the party that had to measure itself against Ambrose over the affair of the Altar of Victory, and his son-in-law had joined the Church. Macrobius does not mention Christianity at all, and his friend Praetextatus was initiated into as many of the mysteries as he could compass.[1] Symmachus, aristocrat and senator, was a rhetorician, and wrote letters to his friends for the admiration of his contemporaries and of posterity. He was no philosopher, but he had learned his rhetoric at Bordeaux.[2] It was inevitable, therefore, that he should write verses and append them to his letters. We see him composing with much care his polished trifles, and sending them to his father for criticism.[3] The father praises them without reserve: 'quid enim concinnius epistula tua, quam nuper accepi? quid versuum admixtione iocundius? vere dicam tibi, plura legere volentibus celeriter terminata est.' And he sends him in return some of his own epigrams, which he is composing to help him to lay aside the memory of his troubles.[4] But by far the ablest of the secular poets of this time, and, as it has seemed to many, the last authentic voice of the poetry of the old world, was Claudius Claudianus, an Oriental Greek, who spent his childhood in Alexandria. From about 395 to 404 he appears in Italy, producing a substantial body of poetry in his efforts to win the favour of the men—imperial, barbarian, or aristocratic—who had rewards to bestow on those who flattered them. Although Greek was his mother-tongue and he wrote poems in Greek, he gained a complete mastery over Latin, which must have been as much the result of unremitting study as of the development of a remarkable talent. For Claudian

[1] It was Praetextatus of whom Jerome tells the story that he used to say to Pope Damasus, 'Make me Bishop of Rome, and I will be a Christian at once.'

[2] Symmachus, *Epist.* ix. 88.
[3] *Symmachi epistolae*, i. 1, *M.G.H.*, *Auct. Antiq.* vi. 1, ed. Seeck; cf. also i. 8.
[4] ib. i. 2.

is one of the ablest of the poet-rhetoricians that ever used the Latin tongue. His themes were mostly such as asked for nothing more than rhetorical treatment, but Claudian knew how to construct a poem so that it should not be a mere string of disconnected episodes. There is a vigour, a hardness, a competence about his work that moves our admiration, even if we are never deceived into thinking that we are dealing with pure poetry.

The work of Claudian falls naturally into three classes[1]—the political poems, the mythological pieces, and the smaller poems. The political poems consist of panegyrics and invectives. In 395 Claudian celebrated the consulship of the brothers Anicius Probinus and Anicius Hermogenianus Olybrius. They were hardly more than boys, but their father had held the highest offices under Theodosius, and the honour of the consulate came to the sons almost as a matter of course.

Claudian begins his poem by invoking the Sun to lead on the year more joyfully, though it is quite usual for him to usher it in with one of the Anician gens as consul. Then the family is praised and, in particular, Probus, the dead father of the youths. The poet makes the usual geographical excursions in telling of the extent of his fame and makes the usual demand for a hundred mouths and a hundred breasts—but these would be quite unequal to the task of describing the deeds of Probus. Yet the glory of the sons is greater than that of their father— they *begin* their career with the consulship.

The poet is warming to his work. He asks his Muse to tell him—the ignorant bard—how this marvellous thing came about. Now is the place to introduce the allegorical and mythological episode which is to be the very centre and substance of the panegyric. Theodosius had just returned victorious from the battle of the river Frigidus. Rome herself— her winged chariot had been yoked by her servants, Impetus and Metus—flew to meet him to ask a favour for the sons of Probus. But first Claudian must, as any rhetorician would, describe in detail the appearance of Rome, who adopts for this occasion the disguise of Minerva. Then he pictures her flight, and tells how she finds Theodosius resting on the grass beneath a tree, still covered with sweat of battle and panting from the fight. The Emperor addresses her first, and asks the reason of her coming. He promises to fight, on her behalf, beneath Libyan heat or Caucasian cold, to march to Meroë in

[1] Cf. Schanz, iv. 2, p. 5.

summer or to the Danube in winter. The 'queen' answers him
in a long speech. There are two boys who are her especial care;
to them she would not prefer the heroes of old—Decii, Metelli,
Scipiones, or Camilli. They have the wisdom of age with the
heart of youth. They ought to have the next consulship.
Theodosius is delighted and says that he had already intended
to reward their father's merit and their own in this way.

The scene shifts to Rome where Proba, the aged mother, is
herself embroidering the consular togas for her children. Now
they are assuming office. Tiber rises from his bed and wonders
at the spectacle. The river-god is now described even to the
colour of his grey-blue eyes. The sight was too amazing even
for the god. He could not speak at first, but at last he began:

> respice, si tales iactas aluisse fluentis,
> Eurota Spartane, tuis. quid protulit aequum
> falsus olor, valido quamvis decernere caestu
> noverit et ratibus saevas arcere procellas?

The comparison with the children of the 'feigned swan' suggests to father Tiber that Olybrius and Probinus might very
well take the place of the heavenly twins in the sky as guides
to seamen. But in any case it is now time for feast. The
drunken river (*ebrius amnis*) should roll wine. All the other
rivers must come to the banquet—Tiber gives their names with
appropriate epithets. The Nymphs hasten to get everything
ready for the under-water feast—the damp palace is bright
with jewelled tables! The poem ends with the hope of a happy
year, with clement winter, quiet spring, and bountiful summer
and autumn.

Claudian was an Oriental; this is perhaps why in this and in
all his panegyrics no exaggeration, however gross, suggested
to him that here he must, for the sake of decency, draw the
line. His resources were so varied and his skill so certain that
he never looked back or troubled about the way he was going.
There were no secrets of rhetoric unknown to him. He composed an invective in two books against Rufinus, the man to
whom had fallen the care of the Eastern half of the Empire
and the guardianship of the young Arcadius. On the advice
of Rufinus, Arcadius had recalled the troops which, under the
leadership of Stilicho, were about to attack Alaric and his
Visigoths in Thessaly. Stilicho, the great soldier, a Vandal by
birth, was Claudian's patron and idol. Rufinus was already
dead—murdered by the soldiers of Gaïnas—when Claudian
wrote his poem, presenting Stilicho as the pattern of excellence

and Rufinus as a monster of all depravity. Claudian uses the
same devices as in his panegyrics; but instead of the gods, he
introduces the Furies. Allecto is jealous of the peace and prosperity of men, and calls a council of the 'innumerable pests of
Erebus'—here they are in their conventional array:

> nutrix Discordia belli,
> imperiosa Fames, leto vicina Senectus
> impatiensque sui Morbus Livorque secundis
> anxius et scisso maerens velamine Luctus
> et Timor et caeco praeceps Audacia vultu
> et Luxus populator opum, quem semper adhaerens
> infelix humili gressu comitatur Egestas,
> foedaque Avaritiae complexae pectora matris
> insomnes longo veniunt examine Curae.[1]

Megaera has a scheme ready for destroying the peace of men.
Rufinus shall be let loose on the world—he is her own child,
but she is not his equal in fierceness and guile. 'He alone has
more wickedness than we have collectively.' There is no need
to describe the tedious course of the myth, how Megaera
appears to Rufinus, and how events move, partly in the world
of the supernatural and partly (but obscurely) in the realm of
history. In the course of his invective Claudian finds room
for a digression on the virtue of the simple life, a piece of
school-exercise which still—it appears—retained its freshness
for contemporary hearers or readers, and was doubtless
appreciated in the Middle Ages. The moral of the contrast
between the cottage and the palace, herbs and a banquet,
Tyrian dyes and the lilies of the field, luxurious beds and the
soft grass is that 'nature has given to all the possibility of
being happy, if they only knew how to make use of it'. The
invective ends with the solitary punishment of Rufinus in the
lowest depths of Hell. He is too evil to mix with the worst
criminals in the realm of the dead.

It will be clear that Claudian has no gift for satire. He gains
his effects by elaboration, and not as Juvenal does, by concentration. Juvenal might have written grimly about the eunuch
Eutropius, who became consul at Constantinople in 399.
Claudian devoted two books to the theme—and at the end he
has proved very little; but he has poured out a torrent of the
vilest abuse and has made his victim guilty of every abomina-
tion that he can think of. Doubtless the poet is ingenious;
he is pleasant about the visit of Eutropius to a Christian seer

---

[1] *In Rufinum*, i. 30-8.

in Egypt at a time of trouble. He calls him 'spado Teiresias enervatusque Melampus', creeping back with oracles from the far-off Nile.[1]

All the 'political' poems—such as the two panegyrics on the consulships of Honorius, that on Stilicho's consulship, that on the Gothic war—show the same technique and the same apparatus of allegory and myth, which were needed to give some substance to the theme of praise. Rome often appears in the person of a woman-goddess. In the poem on the war against Gildo[2] she comes to Olympus to complain of the shortage of corn, which is due to the action of the Count of Africa, who kept back the ships. Rome asks of Jove—'Why did you give me seven hills and a population which cannot be fed on a small amount of corn?' She asks other rhetorical questions, and makes skilful use of a host of allusions from her past history.

Enough has been said perhaps to convey the sense of tedium that falls upon the reader of these remorselessly competent, hard, and glittering verses. The historian must give them every care, in the hope of extracting—if it is to be found—some precious grain of fact. For the rest, they demonstrate the ultimate result of the unbridled passion for the spoken word that dominated the ancient world. It is the end of the poetry of antiquity. Claudian has killed it by exaggeration, an exaggeration so gross that he could have no competitors, though he had a few feeble imitators.

But there is another side to the picture. Claudian continued something that was good and fruitful in the rhetorical tradition, the emphasis on sustained description. In this respect he is superior to Ausonius, and goes back to the example set by Statius. In the *Epithalamium* in honour of Honorius and Maria (398) there is a description of the home of Cyprian Venus, which is a prototype of all those 'bowers of bliss',

> amongst wide waves set like a little nest,

or

> midmost the beating of the steely sea.

For the poets of the Renaissance and of after-times did not invent these glowing pictures of paradises inaccessible—except for strange chances—to mortal men. Claudian himself had examples before him, but he painted his picture boldly, careless of concealing those cruder touches which betray the rhetorician. Here is his picture:

---

[1] i. 315–16.

[2] *De Bello Gildonico*, 17 sqq.; Rome appears to Honorius in *In Eutropium*, i. 371 sqq.

mons latus Ionium Cypri praeruptus obumbrat,
invius humano gressu, Phariumque cubile
Proteos et septem despectat cornua Nili.
hunc neque canentes audent vestire pruinae,
hunc venti pulsare timent, hunc laedere nimbi.
luxuriae Venerique vacat. pars acrior anni
exulat; aeterni patet indulgentia veris.
in campum se fundit apex; hunc aurea saepes
circuit et fulvo defendit prata metallo.
Mulciber, ut perhibent, his oscula coniugis emit
moenibus et tales uxorius obtulit arces.
intus rura micant, manibus quae subdita nullis
perpetuum florent, Zephyro contenta colono,
umbrosumque nemus, quo non admittitur ales,
ni probet ante suos diva sub iudice cantus:
quae placuit, fruitur ramis; quae victa, recedit.
vivunt in Venerem frondes omnisque vicissim
felix arbor amat; nutant ad mutua palmae
foedera, populeo suspirat populus ictu
et platani platanis alnoque adsibilat alnus.[1]

The long unfinished poem on the Rape of Proserpine lent
occasion for many such descriptive passages. Claudian begins
it by professing to sing from a 'full heart'—'mens congesta
iubet'. But he gives us nothing beyond the old devices of
descriptions and speeches. The island of Sicily is, of course,
described, and Mount Aetna as well. What is the cause of the
strange phenomena which the poet records? Is the wind, or
does the sea flow into the entrails of the mountain and turn
into fire? Claudian confesses that he does not know.[2] On
another occasion, when he was celebrating the hot springs of
Abano (near Padua), in a similar long description, he specu-
lated again on the causes of a mysterious phenomenon. Was it
that the fires from the infernal streams had made their way
to the world above, or does a cold river of earth go down into
veins of sulphur and come up on fire? Or does the mountain
itself call the elements together, and mix up fire and water in
equal quantities? Well, whatever the reason, the medicinal
fount does not flow without design. The final cause is the will
of 'the Father of all things'. As we shall see, medicinal waters
found their poets in the Middle Ages, and they, no less than

[1] *Epithalamium*, 49–68. There is
another interesting descriptive passage
in this poem, in which Venus, looking
at Maria, catalogues, in wonder, her
various beauties,

non labra rosae, non colla pruinae,
non crines aequant violae, non lumina flammae, etc. (265 sqq.).
[2] *De Raptu Proserp.* i. 142–78.

Claudian,[1] did not mind employing the Muse to sing of un-poetical bodily symptoms.

The *De Raptu Proserpinae* contains two detailed descriptions of embroidered fabrics. The first is the work at which Proserpine, left by Ceres, sits in the ivory palace. It is to be a present for her mother; it pictures the beginning of all things, how Nature brought order out of chaos, how the 'seeds of things' passed, the light being borne upwards and the heavy falling down. Air, fire, sea, and earth were pictured. But the embroidery was not all in one colour. The girl 'kindled the stars with gold, and poured out the seas with purple'. It was so realistic that you would have been tempted to think that you actually saw the seaweed cast up against the cliffs and heard the hoarse murmur of the waves on the thirsty sands. The zones of the earth were also in the picture, and the house of her uncle Dis. At this part of the work her cheeks were wet with prophetic tears.[2]

But Proserpine herself wore an embroidered robe, and this, at the appropriate time, must also be described. It was the work of her own needle; and the subject was cosmological again—the births of the Sun and Moon, and the new-born god and goddess being carried on the shoulders of Tethys. 'Tali luxuriat cultu', says the poet of the maid who wore the dress.[3] The plain of Henna has its full measure of praise; its trees are catalogued, and there is a list of the flowers that were gathered on that spring morning.[4] Pluto himself, after he has wiped away—with his dusky cloak—the tears that came to his eyes at the sight of his bride's distress, gives a good rhetorical description of the underworld:

> sunt altera nobis
> sidera, sunt orbes alii, lumenque videbis
> purius Elysiumque magis mirabere solem
> cultoresque pios; illic pretiosior aetas,
> aurea progenies habitat, semperque tenemus
> quod superi meruere semel.

But this theology was already antiquated in Claudian's day, even among the heathen. For most men heaven was above the stars.[5] Pluto proceeds to tell with what state Proserpine

---

[1] Cf. *Aponus* (Abano), 95–8:

quodsi forte malus membris exuberat
    umor
  languida vel nimio viscera felle
    rubent,
non venas reserant nec vulnere vul-
    nera sanant

pocula nec tristi gramine mixta
    bibunt.

[2] i. 246–68.   [3] ii. 36–55.
[4] ii. 88–136.
[5] See Cumont, *Astrology and Religion among the Greeks and Romans*, London 1912, pp. 195 sqq.

shall rule in Hell. 'Thou shalt be queen of blessed autumn and ever enriched with golden fruit.'[1] Here we may leave the poet, who has yet to tell of the wrath and grief of Ceres. The interest of the poem has gone—perhaps because Claudian did not live to revise it and give it the final polish.

The collection of shorter poems is of much interest because it shows how the example set by the poets of the 'silver age' was still followed, and how it was handed on to the medieval poets. The constant stream of this minor verse is undoubtedly of great importance for the study of secular poetry in the Middle Ages. The choice of subjects, dictated at first by convention, was wide enough to suggest new possibilities, and these exercises tended to keep the versifier close to things that had a real meaning and relevance—a landscape, a river, a building, a statue, or even an unusual phenomenon of nature. Claudian's collection of small poems covers the most diverse subjects. In five hexameters he describes the harbour at Smyrna; then he gives the merest sketch of another harbour,

> Est procul ingenti regio summota recessu,
> insula qua resides fluctus mitescere cogit
> in longum producta latus, fractasque per undas
> ardua tranquillo curvantur brachia portu.[2]

He saw a marble charioteer and horses—carved from a single block. What an opportunity for saying how 'the chariot melts into the charioteer', 'the horses come out of the car, and out of one another', and

> mons patiens ferri varios mutatur in artus.[3]

The Porcupine is minutely described in another poem. After studying its habits the poet concluded that there was less reason to doubt the fable of the Stymphalian birds which shed fatal arrows as they flew. The description is wonderful; the small animal is treated with the reverence and wonder due to Leviathan. This creature, he says, carries with him his whole armament. He is at once his own quiver, his own arrow and his own bow. One animal owns all the varied artifices of war. It must have been from him that the Cretans learned how to use the bow and the Parthians to shoot while in flight.

The Lobster[4] is dismissed in four verses:

> Horret apex capitis; medio fera lumina surgunt
> vertice; cognatus dorso durescit amictus.

---

[1] This is Mr. Platnauer's attractive rendering, in the Loeb edition of Claudian, ii, p. 339, of

> fortunatumque tenebis

autumnum et fulvis semper ditabere pomis.

[2] Epigr. v (Teubn.).   [3] ib. vii.

[4] ib. xxiv.

        armavit natura cutem dumique rubentes
        cuspidibus parvis multos acuere rubores.

Other subjects are the Electric Ray (*torpedo*), the Magnet, the Shell, and the Crystal enclosing a drop of water. *The Phoenix* is an undistinguished poem, and not worthy to be compared with the charming piece ascribed to Lactantius, which Claudian had in his mind as a model. The favourite theme of the description of a river is not neglected by Claudian. The Nile had already been described at some length by Lucan in a long speech put into the mouth of the Egyptian priest Achoreus.[1] Claudian knew this passage well, and in his own poem made use of some of the ideas suggested by it. Like Lucan he is concerned with the strange law that governs the inundation, an overflow that arises from no law holding good for other rivers. Lucan says,

        inde etiam leges aliarum nescit aquarum,[2]

and Claudian echoes him,

        nec vero similes causas crescentibus undis
        aut tempus meruit.

The Nile, as we have seen,[3] fascinated also the Christian poets, who, making it one of the four rivers of Paradise, had to set forth at some length its wonders.

    The *Epithalamium* for the marriage of Honorius has been already mentioned. In the Fescennine verses prefixed to it Claudian begins with a series of rimes. It should be noted that these rimes are precisely after the manner of the rimes employed in rhetorical prose, and they show how easy it was to transfer this adornment to verse, though poets had, on the whole, avoided doing so. The lines in question are at the beginning of the poem:

        Princeps corusco sidere pulchrior,
        Parthis sagittas tendere doctior,
        eques Gelonis imperiosior,
        quae digna mentis laus erit arduae?
        quae digna formae laus erit igneae?

    Claudian is really the last poet of the heathen world, though for some time to come there were Christian poets who, even after their school days, continued to versify outworn themes derived from pagan mythology. Claudian himself paid lip-service to the new religion, and wrote a coldly orthodox poem

[1] *Bell. Civ.* x. 194 sqq.   [3] p. 70, above.
[2] ib. x. 228.

on the Saviour.[1] In his poem to James, the *magister equitum*, whom he accuses of 'pulling his verses to pieces', he gives a playful catalogue of saints.[2]

> Per cineres Pauli, per cani limina Petri,
>   ne laceres versus, dux Iacobe, meos.
> sic tua pro clipeo defendat pectora Thomas
>   et comes ad bellum Bartholomaeus eat.

But to Augustine and to Orosius, Claudian was an alien from the faith ('a Christi nomine alienus'),[3] though his merits as a poet were recognized, and he was read and admired by succeeding generations.

The rest of the poetry of fifth-century Italy belongs to the Church. In the fourth century a few polemical poems had appeared—the *Carmen ad Senatorem* (addressed to a Senator who had fallen away from the Christian religion),[4] the *Carmen adversus Flavianum*,[5] and the *Carmen adversus Marcionitas*.[6] There are also the Christian centos, to which reference has been already made, and the inscriptions of Damasus, which hardly belong to the history of poetry.

Most important are the hymns of Ambrose, which stand alone, almost free from the stamp of rhetoric that marks nearly all the compositions of this time.

The rhetorician appears in the *Eclogue* of Severus Endelechius, who, strangely, writes in asclepiads;[7] and in Honorius Scholasticus also, who wrote in elegiacs *Contra Epistolas Senecae*.[8] Sedulius,[9] the author of the *Carmen Paschale*, and of the celebrated alphabetical hymn, *A solis ortus cardine*, was well schooled in rhetoric, as his prose dedication to the *Carmen* shows.

During the fifth century the political and social conditions were so adverse to literature and to culture generally that little was written with any other intention than that of practical service or of theological controversy. The real life of the Empire was, as it had been for a long time, in the provinces.

---

[1] *De Salvatore* (no. xxxii). It begins:
  Christe potens rerum, redeuntis conditor aevi.
There is no real reason to doubt that Claudian is the author; see Schanz, iv. 2, p. 32.
  [2] *In Iacobum magistrum equitum* (no. l).
  [3] August., *De Civ. Dei*, v. 26; cf. Orosius, *Contra Paganos*, vii. 35: 'unus

ex ipsis (i.e. of the enemy) poeta quidem eximius, sed paganus pervicacissimus.'
  [4] *C.S.E.L.* xiii, pp. 227 sqq.
  [5] Riese, *Anth. Lat.*, no. 4.
  [6] Tertull., ed. Oehler, ii. 781 sqq.
  [7] Riese, no. 893.
  [8] Riese, no. 666.
  [9] See *Christian-Latin Poetry*, pp. 108 sqq.

Italy was still, in spite of the Church, in a condition of spiritual unrest;

> Wandering between two worlds, one dead,
> The other powerless to be born,

and this malady was, it would seem, recurrent. The fifth century began with promise and dragged on in gloom. The end of that century saw the establishment of the kingdom of the Ostrogoths; the first half of the sixth witnessed its glory and its decline.

§ 6. *Poets in Spain and Africa.*

As we have already mentioned Juvencus and have estimated the significance of Prudentius in the specifically Christian contribution to the development of lyrical poetry, there is little to say of the Spanish verse of the time which we are considering. Spain had been thoroughly Romanized for generations, and it was now being no less thoroughly Christianized. It was a rich country with flourishing cities and good schools. The Church was powerful, and the people clung with a fierce ardour to their own local martyrs, who were now the recognized protectors of the cities which they had honoured by their sufferings or by the deposit of their bones, and where they still, in a fashion, were present as fellow-citizens with those who did them service.

Spain was the home of the family of Theodosius, but besides emperors it produced able officials. Such was Prudentius, and such was Flavius Merobaudes, likewise an official and a poet. The latter was honoured with a statue in the Forum of Trajan; from its inscription we learn that Merobaudes was a 'vir spectabilis' and 'comes sacri consistorii', that he was equally famous as a man of letters as a soldier—'ingenium ita fortitudini ut doctrinae natum stilo et gladio pariter exercuit'. Just as Claudian made Stilicho his hero, so Merobaudes sang the praises of Aëtius. The merest fragments of his work remain.[1] There is part of a prose panegyric on the second consulship of Aëtius (437) and part of a verse panegyric on his third consulship (446). A lighter piece on the second birthday of Aëtius' son begins:[2]

> Annus panditur ecce iam secundus,
> et festum puero diem reducit,
> quo vitalibus inchoatus auris

[1] Ed. Vollmer, *Fl. Merobaudis reliquiae*, M.G.H., *Auct. Antiq.* xiv, pp. 3 sqq.

[2] p. 5. The influence of Statius is apparent here.

infusi bibit aetheris vigorem.
omnes nunc Latiae favete Musae,
omnes nunc Latiae virete silvae:
vernent limina laureisque sertis
inserpant hederae vagante nexu;
exultet placido tumore Thybris,
et nulla rutilus nec asper unda
hibernis vada molliat serenis.
laxet pectora bellicosa ductor
(est dignus rude) lacteamque prolem
nodosis ferus ambiat lacertis.

The poet then introduces the mother, and contrasts her lot with that of Thetis and her wondrous child. For the son of Aëtius was plunged beneath the waters of baptism,

qua puri deus arbiter lavacri
arcana laticum receptus unda
pellit crimina nec sinit fuisse,
et vitam novat obruitque poenam.
his te primitiis, puer, sacratum
excepit gremio micante Roma.

Merobaudes is, therefore, more than a Christian merely in name, although he makes use of the old mythology, after the manner of Claudian.[1] But, if we can judge by fragments,[2] he is not the equal of Claudian, though he avoids the worst excesses of rhetoric and gives the impression of sincerity.

When we have mentioned the metrical inscriptions of Pope Damasus (c. 305–384), who was a Spaniard by birth, we have nothing more to say of Spanish poetry until we reach the seventh century.

From Spain we pass to Africa. These two countries were connected by close ties both of commerce and of intellectual intercourse, and when finally Roman civilization disappeared from Africa it was in Spain that the last Latin writers of that unhappy province were affectionately treasured and read.[3]

Latin civilization in Africa belonged almost solely to the cities. There it maintained a more or less artificial existence, while outside the walls the population bore the indelible marks

---

[1] I feel compelled to abandon the view expressed in *Christian - Latin Poetry*, p. 125, that Merobaudes was 'almost a pagan at heart'.

[2] A religious poem, *de Christo*, in thirty hexameters is ascribed to Merobaudes; see Manitius, *Christl. Lat. Poesie*, p. 325 sq.; Schanz, IV. ii, p. 43. Text, Riese, no. 878; Vollmer, p. 19.

[3] Dracontius was re-edited by Eugenius of Toledo; on the role of Spain in the survival of Dracontius see Schanz, IV. ii, p. 60; the *codex Salmasianus* is, according to Traube, of Spanish origin (Schanz, ib., p. 70); Corippus was read in Spain, ib., p. 81; and Verecundus of Junca also, ib., p. 395.

of other cultures—Berber or Punic. But the very artificiality of
this civilization of the cities seemed to yield it an intenser life.
Fashions borrowed from elsewhere were here carried to an
extreme which made of them what was almost a new creation.
In Apuleius or in Tertullian this waywardness turns into the
path of genius; in Nemesian and in Pentadius it descends to
the lowest perversity. In Augustine the extremes meet—now
he gives way to the always-present temptation of rhetorical
triviality, now he reasserts his greatness and creates a phrase
that is to endure for ever.

In general there is something harsh and restless about these
later Africans. Cyprian, although he loved the rhyming periods
and other devices of the 'Asiatic' school, had yet about him
a trace of the old Roman *gravitas*, the dignity of a bishop, as
he was to win the glory of a martyr. But many of the others
had sunk into an intellectual darkness, deepened by the literary
obscurity which they cherished for its own sake. Macrobius[1]
and Martianus Capella, two heathen writers, illustrate the
hopelessness into which the art of letters had sunk among
those who still clung to the old ways in Christian Africa. With
the *Saturnalia* of Macrobius we have here nothing to do,[2] but
Martianus Capella mingled poetry with prose in his fantastic
treatise, *De Nuptiis Philologiae et Mercurii*.[3] He was born at
Madaura and lived mainly at Carthage in the first half of the
fifth century. He composed this school book wrapped in a
fable for the benefit of his son Martianus, in order to introduce
him to the liberal arts without tears. He could not guess that
he was writing also for generations of schoolboys, and that his
book would be gravely annotated by learned men like John the
Scot, Dunchad,[4] and Remigius of Auxerre.

This mixture of verse and prose goes back, as we have seen,
to the Menippean satire, and Martianus Capella as much as

[1] It is not certain, but it is probable that Macrobius was an African; Schanz, IV. ii, p. 191; Monceaux, *Les Africains*, pp. 426 sqq. He was proconsul at Carthage 409–10.

[2] But we may call attention to the remarks in Schanz (IV. ii, p. 193) in which is summarized the character of Macrobius's work. 'Wenn wir das Werk des Macrobius richtig beurteilen wollen, so müssen wir daran festhalten, dass nur die Einkleidung ihm angehört, der Inhalt dagegen fremdes Eigentum ist. Es werden viele Autoren citiert, allein wir würden sehr irren, wenn wir annehmen wollten, unser Autor hätte umfassende Studien gemacht und die von ihm citierten Schriftsteller alle gelesen. Seine Quellen sind nur wenige, und charakteristisch für ihn ist, dass er diese Quellen dem Leser nicht offen kundgibt; so werden Gellius und Plutarch, die er stark benutzt, niemals von ihm erwähnt.'

[3] Ed. F. Eyssenhardt, Leipzig 1866.

[4] On Dunchad, see Manitius, *Gesch.* i. p. 525 sq.

Boëthius helped to transmit this literary form to the Middle Ages. He transmitted as well a taste for his involved and tortuous sentences, on which Alan of Lille and others modelled themselves in the twelfth and thirteenth centuries.

Capella was an old man when he wrote this fable, worn out, he seems to suggest, by a life of advocacy which involved him in much labour and brought but little reward. The concluding poem, which is in part an autobiography, almost reconciles the weary reader to the pedantic and unintelligent romancer, but he will not praise him for grace or lucidity. Capella says in effect: 'Here is the old man's allegory, which Satire, that "various" thing, has inspired me to create in lamplit hours. My aim has been to teach our Pelasgi arts hardly fit for Attic feasts, and it has extended to nine volumes. Well, Satire is a gossip who does not know when to stop, mixing learned with unlearned, things worth saying with things that should not be talked about, Muses and gods, and by a rustic figment has represented the arts as chattering in an illiterate fashion.' Then Capella proceeds to mention his troubles as a lawyer, though it is now *Satura* who speaks, complaining that her style is settled by one who has to growl like a dog in the law courts before the proconsul. Old age is upon him and his hairs are white; he is full of cares and his gains are scanty. How can a decent style be expected from him? So, with this explanation, he asks his son to read his trifles with an indulgent eye. This is his apology in imperfect iambics:[1]

> Habes senilem, Martiane, fabulam,
> miscilla lusit quam lucernis flamine
> Satura, Pelasgos dum docere nititur
> artes creagris vix amicas Atticis,
> sic in novena decidit volumina.
> haec quippe loquax docta indoctis adgerans
> fandis tacenda farcinat, inmiscuit
> Musas deosque, disciplinas cyclicas
> garrire agresti cruda finxit plasmate.
> haec ipsa nauci rupta conscientia
> turgensque felle ac bile 'multa chlamyde
> prodire doctis adprobanda cultibus
> possemque comis utque e Martis curia,
> Felicis' inquit 'sed Capellae flamine,
> indocta rabidum quem videre saecula
> iurgis caninos blateratus pendere,
> proconsulari verba dantem culmini,

---

[1] Eyssenhardt, p. 374 sq.

ipsoque dudum bombitante flosculo
decerptum falce iam canescenti rota,
beata alumnum urbs Elissae quem videt
iugariorum murcidam viciniam
parvo obsidentem vixque respersum lucro,
nictante cura somnolentum lucibus—
ab hoc creatum Pegaseum gurgitem
decente quando possem haurire poculo?'
testem ergo nostrum quae veternum prodidit
secute nugis, nate, ignosce lectitans.

The treatise consists then of nine books. In the first two Capella tells the story of the marriage of Mercury and Philology; in the remainder the stage is occupied by the liberal arts. The story is too tedious to relate at any length, though it begins in a promising manner. Capella is singing to himself what sounds like a wedding-song, and his son overhears him. He has to explain to the young Martianus that it refers to a marriage which is the subject of a book that Satire has dictated to him. The boy listens, glad to learn that his first conjecture—that his father had taken leave of his senses—is not true. Then the allegory beings. Mercury, a bachelor among so many married gods, wants a bride. He fails to win Sophia, Mantice, or Psyche. Virtus advises him to obtain the assistance of Apollo. This is good advice, for the god at once describes in verse a learned virgin,

est igitur prisci generis doctissima virgo,[1]

whose name is Philologia. But before the betrothal can take place Jove must give his consent. In the end the married gods and the older goddesses meet in council to decide this grave business. Discordia and Seditio are kept away. Jove opens the assembly in verse, and the gods applaud his proposal that the union of the god and the mortal shall be approved, but that like her, other mortals whose merits had raised them to the stars should henceforth be exalted to the ranks of the gods.[2] A 'grave and noble woman, called Philosophy' was instructed to inscribe this decree on brazen tablets for the instruction of mankind.

In book two Philosophy appears. She consults the future in anxiety about her marriage, and the result is favourable. Then Phronesis arrays her in her bridal dress, while each of the Muses sings a poem in her honour.[3] Here is the song of Euterpe, in adonics:

---

[1] op. cit., p. 10.   [2] p. 26.   [3] pp. 32 sqq.

Virgo perite
praevia sortis,
quae potuisti
scandere caelum
sacraque castis
dogmata ferre,
noscere semet
quis valuere,
quisque videntes
lumine claro
numina fati
et geniorum
cernere vultus
quaeque Platonis
Pythagoraeque
esse dedisti
sidera mentes,
tuque caducis
mortalibusque
nube remota
cernere iusti
numina caeli:
iure senatum
scande Tonantis,
quam decet unam
Mercuriali
foedere iungi.
scande caeli templa virgo digna tanto foedere.
te socer subire celsa poscit astra Iuppiter.

While the singing is going on four grave matrons appear in the chamber; they are the four cardinal virtues. After them come the Graces to salute the bride. Athanasia next is seen, whose task is to bring Philologia to the courts of heaven. But she cannot do this until the learned Virgin has removed a load from her breast—this she does by vomiting what is seen to be a whole parcel of books of all kinds. The Muses help to gather them up, but Philologia, after drinking the cup of immortality, which Apotheosis, the mother of Athanasia, offers, goes up to heaven in a litter. Juno Pronuba meets her, and she arrives at last at Jove's palace in the milky way. Mercury is waiting, the *lex Papia Poppaea* is read, and the presents are now to be given. Phoebus brings forward seven damsels who are the gift of Mercury to his bride. These are the seven liberal arts, and with their appearance the serious aim of the treatise makes itself felt, though an attempt is made to retain something of the fiction that a story is being told. The Arts—Grammar, Dialectic, Rhetoric, Geometry, Arithmetic, Astronomy, and

Music—in appropriate costume and with their proper attributes, declaim at great length, each on the subject which she represents. The assembled gods listen to these expositions, taken from Varro or from Pliny, and approve or disapprove until it is time for the nuptial hymn. Music (Harmonia) is concluding her discourse on number and melody:

Quae cum Harmonia intentis tam divis quam heroum populis augusta quadam suavitate percurreret, ad cantus carminumque dulcedinem decenter regressa conticuit. tuncque Iove adsurgente divisque praeambulis κοίμησιν modulata in thalamum quoque virginis magna cunctorum voluptate pervenit.[1]

M. Paul Monceaux[2] long ago pointed out how much Martianus Capella owed, in the conception of his work, to the *Metamorphoses* of Apuleius, and, in particular, to the episode of *Cupid and Psyche*. Capella had also studied the subtly-fashioned sentences of his famous fellow-citizen; but, just as he could do no better than produce a dead and colourless series of abstractions, so over his bizarre periods there is no breath that really blows from the pages of Apuleius. But the very fortune of his book lay in its obtrusive allegory and its didactic aim. These characteristics were its commendation to the teachers in the monastic schools. In the tenth century Notker Labeo, a monk of S. Gall, took what was then the unexampled step of translating the book into the German tongue,[3] and for his pupils, as of those of many a teacher before and after him, Martianus Capella was a main source of information about such diverse subjects as rhetoric and geometry, astronomy and music.[4]

And the poems too had their influence, though this is harder to trace than the influence of the verse of Boëthius, who also chose a 'mixed form' for his most famous treatise.

The *Confessions* of Augustine, his *De Doctrina Christiana*, and other of his works give a clear idea both of the flourishing state of the schools in Africa and of the manner in which a Christian education was being developed beside or grafted on to the pagan, for the purpose of training the clergy as well as laymen.

[1] op. cit., p. 374.

[2] *Les Africains*, p. 453 sq.

[3] J. M. Clark, *The Abbey of S. Gall*, Cambridge 1926, pp. 96 sq., 249 sq.

[4] Cf. Gregory of Tours, *Hist.* x. 30: 'Quod si te, sacerdos dei quicunque es, Martianus noster septem disciplinis erudiit, id est, si te in grammaticis docuit legere, in dialecticis alterca- tionum propositiones advertere, in rhetoricis genera metrorum agnoscere, in geometricis terrarum linearumque mensuras colligere, in astrologicis cursus siderum contemplari, in arithmeticis numerorum partes colligere, in harmoniis sonorum modulationes suavium accentuum carminibus concrepare, ut tibi stilus noster sit rusticus,' etc.

Rhetoric ruled here as elsewhere. Indeed, Africa seems to have
rivalled Gaul as a producer of rhetoricians. The schools of
Carthage were especially famous. 'Latinarum litterarum artifices Roma atque Carthago', says Augustine,[1] and Salvian[2]
towards the middle of the fifth century speaks of 'the schools
of the liberal arts, the lecture rooms of the philosophers, in
short, all the institutions for training students either in literature or in morals'.[3]

The Vandal invasion broke rudely upon the prosperity and
careless luxury of the African provinces. The sources tell of
cities destroyed, of orchards ruined, of wholesale confiscations
and the enslavement of the people. But it is not long before
we find the schools again well established and men of letters
welcomed at the Vandal court. Among those who had a share
in the restoration of the interrupted tradition of learning was
a grammarian named Felicianus, whom his pupil Dracontius,
in faulty verses, pictures as instructing both 'Romans' and
barbarians in the school of Carthage:

> sancte pater, o magister, taliter canendus es,
> qui fugatas Africanae reddis urbi litteras,
> barbaris qui Romulidas iungis auditorio,
> cuius ordines profecto semper obstupescimus,
> quos capit dulcedo vestri, doctor, oris maxima.[4]

The upper-class Vandals found it necessary, of course, to have
their children taught Latin, and they appear to have entered
into the life of the cities to a greater extent than other barbarians in the Empire.[5] The period of the Vandal dominion
saw what might almost be called a revival of poetry in Africa,
a revival which is shared by the old and the new, the profane
and the Christian tradition. Dracontius as a Christian poet
can hold his own with the 'epic' poets of fifth-century Gaul,
and in his profane verses he is simply a poet of the schools like
most of the contributors to the 'African anthology' which was
compiled in the last days of the Vandal kingdom.

Blossius Aemilius Dracontius was a lawyer and 'vir clarissimus'. As he loved rhetoric, he wrote and recited poetry, and
this led to his downfall. For he seems to have sung the praises
of the Roman Emperor instead of those of King Gunthamund,

[1] *Epist.* cxviii. 2. 9 (*C.S.E.L.* xxxiv.
p. 674), quoted by Schanz, IV. ii, p. 315.
[2] *De Gubernatione Dei*, vii. 16.
[3] I use Hodgkin's translation, *Italy
and her Invaders*, ii. 243, note 1.

[4] Dracontius, ed. F. Vollmer, *Poet.
Lat. Min.* v, Leipzig 1914, p. 108.
[5] Cf. the poem of Florentinus in
praise of King Thrasamund, Riese, no.
376, described below, p. 113.

his real lord and master.[1] He was cast into prison and his family with him. His sufferings were severe, but he was able to lighten the load of his imprisonment by writing verses. In the *Satisfactio*, an elegiac poem, he asks forgiveness of God and of the king, and hopes that he may win release from his bonds. There is a good deal of ordinary school rhetoric in this poem, especially in the passage in which the mixture of good and evil in this world is described. God might have made the world an entirely pleasant place if He had so chosen. but actually He created good mixed with evil and evil mixed with good. This fact is exemplified throughout the creation:

> sic elementa potens contraria miscuit auctor,
> humida cum siccis, ignea cum gelidis.
> littera doctiloquax apibus cognata refertur,
> quis datur ut habeant vulnera, castra, favos:
> cera dat ingenium pueris, primordia sensus,
> inde fit ut praestet littera vel noceat.
> aspis habet mortes, habet et medicamina serpens,
> vipera saepe iuvat, vipera saepe nocet.
> cerva salutares pasto serpente medullas
> conficit et pellunt ipsa venena neces.
> materies ferri simplex et noxia fertur,
> impius inde nocet, rusticus inde placet.
> ipsa parit gemmas pretiosos terra lapillos,
> ipsa dat et vepres, spinea ligna, rosas.[2]

But the catalogue is too long to quote in full. It is typical of the rhetorician that he does not know how to select; he must go through the whole list of examples. So in the long 'epic', *De Laudibus Dei*, the theme of which is the greatness and goodness of God illustrated in His dealings with man, Dracontius, after describing the creation, sets out in full the distribution of beasts, of plants and of precious stones in the various countries of the world.[3]

---

[1] Cf. *Romulea*, vii. 70 (op. cit., p. 137), 'dederant quia carmina clades', and *Satisfactio*, 93–4 (p. 98):

> culpa mihi fuerat dominos reticere modestos
> ignotumque mihi scribere vel dominum, etc.

[2] *Satisfactio*, 59 sqq. (p. 97 sq.).

[3] *De Laudibus Dei*, i. 292 sqq. (p. 14 sq.). Another rhetorical passage is in praise of light (i. 118 sqq., p. 6):

> lux datur ante polum, lux clari causa diei,
> lux iubar aetherium, lux noctis limes et umbris,

lux facies rerum, dux lux cunctis elementis, etc.

Cf. also ii. 263 sqq. (p. 45 sq.) on man's cruelty in hunting beasts that are harmless when left alone:

> quid pisces meruere freti, quid turba volucrum?
> pervasit gens nostra fretum, pervaditur aer,
> ut capiantur aves ex nulla parte nocentes.

What is all this but the rhetorical frivolity of the school-exercise? In Book iii, 689 sqq., there is a long description of the reclothing with sinews and flesh

In these poems, Dracontius shows that he had drunk deep of the Christian spirit, but that did not prevent him from collecting, perhaps while he was still in prison, his profane verses under the title of *Romulea*.[1] These are mainly, if we except the two epithalamia, school-exercises for declamation,[2] and even the epithalamia are written according to rule. The first of these latter is in honour of the marriages of two brothers, Victorianus and Rufinianus,[3] and it makes use of the ordinary mythological apparatus, with those personifications— Risus, Amplexus (iusta), Libido (moderata), Voluptas, Fides, Petulentia—which had become indispensable. The other epithalamium, for the marriage of Joannes and Vitula, which was written while Dracontius was still in prison,[4] is likewise in the form of a myth, in which Venus and Cupid play their part.

Several of the remaining poems are narratives in verse on some mythological theme such as was often set for an exercise in the schools. The first is the fable of Hylas and the nymphs:

> Fata canam pueri Nympharum versa calore
> in melius; sic Musa mones. quis casus ademit
> Alcidi comitem, solamen dulce malorum?[5]

Venus embraces Cupid and asks a favour of him. Cupid says that he will grant it whatever it is:

> audeo si cupias ipsum flammare Tonantem
> et dominum caeli facie vestire iuvenci
> oblitumque poli rursus mugire per herbas
> conversum per prata bovem: cadat aureus imber,
> divitias ut tecta pluant. . . .

Cupid continues in a strain yet more frivolous, and in a manner which shows why Augustine spoke so harshly of the learning

of the dry bones over which Ezekiel prophesied (Ezek. xxxvii) in the valley:

> nascuntur venae, iam nervis membra
>   ligantur,
> iam tegit ossa cutis multos distenta
>   per artus;
> quaerit colla caput, constringit gut-
>   tura cervix,
> verticis eximii replentur et ossa
>   cerebro,

and so on, in great and useless detail. On rhetoric in Dracontius, see Manitius, *Christl. Lat. Poesie*, p. 337, and note 3.

[1] 'Romulea soll wohl den Gegensatz klassischer Poesie zu christlicher Dichtung ausdrücken,' ib., p. 338, note 4;

but as we have seen above (p. 105) Dracontius uses Romulidae in the sense of Romans, i.e. as opposed to barbarians.

[2] Dracontius did declaim at least one of them in public, as we know from a note in the MS.:

Explicit controversia statuae viri fortis, quam dixit in Gargilianis thermis Blossius Emilius Dracontius, vir clarissimus et togatus fori proconsulis almae Karthaginis, apud proconsulem Pacideium (Vollmer, op. cit., p. 130).

[3] ib., pp. 130 sqq.
[4] Cf. verse 134, 'at cum liber ero, etc.' (p. 139).
[5] p. 109.

of the schools. But all that Venus wants is that the Nymphs shall be stricken with love of Hylas, and that Hercules shall thereby lose his favourite. This is what happens, and Hercules wonders who will now wipe off the sweat from his weary body after the battle, who will be his companion when his step-mother makes fresh labours for him? What shall he say to the boy's mother when he meets her? Well, after all, he can make her look on the bright side of things:

> exulta, genetrix, nimium laetare, beata,
> ante parens hominis, pulchri modo numinis auctor.[1]

She was once the mother of a mortal, now she is the mother of a demi-god.

Another poem has for its subject, 'the words of Hercules when he saw the heads of the hydra sprouting again after he had cut them off'. He, not unnaturally, invoked almighty Jove,

> Iuppiter omnipotens, celsi moderator Olympi,
> cur mihi viperei fetus mala fata minantur?[2]

and complained rhetorically that his sword instead of destroying creates new enemies,

> saevos gladius mihi suggerit hostis,
> non rapit ecce meus, sed proelia victa reformat.

This is of course the usual rhetorical imaginary theme, as is the versified 'deliberation of Achilles whether he shall sell the body of Hector'.[3] The debate is conducted after the fashion of a *suasoria*. There is a prologue, in which Achilles is asked to give up the body, and the usual philosophical arguments are brought forward to persuade him. These arguments show how the popular philosophy, taught for centuries in the schools, still survived in all its uselessness. The pupil must still learn to argue about the fate of the soul after death:

> quid prohibes tumulos, quamvis iactura sepulchri
> temnitur et nihil est quodvis in morte periclum?
> si sensus post fata perit, cur busta negantur?
> si mens ulla manet, iam rectius ergo putatur
> non requies sed poena rogus: tormenta sepulchrum
> ingerit et manes tolerant per membra dolorem.
> sed sensum cum luce simul post fata perire
> segnibus et pueris mentitur fama relatrix.
> sunt animae post membra piae; quas ignea virtus
> tollit ad astra micans et solis in orbe recondit

---

[1] op. cit., p. 114.   [2] p. 116.   [3] pp. 162 sqq.

lunares non passa globos; ac desuper orbem
expectant stellasque vagas et signa leonis
Augusto quid mense parent, quid cetera temptent
ornamenta poli.   rident sua membra videntes,
funeris abiecti fragiles et corporis usus,
ut doleant animae iam libertate recepta
corporibus vixisse suis et clausa tulisse
carceris angusti.   tumulos aut ossibus urnas
dedignant animae, non curant vile sepulchrum
et plangunt non esse simul, quos urna polorum
claudit et aetherium Phoebus suspendit ad axem.[1]

This passage is reminiscent of Lucan, and bears the stamp of
the orientalized Stoicism which was one of the elements con-
tributing, as we have already seen, to the religious outlook of
the later Empire.[2] These conceptions were always rooted in the
schools, and they survived as material for poetry for many
centuries.

The next section of the poem is a reply to a possible objection; 'at inquies: si post vitam animae corpora sua despiciunt,
pro Hectore cur rogamus?' This has to be answered by a
pathetic appeal to the tears of Hector's wife, his child, and
friends.   But there is yet another objection; 'at inquies:
dolorem meum leniam, percussorem Patrocli canibus et volu-
cribus si dedero laniandum.' Some of the arguments adduced
in reply to this are curious, and are such as only a rhetor could
have devised.   If Achilles gives the body to be torn by dogs,
he thinks he is doing it a wrong, but the Medes and Persians
think it an honourable thing that birds shall tear the members
of the dead.   Also if Hector's body is left to decay, it will be
a source of infection,

> Hector in hoste fuit saevus, cum vita maneret:
> plus post fata nocet.

The poem ends with a peroration, a final appeal to Achilles.

It was doubtless recited in public, like the versified *contro-*
versia,[3] *De statua viri fortis*, which illustrates the way in which
these imaginary situations had still retained their popularity.

[1] p. 163 (verses 10–30).
[2] Cf. Cumont, *Astrology and Religion
among the Greeks and Romans*, p. 178.
He quotes the epigram in Buecheler,
Carmina Epigr., no. 611: 'My divine
soul shall not descend to the shades;
heaven and the stars have borne me
away; earth holds my body, and this
stone an empty name.'

[3] See above, p. 107; text of the
controversia in Dracontii *Opera*, pp. 118
sqq. There is another versified *contro-*
versia in the 'African Anthology'
(Riese, no. 21), the subject of which is,
'Sacrilegus capite puniatur.' 'De templo Neptuni aurum perit. interposito
tempore piscator piscem aureum posuit
et titulo inscribsit "De tuo tibi Nep-
tune". reus fit sacrilegii. contra dicit.'

There are two men at enmity in a city; one is rich and the other is poor. The city is at war. The rich man performs brave deeds, and asks and obtains as his reward a public statue; for he is to have whatever he desires. Once again, he does bravely; this time, he asks that a right of asylum shall be attached to his statue. This also is granted. For the third time, he distinguishes himself in war, and now he asks for the head of his enemy, a poor man. The latter flees for refuge to the rich man's statue. Is the right of asylum to hold good or not? The subject is debated for more than three hundred verses of rhetorical question and answer, with the usual historical and mythological parallels and the usual false pathos. The weeping figure of the *patria* herself is introduced, to move the rich man to pity:

> haec simulacrorum vox est Patriaeque gementis
> audi verba tuae: 'merito te laeta creavi,
> infantem gremio tenui, simul ubera parvo
> Vrbs mater tremibunda dedi cunabula praestans,
> quem praetextatum iaculis proludere iussi:
> impubes iam fortis eras, invictus adultus
> et iuvenis victor.[1]

So the long appeal proceeds. It is tedious enough, but it seems to have delighted the audience that crowded to hear it in one of the great halls of the baths at Carthage. The other pieces are declamations in narrative form, on mythological subjects. The *Hylas* has already been mentioned; and the *Hercules*. Besides these, there are a *Rape of Helen*, a *Medea*, and an *Orestes*. The *Helen* begins with a setting forth of the enormity of the crime of Paris, which is such that the poet feels the need of invoking Homer to aid him:

> ergo nefas Paridis, quod raptor gessit adulter,
> ut monitus narrare queam, te, grandis Homere,—
> mollia blandifluo delimas verba palato.[2]

It is unnecessary to follow the narrative in detail. It is enough to say that it is wholly rhetorical in conception. In a storm at sea Paris gives a long declamation on the advantages of a shepherd's life,

> felici sorte creati
> pastores, quos terra capit, quos nulla procella
> concutit.

Then the pastoral delights are detailed, one by one—and a great wave comes which wrecks the fleet.

---

[1] Vollmer, op. cit., p. 128 sq.   [2] p. 140.

The *Medea* is likewise a rhetorical narrative. In it there are lines of ingenious emptiness:

> sic puer Idalius spargebat plausibus ignes:
> piscis aves armenta pecus fera pastor anhelant
> flammigero surgente deo   (110–112.)

or

> iuvenemque Pelasgum
> diligat optet amet cupiat suspiret anhelet   (141–2.)

or

> dives pauper inops raptor pirata sacerdos
> advenient sub lege pari, non sorte sub una.   (411–12.)

A similar device is employed in the *Orestes*,

> pectora cor sensus animum praecordia mentem
> conturbat pietas dolor angina maeror origo
> affectus natura pudor reverentia fama.   (558–60.)

Embedded in this last piece is a long *controversia*, the speech of Molossus, accusing Orestes before the Areopagus, and the equally studied reply of Orestes in his own defence.[1]

All these secular poems are interesting mainly as showing how under the Vandal regime the old life of the schools continued, and men could think of nothing better to aim at than what had been done unimaginatively for centuries. There are evidences, indeed, in Dracontius of the decline of the old prosody,[2] and even the casual reader will note signs of 'medievalization' in the speech of the poet.[3] It was as a Christian poet that Dracontius lived in the affection of Spanish readers, and it was largely on account of Bishop Eugenius of Toledo's recension of his *Laudes Dei* that he became known at all to later ages. A not unpleasing little poem, called *Aegritudo Perdicae*[4] has been ascribed to Dracontius, but it has in parts a freshness which is lacking in his school exercises, and it moves occasionally, amid its rhetoric, with a little show of grace. It appears, however, to be an African product of about this time. It tells of the love of Perdica for his own mother Castalia; and of his suicide in his despair. There are, of course, rhetorical speeches, and a long description of how Hippocrates diagnoses the boy's strange malady, after the other physicians had failed. The various organs that they had vainly sounded are

---

[1] This is the only place in which Molossus appears as Orestes' accuser; see Schanz, IV. ii, p. 67, note 1.

[2] See Schanz, IV. ii, p. 68.

[3] E.g. the use of *quia*, 'agnovi quia furta paras', *Medea*, 346 (p. 183) and 350; for other examples, see Schanz, IV. ii, 68 and the literature there cited.

[4] Vollmer, op. cit., p. 238 sq.

catalogued. The boy's behaviour in the presence of his mother reveals the cause. The famous doctor says:

> causa subes, mater: medicinae munera cessant;
> hic animi labor est: hebeo. iam cetera di dent![1]

After this Amor and Pudor conflict in the soul of Perdica. In vain are beautiful women brought to cure him of his passion. 'Nulla tamen matri similis!' he says. At this stage the poet calls on Calliope to aid him; else he cannot describe the state to which the hero of his poem was reduced. He has recourse to the usual device of minute description:

> primis languentes pallor perfuderat artus,
> tempora demersis intus cecidere latebris
> et graciles cecidere modo per acumina nares,
> concava luminibus macies circumdata sedit
> longaque testantur ieiunia viscera macra,
> arida nudati distendunt bracchia nervi,
> ordine digestae consumpto tegmine costae
> produnt quidquid homo est et quod celare sepulchris
> mors secreta solet. sat erit tibi, saeve Cupido?[2]

How shall he die? Perdica decides finally for the noose, and this is to be his epitaph:

> hic Perdica iacet secumque Cupido peremptus.

The revival of African poetry in the fifth century had its culmination in the appearance of a collection of smaller Latin poems towards the end of the Vandal dominion in Africa. This so-called 'African Anthology'[3] was gathered together by an unknown editor, who chose things old and new, foreign and native; but, in general, the collection bears an African stamp. It is preserved in a manuscript (Codex Paris. 10318) which was the property of the great Salmasius (it was hence called *Codex Salmasianus*) and is an uncial of the seventh or eighth century.[4] Its lacunae are supplemented by other manuscripts, and the whole collection consists of nearly five hundred pieces. The correct title is *libri epigrammaton*, and perhaps we may take the ninetieth epigram as setting forth the spirit in which the compiler would have wished his book to be read:

[1] ib., p. 245.
[2] p. 249.
[3] The best short account of this collection is in Schanz, IV. ii, pp. 69 sqq. The collection contains poems which mention the Vandal kings Thrasamund and Hilderich (496–530); it also appears to refer to events of the year 532. The Vandal kingdom ended in 534.
[4] It is important to note that Traube considered this MS. to be of Spanish provenance. Riese, pp. xiii sqq., describes the MS.

> Parvola quod lusit, sensit quod iunior aetas,
> quod sale Pierio garrula lingua sonat,
> hoc opus inclusit.   tu, lector, corde perito
> omnia perpendens delige quod placeat.[1]

For, in some sort, this anthology is a book of youth, compiled for youth's delight. It ranges from pieces ascribed to Virgil, Ovid, or Seneca, through the brilliance of Petronius to the *Pervigilium Veneris*, the *Medea* of Hosidius Geta, and the poets of the editor's own day. Not only single epigrams but whole groups assigned to particular authors are gathered in. The last book, for instance, is a collection of the epigrams of Luxorius, and there are a number of riddles under the name of Symphosius. Here are epanaleptic verses and centos, epigrams of excessive obscenity and, by their side, those descriptions of works of art or of nature which afforded endless material for the imitative poet.

One curiosity is a prose *Preface*[2] which is composed of unusual words taken from the dim recesses of glossaries. It begins:

Hactenus me intra vurgam animi litescentis inipitum tua eritudo, instar mihi luminis extimande, a te normam reduviare conpellit.

This fashion must have arisen among the pedantic grammarians of the schools. It found a home in Spain and Gaul and thence, perhaps, it spread to England and Ireland.[3]

It has been pointed out[4] that many of the poets of the anthology are grammarians; the names of a good number are known, and it is possible to arrange some of them roughly in order of date.[5] There are, in the first place, those that belong to the reign of King Thrasamund, 496–523.[6] To this tolerably enlightened monarch Florentinus addressed a poem of praise[7] in thirty-nine hexameters. The king is lauded first,

> Regia festa canam sollemnibus annua votis.
> imperiale decus Thrasamundi gloria mundi,
> regnantis Libyae; toto sic clarior orbe
> sol radiante micans cunctis super enitet astris.
> in quo concordant pietas prudentia mores
> virtus forma decus animus sensusque virilis
> invigilans animo sollers super omnia mens est.

---

[1] *Anthol. Lat.*, ed. Riese, Leipzig 1894, no. 90.   [2] ib., no. 19.
[3] See below, p. 153 sqq.
[4] Schanz, IV. ii, p. 70.
[5] Schanz, IV. ii. p. 71, whose classification I follow.
[6] There is, it is true, a short piece (no. 387) by one Cato, a grammarian, which mentions King Hunnerich, 477–84.
[7] No. 376.

The rest of the poem depicts the flourishing state of Carthage and of Aliana, the daughter-city:

> te regnante diu fulgent Carthaginis arces,
> filia quam sequitur Alianas inpare gressu.

A poet named Felix wrote five epigrams[1] on the baths of Aliana, which had been constructed by the command of the king. 'The last of these epigrams consists of twelve hexameters; each verse contains thirty-seven letters, and possesses an acrostic, a mesostich, and a telestich, which make up the sentence: *Thrasamundus cunta innovat vota serenans.*'[2] As the epigram is short it is given in full as an example of the continuance of this kind of versification:

> Tranquillo nymfae deCurrite fluminis ortV.
> Huc proba flagranti sVccedite numina FoebO
> Rupibus ex celsis, ubi Nunc fastigia surgunT
> Aequanturque polo toTis praecelsa lavacrA
> Sedibus. hic magnis exArdent marmora signiS,
> Ardua sublimes praevIncunt culmina termaE
> Muneraque eximius taNti dat liminis auctoR
> Vnica continuae praeNoscens praemia famaE
> Non hic flamma nocet. vOtum dinoscite carmeN,
> Discite vel quanto viVat sub gurgite lymphA.
> Vandalicum hic renovAt caro de semine nomeN,
> Sub cuius titulo meriTis stat gratia factiS.

The author of this piece is perhaps the Flavius Felix, 'vir clarissimus', who addressed twenty elegiac distichs to the 'primiscrinarius Victorinianus', not, as he says, that he might receive perishable honours or riches, but only a modest ecclesiastical prebend on which he might live out his days, for he had fallen on hard times:[3]

> adnue poscenti, miserum sustolle ruinae;
> clericus ut fiam, dum velis ipse, potes.

Thrasamund was succeeded in 523 by Hilderich, who reigned until 530. Luxorius, a grammarian, 'vir clarissimus et spectabilis', belongs to his reign; he was a Carthaginian, a Christian, and a prolific poet. The 'African Anthology' contains a whole book of his youthful[4] epigrams—*liber epigrammaton*—dedicated to his master Faustus,

> tantus grammaticae magister artis.

Many of these works of his youth display to the full that

---

[1] Nos. 210 sqq.
[2] I quote Schanz, IV. ii. p. 72; *cunta* is for *cuncta*, on which see W. Corssen, *Über Aussprache, Vokalismus und Betonung der latein. Sprache*, i[2], Leipzig 1868, p. 36. [3] No. 254.
[4] No. 287, *Ad Faustum*; cf. verse 5, quos olim puer in foro paravi | versus.

obscenity[1] which by long association had come to be in-
separable from the epigram. It was part of the recipe, and
must not be left out. The subjects were no longer taken from
life; they were stale imitations of what had often been said
before, such imitations as we shall see in the almost contemporary work of Ennodius in Italy.[2] Imitative likewise are the
pieces on works of art or on gardens, though here the poet may
have had 'his eye on the object'. There are pleasant lines, for
instance, on the garden of Eugetius, which show how the
pleasures of life were maintained under the Vandal kings:[3]

> Hortus, quo faciles fluunt Napaeae,
> quo ludunt Dryades virente choro,
> quo fovet teneras Diana Nymphas,
> quo Venus roseos recondit artus,
> quo fessus teretes Cupido flammas
> suspensis reficit liber pharetris,
> quo se Laconides ferunt puellae,
> cui nunquam minus est amoena frondis,
> cui semper redolent amoma verni,
> cui fons perspicuis tener fluentis
> muscoso riguum parit meatu,
> quo dulcis avium canor resultat . . .
> quidquid per varias refertur urbes,
> hoc uno famulans loco subaptat.

More charming still are some verses on a lap-dog, a 'pretty
trifle', which was imitated once in the Middle Ages:[4]

> Forma meae catulae brevis est, sed amabilis inde,
>   hanc totam ut possit concava ferre manus.
> ad domini vocem famulans et garrula currit,
>   humanis tamquam motibus exiliens.
> nec monstrosum aliquid membris gerit illa decoris;
>   omnibus exiguo corpore visa placet.
> mollior huic cibus est somnusque in stramine molli,
>   muribus infensa est, saevior atque catis.
> vincit membra nimis latratu fortia torvo;
>   si natura daret, posset ab arte loqui.

Besides this book of epigrams there is a collection of epanaleptic distichs on mythological subjects which are almost certainly
to be assigned to Luxorius, as they are preceded by this couplet:

> Priscos, Luxori, certum est te vincere vates;
>   carmen namque tuum duplex victoria gestat.[5]

---

[1] The obscene *Epithalamium Fridi* (no. 18), a Virgilian cento like that of Ausonius, belongs to Luxorius.

[2] See below, p. 120.

[3] No. 332; there are similar descriptions in nos. 346, 350, 360.

[4] No. 359; see Gaselee, *Transition from the Late Latin Lyric to the Medieval Love Poem*, Cambridge 1931, p. 8, where there is a graceful translation.

[5] No. 37.

They have, of course, no poetical merit, but they exhibit the persistence of a perverse form which was seriously accepted by later poets. One example will suffice:[1]

De Apolline.
Gratia magna tibi, Paean, qui pectora conples.
lector, si faveas, gratia magna tibi.

Coronatus, another 'vir clarissimus' and grammarian, wrote a poem on the Virgilian theme,

vivo equidem vitamque extrema per omnia duco.[2]

Calbulus wrote on Christian themes,[3] as did Peter the Referendarius.[4] Besides these there is a whole series of minor poets, represented by one or, at most, by two or three epigrams. Here is a specimen of the 'wit' of Tuccianus.[5]

Cantica gignit amor et amorem cantica gignunt.
cantandum est, ut ametur, et ut cantetur, amandum.

Lastly, the 'anthology' contains a collection of a hundred versified riddles which are the work of Symphosius, a *scholasticus*, who may possibly have been a contemporary of these later poets of the Vandal kingdom.[6] In any case the author can hardly be speaking the truth when he says that he composed them on the spur of the moment at a convivial gathering during the Saturnalia. Many of them are obviously 'chestnuts'. Here is the 'Chicken in the Egg':[7]

Pullus in ovo.
Mira tibi referam nostrae primordia vitae.
nondum natus eram nec eram iam matris in alvo.
iam posito partu natum me nemo videbat.

The importance of Symphosius lies in the fact that his collection was the basis directly or indirectly of Anglo-Saxon books of riddles, and especially of Aldhelm's.[8] Here the poetry of the Vandal kingdom has its end. In June 533 a fleet sailed from the Bosphorus under the leadership of Belisarius. On the 15th of September in the same year the soldiers of the Emperor entered Carthage, and the Vandals disappeared from history.

---

[1] Riese, No. 79.
[2] No. 223; *Aen.* iii. 315; 226 and 228 also are by Coronatus.
[3] No. 378.
[4] No. 380.
[5] No. 277.

[6] See Schanz, IV. ii. p. 75. The lack of positive evidence makes it difficult to date these poems.
[7] No. 286 (xiv).
[8] Cf. Manitius, *Christl. lat. Poesie*, pp. 484, 487 (Aldhelm); 502 (Tatwine and Eusebius).

III

THE SIXTH CENTURY

§ 1. *Italy: Ennodius, Boëthius, Maximian.*

THE most important political event of the sixth century was the establishment of the Franks in Gaul. The foundations were then laid of a power which was to exercise a decisive influence on Western civilization. At the beginning of the century learning in Gaul was suffering severely from the breakdown of the system of public schools, and it did not really recover until the time of Charles the Great. In Africa the Vandal kingdom gave place to a restoration of the imperial power under Justinian and his successors, and the schools remained until the final deluge of the Arab conquest. In Spain the Byzantines gained a foothold in the south and east, but they were not sufficiently strong to prevent the establishment of a progressive state in the remainder of the peninsula after the conversion of the Visigoths from the Arian heresy to Catholicism.

In Italy there was, as in Africa, an imperial restoration after a series of wars in which the Ostrogothic kingdom dissolved in ruins. This was the end of a promising epoch, in which the great king Theodoric appeared to be laying the foundations of an era of prosperity and of intellectual revival. For in Italy the peaceful revolution of A.D. 476, and the substitution in 493 of one barbarian ruler for another, involved no fundamental change in the political and social life of the country. There were, of course, the barbarian settlers with their own laws and customs, and, what was far more serious, their Arian priests and bishops. In spite of the encouragement given by Theodoric to the schools[1] and his sense of the value of learning it was impossible for the Goths to mix sufficiently with the Italians to imbibe much of Roman culture, and they remained to the end, because of the impassable barrier of religion, strangers in the land. Neither they nor their kinsmen the Visigoths seem to have made any specific spiritual contribution to the civilization into which they had come as settlers.

But the first half of the sixth century in Italy witnessed the career of a man whose influence was destined to reach far beyond that of kings or princes, a man by whose work the

[1] Roger, *L'Enseignement des lettres classiques*, p. 170 sq.

Roman spirit lived on in the accomplishment of the task of preserving the elements of civilization amid a deluge of barbarism. Benedict of Nursia is for us at this distance of time one of the great figures of the first half of the sixth century in Italy. He performed no immediate service to learning, but he definitely avoided, in his monastic Rule, any pronounced tendency towards a hostile attitude to letters.[1] The story of Benedictine learning belongs to later centuries, but the sixth century saw the foundation by Cassiodorus Senator (c. 490–c. 583) of the monastery of Vivarium, where the first example was given of the establishment in monasteries of a system of education which gave a prominent place to the liberal arts. In the library at Vivarium were collected, as opportunity offered, the literary and scientific treasures of the ancient world, as well as the indispensable works of theology and devotion. It is hard to overestimate our debt to Vivarium and to Cassiodorus. This library it was that handed on many precious codices to the libraries of Bobbio and of Verona, and through them, and other libraries, to the Carolingian scribes.[2]

But all this was work for the future. In contemporary Italy the schools still persisted and produced rhetoricians and poets according to pattern. Of the three poets whom we have to consider, Ennodius and Maximianus were certainly according to pattern, but Boëthius was a man of original power.

Magnus Felix Ennodius (474–521) was a Gaul by birth, but he seems to have received most of his education in Italy. He was betrothed to a rich lady at a time when he had fallen into poverty. But her fortune declined and both turned to religion. Ennodius became a deacon in 493; a career opened before him in the city of Milan, where he was closely associated with the Bishop, and, at the same time, he continued his tireless pursuit of rhetoric and the fashioning of verses. He was shrewd enough to make the most of the chances that came his way, and he crowned his career by becoming Bishop of Ticinum. In this office he conducted himself with prudence, and after his death in 521 he was reckoned among the saints. Rhetoric was the master-passion of his life. In a *Paraenesis didascalica*, a didactic treatise addressed to two young men, Ambrosius and Beatus, he sets forth his educational ideal.[3] Ennodius was

[1] See on this subject Hörle, *Frühmittelalt. Mönchs- und Klerikerbildung in Italien*, Freiburg-i-B. 1914, p. 48; the remarks of Roger, p. 173, deal with the exaggerated ideas once current of what the *Rule* did for learning.
[2] See Hörle, pp. 9 sqq.
[3] Works in *C.S.E.L.*, ed. Hartel, pp. 401 sqq.; also Vogel, *M.G.H., Auct. Antiq.* vii (my references are to Hartel).

doubtful whether he should write in verse or in prose; he
finally decided to write in a mixture of both—'quia et praeci-
pientem decet fortis elocutio et pressis admonitione mentibus
mollioris stili cura subvenitur'. After a short poem in praise of
poetry he gets back to business for a little, and speaks of the
three virtues, Verecundia, Castitas, and Fides, but each of them
has to introduce herself with a little poem. These virtues are
the foundation of learning; on them the fabric of the liberal
arts is to be raised. Grammar appears and speaks pleasantly
in trochaic tetrameters, but Rhetoric speaks, of course, in
elegiacs, as befits the art of arts:

> sit noster tantum, non stringunt crimina quemquam.
>   nos vitae maculas tergimus artis ope.
> si niveo constet merito quis teste senatu,
>   cogimus hunc omnes dicere nocte satum.
> et reus et sanctus de nostro nascitur ore:
>   dum loquimur, captum ducitur arbitrium.
> lana Tarentinae laus urbis, gemma, potestas
>   quid sunt ad nostrum iuncta supercilium?
> qui nostris servit studiis, mox imperat orbi.
>   nil dubium metuens ars mihi regna dedit.[1]

Rhetoric is the great source of poetry as of other arts and
studies—'poetica, iuris peritia, dialectica, arithmetica, cum
me utantur *quasi genetrice*, me tamen adserente sunt pretio'.
This is fine teaching for one who was in orders and a director
of souls. But Ennodius was merely repeating what he had been
taught and what he firmly believed to be true. Like Sidonius
he had acquired that literary frivolity which never deserts a man
who has once received its mark upon him. Yet, like Sidonius,
when the Church had claimed him, he served her well and
faithfully, and tended with diligence the flock entrusted to his
charge.[2] In his *Eucharisticum de Vita sua*,[3] a confession to God
in which he tells how he was led by the divine goodness out
of a life of sin, Ennodius describes in his dull and tortuous
manner his early love of verse:

Nam elevatus insanis successibus poetarum me gregi ignarus venerandae
professionis indideram: delectabant carmina quadratis fabricata particulis
et ordinata pedum varietate solidata: angelorum choris me fluxum aut
tenerum poema miscebat, et si evenisset, ut essem clarorum versuum servata
lege formator, sub pedibus meis subiectum quicquid caeli tegitur axe cerne-
bam.[4]

[1] Hartel, p. 408.
[2] On Ennodius as a Bishop see
Grisar, *History of Rome and the Popes*
in the Middle Ages, ii. p. 245.
[3] Hartel, pp. 393 sqq.
[4] ib., pp. 394–5.

But none of the verses that Ennodius composed in youth or age has the least claim to distinction. The epigrams—and many of them so obscene that they must belong to the time before he took orders—are obscene to the limit of pointlessness, and it is hard to choose one that will give a favourable idea of the poet's skill. He composed a couplet 'on a fool who had the name of Virgil':

> In tantum prisci defluxit fama Maronis,
> ut te Virgilium saecula nostra darent.[1]

Not content with this, he produced four equally fatuous epigrams on the same theme:

> Si fatuo dabitur tam sanctum nomen homullo,
> gloria maiorum curret in obprobrium.

Aliter

> Captivo stultus congaudet stemmate vatis.
> non est Virgilius, dicitur iste tamen.

Aliter

> Externo quotiens vocitaris nomine, demens,
> si tibi sunt sensus, prospice ne venias.

Aliter

> Cur te Virgilium mentiris, pessime, nostrum?
> non potes esse Maro, sed potes esse moro.

The longer poems, such as the *Epithalamium* for Maximus,[2] show that Ennodius had no constructive capacity. The *Epithalamium* is a polymetric poem,[3] and the variety of metres tends to destroy the small amount of unity the piece might otherwise have possessed. The theme, if there is a theme, is the reluctance of Maximus to follow the bidding of nature and get married. Venus is described, naked and beautiful; to her Cupid laments the coldness of the race of men:

> perdidimus, genetrix, virtutis praemia nostrae.
> iam nusquam Cytherea sonat, ridetur Amorum
> fabula, nec proles nascenti sufficit aevo.

[1] Hartel, p. 598; Vogel, p. 242. Efforts have been made, without success, to prove that this Virgil is the famous Virgilius Maro Grammaticus; who would thus belong to the end of the fifth century; see Huemer, *Berlin. Sitzungsber.* cxix (1882), p. 511. Zimmer (see below, p. 154) accepts this view.

[2] Hartel, p. 512; Vogel, p. 276.

[3] Another polymetric poem is in praise of Faustus, consul in 490; Hartel, pp. 524 sqq.; Vogel, pp. 27 sqq. It ends in adonics:

> Lux mea, Fauste,
> spesque salusque,
> litterularum
> munera parva
> suscipe laetus, etc.

frigida consumens multorum possidet artus
virginitas: fervore novo sublimia carnem
vota domant: mundus tenui vix nomine constat.

This is far enough from the spirit of the verses in which Saint
Paulinus had blessed the union of Julianus and Titia,[1] and it
sounds strangely on the lips of a deacon of the Church. But
Ennodius knew that he would not be taken seriously; any
school-boy at that time might have had to compose a speech
on the same theme—'Cupid complains that young people are
reluctant to marry.' And how else could Cupid be made to
speak than in tones of rhetorical excess? Well, it is decided
that Maximus is to be the victim, along with the maiden whom
he is to wed. The transfixing of the lovers by Cupid's arrows
is described, and the poem ends.

The other poems are of little interest. There are a few
'itineraries',[2] but they never develop into a narrative and
hardly ever forsake the obscurity in which Ennodius loved to
move, or from which he was unable to escape. He is no happier
when he attempts the composition of hymns to supplement,
perhaps, for use in the Milanese Church, the modest and
beautiful legacy of Ambrose.[3]

The greatest mind of his age was Anicius Manlius Severinus
Boëthius.[4] He was born about 480 and was brought up in the
family of Q. Aurelius Symmachus, whose daughter he married.
He was devoted to learning and especially to natural science
and philosophy, as they were understood by the Neoplatonists:

hic quondam caelo liber aperto
suetus in aetherios ire meatus
cernebat rosei lumina solis,
visebat gelidae sidera lunae
et quaecumque vagos stella recursus
exercet varios flexa per orbes,
comprensam numeris victor habebat.
quin etiam causas unde sonora
flamina sollicitent aequora ponti,
quis volvat stabilem spiritus orbem
vel cur hesperias sidus in undas
casurum rutilo surgat ab ortu,
quid veris placidas temperet horas,
ut terram roseis floribus ornet,

[1] *Christian-Latin Poetry*, pp. 105–6.
[2] Hartel, p. 507, *A Journey to Brian-*
çon; ib., p. 517, *A Journey over the*
Po; on works of art, no. 18, Hartel,
p. 564; also no. 98, Hartel, p. 590; on
a garden of Theodoric, no. 111, Hartel,

p. 595.
[3] *Christian-Latin Poetry*, p. 116, and
note 3.
[4] On Boëthius see Manitius, *Gesch.* i.
pp. 22 sqq.

quis dedit ut pleno fertilis anno
autumnus gravidis influat uvis
rimari solitus atque latentis
naturae varias reddere causas . . .[1]

This curiosity about natural things led Boëthius on to the
great problems of philosophy.[2] He knew Plato and Aristotle
better than any of his contemporaries. He translated Aristotle's
Organon, and it was his ambition to provide a Latin version of
all his works, with an adequate commentary. He would perform a like service for the dialogues of Plato, and then, again
in the Neoplatonic spirit, he would attempt a reconciliation of
the systems of these two great thinkers. Arithmetic and music
attracted his attention, and he composed theological treatises.
With all this he was impelled by a sense of duty and family
tradition to follow the course of public office, and he became
consul in 510. His good fortune lasted until 524, when he fell
under the suspicion of treason, was imprisoned at Pavia, and
finally murdered by the command of Theodoric. It was in
prison that he wrote the *Consolation of Philosophy*, 'a golden
volume' as Gibbon called it, unmasking, in the words of Dante,
'the deceitful world to those who give it good hearing'. It is
'the supreme essay of one who throughout his life had found
his highest solace in the dry light of reason',[3] and it is a brave
construction from the best that his studies and his own reflection had taught him. The consolation is the consolation of
Philosophy and not of Religion. The final consolation he
possessed, no doubt, though there was apparently little of
mysticism in his nature.

Boëthius knew and loved the poets well, and the verses
scattered through the book have an impressive strength and
competence. In his youth he had written in another strain:

Carmina qui quondam studio florente peregi,
flebilis heu maestos cogor inire modos . . .[4]

Now the argument is higher, though the purpose of the verses
in the *Consolation* is to soften the austerity of its relentless
dialectic. 'Sed video te,' says Philosophy, 'iam dudum et
pondere quaestionis oneratum et rationis prolixitate fatigatum

---

[1] *De Consolatione*, i, metr. ii (p. 134,
ed. Stewart and Rand, *Loeb Library*).
[2] For his philosophical writings see
Ueberweg-Geyer, 'Die patristische und
scholastische Philosophie', in *Grundriss*

der Geschichte der Philosophie, Berlin
1928, ii, pp. 135 sqq.
[3] Stewart and Rand, p. x.
[4] *De Cons*. i, metr. i, p. 128.

aliquam carminis expectare dulcedinem. accipe igitur haustum quo refectus firmior in ulteriora contendas.'[1]

It is almost useless to quote the poems apart from their context, but there is one piece which might stand by itself—the fable of Orpheus and Eurydice, as the allegory of the soul that looks backward from the highest Good:[2]

Felix qui potuit boni
fontem visere lucidum,
felix qui potuit gravis
terrae solvere vincula.
quondam funera coniugis
vates Threicius gemens
postquam flebilibus modis
silvas currere mobiles,
amnes stare coegerat,
iunxitque intrepidum latus
saevis cerva leonibus,
nec visum timuit lepus
iam cantu placidum canem,
cum flagrantior intima
fervor pectoris ureret,
nec qui cuncta subegerant
mulcerent dominum modi,
inmites superos querens
infernas adiit domos.
illic blanda sonantibus
chordis carmina temperans
quidquid praecipuis deae
matris fontibus hauserat,

quod luctus dabat impotens,
quod luctum geminans amor,
deflet Taenara commovens
et dulci veniam prece
umbrarum dominos rogat.
stupet tergeminus novo
captus carmine ianitor,
quae sontes agitant metu
ultrices scelerum deae
iam maestae lacrimis madent.
non Ixionium caput
velox praecipitat rota
et longa site perditus
spernit flumina Tantalus.
vultur dum satur est modis,
non traxit Tityi iecur.
tandem, 'vincimur,' arbiter
umbrarum miserans ait,
'donamus comitem viro
emptam carmine coniugem.
sed lex dona coerceat,
ne, dum Tartara liquerit,
fas sit lumina flectere.'

quis legem det amantibus?
maior lex amor est sibi.
heu, noctis prope terminos
Orpheus Eurydicen suam
vidit, perdidit, occidit.

vos haec fabula respicit
quicumque in superum diem
mentem ducere quaeritis.
nam qui Tartareum in specus
victus lumina flexerit,
quidquid praecipuum trahit
perdit, dum videt inferos.

From that highest Good Boëthius never looked back, and it is with the vision of the providence and eternity of God that the *Consolation* ends. 'There remaineth also a beholder of all things which is God, who foreseeth all things, and the eternity

---

[1] ib., iv. 6, p. 352.   [2] ib., iii. 12, p. 294.

of His vision, which is always present, concurreth with the future quality of our actions, distributing rewards to the good and punishments to the evil. Neither do we in vain put our hope in God or pray to Him; for if we do this well and as we ought, we shall not lose our labour or be without effect. Wherefore fly vices, embrace virtues, possess your minds with worthy hopes, offer up humble prayers for the highest things. There is, if you will not dissemble, a great necessity of doing well imposed upon you, since you live in the sight of your Judge, who beholdeth all things.'

Such was the greatness of Boëthius's fame in after-days that a recent writer[1] has said that 'after Augustine he appears as the great teacher and weighty authority for the early Middle Ages'. He was 'noster summus philosophus'. The *Consolatio* was a concentration of the best of Neoplatonic, Augustinian and Aristotelian thought in a system admirably adapted to the common intelligence of medieval students. The poems were studied with care, and some of the simpler metres were imitated. Hugh of S. Victor is said to have commented on them and those of Martianus Capella in his Treatise on metres.[2] For many centuries commentaries and translations were produced in quick succession, and at the present day Boëthius does not fail of readers.

Boëthius had a young friend named Maximianus, a gifted student, obviously of high birth and perhaps of old Etruscan lineage. Maximian was much given to poetry, but it was not until he was an old man that he conceived the idea of reviving the Roman elegy in a collection of verses the main theme of which is the painfulness and weakness of age.[3] It is true that there are love adventures as well, but they do not end happily. In the third elegy Maximian tells how when he was a young man he fell in love with a girl named Aquilina. Just as Ovid might have done, he resorts to epanalepsis to emphasize his madness:

> captus amore tuo demens, Aquilina, ferebar
> pallidus et tristis, captus amore tuo.

The love was mutual; both were young and inexperienced, and they had to keep their love secret. But the girl's mother knew, and the lovers had to suffer. It was Boëthius who came to the rescue—'magnarum scrutator maxime rerum', as Maximian

[1] [Ueberweg]-Geyer, p. 137.
[2] Manitius, *Gesch.* i. p. 34.
[3] *Maximiani Elegiae* in Baehrens,

Poet. Lat. Min. v; *Eleg.* v. 5, 'me . . . Etruscae gentis alumnum': cf. ib. 40 (p. 341).

finely calls him. He noticed the pale and sad visage of his young friend, and made him confess the cause. How he cured him of his malady is perhaps best left to be told in the very word of Maximian, who ends by saying:

> sic mihi peccandi studium permissa potestas
> abstulit atque ipsum talia velle fugit.

It is profitless to speculate on the amount of *Wahrheit* mixed with the *Dichtung* of these elegies. But there is clearly something historical in this curious tale, as in the tale of Maximian's adventure with a Greek lady on the occasion of his visit to Constantinople as an ambassador to the Emperor.[1] Highly improper as the story may appear, it has an ingenious ending in a speech by the Greek courtesan, in which an idea is developed[2] with a persistence that would seem shameless if it were not clearly a mere exercise in rhetoric.

Similarly, in his other elegies, the laboured onslaught on old age was not intended by Maximian to win the sympathy but the admiration of his friends. It was not his misfortunes, but his literary talents that were to be given the first place:

> Aemula quid cessas finem properare senectus?
> cur et in hoc fesso corpore tarda venis?
> solve precor miseram tali de carcere vitam:
> mors est iam requies, vivere poena mihi.
> non sum qui fueram: periit pars maxima nostri;
> hoc quoque quod superest languor et horror habent.[3]

This is how he begins; so he labours on, and so with Maximian the Roman elegy has its inglorious end.

Maximian is, therefore, in some sort, the last of the Roman poets. There is no trace of Christianity in his elegies,[4] or of any other discipline than that of the secular schools. Right

---

[1] *Elegy* v (Baehrens, v. pp. 340 sqq.); the motif is the same as that of Ovid, *Amores* iii, 7. The date of the embassy seems to be round about the year 550, i.e. during the Gothic wars.

[2] *Elegy* v. 107 sqq. (p. 345):

'dum defles nostri languorem, femina, membri,
  ostendis morbo te graviore premi.'
illa furens: 'nescis, ut cerno, perfide, nescis:
  non fleo privatum, sed generale chaos.
haec genus humanum, pecudum volucrumque, ferarum

et quidquid toto spirat in orbe, creat.
hac sine diversi nulla est concordia sexus,
  hac sine coniugii gratia summa perit.
haec geminas tanto constringit foedere mentes,
  unius ut faciat corporis esse duo'.

This extract should be enough to show the thoroughly artificial and scholastic character of the elegy.

[3] *Elegy* L (p. 316).

[4] There are a few turns of phrase which may be unconscious adaptations of Christian thought.

on into the middle of the sixth century, in spite of the Gothic invasion, in spite of the great religious changes, the old custom of public recitations had persisted. As we have seen,[1] these recitations went on in Africa during the Vandal domination, and in Rome the *Aeneid* was still declaimed in the Forum of Trajan.[2] On the 6th of April in the year 544 a curious scene took place in the presbytery before the *confessio* in S. Peter's. Pope Vigilius, surrounded by Bishops and other clergy, received in state a middle-aged subdeacon, who presented an epic poem in two books on the *Acts of the Apostles*. This subdeacon, whose name was Arator, had been in his boyhood a friend of Ennodius, who had celebrated his beauty and talents in prose and verse.[3] The Pope courteously listened while a part of the poem was read, and ordered Surgentius, the *primicerius*, to keep the manuscript in the archives of the Roman Church. But, so we are told, all the most learned among the citizens continually demanded a public recitation. The Pope or his notary agreed, and the clergy and people gathered to hear it in the church of S. Peter *ad Vincula*. It is astounding to learn that the poet spent four days reading and re-reading his poem, 'propter repetitiones assiduas, quas cum favore multiplici postulabant'. For Arator had drunk about as deeply as Ennodius of the spring of poetry. But the Romans had not lost their love of rhetoric, and they still applauded the old points, however feebly they were made. Yet we can well believe that the recitation of Arator was one of the last that ever echoed in forum or church in Rome. The fall of the Gothic kingdom was not compensated by the imperial restoration, and, before long, the dreaded Lombards were again reducing Italy to ruin. A new order had begun, which is represented by the pontificate of Gregory I (590–604). This great and noble figure, grand and melancholy, stands between the two worlds. He received the old education from the public schools, he had followed the usual career of those born to riches, and in 573 he became Prefect of the city. But as soon as his father died he bestowed his goods on the Church, and became a monk in his ancestral palace on the Coelian, which now bore the name of S. Andrew. In 590 he became Bishop of Rome, and in his

[1] Above, p. 107.
[2] Fortunatus, *Carmina*, vii. 8, verse 26 [cf. iii, 18, verses 7–8].
[3] See the references in Ennodius, ed. Hartel, p. 615. Ennodius composed *ex tempore* an epigram 'in natalem infantis

Aratoris' (Hartel, p. 593; ii, 105):
  iure colis proprium natalem, pulcher Arator.
  qui si non coleres, numquid arator eras?

pontificate of a few brief years he left an ineffaceable impression on the Western Church. It is significant that in his writings Gregory never condescended to quote from a heathen author, but, in spite of his famous remarks on the study of grammar, he himself wielded a style which, being all his own, threw aside all the borrowed devices that were the stock-in-trade of others, and went straight to the point with a terrible and gloomy certainty. Here again we have the consciousness that what was new and real in thought and in expression was rising from those springs of life which had their source in the ground of the Christian Church. The darkness, indeed, seemed to be falling for ever on Western civilization at the end of the sixth century, but it was not to be thick darkness, and morning was near. This darkness and this promise are alike symbolized by the powerful and pathetic words with which Gregory closed his twenty-one Homilies on the prophet Ezekiel:

> Nemo autem me reprehendat, si post hanc locutionem cessavero: quia sicut omnes cernitis, nostrae tribulationes excreverunt: undique gladiis circumfusi sumus, undique imminens mortis periculum timemus. Alii truncatis ad nos manibus redeunt, alii captivi, alii interempti nuntiantur. Iam cogor linguam ab expositione retinere: quia taedet animam meam vitae meae. Iam nullus in me sacri eloquii studium requirat: quia versa est in luctum cithara mea, et organum meum in vocem flentium. Iam cordis oculus in mysteriorum discussione non vigilat: quia dormitavit anima mea prae taedio. Iam minus lectio animo dulcis est: quia oblitus sum manducare panem meum a voce gemitus mei. Cui autem vivere non licet, de scripturae sacrae sensibus loqui mystica qualiter libet? Et qui cogor quotidie amara bibere, quando possum dulcia propinare? Quid igitur restat, nisi ut inter flagella quae ex nostris iniquitatibus patimur, cum lacrymis gratias agamus? Ipse etenim qui nos creavit, etiam pater nobis factus est per adoptionis spiritum quem dedit. Et aliquando filios pane nutrit, aliquando flagello corrigit: quia per dolores et vulnera ad hereditatem perpetuam erudit. Sit itaque gloria omnipotenti domino nostro Iesu Christo, qui vivit et regnat cum patre in unitate spiritus sancti deus, per omnia saecula saeculorum. Amen.

§ 2. *Gaul: Venantius Fortunatus*, A.D. 540–c. 600.

When Clovis died in 511 he was master of the greater part of Gaul;[1] he had laid the foundations of a strong monarchy, and had begun the work of organization necessary for the establishment of Frankish rule. But on his death his dominions were divided between his sons, who were soon conspiring each against the other. After a series of deaths and murders Chlotar alone was left in the year 558. In the meantime, however, the kingdom of Burgundy was overrun and dismembered, and the

---

[1] Cf. C. Pfister in *C. Med. Hist.* ii. pp. 118 sqq.

Ostrogoths were driven out of Provence. Only Septimania remained, obstinately held by the Visigoths of Spain. In the extreme west there was a settlement of Celts who had crossed the sea from Britain and established themselves in a state of precarious independence.

North-eastwards the Franks spread as far as they were able, conquering the Thuringians and threatening the Saxons. But with the death of Chlotar in 561 the kingdom was again divided, Charibert became king of Paris, Sigebert king of Metz, and Chilperic king of Soissons. Guntram was king of Orleans and Burgundy. The history of these years, with its tale of treachery and murder, of personal tragedy and public misery, is reflected unforgettably in the pages of Gregory of Tours. As Montalembert so eloquently put it:[1]

> Ce contraste confus de tant de forfaits avec tant de vertus: ces filles de rois francs et germains, les unes transfigurées par la foi et la poésie, les autres subissant ou infligeant les plus infâmes outrages; ces rois, tour à tour féroces et complaisants; ce grand évêque debout près du tombeau de son immortel prédécesseur et prêchant à tous l'ordre et la paix; les meurtres et les sacrilèges, en face du culte passionné des reliques les plus vénérables; l'audace et la longue impunité du crime, à côté de tous ces prodiges de ferveur et d'austérité: en un mot, toute cette mêlée de saints et de scélérats offre la plus fidèle peinture du long combat que livraient la vertu et la dignité chrétienne à la violence des Barbares et à la mollesse des Gallo-Romains.

There is, indeed, a measure of truth in this impression derived from Gregory's great *History*. But if we turn aside from the courts of the kings and the stories of bloodshed and revenge we see the other side of the picture. The remains of the old Gallo-Roman aristocracy were not entirely effete. The great senatorial families provided bishops and administrators. These latter took their place beside the new official Frankish aristocracy. Nicetius of Treves had a mighty castle overlooking the Moselle, and there were still luxurious villas where bishops or country gentlemen could spend a more or less carelesss leisure. But the towns kept their fortifications. Inside were concentrated the riches of the merchants and the misery of the poor. The churches and monasteries increased in splendour. Outside, the roads were not always safe; but there was plenty of trade, especially along the excellent water-ways. The countryside was rich in corn and wine, and everywhere there stood the mighty ruins of an older day.

It was into this new Gaul of the Franks that a young Italian, Venantius Honorius Clementianus Fortunatus, came about the

---

[1] *Les Moines d'Occident*, ii. 345; cf. Tardi, *Fortunat*, p. 132.

year 565. He was born near Treviso and had studied in the schools of Ravenna. There he began the practice of poetry, addressing verses to Bishop Vitalis and celebrating the latter's new church of S. Andrew.[1] Urged perhaps by the growing difficulties of life in Italy, and also by the desire to fulfil a vow of pilgrimage to Tours in gratitude to S. Martin, by whose intercession his eyes had been healed, he crossed the Alps and made his way to Mainz,[2] and thence to Cologne.[3] It was his policy to win the favour of the Bishops by neatly turned verses in their praise, or by epigrams such as no Gallic skill could fashion in those times. At Treves he composed an elegy on the dead Bishop Nicetius,[4] and celebrated his castle above the Moselle in a 'description' which was written in the Bishop's lifetime.[5] Such descriptions had been a favourite kind of composition for centuries, and Fortunatus had done such things before.

Mons in praecipiti suspensa mole tumescit
    et levat excelsum saxea ripa caput:
rupibus expositis intonsa cacumina tollit
    tutus et elato vertice regnat apex.
proficiunt colli quae vallibus arva recedunt:
    undique terra minor vergit et iste subit,
quem Mosella tumens, Rodanus quoque parvulus ambit,
    certanturque suo pascere pisce locum.
diripiunt dulces alibi vaga flumina fruges:
    haec tibi parturiunt, Mediolane, dapes.
quantum crescit aquis, pisces vicinius offert;
    exhibet hinc epulas, unde rapina venit.
cernit frugiferos congaudens incola sulcos,
    vota ferens segeti fertilitate gravi.
agricolae pascunt oculos de messe futura,
    ante metit visu quam ferat annus opem.
ridet amoenus ager, tectus viridantibus herbis,
    oblectant animos mollia prata vagos.
hoc vir apostolicus Nicetius ergo peragrans
    condidit optatum pastor ovile gregi;
turribus incinxit ter denis undique collem,
    praebuit hic fabricam, quo nemus ante fuit.
vertice de summo demittunt brachia murum,
    dum Mosella suis terminus extet aquis.
aula tamen nituit constructa cacumine rupis,
    et monti inposito mons erit ipsa domus.

[1] *Venanti Honori Clementiani Fortunati opera poetica*, ed. F. Leo, *M.G.H.*, *Auct. Antiq.* IV. i, pp. 7 sqq.

[2] For the route, see *Vita Martini*, iv. 630 sqq. (p. 368 sq.), where the itinerary is given in reverse order; cf. also p. 2,

Praefatio. At Mainz he addressed the Bishop Sidonius in verse, p. 215.

[3] Poem to Bishop Carentinus of Cologne, p. 67 (iii. 14).

[4] p. 63 (iii. 11).

[5] p. 64 sq. (iii. 12).

conplacuit latum muro concludere campum,
  et prope castellum haec casa sola facit.
ardua marmoreis suspenditur aula columnis,
  qua super aestivas cernit in amne rates.
ordinibus ternis extensaque machina crevit,
  ut, postquam ascendas, iugera tecta putes.
turris ab adverso quae constitit obvia clivo,
  sanctorum locus est, arma tenenda viris.
illic est etiam gemino ballista volatu,
  quae post se mortem linquit et ipsa fugit.
ducitur inriguis sinuosa canalibus unda,
  ex qua fert populo hic mola rapta cibum.
blandifluas stupidis induxit collibus uvas,
  vinea culta viret quo fuit ante frutex.
insita pomorum passim plantaria surgunt
  et pascunt vario floris odore locum.
haec tibi proficiunt quidquid laudamus in illis,
  qui bona tot tribuis, pastor opime gregis.

The modern historian cannot help being pleased with the
ordered precision of these rhetorical descriptions. Here we see
the vast frowning fortress, with the river below; the mighty
towers contrasting with the peace of field and vineyard; the
threatening ballista and the fruitful orchards. The insecurity
of the times was turning the Bishop into a feudal lord, whose
business it was to defend the land and protect his people.

From Cologne the poet proceeded to Metz, the capital of
Sigibert. Here in 566 he celebrated the king's marriage to the
Spanish princess Brunhildis in a long hexameter poem, preceded by an elegiac introduction which pictures the gracious
spring of the year when the wedding took place.[1] In the
epithalamium itself Fortunatus displays in honour of these
Christian 'barbarians' all the treasures of pagan mythology.
He uses the allegorical setting which Claudian had used before
him, and introduces Cupid and Venus conspiring to bring about
the marriage. Cupid says to his mother,

mater, mea bella peregi:
pectore flagranti mihi vincitur alter Achilles,
Sigibercthus amans Brunichildae carpitur igne,

and they dispute about the merits and beauty of the king and
the princess. It is only in a second poem that Fortunatus
speaks of Brunhildis as Christ's gift to the pious king, and
mentions her conversion to the Catholic faith.[2]

At Metz the poet made many new friends. There was, first
of all, the Bishop Vilicus, whom he praised as the true shepherd

[1] pp. 124 sqq. (vi. 1).   [2] p. 130 (vi. 1 a).

of his sheep. In a pleasant poem Fortunatus prefaces his flattery of the Bishop with a picture of the city of Metz in the style of which he was a master:[1]

> Gurgite caeruleo pelagus Mosella relaxat
>   et movet ingentes molliter amnis aquas;
> lambit odoriferas vernanti gramine ripas
>   et lavat herbarum leniter unda comas.
> hinc dextra de parte fluit qui Salia fertur,
>   flumine sed fluctus pauperiore trahit;
> hic ubi perspicuis Mosellam cursibus intrat,
>   alterius vires implet et ipse perit.
> hoc Mettis fundata loco speciosa coruscans
>   piscibus obsessum gaudet utrumque latus.
> deliciosus ager ridet vernantibus arvis;
>   hinc sata culta vides, cernis at inde rosas.
> prospicis umbroso vestitos palmite colles,
>   certatur varia fertilitate locus.
> urbs munita nimis, quam cingit murus et amnis,
>   pontificis merito stas valitura magis . . .

In another poem, which belongs to a later visit to Metz, Fortunatus describes a river journey along the Moselle which he made in company with the king. He was mindful, no doubt, of Ausonius's idyll, which he could hardly hope to equal, but it was with his 'eye on the object' that he tried to picture the river scene with the vine-clad slopes and the frowning rocks which nourish the grapes as well:[2]

> undique prospicimus minitantes vertice montes,
>   nubila quo penetrans surgit acuta silex,
> qua celsos scopulos praerupta cacumina tendunt,
>   hispidus et tumulis crescit ad astra lapis.
> nec vacat huc rigidis sine fructibus esse lapillis:
>   denique parturiunt saxaque vina fluunt.
> palmite vestitos hic respicis undique colles
>   et vaga pampineas ventilat aura comas;
> cautibus insertae densantur in ordine vites
>   atque supercilium regula picta petit;
> culta nitent inter horrentia saxa colonis:
>   in pallore petrae vitis amoena rubet,
> aspera mellitos pariunt ubi saxa racemos,
>   et cote in sterili fertilis uva placet,
> quo vineta iugo calvo sub monte comantur,
>   et tegit umbrosus sicca metalla viror;
> inde coloratas decerpit vinitor uvas,
>   rupibus adpensis pendet et ipse legens . . .

But if his eye was on the object, he did not forget what was expected of him in the way of rhetorical ingenuity. Yet who

---

[1] p. 65 (iii. 13).   [2] pp. 242 sqq. (x. 9).

shall say that this ingenuity is misplaced? We are pleased with this picture of the Moselle in the sixth century, unchanged since the time of Ausonius, and not entirely transformed at the present day.

In another earlier poem Fortunatus tells with humour how the king's cook commandeered his boat and he had to come to Nauriac in a crazy skiff.[1]

The Bishop had a table decorated—perhaps in mosaic—with a picture of a vine. Here Fortunatus had doubtless sat, drinking the bishop's wine; for he wrote:[2]

> Vitibus intextis ales sub palmite vernat
> et leviter pictas carpit ab ore dapes.
> multiplices epulas meruit conviva tenere:
> aspicit hinc uvas, inde Falerna bibit.

And again, a poor poet who has to live on the liberality of the great, he asks for his daily bread:

> Currit ovis repetens a te sua pascua, pastor:
> qui cibus esse soles, da mihi panis opem.

There were others also whose favour it was necessary to win if Fortunatus were to establish himself securely at court. First of all there was the eloquent Gogo, the king's trusted adviser,[3] with whom Fortunatus formed a friendship that was to endure. If the great man invited him to supper he replied with a playful epigram:[4]

> Nectar vina cibus vestis doctrina facultas—
> muneribus largis tu mihi, Gogo, sat es;
> tu refluus Cicero, tu noster Apicius extas:
> hinc satias verbis, pascis et inde cibis.
> sed modo da veniam: bubla turgente quiesco,
> nam fit lis uteri, si caro mixta fremat.
> hic, ubi bos recubat, fugiet puto pullus et anser:
> cornibus et pinnis non furor aequus erit.
> et modo iam somno languentia lumina claudo:
> nam dormire meum carmina lenta probant.

In late years Fortunatus, settled at Poitiers, remembered his friend, and wondered whether he was netting the salmon in the

---

[1] p. 148 sq. (vi. 8). He humorously curses the cook in these terms:

> corde niger, fumo pastus, fuligine tinctus,
> et cuius facies caccabus alter adest,
> cui sua sordentem pinxerunt arma colorem,
> frixuriae cucumae scafa patella tripes,
> indignus versu potius carbone notetur,
> et piceum referat turpis imago virum.

[2] p. 67 (iii. 13 b). [3] p. 153 (vii. 1).
[4] p. 154 (vii. 2).

Rhine, or walking above the Moselle in the shade of the vines, or perhaps by the Meuse, famed for its birds, fishes, and river-traffic,

> triplice merce ferax (alite pisce rate).

Or is he cultivating his estate, or presiding, perhaps, in the royal school?[1] Wherever he is, may the winds bear him the message of his loyal friend.

Next there is Duke Bodegisel, a great official and a just administrator, with Palatina his wife, a bishop's daughter.[2] Duke Lupus stands, perhaps, above them all; of him Fortunatus could say,

> antiqui proceres et nomina celsa priorum
> cedant cuncta, Lupi munere victa ducis.
> Scipio quod sapiens, Cato quod maturus agebat,
> Pompeius felix, omnia solus habes.
> illis consulibus Romana potentia fulsit,
> te duce sed nobis hic modo Roma redit . . .

And, indeed, the Duke seems to have had great qualities as soldier and administrator. He made at any rate a deep impression upon the poet, whose flatteries cannot be regarded merely as insincere trifles. For Fortunatus appears to have won his right to the friendship of these men on even terms. He sat at their tables and recited his poems after dinner, or perhaps composed impromptu epigrams. The Franks had taken over the externals of the civilization into which they entered. King Chilperic was something of a scholar, though Gregory of Tours speaks with contempt of the verses of the man whom he called 'the Nero and the Herod of our time'.[3] It is clear that many of these Frankish nobles, especially those of the new official class, had been educated in the Gallic schools, and so at the Austrasian court they formed, with the bishops, a circle of men who recognized the value of learning and the merits of a brilliant young poet from Italy.

But Fortunatus did not wish to remain for ever a poet at the northern court. By means of his scattered verses we trace his progress through Verdun,[4] Reims,[5] and perhaps Soissons[6] to Paris, the capital of the Neustrian kingdom. The clergy of

---

[1] p. 155 sq. (vii. 4). The school is not a Court school proper, but clearly for the young boys sent to the Court for the royal service; cf. Köbner, *Fortunatus*, p. 36, note.

[2] pp. 156–8 (vii. 5).

[3] *Hist. Franc.* v. 44; vi. 46.

[4] Leo, op. cit., p. 73 (iii. 23). But Köbner (p. 21), perhaps rightly, regards these visits as made by Fortunatus moving with Sigebert's court in 566–7.

[5] p. 68 (iii. 15).

[6] p. 44 (ii. 16, poem on S. Medard); but on this see Meyer, p. 15.

Paris received him, and he rewarded them with his praises—
praises for them, for their venerable Bishop Germanus, and
for their grand church which rivalled the temple of Solomon.[1]
He professed to be taking up reluctantly his long unused lyre,
but he was soon addressing a long panegyric to King Charibert,[2]
with compliments of this kind,

> cum sis progenitus clara de gente Sigamber,
> floret in eloquio lingua Latina tuo.
> qualis es in propria docto sermone loquella,
> qui nos Romanos vincis in eloquio ?[3]

He paid a visit to the aged Ultrogotho, the widow of Childe-
bert I,[4] living under the protection of Charibert, with her two
daughters, devoted to good works, to prayer, and perhaps to
the care of her garden. This garden Fortunatus celebrated in
a little poem.[5] He begins with the vines, the flowers, and
the fruit trees, but the main point of the poem is its flattery
of the queen through praise of her royal husband, who, as
Gregory of Tours tells us, was buried 'in the basilica of the
blessed Vincent, which he himself had built'.[6] It was near
this church that the garden lay:

> Hic ver purpureum viridantia gramina gignit
> et paradisiacas spargit odore rosas;
> hic tener aestivas defendit pampinus umbras,
> praebet et uviferis frondea tecta comis,
> pinxeruntque locum variato germine flores,
> pomaque vestivit candor et inde rubor.
> mitior hic aestas, ubi molli blanda susurro
> aura levis semper pendula mala quatit.
> haec magno inseruit rex Childebercthus amore;
> carius ista placent quae manus illa dedit:
> de cultore trahit mellitum planta saporem,
> forsan et hic tacitos miscuit ille favos.
> regis honore novis duplicata est gratia pomis,
> nari suavis odor, dulcis in ore sapor.
> qualiter ille hominum potuit prodesse saluti,
> cuius et in pomis tactus odore placet!
> felix perpetua generetur ab arbore fructus,
> ut de rege pio sit memor omnis homo.
> hinc iter eius erat, cum limina sancta petebat,
> quae modo pro meritis incolit ille magis.
> antea nam vicibus loca sacra terebat amatus,
> nunc tamen assidue templa beata tenet.
> possideas felix haec, Vltrogotho, per aevum,
> cum geminis natis tertia mater ovans.

[1] Leo, pp. 37 sqq. (ii. 9).
[2] pp. 131 sqq. (vi. 2).
[3] p. 133.
[4] Cf. Tardi, *Fortunat*, p. 116.
[5] Leo, p. 146 sq. (vi. 6).
[6] *Hist. Franc.* iv. 20.

Fortunatus was now well established in Gallic society. Wherever he went he had access to the bishops and to the great, and he probably had no need to invite himself or to insinuate his way into their houses. He came, at any rate, not like a needy adventurer, but as the equal and friend of those on whom he lavished his verse.

His path now lay southwards, for he had not forgotten his vow to S. Martin. He knelt before the shrine at Tours which held the precious relics and he was kindly received by Bishop Euphronius. We do not know what impression the great basilica of Perpetuus made upon one who knew the churches of Ravenna; for the poem which Fortunatus addressed to Euphronius[1] tells us nothing of this. But in a letter of a later date he remembers his visit and his holy patron, asking the bishop to pray for him, 'your humble son and servant at his blessed sepulchre, and of your goodness to intercede on my behalf for the remission of my sins'.[2]

It was hardly this visit to S. Martin that brought back to Fortunatus the claims of divine things. He was still a layman, free from any kind of obedience or control, a 'wandering scholar', whose life was spent passing from house to house, seeking new faces and new experiences. And now the crowning experience of his life was to come. In 567 he came to Poitiers. No visitor could fail to be curious about the monastery where Radegunde, once the wife of Chlothar, lived a life of utter renunciation and devotion, with Agnes, her spiritual daughter, the young Abbess.

At the age of eight Radegunde had been taken from her home and the wreck of her father's kingdom of Thuringia to be reared as a bride for king Chlothar. But her heart was soon set on heavenly things, and although she was married to Chlothar in 538, she forsook him at last and, with the help of Bishop Medard, withdrew from the world. The monastery which she founded attracted noble and cultivated women of the old Gallo-Roman families and of the Frankish aristocracy.[3] It was planned with the still familiar luxuries of the great Gallic villas—with gardens and baths and all that could make life pleasant. But the Queen herself lived in great humility, performing the most menial services, and practising the most severe asceticism. Her biographers set forth in minute and terrifying detail the tale of her austerities. She tended the

---

[1] Leo, p. 51 (iii. 3).
[2] p. 50; a prose letter.
[3] Cf. Dill, *Roman Society in Merovingian Gaul*, p. 374.

poor and diseased with her own hands. She nourished her vigorous mind on hard readings from the Fathers and even practised the composition of verse. To those who knew her she seemed to live on this earth the life of the angels, and her charity was such that she did not attempt to impose her own self-discipline upon others.

Fortunatus seems to have found no difficulty in making himself known to Radegunde and the Abbess Agnes. His fame had doubtless preceded him, and he took care that his flatteries and his courtesies should not fail of their effect. But if he came under the impulse of the curiosity that had driven him of old, he remained a spell-bound captive to the charm of a new existence. Poitiers became his home until his death about the year 600. The centre of this new existence was the society of Radegunde and Agnes. The ladies admired his learning, his poetry, and his southern courtesy; and he doubtless placed his services at the disposal of the monastery for the transaction of business and the conduct of correspondence with the great ones of the outside world. They showed their affection by sending him the choicest dishes prepared in their kitchen, the most delicious fruits and the best wines. Fortunatus was a frequent visitor and he dined on occasion with Radegunde and the Abbess. In one of the poems we have a picture of the preparations that were made to receive such an honoured guest:[1]

> Respice delicias, felix conviva, beatas,
>   quas prius ornat odor quam probet ipse sapor.
> molliter adridet rutilantum copia florum;
>   vix tot campus habet quot modo mensa rosas,
> albent purpureis ubi lactea lilia blattis
>   certatimque novo fragrat odore locus.
> insultant epulae stillanti germine fultae;
>   quod mantile solet, cur rosa pulchra tegit?
> conplacuit melius sine textile tegmine mensa,
>   munere quam vario suavis obumbrat odor;
> enituit paries viridi pendente corymbo:
>   quae loca calcis habet, huc rosa pressa rubet.
> ubertas rerum tanta est, ut flore sereno
>   mollia sub tectis prata virere putes.
> si fugitiva placent, quae tam cito lapsa recedunt,
>   invitent epulae nos, paradise, tuae.
> Daedalicis manibus nituit textura sororis;
>   tantum digna fuit mater habere decus.

But more often the poet dined alone on the good things sent

from the monastery. If the ladies enquired 'with charitable solicitude'[1] how their friend enjoyed the abundant dishes sent in quick succession, Fortunatus would reply with verses committed to his tablets then and there, and polished perhaps at his leisure later on:[2]

> Sollicita pietate iubes cognoscere semper,
>   qualiter hic epulis te tribuente fover.[3]
> haec quoque prima fuit hodiernae copia cenae,
>   quod mihi perfuso melle dedisti holus;
> nec semel aut iterum, sed terque quaterque cucurrit,
>   cuius me poterat pascere solus odor.
> portitor ad tantos missus non sufficit unus;
>   lassarunt totiens qui rediere pedes.
> praeterea venit missus cum collibus altis
>   undique carnali monte superbus apex,
> deliciis cinctus quas terra vel unda ministrat;
>   conpositis epulis hortulus intus erat.
> haec ego nunc avidus superavi cuncta gulosus:
>   et mons et hortus ventre tenetur iners.
> singula nec refero, quia me tua munera vincunt:
>   ad caelos victrix et super astra voles.

But Fortunatus could repay these *eulogiae*, as he called them, these gifts of affection, by humbler presents of his own. He learned to weave osier baskets,[4] which he filled with chestnuts, and sent them to his friends. Or he gathered the flowers in his poor little garden or in the fields. As the season will not yield lilies or roses he sends the purple violet, which perhaps they will not disdain.[5] Or he has gathered some wild plums in the woods. They need not be afraid of them as though they were mushrooms gathered on the ground; he would not send them anything that would do them harm:[6]

> hoc quoque non metuas quod ramo umbrante pependit:
>   non tellus fungos, sed dedit arbor opes.
> non ego crudelis, qui matri incongrua praestem:
>   ne dubites puros sumere fauce cibos.

When the season of Lent came, Fortunatus and his friends were parted. This absence was hard for the poet, who could not imitate the austerities of a monastic retreat. But Easter brought back for him a double joy; it was Spring indeed, but

---

[1] Tardi, p. 173.
[2] Leo, p. 262 (xi. 9); other poems of the same kind follow.
[3] ? *fruar*.
[4] p. 264 (xi. 18):
Ista meis manibus fiscella est vimine texta:

credite mi, carae, mater et alma soror;
et quae rura ferunt, hic rustica dona ministro,
castaneas molles, quas dedit arbor agris.

[5] p. 193 (viii. 6).
[6] pp. 266 sqq. (xi. 18).

Summer and Autumn as well. For Radegunde returned from the Winter of her immurement, and with her came the harvest and fulfilment of the year.[1]

> Unde mihi rediit radianti lumine vultus?
>   quae nimis absentem te tenuere morae?
> abstuleras tecum, revocas mea gaudia tecum,
>   paschalemque facis bis celebrare diem.
> quamvis incipiant modo surgere semina sulcis,
>   hic egomet hodie te revidendo meto.
> colligo iam fruges, placidos compono maniplos:
>   quod solus Augustus mensis, Aprilis agit;
> et licet in primis modo gemma et pampinus exit,
>   iam meus autumnus venit et uva simul.
> malus et alta pirus gratos modo fundit odores,
>   sed cum flore novo iam mihi poma ferunt.
> quamvis nudus ager nullis ornetur aristis,
>   omnia plena tamen te redeunte nitent.

These occasional poems are the last expression of that refinement of manner, that cult of friendship and literature which was one of the civilizing gifts of the ancient world. Fortunatus came out of Italy, where no violent changes had availed to sweep away the public schools, and no barbarian settlement had been able to obscure the Roman civilization of the great cities. At Poitiers rather than at Metz he found a society suited to the needs of his nature. It was a small society of cultivated women who became for many years an ever ready audience for his verse. The situation seems, perhaps, strange to us, as it has seemed to many critics. But how admirably adapted it was to bring out the best that Fortunatus could give! He was a rhetorician, and he had now to use his rhetoric in the service of what became the closest and most exacting friendship. For at the command of Radegunde Fortunatus must write a long poetical letter to be directed to Constantinople in the hope of discovering her nephew Amalfrid, who was seeking his fortune in exile. The poet must revive the passionate memories of their lost Thuringian home, the horrors of the murder and rapine in which her father's kingdom perished; and he did this, as best he could, in the long piece entitled, *de excidio Thoringiae*.[2] It was difficult to reproduce in verse the passion of Radegunde's yearning for some living link with the Thuringian past. But Fortunatus wrestled bravely with the problem and not without success. No answer came, it seems, from distant Byzantium—or wherever the young soldier had wandered:

[1] p. 195 sq. (viii. 10).   [2] pp. 271 sqq. (appendix).

> quae loca te teneant, si sibilat aura, requiro,
>   nubila si volitant pendula, posco locum:
> bellica Persidis seu te Byzantion optat
>   ductor Alexandrae seu regis urbis opes?
> an Hierosolymae resides vicinus ab arce,
>   qua est genitus Christus virgine matre deus?

News came, somehow or other, that the young soldier was dead. So Fortunatus must compose another letter in her name, this time to another nephew, Artachis,[1] who lived somewhere in Gaul, and might be persuaded to write frequently.

And who but Radegunde would have chosen the pitiful story of Galeswintha as a subject for the poet's verse? A sister of Queen Brunhildis, Galeswintha was sent from her Spanish home to marry King Chilperic. She was brutally murdered not long after her marriage, but Fortunatus does not say so in his poem. He presents the princess as the victim of fortune or fate. She sets out from Spain amid the wildest demonstrations of sorrow, already doomed to misery and to death. Fortunatus packs the pathos of his story into a series of rhetorical speeches joined together by a modicum of narrative and relieved by a little description. First there are the passionate speeches of farewell between Galeswintha and her mother; there is the nurse's speech after the murder, the lament of Brunhildis, and the final despairing cry of the bereaved mother. The poet does his best to heighten the pathos, but he cannot help setting out the route of the journey and he must linger to celebrate the glory of Poitiers and its saint.

In this and in other pieces Fortunatus was nevertheless moving away from the triviality of his earlier manner. If he still had to praise—at the council of Braine—the royal pair, Chilperic and Fredegund,[2] and console them another time for the death of their children,[3] he might be excused by the formality of the occcasion or by the requirements of policy. He was happier when, in the service of Radegunde, he could sing the praise of the religious life. He had begun with a long and elaborate festal poem which he recited at the installation of Agnes as Abbess.[4] This was a panegyric in praise of virginity, and a presentation of the glories of a life which was already raised above the life of this lower world, and was a foretaste of the joys of heaven. Instead of the conventional picture of Olympus and its inhabitants, with which Fortunatus was as

---

[1] p. 278 sq. (appendix).
[2] pp. 201 sqq. (ix. 1).
[3] pp. 205 sqq. (ix. 2).
[4] pp. 181 sqq. (viii. 3).

familiar as Sidonius, here is the throne of God, and 'all the
company of heaven'; here are the choirs of angels—

> alternis vicibus divina poemata psallunt
> atque creatori mystica verba canunt,

and here the patriarchs, apostles, martyrs, and virgins:

> Eufemia illic, pariter quoque plaudit Agathe,
> et Iustina simul consociante Thecla.
> hic Paulina Agnes Basilissa Eugenia regnant,
> et quascumque sacer vexit ad astra pudor.
> felices quarum Christi contingit amore
> vivere perpetuo nomina fixa libro!

The poem as it proceeds becomes a mystical epithalamium,
at which angels and prophets, patriarchs and saints—catalogued in long and impressive order—assist. Then with the aid
of the sensuous imagery of the Song of Songs transmuted into
Latin rhetoric, Fortunatus attempts to show the passionate
emotion of the cloistered life as he had learned to know it at
Poitiers. But the contrasting picture of the married state with
which, by a grievous error of taste, Fortunatus continued his
poem shows that we are still in the circle of ancient rhetoric,
and that the poet cannot escape from the prison of the past.

And yet on rare occasions he won a brief and precarious
freedom. In the verses *de cruce domini*[1] and in those *ad Felicem
episcopum de pascha*[2] he had sung of the tree of life,

> fertilitate potens, o dulce et nobile lignum,

and of the spring of the year when all things rose with Christ.
But his full triumph was in those hymns which he wrote for
Radegunde when the relic of the true Cross came from the
Emperor Justin II and his wife, to shed its glory on the
monastery. Fortunatus had praised these great and generous
givers in the name of his princess,[3] and in a happier moment
he wrote those festal hymns—which the Church has embalmed
in the pages of her liturgy for ever. Here for the first time the
ancient Latin rhetoric suffered a transformation

> into something rich and strange.

The strains of a new music were heard in lines like these,

> arbor decora et fulgida,
> ornata regis purpura,
> electa digno stipite
> tam sancta membra tangere . . .[4]

---

[1] p. 27 (ii. 1).
[2] pp. 59 sqq. (iii. 9).
[3] pp. 275 sqq. (Appendix, ii).
[4] p. 34 (ii. 6), *Vexilla regis*.

and by a wonderful new fantasy what began as rhetoric was sublimated into intensity and vision:

> hic acetum fel harundo sputa clavi lancea,
> mite corpus perforatur, sanguis, unda profluit,
> terra pontus astra mundus quo lavantur flumine.
>
> crux fidelis, inter omnes arbor una nobilis,
> nulla talem silva profert flore fronde germine,
> dulce lignum, dulce clavo dulce pondus sustinens!
>
> flecte ramos, arbor alta, tensa laxa viscera,
> et rigor lentescat ille quem dedit nativitas,
> ut superni membra regis mite tendas stipite.[1]

It is profoundly significant that these poems were composed in 'popular' measures, one in the metre chosen by Ambrose and the other by Hilary of Poitiers for the earliest Latin hymns. These, too, were the metres that lent themselves most easily to rhythmical schemes and to the ornament of rime. In the *Vexilla regis* Fortunatus broke naturally into rimed couplets; in the *Pange lingua* it is the rhythm of the Roman soldiers' marching songs that becomes the music of his processional.

It is here that we might fittingly take leave of Fortunatus. His much loved friends died about the year 587, but he did not care to leave the city where he had spent such happy years. He still wrote verses, the last which can be dated belonging to the year 591, when he celebrated the ordination of Bishop Plato. But before long Plato died, and Fortunatus became his successor, dying in his turn after a brief episcopate.

Fortunatus has been called an 'occasional' poet;[2] and it is, indeed, through his occasional verses that we are able to see the other side to that grim picture of the world which his friend Bishop Gregory was painting as he looked from the window of his palace at Tours. We know that the sun shone on the bright fields, and that the fruits of the earth were gathered in. Fortunatus rejoiced in the spring of the year and he asks us to rejoice with him,

> mollia purpureum pingunt violaria campum,
> prata virent herbis et micat herba comis.

He charms us, too, by those traits of originality that mark his character. The critics who have praised or blamed him have paid him a sufficient tribute in the infinite pains they have

---

[1] p. 28 (ii. 2), *Pange, lingua.*   [2] W. Meyer, *Der Gelegenheitsdichter Fortunatus*, Berlin 1901.

taken to draw a picture of the man as they have seen him in his writings. To some he has appeared, fantastically, as a Rabelaisian figure or as a consummate voluptuary. Others have preferred to dwell upon his servile flattery of the great and his self-complacent rhetoric. It is better to be content to follow with admiration the long adventure of his life from the early schooldays at Ravenna to the seat of S. Hilary, and to watch the transformation of the Italian rhetorician into the renowned poet and saint, whose epitaph was penned by Paul the Deacon, the Lombard scholar who visited his tomb at the end of the eighth century.

He was read as a classic until the later years of the eleventh century, when he was almost forgotten,[1] living only in his hymns until his poems were printed in the sixteenth century.[2]

§ 3. *Spain and Africa.*

The literary record of Spain in the sixth century is indeed barren. There were no poets left who worked according to the old models. Heathenism and its memories were dead. The Visigoths had definitely made Spain their home, but their Arian faith was the cause of great bitterness, and, in the south, the presence of Byzantine garrisons was also a menace to political union. But Leovigild (570–86) began the solid work of building up the state, and his son Reccared (586–601) took the one further step necessary when he became a Catholic. The seventh century saw a literary revival. The only name in poetry which belongs to the sixth is that of Archbishop Martin of Bracara, who died in 580. He was a Pannonian by birth, and all we possess of his poetry is three small poetical inscriptions.[3]

Of African poets there is more to say, although the destruction of the Vandal kingdom in 534, and the union of Africa with the Eastern Roman Empire, were not an unmixed blessing. The yoke of Byzantium was heavy, as the African bishops found who dared to oppose the will of Justinian in the matter of the Three Chapters.[4] Verecundus, Bishop of Junca in

---

[1] Manitius, *Gesch.* i. p. 179.

[2] My own copy, printed in Venice in 1578, bears the words 'nunc primum in lucem emissi . . .', but Tardi, p. vii, refers to editions of 1573 and 1574 at Cagliari. Bröwer's edition, Mainz 1603, was the first edition which can

be considered at all satisfactory until Luchi's edition, Rome 1786–7 (=Migne lxxxviii).

[3] See Manitius, *Christl. lat. Poesie,* p. 409 sq.

[4] *Christian-Latin Poetry,* p. 99.

Byzacene, who was haled to Constantinople along with Pope
Vigilius to answer for his presumption, set out his view of
life in a poem, *de satisfactione poenitentiae*, which Isidore of
Seville in the next century called a 'lamentabile carmen'.[1]

But other poets found it possible to sing the praises of their
new masters. The great grammarian, Priscian, had settled in
Constantinople in the reign of Anastasius (491–518). He was
born in Caesarea of Mauretania, but went to the capital of the
Eastern Roman Empire as a professor of Latin. Besides his
Institutio Grammatica and other technical works he wrote
poems, two of which have survived, a panegyric on the
Emperor Anastasius and a translation from the Greek of the
Periegesis of Dionysius.[2] The first poem was written about the
year 512. The introduction is in iambic senarii and the pane-
gyric itself in hexameters. Priscian sings the praises of the
Emperor in war and peace; he is greater than his ancestor
Pompey,

> sed tamen egregio, Pompei, cede nepoti.

For Pompey left the mountaineers of the Taurus unconquered,
and it was Anastasius who tamed them. Anastasius possesses
all the virtues, says Priscian:

> in cuius vita virtutes cernimus omnes:
> est iustus, sapiens, castus fortisque piusque,
> est clemens, stabilis, moderatus, mitis, honestus,
> et, loquar ut breviter quod sentio corde sub imo,
> possidet hic veterum quidquid laudatur in ullo:
> Antoninum huius pietas, sapientia Marcum,
> et mitem Nervam lenissima pectora vincunt,
> promeruitque Titus non tantum mente benigna;
> gloria magnanimi Traiani cesserit isti.

It is easy to see that Priscian wrote poetry as a grammarian
who knew the rules and had read a great deal might be expected
to write it. There is not much more to be said for Corippus,
who was also a grammarian by profession, and composed an
epic, about 550, in praise of John, the *magister militum*, who

[1] *Christian-Latin Poetry*, p. 99.
[2] Baehrens, *Poet. Lat. Min.* v. 264
sqq. It is hardly necessary to stress
the influence which Priscian had on
grammatical studies in the Middle
Ages. A MS. of Orleans has in a collection of treatises on grammar the
following lines:

Prisciani quicumque boni per gram-
    mina curris,

grammaticos flores collige mente,
    puer,
ut vivas sapiens per secula, dogmate
    vitae
plenus, et ingenio exuberans liquido.
sicut apis sollers studioso pectore sic sic
    per campos sophiae mellea verba
    cape.
(*Notices et Extraits des mss.*, XXXI, i,
                        p. 388.)

had subdued the Moors. It seems that Corippus made his way
from Carthage to Constantinople, and that there he found himself in distress, from which he attempted to deliver himself by
means of a poetical panegyric on the Emperor Justin (565–78).

The epic, entitled *Johannis*, is in eight books.[1] In the preface
Corippus, who appears to have recited the whole poem before
an audience at Carthage, says that he is essaying a task like
that of Virgil, but that while John is easily superior to Aeneas,
he himself cannot claim to compete with Virgil. The first part
of the preface is perhaps worth quoting. It is addressed to the
chief citizens of Carthage:

> Victoris, proceres, praesumpsi dicere lauros:
>   tempore pacifico carmina festa canam.
> scribere me libuit magnum per bella Iohannem,
>   venturo generi facta legenda viri.
> omnia nota facit longaevo littera mundo,
>   dum memorat veterum proelia cuncta ducum.
> quis magnum Aeneam, saevum quis nosset Achillem,
>   Hectora quis fortem, quis Diomedis equos,
> quis Palamedeas acies, quis nosset Ulixem,
>   littera ni priscum commemoraret opus?
> Smyrnaeus vates fortem descripsit Achillem,
>   Aeneam doctus carmine Vergilius.
> meque Iohannis opus docuit describere pugnas,
>   cunctaque venturis acta referre viris.
> Aeneam superat melior virtute Iohannes,
>   sed non Vergilio carmina digna cano.[2]

And so on. The epic itself is well conceived, and is written
without any parade of learning or of obscurity. Occasionally
there are historical and mythological allusions, as in the passage
which describes how the fleet, sailing from Byzantium for the
conquest of the Moors, passes by the site of ancient Troy,
'litus lacrimabile Troiae', and Peter, the son of the illustrious
John, listens in boyish wonder to the names of Priam, Achilles,
Hector, and Aeneas.[3]

Corippus is a devout Christian, and, when he feels tempted
to introduce a heathen fable in order to adorn a simile, qualifies
it in this way:

> ut veteres aiunt gentili carmine vates.[4]

He employs all the usual epic devices, such as the catalogue
of heroes and the long narrative which brings before the reader

[1] *Corippi Africani grammatici libri qui supersunt*, ed. I. Partsch, *M.G.H.*, *Auct. Antiq.* iii. On Corippus's distress see *In Laudem Iustini, Praefatio*, 41 sqq. (p. 116).
[2] Partsch, p. 1.
[3] ib., p. 7 (*Johann.* i. 170 sqq.).
[4] *Johann.* i. 451.

the events that took place before the action of the poem opens. For this purpose the tribune Liberatus Caecilides[1] obligingly recites the whole of the events leading up to the present campaign.

The long poem *In laudem Justini*,[2] in praise of Justin II, the successor of Justinian, is even more interesting, as, in the words of a modern historian, 'it paints the character and policy of Justin as he himself wished them to be portrayed. His conception of his imperial duty was the ideal of the unbending Roman whom nothing could affright. This spirit of exalted self-possession had been shown at its height when the senate was leader of the State, and it was not without a definite purpose that the role of the senate is given marked prominence in the poem of Corippus.'[3] The poem contains a great deal of historical material as it treats in detail of a few events—the death of Justinian, the accession of Justin, an embassy from the Avars, and the assumption of the consulship by the new emperor. The usual mythological or allegorical machinery of the panegyric is not dispensed with,[4] and there are also rhetorical descriptions, like that of the palace of Justin,[5] or that of the court in all its splendid array.[6]

The voice of Corippus declaiming in the halls of a Byzantine palace the language of Virgil learned in his native Africa comes to us strangely across the centuries. He spoke still of hope in the Roman name and in the eternity of the Empire. In the *Johannid* he had put words such as these into his hero's mouth:

> nos Parthica regna,
> nos Lazos, Unnos, Francosque Getasque domamus,[7]

[1] *Johann.* iii. 54 sqq. (Partsch, p. 29).
[2] Partsch, pp. 115 sqq.
[3] Norman H. Baynes, in *Camb. Med. Hist.* ii. p. 264.
[4] Cf. *Johann.* i. 36 sqq. (p. 119).
[5] i. 97 sqq. (p. 120).
[6] iii. 159 sqq. (p. 141):
> iamque ordine certo
turba decanorum, cursorum, in rebus agentum,
cumque palatinis stans candida turba tribunis
et protectorum numerus mandante magistro
omnis sacrorum vis adfuit officiorum
ornatu vario cultuque habituque modoque, etc.

There is another long description of the felling of trees in connexion with the preparations for the public show on the occasion of Justin's consulship. The trees are laboriously catalogued (iv. 13 sqq., p. 148).

[7] ii. 382–3 (p. 25); cf. also preface to *In Laudem Iustini* (p. 115):
> deus omnia regna
sub pedibus dedit esse tuis . . .
quis totiens victos numeret per proelia Francos
edomitosque Getas ? captos stratosque tyrannos ?
Langobardorum populos Gipidumque feroces . . . ?
Also in Justin's speech to the Avar envoy (iii. 383 sqq.):
> quid noster senior potuit pater, inscie, disce,
sub quo Vandalici ceciderunt strage tyranni
edomitique Getae, pubes Alamannica, Franci
totque aliae gentes.

and the boast was, so far, not remote from the truth. But the
Latin speech was to perish for ever from Roman Africa. For
though the Vandals fell before Belisarius, and great chains of
fortresses were constructed to hold back the desert tribes, the
next century was to see the end of this ancient civilization at
the hands of fierce conquerors from the East.

THE AGE OF TRANSITION

§ 1. *Spain, Gaul, and Italy.*

THE period between the death of Gregory the Great (604) and the establishment of the Frankish Empire is one that might be described with some justice, so far as the western part of the continent of Europe is concerned, as an age of intellectual barrenness and decline. Here, for the first time, the direct contact or continuity with classical antiquity appears to be on the point of vanishing. A world which bears all the marks that we are accustomed to associate with the Middle Ages is making its appearance. A significant fact is the emergence as leaders of culture of the Irish and the Anglo-Saxon peoples, who received the Latin language and the civilization of which it was the symbol as something which was not their natural heritage. So that while on the continent the level of culture was slowly sinking, the peoples who were to have a large share in its revival in the eighth and ninth centuries had acquired their cultures as it were at second hand.

At the same time the political face of Europe had suffered a remarkable change. The Angles and Saxons had mastered most of England, and were being converted by Roman and Irish missions. Gaul was now the home of the Franks, who expanded their power by degrees in all directions. The Visigoths felt their pressure in the south, but it was another foe, the dreaded Saracens, who brought the power of the Visigoths to an end in the early years of the eighth century. In Italy the Lombards were settled in the place of Ostrogoths and East Romans. Carthage had fallen to the Saracens in 698, and Roman Africa was only a memory.

The Church endured, as strong in the last resort as ever, in spite of the difficult adjustments which had to be made with the governments of the new barbarian kingdoms. All signs of weakness were, in truth, superficial; the progressive expansion of monasticism was a sure guarantee of vigorous life, and although in the eighth century Frankish kings had to undertake a drastic reform of the Church, there was good material to work on and results were not long in appearing.

But the Church might be strong in the midst of intellectual poverty, and this was actually, to a great extent, the case.

Political troubles and continual wars produced conditions under which the cause of civilization laboured heavily and was likely to sink, unless power should ultimately be concentrated in strong and wise hands. These are perhaps not the only considerations which might be adduced to explain the intellectual exhaustion that had overtaken most of Western Europe.

If we turn in the first place to Spain and read the record of the seventh century we find that here much of what Roman Africa had left is gathered up and cherished,[1] and that a dim glow of antiquity still lingers over some of the products of the age. Isidore of Seville (*circ.* 570–636) went to the ancients for his encyclopaedic compilations, but he seems far removed from Ennodius or from Dracontius, who bore upon them the indelible stamp of the old schools. Yet he was of good Roman provincial stock from Cartagena, and, although his elder brother Leander, who preceded him as Bishop of Seville, supervised his education on strict and somewhat narrow lines, the methods must have borne some relation to those practised in the schools of grammar and rhetoric. Isidore was in any case a remarkable man; he had, as Manitius has pointed out,[2] a passion like that of Cassiodorus for the collection of books and for the making of abstracts. Not that he had read all the authors whom he cites or had always fully comprehended their meaning. But he stands as a dispenser of knowledge to the later centuries. With Gregory the Great and Bede he is one of the significant figures of the somewhat dark times between the departure of antiquity and the beginning of the true Middle Ages. His love of books is expressed in the *Versus in bibliotheca*,[3] an elegiac poem in which he describes the contents of his library. The reader of this poem will feel that there is a kinship between this Spanish poetry and that of the Carolingian revival of the next century:

> Sunt hic plura sacra, sunt hic mundalia plura:
> ex his si qua placent carmina, tolle, lege.
> prata vides plena spinis, et copia florum.
> si non vis spinas sumere, sume rosas.
> hic geminae radiant veneranda volumina legis,
> condita sunt pariter hic nova cum veteri.

The books are catalogued from the Fathers onwards with appropriate comments. The profane poets mentioned are

[1] See above, p. 112, n. 4.
[2] *Gesch.* i, p. 52.
[3] Migne, lxxxiii, col. 1107 sqq. I think that we can safely say, with

Manitius, *Gesch.* i, p. 70, that Isidore's authorship of these verses is highly probable.

Virgil, Horace, Ovid, Persius, and Lucan; by their side are placed, for those who have no taste for fables, the Christian poets—Prudentius (*eximio dulcis Prudentius ore*), Avitus, Juvencus, Sedulius. There are books also of law and of medicine and, apparently, there is a cupboard for spices:

> vascula concreta fragilis de pulvere terrae
> pigmenta gerimus, pocula nulla damus.

For all its failing sense of prosody this is a pleasant poem because it is clear and true. It made a great appeal for several centuries, and English and Frankish poets felt its influence.[1]

A long line of Spanish bishops followed Isidore in the composition of verses. First in order is his friend Braulio of Saragossa[2] (d. 651) to whom he dedicated his great Realenzyklopädie, the *Etymologiae*.[3] Besides a hymn in iambic trimeters with much rime Braulio wrote an epitaph in distichs on Bishop Maximus of Saragossa.[4] Taio, Bishop of the same city, wrote an 'epigram' in hexameters as an introduction to his own prose work of *Sententiae*, a theological treatise.[5] Both Ildefonsus and Julian of Toledo were versifiers; the poetical work of the latter has perished,[6] but a few trifling lines of the former have survived.[7]

Eugenius of Toledo, who preceded both Ildefonsus and Julian, and was Archbishop from 646 to 658, is a figure of much greater importance. He is a witness to the persistence of the rhetorical tradition, and like Isidore a link between the old world and the new. Weak in body and a devoted student, he had become a monk against the wishes of his family, who belonged to the Visigothic race. But Bishop Braulio of Saragossa made him his archdeacon, and so loved him that it was only in deference to the wishes of King Chindaswinth that he parted with him when Eugenius was elected to the see of Toledo. The king himself was interested in poetry, and it was in response to the royal request that Eugenius revised and re-edited the popular poem of Dracontius

---

[1] e.g. Eugenius of Toledo (ed. Vollmer, *M.G.H.*, *Auct. Antiq.*, p. 238) described his library (*bibliotheca*), i.e. the Bible.

[2] *Christian-Latin Poetry*, p. 127.

[3] This work can now, fortunately, be studied in W. M. Lindsay's admirable edition, Oxford 1911, 2 vols.

[4] Migne, lxxx, col. 614:

Maximus hic situs est, dictus cognomine Marcus,
    nobilis historicus, praeco, poeta,
    vigil, etc.

The hymn is in *Anal. Hymn.* xxvii, p. 125.

[5] Migne, lxxx, col. 731.

[6] See Manitius, *Christl. lat. Poesie*, p. 423.   [7] ib., p. 422.

on the Creation.[1] Eugenius took himself seriously as a poet, as his preface to his collected poems shows.[2] And, as he had read widely and intelligently among the classical poets and among his immediate predecessors, he was able to command a variety of metres and of subjects. He admired, it seems, the foolish devices which had lingered in the schools—acrostic, telestich, epanalepsis. So he composed his own epitaph in acrostic and telestich:[3]

> Excipe, Christe potens, discretam corpore menteM
> Ut possim picei poenam vitare barathrI.
> Grandis inest culpa, sed tu pietate redundaS.
> Elue probra, pater, et vitae crimina tollE.
> Non sim pro meritis sanctorum coetibus exuL;
> Iudice te prosit sanctum vidisse tribunaL.
> Vis, lector, uno qui sim dinoscere versV;
> Signa priora lege, mox ultima nosse valebiS.

There are many moral and religious pieces among the poems, some of which, such as the verses *Contra Ebrietatem* and *Contra Crapulam*,[4] are merely adaptations of rhetorical themes. Others are pieces on churches, not descriptive, but written to inform the reader of the virtues of the saint whose bones repose there. In two poems, one of them polymetric, Eugenius laments the coming of old age, and here again he was exercising a well worn theme.[5] The sapphics in which he gives us a picture of his pain-racked life are interesting as a continuation of the tradition of the personal poem which was to bear fruit again in Carolingian times:[6]

> Nosse quicumque cupis aut requiris,
> quae mei causa fuerit laboris,
> huius ut vitae mala funerarem,
>   disce benigne.
> dum quaterdenos simul et novenos
> vita non felix agitaret annos
> dumque me pigra peteret senectus
>   praepete cursu,
> accidit lasso gravis aegritudo,

---

[1] It seems that this part of the *De Laudibus Dei* circulated in Spain as a separate poem; Manitius, *Christl. lat. Poesie*, p. 425. Eugenius also edited the *Satisfactio* and worked it on to his revision of the *Creation*.

[2] Eugenii Toletani Episcopi, *Carmina*, ed. Vollmer, *M.G.H.*, *Auct. Antiq.* xiv, p. 231 sq.

[3] *Opera*, p. 246. He wrote three other epitaphs for himself, one in sapphics and two in elegiacs; see p. 246 for another acrostic and telestich, also p. 252.

[4] ib., pp. 236–8. The latter begins:
> Propense stomachum qui farcit dape ciborum,
>   viscera crassa vehit, sed macra corda gerit.
> decrescit sensu, grandescit corporis auctu,
>   carnea fit moles membra caduca ferens.

[5] ib., pp. 243 sqq. [6] ib., p. 245.

quae ferae mortis minitaret ictum
ac diu fessa cruciaret acri
 membra dolore.
febris incerta terebrabat ossa,
languida morbis caro defluebat,
nulla quassatum recreabat esca,
 potio nulla.
tanta me crebro mala dum ferirent,
mortis horrendae trepidus pavore
labilem cursum fugientis aevi
 carmine planxi.

Is there a slight trace in the verses on the nightingale[1] of a new note, of a new feeling? It is perhaps a question that admits of no certain answer, but the last distich is not without significance:

Vox, philomela, tua cantus edicere cogit,
 inde tui laudem rustica lingua canit.
vox, philomela, tua citharas in carmine vincit
 et superas miris musica flabra modis.
vox, philomela, tua curarum semina pellit,
 recreat et blandis anxia corda sonis.
florea rura colis, herboso caespite gaudes,
 frondibus arboreis pignera parva foves.
cantibus ecce tuis recrepant arbusta canoris,
 consonat ipsa suis frondea silva comis.
iudice me cygnus et garrula cedat hirundo,
 cedat et inlustri psittacus ore tibi.
nulla tuos umquam cantus imitabitur ales,
 murmure namque tuo dulcia mella fluunt.
dic ergo tremulos lingua vibrante susurros
 et suavi liquidum gutture pange melos.
porrige dulcisonas attentis auribus escas;
 nolo tacere velis, nolo tacere velis.
gloria summa tibi, laus et benedictio, Christe,
 qui praestas famulis haec bona grata tuis.

Eugenius was much read in his own day, and his poems passed quickly to England, where they were known to Aldhelm and Bede.[2] It is supposed that Alcuin took them over to Frankish soil, where the Carolingian poets admired and imitated them.

[1] *Opera*, p. 254.
[2] Manitius, *Gesch.* i. p. 197. A contemporary of Eugenius was Bishop Fructuosus of Braga, who may be the author of three rhythmical poems printed in Migne, lxxxvii, col. 1129–30. Two are in rhythmical hexameters; one of them, addressed to King Sisenand (631–6) runs as follows:

quid Sisenandum recolam gratia praecipua regem
populos qui rite rexit, cunctosque refovit.
illustrium si exeam generoso fomite pompas,
ignosce ipse proprias stirpis inclite venas.
bonum propagine geminae refulgere lucernae.

Parallel to this array of poet-bishops is a more modest line of poet-kings, Sisebut, Chintila, Reccesvinth, and Wamba. Sisebut reigned from 612 to 620, and was a man of great ability. He drove back the Byzantines in the south and kept order in his kingdom with a strong hand. A friend of the Church, he had a passion for learning and shared the ideals of Bishop Isidore, to whom he addressed a curious poem on eclipses of the sun and moon.[1] The first few lines will show that he had acquired a measure of skill in composition, and also, perhaps, arouse some sympathy for the king who was torn between the demands made by camp and forum and the love of his books and verses. He is addressing Isidore who, unlike the poor king, has leisure to cultivate his muse:

> Tu forte in lucis lentus vaga carmina gignis
> argutosque inter latices et musica flabra
> Pierio liquidam perfundis nectare mentem.
> at nos congeries obnubit turbida rerum
> ferrataeque premunt milleno milite curae.
> legicrepi tundunt, latrant fora, classica turbant,
> et trans Oceanum ferimur porro, usque nivosus
> cum teneat Vasco nec parcat Cantaber horrens.[2]
> en quibus indicas, ut crinem frondea Phoebi
> succingant hederaeve comas augustius umbrent!
> en quos flammantem iubeas volitare per aethram!
> quin mage pernices aquilas vis pigra elephantum
> praecurret volucremque pigens testudo molossum,
> quam nos rorifluam sectemur carmine lunam.
>
>   sed tamen, incurvus per pondera terrea nitens,
> dicam, cur fesso livescat circulus orbe
> purpureumque iubar nivei cur tabeat oris.

We need not follow Sisebut in his excursion into astronomy. The poem was read by the Anglo-Saxons, as its citation by Aldhelm shows, and in later days it is referred to and quoted by Clement the Irishman.[3] There is much in it that resembles Aldhelm's manner, and, as we have seen, the Spanish poets exercised a considerable influence over English readers.[4] King

---

at Lupus Brutioque tui germani decori
quibus clarissimo ditatus Brutio natu obtinuit legali Iustam aequitate matronam.
mihique videlicet extat unicus error unicum sortita pignus mirabile nobis in quo retentans pii gaudia magna viri.
The text is clearly defective.
[1] Riese, no. 483 (ii. p. 9); Baehrens,

Poet. Lat. Min. v. pp. 357 sqq.
[2] Sisebut crushed an insurrection of the Basques and also built a fleet (Oman, *Dark Ages*, p. 223; *Camb. Med. Hist.* ii. 173).
[3] Manitius, *Gesch.* i. p. 188.
[4] On the rapidity with which Spanish MSS. spread to Britain see C. H. Beeson, *The Ars Grammatica of Julian of Toledo, Miscellanea Ehrle*, i, pp. 50 sqq., Rome 1924.

Chintila (636–40) wrote an inscription for a gift which he sent to S. Peter's at Rome,[1] and Reccesvinth and Wamba are said to have practised similar compositions, unless, indeed, the inscriptions were simply composed in their names.[2] Almost the whole of this Spanish poetry is in classical metres, and it derives its form and expression from what remained of the methods and practices of the ancient schools. The decline in skill and even in taste is apparent; there is a defective sense of quantity, and a lack of discrimination in the choice of words. But these poets had one merit—they helped to keep alive for better days the love of poetry and of the old authors. They had little or no inspiration of their own; for real passion and feeling we must turn to the Mozarabic hymnary,[3] that collection of hymns composed for the most part in the days when the Arabs were masters of the land, and the Church had lost her high position and for a time her external splendour.

If we pass northwards from Spain into Gaul we are met by the curious and enigmatic figure of Virgilius Maro, the grammarian, who belongs, perhaps, to Toulouse and to the latter part of the sixth century. An enigma he remains in spite of the attention which he has attracted since Cardinal Angelo Mai introduced him to a wondering world of scholars. We have called Virgil a grammarian. Was he a pure charlatan, or a miserable pedant purveying scraps of debased learning in the darkest corner of Europe? Or, again, was he a 'mystificateur', who is not worth our attention?[4] He writes in a strange language which suggests at once a *Geheimsprache* such as the African Octavian[5] used,

---

[1] Riese, no. 494; Baehrens, *Poet. Lat. Min.* v. 363, note. It runs:

Discipulis cunctis domini praelatus amore,
    dignus apostolico primus honore coli,
sancte, tuis, Petre, meritis haec munera supplex
    Chintila rex offert: pande salutis opem.

The MS. note is: 'in velo quod a Chintilane rege Romae dicatum est.'

[2] Reccesvinth, Migne, lxxxvii, col. 402; Wamba, ib., col. 401.

[3] *Christian-Latin Poetry*, p. 128.

[4] D. Tardi, *Les Epitomae de Virgile de Toulouse*, Paris 1928, p. 10. This is a very valuable study; see besides, Huemer, 'Die Epitomae des Grammati-

kers Virgilius Maro nach dem Fragmentum Vindobonense 19556', *Wiener Sitzungsber*. xcix (1882), pp. 509 sqq.; Roger, *L'Enseignement des lettres classiques*, pp. 110 sqq. Text, ed. Huemer, *Virgilii Maronis grammatici opera*, Leipzig 1886. I am much inclined to the view that Virgil was a badly educated, clever man, whose brain had taken an unhealthy and eccentric turn. He was taken seriously by Irishmen and others, but hardly by his contemporaries in Toulouse.

[5] For the *Preface* in the Latin Anthology (no. 19), which has been ascribed to Octavian, the author of no. 20, see above, p. 113. Virgil does, indeed, discuss the 'art of cutting up words' (*de scinderatione fonorum, Epit.* xiii), which

and such as at a later date the Irish and the Anglo-Saxons loved.[1]

It is on the late testimony of Abbo of Fleury (d. 1004) that Virgil is placed in Toulouse, but this testimony is confirmed perhaps by the words of the grammarian himself who says in his second epitome, 'bigerro sermone clefabo'—'I will speak in the vulgar tongue of Bigorre.' The works of Virgil consist of fifteen *epitomae* and eight letters, dealing with grammatical questions, and revealing a strange world which is a mixture of the real and the fantastic, of the probable and the palpably false. Virgil has a good deal to say about the scholars who were his masters or his friends, and he mentions others who lived in past ages and were still renowned. But none of these figures belongs to the history of literature as it has come down to us in the ordinary way. In the fifteenth epitome, the subject of which is a List of Grammarians, he says:

> The first then was an old man named Donatus, who lived at Troy, it is said, for a thousand years. When he came to visit Romulus, by whom Rome was founded, he was cordially received, and stayed there for four years, setting up a school and leaving innumerable works. . . . There was also at Troy one Virgil, a pupil of this same Donatus, who was an industrious prosodist, and wrote seventy volumes on metre and a letter *de verbi explanatione* which he sent to Virgil of Asia. I am the third Virgil.
>
> Now Virgil of Asia was the pupil of the first Virgil. . . . I have seen him with my own eyes. He set me my copies when I was a child. He wrote a well-known book about the twelve kinds of Latin, which he called by these names: usitata, assena, semedia, numerosa, metrofia, lumbrosa, sincolla, belsavia, presina, militana, spela, polema . . .

Then there was Istrius the Spaniard; Gregory the Egyptian, who wrote three thousand books on Greek history; three Lucans, of Arabia, India, and Africa, who taught Virgil's own master Aeneas. This Aeneas mentioned in one of his books a Maro who lived about the time of the Flood, and as he thought that his young pupil showed promise, he said, 'This

was the invention, he says, of Aeneas; the reasons for employing such means of mystification are: 'prima . . . ut sagacitatem discentium nostrorum in inquirendis atque inveniendis his quaeque obscura sunt adprobemus, secunda est propter decorem aedificationemque eloquentiae, tertia ne mystica quaeque, et quae solis gnaris pandi debeant, passim ab infimis ac stultis facile repperiantur, ne secundum canticum antiquum sues gemmas calcent.' These

reasons are at the root of all such writings and especially of the *Hisperica Famina*.

[1] Aldhelm and Bede knew the works of Virgil the Grammarian, Roger, p. 111. Zimmer, 'Über direckte Handelsverbindungen Westgalliens mit Irland' (*Berlin. Sitzungsber.* 1909), held that Virgil came to Ireland at the end of the fifth century (pp. 1031 sqq.) and exercised an influence over all later Irish writers. It is difficult to take his arguments seriously.

my son shall be called Maro, for in him the spirit of the ancient Maro lives again.'

We are introduced as well to Galbungus, Gelbidius, and Glengus; to a Cicero who did not come from Arpinum, and to a host of other scholars with strange or famous names. For the most part they talk nonsense, as when Galbungus and Terrentius spent fourteen days and as many nights in disputing whether *ego* had a vocative case,[1] or Regulus the Cappadocian and Sedulus the Roman nearly came to sword-blows in their heated discussion over frequentative verbs, in which they spent fifteen days and nights without food or sleep, and each kept three armed men to come to his assistance, if the need arose![2]

Enough has been said to show how difficult it is to use the writings of Virgilius Maro as evidence for the condition of culture in southern Gaul at the end of the sixth and in the early seventh century. But Virgil says something about metre and gives some examples of what he claims to be contemporary poetry. It is hard to believe that he had any serious knowledge of quantitative verse,[3] and it is impossible to make any sense of what he says about metre in general.[4] It is significant, however, that the verses he quotes are to be classed as rhythmical and that they have a well developed rime. Here are some examples:

i. By the poet Aeneas,

> Phoebus surgit, caelum scandit,
> polo claret, cunctis paret.

ii. By Varro,

> festa dium sollemnia
> pupla per canam conpita,
> quorum fistilla modela
> poli persultant sidera.

iii. By Cato, 'rhetor elegantissimus',

> bella consurgunt poli praesentis sub fine,
> precae temnuntur senum suetae doctrinae.
> regis dolosi fovent dolosos tyrannos,
> dium cultura molos [=multos] neglecta per annos.

---

[1] Huemer, p. 123.
[2] ib., p. 138.
[3] It is true that he says (*Epist.* iv, p. 25) that in one of the twelve letters which he sent to Donatus at Rome he had written on sapphics and on heroic verse, but the letters are probably mythical and, in any case, he knew nothing about the subject.

[4] I refer the reader to the Abbé Tardi's translation of *Epit.* iv. (*De metris*), op. cit., p. 46, and to Roger, op. cit., p. 118 sq., and to P. Lejay, 'Le Grammairien Virgile et les rythmes latins', *Revue de Philologie*, xix (1895), pp. 45 sqq.

iv. By Lupus, a Christian poet,

> veritas vera,
> aequitas aequa,
> largitas lauta,
> fiditas fida
> diurnos dies tranquilla
> tenent tempora.

v. By Don, brother of Donatus, Virgil's master, in praise of Arcas, king of Arcadia,

> Archadius rex terrificus,
> laudabilis laude dignissimus.

vi. By Gergesus,

> Sol maximus mundi lucifer
> omnia aëra inlustrat pariter.

vii. By Sagillius,

> mare et luna   concurrunt una
> vice altante   temporum gande.

viii. By Vitellius,

> mea, mea Matrona, tuum amplector soma,
> nobis anima una heret, aquae arctura.

All these examples are from the epitome *de metris*, but there are three quotations in the other sections. Thus Virgil of Asia wrote,[1]

> summa in summis
> potens caelis
> celsaque cuncta
> gubernat celsa;

and Donatus,

> nostras omnis familia,
> nostrates quoque pecora
> evadant imminentia
> hostilium pericula;[2]

and Plastus, 'elegantissimo carmine',[3]

> limo solubili
> lympha meabili,
> igne ardibili,
> aura mutabili,
> mundus visibilis
> sumptus initiis,
> cuius terribilis
> pendet tristities.

It does not matter whether Virgil himself forged these verses or whether some of them are actually the work of his contem-

---

[1] *Epit.* xv (p. 91).   [2] *Epist.* ii (p. 126).   [3] ib. iii (p. 151).

poraries. They are reasonable evidence of the characteristic poetical activity of southern Gallic writers, and, as Wilhelm Meyer has pointed out, they show a developed rhythm and observe the rule of hiatus. He further draws attention to the fact that there is no sign of strophic structure, and that the rime joins only pairs of verses.[1] Some of the verse-forms bear a resemblance to those employed by Irish poets.

Our brief study of Virgilius Maro has shown that in the sixth century the *rhythm* had established itself as a recognized verse-form by the side of the old classical prosody. It was known, of course, before; but it was now beginning to find recognition in treatises[2] and to be practised in the schools. Among the scanty remains of Gallic verse of the seventh century are two rhythmical poems, which may be the work of Theodofrid, a monk of Luxeuil, who became Abbot of the newly-founded monastery of Corbie in 657.[3] The first bears the curious title, *De sex aetatibus mundi*.[4] It is an alphabetical poem, based on the iambic trimeter, and, as regards its material, derived largely from Isidore. It is really a survey of human history from the creation to the crucifixion, with a final strophe on the last judgement. The first two strophes will give the reader an idea of the structure of the verse, with its refrain:

> Ante secula   et mundi principio
> tu, pater sancte,   genuisti filium,
> qui tecum regnat   cum sancto espiritu ;
> novem fecisti   ordines angelicos,
> deus qui iustus   semper es laudabilis.
>
> Aspice, deus,   de supernis sedibus
> quos Theodofridus   condedit versiculos
> de sex aetatis   et mundi principio
> a protoplausto   usque in novissima.
> deus qui iustus   semper es laudabilis.

The original title of the second poem is, it seems, *De Asia et de universi mundi rota*.[5] It depends a great deal upon Isidore,

---

[1] *Rythmik*, i. pp. 199 sqq.

[2] Flavius Mallius Theodorus, in his *De metris* (Keil, *Grammatici Latini*, v. 586), written *circ.* 400, says: 'scribimus ita de metris, ut ab his rhythmos procul removeamus, atque in his omnino nullum sit, in quo non pedum defixa ratio cum dulcedine adsociata atque permixta sit.'

[3] Manitius, *Gesch.* i. pp. 200–1. In 681 he was a bishop, perhaps of Amiens.

[4] Ed. Dümmler, *Zeitschr. f. deutsch.*

Alt. xxii (1878), pp. 423 sqq. (see also xxiii, pp. 280 sq.) ; also *Poet. Lat. Aevi Car.* iv, pp. 559 sqq.

[5] Text in Pertz, 'Über eine fränkische Kosmographie des siebenten Jahrhunderts', *Abhdl. d. kgl. Akad. d. Wiss. zu Berlin*, 1845, pp. 253 sqq.; critical text by K. Strecker, *Der Rythmus De Asia et de universi mundi rota*, Berliner Progr. 1909, pp. 13 sqq., and in *Poet. Lat. Aevi Car.* iv, pp. 545 sqq.

and purports to be a description of the three known continents. Actually our text provides a description of Asia and Europe, with a fragment about Africa and the islands. It begins:

> Asia ab oriente   vocata antiquitus
> a regina, cuius nomen   funxit in imperio;
> hec in tertiaque parte   orbis est disposita.
>
> ab oriente ortu solis,   maris a meridie,
> ab occiduoque mare   Tyrreno coniungitur,
> septentrione fluviale   Tanaeque cingitur.
>
> habet primum paradisi   hortorum dilicias,
> omni genere pomorum   consitus qui graminat,
> habet etiamque vite   lignum inter medias.
>
> non est aestas neque frigus,   sincera temperies,
> fons manat inde perennis   fluitque in rivolis.
> post peccatum interclusus   est primevi hominis.

From the earthly Paradise the poet passes to India and Ceylon, with all their marvels of ivory and precious stones, and the golden mountains guarded by fabulous beasts. Next come Parthia, Assyria, Babylonia, Palestine, and Egypt, with many other countries, until it is time to 'hasten to Europë, the daughter of Agenor, whom Jove bore away into Greece'. Here the poet forgets his mythology and confounds her with Danaë— 'she was corrupted by gold and gave her name to a country'. The Franks are mentioned as once fierce, but now Christians by God's grace, and the Irish win the poet's favour for learning and for the freedom of their land from snakes and bees:

> Hibernia maxima floret   multa sapientia,
> vermiumque sic purgata,   apium aculia.

It is only fair to say that the poet is not relying on his own knowledge, but merely upon Isidore, who writes: 'illic nulla anguis, avis rara, apis nulla'.[1]

This is the sorry tale of Gallic poetry in the century before the Carolingian renaissance, and the story of Italy is not dissimilar. As in Gaul, so in Italy political conditions were adverse; the Lombard kings were struggling with the forces which made for disintegration—the turbulent nobles, the heathen Avars, or the Byzantine exarch. The towns, of course, were still the shelters of civilization, and there were still lay schools for those who could make use of them.[2] We hear (*circ.* 680) of a 'grammarian', Felix of Pavia, whom King Cunincpert

---

[1] *Etym.* xiv. 6.

[2] Cf. Hörle, *Frühmittelalterliche*   *Mönchs- und Klerikerbildung in Italien,* p. 36.

'so loved that he gave him amongst other gifts a staff adorned with silver and gold'.[1] Rome was not in those days a centre of learning. The output of epitaphs is poor in quality, and there is only one poem worth mentioning—by Honorius I (625–38)—a series of distichs on the Apostles gazing at Christ ascending into heaven.[2] The northern towns were the homes of what remained of the old culture. Writing to his pupil Maurus, Crispus, a deacon of Milan, reminds him that he brought him up almost from his cradle and instructed him in the seven liberal arts ('septiformis facundiae liberalitate ditavi'). This is evidence that clerical education was by no means neglected, and if this Crispus is, as seems probable,[3] identical with Benedict Crispus who was Archbishop of Milan from 681 to 725, he was able to use his high position to further the cause of education. It was to his pupil Maurus that Crispus dedicated a poem in which a number of medicinal remedies were set forth after the pattern of Serenus Sammonicus. It is in fairly good hexameters; 'heroico te melle pascere cupio,' says the author in his dedication, 'ut paulatim ad artis amorem adducam'.[4] But more interesting is the epitaph which Crispus wrote for Caedualla, the king of the West Saxons, who after his baptism came to Rome, and, dying, was buried in S. Peter's.[5]

A contemporary of Crispus, a Master Stephen, wrote a rhythmical poem about the Synod of Ticinum (*circ.* 698) which was called in order to deal with a schism.[6] Stephen says that he wrote it at the request of King Cunincpert, and, as it is not in metre, he calls it simply prose. And this indeed it was according to the strict canon of the time, although the scheme is that of the twelve-syllabled iambic trimeter. The only principle observed is that of syllabic equality, but there is a sporadic assonance or rime, and a curious acrostic—Stefanus M.—in which the initial letter is repeated in the following strophe. The first two strophes will serve to illustrate this as well as the rhythmic scheme:

> Sublimis ortus in finibus Europe
> Langibardorum regali prosapia,

[1] Paulus Diaconus, *Hist. Lang.* vi. 7.
[2] Migne, lxxx, col. 483.
[3] Hörle, p. 38.
[4] A. Mai, *Class. Auct. e Vatic. Codd.*, Rome 1833, v. p. 392.
[5] It is quoted in Bede, *H.E.* v. 7.
[6] It was the old Three Chapters schism. King Cunincpert had been almost deposed by the rebellious Duke Alahis, who incautiously supported the schismatics. This led to the Duke's downfall in battle, after which the Synod was held at Ticinum (Pavia) to enforce orthodoxy; see *Camb. Med. Hist.* ii. 206. The text of the poem is in *M.G.H., Script. Rer. Langob.*, pp. 189 sqq.; and *Poet. Lat. Aevi Car.* iv. 728 sqq.

rex Haribertus pius et catholicus
Arrianorum abolevit heresem
et Christianam fidem fecit crescere.
Subolis item Bertharith in solium
regni suffectus, imitatus protinus
exempla patris, ad fidem convertere
Iudaeos fecit baptizandos, credere
qui renuerunt, gladium peremere.

This is poor enough, as the modest poet himself realized. Yet
he had read Virgil, and ventured to insert a reminiscence of
the *Aeneid* in his poem.[1]

To the reign of King Luitprand (712–44) belongs a more
interesting but not more inspired rhythm, *de Mediolano civitate*,[2] written by a Milanese cleric, who was especially proud
of the great churches in his city and of the holy relics which
they contained. It is alphabetical, the scheme is that of the
trochaic tetrameter catalectic, and there is frequent hiatus.
It begins,

Alta urbs et spaciosa manet in Italia,
firmiter edificata opere mirifico,
que ab antiquitus vocatur Mediolanum civitas.

Bonum retinet decoris speciem et variis
rutilat culture modis ornata perspicue;
locus ita fructuosus constat in planicie.

Celsas habet opertasque turres in circuitu,
studio nitentes magnas scultantes forinsecus ·
que introrsus decorata manet edificiis.

. . . . . .

Haec est urbium regina, mater adque patrie,
que precipuo vocatur nomine metropolis,
quam conlaudant universi naciones seculi.

Then the devotion of the citizens is described, and the names
of the saints are set forth whose bones rest in the churches—
Victor, Nabor and Felix, Gervasius and Protasius, and, of
course, Ambrose.

O quam felix et beata Mediolanum civitas,
que habere tales sanctos defensores meruit,
precibus invicta quorum permanet et fertilis.

We have here a foretaste of the possibilities of this rhythmical
scheme when it was handled by a really competent poet. Such
was the author of the beautiful *Urbs beata Hierusalem*, who

[1] Verse 56; cf. *Aen.* ii. 6; see Mani-
tius, *Christl. lat. Poesie*, p. 398, note.   [2] Text in *Poet. Lat. Aevi Car.* i.
24 sqq.; also in Traube, *Karolingische
Dichtungen*, pp. 119 sqq.

wrote perhaps in the same century as the versifier who composed this rhythm.[1]

This survey of poetry in what is usually regarded as the dark age of medieval civilization shows, beyond the almost irrelevant fact of decline, that there was still enough left of the old classical tradition to make a revival possible, and that there was in addition a decided tendency to experiment with rhythmical and rimed verse. The principle of syllabic equality had not yet been completely united with that of a regular rhythm based on the word-accent, and rime was still imperfect and sporadic. But the way was open to new developments, though progress was destined to be slow and difficult.

§ 2. *Ireland.*

Ireland remained always beyond the limits of the Roman Empire and received the Latin language only through the Church. Christianity had made its way there before the days of Patrick, and there was considerable intercourse between Ireland and the sea-ports of Gaul,[2] including Bordeaux, which, as we have seen, was one of the chief centres of Roman culture in the later Empire. Patrick himself brought no learning, as his writings show, but there were doubtless among his colleagues men who had received an education approaching that of the continental clergy. These may be the *rethorici*, the rhetoricians before whom the saint appeared as a fool for Christ's sake.[3] But, if we are to judge from the meagre specimens of literature which have survived from fifth- and sixth-century Ireland, there was no real study of Latin authors, still less any serious acquaintance with Greek. Irish monks and clergy had to acquire Latin with the aid of the usual grammars, and possibly with the addition of a few classical authors. But the language of the Latin scriptures and of the Latin Fathers seems to have been a more potent influence, though there were other influences at work in the fashioning of the strange speech which was employed by some of the early writers of hymns. The old prosody did not make much appeal

[1] See *Christian-Latin Poetry*, p. 362 sq.; *Anal. Hymn.* li, p. 110.

[2] H. Zimmer, 'Über direkte Handelsverbindungen Westgalliens mit Irland', *Berlin.Sitzungsber.* 1909–10 (Sonderabdruck).

[3] I see no reason for regarding these as bards, as Roger suggests, *L'En-seignement des lettres classiques*, p. 220; the context, *Confessio*, 13 (ed. N. J. D. White, London 1918, in *Libri Sancti Patricii*), suggests that the rhetoricians are Christians and not heathen; it is possible, of course, to think of them as Gallic rhetoricians teaching Latin to the Irish.

to the first generations of Irish students, who found, especially for religious verse, that the rhythm, with the adornment of rime, was more to their taste.

It is clear that even in the sixth century when we hear of numerous monastic schools, there was no comprehensive and systematic organization of studies such as we meet with later at York and Canterbury. *Lectio sacra* must have been the chief preoccupation, with a certain amount of profane literature and occasionally metrical composition. In the latter half of the sixth century Columbanus, who was a monk of Bangor when Comgall was abbot, had read a large number of authors, including Virgil, Horace, Ovid, Statius, Juvenal, Ausonius, Claudian, Juvencus, Sedulius, Prudentius, and Dracontius. It is possible that, as his poems were written in his old age in the days of his wanderings on the continent, he owed neither his acquaintance with these poets nor his metrical skill to the schools of his native country. But it seems reasonable to assume that at Bangor a clever scholar had an opportunity of mastering the elements of prosody and of reading the best among the classical and the Christian poets.

Most of the Latin poetry of Irish origin can be included under the general description of hymns.[1] We are concerned with it only in so far as it represents a stage in the development of rimed and rhythmical poetry. The oldest-known example of Irish Latin verse is the hymn of S. Sechnall or Secundinus on Patrick. It is alphabetical like many other Irish hymns, and here the example of Augustine and of Hilary was followed.[2] The rhythmic scheme is based on the trochaic tetrameter, and there is much elision and no hiatus.[3] What rime exists is accidental.

Later hymns show much assonance and rime, along with alliteration. Rhythm does not advance much beyond the old rule of equality of syllables. The strange and powerful *Altus prosator*, ascribed to Columba, has this rudimentary rhythm with sporadic rime. Its power is derived from the flavour of its strange speech, a mixture of ecclesiastical and biblical Latin with the odd words found in glosses or in the writers of the *Hisperica Famina*.[4] Who can deny that something new and

---

[1] It is conveniently collected in *Analecta Hymnica*, li, pp. 259 sqq.

[2] Perhaps the hymn of Sedulius was also known; text of Sechnall's hymn, *Liber Hymnorum*, i. 7 (*Henry Bradshaw Society*, 1898, 2 vols.); *Anal. Hymn.* li,

pp. 340 sqq.

[3] See Engelbrecht, 'Der heilige Augustinus als Volksdichter', *Zeitschr. f. d. österreich. Gymnas.* lix (1908), p. 593.

[4] See below, p. 167.

grand had come into being, something that could not have grown on Latin soil, where the memories of the past had a stronger hold than they could ever gain in a land beyond the Roman frontiers?

Quis ad condictum domini	Vagatur ex climactere
montem conscendit Sinai,	Orion celi cardine
quis audivit tonitrua	derelicto Virgilio,
ultra modum sonantia,	astrorum splendidissimo,
quis clangorem perstrepere	per metas Tithis ignoti
inormitatis bucinae,	orientalis circuli;
quis quoque vidit fulgora	girans certis ambagibus
in giro coruscantia,	redit priscis reditibus,
quis lampades et iacula	oriens post biennium
saxaque collidentia	Vesperugo in vesperum;
preter Israhelitici	sumpta in proplesmatibus
Moysen iudicem populi?[1]	tropicis intellectibus.[2]

But verse of this grandeur is rare. The so-called *Bangor Antiphonary* contains a collection of hymns of which some are of great merit. The strong feeling for rime is remarkable, and the poets can on occasion handle two-syllabled rimes with considerable skill. In the *Versiculi Familie Benchuir*,[3] a poem in praise of the monastic rule of Bangor, there are verses like the following:

> Munther Benchuir beata,
>   fide fundata certa,
> spe salutis ornata,
>   caritate perfecta.
>
> navis nunquam turbata,
>   quamvis fluctibus tonsa,
> nuptiis quoque parata
>   regi domino sponsa.

And in the *Book of Cerne*[4] we have a rhythmical prayer which is almost certainly of Irish origin, and shows a similar use of the two-syllabled rime:

> sancte sator   suffragator,
> legum lator   largus dator, etc.

It is clear that the Irish poets did much to further the development of rimed and rhythmical verse. They took it in its rudimentary form from the continental poets and gave it a whole-hearted welcome. They were familiar with rime, not

---

[1] *Lib. Hymn.* i, 78; *Anal. Hymn.* i, p. 277.

[2] *Lib. Hymn.* i, 79; *Anal. Hymn.* li, p. 278.

[3] *The Antiphonary of Bangor* (Henry Bradshaw Society, 1893-5), ii, 28; *Anal. Hymn.* li, p. 356.

[4] Ed. A. B. Cuypers, Cambridge 1902, p. 131; *Anal. Hymn.* li, p. 299.

only in hymns but in the rhetorical prose of ecclesiastical writers, and in the *contestationes* or prefaces of their mass-books. The writings of Isidore and of other Spanish churchmen must have been well known in Ireland in the seventh century,[1] and Columbanus knew all the devices of rimed prose. This love of rime passed from the Irish to the Anglo-Saxons, and thence back again to the continent.

Columbanus has already been mentioned as the author of metrical poems. They are the oldest surviving quantitative verses of Irish origin.[2] One poem is in adonics, an epistle addressed to his friend Fedolius, and its model is perhaps to be found in Boëthius.[3] It is very long, but its lightness of spirit—it is a work of the old age of this heroic toiler—makes it pleasant reading:[4]

Columbanus Fidolio fratri suo.

Accipe, queso,
nunc bipedali
condita versu
carminulorum
munera parva:
tuque frequenter
mutua nobis
obsequiorum
debita redde.
nam velut aestu,
flantibus austris
arida gaudent
imbribus arva,
sic tua nostras
missa frequenter
laetificabat
pagina mentes . . .

Then later he explains how the metre is constructed, which, he says, was used by the 'famous poetess of the Greeks, Sappho by name':

[1] On rime in Isidore see Polheim, *Die lateinische Reimprosa*, Berlin 1925, pp. 292 sqq.; on the Irish and rime, pp. 312 sqq.; on rime in the prose of Columbanus, p. 313 sq.

[2] See Gundlach,'Über die Columban-Briefe', *Neues Archiv*, xiii (1888), pp. 514 sqq., who decides that we have four genuine poems of Columban—two poems in hexameters, one in adonics, and one a rhythmical piece; see also *Christian-Latin Poetry*, p. 139. He may also have

written the boating-song (given in *Neues Archiv*, vi (1881), p. 190 sq.).

[3] Or ought we not rather to say Martianus Capella?—see above, p. 103. On the tradition of the adonic among the Irish see B. Bischoff, 'Anecdota Carolina', *Studien zur lateinischen Dichtung des Mittelalters, Ehrengabe für Karl Strecker*, Dresden 1931, p. 9.

[4] Text, ed. Gundlach, *M.G.H., Epist.* iii, pp. 186 sqq.

> si tibi cura
> forte volenti
> carmina tali
> condere versu,
> semper ut unus
> ordine certo
> dactilus isthic
> incipiat pes;
> inde sequenti
> parte trocheus
> proximus illi
> rite locetur.
> saepe duabus
> claudere longis
> ultima versus
> iure licebit.

And the charming old man ends with six hexameters, in which he tells how he is bowed by age and sickness and is near his end:

> haec tibi dictaram morbis oppressus acerbis,
> corpore quos fragili patior tristisque senecta;
> nam dum praecipiti labuntur tempora cursu,
> nunc ad olympiadis ter senos venimus annos.
> omnia praetereunt, fugit inreparabile tempus:
> vive, vale laetus tristisque memento senectae.

But the saint left behind him as his most lasting memorial the cloister of Bobbio in the Apennines, which in days to come was to be a place of light and of learning as well as of zeal and piety.

Before we close the story of early Irish poetry we must note two collections of riddles. The first is entitled *Versus cuiusdam Scoti de Alphabeto*,[1] and it consists of riddles on the various letters of the alphabet, in this fashion:

> A. Principium vocis veterumque inventio mira
> nomen habens domini sum felix voce pelasga;
> exsecrantis item dira interiectio dicor.

> B. Principium libri, mutis caput, alter et ordo,
> tertia felicis vere sum syllaba semper;
> si me graece legas, viridi tum nascor in horto.

The second collection of riddles is contained in a manuscript at Berne, and was probably the work of an Irish monk at Bobbio in the seventh century.[2] It is in rhythmic hexameters, one specimen of which will suffice.

---

[1] Baehrens, *Poet. Lat. Min.* v. pp. 375 sqq. The date is about the middle of the seventh century; Manitius, *Gesch.* i. p. 192.

[2] Manitius, *Gesch.* i. p. 193; Text, Riese, *Anthol. Lat.* no. 481. The riddles show the influence of Symphosius.

De piscibus.

Nullo firma loco manens consistere possum
et vagando vivens nullo conspicere quemquam.
vita mihi mors est, mortem pro vita requiro
et volanti domo semper amica delector.
numquam ego lecto volo iacere tepenti,
sed vitalem mihi torum sub frigore condo.[1]

Taking Irish literary culture as a whole we see that it owed much to contact with what Spain and Gaul had immediately to offer both of old and of new. It made use as best it could of both, but the time of its full development was yet to come. The next and necessary stage in the story is that of the emergence of the Anglo-Saxons to the forefront of western civilization.[2]

§ 3. *British and Anglo-Saxon Culture.*

The British Church sent the Bishops of London, York, and Caerleon[3] to the Council of Arles in 314. It was in close touch with the ecclesiastical life of the West, and, if the more learned among its leaders got their education abroad, the native clergy must have had some fairly adequate instruction at home. The Saxon invasions drove the remains of what was now an isolated native Church into the south and west. There it maintained its existence and shared something like a common culture and practice with the Irish Church. We hear of British monks and British schools, and out of the mists emerges the figure of Gildas (*circ.* 547), the author of the *de excidio et conquestu Britanniae*, a melancholy tract in which the British monk lays upon the sins of his people the responsibility for their disasters. He wrote 'vile quidem stilo', as he himself says,[4] but he had

[1] Riese, i, p. 301; also W. Meyer, *Rythmik*, ii, p. 169 sq. Meyer regards these rhythmical hexameters as specifically 'Lombardic', pointing out that there are a number of grave-inscriptions of Lombard princes and clerics (*circ.* 700–50) which are composed in rhythmic hexameters. These are referred to below, p. 219, and are printed in *Poet. Lat. Aevi Car.* iv. pp. 718 sqq. Meyer relates also to the Lombardic school the rhythmical hexameters of the poem *Exhortatio poenitendi* (text, *Rythmik*, ii, pp. 183 sqq.), which had usually been regarded as of Spanish origin. At the end of the Berne riddles in the Leipzig MS. is a riddle, *de vino*, with the acrostic PAULUS, which Neff (*Gedichte des Paulus Diaconus*, p. 83)

thinks is the work of Paul the Deacon.

As Meyer points out, the rhythmical hexameter was not much cultivated because it presented exceptional difficulties. Its composers were divided between attempts to keep syllabic equality, to imitate the stresses of the metrical model, and to pay some regard (especially at the end of a verse) to quantity.

[2] Poems 739, 791, 941, in Riese seem to be Irish; also the poem in Pitra, *Spicil. Solesm.*, iii (1855), pp. 399 sqq.; see Kenney, *Sources for the Early History of Ireland*, i, 733 sq.

[3] Haddan and Stubbs, *Councils*, i, p. 7. The reading 'Caerleon' is not quite certain.

[4] Cf. Manitius, *Gesch.* i. p. 209.

read Orosius and other ecclesiastical authors, and of the poets
he knew Virgil, perhaps Juvenal and Persius, and Claudian.
He is associated with two rhythmical poems, one the famous
Lorica, and the other—also a charm against misfortune—*pro
itineris et navigii prosperitate*. We are concerned here only to
note that these poems show the Irish love of rime and of
rhythmical construction, along with the use of strange words
belonging to a mysterious speech, a *Geheimsprache*, which
Britons and Irish wrote in the sixth century. Here is a specimen from the *Lorica*:[1]

> Deus, inpenetrabili tutela
> undique me defende potentia.
> mei gibrae[2] pernas[3] omnes libera
> tuta pelta protegente singula,
> ut non tetrae daemones inlatera
> mea librent ut solent iacula.
> gygram[4] cephalem cum iaris et conas
> patham liganam sennas atque michinas
> cladam crassum madianum talias
> bathma exugiam atque binas idumas.[5]

The origin of this strange speech, with its mixture of recognizable Hebrew and Greek, along with vulgar Latin and words of
no known origin, is still obscure. That it was taken seriously
we cannot doubt, and it exercised a fascination over the mind
of Aldhelm and over generations of Irish scholars. It is tempting to associate it with some such circle as that in which the
grammarian Virgilius Maro may be expected to have moved,[6]
but the connexion is difficult to establish. If the chief specimen
—called *Hisperica Famina*—is not of Irish origin, it may have
been produced in south-west Britain in the sixth century. The
Hisperica Famina is a collection of episodes, very loosely

---

[1] Text, F. J. H. Jenkinson, *The
Hisperica Famina*, Cambridge 1908,
p. 52; also *Anal. Hymn.* li, p. 359; cf.
also the curious alphabetical hymn in
the S. Omer and Cambridge MSS. It
is rimed and is a mixture of Greek and
of 'Hisperic' and ordinary Latin (Jenkinson, p. 61). It begins:

> Adelphus adelpha meter
> alle pilus hius tegater
> dedronte tonaliter,
> Blebomen agialus
> nicate dodrantibus
> sic mundi vita huius.

[Brother, sister, mother, father (?), son,
daughter die together; we see the shore
beaten by the waves, so is the life of
this world.]

[2] *hominis.*

[3] *membra.*

[4] *caput.*

[5] *manus.*

[6] Zimmer, 'Der Gascogner Virgilius
Maro Grammaticus in Irland', *Berlin.
Sitzungsber.* 1910, pp. 1031 sqq.; Roger,
L'Enseignement des lettres classiques,
p. 242, and note 1.

joined together, as the following analysis, derived mainly from Jenkinson,[1] shows:

1-48, glorification of the rhetors or *sophiae arcatores* and their school, and of the speaker himself as a match for any of his contemporaries.

49-86, a would-be scholar, a grazier, who has mistaken his vocation, is recommended to go home to his family.

87-115, the speaker illustrates the superiority of his Latin.

133-357, a day and its occupations are described. Then follow passages on various subjects, sky, sea, fire, wind, etc.

Perhaps the best passage to choose for quotation is that in which the dawn is described at the beginning of the scholars' day:

Titaneus olimphium | inflammat arotus tabulatum·
thalasicum | illustrat vapore flustrum ;
flammiuomo secat polum corusco supernum·
Almi | scandit camaram firmamenti·
Alboreum febeus | suffocat mene proritus·
Cibonea | pliadum non exhomicant fulgora·
Merseum solifluus | eruit neuum †tractus (tactus)·
Densos phetoneum | extricat sudos incendium·
Roscida | aret rubigine stillicidia·
Nec oliuatus frondea | oliuat nimbus robora·
Fẹnosas | dividat imber uuas·
Micras uricomus | apricat lacunas rogus
mundanum | que torret iubar girum·
Aligera placoreum | reboat curia concentum·
Tinulas patulis | mormurant armonias rostris·

The reader, even if he has not had the courage to attempt to construe this passage closely, will feel that it is poetically conceived, whether it is to be called verse or prose. It consists of rimed 'cola'; the caesura occurs after any syllable from the second to the eighth, and there is no law governing the length of the 'cola',[2] though there are signs that the classical hexameter had some vague influence on the form of the verses.[3]

The *Hisperica Famina* is of importance to our study for two reasons. In the first place it bears witness to the existence of schools in the sixth century in which something more than purely religious studies were made, and secondly it helps to bring before us part of the atmosphere of this kind of twilight

[1] op. cit., p. xi; this is taken from what is known as the A-text (Cod. Vat. Regin. Lat. 81); see also E. K. Rand, 'The Irish flavour of *Hisperica Famina*', *Studien zur lateinischen Dichtung des Mittelalters, Ehrengabe für K. Strecker*, Dresden 1931, p. 137 sq.

[2] See Polheim, *Lateinische Reimprosa*, p. 286; Jenkinson, p. xviii, 'We are left to wonder how such a vocabulary came to be associated with such artistic feeling.'

[3] Jenkinson, p. xvii.

between the ancient and the medieval world, in which new thoughts were struggling for expression and new literary experiments were being tried. The author of the *Hisperica Famina* had said, in his opening verse:

ampla pectoralem | suscitat vernia[1] cavernam.

A new breath was indeed to blow upon the island, the greater part of which was as yet given over to those who appeared in British eyes to be wildest heathen.[2] In 597 came the Roman mission, which was followed by the conversion of Kent. The north was evangelized by Irish monks. In 635 Oswald of Northumbria sent to Iona for a bishop, and Aidan came to the see of Lindisfarne. The number of Irish monks increased, churches were built, the king gave money for monasteries, and the children of the English were taught by Irish masters even to the extent of compassing *maiora studia*.[3] This is what Bede tells us; from it we must conclude that monastic education, as it was understood in Ireland and with the limitations that accompanied it, was reproduced in Northumbria.

The really decisive event in the history of Anglo-Saxon education was the appearance of Theodore of Tarsus and Hadrian, two learned monks, whom Pope Vitalian sent in 667 at the request of the kings of Northumbria and Kent to reform the English Church.[4] These were indeed remarkable men. Theodore had studied at Athens, and he had at his command Latin and Greek, and authors sacred and profane, presumably in both tongues. Hadrian was by birth an African, and he also was learned in those two languages. It is clear that these men had received a systematic training in grammar and rhetoric, and had acquired in addition not only the elements of the other liberal arts, but had had the advantage of a serious study of the Greek Fathers. They were competent, therefore, to reorganize the monastic schools on continental models; but, if Bede's testimony is to be relied on, they set up a standard considerably higher than that of any monastic school in the West. For Bede says that, besides the study of Holy Writ, they instructed their pupils in 'the metrical art' and in astronomy and arithmetic. 'A proof of this', he says, 'is seen in the fact that at the present day there are living some of their pupils, who are as skilled in Latin and in Greek as in their native tongue.'[5] How long this knowledge of Greek, a

[1] = *laetitia*; see Echternach Gloss., Jenkinson, p. 36.
[2] Cf. Gildas, *De excidio*.
[3] Bede, *H.E.* iii. 3.
[4] ib. iv. 1.
[5] ib. iv. 2.

thing so unusual in the West, survived we do not know. But
it seems to have passed from England to Ireland, where it
gave a new stimulus to the small amount of Greek study which
still, perhaps, persisted there.

The Anglo-Saxons took a great interest in grammatical and
metrical questions, and their new masters were able to give
them access not only to the standard treatises—some of which
were already known to the Irish—but to direct their attempts
at the composition of quantitative verses.

Canterbury, where Theodore was Archbishop, was the great
school in the south. In the north Benedict Biscop (d. 690),
who had once been the master at Canterbury, set up in his
foundations of Wearmouth and Jarrow a similar discipline.
Authors profane as well as sacred were studied, though there
was still a feeling that no encouragement should be given to
the reading of heathen poets.[1] The Christian poets now took
equal if not superior rank to the classical poets. This was all
to the good, as it helped to keep alive the achievement of men
like Prudentius and Paulinus of Nola, and provided a healthy
influence for poets who breathed the Christian air.

While there was, on the one hand, a distinct revival of
metrical verse, the old Irish and British influence, still strong
in western Britain and kept alive by continuous intercourse with
Irish schools, did not allow the tradition of rhythmical verse
to die.

Most of this verse, of both kinds, was purely religious, and
does not require detailed consideration here; but it has importance as a link in the historical chain.

Aldhelm (b. *circ.* 650) is the first poet. It was at Canterbury
under Hadrian that he laid the foundation of his wide acquaintance with Latin authors and acquired as well some little
Greek. Yet he had begun his studies at Malmesbury under an
Irishman named Maeldubh, and to the end he professed a great
admiration for the Irish schools.[2] For his mind was really set
in the British and Irish mould. He loved the tortuous and the
obscure; and the *Hisperica Famina* probably pleased him
more than the plain speech of the older masters of the Latin
tongue. This is how Aldhelm, 'exiguus in domino', begins an
epistle to Aelfrid:[3]

[1] Cf. Bede, *De arte metrica* (Keil,
Grammatici Latini, vii. p. 258):' reperiun-
tur quaedam et in insigni illo volumine
Porphyrii poetae, quo ad Constantinum
Augustum misso meruit de exilio libe-

rari, quae, quia pagana erant, nos tan-
gere non libuit.'

[2] *Aldhelmi opera*, ed. Ehwald,
M.G.H., Auct. Antiq. xv, p. 492.

[3] ib., p. 488.

Primitus pantorum procerum praetorumque pio potissimum paternoque praesertim privilegio panagericum poemataque passim prosatori sub polo promulgantes stridula vocum simphonia et melodiae cantilenaeque carmine modulaturi ymnizemus. . . .

This Irish alliteration[1] was taken up later by Carolingian poets and culminated in Hucbald's famous poem in praise of baldness.[2] This and other elements in Aldhelm's prose style show how little fitted he was to take advantage of the best that the school of Canterbury had to offer, though to his own and to succeeding generations he appeared as a prodigy or even a genius.[3]

His metrical verse shows, indeed, how he had profited at Canterbury by the library of profane and Christian poets to which he had access, and, although he uses 'Hisperic' words and words curiously sought for in glossaries, his meaning is not wrapped up in the obscurity which dominates his prose. The study of metre interested him greatly. The Epistle to Acircius[4] (Aelfrid, King of Northumbria) begins with a discussion of the number seven and its mystical meaning, and branches off into a dialogue between a master and his pupil on metre and the 'rules of feet'. It contains also the famous collection of versified riddles, in which Aldhelm took as his models Symphosius and the author of the Berne collection,[5] though he did not follow them at all slavishly. Some of the riddles are of considerable length. It is amusing to see Camillus and camellus (i.e. camelus) associated in one of the pieces:

Camellus.

Consul eram quondam, Romanus miles equester
arbiter imperio dum regni sceptra regebat;
nunc onus horrendum reportant corpora gibbi
et premit immensum truculentae sarcina molis.
terreo cornipedum nunc velox agmen equorum,
qui trepidi fugiunt mox quadrupedante meatu,
dum trucis aspectant immensos corporis artus.[6]

The subjects of the riddles are mostly works of nature or of men. In his introductory poem (an acrostic and telestich each containing the line

Aldhelmus cecinit millenis versibus odas)

---

[1] Cf. Ehwald, p. 488, note 1.
[2] Below, p. 249.
[3] See Bede's estimate, *H.E.* v. 18, 'vir undecumque doctissimus.'
[4] Ehwald, pp. 61 sqq.
[5] See above, p. 165; Isidore and

Eugenius of Toledo provided material, Manitius, *Gesch.* i. p. 489. It is important to note the knowledge of African and Spanish authors in Britain. The Irish knew them as well.
[6] Ehwald, p. 145.

the author tells us that he is not calling on the Castalian nymphs, neither, in the words of Persius, has he seen visions on Parnassus.[1] The long poem *De Virginitate* belongs to religious verse. It is in hexameters and is a versification of Aldhelm's long prose treatise on the same subject. The latter contains a small specimen of his rhythmical verse. He is speaking of John beneath the Cross:

> Verax medicus . . . maternae memor reverentiae discipulo inter discrimina perfidorum militum eventus rerum praestulanti genetricem pie praecepit tuendam, ut non inconvenienter carmine rithmico dici queat.

> Christus passus patibula
> atque leti latibula
> virginem virgo virgini
> commendabat tutamini.[2]

This is precisely the kind of rhythmical verse that was most cultivated by the Anglo-Saxons at this time. A group of five rhythmical poems has been preserved in the ninth-century manuscript of Boniface's Epistles, now at Vienna (no. 731),[3] and all are composed in this measure, which is clearly derived from Irish prototypes. They show a similar choice of 'Hisperic' and rare or fantastic words, with a mixture of Graecisms. The first is the work of an unknown clerk and is addressed to Aldhelm, his master. The others were composed by another pupil of Aldhelm, Aethelwald, who became king of Mercia.[4]

The first poem describes a journey and a storm very much as Columba would have done.[5] The second deals likewise with a journey, but it is a pilgrimage across the seas to Rome. Three men, two of them brothers, set out for Italy; one dies during their stay in Rome and the other two finally reach home bringing back all kinds of wondrous things. The descrip-

---

[1] Ehwald, p. 98; cf. *De Virginitate*, 23 sqq. (p. 353).

[2] ib., p. 235; another example (Ehwald, p. 521) is found at the end of a charter to which Aldhelm's name is attached:

> Pax cunctis ⟨sit⟩ legentibus consensumque prebentibus
> sitque laus utentibus luxque perpes credentibus.
> virtus vita faventibus rite constet senatibus
> Anglorum atque coetibus qui dona firment nutibus.

Ehwald also quotes a prose passage from the *De Virginitate* (c. 23) which falls into this same rhythm.

[3] ib., pp. 519 sqq.

[4] Henry Bradley, 'Some Poems ascribed to Aldhelm', *E.H.R.*, 1900, xv, p. 291, ascribed them all to Aethelwald; I follow Ehwald's view, which seems more likely (pp. 521 sqq.). See Traube, *Karolingische Dichtungen*, pp. 130 sqq.

[5] I have given extracts and a summary in *Christian-Latin Poetry*, p. 144 sq.

tion of these latter will give an idea of the compass of the
poet's art and of the strange language he uses:[1]

```
en vehebant volumina     numerosa per agmina
multimodis et mysticis    elucubrata normulis,
quorum auctori aius[2]    adesse constat alitus;
quae profetae, apostoli    doctiloqui oraculi
indiderunt pergaminae    almo inflati flamine.
nunc vestium velamina     bella produnt ornamina,
mirifico quae munere     proferebant praepropere
quaeque ita inormia     eliciunt exordia:
'pulchra prorsus propagine     deprompta in origine
gnari quaedam genimina     vermis[3] feruntur minima,
foliis quique vescitur,     brumae meatu moritur;
cumque proles progreditur,     ovorum alvo oritur,
neque illos qui genuit     vermis, idem recaluit.
foetus fluunt ex semine     imo naturae germine;
sed quod magis mirabile     mundo et desperabile:
ova viri et feminae     calificata calore
parturire progenitum     foetum vellere vegetum.
lana ostri elabitur     vermiculo, cum vertitur,
spissam ceu aranea     telam texit muscarea;
tumque lana, latratibus     fusi valde volantibus
filatim quae revolvitur,     veluti setis torquitur.'
inde sumuntur syrica,     quae portabant, promiscua,
quorum persplendit species:     pulchra ceu planities
paradisi puniceis     purpurata cum rosetis,
quibus inter eburnea     lilia lucent linea;
sic, sic sane sanguinea     Syricorum insignia,
pulchre picta perniveo     colore atque croceo;
viridi, fulvo, floreo     fucata atque blaveo
ut peplorum per pallia     pulchra pandunt ornamina!
```

This is a lively and, it seems, perfectly accurate description of
the ways of the silkworm and of how the silken thread is made,
from which the precious stuffs are woven.[4] The poet goes on
to describe some of those marvellous oriental *pallia* which were
at that time making their way into the West for the adornment
of the churches.

The next poem is a prayer to God, and the fourth is addressed
to Aldhelm in a flattering strain. The last is, it seems, directed
by Aethelwald to Hova, a nobleman of some account, whose
personal charms are described in much detail:

```
manus, manus mirabiles,     multum pedes placabiles,
tibiae cursu teretes     tam fortes, ut sonipedes
saepe sequantur cursibus     salientes praepetibus, etc.[5]
```

[1] Ehwald, p. 531.
[2] ἅγιος.
[3] The silk-worm; silk stuffs are being

described.
[4] See Ehwald, p. 532, note to 145.
[5] ib., p. 537.

These poems show what a profound impression the Irish rhythmical and rimed verse had made upon the Anglo-Saxons. Not merely the form—the line of sixteen syllables with the internal rime—but the continuous alliteration and the very vocabulary are taken over from the Irish examples.

Yet there were other rhythmical models in existence, which had been developed on the continent in closer contact with the old classical versification. These made a greater appeal to Bede, who was a pupil of the Northumbrian schools, which were kept so closely in touch with continental methods by the continued visits of Abbot Benedict Biscop to Gaul and to Rome. In his treatise *De arte metrica*,[1] Bede devotes a brief section to 'rhythm'.[2] He says that the characteristic of rhythmic verse is that it is isosyllabic—

verborum modulata compositio, non metrica ratione, sed numero syllabarum ad iudicium aurium examinata, ut sunt carmina vulgarium poetarum.

He proceeds:

et quidem rhythmus per se sine metro esse potest, metrum vero sine rhythmo esse non potest, quod liquidius ita definitur: metrum est ratio cum modulatione, rhythmus modulatio sine ratione. plerumque tamen casu quodam invenies etiam rationem in rhythmo, non artifici moderatione servata, sed sono et ipsa modulatione ducente, quam vulgares poetae necesse est rustice, docti faciant docte. quo modo et ad instar iambici metri pulcherrime factus est hymnus ille praeclarus,

> Rex aeterne domine,
> rerum creator omnium,
> qui eras ante saecula
> semper cum patre filius,

et alii Ambrosiani non pauci. item ad formam metri trochaici canunt hymnum de die iudicii per alphabetum,

> Apparebit repentina dies magna domini,
> fur obscura velut nocte improvisos occupans.

It is clear that the ears of Bede were thoroughly attuned to the music of this rhythmical verse, and M. Roger is probably right in his suggestion that they could hardly distinguish between classical verses and rhythmical verses fashioned on the same model.[3] The preference of Bede for rhythmic verse which seemed to reproduce the character of the verse of antiquity is very significant. The Irish compositions must have seemed, on the whole, 'rustic', not to say barbarous, to one

[1] Ed. Keil, *Grammatici Latini*, vii. pp. 227 sqq. On the popularity of Bede's treatise in the Middle Ages and on its use by the Carolingian grammarians see Manitius, *Gesch.* i. p. 510. Remigius of Auxerre wrote a commentary upon it.

[2] ib., pp. 258–9.

[3] Roger, *L'Enseignement des lettres classiques*, p. 382 sq.

who had studied the classical Christian poets with such care.[1]
Bede wrote a book of hymns, some of which were rhythmical.
The book has perished, but Dreves has tried to prove that
a number of these rhythmical hymns have survived.[2] If they
are really Bede's they are written in the form that we should
expect—the rhythmic iambic dimeter.

Bede's other poems are in classical metres. Once he borrows
the epanaleptic form from Sedulius, in a hymn on S. Ethel-
dreda of Ely, combining it with the alphabetical, in order still
further to test his skill.

His merit lies in the industry with which he ministered to
the necessary studies of the monastic school. The foundation
of all was the Latin tongue, which had to be painfully acquired
by Anglo-Saxons, to whose native language it bore no resemblance. If even the Christian poets were to be read, metre
must be studied, and it was now necessary also to include the
rules of rhythm, since there were so many rhythmical hymns
in common use. Bede also realized the value of history, sacred
and profane, and did not neglect chronology, natural history,
or arithmetic. He aimed, in effect, at something which did
not fall far short of a liberal education as it was understood in
late antiquity, although, of course, his methods were un-
critical, and he had to work to a great extent at second-hand.
His treatise on metres remained a text-book for centuries, but
by its emphasis on quantity, tended to obscure from sight
the other things necessary to the composition of readable verse.
Exceptional or debased uses tended to become elevated to the
position of rules, and, as M. Roger has said,[3] the artificial
character of prosodic versification was thereby exaggerated
with harmful but perhaps unavoidable results.

The Anglo-Saxons seem to have had a preoccupation with
metre in its mechanical aspect.[4] They appear to have imagined

[1] It is from the Christian rather than from the profane poets that Bede likes to draw his examples in his *De arte metrica*.

[2] *Anal. Hymn.* l, pp. 96 sqq.

[3] op. cit., p. 383.

[4] They liked also to describe the metre they were using (cf. the example of Columbanus, p. 164 above); thus Aldhelm, *De Virginitate* (45 sqq.; Eh-wald, pp. 354-5):

en promissa novo scribantur carmina versu!

garrula virgineas depromat pagina laudes
colaque cum pedibus pergant et commata ternis:
dactilus excepto decurrat fine metrorum,
spondei quintam contemnat sillaba partem;
ultima sic trochei concludat littera versum,
extremus iugiter qui gaudet calce teneri.
sic ternis pedibus properent epigrammata metri!

that a verse was well constructed if it were a succession of accurate quantities. Accuracy for them was guaranteed by precedents set, however doubtfully, by any poet, Christian or profane.

The spirit of the Northumbrian schools passed into the school of York, where Archbishop Egbert and his successor Aelbert followed what was in all essentials the ideal of Bede. Like Benedict Biscop, Aelbert visited the continent and met learned men abroad. The career of his famous pupil, Alcuin, belongs to the story of the Carolingian renaissance.

Other Englishmen, like Boniface and his friend Lul, wrote rhythmical verse in the Irish manner, and helped to make this fashion popular on the continent.[1] Boniface was of West-Saxon birth, and he came naturally into contact with the tradition of Aldhelm. So he delighted in acrostics and riddles, and in the mysteries of prosody, which, along with grammar, he taught in the monastic school before he was called to the missionary labours which ended in his martyrdom.[2]

Boniface's riddles are all on Christian subjects, a kind of pious play, in which he gathered a few flowers from the old poets, and set forth the virtues and vices for the edification of his sister. There are ten virtues,

> aurea nam decem transmisi poma sorori,
> quae in ligno vitae crescebant floribus almis,

and the vices follow,

> sunt alia alterius ligni acerbissima mala,
> pestifero vernant quae in ligno mortis amara.

These riddles of Boniface are, fortunately, hardly riddles at all, and this is perhaps why they escape the tediousness attached to the riddles of Tatwine and Eusebius, who are here mentioned because they followed Aldhelm's example, and seem also to have been influenced by Boniface.[3]

The remainder of Anglo-Saxon poetry up to the Norman conquest is religious in character, and is mainly metrical.[4] The Irish influence did not wholly die away, for in the tenth century Dunstan studied at Glastonbury under Irish masters.

---

[1] *Christian-Latin Poetry*, p. 149 sq.; texts in Tangl, *Die Briefe des heiligen Bonifatius und Lull*, M.G.H., *Epist. Select.* i, Berlin 1916.

[2] See the references in *Poet. Lat. Aevi Car.* i, p. 1, note 1.

[3] This is probably true, at any rate, of Tatwine; see Manitius, *Gesch.* i. p. 205; for other English riddles, *Poet. Lat. Aevi Car.* i. pp. 20 sqq.

[4] See *Christian-Latin Poetry*, pp. 150 sqq.

In the middle of the same century Frithegode wrote a metrical life of S. Wilfrid in which occur the peculiar mannerisms associated with the Irish school.[1] The eleventh century, so far as poetry is concerned, is an age of decline, and it was not until the Normans were well established in the country that a revival of letters took place.

[1] ib., p. 152.

THE CAROLINGIAN REVIVAL

§ 1. *Poets of the Court Circle.*

IN his long poem on the Saints of the Church of York[1] Alcuin
has a good deal to say about the studies in the school of
which he was once the most illustrious ornament. He is speaking about his beloved master Aelbert, who was to his pupils
a father, a counsellor, and a friend. To him Archbishop Egbert,
who had been the pupil of Bede, entrusted the care of the
school which under his own guidance had risen to such
renown. Alcuin goes over in detail the curriculum of the school
as it was in Aelbert's time:[2]

> . . . Euborica praefertur in urbe magister.
> ille ubi diversis sitientia corda fluentis
> doctrinae et vario studiorum rore rigabat,
> his dans grammaticae rationis gnaviter artes,
> illis rhetoricae infundens refluamina linguae;
> illos iuridica curavit cote polire,
> illos Aonio docuit concinnere cantu,
> Castalida instituens alios resonare cicuta,
> et iuga Parnassi lyricis percurrere plantis.
> ast alios fecit prefatus nosse magister
> harmoniam caeli, solis lunaeque labores,
> quinque poli zonas, errantia sidera septem,
> astrorum leges, ortus simul atque recessus,
> aerios motus pelagi terraeque tremorem,
> naturas hominum, pecudum, volucrumque ferarum,
> diversas numeri species variasque figuras,
> paschalique dedit sollemnia certa recursu,
> maxima scripturae pandens mysteria sacrae,
> nam rudis et veteris legis patefecit abyssum.

It seems, then, that the circle of studies included grammar,
rhetoric, law, poetry, astronomy, natural history, arithmetic,
geometry, the methods of calculating the date of Easter, and
the study of the Scriptures. We need not examine the extent
to which this programme falls short of the cycle of the liberal
arts as understood by late antiquity.[3] What we are concerned
to notice is the fact that the composition of Latin verses had
an important place in the studies of the school.

---

[1] *Poet. Lat. Aevi Car.* i. 169 sqq.
[2] ib., p. 201 sq.

[3] Roger has done this in *L'enseignement des lettres classiques*, p. 315.

There was an excellent library, and fortunately Alcuin thought it worth while to say something about its contents:[1]

illic invenies veterum vestigia patrum,
quidquid habet pro se Latio Romanus in orbe,
Graecia vel quidquid transmisit clara Latinis,
Hebraicus vel quod populus bibit imbre superno,
Africa lucifluo vel quidquid lumine sparsit.
quod pater Hieronymus, quod sensit Hilarius atque
Ambrosius praesul, simul Augustinus, et ipse
sanctus Athanasius, quod Orosius edit avitus:
quidquid Gregorius summus docet et Leo papa:
Basilius quidquid Fulgentius atque coruscant.
Cassiodorus item, Chrysostomus atque Iohannes.
quidquid et Althelmus docuit, quid Beda magister,
quae Victorinus scripsere Boetius atque
historici veteres, Pompeius, Plinius, ipse
acer Aristoteles, rhetor quoque Tullius ingens.
quid quoque Sedulius, vel quod canit ipse Iuvencus,
Alcimus et Clemens, Prosper, Paulinus, Arator,
quid Fortunatus, vel quid Lactantius edunt.
quae Maro Virgilius, Statius, Lucanus et auctor,
artis grammaticae vel quid scripsere magistri:
quid Probus atque Focas, Donatus Priscianusve,
Servius, Euticius, Pompeius, Comminianus.
invenies alios perplures, lector, ibidem
egregios studiis, arte et sermone magistros,
plurima qui claro scripsere volumina sensu;
nomina sed quorum praesenti in carmine scribi
longius est visum, quam plectri postulet usus.

The list of authors is not, as Alcuin warns us, anything like complete. We cannot therefore safely assume that he has not omitted many of the poets who were of first importance. If he omits Horace it was probably because no manuscript of his poems existed at York,[2] and yet, in later years, Alcuin himself bore the name of Flaccus in the 'academy' of Charles the Great.[3]

---

[1] *Poet. Lat. Aevi Car.* i. 203 sq.

[2] Alcuin does not seem to have read Horace. This was Hauck's view (*Kirchengesch. Deutschlands*, ii. 127, note 1), but Dümmler, 'Alchuinstudien', *Berlin. Sitzungsber.*, 1891, p. 506, and note 2, tried to prove otherwise; Manitius also, *Analekten zur Geschichte des Horaz im Mittelalter*, pp. 18 sqq. Winterfeld, 'Wie sah der Codex Blandinius vetustissimus des Horaz aus?', *Rhein. Mus.* lx (1905), pp. 31 sqq., shows that all the quotations from Horace made in the genuine works of Alcuin are at second hand from Augustine, Jerome, etc. His

conclusion is that it was the Irish, about the middle of the ninth century, who brought Horace into the Frankish Empire. The famous Berne Horace is Irish. Columbanus knew Horace, and so did Sedulius Scottus, Heiric of Auxerre, and Notker Balbulus, the first two being Irish, and the two latter in contact with Irish influence.

[3] But as Winterfeld says (*Rhein. Mus.* lx, p. 33): 'Dass Alcuin Flaccus genannt ward, beweist für Kenntniss des Horaz genau so viel und genau so wenig wie Angilberts Beiname Homer für Kenntniss der Ilias und Odyssee.'

It was Virgil whom he studied most among the heathen poets, though he knew Ovid, who is not mentioned in the verses just quoted.[1] It is characteristic of Alcuin that he lays great stress on the Christian poets. Here he follows the example set by Bede, who admitted the great religious poets to an equality with the classical poets of antiquity. During the whole of the Carolingian age their right to that position was never questioned.

Like Alcuin the Englishman, Theodulf, the Goth from Spain, has left a poem in which he sets forth the contents of a library, his own. The title of the poem is *de libris quos legere solebam et qualiter fabulae poetarum a philosophis mystice pertractentur.*[2] Theodulf plunges into the midst of his subject at once:

> Namque ego suetus eram hos libros legisse frequenter,
> extitit ille mihi nocte dieque labor.
> saepe et Gregorium, Augustinum perlego saepe,
> et dicta Hilarii seu tua, papa Leo.
> Hieronymum, Ambrosium, Isidorum,[3] fulvo ore Iohannem,
> inclyte seu martyr te, Cypriane pater,
> sive alios, quorum describere nomina longum est,
> quos bene doctrinae vexit ad alta decus.
> legimus et crebro gentilia scripta sophorum,
> rebus qui in variis eminuere satis,
> cura decens patrum nec erat postrema piorum,
> quorum sunt subter nomina scripta, vide:
> Sedulius rutilus, Paulinus, Arator, Avitus,
> et Fortunatus, tuque, Iuvence tonans;
> diversoque potens prudenter promere plura
> metro, o Prudenti, noster et ipse parens;
> et modo Pompeium, modo te, Donate, legebam,
> et modo Virgilium, te modo, Naso loquax.

These were the authors whom Theodulf read in his native Spain, where Christian schools still existed, carrying on to some extent the old traditions of the days of Isidore and Eugenius. He gives us, in fact, the impression that he belonged to an older civilization. He thinks quite naturally of Prudentius as a poet of his own country,[4] and he has a fine feeling for

---

[1] Besides Virgil and Ovid, Alcuin knew others, but many of them, it seems, only at second hand. It was the Christian poets that he knew best. Porphyrius Optatianus, however, was known to him (see *Poet. Lat. Aevi Car.* ii. p. 691, col. 2).

[2] *Poet. Lat. Aevi Car.* i. 543.

[3] Alcuin also knew Isidore, though he does not put him in the list of

Aelbert's books; see Roger, *L'Enseignement des lettres classiques*, pp. 317–18.

[4] Or even of his own town (Saragossa, in that event), cf. Cuissard, *Théodulfe évêque d'Orléans*, Orleans 1892, p. 45. Theodulf never lost an opportunity of referring to Prudentius; he quoted him even in his theological works. See Manitius, *Gesch.* i. 542–3. Eugenius of Toledo was also a favourite.

works of art and a love of precious things. It is noteworthy
that the fathers and the Christian poets occupy an important
place in the 'libraries' of both Alcuin and Theodulf, and that
Horace was as unknown to the Spaniard as to the Englishman.
They brought to the Frankish kingdom learning of much the
same compass, but Theodulf came from schools which had an
unbroken tradition from the days of Isidore and indeed from
far beyond. His contribution, therefore, represents something
that must be seriously considered in the history of the Carolingian revival. It was probably Theodulf who brought from Spain
the poems of his fellow-countryman, Martial,[1] and certainly
Cyprian, with whom he claims acquaintance in the poem just
quoted, was far from well known in the West.

If we turn to the Italians and Lombards who came to the
court of Charles, we find no catalogue of authors set out in
verse, but if Paul the Deacon had composed a poem in which
he called up memories of his youthful studies in the court
school of King Luitprand, his list would not have differed
greatly from that of Alcuin or of Theodulf. This is true, at any
rate, as regards poets.[2] Paul the Deacon knew Lucan and
Calpurnius, as well as Virgil and Ovid. He seems also to have
known Nemesian.[3] But, like Alcuin and Theodulf, he paid
much attention to the Christian poets—to Sedulius, Fortunatus,
Juvencus, and Arator. Ausonius seems to have been neglected
entirely by the first generation of Carolingian scholars, Paulinus
of Nola also; though, like Horace, they were known to the
Irish and to the next generation of Frankish scholars, who were
in closer contact with Irish influences.

In general we may say that the poetry of the court circle
bears most directly the impress of Virgil, of Ovid, and of
Fortunatus; though there are numerous reminiscences of
Juvencus, Sedulius, Aldhelm, and Arator. We should imagine
that Italy was still the great storehouse of manuscripts,
and that many codices were carried northwards across the
Alps.[4] This was actually the case, and it was owing largely
to the care of Paul the Deacon and Peter of Pisa that the

---

[1] Manitius, *Gesch.* i. 541, note 2;
Neff, *Gedichte des Paulus Diaconus*,
Munich 1908, p. 3.

[2] For the numerous prose-writers
known to Paul see Hörle, p. 45.

[3] Manitius, *Gesch.* i. 270, note 5, con-
jectures that it was Paul who brought
this 'bucolic corpus' (Nemesian, Calpurnius) into the Frankish kingdom.

[4] See Hörle, p. 42; Manitius, *Gesch.*
i. 250. In this age, too, we have to
reckon with the existence of *Florilegia*,
collections of extracts from the poets
for use in school (for purposes of prosody). One such *Florilegium* came from
Lombardic Italy, *circ.* 800, to Reichenau, where it received additions.

monastic scribes had material to keep them busy for a long time.

From Italy, too, came, as much as from England, the example of rhythmical verse. Alcuin may himself have produced rhythms;[1] but, if he did, he made no impression on his contemporaries. Insular influence in this direction was not strong until the coming of the Irish in full force in the ninth century. But Paulinus of Aquileia brought or sent into Frankish circles his own rhythmical verses composed on the Italian or Lombardic model. He used the trochaic tetrameter or the iambic trimeter, just like his predecessors,[2] but with more success. The other rhythms of the Carolingian age are discussed in the next section.

Alcuin, Theodulf, Paul the Deacon, and Peter of Pisa represent the most active influences in the revival of letters that took place under the presidency, as it were, of Charles the Great.[3] For Charles at his accession had a twofold task before him. He had to continue the political reorganization begun by his predecessors, and he had to carry on to its logical conclusion the reformation of the Church which Boniface had commenced in the days of Pippin and Carloman. But what Charles aimed at now was a Church that should be a pattern to the rest of Christendom, a Church in which the bishops and clergy should possess the education and intelligence which alone could fit them for the service of God and of the commonwealth. There was no superstition mingled with Charles's unbounded love of learning. He delighted in the thought that he had round him a band of scholars; but he saw, perhaps more clearly than they, the urgency of the problem which often stirred him to impatience, and the magnitude of the task which called for more than the resources immediately available.

The central institution for the propagation of learning was the royal school, which moved about with the court. The children of the king, male and female, were pupils, and Charles himself, according to Einhard,[4] took lessons in grammar from the aged Peter of Pisa, and in the other arts from Alcuin,

---

[1] Strecker, with reservations, ascribes three to Alcuin, *Poet. Lat. Aevi Car.* iv. 904 sqq.; but there is no entirely adequate reason for the ascription. They do not follow the models of the Irish or English school, though the author knew the Irish hymns.

[2] See above, p. 160.

[3] M. L. W. Laistner, *Thought and Letters in Western Europe*, A.D. 500–900, London 1931, gives an excellent account of learning and poetry in the Carolingian Age. For libraries and *scriptoria* see pp. 180 sqq. of that work, and for the study of Greek pp. 191 sqq.

[4] *Vita Karoli*, 25.

who was the master of the school. The men of learning
whom Charles had gathered round him formed a circle of
friends, over whom the king presided as their David and their
Solomon, while they adopted names derived from antiquity
or from Holy Writ. Alcuin was Flaccus, Angilbert Homer,
though neither had read the *Odes* or the *Iliad*. Einhard was
Bezaleel, Theodulf Pindar, Paulinus Timotheus, Modoin Naso,
and they had besides a Menalcas, a Thyrsis, and a Corydon.

If in the school the Christian poets and the Fathers had a
prominent place, there was room enough for classical studies,
as the example of Einhard shows. He had read Suetonius with
such care that in his life of Charles the Great he was able to
reproduce with amazing skill not only his arrangement of
material—'neque per tempora sed per species'[1]—but his general
manner, even to his characteristic disregard of probability or
of truth. The book is a delight to read after the confused
obscurities of his predecessors, but it is none the less a solitary
phenomenon, not on the main line of medieval development.

Yet Einhard does represent in some way the partial secularization of studies, which reveals itself also in the poetry of
the court circle. Much of the poetry of Alcuin and of his
colleagues sprang, like that of Columban and Boniface, from
the personal or epistolary intercourse of friends. Here they
followed the example of Eugenius and of Fortunatus, and,
instead of taking their subjects from the threadbare suggestions
of school themes, they were able to find them in the things
around them. This occasional poetry is, indeed, the successor
of the old rhetorical exercises known to Fortunatus and to
Eugenius, and we must remember that the African Anthology
and Ennodius were probably available to our Carolingian
poets.[2] Alcuin doubtless had the example of Columbanus in
mind when he wrote to his English friend Credulus,

> nunc bipedali
> carmine laudes,
> Credule, dulces,
> mi tibi nate
> care, canemus;[3]

but when he fashioned his little poem on the nightingale that

[1] Cf. Suet. *Vit. Octaviani,* ix. On
Suetonius and the Carolingians see
E. K. Rand, *Harvard Studies in Classi-
cal Philology,* xxxvii (1926), 1 sqq.

[2] Manitius, *Gesch.* i. 728, refers to
Alcuin, Amalar, and Theodulf as know-

ing the Anthology; and p. 26 to Paul's
knowledge of Ennodius (his *Vita Epi-
phanii* only, but doubtless he also knew
the poems).

[3] *Poet. Lat. Aevi Car.* i. 266; cf.
Columbanus to Fedolius, p. 164 above.

stayed for so brief a time, he may have thought of Eugenius and his bird of long ago in Spain, but the matter is altogether his own:

> Quae te dextra mihi rapuit, luscinia, ruscis,
>   illa meae fuerat invida laetitiae.
> tu mea dulcisonis implesti pectora musis,
>   atque animum moestum carmine mellifluo.
> quapropter veniant volucrum simul undique coetus,
>   carmine te mecum plangere Pierio.
> spreta colore tamen fueras non spreta canendo;
>   lata sub angusto gutture vox sonuit,
> dulce melos iterans vario modulamine Musae,
>   atque creatorem semper in ore canens.
> noctibus in furvis nusquam cessavit ab odis
>   vox veneranda sacris, o decus atque decor.
> quid mirum, cherubim, seraphim si voce tonantem
>   perpetua laudent, dum tua sic potuit?
> felix o nimium, dominum noctemque diemque
>   qui studio tali semper in ore canit.
> non cibus atque potus fuerat tibi dulcior odis,
>   alterius volucrum nec sociale iugum.
> hoc natura dedit, naturae et conditor almus,
>   quem tu laudasti vocibus assiduis,
> ut nos instrueres vino somnoque sepultos
>   somnigeram mentis rumpere segniciem.
> quod tu fecisti, rationis et inscia sensus,
>   indice natura nobiliore satis,
> sensibus hoc omnes magna et ratione vigentes
>   gessissent aliquod tempus in ore suo.
> maxima laudanti merces in secla manebit
>   aeternum regem perpes in arce poli.[1]

There are in this poem a few harmless rhetorical touches,[2] but its whole construction gives a general impression of simplicity. The form of the Ovidian couplet is reproduced and this by itself is restriction enough. The Virgilian reminiscence in 'vino somnoque sepultos' is curious in its inaptness, and there is some redundancy in 'O decus atque decor'. Alcuin follows an old and respectable tradition in his use of 'tonans', the epithet of Jove. Boëthius had spoken so of the supreme God:[3]

> Si vis celsi iura tonantis
> pura sollers cernere mente,

and Dracontius used 'tonans' indifferently for Jove and the

---

[1] *Poet. Lat. Aevi Car.* i. 274–5.
[2] Cf. the beginning, 'quae te dextra ... ruscis'.
[3] *De Cons.* iv. Juvencus also used

'tonans' for God (ii. 795; iv. 553, 671, 785). Commodian uses it only of Jove, *Instruct.* i. 15. 4.

Christian Deity.[1] The later Spanish poets had handed on the
use to the Anglo-Saxons, and, because of its metrical convenience, it was generally accepted. But it would be wrong
to inquire too closely into the mechanism of Alcuin's verse;
for what shines forth is the poet's gentle and harmless spirit
exercised on these simple themes. [A pupil whose name was
Dodo had left him, having loved wine and other good things
too dearly. Alcuin mourns him in a pastoral, a lament for the
cuckoo that will never wait for the summer's end:[2]

> Plangamus cuculum, Dafnin dulcissime, nostrum,
>   quem subito rapuit saeva noverca suis.
> plangamus pariter querulosis vocibus illum;
>   incipe tu senior, quaeso, Menalca prior.
>
> heu, cuculus, nobis fueras cantare suetus,
>   quae te nunc rapuit hora nefanda tuis?
> heu, cuculus, cuculus, qua te regione reliqui,
>   infelix nobis illa dies fuerat.
>
> non pereat cuculus, veniet sub tempore veris,
>   et nobis veniens carmina laeta ciet.
>
> heu mihi, si cuculum Bachus dimersit in undis,
>   qui rapiet iuvenes vortice pestifero.
> si vivat, redeat, nidosque recurrat ad almos,
>   nec corvus cuculum dissecet ungue fero.

Did not Alcuin feel sure that the cuckoo would come back
again to his nest at Tours 'in the sweet spring-days'?

> tempus adest veris, cuculus modo rumpe soporem . . .

The Abbot speaks as gently as that other Abbot, the great
Bernard, who had once to entice back a little monk who had
left him, but the Abbot of Clairvaux never thought of composing a pastoral. Alcuin wrote a letter as well to Dodo—the
'vernalis avis', as he used to call him playfully in happier
days[3]—a letter of admonition mingled with tenderness.[4]

> Do do iuxta nomen tuum, tu mihi da da.
>   do tibi me totum; sed tu, Dodo, mihi te da.

This is how he commences, but it is only that he may win from
Dodo the smile that shall be a beginning of his repentance.
For he proceeds with paternal seriousness: 'karissimo filiolo
meo, quem et sero genui. Nec bene ablactatus raptus est ab
uberibus meis; inmitiorque noverca tam tenerum de paterno

[1] See *Index* to Dracontius, ed. Vollmer (1914), pp. 266 sqq.
[2] *Poet. Lat. Aevi Car.* i. 269.

[3] *Monumenta Alcuiniana*, p. 609,
Epist. 167 (*circ.* 801).
[4] ib., p. 866, *Epist.* 286 (before 804).

gremio per libidinum vortices caro rapuit.' 'Be a man in courage,' says Alcuin, 'though in body thou art but a boy. Pray every day with tears, that He may help thee who has redeemed thee; that He may guard thee who has adopted thee to be His son. . . . For He has granted unto us freely that we should be children of God.' And, at the end, to remind the ungrateful Dodo of his delightful lost hours of study, Alcuin makes an appeal in elegiacs such as master and pupil had often fashioned together. The cuckoo was clearly much loved, for Bishop Arno also writes to him—'carissimo avi Cuculo Aquila salutem'[1]—reminding him of the vows he had made and urging him to be 'sweet and obedient to our father', and to strive against the flesh. 'Arise, arise, sweet bird, for the winter is past. The rain is over and gone. The flowers have appeared in the land, the time of singing has come.'

> adveniant aquilae cuculi, rogo, carmina nostri,
> audiat ut cuculi prospera cuncta sui.
> mellifluum turdus variat de gutture carmen,
> ecce tuum resonat semper in aure mea.

After this Alcuin's letters are silent on the subject of the cuckoo. The Abbot had not long to live, but perhaps the wayward bird listened to the Eagle and came back to Tours.

Winterfeld has called Alcuin a pedant,[2] but if he was a schoolmaster he wore his learning lightly in his intercourse with his pupils and his friends. How charmingly he writes to Angilbert, his 'son' and 'brother'—for his pupil was now Abbot of S. Riquier and a man of great account in the kingdom. Angilbert was, as we have said, the 'Homer' of the court circle. Alcuin writes to him, as he is on his way to Rome in 796:

Do not forget the relics of the saints. Do not neglect to lay hold of any objects of beauty for church use that come your way. Our 'rusticity' is greedy of such things; your magnificence is generous in all things. Remember that poetical prophecy:

> si nihil adtuleris, ibis Homere foras.[3]
> (If you bring nothing, Homer, out you will go!)

Who can doubt that this is a prophecy about you and your journey? If the Sibyl predicted the coming of Christ and His passion, why should not Ovid foretell Homer and his travels?

See how for the refreshment of my soul I have indulged in a little rhetorical playfulness.

But—to return to my train of thought with serious brow—I ask and

---

[1] *Monumenta Alcuiniana*, p. 870, *Epist.* 287.

[2] *Rhein. Mus.* lx. 36.

[3] Ovid, *Ars Amat.* ii. 280.

beseech you that you pray God through the aid of the holy apostles to grant counsel for the salvation of our souls.

The cult of friendship which Fortunatus and his circle had endeavoured to set up was in the court of Charles a reality based on a common good humour, a common piety, and a common love of learning and of poetry.

It was to please his friends that Alcuin, when the school or his monastery ceased for a brief time to call him, dictated his little poems. Now it is a riddle, now it is the praise of his beloved master 'David'; or it is a prayer or an inscription, or even a dreadful picture-acrostic, which Dümmler will not allow us to assign to Joseph the Irishman.[1]

Theodulf called Alcuin 'nostrorum gloria vatum'; but really that high position was his own by right of achievement. For the able and learned Bishop of Orleans, with all his solidity of intellect and his practical wisdom, was also a more considerable poet than the Abbot of Tours. He is best known, of course, as the author of the Palm Sunday poem,

> Gloria, laus et honor tibi, sit, rex Christe, redemptor,

which has provided the material of a famous hymn. But he was not pre-eminently a religious poet, though he was often attracted by moral subjects, which he treated like Christian counterparts of the old rhetorical exercises of the schools. He takes a motto from Lucan—'quod potestas impatiens consortis sit'[2]—and writes a little poem with mythological and historical examples to prove a point which had a real bearing on the troubles that followed the death of Charles. The rule among most peoples was, he says, that of royal brothers one only should wear the crown:

> Assyriis, Phariis, Hebraeis mos fuit iste,
>   genti et Achaemeniis quae fuit ante locis.
> morem hunc Parthus habet, hunc Atticus atque Quiritis,
>   decolor hunc Indus, hunc Agarenus habet.
> mos fuit iste Getis, Hunis, Maurisque nigellis,
>   et reor Aethiopas mos habet iste tetros.
> Thracibus et Phrygibus, tibi seu, Laecedaemona tellus,
>   gens si qua aut modo fert sceptra vel ante tulit.

These verses have been quoted to show how Theodulf carries on the rhetorical tradition, not merely by his imitation of Ovid or of Fortunatus, but because his early education was in schools which had not changed much since the days of Isidore.

---

[1] Cf. the *Versus ad Carolum regem*,   [2] ib., p. 526; Lucan, i. 92–3.
Poet. Lat. Aevi Car. i. 227.

Another poem has for title *de septem liberalibus artibus in quadam pictura depictis*,[1] a subject which might have inspired a poet at any time during the preceding six hundred years. It is too long to quote in full; but the first few verses will show that Theodulf was following the old methods of this kind of descriptive poetry:

> Discus erat tereti formatus imagine mundi,
>   arboris unius quem decorabat opus.
> huius Grammatica ingens in radice sedebat,
>   gignere eam semet seu retinere monens.
> omnis ab hac ideo procedere cernitur arbos,
>   ars quia proferri hac sine nulla valet.
> huius laeva tenet flagrum, seu dextra machaeram,
>   pigros hoc ut agat, radat ut haec vitia.
> et quia primatum sapientia gestat ubique,
>   compserat illius hinc diadema caput.
> et quia te sensus bonus, aut opinatio gignit,
>   ambae hic adsistunt, celsa Sophia, tibi.
> arboris illius recto de stipite rami
>   undique consurgunt e regione sibi;
> dexter Rhetoricam habet et, Dialectica, temet,
>   virtutes laevus quatuor atque gerit.

Rhetoric, dialectic, and the rest of the arts are described with their appropriate symbols in a manner which suggests that the poem was designed, like the picture it describes, for scholastic use. This poem is followed by another of similar character— *alia pictura, in qua erat imago terrae in modum orbis comprehensa*.[2] Other titles, which give some idea of the range of Theodulf's verse and of its relation to the poetry of the schools, are: *de equo perdito; de bilingue; ad quendam de mulieribus; de talamasca; quod Deus non loco quaerendus sit, sed pietate colendus; de siccitate cuiusdam fluvii; de pugna avium*. The best of these occasional poems is one that tells how the monks of Charroux found out who was stealing their hens.[3] The monastery and its story are first solemnly described:

> hoc fulvo argento, gemmisque exornat[4] et auro,
>   affluit et libris, vestibus atque sacris.
> praedia, prata, domos, silvas, vineta, colonos,
>   et pecora et pecudes et bona quaeque dedit . . .

Christ Himself was the defender of this holy place, but the fowls disappeared and the simple monks could not discover the reason. One day, however, a fox was seen hanging, caught

[1] *Poet. Lat. Aevi Car.* i. 544.   [4] sc. the founder, Count Rothar.
[2] ib., p. 547.   [3] ib., p. 551.

by a stake of wood, with a fowl in its mouth and writhing in
terror. The monks ran out to see this sign of God's favour:

> his visis gaudet monachorum turba fidelis,
>   admiranda videns signa favente deo.
> fur, procul atque procul hinc omnis abesto, profane,
>   daemonis error abi, angelus alme veni.
> invidiae pressis habitet concordia telis,
>   inque isto regnet spesque fidesque loco.
> prospera quaeque deus tribuens adversa repellat,
>   pascantur mentes nectare, Christe, tuo.

Among the longer poems is a 'consolation' for the death of
a certain brother,[1] in which Theodulf imitates the poem
addressed by Fortunatus to King Chilperich. The argument
of the poem is this. If there were anything out of the natural
order of things implied in the death of this brother, then it
might call for some special attitude to be adopted towards it.
But since the world came out of chaos, such has been the condition of things and so it will be at the end. There the poem
might well have ended, but Theodulf will not let his reader off
so lightly. He thought that he could reinforce his argument
by running through a list of famous men of the Old Testament
and of Apostles of the New who went the same way to death.
The list is long; it begins with Adam, Abel, and Enoch, ending
with Peter, Paul, John, and the multitude of martyrs, confessors, and virgins. Theodulf exhibits the relentless persistence
of the rhetorical method when he introduces into the list the
Saviour as at once the victim, and the conqueror, of death:

> sed, fera mors, quid ages, aliis trux, improba, saeva,
>   cum vitae auctorem pernitiosa petis?
> qui te morte sua pressit, curvavit, abegit,
>   et vitae surgens qui patefecit iter,
> auctoremque tuum tenebrosa in Tartara mersit,
>   montibus exemptum conlegiisque piis.

At the end of the poem he versifies the words of David in the
Psalm: 'Quis est homo qui vivet et non videbit mortem eruet
animam suam de manu inferi?'

Two of Theodulf's poems are of great historical interest, and
they illustrate as well the poet's methods and the manner in
which he followed the example set by Fortunatus. They are
the verses *Ad Carolum regem* and the *Versus contra iudices.*
The first poem gives a very lively impression of the Court and
home-life of Charles about the year 796.[2] Theodulf begins with

---

[1] *Poet. Lat. Aevi Car.* i. 477.

[2] See Hodgkin, *Italy and her In-*   *vaders,* viii. 160 sqq., on this poem.
Text, *Poet. Lat. Aevi Car.* i. 483.

the praises of the king. If the Meuse, Rhine, Saône, Rhone, Tiber, and Po could be measured, then the praise of Charles might have bounds set to it. So the prelude continues, with proper reminiscences of Fortunatus, and without neglecting the head, the chin, the neck and the various members of the king— 'est non laudabile cui nil'. The triumphs of Charles and his recognition by the whole earth are next celebrated. From east to west his power is known. It is a time of peace; embassies come from all directions telling of prosperity. The year is at the spring:

> en renovatur ovans aeternis legibus annus,
>   et sua nunc mater germina promit humus.
> silvae fronde virent, ornantur floribus arva,
>   sicque vices servant, en, elementa suas.

The court is gathered in the palace at Aachen, half palace, half country villa. There are prayers in the domed basilica near by, and, when they are over, the king goes back into his house. The common people crowd in the outer courts; only a few can enter the palace. Charles, who loved to have his children about him, is surrounded by his family. There are the boys, Charles and Louis (Hludowic), in all the promise and strength of youth. The girls are Bertha, Hrotrud, Gisla, and three others. The queen Liutgarda is with them. The boys and girls crowd round their father. The young Charles takes his double cloak, Louis his sword. He sits down and the girls embrace him; they wait upon him with flowers and apples, bread and wine:

> Berta rosas, Chrodtrudh violas dat, lilia Gisla,
>   nectaris ambrosii praemia quaeque ferat;
> Rothaidh poma, Hiltrudh Cererem, Tetdrada Liaeum.[1]

The magnificence of their dresses is described; they entertain their father with soft words, with gentle pleasantries, and with dance. But the grave figure of Gisla, the king's sister, breaks upon the scene. She is vowed to Christ, and, after embracing the king, she asks him to expound to her some passage of holy writ—so the king teaches her what God Himself has taught him.

Next the courtiers come in. First the bald Thyrsis, the chamberlain, who is kept busy listening to the pleas of those who wish to enter, admitting some and sending others tactfully away. The bishop, of course, is there, who has to bless

[1] This is based on the poem, *Anth. Lat.*, Riese, 393, verse 8.

the king's meat and drink. Then comes Alcuin (Flaccus), the great poet, learned in divine things, and clever at riddles and at mathematics. Richulf, bishop of Mainz, is there, but Homer (Angilbert) is absent,

> dulce melos canerem tibi, ni absens, dulcis Homere,
> esses, sed quoniam es, hinc mea Musa tacet.

After Ercambald, the chancellor, and 'Lentulus', comes Nardulus, the famous Einhard, who runs to and fro like an ant, a great mind in a tiny body ('cuius parva domus habitatur ab hospite magno'). He is bringing in large books, and his arrows are for the destruction of a certain Irishman.

These pilgrims from beyond the seas, with their outlandish manners and their air of superior learning, seem to have annoyed the gentlemanly Spaniard, who gives vent to his irritation in what may pass as a piece of satirical invective. He deals thus with the Irishman:

> cui dum vita comes fuerit, haec oscula tradam,
> trux, aurite, tibi quae dat, aselle, lupus.
> ante canis lepores alet aut lupus improbus agnos,
> aut timido muri musio terga dabit,
> quam Geta[1] cum Scotto pia pacis foedera iungat,
> quae si forte velit iungere, ventus erit.
> hic poenasve dabit fugietve simillimus Austro,
> utque sit hic aliud, nil nisi Scottus erit.
> cui si litterulam, quae est ordine tertia, tollas,
> inque secunda suo nomine forte sedet,
> quae sonat in 'caelo' prima, et quae in 'scando' secunda,
> tertia in 'ascensu', quarta in 'amicitiis',
> quam satis offendit, pro qua te, littera salvi,
> utitur, haud dubium quod sonat, hoc et erit.

Here we have the jest of Scottus and *sottus*, usually ascribed to Charles the Bald, who it appears, only borrowed it from Theodulf.

The poet's good humour soon returns. He playfully says that Osulf, Einhard, and Ercambald—all small men, but of different weight—might easily be the three legs of one table. For the time of the banquet has come, and we meet 'Menalcas', who controls the kitchen, and Eberhard the butler. 'Father' Alcuin dispenses his learning, but he does not neglect the good fare. 'His instruction is better and his reed has a better tune if he moistens the caverns of his learned chest.' After the banquet the Muse of Theodulf has to play her part; but she has one enemy, Wibod the 'hero' (perhaps the Count of

---

[1] i.e. Theodulf, the Goth.

Perigueux), who shakes his thick locks when he hears the voice of Theodulf; yet, when the king summons him, goes trembling with round belly and the gait of Vulcan, though his voice be great like Jove's. Wibod thus disposed of, Theodulf turns once more to the nameless Irishman, and having rent him asunder with wild invective ends his poem with a prayer, in the name of charity, for pardon if he has offended anyone—for 'charity suffereth long and is kind'.

The largeness of Theodulf's own charity, and the strength of his grasp of what the Church had to offer to and, indeed, to impose on the barely-civilized Franks, are shown in the long poem of exhortation addressed to the judges of the kingdom.[1] We are not here much concerned with the historical setting of the piece; it is enough to say that it arose out of Theodulf's own experience as one of the *Missi Dominici*, sent on tour to correct abuses and administer justice in the king's name. It is the structure of the poem that demands attention, and the manner in which it carries on the rhetorical tradition in the collection and arrangement of episodes and in the details of their treatment. Like most of the other poems of Theodulf it is in Ovidian elegiacs.

It begins with a general exhortation to justice, reinforced by promise of eternal rewards for those who listen, and of eternal pains for those who disobey; and it goes on to present a series of examples of righteousness gathered from the Old Testament. Moses and Samuel head the list, and David is introduced in lines of studied rhetoric:

> quid referam resono modulantem carmine regem,
>   qui tota studuit mente placere deo?
> cui bene cuncta simul parent in laude tonantis
>   ars, caro, mens, plectrum, vox, lyra, chorda, chorus?
> cantibus et gestis et totis nisibus iste
>   probra cavenda monet, iura tenenda docet.[2]

For it was David who said, in one of the earliest admonitions to judges: 'usquequo iudicatis iniquitatem, et facies peccatorum sumitis? iudicate egeno et pupillo: humilem et pauperem iustificate.'[3] David is followed by Solomon, at once an example and a warning, and by Hezekiah and Josiah, righteous kings.

---

[1] *Poet. Lat. Aevi Car.* i. 493; Dümmler chose for the poem the title *Versus Teudulfi espiscopi contra iudices* (from the *explicit* of the Paris MS.), but the title invented by Daniel, the first editor, is, as G. Monod points out, more exactly descriptive—*Paraenesis ad iudices* (*Revue Historique*, xxxv (1887), p. 3, note 1).

[2] *Poet. Lat. Aevi Car.* i. 494–5.

[3] Ps. lxxxi.

Concluding his prelude Theodulf says that, while he strives to keep others in the right way and reproves those who act with venality or injustice, he is often himself suspected or accused of being accessible to bribery. He has many things that defile him, but he is, at any rate, free from this.

The next section of the poem describes the province in which his functions as *Missus Dominicus* are exercised. The rivers which water it are catalogued in a way that the old rhetoricians would have appreciated—the Saône, Gard, Rhône, Allier, Aude, Ebro—and there is a list, too, of famous cities, each with the little learned or topographical fact to set it off. It is, of course, the ordinary description of a journey, a *genre* that we have often met already:

> iam, Lugdune, tuis celsis post terga relictis
>   moenibus, adgredimur, causa quod optat, iter.
> saxosa petimus constructam in valle Viennam,[1]
>   quam scopuli inde artant, hinc premit amnis hians.
> inde Valentinis[2] terris urbique iacenti,
>   rupee, nos dedimus hinc, Morenate,[3] tibi.
> post et Arausinas[4] terras et Avennica rura[5]
>   tangimus et fines, quos tenuere Getae.[6]
> inde Nemausiacas sensim properamus ad arces,[7]
>   quo spatiosa urbs est resque operosa satis.
> hinc Madalona habuit laevam, Sextatio dextram:[8]
>   hec scabris podiis cingitur, illa mari.

At Narbonne Theodulf is greeted by a joyful throng of his own people, Visigoths and Spaniards; and everywhere he and his colleague, Leidrad, Archbishop designate of Lyons, are met by crowds of all classes and ages,

> parvulus, annosus, iuvenis, pater, innuba, celebs,
>   maior, ephoebus, anus, masque, marita, minor.

They all proffer gifts, and each thinks that he will gain the desired issue of his suit if only his gifts are accepted. The description of the journey is now completed. Theodulf turns to another theme, and one that has for him a special pleasure. He describes at length the precious works of art, of antique craftsmanship or imported from the East, that were held up before his eyes to tempt him to grant the miserable requests of the litigants. 'One promises a crystal, and jewels from the East, if only he may win possession of another's lands. Another

---

[1] Vienne.	[2] Valence.	[3] Rochemore.
[4] Orange.	[5] Avignon.	[6] The Visigoths.
[7] Nîmes.	[8] Magnelonne, and Soutancion.	

brings rich store of golden coins inscribed with Arabic letters, or "Roman" coins of pale silver; he desires estates and villas. Another comes, and in a low voice murmurs that he is the possessor of a wonderful and precious vase of antique workmanship.'[1] The vase is lovingly described in more than thirty lines of verse—Theodulf had evidently examined this and other vases very carefully, for he describes it with the eye of a connoisseur. The man begins:

> est mihi vas aliquod signis insigne vetustis,
> cui pura et vena et non leve pondus inest . . .

This should be enough to whet the curiosity of any collector. What follows might have taken its place as an occasional poem 'on an antique vase'; for the scenes pictured upon the vase, taken from the labours of Hercules, are set forth as they would catch the eye of the man who held it and turned it round in his hands. The outside surface of the vase was worn with age, and the figures were hard to discern.

The next petitioner presented woven stuffs from the East,

> . . . mihi sunt vario fucata colore
> pallia, quae misit, ut puto, torvus Arabs.

Here with marvellous skill are pictured a calf following his mother, and a heifer following the bull. The other presents are catalogued in more summary fashion—swords, helmets, shields, mules, horses, shoes, gloves, hats. When the petitioners find that the Bishop will have none of their gifts they gather them up, and justice takes its course. But Theodulf does not churlishly refuse little simple gifts of food—fruit, eggs, wine, bread, and some hay for his horses. He will take also a few fowls and other birds, 'whereof the bodies are small, but good to eat'. These were gifts of courtesy and affection, which it was proper to take with gratitude.

The real admonition to the judges now begins. The day in the courts should be prefaced by prayer in the church. The poor man who makes his voice heard above the tumult outside the court shall be given justice first. 'Begin your day early'— is Theodulf's advice.[2] This maxim is the text for a satirical piece, which is of considerable interest, for its method and its exaggerations owe as much perhaps to the ecclesiastical sermons, and through them to the *diatribe*, as to the classical

---

[1] *Poet. Lat. Aevi Car.* i. 498 sq.
[2] ib., p. 503: 'accipe consilium, "mane venito", meum.'

satirists, who themselves were strongly influenced by Stoic and
Cynic popular literature:

> I have seen judges slow in performing their duties; but not slow, I must
> admit, when it was a question of receiving bribes. They come at the fifth
> hour, and go away at the ninth, or if they begin at the third, they don't
> stay beyond the sixth. For if it is they who have to give, the ninth hour is
> good enough; if it is a question of taking, they come at the first.

The poet pictures the judge who comes into court after a
drunken sleep and cannot keep awake sufficiently to follow
the case:[1]

> marcidus et segnis et sine mente sedet.

There are no brilliant touches in the picture: Theodulf merely
uses the ordinary resources of the rhetoric which came most
easily to him:

> ille piger, madidus, ructans, temulentus, anelus
> oscitat et marcet, nauseat, angit, hebet.

This is how he describes the drink-sodden judge, and then the
greed of the door-keepers draws him on to a moralizing section
on the universality of avarice, which spares neither age nor
class nor sex. It taints all, 'the girl, the boy, the old man,
both sexes alike'.[2]

At last Theodulf has got the judge seated in the curule chair.
We must imagine him in a great hall, a basilica now venerable
with age, from its Roman past, in Arles or in Narbonne. The
very chair was once used by a Roman magistrate or governor.
Everything tempts to pride, and Theodulf again keeps us
waiting until he has described a kind of minor *Psychomachia*,
a conflict in the judge's soul.[3] The allegory of Prudentius
provided the suggestion; for Theodulf describes Superbia, not
indeed with traits borrowed from the *Psychomachia*, but still
as a warrior-demon,

> torva oculos, horrenda manus, fedissima rictus,
> vipereumque caput corpus et omne tumens,
> mens tumefacta cui, levis actio, turgida vox est,
> cui cibus et potus atra venena manent.

Humility and Prudence, 'a noble pair', are to fight against her,
after making the usual speech that is the preliminary to the
combat.[4] The battle over, there is a long homily on death and
judgement, which rounds off the episode; and now the real
business of the court can begin. The judge orders his servant

---

[1] *Poet. Lat. Aevi Car.* i. 504.   [3] ib., p. 505.
[2] ib., p. 504.   [4] Cf. the *Psychomachia*, passim.

to call first those who have come from a distance, then the poor, and then those who are in the hall, so that there may be no confusion of people coming and going.[1] After a quotation from Job, Theodulf gives good advice on how to deal with cases; the judge must go neither too fast nor too slow, he must deal gently with the timid, and have a special care for the fatherless and the widow. Firmness is often needed, and often enough a little guile is useful.

Even when the judge has gone back to his house, his difficulties are not yet over. The litigants have found out his wife and are holding their tempting presents before her eyes.[2] In describing the scene that follows Theodulf creates a satirical picture with deft touches of exaggeration. The wife embraces the knees, the hands, the neck, and the cheeks of her lord; she speaks soft words, knowing well how to arm her own prayers with such poison as that wherewith an archer tips his arrows. If you are proof against all this, she will come back again with feigned sighs, complaining with tears that her prayers weigh nothing with you. Then a servant, or a nurse, or a handmaid joins in: 'Why do you refuse what my lady asks?' The lady herself sobs quietly. 'Other women get what they want. I alone never get anything.' The maid servants pull her towards her husband. 'Give him a kiss,' they say, and, to the husband, 'Why do you upset her?' This, says Theodulf, in effect, is the hardest trial the judge has to face. If he can resist feminine guile he can do anything.

The rest of the poem is concerned with advice for dealing with witnesses, and with a deeply interesting discussion of the Teutonic practice of oath-helping, which in Theodulf's eyes was a licensed perjury. The cruel and unequal penalties imposed by the law filled him with horror. Over against the barbarous custom of men he set the commandment of Christ. It is on this that a judge must fix his eyes. With a noble exhortation to the rich to remember what they owe to the poor, and what their duty is to those who are 'blessed by the same holy baptism, anointed with the same oil, and fed with the flesh and blood of the Lamb',[3] Theodulf ends his long poem,

hic submittantur transacti carbasa libri,
litore in hoc teneat anchora iacta ratem.

Ovid is the model for his verse, but the poem belongs, structurally, to the tradition which we can follow most easily from Statius through Ausonius to Fortunatus. It is a collection of

[1] *Poet. Lat. Aevi Car.* i. 509.   [2] ib., p. 511.   [3] ib., p. 517.

episodes and digressions, managed with a fair amount of skill, and with no attempt at dazzling the reader by a display of useless learning. The poem shows how real was the Spanish contribution to Carolingian culture; and suggests that the Spanish schools had something to give which the Anglo-Saxons could not offer so fully, something based on the long Spanish connexion with Latin speech and Latin civilization. Theodulf came to the Franks as the countryman of Martial and Prudentius.

The three Lombards who taught in the Court school were Peter of Pisa, Paul the Deacon (Warnefrid), and Paulinus of Aquileia. Of these, Peter of Pisa was the first comer, and it was he who, in his venerable old age, taught grammar to Charles himself.[1] There was, perhaps, something dry and pedantic about the old professor, and although the king loved him, he does not seem to have been much liked by the rest of the court circle.[2] Paul the Deacon was probably his closest friend. The political career of this young Lombard noble had been cut short by the Frankish invasion of Italy, and he lived in banishment at Monte Cassino, while his brother languished in prison in France. Paul appealed to the conqueror's mercy in a Latin elegy,[3] which revealed a scholar who must be retained at the palace school. Charles seems to have given Peter the task of winning over the disappointed patriot to a new master. Peter composed a poem[4] in the favourite Lombardic rhythmical measure, the trochaic tetrameter catalectic, in which he praised Christ for the presence in the Frankish kingdom of such a man as Paul, 'most learned of poets and bards', the master of several languages,

> Graeca cerneris Homerus, Latina Vergilius,
> in Hebraea quoque Philo, Tertullus in artibus,
> Flaccus crederis in metris, Tibullus eloquio.
> tu nos gestu docuisti exemplorum credere,
> quod amoris agro nostri plantatus radicitus
> tenearis nec ad prisca cor ducas latibula.

There was evidently a fear in the mind of Charles that before long Paul would slip back to Italy and to his own people. For Peter went on to say,

> cum grammaticae Latinis fecundare rivulis
> non cesses nocte dieque cupientis viscera
> partiumque satione Graecorum sub studio,

[1] Einhard, 25, 'in discenda grammatica Petrum Pisanum diaconem senem audivit.'
[2] Cf. Manitius, *Gesch.* i. 452.
[3] Neff, *Die Gedichte des Paulus Diaconus*, Munich 1908, p. 53.
[4] ib., p. 60.

haec nos facit firmiores doctrina laudabilis
vestra de permansione qua fuit dubietas,
quod te restis nostrae cinxit nec dimittit anchorae.

In adding the fame of a knowledge of Hebrew to the certainty of Paul's moderate acquaintance with Greek, Peter felt that he was really carrying out the spirit of Charles's instructions. In the Emperor's name, at the close, he clinched the matter.

You know that by Christ's bidding our daughter is going across the sea with Michael the Greek ambassador to become a queen. For this reason you are teaching Greek grammar to our clerks, so that, remaining in her service, they may appear skilled in the tongue of the Greeks.

Paul is depicted in this way as an indispensable member of the court. That he took in the situation to the full, is shown by his clever and essentially non-committal answer.[1] He professed to see in this poem, sent in the name of the king, nothing more than a piece of ironical ridicule,

totum hoc in meam cerno prolatum miseriam,
totum hoc in meum caput dictum per hyroniam.
heü, laudibus deridor et cachinnis obprimor.

'I am said to be like Homer, Horace, and Virgil, I am likened unto Tertullus, and Philo of Egypt, and I am compared with thee, O Tibullus of Verona. May I perish, if I desire to imitate any one of these, who went astray from the path; nay, rather, I will liken them to dogs. I know not Greek, I am quite ignorant of Hebrew.'

And so on, until Paul has in the end to say something to please the king:

It is only the anchor of your affection that holds me here. I have no wish to win the praise of a vain glory from my learning. I am glad that your daughter is going across the sea for a crown; but [he adds somewhat maliciously] if the clerks who go with her can't produce there more Greek than they have learned from me, they will be laughed at as dumb statues. But to avoid the reproach that I am entirely illiterate, I will append a few verses that I learned when a child.

What follows is a translation from a Greek epigram, but Paul does not allow us to infer that it is his own:[2]

De puero qui in glacie extinctus est.
Trax puer adstricto glacie dum ludit in Hebro,
    frigore concretas pondere rupit aquas.
dumque imae partes rapido traherentur ab amni,
    praesecuit tenerum lubrica testa caput.
orba quod inventum mater dum conderet urna,
    'hoc peperi flammis, cetera', dixit, 'aquis'.

---

[1] Neff, p. 64.   [2] Cf. Neff, pp. 67–8.

We do not know what impression this rather ungracious composition made on the mind of Charles. But the poetical correspondence continued, and in the end Paul seems to have become more reconciled to his exile from Italy, and more ready to acknowledge the claim of Charles to his affection and loyalty. He contributed riddles for the amusement of his master, composing them both in rhythmical and in metrical hexameters, and also seems to have introduced the 'Berne collection' of riddles in rhythmical hexameters, which took their place by the side of the riddles brought over by the Anglo-Saxons.[1]

The poems of Peter and Paul show how, besides the purely classical verse, the specifically Lombardic contribution came to the Frankish schools in the shape of the rhythmical trochaic tetrameter, and perhaps of the rhythmical hexameter. We shall see in the next section that the actual contribution was much larger than the small output of these two grammarian-poets, but the strength of the Lombardic influence is very aptly illustrated by the example of these scholars, who quite naturally gave the rhythmical an equal place beside the metrical verse. The same influence is seen even more strongly at work in the poetry of Paulinus, another Lombard grammarian who took service under Charles and taught in the palace schools. He became a firm friend of Alcuin, and when, in 787, Charles made Paulinus Patriarch of Aquileia, they parted with sorrow, and Alcuin asked the Bishop, in pathetic verses, to remember him as he stood at the holy altar, and pray thus for him with tears—'Have mercy, O God, in Thy goodness, upon this our friend, and be pleased to grant him forgiveness of his sins, that He may praise Thee with Thy saints ever world without end.'[2]

Paulinus was a poet of no mean order. If he chose rhythmical verses partly because of his lack of metrical skill, he must also have felt that in rhythmical schemes his conceptions could flow on unfettered by classical reminiscence and the exigencies of custom. The lament which he composed for his friend Duke Erich of Friuli, who fell in battle in 799,[3] is written with a great smoothness in rhythmical iambic trimeters. Certainly it begins conventionally, with a list of rivers and towns and mountains that are to join with the poet in his dirge:

> Mecum Timavi saxa novem flumina
> flete per novem fontes redundantia,
> quae salsa gluttit unda ponti Ionici,

[1] Neff, pp. 83 and 84 sqq.; see above, p. 165.

[2] *Poet. Lat. Aevi Car.* i. 240.

[3] ib., p. 131. Prudentius had grouped his iambic trimeters into five-lined stanzas, and Paul follows his plan.

Istris Sausque, Tissa, Culpa, Marua,
Natissa, Corca, gurgites Isontii.

Hericum mihi dulce nomen plangite,
Sirmium, Pola, tellus Aquileiae;
Iulii Forus, Cormonis ruralia,
rupes Osopi, iuga Cenetensium,
Attensis humus ploret et Albenganus.

But the poem gathers wings as it proceeds, and reaches its
final flight in lines which demonstrated beyond all doubt that
the Christian feeling, wedded to rhythm, was to give the new
verse-forms such a sureness and strength that they could not
fail to triumph in the end.

Deus aeterne, limi qui de pulvere
plasmasti tuam primos ad imaginem
parentes nostros, per quos omnes morimur,
misisti tuum sed dilectum filium,
vivimus omnes per quem mirabiliter,

sanguine cuius redempti purpureo
sumus, sacrata cuius carne pascimur;
Herico tuo servulo mellifluo
concede, quaeso, paradisi gaudia
et nunc et ultra per inmensa saecula.

The same strength and the same uplifting of the poet's wings
are apparent in the verses on the Apostles Peter and Paul,
which are probably, but not certainly, the work of Paulinus:[1]

Felix per omnes festum mundi cardines
apostolorum praepollet alacriter
Petri beati, Pauli sacratissimi,
quos Christus almo consecravit sanguine,
ecclesiarum deputavit principes.

.   .   .   .   .

O Roma felix, quae tantorum principum
es purpurata precioso sanguine,
excellis omnem mundi pulchritudinem
non laude tua, sed sanctorum meritis
quos cruentatis iugulasti gladiis.

This is doubtless, in some sort, 'learned' poetry, and the author
was no mean rhetorician. But he had a secret denied to most
of his contemporaries, and he remains one of the first masters
of rhythmical verse.

Alcuin, Theodulf, and the three Lombard scholars were the
great and impressive figures in and around the Court school.
Among the Franks the man who stood above all others as a
product of the revival of learning was Angilbert,[2] who was

[1] *Poet. Lat. Aevi Car.* i. 136–7.   i. 543 sqq.; *Poet. Lat. Aevi Car.* i.
[2] On Angilbert see Manitius, *Gesch.*   355 sqq.

a favourite pupil of Alcuin and enjoyed as much as any one the close confidence of Charles.

Angilbert was of noble birth, and his progress in the Court school revealed talents which were soon seen to be of the right order for employment in the service of the State. He was *Primicerius Palatii* to the young King Pippin in Italy; he was employed on important missions to Rome; and he was rewarded, though a layman, with the Abbey of S. Riquier (Centula), which he enriched with stately buildings and a splendid library. He had two sons by Charles's daughter Berta, whom her father kept at Court; for he could not bring himself to give her away in marriage. Angilbert was a man of affairs, and he loved the classical authors in a way that could not have altogether commended itself to Alcuin. He was called Homer in the court circle, and it has, therefore, been conjectured that he is the author of an epic fragment, commonly called *Karolus Magnus et Leo Papa*,[1] but there is no real evidence to support this view. Whoever the author was, he belonged to the first generation of Carolingian poets,[2] and he made considerable borrowings from the poets who were then most read—Virgil, Ovid, Lucan, and Fortunatus. The poem contains a long description of Charles and his family hunting in the royal park. Much is said about the rich garments worn by the ladies, and the whole episode is rhetorically conceived, as is the scene which follows, in which Charles sees in a dream the unhappy plight of Pope Leo, who had been ferociously attacked by the Romans.[3]

The most important of the authenticated poems of Angilbert are one in elegiacs addressed to Pippin, King of Italy, and an 'eclogue' to Charles.[4] The first is full of reminiscences from

---

[1] Text, *Poet. Lat. Aevi. Car.* i. 366 sqq.

[2] He was evidently in close contact with the Court, as the poem shows. Although he exaggerates Charles's learning, he knows all about the multifarious interests of the king. He says (ib., p. 368),

> summus apex regum, summus quoque
>   in orbe sophista
> extat et orator, facundo famine pollens;
> inclita nam superat praeclari dicta
>   Catonis,
> vincit et eloquii magnum dulcedine
>   Marcum,
> atque suis dictis facundus cedit
>   Homerus,

et priscos superat dialectica in arte
     magistros.

Angilbert would hardly have spoken like this. But the author, like Angilbert, knew the members of the royal family well, as his descriptions show. His picture of Berta, however, does not suggest the work of Angilbert. The author was someone who, like Einhard, had drunk deeply of the classical authors and loved them for their own sake.

[3] There is also a long and well-sustained description of the works at Aachen (ib., pp. 368–9).

[4] ib., 358 sqq.

Ovid, and it, too, describes a dream, in which Pippin appeared to Louis announcing his return from the campaign against the Avars. The 'eclogue' is in praise of 'David':

> Surge, meo domino dulces fac, fistula, versus.
> David amat versus, surge et fac, fistula, versus.
> David amat vates, vatorum est gloria David . . .

Angilbert writes as one who was of the household of Charles. For his refrain runs, once more,

> surge, meis caris dulces fac, fistula, versus.

He mentions Gisla, the dedicated virgin, sister of Charles; Hrotrud, 'mentis clarissima virgo'; and Berta, whom he loved. Then, after saluting some of the courtiers by name, he directs his poem to those pleasant walled gardens where his two boys play in safety, waiting for 'Homer' to return to them.

In these poems Angilbert appears as the brave and capable man he was, one who met to the full the demand of Charles that his school should produce men of education and character, who could serve the needs of Church or State.

Amalar was another pupil of Alcuin who rose to high position in this double service. Charles sent him on an embassy to Constantinople along with Peter, Abbot of Nonantola. In a poem addressed to his companion he revives the memories of their unpleasant voyage. These *versus marini*,[1] as Amalar calls them, describe the sea-voyage as far as Dyrrachium, and the sufferings of an unfortunate companion named Gregory. At Constantinople the ambassadors were kept closely shut up, with guards to watch them:

> continuo statuunt vigiles, qui limina claudant,
> ne monachus forsan per opaca evaderet urbis,
> sed sancti potius cursus psallat Benedicti:
> aut fors, ut potiusque forent ignota nefanda
> illius nobis urbis.

So Amalar humorously ruminates. At last the new Emperor Leo received them, but their journey home was as bad as the outward voyage. They reached Italy, however, in safety, and the Abbot got back to his monks at Nonantola, who wept tears of joy at seeing their father again.

Amalar is not much of a poet. His obscurity is due mainly to his lack of skill, and as Manitius points out,[2] he airs his small knowledge of Greek by introducing a few words of that tongue into his poem (*agius, basileus, protus*).

We are already among the minor poets, but Modoin, Bishop

---

[1] *Poet. Lat. Aevi Car.* i. 426.   [2] *Gesch.* i. 399.

of Autun (815), was regarded as more than a minor poet in his own day. He was 'Naso' at the court of Charles, and a friend of Theodulf, who turned to him for consolation in the day of trouble. Modoin is a link between the great days of Charles and the literary movement of the following half-century. For when Theodulf and Angilbert had departed this life, he found new friends in Walafrid Strabo and Florus of Lyons.

Two only of Modoin's poems have survived. One is his reply to Theodulf, who had addressed to him a political complaint in the time of exile, when the Bishop of Orleans was suffering for his supposed share in the conspiracy against Louis the Pious.[1] Modoin begins by modestly commenting on his own lack of learning:

> fac, Theodulfe, meos versus adverte benigne,
> nec sint dispecta carmina nostra tibi.

He has often bewailed his friend's misfortune, for he was convinced of his innocency. Remembering what Ovid had said of his own exile, he assures Theodulf that it was his 'genius' (*ingenium*) that was the reason for his fall:

> laesus ab ingenio es, pater alme, tuo.[2]

The passage which follows is a curious list of eminent persons, heathen and Christian, who had unrighteously suffered from the envious malice of their enemies. These are Ovid, Boethius, Virgil, Seneca, S. John the Apostle, Hilary of Poitiers, S. Peter, and S. Paul. The whole passage is worth quoting as showing how the classical and the Christian abode together in the thought of the Carolingians. But those who belong to the Christian dispensation are alone *nostri*:[3]

> pertulit an nescis quod longos Naso labores?
>   insons est factus exul ob invidiam.
> ipse Severinus magna est deiectus ab urbe,
>   consul Romana clarus ab arce procul.
> magnus ab infesto est agitatus milite vatis
>   Virgilius propriis exspoliatus agris.
> vulnera saeva suo fertur sumpsisse tyranno
>   Seneca praecipuus, caede Neronis obit.
> quid memorem ex nostris plures sudasse nefandum
>   pro nostra exilium religione pia?
> qui magis a magno colitur pius ipse magistro,
>   Iohannes durum pertulit exilium.

---

[1] *Poet. Lat. Aevi Car.* i. 563 sqq., 569 sqq.

[2] Cf. *Trist.* ii. 2, 'Ingenio perii qui miser ipse meo'; iii. 3. 74, 'ingenio perii Naso poeta meo'.

[3] Boethius (Severinus) is here classed among the heathen. As Manitius remarks (*Gesch.* i. 551, n. 3), his theological works cannot have been well known at this time.

Hilarius, sensisti ergastula, tu quoque, dira,
　　missus in ignotum rege iubente locum.
claviger ipse Petrus nam, necnon et populorum
　　doctor erat Paulus carceris in gremio.

The consolation over, Modoin gives good advice. If Theodulf
will only confess to Caesar that he has sinned, Caesar will forgive. Theodulf may have taken the wise course suggested by
his friend, for in 821 he was set free from his confinement in
the monastery of S. Aubin at Angers.

Modoin's other poem belongs to an earlier time. It is an
Eclogue in two parts, dedicated to Charles.[1] Modoin had carefully studied the Latin bucolic poets. Besides Virgil he knew
Calpurnius and Nemesian, but he never forgot his favourite
Ovid. The first part of the Eclogue is a dialogue between a
boy and an old man. The latter is, it seems, an established
member of the court circle, and a poet of renown. The boy is
a new comer who has yet to win the full favour of Palaemon—
for it is in the guise of a shepherd that the Emperor has to
appear in this pastoral. The old man is not very encouraging.
He does not think that Palaemon will listen for a moment to the
hoarse piping of this youthful poet, who now, in his turn, takes
up the song and dilates on the good fortune of the aged bard
who lives at ease in this second Rome, the imperial city of
Aachen. The old man is not appeased ; he reminds the boy of
the fate of Ovid—'Naso loquax'—who, having incurred the
anger of Caesar, could never regain his favour, however sweetly
he might sing. But the boy is not at a loss. He retorts with the
example of Virgil, who came to Rome, regained his paternal
fields, and established his fame. Lucan too, and Ennius, won
riches, and so did many others. Lastly,

in our own day, you can see the same thing happening. See how my
Homer (Angilbert) with his studious songs is wont to please the ear of
Charles. If Flaccus (Alcuin) had not known how to pipe his songs, he would
not have gained so many rewards in this present life. Theodulf, this long time
since, has been playing on his slender reed: he has won the right to take part
in affairs of State. See how Nardus (Einhard), who was wont to recite his
Aonian songs, now rejoices in the highest honours. Yield, O sage, o'ercome
at last by a boy. Be sure that our Master loves the Muses well.

The second part of the Eclogue is again a dialogue. The
characters are Micon and Nectilus,[2] in whom we see again an
old man and a youth. They are reconciled now, and Mico
begins with a picture of a summer landscape in the burning

---

[1] *Poet. Lat. Aevi Car.* i. 384.
[2] This name appears in Nemesian and Calpurnius.

noon, which, if it owes something to Virgil and to Calpurnius, has none the less some lively touches of the poet's own making:

> aurea rura, puer, ridentia flore videto.
> nunc apium omnis ager fervet passim agmine laeto;
> ore legunt flores, lentis stridentibus alis
> per tima summa volant, apibus populatur agellus,
> his mixtis pariter nam murmurat ore susurro.
> frondea tecta canunt, ave silvae multa resultant.
> arboreis subeunt iamdudum animalia tectis.
> pallet ager rabido solis fervore perustus,
> aestuat indomito sol aureus igne calescens.
> monte pecus nemorosa petit loca, frigus opacum.
> rara vides nudis errare animalia campis. . . .
> vicinumque nemus, frater, quaeramus opacum,
> quo tegit ulmus aquas, ventos ubi currere cernis,
> summatim blando foliis incumbere motu,
> herba comis viridis quo stat densata sub ipsis,
> molliter aspirans ubi se fert flatibus Eurus.

Then, as they lie in the shadows, Nectilus praises Mico, who has won riches and security, Mico whose song charms the beasts of field and forest, so that they leave their pastures and come to hear him. The beasts are at peace with him and with one another; so, it would seem, there is here a foretaste of the coming age of gold, and the lines cut by some divine hand upon a tree have a prophetic import—they cry and the forest resounds, 'Peace upon earth. Let cruel war depart!'

Yes, replies Mico, these words were graven on this beech not by human art but by a hand divine. A golden sun shines without a cloud, and Saône, Rhône, Loire, Meuse, and Rhine rejoice in its brightness. It has subdued savage people, arrested sedition, and pacified the world:

> aurea securis nascuntur regna Latinis.

Naso is the poet of the restored Empire, and he takes up the part of Virgil, singing of Charles the new Augustus. The events of the year 800 called for such a celebration, and it is to Naso's credit that he saw his opportunity and to Charles's that he rewarded his faithful poet.

Somewhat on the fringe, perhaps, of the inner circle of scholars at the court, hung the Irish group. They had an air which marked them out from the rest. There was something outlandish about them, and although no one could call their piety or their learning in question, they were not entirely acceptable to the more exacting among the king's scholars. They came in poverty and had to make their way by persistence.

Notker tells the story of two 'Scots' who came to Gaul and instead of exhibiting wares to the crowd, cried with a loud voice, 'Ho, every one that desires wisdom, let him draw near and take it at our hands; for it is wisdom that we have for sale.' This came to the ears of Charles, who saw that they were not, as some supposed, fools or madmen. He asked them whether it was true that they had brought wisdom with them, and he was delighted when, in response to his question—what price they asked for it—they declared 'We ask no price, O king: but we ask only for a fit place for teaching and quick minds to teach; and besides, food to eat and raiment to put on, for without these we cannot accomplish our pilgrimage.'[1] For the Irish came as pilgrims, and gradually their influence permeated a great number of the western monasteries. But it was in the century following the death of Charles the Great that this movement reached its fullest extent.

Clement the Grammarian[2] was one of the first Irishmen to become a teacher at the Court school. According to Notker, he was one of the two 'Scots' who came selling wisdom. There was another Irishman named Joseph, who had studied at Clonmacnois and then under Alcuin at York. Charles made him an abbot, and accepted at his hands a number of ingenious figure poems after the manner of Porfirius Optatianus.[3] Joseph was on friendly terms with S. Leger, the missionary to the Frisians, for he addressed to him a pleasing little poem, full of his praises and asking, at the end, for his prayers on behalf of the poet who had praised him 'in these brief odes', and—the gift of a staff:

> fors haec mercedula vati
> concordat modico.   felix sine fine valeto!

Smaragdus, the celebrated grammarian and Abbot of S. Mihiel, may also have been an Irishman.[4] His most important work is the *Liber in partibus Donati*. Just as Bede preferred in his book on metres to take his examples from Christian poets, so Smaragdus neglected Virgil and Cicero and tried to illustrate his grammar from the inspired writers of the Old and New Testaments.[5] He wrote a long preface to the book, in elegiacs, explaining his intention:

> muneribus sacris plenus est iste libellus,
> scripturam retinet, grammatica redolet.

[1] *Gesta Karoli* i. 1; trans. A. J. Grant, London 1905, p. 60.
[2] Manitius, *Gesch.* i. 456.
[3] Joseph's poems are in *Poet. Lat. Aevi Car.* i. 150 sqq.
[4] Manitius, *Gesch.* i. 461; poems, *Poet. Lat. Aevi Car.* i. 605 sqq. Dom Wilmart tells me that it is very doubtful whether Smaragdus was an Irishman.
[5] Cf. Manitius, *Gesch.* i. 464.

Each of the fifteen parts into which the treatise is divided has a prefatory poem, dealing with the matter in hand. The last poem ends with a pious wish:

> carminis hic statuo finem defigere nostri,
> ut teneam requiem iam tribuente deo.

Last comes Dungal,[1] unmistakably Irish, an exile from his country, as he styled himself, and conscious that though in Ireland he had had a position which entitled him to esteem, he was now at the mercy of patrons upon whom he relied for his daily bread.[2] But Charles loved him for his learning, and when Alcuin died it was to Dungal that the king turned for enlightenment on curious problems of astronomy and other 'naturales questiones'. Dungal answered, to the best of his ability, out of Macrobius or Pliny.

The best of his poems is a kind of dialogue between the poet and his Muse.[3] The poet begins: 'Kings receive rich gifts (Dungal enlarges on the splendour of these gifts). What gifts, O Muse, are ours to give?' 'We must give our songs,' the Muse replies. 'But,' says the poet, 'are you putting songs on a level with riches? What value can *they* possess?' This leads the Muse to celebrate the eternity of song, in verses which have in them the ring of a true nobility. Dungal feels that he is in the long line of those who were nourished by the Muses:

> dic nunc [he says], veterum vatum mihi maxima nutrix,
> quae nostrae laudis concludent saecula finem?

And the Muse replies:

> sidereae summus dum sphaerae volvitur axis,
> et nox obscura claris dum pellitur astris,
> splendidus ex imis surgit dum phosforus umbris,
> et celer aequoreas ventus dum verberat undas,
> in mare dum properant spumosis cursibus amnes,
> nubila dum tangunt minaci vertice montes,

[1] On the four Dungals whom it was customary to regard as one see Traube's note, *Dungali*, in *Abh. d. kgl. Bayer. Akad.* xix (1891), ii, p. 332 sqq. Traube showed that our Dungal was the *Hibernicus exul*, whose poems are in *Poet. Lat. Aevi Car.* i. 395 sqq., and for the first time sorted out Dungal's genuine verses (*op. cit.*, p. 335). The other Dungals (all Irish) are (i) Dungal, who taught in Pavia (825); (ii) Dungal the companion of Sedulius Scotus, and author of a poem to a master Baldo (*Poet. Lat. Aevi Car.* i. 412); (iii) Dungal monk of Bobbio, not earlier than the eleventh century. But M. Esposito, 'The Poems of Colmanus "Nepos Cracavist"', and 'Dungalus "Praecipuus Scottorum"', *J.T.S.* xxxiii (1932), pp. 113 sqq., rejects (p. 125) the identification of Dungal with the *Hibernicus exul*, whom he prefers to identify with Dicuil.

[2] For his letters, some of which are of a begging sort, see *M.G.H. Epist.* iv.

[3] *Poet. Lat. Aevi Car.* i. 396.

atque iacent humiles limoso limite valles,
aut summi extollunt praerupta cacumina colles,
regumque obrizo candor dum fulminat auro,
munera musarum saeclis aeterna manebunt.
his regum veterum clarescunt inclita gesta,
praesentum et saeclis narrantur facta futuris.

So the transition is made to the deeds of the king, in whose
service the Muse is to labour; and in particular the rebellion
of Tassilo, Duke of Bavaria, the ungrateful vassal of Charles,
is made the subject of the song.[1]

This is the place, perhaps, to speak of the *Conflictus veris et
hiemis*, if we are, with Winterfeld,[2] to deprive Alcuin of its
authorship, and assign it to an unknown Irishman. It is safer
to say that we have no sure evidence at all as to its authorship.
It is a *Streitgedicht*, a poetical debate between Spring and
Winter, and the question is: Shall the cuckoo come or not?
The cuckoo is our northern bird of Spring—for Germany as
for England or for Ireland. The idea of the poetical *debate*
goes back to antiquity—to Aesop, who has somewhere actually
a dispute of these two seasons,[3] to the Stoic-Cynic diatribe,
to the feigned lawsuits of the schools, and, more surely, to the
Greek and Latin *Eclogues* and their offshoots. There is Vespa's
Contest of Cook and Baker, which has already been mentioned,
and among the Carolingians Calpurnius and Nemesian
were favourites. But we cannot doubt, too, that the cuckoo
had already played his part in popular story, and in the rude
songs of the peasants. Here, however, in our poem, it is
Daphnis and Palaemon who come down from the hills in the
spring sunlight, the old and the young shepherd from the
classical eclogues. But Spring with his coronet of flowers, and
Winter with his frozen locks are figures of the north. They
hold their contest; Palaemon and Daphnis sit above them,
with the other shepherds, judges of debate. The sentence is
given with a triumphant shout:

desine plura, Hiems—rerum tu prodigus, atrox—
et veniat cuculus, pastorum dulcis amicus.

[1] Tassilo was deprived of his duchy in 788, and was immured in the monastery of Jumièges.

[2] *Rhein Mus.* lx, p. 35. The author knew Horace, and Alcuin did not. The Irish did; therefore, it is argued, the author was probably Irish. Winterfeld's view was that it was the Irish who made Horace known again on the continent. The text of the Eclogue is in *Poet. Lat. Aevi Car.* i. 270 sqq. The references to Horace are: *Epod.* xvi. 49, 'veniunt ad mulctra capellae' (verse 50, 'veniant ad mulctra capellae'), and *Od.* i. 1, 2, 'dulce decus meum' (verse 55, 'dulce decus').

[3] H. Walter, *Das Streitgedicht in der lateinischen Literatur des Mittelalters*, Munich 1920, p. 5.

collibus in nostris erumpant germina laeta,
pascua sint pecori, requies et dulcis in arvis,
et virides rami praestent umbracula fessis,
uberibus plenis veniantque ad mulctra capellae,
et volucres varia Phoebum sub voce salutent.
quapropter citius cuculus nunc ecce venito!
tu iam dulcis amor, cunctis gratissimus hospes:
omnes te expectant pelagus tellusque polusque,
salve, dulce decus, cuculus, per saecula salve.

§ 2. Carolingian Rhythms.

An account of the poetry of the Carolingian age which dealt
only with the learned verse of the court circle would afford a
very incomplete idea both of the influences at work and of the
actual achievement. Besides the classical poetry, there is a
large body of 'rhythms' of the most diverse character, the
product, for the most part, of the humble versifiers who lived
in the Frankish monasteries. While it is not always possible to
assign a precise or even approximate date to these compositions,
it seems clear that many of them were collected in S. Gall
before the death of Charles the Great,[1] and that they are the
work of Frankish or of Italian authors. One striking feature
of this collection is the large number of alphabetical poems.
This was an almost universal form, cultivated in Italy and Spain
as well as in Ireland or in England, and its appearance here cannot be traced to any one particular influence. The favourite
rhythmic form is one based on the trochaic tetrameter $(8+7)$;
elision is fairly common, and in many cases there is no definite
principle of structure beyond that of equality of syllables.
Rime is, of course, frequent, but it is often sporadic and un-
developed, though occasionally the two-syllabled rime is
employed without being carried consistently throughout a
poem. Another feature of this collection is the wide variety
of the subjects chosen. Much of the verse is religious, but
the poets broke new ground in choosing for their rhythms
subjects like Judith and Holofernes, Enoch and Elias, Jacob
and Joseph, or the siege of Jerusalem by Vespasian and
Titus.

Standing apart from this group are three poems (though the
last is actually included in the S. Gall collection) which possess
a more individual character. The first is a celebration of the
victory of King Pippin over the Avars in 796. Pippin, son of

---

[1] *Poet. Lat. Aevi Car.* iv. 454.

Charles the Great, had been crowned king of Italy while still a child (781). It was really Erich, duke of Friuli, who was in charge of the campaign and made his way into the great Avar fortress and carried off their fabulous treasures. The young Pippin came after him and received the submission of the Avar king.[1] The song of victory composed by an unknown poet has a certain vividness and strength. It is reproduced here with all the crudeness of its original form and spelling:[2]

> Omnes gentes qui fecisti, tu Christe, dei sobules,
> terras, fontes, rivos, montes et formasti hominem,
> Avaresque convertisti ultimis temporibus.
>
> multa mala iam fecerunt ab antico tempore,
> fana dei destruxerunt atque monasteria,
> vasa aurea sacrata, argentea, fictilia.
>
> vestem sacram polluerunt de ara sacratissima,
> linteamina levitae et sanctaemonalium
> muliebribus tradata suadente demone.
>
> misit deus Petrum sanctum, principem apostolum,
> in auxilium Pippini magni regis filium,
> ut viam eius comitaret et Francorum aciem.
>
> rex accinctus dei virtute Pippin, rex catholicus,
> castra figit super flumen albidum Danubium,
> hostibus accingens totum undique presidia.
>
> Unguimeri satis pavens, Avarorum genere,
> regi dicens satis forte: 'tu Cacane perdite!
> atque Catunae mulieri, maledictae coniugi:
>
> regna vestra consummata, ultra non regnabitis,
> regna vestra diu longe cristianis tradita,
> a Pippino demollita, principe catholico.
>
> adpropinquat rex Pippinus forti cum exercitu,
> fines tuos occupare, depopulare populum,
> montes, silvas atque colles ponere presidia.
>
> tolle cito, porta tecum copiosa munera;
> sceptrum regis adorare, ut paullum possis vivere,
> aurum, gemmas illi offer, ne te tradat funeri.'
>
> audiens Cacanus rex, undique perterritus,
> protinus ascendens mulam cum Tarcan primatibus,
> regem venit adorare et plagare[3] munere.
>
> regi dicens: 'salve princeps, esto noster dominus,
> regnum meum tibi trado cum festucis et foliis,
> silvas montes atque colles cum omnibus nascentiis.

---

[1] Hodgkin, *Italy and her Invaders* viii. 5. 183. Erich was killed by the Croatians in 799. Paulinus of Aquileia wrote a fine rhythmical dirge to his memory, *Christian-Latin Poetry*, pp. 168–9.

[2] *Poet. Lat. Aevi Car.* i. 116 sqq.

[3] i.e. placare.

tolle tecum proles nostras, parent tibi obsequia,
de primatibus nec parcas, terga verte acie,
colla nostra, proles nostras dicioni tradimus.'

nos fideles cristiani deo agamus gratiam,
qui regnum regis confirmavit super regnum Uniae,
et victoriam donavit de paganis gentibus.

vivat, vivat rex Pippinus in timore domini,
avus regnet et senescat et procreet filios,
qui palatia conservent in vita et post obitum.

qui conclusit regnum crande,[1] amplum, potentissimum,
quae regna terrrae non fecerunt usque ad diem actenus,
neque cesar et pagani, sed divina gratia.

gloria aeterna patri, gloria sit filio.

This adaptation of the trochaic tetrameter, with sporadic
rimes, does not mark any advance over the earlier productions
of a similar character which have already been noted. It is
the subject matter that is of particular interest. We can only
guess its relation to the vernacular songs known to these
poets who were writing in the learned language, in which they
were never entirely at ease. So the author of the *Planctus de
Obitu Caroli*[2] succeeded in bringing into his Latin chant a
mixture of the popular dirge with some of the rhetorical
devices he had learned in the schools. The ninth stanza, for
instance, shows how widely the Irish and Anglo-Saxon example
of alliteration had spread:[3]

1. A solis ortu usque ad occidua
   littora maris planctus pulsat pectora.
        heu mihi misero!

2. ultra marina agmina tristitia
   tetigit ingens cum merore nimio.
        heu mihi misero!

3. Franci, Romani atque cuncti creduli
   luctu punguntur et magna molestia.
        heu mihi misero!

4. infantes, senes, gloriosi presules,
   matronae plangunt detrimentum Caesaris.
        heu mihi misero!

---

[1] i.e., grande.
[2] *Poet. Lat. Aevi Car.* i. 435 sq.
[3] The author was perhaps a monk of
the Irish foundation of Bobbio; ib.,
p. 434; cf. also stanza 17 with its
reference to Columbanus. The device
of the refrain appears in the famous

hymn, 'Apparebit repentina dies magna
domini', each stanza of which ends
with
      in tremendo die iudicii. (ib., iv. p. 507.)
The long poem on the last things (ib.,
p. 491), called *de Enoch et Haeliae*,
has a series of impressive refrains.

5. iamiam non cessant lacrimarum flumina,
   nam plangit orbis interitum Karoli.
      heu mihi misero!

6. pater communis orfanorum omnium,
   peregrinorum, viduarum, virginum,
      heu mihi misero!

7. Christe, caelorum qui gubernas agmina,
   tuo in regno da requiem Karolo.
      heu mihi misero!

8. hoc poscunt omnes fideles et creduli,
   hoc sancti senes, viduae et virgines.
      heu mihi misero!

9. imperatorem iam serenum Karolum
   telluris tegit titulatus tumulus.
      heu mihi misero!

10. spiritus sanctus, qui gubernat omnia,
    animam suam exaltet in requiem.
       heu mihi misero!

11. vae tibi, Roma, Romanoque populo
    amisso summo glorioso Karolo.
       heu mihi misero!

12. vae tibi, sola formonsa Italia,
    cunctisque tuis tam honestis urbibus.
       heu mihi misero!

13. Francia diras perpessa iniurias
    nullum iam talem dolorem sustinuit,
       heu mihi misero!

14. quando augustum facundumque Karolum
    in Aquisgrani glebis terrae tradidit.
       heu mihi misero!

15. nox mihi dira iam retulit somnia,
    diesque clara non adduxit lumina,
       heu mihi misero!

16. quae cuncti orbis christiano populo
    vexit ad mortem venerandum principem,
       heu mihi misero!

17. o Columbane, stringe tuas lacrimas,
    precesque funde pro illo ad dominum,
       heu mihi misero!

18. pater cunctorum, misericors dominus,
    ut illi donet locum splendidissimum.
       heu mihi misero!

19. o deus cunctae humanae militiae
    atque caelorum, infernorum domine,
        heu mihi misero!

20. in sancta sede cum tuis apostolis
    suscipe pium, o tu Christe, Karolum.
        heu mihi misero!

There is, after all, little enough to suggest that this is anything but a humble effort of some monastic versifier, who had a good grasp of the principles of rhythmic composition, and saw how a refrain, breaking into his sentences, could be used with effect. He very wisely did not adopt the alphabetical form.

The same temptation was resisted by the author of a rhythm on the City of Verona,[1] written in the days when Charles's son, Pippin, was king of Italy. The 'ut docet Isidorus' of the opening strophe is delightful, but Isidore, we are told, actually never mentions Verona.[2] Anyhow the poet thought that he could not do better than introduce Isidore as guarantee of a geographical fact:

Magna et praeclara pollet urbs haec in Italia
in partibus Venetiarum, ut docet Isidorus,
que Verona vocitatur olim ab antiquitus.

The poem describes the buildings of Verona, the amphitheatre, the walls, the temples, the churches, and celebrates, of course, the saints and martyrs whose relics are the glory and the protection of the city.

o felicem te, Verona, sic ditata et inclita,
qualis es circumvallata custodibus sanctissimis,
qui te defendant et expugnent ab hoste iniquissimo.

These three poems are, in a measure, all of a patriotic character, evidences of civic and national feeling. There is something in them which sets them apart from ancient elegy, epitaph, or rhetorical description. What is new comes either from the Christian outlook,[3] or from the new loyalties that had arisen to take the place of the old loyalty centering round Rome, the mother of the peoples. It was instinctively felt, besides, that the rhythmic verse was nearer to these real and vivid things which demanded expression in a manner different from mere variations on themes borrowed from the schools. This freshness and vividness cannot fail to be felt by the reader of the

---

[1] *Poet. Lat. Aevi Car.* i. 119 sqq.; the verses *de Mediolano civitate*, p. 160. above, are alphabetical.

[2] ib., p. 119, note 3.

[3] Hörle, *Frühmittelalterliche Mönchs-* *und Klerikerbildung in Italien*, p. 43, notes that this poem contains scriptural reminiscences, but none of any classical author.

verses on the battle of Fontenoy (841), composed by one Angilbert, who on that day of fratricidal strife was in the foremost ranks, and at the end of the fight stood alone among the dying and the dead:[1]

> gramen illud ros et ymber nec humectat pluvia,
> in quo fortes ceciderunt, proelio doctissimi,
> pater, mater, soror, frater, quos amici fleverant.
>
> hoc autem scelus peractum, quod descripsi ritmice,
> Angelbertus ego vidi pugnansque cum aliis,
> solus de multis remansi prima frontis acie.

With some such considerations as we have just described in mind, we can approach with proper sympathy the varied collection of rhythms associated, as regards their compilation rather than their origin, with the monastery of S. Gall. It will hardly be wrong to say that they represent a crucial stage in the great experiment with rhythmical poetry which filled so many years, from its uncouth and yet deeply impressive beginnings to its clear and wonderful music in the great medieval centuries. Here we see the rhythm, pure and simple, with little or no conscious seeking for rime. Or we have a lovely poem, the 'hymn of Charity', which begins without rime and then develops assonance and the finest of rhetorical rimes.

> Nos alterutrum amemus   et in die,
> sicut decet, ambulemus   lucis fili!
> ubi caritas est vera,   deus ibi est.
>
> .   .   .   .   .
>
> karitas est summum bonum, amplum donum.[2]

An alphabetical poem, *de passione et resurrectione domini*[3] is full of two-syllabled rimes, more or less perfect:

> Audite, omnes gentes,   ... Ducitur salvator,
> et discite prudentes   ut impiis tradetur,
> de passione Christi,   quem Iudas tradidit reus
> per quem redempti estis.   propter triginta argenteus.[4]

> Zelus bonus et magnus!
> Christus passus ut agnus;
> surrexit de sepulchro,
> vivus ascendit sursum.
> iam Christus resurrexit!

[1] *Poet. Lat. Aevi Car.* ii. 138 sq.

[2] *Poet. Lat. Aevi Car.* iv. 527; on this hymn see *Christian-Latin Poetry*, p. 157 sq.

[3] *Poet. Lat. Aevi Car.* iv, p. 501; cf. also *Versum de Castitate*, ib., p. 573:

> Cecos tu inluminasti,
> paraliticos curasti,
> Lazarum quadriduanum
> de monumento suscitasti, etc.

[4] *u* for *o*, as elsewhere in this poem.

The long narrative poems belong mostly to the history of religious verse. They owe little or nothing to the rhetorical tradition, but are rather allied to the historical poems which were being written at the time. They adopt the direct manner of the ballad, and do not pretend to do anything more than tell their story plainly. The tale of Judith and Holofernes begins:

> Anno tertio in regno   cum esset et decimo,
> Nabuchodonosor coepit   excitare proelia
> contra gentes atque regna   usque Hierosolimam.[1]

The *versus de Iacob et Ioseph* commence, it is true, with something more imaginative, but it is merely the prelude to a sober narrative:

> Tertio in flore mundus   adhuc dum pubesceret,
> in decore iuventutis   seculum pulchresceret
> atque proles subter omnes   latos caeli cardines
> germinando pullularet   humana feliciter,
>
> natus est homo in mundum,   patriarcha nobilis,
> Abraham dei amicus,   puer fidelissimus;
> Heber aurea de stirpe   oriundus extitit,
> a quo coepit Hebreorum   diffamari populus.[2]

The *versus de contemptu mundi*[3] adopt the alphabetical form and the refrain; their peculiar interest lies in the way in which they anticipate the theme of much later moralizing verse, half religious and half-secular, primarily of monastic inspiration though afterwards becoming part of the stock-in-trade of poets of any kind:[4]

> Audax es, vir iuvenis,
> dum fervet caro mobilis;
> audenter agis, perperam
> tua membra coinquinas.
>   adtende homo, quod pulvis es
>   et in pulverem reverteris.
>
> Brevis est tempus, iuvenis,
> considera, quod moreris,
> venitque dies ultimus
> et perdes florem optimum.
>   adtende homo, quia de terra factus es
>   et in terra ponendus eris.

---

[1] ib., p. 459. Another narrative is that of Placidas (S. Eustasius) and the stag, ib., p. 593.

[2] *Poet. Lat. Aevi Car.* iv. 462.

[3] ib., p. 495.

[4] Cf. also the verses, ib., p. 612, beginning:

> qui signati estis Christo,
> mementote repromisso,
> quod daturum se in caelo
> vobis dixit in futuro.
> abicite vana loqui.

Stanza 9 commences with a good couplet,

> nuptias Christus paravit,
> ad quas omnes invitavit.

There is a fragment of an alphabetical poem on Alexander the Great, full of the wonder with which his life had long been invested, but containing details that can be referred to no known source:

Alexander puer magnus	circumivit patriam
usque ad mare oceanum,	civitates(?) insulas(?),
antequam Christus fuisset natus	ex Maria virgine.
Bonus fuit puer magnus,	natus fuit in Africa,
patrem habuit Philisteum,[1]	matrem de Bethania.
totum mundum circumivit,	fecit Alexandriam.
Cum totum mundum circumiret,	introivit in tenebras,
unde gemme speciose	exierunt sine numero,
unde reges et potentes	ornati sunt in seculo.[2]
Dum in heremo esset, cepit	bestiam dissimilem,
corpus habuit ut caballus,	caput sicut bubalus;[3]
centum leuvas[4] mane currit,	vespere renuntiat.

We cannot follow the poet into his further obscurities, which are increased by the fragmentary condition of the text. Who were his readers? The pupils of the monastic school, who had to study the various ages of the world, and may have memorized these verses as part of their lesson in history.

A marvellous example of the alphabetical principle carried to extremes is the poem *de accipitre et pavone*,[5] the rhythm of which is based on the Adonic:

Avis hec magna	Contectas plumis
Ad astra tendit	Concussit pennas.
Alta, sublimes	Cauda coruscat
Aspergens voces	Colore fulgens.
Agnum conlaudat	Cantum emittit,
Auctorem cunctis.	Cunctis precellit.
Bonus plasmator	Dilatat pavo
Bene laudetur.	Dignis triumphis
Bona per orbem	Diversis modis
Bene formavit,	Duo in rotis,
Bona percomplens	De parvis membris
Benigne tegit.	Decior cunctis.

---

[1] Strecker is unwilling to change this into Philippum.

[2] Strecker (*Poet. Lat. Aevi Car.* iv. 600) quotes the Pseudocallisthenes, cap. 39: καὶ πάλιν ὁδεύσαντες ἤλθομεν ... εἰς τόπους, ὅπου ἥλιος οὐ λάμπει ... καὶ ἐξελθόντων ἡμῶν πρὸς τὸ φῶς εὑρέθησαν χρυσίον δόκιμον λαβόντες καὶ μαργαρίτας μεγάλους τιμῆς ἀξίους.

[3] Here Strecker suggests (following Zarncke) that our poet has found it possible to confuse Bucephalus and the ὀδοντοτύραννος, the Indian *worm* mentioned in Aelian, *N.H.* v. 3.

[4] i.e., *leugas*, leagues.

[5] *Poet. Lat. Aevi Car.* iv. 610; *Anal. Hymn.* xlvi, p. 384.

Extrema die	Fortis acceptor,[1]
Extincto sole	Firmior pavo:
Excelsus subens	Ferocem sive
Evadat mala,	Fidus despexit;
Extendens plumis	Felix invictus
Evolat summis	Firmus permansit.

The poem goes on, with the obscure unfolding of the virtues of the peacock, until we realize at last that it is a type of Christ,

> Verus occisus
> Verus aeternus,
> Volans ad celum,
> Vivens aeternus.

It is a strange transition from the *Hawk and the Peacock* to a real drinking song, concerning an abbot of Angers who had an unquenchable thirst.[2] This poem is in a ninth-century manuscript of Verona, but it had its origin in some monastery of the Frankish Kingdom or Italy where there was a poet who loved rhythms set to music, and had no fear of the censure of his superiors. Or was it a song that reached the monastery from the outside world, somehow or other, and found its way, by one of those chances which later were to be more frequent, into the monastic collection of rhythms? At any rate, it is about an abbot of Angers, whose name was Adam. The Latin is as bad as it can be, that is to say, it is properly adapted to the theme:[3]

Andecavis	abas esse dicitur,
ille nomen	primi tenet hominum;
hunc fatentur	vinum vellet bibere
super omnes	Andechavis homines.
Eia eia eia laudes,	
Eia laudes dicamus Libero.	
iste malet	vinum omni tempore;
quem nec dies	nox nec ulla preterit,
quod non vino	saturatus titubet
velut arbor	agitata flatibus.
eia eia eia laudes,	
eia laudes dicamus Libero.	
iste gerit	corpus inputribile
vinum totum	conditum ut alove,
et ut mire[4]	corium conficitur,
cutis eius	nunc con vino tinguitur.

---

[1] i.e. *accipiter.*

[2] *Poet. Lat. Aevi Car.* iv. 591.

[3] Mr. Gaselee suggests that the last *eia* should end the preceding verse, giving a trochaic and iambic scheme, the last two verses being

$$-\cup \mid -\cup \mid -\cup \mid \cup - \mid -\bar{\cup}$$
$$\cup - \mid \cup - \mid \cup - \mid \cup -$$

and the others

$$-\cup \mid -\cup \parallel -\cup \mid -\cup \mid -\cup \mid \underset{\smile}{}$$

But it is clear, I think, that each *Eia* is to be read as having three syllables, and we therefore get, throughout, verses of eleven syllables in a trochaic scheme.

[4] *myrrha.*

eia eia eia laudes,
eia laudes dicamus Libero.

iste cupa	non curat de calicem
vinum bonum	bibere suaviter,
set patellis	atque magnis cacabis
et in eis	ultra modum grandibus.

eia eia eia laudes,
eia laudes dicamus Libero.

hunc perperdet	Andechavis civitas,
nullum talem	ultra sibi sociat,
qui sic semper	vinum possit sorbere;
cuius facta,	cives, vobis pingite!

eia eia eia laudes,
eia laudes dicamus Libero.

This rhythm has no fellow until the time of the *Cambridge Songs*. It stands, therefore, as a lonely landmark, suggesting, on second thoughts, the same Teutonic humour[1] which gave birth to several of the songs in that collection. It is also a witness, if we read its evidence aright, to a continuous stream of Latin secular song.

To none of the rhythms that we have considered is the name of the author attached. They remain in their more or less humble anonymity and make their appeal on their bare merits. It is, therefore, with a feeling of surprise and perhaps of expectation that the reader comes across the name of a woman as the author of a number of rhythms embedded in a manual of moral instruction.[2] Dhuoda, a noble lady, married Bernard, a Frankish count, in 824, and they had a child named William. The husband, a man of rough nature, took the child away from his mother, and when a second son was born, he removed him likewise, actually before baptism. To console herself in her sadness and to attempt, in some sort, to make up for the lack of a mother's care, Dhuoda addressed to the elder boy a manual of good counsels, with a few rhythms of interesting structure. The first is addressed to William, 'Dhuoda

---

[1] Another example is the story in hexameters, from S. Gall MSS. (*Poet. Lat. Aevi Car.* ii. 474), of the three brothers who inherited from their father nothing but a goat. Instead of dividing it they agreed that the one who could conceive the greatest and most fantastic wish about a goat should have it. The wishes are given, but the point of the story lies in the end:

at quicumque sibi sapiens quicumque

videtur,
decernat horum quis victor iure putetur
et teneat hircum felici munere pulchrum.

The story comes, of course, from popular tradition; see P. von Winterfeld, *Die Dichterschule St. Gallens und der Reichenau, Neue Jahrb.*, 1900, p. 348.

[2] *Poet. Lat. Aevi Car.* iv. 705.

dilecto filio Wilhelmo salutem. Lege.'; so the acrostich runs. The last stanza will give a sufficient idea of the rhythmical scheme:

Lector qui cupis	formulam hanc nosse,
capita perquiras	apta versorum;
Exin valebis	concito gradu
sensu cognosci,	que sim conscripta.
Genetrix duorum	masculini sexus
rogo, ut ores	conditori almo.
Erigat ad summum	genitorem prolis
meque cum illis	iungat in regnum.
A littera Delta	incipe legendo
Moida[1] hac tenus	conclusa sunt⟨o⟩.

Traube[2] considered that Dhuoda's verses were to be regarded as Adonics of rather free construction, but the poems show such irregularity in the numbering of syllables that this theory is untenable. Each verse is divided into two parts; the number of syllables in each part varies from five to seven, though occasionally there are half-verses of four and verses of eight syllables. But the number of stresses in each half-verse is two, and this is the principle that gives unity to the scheme. Such at any rate is Wilhelm Meyer's theory, and we are asked to see here the influence of the German vernacular rhythm.[3]

Among the mass of other Carolingian rhythms is a series of 'computistic rhythms'—rhythms, that is, relating to the calendar; these exhibit no special structural characteristics, and only those curious about things pertaining to the *ars computandi* as it was understood in the Middle Ages are likely to study them.[4] It seems that the collection had its origin in the monastery of Monte Cassino.[5]

A group of Lombard rhythms[6] consists of 'hexameters' somewhat mysteriously fashioned, though Wilhelm Meyer has professed to explain their structure.[7] There is also a versification of the famous *Cena Cypriani*, which is the work of one John the Deacon, a contemporary of Charles the Bald.[8] The *Cena* itself is a narrative about the marriage feast of King Johel at Cana of Galilee, to which persons of all kinds from the

---

[1] Moida, used by Dhuoda for M (μū); see *Poet. Lat. Aevi Car.* iv. 708, note.

[2] *Karolingische Dichtungen*, p. 136.

[3] 'Ein Merowinger Rythmus und altdeutsche Rythmik in lateinischen Versen', *Gött. Nachr.* 1908, pp. 31 sqq.

[4] *Poet. Lat. Aevi Car.* iv. 667 sqq.

[5] K. Strecker 'Zu den komputistischen Rhythmen' *Neues Archiv*, xxxvi (1911), pp. 319 sqq., with text of an interesting rhythm by Hirenicus.

[6] ib., pp. 718 sqq.

[7] *Rythmik*, i. 229 sq.; ii. 11 sq.

[8] *Poet. Lat. Aevi Car.* iv. 857. On John the Deacon, a man of great importance in the Roman Church and of considerable learning, see Manitius, *Gesch.* i. 689 sqq.

Old and the New Testament are invited. All these people are introduced with the characteristics they possess or the actions they perform in their biblical setting; so that the whole composition, puerile in itself, might serve the purpose of instruction, if it did not rather move those who heard it recited to unseemly laughter.[1] John the Deacon's versification of the *Cena* seems, at any rate, to have been produced as a *jeu d'esprit* for the amusement of Pope John VIII, to whom it is dedicated. For the author says in his versified postscript,

> qui risum poterit stringere marmor erit,

and if the humour seems rather dull to us, it was good enough for John's contemporaries:

Adam pater sedit primus	cunctorum in medium,
Eva mater heu lasciva	fici super folium,
et Cain super aratrum,	Abel in mulctrarium,
super arcam sedit Noe,	Iafet super laterem,
Isaac super altare,	Abraham sub arbore,
Iacob sedit super petram	et Loth secus (h)ostium,
Moyses super lapillos,	Helias in pellibus

Petrus sedit in cathedra,	Iudas super loculum,
Samson sedit in columpnas,	super rete Iacobus,
Heli senex super sellam,	Rachel super sarcinam.
patienter stabat Paulus,	murmurabat Esau,
et dolebat Iob, sederet	quod solus in stercore.[2]

So the catalogue continues interminably with variations, relieved only by a few crude jokes and a grain of obscenity.

The poet has used his rhythmical trochaic tetrameters with a fair amount of skill; there is a good deal of rime, but it is not consciously sought. Like most of the Italian rhythms it is on the whole superior in execution to those produced by the Franks. For it was from Italy that the example of the rhythmic trochaic tetrameter appears to have passed into the Frankish Kingdom. Indeed we may say that the Lombardic or Italian influence on the development of rhythm was stronger than that which came from England and Ireland. For the rhythms which we have been considering are manifestly, in the main, of continental origin. The English influence was, on the whole, confined to the Court school, and it was not until the ninth century that invasion by Irish scholars took place on a large and effective scale. Then, indeed, Irish rhythmical poetry came to be read

---

[1] Actually, it would seem, the piece was composed to be recited at table, following the advice given in a tract by Bishop Zeno of Verona, entitled *ad* *neophytos post baptisma* (for text see *Poet. Lat. Aevi Car.* iv. 861 sq.), and once ascribed to Cyprian.

[2] ib., p. 873-5.

and imitated, but it left its mark chiefly in a rich development of rime, which was of incalculable importance for the future of lyrical poetry.

§ 3. *The Ninth Century.*

(i) *Ermoldus, Raban, Gottschalk, and Walafrid.*

After the death of Charles the Great the Court school gradually lost its supremacy as the dispenser of learning to the Frankish kingdom. 'David' was gone, and before him Alcuin, Paul the Deacon, and Paulinus had departed. Theodulf survived in a colder world, a world from which the glory had faded. The new Emperor was weak, and although he knew Latin well and had some acquaintance with the Greek tongue, he never became the centre of a literary circle. The Court school continued under Clement, an Irish grammarian, and Ermoldus Nigellus made an attempt to keep up the tradition of Court poetry.

Ermoldus was perhaps a secular clerk,[1] and he seems to have been a native of Aquitaine. Before the death of Charles he was, it seems, attached to the court of Louis in Aquitaine, and when Louis became Emperor, Ermoldus remained with his son Pippin, whom he accompanied in 824 on an expedition against the Bretons. He was not intended by nature for a soldier,

> nemo me feriente dolet.

No one suffered from his taking up of arms, he said. And seeing this, Pippin smiled, wondered, and said: 'Put away your arms, brother, and get back to your books!'[2] But Louis was told that Ermoldus exercised no good influence over his son, and relegated him to the surveillance of Bishop Bernold of Strasbourg. Ermoldus now had to set about obtaining his pardon. To this end, in 826, he began a long elegiac poem in four books—'in honorem Hludowici Christianissimi Caesaris Augusti'.[3] The details of the poem need not concern us; they are of considerable interest to the historian, who finds in the poem much material which is not available elsewhere. Ermoldus chose the elegiac couplet rather than, with the author of the poem about Charles and Leo, venture on the heroic measure.

---

[1] This suggestion of Manitius, *Gesch.* i. 553, seems justifiable in all the circumstances; a monk would hardly have had the intimate knowledge of affairs which Ermoldus evidently possessed.

[2] *Poet. Lat. Aevi Car.* ii. 62.

[3] *Poet. Lat. Aevi Car.* ii. 5 sqq.

He begins by confessing the smallness of his merit in comparison with the greatness of his theme, and in doing so he quotes the names of a number of authors, with some of which he was reasonably familiar:

> non ego gestorum per singula quaeque recurram:
>   nec fas, nec potis est, nec valet ingenium.
> si Maro, Naso, Cato, Flaccus, Lucanus, Homerus,
>   Tullius, et Macer,[1] Cicero, sive Plato,
> Sedulius nec non Prudentius atque Iuvencus,
>   seu Fortunatus, Prosper et ipse foret,
> omnia famosis vix possent condere cartis,
>   atque suum celebre hinc duplicare melos.

This is one more evidence of the way in which the Christian poets had taken their place beside the poets of antiquity. Ermoldus was conscious of himself as a successor of Fortunatus as well as of the poet who celebrated Charles and Pope Leo. In his poem he employs the usual resources of such poets. Thus in the fourth book he gives an account of a visit of Louis and his wife Judith to Ingelheim:

> Engilin—ipse pius placido tunc tramite—heim
>   advolat induperans coniuge cum, sobole.[2]

There the Emperor had a palace, quite close to Mainz. Near at hand was the basilica of S. Alban, and of this church Ermoldus gives a detailed description, after the manner in which rhetorical poets had learned, throughout the centuries, to attack such a theme. The method is, of course, that of the catalogue. He is telling of the pictures which adorn the walls of the church, and he gives a distich to each subject until he has exhausted the list. On the left side are the 'gesta Dei' from the Old Testament; on the right the 'vitalia gesta' of Christ. The scenes are much the same as those in the *Dittochaeon* of Prudentius. Then there are inside the palace scenes from ancient history—Cyrus and Ninus, Phalaris, Romulus and Remus, Hannibal, Alexander—largely taken from Orosius. Lastly, there are scenes from the history of the Christian Empire, in which Constantine, Theodosius, Charles, and Pippin appear.

There is, as in the poem about Charles and Leo, a hunting scene set forth in detail. This, like much of Angilbert's narra-

---

[1] This is Aemilius Macer, the friend of Virgil; Manitius, *Gesch.* i. 554, note 5, doubts whether any of his poems survived to Carolingian times.

[2] The infant Charles, the future Emperor, known as Charles the Bald; *Poet. Lat. Aevi Car.* ii. 63.

tive in the earlier work, has the merit of a vivid simplicity.[1]
The poem ends with a prayer for pardon, addressed to Louis
and to his beautiful wife, Judith.

In choosing the elegiac couplet Ermoldus doubtless made his
own task easier, but the metre is not suited to continuous
narrative. He is fond of jingles—'dante tonante' often occurs,[2]
borrowed from Theodulf; also 'miserante tonante'[3] and 'dante
creante',[4] but these faults of taste he shared with his contemporaries.

This long panegyric of Louis did not win Ermoldus his
pardon. So he addressed himself next to King Pippin, his
former master. In the first of two elegies he adopted the device
of Theodulf in his poem to Modoin,[5] and made his Muse,
Thalia, present herself to Louis and his wife at one of the
numerous royal palaces.[6] It was Easter, and they held court.
The poet imagines the dialogue between Thalia and Pippin,
who inquires as to Ermoldus's place of exile. Thalia then
describes Alsace,

> terra antiqua, potens, Franco possessa colono,
>   cui nomen Helisaz Francus habere dedit:

it is between the Vosges and the Rhine; the slopes are covered
with vines and the valleys with corn:

> arva ferunt Cererem, colles dant copia vini,
>   Wasace,[7] das silvas, Rhenus opimat humum.

Then follows a dialogue between Rhine and Vosges, telling
of the benefits they each bestow on the people of Alsace, and

---

[1] The first book (*Poet. Lat. Aevi Car.*
ii. 5 sqq.) contains a description of the
siege and capture of the Saracen strong-
hold of Barcelona, which cannot fail to
hold the interest of the reader. In the
second book there is the meeting of
Louis the Pious and Pope Stephen at
Reims and the banquet which followed
(p. 30 sqq.). In a long speech the Pope
compares Louis to Solomon. Then
(p. 39 sqq.) there is an account of the
reforms of Benedict of Aniane. In the
third book Ermoldus tells of Louis's
dealings with the hostile king of the
Bretons, Murman, to whom the Emperor sent Abbot Wicchar as his envoy
to admonish him. Wicchar (p. 43) in
his speech uses the names of Turnus,
Camilla, Aeneas, Odysseus, Pyrrhus,
Achilles, and Pompey. The war which
followed is described in a very lively

manner. Murman is killed in single
combat with a Frankish knight. They
make the usual speeches before the
fight. The fourth book begins with
Louis's attempt to convert the North-
men (p. 59). He makes a speech to
Ebo, Bishop of Reims, who is to be the
missionary for the purpose, in which he
gives a concise account of man's fall
and redemption. Harold, the King of
the Danes, is converted and comes to
Louis to be baptized. After the festivi-
ties, Louis and Harold go hunting
(p. 71).

[2] p. 28, verse 148; 35, verse 394;
75, verse 596.

[3] p. 56, verse 533.

[4] p. 60, verse 38.

[5] See *Christian-Latin Poetry*, p. 173

[6] *Poet. Lat. Aevi Car.* ii. 79.

[7] i.e. the Vosges.

each belittling the achievement of the other. 'I carry great cargoes, and provide much fish,' says the Rhine, 'The Vosges are shaken by winds and only provide wood for the fire.' But the Vosges answer: 'Palaces are made of our mighty trees, and churches too. Kings hunt in my forests. The stricken deer flees to our pools, and the boar as well. We too have fishes, and are full of small rivers.' And so the contest continues, until Thalia reconciles the disputants.

After the Muse has described Strasbourg, where Ermoldus is kept, and the virtues of the Bishop, Louis speaks the final words. He speaks not of release but of consolation, and in the same terms as those employed by Modoin in his poem of consolation to Theodulf.[1] He invites Ermoldus to recall the names and sufferings of famous men of the past, and the list is practically the same as Modoin's.

In the second poem Ermoldus appeals directly to Pippin, and although he admonishes him as to the proper conduct of a prince, he does this in order to put forward Louis as his exemplar, hoping, we may suppose, that this ingenious flattery, coupled with the admonition to the son, would suggest to the Emperor that after all he might have been mistaken about Ermoldus.

Here we leave Ermoldus Nigellus. His work soon fell into obscurity. It remained unread until historians brought it once more into the light and enabled us to see the author as he here presents himself to us, a man of some charm, not over conscientious or pious, a lover of poetry old and new, and a patient maker of verses according to pattern:

> carminibus prisci quondam placuere poetae,
> carmine Naso placet atque poeta Maro;
> rustica nostra tamen nuper Musella placebat;
> es solitus nostris ludere versiculis.

So he addressed Pippin. His desire was to please, and he doubtless wrote well enough to please his contemporaries, if the taste of later generations rewarded him with neglect.

In the ninth century the homes of learning were the great Benedictine houses of Germany and Lorraine.[2] Here the traditions of Boniface and of Alcuin were carried on, with the somewhat narrower aim that inevitably characterized a monastic school. We have seen Alcuin at the court of Charles, devising riddles, composing epistles, and good-naturedly enjoying the gaiety of the Emperor's dinner-parties. But as Abbot of

---

[1] Above, p. 203.
[2] But Corbie and Fleury in France were also at the height of their fame.

Tours, he ruled the school with great prudence, and did his best to instil into his pupils a preference for the fathers instead of the 'luxuriosa facundia' of Virgil.[1] The great schools of Fulda and Reichenau followed the pattern of Tours; but in spite of all protestations the classical authors were copied and read, and immense care was bestowed on the composition of verses. During this century the copying of manuscripts went on at a great pace, and authors, some of them brought by the Irish, came to be read again after they had fallen out of current knowledge. Fresh waves of Irish immigration broke on the Frankish monasteries of the north and east.[2] The Irish scholars brought not only a knowledge of Greek, but the rimed Latin verse which they had practised at home for several centuries. Thus Raban Maur, the great Abbot of Fulda, the monastery consecrated by the presence of the body of Boniface, had made a study of the Irish rhythmical verses, though he was also acquainted with similar verse composed by the saint himself and by members of his circle. At Fulda rime breaks out exuberantly, not merely in Raban's imitation of the *altus prosator* of Columba, but in the poems of Gottschalk, who spent an unhappy boyhood in the monastic school.

Raban himself had learned the art of composition under Alcuin at Tours. So, in his metrical poems, he borrows from Virgil and Ovid, and is full of reminiscences of the usual Christian poets. He wrote poetical epistles, in which he sometimes relaxed from his accustomed severity, though he was fond of moral commonplace.[3]

In his rhythmical poem, to which we have referred, Raban showed no originality, and did not advance technically beyond what the Irish and Anglo-Saxons had already achieved:

> Deus salus credentium,
> deus vita viventium,
> deus deorum omnium,

[1] *Vita Alchuini*, x, p. 24.

[2] Gougaud, 'L'Œuvre des Scotti dans l'Europe continentale', *Revue d'histoire ecclésiastique*, ix (1908), p. 258, observes that Cambrai was a favourite rendezvous of the 'Scotti' at the end of the eighth and in the early ninth century. They are also found at Reims, Soissons, Laon, and Liége. Erigena stayed at Laon.

[3] See *Christian-Latin Poetry*, pp. 180 sqq.; cf. *Poet. Lat. Aevi Car.* ii. 193 sq., a poem to Hatto, who succeeded him

at Fulda:
> una dies ridet, casus cras altera plangit,
>   nil fixum quomodo tessera laeta dabit.
> aestas clara micat, autumnus conferet umbras,
>   ver floret gemmis, has fera tollit hiems.
> quid porro est quod non properatis effugit alis,
>   et varium non sit quod tegit arce polus, etc.

> deus et princeps principum,
> deus summus amabilis,
> deus inestimabilis,[1]

is the best that he can accomplish. But his young pupil
Gottschalk[2] was a poet of no ordinary gifts. Raban appears
to have used more than ordinary persuasion when the time
came for him to take his vows. On this ground Gottschalk got
a release in 829, at the synod of Mainz. But Raban had this
decision reversed at a synod held in the presence of the Emperor.
Gottschalk was, however, transferred to Orbais, and here he
began his career as a theologian and a poet. He managed to
obtain ordination from the *chorepiscopus* of Reims, and thus
equipped he went about Europe preaching and disputing,
until in 849 he was deprived of his orders and was immured
at Hautvillers. He died in 869 without the sacraments.
Gottschalk made his own unhappiness, and it overflowed into
his song. His poems show how much the stimulus of personal
suffering could avail to intensify the lyrical feeling which was
his by nature. For Gottschalk naturally took a classical metre,
and by adding rime made something new and strange. He is
a significant witness to the history of the Latin lyric, for his
example proves that whenever the personal conditions were
present which were propitious to the expression of intimate
feeling there was a possibility of lyrical poetry. In this sense
the lyric has no continuous history. A Petronius appears, and
after him a few scattered voices, and then a Gottschalk who
points the way to the future. Not that Gottschalk is the equal
of Petronius but, like Petronius, he is a landmark in literary
history, a poet above his contemporaries. His mastery of rime
and even of rhythm was far from complete,[3] but he poured his
whole spirit into the mould of his verses:

> Christe, mearum
> lux tenebrarum . . .

[1] *Poet. Lat. Aevi Car.* ii. 197.
[2] On the career of Gottschalk we
must now consult Dom G. Morin,
'Gottschalk retrouvé', *Rev. Bénéd.* xliii
(1931), pp. 303 sqq. Morin has found
a collection of Gottschalk's theological
writings, which contain material of
biographical interest. We learn for instance that Gottschalk was at Reichenau before the end of 824 and, with his
friend Walafrid, studied under Wettin.
There is also some information about
his wanderings in Dalmatia. Morin
suggests that the eight pieces on the
canonical hours in *Anal. Hymn.* xlvi.
9 sqq., which follow the writings of
Gottschalk in the Berne MS. (the only
MS.), may be his also.
[3] Cf. W. Meyer, *Rythmik*, ii. 365,
'Selbst der Feuergeist des Gottschalk,
der immer neues und selbständiges
suchte, der Reim und Gesang liebte,
in welch armseligen Formen ergiesst er
seine tief empfundenen Klagen!'

respice nunc me,
da, sequar ut te:
iam miserere
iamque medere,
et tibi fac me
iamque placere.[1]

Or he adapts the sapphic measure to rime,

fac mihi signum,   pie rex, benignum,
quin et indignum,   rogo, redde dignum,
ut canam laudum   tibi, Christe, metrum
         nunc et in aevum.[2]

But he sings his clearest note in the lovely poem he wrote in
his exile for a young friend, whom he had, perhaps, known at
Orbais. The young man had asked him for a song, but how
can he sing in a strange land?

Ut quid iubes,   pusiole,
quare mandas,   filiole,
     carmen dulce   me cantare,
     cum sim longe   exul valde
         intra mare?
     o cur iubes canere?

magis mihi,   miserule,
flere libet,   puerule,
     plus plorare   quam cantare
     carmen tale,   iubes quale,
         amor care.
     o cur iubes canere?[3]

The arrangement and the richness of the two-syllabled rimes
are very striking, and the rhythmical scheme is entirely
original. Each stanza consists of six verses. The first two
are iambic and the remainder trochaic in rhythm.[4]

The impression of strange and pathetic beauty which this
poem makes at first is not diminished on long acquaintance.
These verses remain a memorial of the troubled life of the man
who matched himself against Raban Maur and Hincmar of
Reims, and died still following his own ways. He confessed
once that he owed little to any man's instruction. He was
writing to Ratramnus, and he showed his freedom of spirit

[1] *Poet. Lat. Aevi Car.* iii. 724–5.
[2] ib., p. 727.
[3] ib., p. 731.

[4] See Gaselee, *Oxford Book of Medie-*
val Latin Verse (1928), p. 215.

by writing in hexameters which he adorned at intervals with
leonine rimes:[1]

> . . . nimium metuo tibi respondere, quod imo
> in sensu teneo, quia torpeo pectore bruto
> inscitiae plenus multoque errore volutus,
> sermone incultus, metri quoque iure solutus,
> quamlibet hoc modico usus sim sub tempore pauco,
> namque magisterio vix uno subditus anno:
> nec didici deinceps, dubiis ambagibus anceps,
> stultorum princeps, abrupta per omnia praeceps.
> nemo mihi fuit dux: ideo minime patuit lux
> septo peccatis, quantum pietas nisi gratis
> caelestis tribuit, cui virtus gloria laus sit.
> raro hoc per me fit: per te peto crebrius ut sit.

With this confession we could happily leave Gottschalk, but
it has been suggested that he is the author of the famous
Eclogue which passed under the name of Theodulus[2] and
became a text-book in the medieval schools. The name
Theodulus (Θεοῦ δοῦλος) corresponds, according to this theory,
to Godescalc or Gottschalk,[3] and the fact that the poem is
written for the most part in hexameters with a simple leonine
rime or assonance is adduced as a further argument.[4] But it
is safer to say that the eclogue belongs to the same century as
Gottschalk, and that the author, though he belonged to the
north, is still unknown.

The poem describes a learned contest between Pseustis, a
shepherd who hailed from Athens, and Alithia, a maiden
shepherdess of the lineage of David. Fronesis is the arbitress.
They conduct their poetical strife in quatrains. Pseustis draws
on antique mythology; Alithia answers with as close a parallel
as possible from the Old Testament. The medieval student
who read the eclogue with his master's comments would learn
a great deal of profane and of sacred lore. The author had
drawn upon Ovid, Virgil (with Servius), and Martianus Capella,

[1] Carmen ad Rathramnum, *Poet.
Lat. Aevi Car.* iii. 733 sqq. These are
among the earliest developed leonine
hexameters; for a poem with leonine
rimes included in Walafrid's works,
see ib. ii. 397. If it is not Walafrid's,
it is probably addressed to him by a
pupil.

[2] Theoduli eclogam ed. J. Osternacher, Urfahr, 1902 (*Fünfter Jahres-
bericht des bischöflichen Privat-Gym-
nasiums am Kollegium Petrinum in
Urfahr*, 1901–2).

[3] J. Osternacher, 'Die Überlieferung
der Ecloga Theoduli', *Neues Archiv*,
xl (1915), pp. 331 sqq.

[4] K. Strecker, against Manitius,
Gesch. i. 573, contends that there is a
great difference between the hexameters of Gottschalk and those of
'Theodulus'. Gottschalk, for example,
loves elision, while 'Theodulus' avoids
it; see Strecker, 'Ist Gottschalk der
Dichter der *Ecloga Theoduli?*' *Neues
Archiv*, xlv (1923), p. 18.

and of course he did not neglect the Christian poets.[1] He chose a very agreeable way of reviewing heathen mythology while demonstrating at the same time the superiority and truth of the divine revelation. But the demonstration is in the end wearisome, and when Pseustis calls for mercy, confessing himself beaten, the reader is glad to hear Fronesis telling Alithia that it is time to desist, and hinting that it is possible to have too much of a good thing:

> mortales cuncti quod contendunt adipisci
> nec, si perficiant, vitae discrimina curant,
> ex insperato Dominus tibi contulit ultro:
> ut cessare velis, devictus supplicat hostis.

> Trëicius vates commovit pectine Manes,
> te moveant lacrimae; iam tollit cornua Phoebe,
> sol petit oceanum, frigus succedit opacum:
> desine quod restat, ne desperatio laedat.

About the year 827 there came to the monastery a young man from Reichenau, who was to complete his education under the care of the Abbot, Raban Maur. This was Walafrid Strabo, a Swabian of humble birth, who had passed most of his life in the cloister at Reichenau, and showed such remarkable promise in the arts that he was sent to Fulda to study theology. At the early age of fifteen he had astonished his fellow-monks by his versification of the vision of hell and heaven which had been granted to his dying master Wettin and which Haito had set forth in prose for their edification.[2]

So Walafrid came to Fulda with some reputation as a poet, and it is not surprising that, with his frank and enthusiastic nature, he made friends with Gottschalk. But they were soon parted. Gottschalk wandered away; Walafrid went to the court to teach the young Charles, the son of Louis the Pious. But the friends still exchanged poems, as we learn from a poetical epistle which Walafrid sent after Gottschalk, of whose whereabouts he had no certain news:[3]

> ut requies lasso, sitienti ut dulcis aquae fons,
> lac maternum agnis, pluvia ut squalentibus arvis,
> carcere constrictis ut lucis vena diurnae:
> sic optata palatinas mihi metra tuapte
> scripta manu nebulas vero pepulere nitore.

Walafrid had a genuine poetical gift, and this was perhaps the real bond between him and Gottschalk. He must have loved

---

[1] Manitius, *Gesch.* i. 573. [2] *Poet. Lat. Aevi Car.* ii. 303. [3] ib., p. 363.

his Virgil and Ovid, and like Theodulf and Modoin he dared
to speak of his Muse—his *Scintilla* or 'spark' of genius—as a
poet should. For while he was at Aachen in the service of Louis
he wrote an eclogue, a conversation between himself and his
Muse, on the subject of the statue of Theodoric which Charles
the Great had brought from Ravenna and had set up in front of
his palace. The eclogue begins conventionally with the description of Spring.[1] Walafrid asks his Muse why in the season of
lengthening days and pleasant shade she will not answer to
his desires. He does this with reminiscences of Horace,[2] of
Virgil, and of Lucretius.[3] Scintilla replies that the poets of old
loved the lonely hills, the wooded valleys, or secluded caves.
The tumult and the filth of the city are abhorrent to the Muses.
So he must not be annoyed if she answers her poet briefly.

Then Walafrid asks about the statue which stands before
the palace. Scintilla replies with a description of Theodoric as
a monster of pride and of cruelty. Not only his unorthodoxy,
but his treatment of Boëthius is evidently before the poet's
mind, for a reminiscence of the *De Consolatione* shows that the
martyr-philosopher was in his thoughts.

But after a while Walafrid urges the Muse to change the
subject, for it is time to sing the praises of the 'princes':

> dignum est, ut video, praemissis tristibus ergo
> debita principibus laudum persolvere vota.

Scintilla takes up the tale, and continues to the end with a panegyric on Louis, his family, and his household officials. First
Louis is compared with Moses—though Moses had only the
shadow (the old law), and Louis has the 'body' or the reality.[4]
Moses had only the movable tabernacle; Louis has the great
church which his father built at Aachen, not in a desert but
near the murmuring waters and the green meadows of the
park, where all kinds of animals roam:

> ludunt pecudesque feraeque,
> uri cum cervis, timidis cum caprea dammis.
> si quoque deinde velis, saltabunt rite leones,
> ursus, aper, panthera, lupus, linces, elephanti,

---

[1] On such beginnings with a nature-
description see H. Walther, *Das Streitgedicht in der lat. Lit. des Mittelalters*,
p. 42. He suggests that such beginnings passed from the *Eclogue* into the
poems of the 'wandering scholars' of
later times, but they were more probably of popular origin.

[2] 'Dulce decus' (*Poet. Lat. Aevi Car.*

ii. 370). This is from *Odes*, i. 1, but
Walafrid borrowed it, I think, from the
Conflictus veris et hiemis, as it is un-
likely that he knew Horace at first
hand.

[3] 'Genus omne animantum' (*Lucr.*
i. 4).

[4] Cf. Coloss. ii. 16, 'quae sunt umbra
futurorum: corpus autem Christi.'

rinoceros, tigres venient, domitique dracones,
sortiti commune boumque oviumque virectum.
omnia pacatis animalia litibus assunt,
aeriae summo quercus de vertice laetis
commodulantur aves rostris et suave susurrant.[1]

This is once again the method of the catalogue, which never lost favour. Walafrid, who seems to be speaking, though it is Scintilla who nominally still holds the field, turns at the sound of music to watch the procession. But first he celebrates the hydraulic organ which George the Venetian had installed in the palace. It is for Walafrid not least among the wonders of the world. Louis and his following seem to be passing along the bridge or portico between the palace and the basilica. The Emperor, again designated by the name of Moses, is arrayed in royal state. Is it Solomon or David that the poet sees? Certainly it is not Herod. Then, when he has been able to collect himself, he sees the 'hornèd face of the holy father in its glory', for, like Moses, Louis by his piety had held converse with God.

It is clear that Walafrid had learned the old lesson of the rhetorician—when in doubt throw all restraint to the winds. Louis is invested with the glory of Moses newly descended from the Mount. Lothair, the son who stands at the right of Louis, is Joshua, and Louis the German, who stands at the left, is Jonathan. Pippin is not present; so he occupies only three verses. The longest panegyric is reserved for Judith and her son Charles, for they are nearer to Walafrid than any of the other members of the royal family. They are Rachel and Benjamin. But she is in virtue and piety like the Judith after whom she is named; and, as she plays the organ with skill, she is like Miriam, who 'took the timbrel in her hand, and all the women went out after her with timbrels and with dances':[2]

tympana raucisona pulsavit pelle Maria,
organa dulcisono percurrit pectine Iudith.

The weakness of her sex has its compensation in her intellect, her character, and her piety. Next comes Aaron in his priestly vestments—Hilduin the arch-chaplain, Abbot of S. Denis, a stately figure—and with him is Bezeleel—Einhard, the little man with a great soul, who served Louis as he had served his mighty father. Lastly there is Grimald, Walafrid's beloved master, who here takes Angilbert's title of Homer; he had

---

[1] *Poet. Lat. Aevi Car.* ii. 374.   [2] Exod. xv. 20.

been brought from the peace of Reichenau, where he enjoyed
the company of the Muses, to the cares of the court:

> quamvis subter agas regum tabularia vitam,
> non te praetereo; specubusne latebis, Homere?
> novi namque Sicana tibi spelea placere,
> solus ubi Musis Musarum et amore fruaris.
> saepe tamen magnis victoribus optima cudis
> carmina: tempus erit rutilo te sole calere.[1]

Here the poet thinks to make an end, for he is not equal to
the task of celebrating all the members of the court. But he
is discovered, and is brought, it would appear, into the presence
of the Emperor. Or is it the Muse who has declared her name,
and her business there? In any case the poet is now free to
complete his eclogue with the praise of the pious Emperor, and
to fling a parting malediction at Theodoric, who had been the
occasion of his song:

> Tetrice stulte, vale; quia te suadente canebam,
> non mirum est vitiis nostram sordere Camenam.
> nec mihi materiem nec verba ostendere nosti:
> haec tibi si qua ferat ratio, tum, Musa, nitebis;
> hic calamum placuit, Vesper iam, figere, surgit.

In this poem Walafrid showed that he was well able to carry
on the tradition of the court poets. He is clearly influenced
by his Carolingian predecessors, and especially by Modoin, who
survived into the reign of Louis. But, as Ebert observed long
ago,[2] it is not the Emperor but his wife Judith who is now the
patron of letters. It is to her that Walafrid looks, and to her
that his devotion goes out:

> pacis amatrix,   lucis amica,   quae bona cuncta
> mente tueris,   haec mea clemens   percipe scripta.[3]

This is how he talks to his 'Augusta', the beautiful and accomplished woman whose graciousness and kindness had made his
stay at the court more happy than he could have expected.

For his heart was always drawn again to Reichenau, the
island monastery, and to the memory of his dear masters. And
at last he was allowed to return, this time as Abbot. Here he
had had but little rest when he became involved in the strife
between the sons of Louis. He had to leave his abbey, and did
not return until 842. Seven peaceful years followed. Then in

---

[1] *Poet. Lat. Aevi Car.* ii. 377.   ii. 157.
[2] *Allgemeine Gesch. d. Lit. d. M. A.*   [3] *Poet. Lat. Aevi Car.* ii. 378.

August 849 Walafrid died as he was journeying on a mission to Charles the Bald, his former pupil.

His love of Reichenau[1] is celebrated in the delightful poem *De cultura hortorum* (sometimes called *Hortulus*), in which he describes one by one the flowers and herbs which he had tended in the cloister garden, explaining their medicinal virtues and pointing out their allegorical significance or their mythological relationships. Although Walafrid had read the Columella which he found in the library at Fulda,[2] and although he knew the pseudo-Apuleius *de Herbarum virtutibus*, he wrote unfettered by antiquity, and set forth what he knew from experience or had drawn from the stores of ancestral German wisdom. He dedicated his little work to his old master Grimald, who was then Abbot of Weissenburg. The dedication is a picture of past days, when Grimald had sat in the little garden at Reichenau, under the trees in autumn, near the 'broken shade' of the peach, while the boys gathered the fruit, too large for their small hands, and played happily about their master:

> Something the book may have of use to thee.
> Read it, my father, prune it of its faults,
> And strengthen with thy praise what pleases thee.
> And may God give thee in thy hands the green
> Unwithering palm of everlasting life.[3]

It would be foolish to attempt to compress into a few lines of prose the content of a poem whose charm can be gathered only by leisurely and patient study of its text.[4] In the *De cultura hortorum* we see the best that the Carolingian renaissance could offer in the way, not of pure poetry, but of sincere creation, simple and unaffected by fashions; and the truest witness to this is the delight we take in following the poet about his garden as he expounds the virtues of sage and rue, horehound and fennel, or speaks at length on the marvellous pumpkin whose uses cease not at the table, for the rind can be made

---

[1] This love for the island monastery is expressed also in the Sapphic poem (written from Reichenau in his exile) (ib. ii. 412):

sancta sis semper nimiumque cara
mater, ex sanctis cuneis dicata,
laude, profectu, meritis, honore,
insula felix.

[2] On Columella in the Middle Ages and especially at Fulda see Manitius, *Gesch.* i. 309 sq.

[3] *Poet. Lat. Aevi Car.* ii. 350; this translation is by Miss Waddell (*Medieval Latin Lyrics*, p. 115).

[4] For those who find the Latin crabbed and the allusions obscure, Mr. R. S. Lambert has supplied a sprightly and attractive verse-rendering in *Hortulus*, or *The Little Garden*, London 1923 (printed by the Stanton Press in an edition limited to 132 copies). There is a copy in the London Library.

into a bottle, which will hold 'uncorrupted for a long while the gifts of generous Lyaeus'.[1] A recent writer has said, 'It is Walafrid's *Hortulus* that still is green, while the volumes of the *Glossa Ordinaria* do but gather dust.'[2] Well, it seems that we can now absolve Walafrid of all responsibility for what Dom Wilmart has called 'that poor rhapsody';[3] he is not the author of the *Glossa*, but no one can deprive him of his beloved 'little garden'.[4]

The other poems of Walafrid are mainly religious. Manitius has remarked[5] that Walafrid is the first poet after Boëthius to make use of a great variety of lyrical measures; for he employs asclepiad, glyconic, adonic, and anacreontic verses, besides hendecasyllabics, the iambic dimeter and trimeter, and sapphics. He was diligently read by his contemporaries, who admired him as the best poet of his day. His old master, Raban, writing his epitaph, said:

> nam docuit multos, metrorum iure peritus
> dictavit versus, prosa facundus erat.[6]

Walafrid once singled out among the writers of his time Florus, deacon of Lyons.[7] He was sending a poetical epistle to Agobard, the Bishop of that city, and he praised Florus, who was then the right-hand man of Agobard and a mighty defender of the faith.

Florus, of course, wrote verses, but they are for the most part religious. Although he composed his elegiacs according to the accepted methods, that is to say with frequent borrowings from Ovid, he pretended to frown on the secular tendency of the poems of his friend Modoin, and in a lengthy epistle, in which he drew upon the *Fasti*, the *Remedium Amoris*, the *Metamorphoses*, the *Amores*, and the *Epistolae* of Ovid, he congratulated the Bishop on having forsaken, on one occasion at least, the profane muse:

> crede pater, multo gaudent mea viscera motu,
>   et laetante anima vix mea lingua silet:
> quod me non meritum tanto dignaris amore,
>   tamque pio affaris carmine tamque sacro,
> quod non Assyrii violatur fluminis undis,
>   nec sordescit aquis, turbide Nile, tuis,
> sed liquido potius Iordanis manat ab amne,
>   quo pulcher Christi laetificatur ager.

---

[1] *Poet. Lat. Aevi Car.* ii. 340.
[2] H. Waddell, *Medieval Latin Lyrics*, p. 317.   [3] *Rev. Bénéd.*, 1928, p. 95.
[4] The title *Hortulus* has, however, no authority besides the original *De*
cultura hortorum, which corresponds exactly with the contents of the poem.
[5] *Gesch.* i. 313.
[6] *Poet. Lat. Aevi Car.* ii. 239.
[7] ib., p. 357.

iam nunc Castalii siccetur fontis harena,
    Aoniumque nemus fistula nulla sonet,
Laurus Apollineae marcescat denique silvae,
    cumque suis baccis alba ligustra cadant.[1]

It is plain that in his youth even Florus had wandered in the 'Aonian grove' and had heard the music of the reed, but, like Alcuin, he thought it more prudent to repent, and he looked askance, we may believe, at the Irish scholars who had found their way into the northern monasteries, bringing not only dangerous speculations like those of Erigena, against which he directed a withering treatise,[2] but also manuscripts of Petronius[3] and undisguised delight in Virgil and Ovid.

Outside the southern limits of the Frankish kingdom learning and poetry still lingered among the Spanish Christians. Paulus Albarus, though of Jewish origin, was a staunch defender of the Christian faith. He had been educated by Abbot Speraindeo of Cordova, and in his poems he made use of illustrious predecessors like Eugenius and Isidore. He knew Aldhelm and, significantly, Theodulf of Orleans.[4] He loved to write of the beauty of natural things; and we have three poems of his in praise of the nightingale. But Paul had nothing to say that had not been better said already:[5]

Vox, filomela, tua metrorum carmina vincit
    et superat miris flamina magna modis.
vox, filomela, tua dulcis super organa pergit,
    cantica nam suabe fulgide magna canit.
vox, philomela, tua superat sic gutture Musas,
    ut citharas vincat sivila ter tua, ter.
sicque liras dulces cordarum pollice ductas
    excellis mulcens, corda fobens hominum.
cedat omnigena, tivi vox quoque garrula cedat,
    iudice me carmen fulgeat (h)omne tuum.
nulla certe tivi equeter nunc cantibus ales:
    et victrix hominum voce feras superum.
dic ergo varias blande modulamine voces
    et funde solite gutture sepe melos.
porrige dulcissonum gaudenti pectore plectrum
    et dulce tibias gutture clange sonans.
gloria summa deo dico per secula Christo,
    qui nobis famulis gaudia tanta dedit.[6]

This is the first nightingale poem. The others do little more

---

[1] *Poet. Lat. Aevi Car.* ii. 553.

[2] 'Libellus adversum cuiusdam vanissimi hominis, qui cognominatur Iohannes, ineptias et errores.'

[3] See below p. 239.

[4] Cf. Manitius, *Gesch.* i. 422, 426.

[5] Paulus Albarus' poems are in *Poet. Lat. Aevi Car.* iii. 126 sqq. On his metrical defects see Meyer, *Rythmik*, ii. 13, n. 1.   [6] *Poet. Lat. Aevi Car.* iii. 126.

than repeat the same ideas, and there is but small merit in Paul's epigram on the cock:[1]

> Gallus se excutiens pennis et voce resultat
>   dulcissono crispans gutture, pulcre sonans.
> hic repetit altas nocturno tempore voces
>   et luce previa carmina clare canit.
> hic laudes domino pandit per ora dierum,
>   excitat et pigros sepius hic recinens.

§ 4. *The Ninth Century.*

(ii) *Irish Influence.*

The influx of Irish scholars in the ninth century left its mark on the poetry of the monastic schools. They came, bringing with them, besides an acquaintance with Greek which in most of them did not go very far, the desire to create a favourable impression by a parade of learning, which was tempered by an easy-going attitude on non-essentials and a willingness to take whatever their patrons could be induced to provide. For they came as pilgrims and had to make their way by their wits.

One of them, S. Donatus, who became Bishop of Fiesole (*circ.* 850), and, from his lovely hill-top city, thought often of the country which he had left, composed some verses on the Ireland of his memories, a golden land of peace and valour and faith:[2]

> Finibus occiduis describitur optima tellus
>   nomine et antiquis Scottia scripta libris.
> dives opum, argenti, gemmarum, vestis et auri,
>   commoda corporibus, aere, putre solo.
> melle fluit pulchris et lacte Scottia campis,
>   vestibus atque armis, frugibus arte, viris.
> ursorum rabies nulla est ibi, saeva leonum
>   semina nec unquam Scottica terra tulit.
> nulla venena nocent nec serpens serpit in herba
>   nec conquesta canit garrula rana lacu.
> in qua Scottorum gentes habitare merentur,
>   inclita gens hominum milite, pace, fide.

The same love of the Western island is enshrined in the charming verses of Colman, an Irishman who was settled on the continent in the early ninth century. He bears the curious appellation of 'Colmanus nepos Cracavist' in one manuscript,[3]

---

[1] *Poet. Lat. Aevi Car.* iii. 128.

[2] ib., p. 691; see M. Esposito, *J.T.S.* xxxiii (1932), p. 129 sq., on Donatus of Fiesole. Esposito thinks that Donatus may also be the author of the poem addressed to Abbot Dungal, printed by

K. Strecker, 'Ein neuer Dungal?' in *Zeitschr. für roman. Philologie*, xli (1921), pp. 566 sqq.

[3] Esposito, p. 116. The verses are on pp. 116 sqq.

and in the poem in question he is addressing his namesake, a Colman who was returning to his native country. With his memories of the pathetic beauty of Virgil's verse and the added memories of his home this Colman holds us as we read his lines and think of him, probably at Reims, too old to cross the sea again, and conscious as well that he was comfortably settled in the Frankish kingdom.

> Dum subito properas dulces invisere terras,
> deseris et nostrae refugis consortia vitae,
> festinas citius precibus nec flecteris ullis,
> nec retinere valet blandae suggestio vocis.
> vincit amor patriae. quis flectere possit amantem?
> nec sic arguerim deiectae taedia mentis.
> nam mihi praeteritae Christus si tempora vitae
> et priscas iterum renovaret ab ordine vires,
> si mihi quae quondam fuerat floresceret aetas
> et nostros subito faceret nigrescere canos,
> forsitan et nostram temptarent talia mentem.
> tu modo da veniam pigraeque ignosce senectae,
> quae nimium nostris obstat nunc aemula votis.
> audi doctiloquo cecinit quod carmine vates:
> omnia fert aetas, gelidus tardante senecta
> sanguis hebet, frigent effetae in corpore vires,
> siccae nec calido complentur sanguine venae.
> me maris anfractus lustranda et littora terrent.
> at tu rumpe moras celeri sulcare carina,
> Colmanique tui semper Colmane memento.
> iam iam nunc liceat fida te voce monere;
> pauca tibi dicam vigili quae mente teneto:
> non te pompiferi delectet gloria mundi,
> quae volucri vento vanoque simillima somno
> labitur et vacuas fertur ceu fumus in auras,
> fluminis et validi cursu fluit ocior omni.
> vade libens patriae quoniam te cura remordet.
> omnipotens genitor, nostrae spes unica vitae,
> qui maris horrisonos fluctus ventosque gubernat,
> det tibi nunc tutas crispantis gurgitis undas,
> ipse tuae liquidis rector sit navis in undis,
> aequore nubiferi devectum flatibus Euri
> reddat ad optatae Scottorum littora terrae.
> tunc valeas fama felix multosque per annos
> vivas egregiae capiens praeconia vitae.
> sic ego praesentis nunc gaudia temporis opto
> ut tibi perpetuae contingant praemia vitae.

John the Irishman, known as Erigena, came to Laon and had a solid knowledge of Greek to offer. If he was not exempt from vanity he had reason to know that he had few superiors

in the world of learning. For who else could write to Charles
the Bald like this?

θαυμαστῷ βασιλεῖ Καρόλῳ ӡωή τε φάος τε.
ὀρθόδοξος ἄναξ φράγγων, τῷ Δόξα τιμή τε.[1]

And who, indeed, could fail to wish to imitate him when he
wrote so learnedly and with such strange words about the
great Dionysius?

> lumine sidereo Dionysius auxit Athenas
>   Ariopagites magnificusque sophos,
> primo commotus Phoebo subeunte Selena,
>   tempora quo stauro fixus erat dominus.[2]
> mox ut conversus mira stupefactus elympsi (v.l. eclypsi),
>   consequitur gaudens Ierothea ducem.
> quo mox edoctus praeclarus namque magister
>   pneumatis excelsi fonte renatus erat.
> nec mora: perfulgens caelestis luce sophiae
>   Attidas edocuit, de quibus ortus adest.
> namque ferunt Paulum, qui Christum sparsit in orbem,
>   ipsi felices imposuisse manus.
> ast mox perfectus doctoris Symmachus instar
>   rexit Cecropidas pervigil archiereus.
> alta dehinc volitans Paulum super astra secutus
>   empyrii caeli tertia regna videt.
> suspicit at seraphym primos sanctosque cherubym
>   aethereosque thronos, quo sedet ipse deus;
> post hos virtutes, dominatus atque potentes
>   agminibus sacris enitet ordo sequens;
> ΑΡΧΩΝ ΑΡΧΑΓΕΛΩΝ ΤΕ ΧΟΡΩΝ ΑΓΕΛΩΝ ΤΕ ΤΕΛΑΥΓΩΝ
>   mentibus oyraniis tertia taxis inest.
> hos igitur numeros terno ter limite septos
>   praedicti patris mystica dicta docent.[3]

The baneful influence of such verses extended to many of the
poets of the ninth century, who had for their masters either
Irishmen or the pupils of Irishmen.[4]   Heiric of Auxerre is a
typical product of Irish influences. He had studied at Laon
under the Irishman, Elias, who had been a pupil of Erigena.
He picked up a little Greek, which he loved to parade in his
verses,[5] and he even provided glosses to his own metrical life
of S. Germain.[6] This poem is of interest to us because each
book is preceded by a *praefatio* in some lyric measure taken
from Prudentius or from Horace.[7] The collection of excerpts

---

[1] *Poet. Lat. Aevi Car.* iii. 546.
[2] 'Dionysius' says that he was in Egypt at the time of the Crucifixion and, along with Polycarp, witnessed the darkness of the eclipse.
[3] *Poet. Lat. Aevi Car.* iii. 548.
[4] A collection of poems in mixed Latin and Greek is to be found in *Poet. Lat. Aevi Car.* iii. 685 sqq.
[5] *Christian-Latin Poetry*, p. 200.
[6] *Poet. Lat. Aevi Car.* iii. 432 sqq.
[7] Cf. Manitius, *Gesch.* i. 503.

from classical authors, which Heiric made under the influence of his Irish masters, is of great importance, and it is with surprise that we come upon a Petronius in the library at Auxerre, whither it had doubtless voyaged from Ireland.

Ermenrich of Ellwangen, who was educated at Fulda, Reichenau, and S. Gall, came finally under similar influences, and if at the same time he made the acquaintance of a large number of classical authors, he allowed his small knowledge of Greek to ruin his Latin verse.[1] It is hard to resist the conclusion that the decline in the standard of verse-composition was in part due to Irish influence.

In a long epistle to Grimald, then Abbot of S. Gall,[2] Ermenrich, while pretending to pay homage to the illustrious master whom he was addressing, made a parade of his own learning by presenting in turn a multitude of subjects in grammar or in theology which he attempted to discuss without acknowledging the sources on which he drew. At one point he has to speak of Virgil, and he breaks off his discussion in this fashion:

> Let us renounce, my father, let us renounce Maro as a liar along with his Sinon, and leave him buried in the bottom of Styx with Apollo and his Muses. There let him embrace his Proserpine, and listen to Orpheus harping for his Eurydice to the infernal gods. . . . Let the heavenly King curse such vain imaginings. And what can I call these same things but the droppings of the horses that draw your cart? Whence not inaptly Ennius the poet, when one asked him what he sought in Virgil, replied: 'I seek gold in dung.'[3] And as you know, just as dung prepares the field to bring forth corn more abundantly, so the words of the pagan poets, foul though they be, since they are not true, are yet of much aid in the comprehension of the divine word.

Ermenrich found them useful, too, the moment he sat down to verse-composition, and he did not hesitate to pillage freely from Ausonius, Theodulf, and Modoin. He borrowed from the Irish the tiresome habit of mixing Greek with his Latin. So in his letter to Grimald, in the course of which he breaks into verse, he writes:[4]

> quod si non cesset [sc. livor] lacerans mea dicta susurro,
>   hoc ipse exponat posco problema tibi:

---

[1] Cf. Manitius, *Gesch.* i. 498.

[2] *M.G.H. Epist.* v, pp. 536 sqq. His testimony to Irish learning is on p. 575, 'Sed neque de Hibernia insula, quae inter Spaniam et Brittanniam iacet, silendum censeo, unde nobis tanti luminis iubar processit', etc.

[3] Our clever author has reversed the names: it was, of course, Virgil who was reading Ennius.

[4] *M.G.H., Epist.* v. 569; for other poems of Ermenrich see *M.G.H., SS.* ii. 32 sq.; x. 11 sqq.; xv. 155.

oenon paleon pimelin gallan eleon,[1]
et nos miraris dulcia nosse tua.
neon ide lalo rema sison ripho ariston:[2]
vescere quis poteris tuque poeta tuis.
phrontistes phronimos phisa philophonia nechros:[3]
hoc fecit Christus primus in orbe deus.

By such means Ermenrich was able to advertise his learning, and Ebert[4] has suggested that nothing else can explain his elevation to the Bishopric of Passau in 865.

Mico of S. Riquier was a better poet than Ermenrich. He took a great interest in prosody, and made a collection of extracts for use in school. Mico based his work on already existing collections which were derived from a Lombardic original. His words are arranged alphabetically—'currit enim,' he says of his work, 'commode per alfabetum, ut facilius inveniatur, quod ab amante requiritur.'[5] Such a collection gives us an idea of the kind of assistance of which the would-be versifier stood in need. Here Prudentius, Sidonius, Prosper, and Fortunatus appear by the side of Horace, Virgil, Martial, and Juvenal. The first word is 'Alfabetum', and the example is:

> hoc discunt omnes ante alfa et beta puellae.
>
> *Juv.* xiv. 209.

The next is 'accidit',

> accidit haec fessis etiam fortuna Latinis.
>
> *Aen.* xii. 593.

And so on. Mico's poems, along with those of Fredegard and Odulf, are gathered together in a collection from S. Riquier.[6] Mico's verse consists mainly of inscriptions and epigrams. In one of the poems he requests a friend to send him his Claudian —not the poet, but the author of *de statu animae*—so that he can correct his own bad copy. He adds that he should like his Fortunatus back, if his friend has it, for he does not know what rascal has purloined it.[7]

---

[1] *Ad marg.* 'Vinum butyrum bibe lac oleum.' Bursian transliterated: οἶνον παλαίον, πιμελήν, γάλαν (for γάλα), ἔλαιον.

[2] *Ad marg.* 'Novum vide loquor verbum move sorbeo prandium.' Traube read: νέον ἴδε λαλῶ ῥῆμα. σεῖσον. ῥυφῶ ἄριστον.

[3] *Ad marg.* 'Curator sapiens suffluat studium mortuus.' Traube read: φροντιστὴς φρόνιμος φυσᾷ φιλοπονίᾳ νεκρός.

[4] Ebert, ii. 184.

[5] *Poet. Lat. Aevi Car.* iii. 279.

[6] 'Carmina Centulensia,' in *Poet. Lat. Aevi Car.* iii. 294 sqq.; nos. 1–67 and 152–71 belong to Mico; 68–119 to Fredigard; 120–51 to Odulf. All three were monks at S. Riquier.

[7] ib., p. 335; he makes the same request about Fortunatus in another poem (p. 363), perhaps addressed to Radbert of Corbie.

He has another piece—*de quodam lurgone meribibulo*—on a gluttonous wine-bibber.[1] It is a sorry tale of one who ate and drank, on the invitation of Bacchus, not wisely but too well. It begins with the conventional nature-picture:

> Inter florigeras laeti dum sedimus herbas,
> nostros se Bachus praetulit ante oculos.

Here Mico is parodying the manner of the Eclogue, but the whole poem is rather an example of the German spirit, with its saturnine humour, making its way into verse. German too in its feeling is Fredegard's poem on the thrush whose song had charmed away his toothache.[2] It is worth quoting because it shows how the example of Eugenius was being improved on; for Fredegard is making a personal poem, not an imitative exercise:

> Iam pridem nimium residebam maestus amoeno
> pomerio chiram levam positam subhabensque
> ad malam nimia dentum pro morte doloris.
> vox subito turdi nostras tunc perculit aures
> invalidas dulcis varios imitando volucres.
> ad sonitum galli resonabat gutture tenso;
> post vero merulae morem milvique sonabat;
> inde simul recinens velut aureolus nitidusque,
> bitrisci vocem frangebat et ipse pusilli.
> talia demirans, confestim diffugit ultro
> improbus ille dolor, qui me vexabat amare;
> deinde petens nidum, memetque laborque revisit.
> quem deus apellat, ne me torquere parumper
> exim iam valeat, submisse flagito, noster.
> discite, lectores, avium cantus variarum;
> segnitiem mentis post rumpite nocte dieque,
> quo iugiter domino laudes depromere dignas
> possitis, summa digne et vos audiat arce
> iudiciique die dicat: 'properate, beati,
> sumite nunc vobis ab origine regna parata
> mundi' de messi latitant quo perpete iusti,
> balsama quo redolent, fragrant et lilia semper,
> quo deus omne bonum meritis clemensque rependit
> clementer famulis, gratis quos condidit ipse.

Fredegard was a man of small learning, although he too liked to parade his little Greek; but, if his execution is clumsy, he does attempt a subject with some promise in it, and so goes a long way towards winning our sympathies. Yet we cannot fail to notice that the standard of S. Riquier is not that of Fulda or of Reichenau.[3]

---

[1] ib., p. 362.   [2] ib., p. 332.   [3] Cf. Manitius, *Gesch.* i. 472.

We have spoken hardly of the Frankish poets who wrote under Irish influence; but there was one among the Irish adventurers who must be reckoned as a poet of the rank of the abler among the Carolingians. Sedulius the Irishman—Sedulius Scottus—appeared in Liége about the year 848, in the midst of winter, and, along with his companions, threw himself upon the hospitality of Bishop Hartgar. This coming of the Irish made the fortune of the school, and after the death of Hartgar, Bishop Franco (854–901) continued to protect and help the Irish colony.

The relations between Hartgar and his Irish friends are depicted in a series of poems which show the talent of Sedulius at its best and happiest.[1] Sedulius appears in these poems as priest and scholar. In his *Liber de rectoribus Christianis*, written at a later date[2] and for the benefit of Lothar II, he says, 'Namque hominis naturam Deus hanc esse voluit, ut duarum rerum ipse homo cupidus et appetens esset, religionis et sapientiae.'[3] And in one of the poems he calls himself and his companions,

> doctos grammaticos presbiterosque pios.[4]

Sedulius was doubtless a man of genuine piety, and he is kind enough to show us that he did not take life hardly, any more than the saintly men who had come from Ireland before him. He did not claim to be anything but a sinner; one who ate, drank, invoked the Muses, said his prayers, and slept well:

> Aut lego vel scribo, doceo scrutorve sophian:
>   obsecro celsithronum nocte dieque meum.
> vescor, poto libens, rithmizans invoco Musas,
>   dormisco stertens: oro deum vigilans.
> conscia mens scelerum deflet peccamina vitae:
>   parcite vos misero, Christe Maria, viro.[5]

Like the Carolingian poets, Sedulius held converse with his Muse; he addresses her in a charming dialogue:[6]

> Sacra Camena, refer: quis te decoravit amictu,
>   quis laetam faciem reddidit atque tuam?
> at quis laurigera cinxit caput, oro, corona,
>   unde micas alba pulchrior en edera?

So the Poet speaks, and the Muse answers. Or, appropriately,

---

[1] *Poet. Lat. Aevi Car.* iii. 166 sqq.
[2] 855–9; see Hellmann, *Sedulius Scottus*, p. 5.
[3] ib., 30–1.
[4] *Poet. Lat. Aevi Car.* iii. 168.
[5] ib., p. 225.
[6] ib., p. 225.

it is the Spring-time, and the poet remembers that the king is coming, and must be duly praised:

> floridus ecce venit: campi, florete patentes;
> florescant silvae: floridus ecce venit.
> tempora veris aves celebrant crispante susurro,
> produnt organulis tempora veris aves.
> obsecro: promo tonos, septimplex fistola Musae;
> exuperans cignos, obsecro, prome tonos.
> rex venit ecce pius: regalem texe Camenam;
> dicite vos, Musae: rex venit ecce pius . . .

But his most sumptuous invocation is on account of Bishop Hartgar, 'through whom refreshment is granted to the needy sons of Ireland'. It was composed in the early days of the sojourn at Liége, when the pilgrims were still in the process of 'settling down':

> florida Thespiadum soror ac praenobilis Eglae
> cignea, mellifluos nunc cane, posco, tropos;
> obsecro: Pegaseo flavum caput erige fonte,
> femina doctiloquax organicumque decus;
> syrmate purpureo glaucisque venusta capillis,
> oscula da labiis Sedulio roseis:
> musigenum plectro cytharizans texito carmen
> permulcens aures nobilis Hartgarii.

The good Bishop, if he did not blush, at any rate tolerantly smiled when he read the praises that followed. In spite of their complaints to him about their draughty lodging, the keys that would not fit, the smoky chimney, and the leaky roof,[1] these Irish scholars were his devoted servants, and they were happier when their father was present. If the Bishop goes away Sedulius begins a poetical complaint. Their shepherd is gone, and Tityrus must pipe a sad ditty:[2]

> Tytirus in silvis ego tristis mente remansi:
> absens pastor erat, nulla quiesque fuit.
> quis vos surripuit? Zefirus? Rhenusne bicornis?
> quadrupedale decus vos rapuitne, pater?
> an vos puniceis nobis avexerat alis
> splendidus Aurorae currus Amorque volans?
> te magis elegit terrarum nobile sidus
> ac Thitona suum sprevit amore tui—
> an mage credendum, quod vos pia dextra tonantis
> angelicusque simul fertque refertque chorus?

Hartgar goes to Rome; Sedulius, in epanaleptic elegiacs,[3] calls

---

[1] *Poet. Lat. Aevi Car.* iii. 169;   [2] *Poet. Lat. Aevi Car.* iii. 167; cf. also
Christian-Latin Poetry, pp. 193–4.   no. v, ib., p. 169.   [3] ib., p. 170.

on the Muses, on the 'daughter of Zion', on Rome, on Father
Tiber to bring him safely back. For the Meuse of his home
weeps for him, and calls for him; the groves murmur, the hills
and valleys lift up their voices, and the woods are full of the
lamentation of the Dryads. The Bishop has to come over the
Alps; but let him come as Hannibal came before, though
Hannibal lost an eye on the journey. May Hartgar find all
things easy—flowers in the fields when the Alps are past,
honey flowing, and no stint of the gifts of Bacchus. May
Aries, Gemini, Cancer, and Leo bring him back. The spring
comes with good omen for his return:

> ver redit ecce novum secum pia gaudia portans,
>   florida cuncta ferens ver redit ecce novum.
> tristibus exoritur nobis nunc sidus amoenum
>   solamenque pium tristibus exoritur.
> nunc et oliva micat, nunc vitis florida gemmat
>   palmaque florescit, nunc et oliva micat.
> cedrus adest Libani non falso nomine dicta,
>   cuncti laetemur: cedrus adest Libani.

There is a great deal more in the same strain, in this and in
another poem.[1] There is also a complaint, no less heartfelt,
from the Irish monks, that they were suffering from the 'twofold beast, hunger and thirst', or to use the order in which
Sedulius puts them, 'thirst and hunger'.[2] They were asked to
drink beer which was yellow indeed, but was never the gift
of Ceres:

> nos sitis atque fames conturbat, bestia duplex,
>   vulnificis rostris nos laceratque suis.
> nec nos oblectat praedives copia rerum,
>   sed nos excruciat horrida pauperies;
> nec nos oblectant dulciflua dona Liei
>   mellifluusque medus domata nostra fugit;
> nec nos oblectat cacavus biscoctaque Mosa,
>   flavicomae Cereris gratia dulcis abest.
> tenuida[3] nos macerat, crudelis bestia, sophos;
>   optime Christe, rogo, respice nos, domine:
> nec gustu facilis, nulli potabilis ipsa
>   est quia nec Cereris dulcida progenies;
> non est Iordanis, non amnis filia Mosae,
>   sed torrens Cedron turbidus hanc genuit.
> haec sophicae mentis cunctas obnubilat artes,
>   laetitiam removet tristitiamque gerit;
> flavicomum Cereris mentitur habere colorem:
>   di, talem terris hanc removete feram;

---

[1] *Poet. Lat. Aevi Car.* iii. 172.   [3] i.e. meagreness of fare.
[2] ib., p. 177.

Laetheo fluvio vosmet summergite monstrum
   seu Stigiis undis condite tale nefas,
illic quo valeat crudeles solvere poenas:
   quae nos excruciat, praemia digna luat.
quid moror in verbis ventosque lacesso querelis?
   o pater, has geminas, obsecro, vince, feras;
large salutiferum contra vulnuscula, praesul,
   Sedulio famulo da cataplasma tuo.
ast his versicolis risit pius ille relectis
   ac sophicis votis prospera cuncta dedit.

How could the Bishop have failed to give them what they
wanted? The next request was for three rams (*multones*), again
in epanaleptic verse.[1] It is Tityrus who sings, and Hartgar is
Daphnis,

Daphnis amoenus adest pastor bonus atque beatus;
   Tytire, plaude manu: Daphnis amoenus adest.

The rams are admonished and made to learn that they are
being sacrificed for good ends. Their fleeces will cover the
scholars in winter, and their skins will make parchment for
immortal verse:

vellere deque tuo pellantur frigora multa,
   nos defende, precor, vellere deque tuo
pellis et exuviis sit kartula famaque perpes,
   nomen sparge polo pellis et exuviis.
despice sic miseram, meliorem delige vitam,
   multo, brevem vitam despice sic miseram.

Yes, the ram may perhaps win a place in the starry skies, a
wondrous immortality:

mox Aries caeli fors eris astrigeri.

'In any case, Ram,' says Sedulius, 'without you I can't write
or compose many songs; without you, I weep, I cannot write.'

scribere non valeo nec multas ferre Camenas:
   te sine, multo, fleo, scribere non valeo.

Well might Sedulius and his companions love their venerable
protector. In 854 he was taken away from them, and Sedulius
dedicated a sapphic ode to his memory:

Heu mihi flenti misero poetae:
vix queo verbis resonare maestum
corde conceptum misero dolorem,
   heu, bone Christe.[2]

---

[1] *Poet. Lat. Aevi Car.* iii. 178.   [2] ib., p. 184.

But the swains had soon to tune their reeds to a song of gladness, to welcome Franco, the new shepherd,

> splendide pastor, ave, Franco, lux aurea cosmi.[1]

and they found him a protector if less indulgent at any rate as effective as the old. Reading these poems of Sedulius we seem to watch something of the Irish monastic idyll being transplanted to the continent.[2] There is no talk of discipline, but much grammatical learning, great boast of Greek, and a delighted acceptance of good food and drink.

> Oscula das pacis felicia pocula donans;
> permulces sophicos, optime Bache, viros.
> hic est libertas, Liber hic liberat omnes:
> liber ut esse queam, Liber adesto pater.[3]

Sedulius had, too, the gift of making himself known and remembered by the great.[4] He attached himself to Margrave Eberhard of Friuli, in whose honour he wrote a sapphic ode,[5] in which he compared him with Hercules. He allowed no opportunity to slip by. When Eberhard lost his son Sedulius consoled him with an elegy. When his noble wife Gisla gave birth to a boy, Sedulius reminded them that they could now turn their sorrow into gladness.[6] So Sedulius followed afar in the steps of Fortunatus, and, in his Irish fashion, became a court poet. He addressed verses to the Emperors Lothar and Charles the Bald in turn, and to Louis, king of Germany. For Lothar, as we have said, he composed his *Liber de rectoribus Christianis*, of which Hellmann unkindly remarks that the author saw in it, more than anything else, a welcome opportunity to parade his literary knowledge before the eyes of the Carolingian scholars.[7] The form of the treatise is interesting; it is composed of mingled prose and verse, after the manner of Martianus Capella and of Boëthius.

Sedulius wrote as well grammatical treatises—a commentary on Eutyches and one on Priscian; and he busied himself with the Epistles of Paul. But it is as a poet that he would have wished to live, the poet of harmless pleasures, the poet of books and of wine, the poet who stages the debate of Rose and Lily, intervening in person at the end, and telling how the

---

[1] ib., p. 185.

[2] There is, I suppose, no direct evidence that Sedulius and his friends were actually monks, but the word 'fratres' continually occurs to describe them.

[3] *Poet. Lat. Aevi Car.* iii. 198.

[4] Cf. Manitius, *Gesch.* i. 316.

[5] *Poet. Lat. Aevi Car.* iii. 202.

[6] ib., pp. 201–2.

[7] *Sedulius Scottus*, p. 8. It is interesting to note that Sedulius knew the *Historia Augusta*.

Spring, their father, reconciles the disputing maidens with a kiss. The title of the eclogue is *De rosae liliique certamine idem Sedulius cecinit.*[1] Here the Irish and the German spirit meet, and the Carolingian pastoral, with its memories of Virgil, of Calpurnius, and of Nemesian, and northern memories as well, reaches its close. What it brought was not forgotten. In a happier hour the poetry of nature was to come again, but with a new music.

§ 5. *The End of the Carolingian Age.*

If the literary and intellectual achievement of the ninth century is regarded as a whole, it is seen to be an achievement of no mean order. In spite of the pessimistic assertions of Walafrid or of Lupus of Ferrières,[2] the work began by Charles the Great was being carried on. The monastic schools were to secure the cause of learning until the torch could be handed on to the cathedral schools and the universities. Grammatical studies were unrelentingly pursued in accordance with the example of the Irish, who also made some small knowledge of Greek available to the more promising pupils in the monastic schools. But, best of all, the copying of manuscripts went on apace. Copies were multiplied, the scribes worked busily at them in Tours and Fulda, in Fleury and S. Gall.[3] It is to such industry that we owe the preservation of the greater part of the works of classical authors which have survived to the present day.

If there were few good poets, the study of Latin verse and its composition were part of the regular routine of the schools, and men like Sedulius and Notker had doubtless a real appreciation of the authors whom they had to expound. Ovid was still the model as much as Virgil, and Fortunatus more than any other Christian poet. After Sedulius Scottus the standard of composition definitely fell; for not until the eleventh century do we meet with poets of a similar order who employed the classical metres.

But in the poetry of the tenth century in the monastic centres of the eastern half of the old Frankish Empire there emerges, more clearly than before, the German note. This poetry is being written by men whose mother tongue is not the

---

[1] *Poet. Lat. Aevi Car.* iii. 230.

[2] Cf. Laistner, *Thought and Letters in Western Europe*, p. 205.

[3] Manitius, *Gesch.* i. 251; Laistner, pp. 180 sqq.

offspring of the vulgar Latin, by men who have other memories, other stories, and other poetry to draw upon than those provided by the old Roman civilization through the medium of the school. The importance of such a factor as this will appear as we trace, so far as the available material allows, the development of the Latin lyric in the Middle Ages.

There is, it is true, little sign of specifically national characteristics in the remaining poets of the Carolingian age—in Hincmar, in Agius of Corvey, or in Hucbald of S. Amand.

Hincmar was born about 806. As a boy he went to school at S. Denys, where, as he recalled in later years, he had read the *Cynegetica* of Nemesian.[1] How he achieved greatness, and, as Archbishop of Reims, had a large share in the consolidation of the western part of what had been the Frankish empire, does not concern us here. Like all his educated contemporaries he wrote verse. His poems are mostly religious, but he did once compose an epigram. Frotarius, Bishop of Bordeaux, in a letter to Hincmar had written,

> Remis equum nobis, mulum Burdegala vobis;

and Hincmar replied,

> Remis equum misit, mulum Burdegala nullum:
> aut mulus veniat, aut equus huc redeat.[2]

From which it would appear that Hincmar had lent his brother bishop a horse, and would have it back, or, in its stead, one of the mules for which Bordeaux was famous.

Hincmar was a much hated man, and one of his enemies, John the Irishman, left him an epitaph, which he composed during the Archbishop's lifetime, with free licence for its use:

> Hic iacet Hincmarus cleptes vehementer avarus:
> hoc solum gessit nobile, quod periit.[3]

But the eleventh-century codex of S. Emmeram which contains the epitaph has this inscription:

> hoc epitaphium composuit Iohannes Scotus licet sapiens hereticus tamen.

So John did not, after all, speak the last word.

Agius of Corvey wrote, some time after 874, a long elegiac poem in memory of Hathumod, the first abbess of Gandesheim.[4]

---

[1] Manitius, *Gesch.* i. 339.
[2] *Poet. Lat. Aevi Car.* iii. 415.
[3] ib., p. 553; see Traube, *Abh. d. kgl. Bayr. Akad.* XIX. ii (1891), p. 362 sq.

Hincmar died in 882.
[4] *Poet. Lat. Aevi Car.* iii. 372; for his 'computistic' poems see, ib. iv. 937 sqq.

The most interesting thing about it is that it is in the form of a dialogue. Agius speaks, and there is a *Responsio* in the name of the sorrowing nuns.

Hucbald of S. Amand is a more important figure. He was born about 840, and was a pupil of Heiric at Auxerre, where, as we have seen, Irish influences were strong. It is not surprising, therefore, that Hucbald's studies embraced a variety of subjects, and that he was, after Hincmar's death, called by Archbishop Fulco to Reims to assist in the reform of the schools.[1] He lived into the tenth century, dying in 930 at the age of ninety. He left a number of books to his old home, S. Amand, among which were works of Plato (Chalcidius's partial Latin version of the *Timaeus*) and Seneca, a Virgil, a Priscian, and writings of Alcuin and Raban Maur.[2]

Hucbald is best known for his amazing *Ecloga de Calvis*,[3] a praise and justification of baldness dedicated to Hatto, the bald-headed Archbishop of Mainz.

This learned and impressive defence of baldness is the only philosophic treatment of the subject which has ever been produced, and it has this peculiarity, that every word of the hundred and forty-six verses of which it is composed begins with the letter *c*. The dedication to Hatto is in more sober hexameters; it is interesting because, in relating how the Muse has brought fame to poets, it puts Porfirius beside Virgil and Ovid, and, after telling a couple of stories borrowed from Macrobius through Milo of S. Amand, it broaches in amusing fashion the subject of the poem:

> taceant si forte Camenae
> dactilicae, calvis quisnam, rogo, carmina laudis
> componet pulchris? quisnam, rogo, plena cachinno
> obstruet ora canum circumlatrantia calvum?
> candiduli calvi, concurrite, ferte iuvamen!
> tuque decus summum, calvorum gloria, Calve,
> nostra ad vota fave perque omnia prospera salve!
> perspice prudenti perlustrans pectore parva
> munera Musarum miris modulata melodis.

We need not follow the poet through the dizzy maze of his alliterations, in the course of which he would prove that the best and greatest men have had the honour of being bald—dignitaries of the Church, saintly eremites, men of learning, poets, kings, soldiers, and physicians, to say nothing of Elisha[4] and

[1] Manitius, *Gesch.* i. 588.
[2] ib., p. 590.
[3] *Poet. Lat. Aevi Car.* iv. 265.

[4] Hucbald (p. 270) works in skilfully the words,
   'conscende citus, conscendito, calve.'

Paul. Perhaps the best passage is that in which Hucbald sets forth the skill of the bald physicians:

> Carmina, clarisonae, calvis cantate, Camenae.
> comperies calvos columen conferre cerebro;
> comperies calvos capitis curare catarrhos;
> comperies calvos caecas curare catervas.
> cronica cum cancro ceditque cacexia calvo;
> cardia cor carpens cassatur, colica cessat.
> contrectans calibem concisa carne cohercet
> corruptum capitis cocta cervice cruorem.
> cur complura cano? clandestina cuncta caduci
> corpore confutat, collapsaque corpora curat.
> carmina, clarisonae, calvis cantate, Camenae.

And so on, imperturbably. After this Hucbald's verses 'on the Egyptian days'[1] are tame. No one ventured to imitate his example, and Porfirius himself might have felt that he had met his match. To the eclogue on baldness a scribe added:

> hoc scriptum carmen complet dulcedine mentem.

The subject of baldness tempted another poet, who had perhaps in mind the fable of Phaedrus about the bald man and the fly.[2]

> Stridula musca volans calvum conspexit euntem.
> 'calve viator', ait, 'quo tendis? cede parumper
> perque tuos iuro qui restant retro capillos
> me gratam liceat rostro decerpere sedem.'
> sic ait et trepidum circumvolat inproba calvum.
> at contra ille timens solito caput armat amictu.
> [quid valet en calvus muscae lassatus ab ictu?]

It would hardly appear fitting to leave the Carolingian age on a note of such frivolity. Its best poetry has a different tone. The base is, indeed, the school exercise, the successor of the old rhetorical theme; but it has something more, something gathered from the freshness of everyday life or, better still, from observation in the open air. The eclogues are not merely stiff and formal, the nature-pictures are not at second hand. Bishop Radbod of Utrecht (d. 917), who had studied at the court school of Charles the Bald, where some of the spirit of the great days still lingered, has left a poem on the swallow that built beneath his eaves. There are a few learned touches and a little rhetorical moralizing; but it is a true German product, worth noting as we try to make out the course of medieval nature-poetry:[3]

---

[1] *Poet Lat. Aevi Car.* iv. 272. *Anth. Lat.* ii. 135.
[2] *Phaedr.* v. 3. The poem is in Riese, [3] *Poet. Lat. Aevi Car.* iv. 172.

Est mihi corporeae species aptissima formae,
   quae fore terrigenûm nulli onerosa queat:
vix etenim digitos numerat mensura quaternos,
   formula qua constat corporis arta mei.
unde dei templis fas est mihi ponere nidos
   inque hominum pullos aede fovere meos.
agricolis autem veniens nova gaudia porto;
   garrula nam 'vacuum scindite' clamo 'solum'.
quorum sub laribus modicam dum congero glebam,
   nequiquam augurio spondeo fausta meo.
at mihi mirandum tribuit natura secretum,
   quo medicans pullis lumina reddo meis;
nam mihi Phytagoras hac coedit in arte magistrae,
   quem frustra caecus, ut reparetur, adit.
inde est quod nostro nomen de nomine nascens
   urbe tenus crassis accipit herba locis;
quid qui nosse velit, Grecos primum ore sequatur,
   mox et hirundineam Roma et hirundo dabit.
ergo iuvat nostrum, lector, tibi dicere morem,
   quo mirere magis cuncta creantis opus.
floriferas auras et frondea tempora capto
   tumque per humanas hospitor ipsa domos
atque ibi spectandum cunctis confingo cubile,
   segnis inersque manus quale patrare nequit.
in quo nata mihi praedulcia pignora servo,
   donec me valeant per spatia ampla sequi.
hunc mihi iungo gregem, et volucres mox explico pennas;
   impigra sic totam duco volando diem,
nec tamen id frustra: dum quippe per ardua trano,
   arrident densis aethera laeta satis;
at, cum limosas pennis contingo paludes,
   tum pluvia et ventis, Aeole, tundis agros.
sole dehinc gelido cum ninguida bruma propinquat,
   seu patria pellor seu fugio ipsa mea,
nec dulces nidos nec hospita limina curans,
   sed propriae sortis indita iura sequens.
sic rigidas auras ignotis vito sub antris,
   sic quoque naturae do paradigma tenax.
heus homo, dum causas rerum miraris opertas,
   ne spernas decoris munera quaeso tui:
tu ratione viges—ego sum rationis egena;
   tu post fata manes—fata ego tota sequor.
his quantum superas, tantum me vince creantis
   imperio parens, iussit ut ipse creans.

VI

THE TENTH CENTURY

§ 1. *The School of S. Gall.*

WHEN Columban, wearied by the persecutions to which he and his monks were subjected in the territory of Duke Cunzo of Alemannia, went southwards to Italy and founded the monastery of Bobbio, he left behind him a tall Irishman, who was called by the name of Gallus. Gallus had pleaded that by reason of the weakness of his body—he was wasted by fever—he could not go with his master, and when he had at last regained his strength he went with a young deacon named Hiltibod to find a lonely place where he could build a hut and an oratory, and spend his days in solitude and prayer. 'With desire,' he said, 'hath my soul desired to abide the length of my days in solitude, even as the psalmist admonishes us, saying: Lo, then I got me away far off, and remained in the wilderness: I waited for Him who should save me.'[1]

He was a fisherman, and by the waters of the Steinach he made up his mind to remain. Satisfied with the quality of the fish, he sought a place for prayer, but he fell over a thorn-bush. The deacon ran to lift up the man of God, but he heard him say, 'Let be! This is my resting place for ever: here will I dwell, for I have desired it.'

The place was hallowed by the presence of the saint and afterwards by his bones. Here arose, in due time, the great abbey that bore his name, with the church that contained his relics—his body, his cross, and his staff. About a hundred years after the death of Gallus, the first abbot was appointed (720).[2] His name was Othmar, and under his rule the monastery began to grow. The Benedictine Rule was gradually enforced, and a school was set up which was to become great and famous.[3] The ninth and tenth centuries were the golden age of the abbey. The monastery had now acquired great possessions, the fame of its patron was spread far and wide, and the school was recognized under Grimald (842–72), Hartmut (872–83), and Salomo (890–920) as second to none in Western Christendom.

---

[1] *Vita Galli auct. Wettino, M.G.H., Script. Rer. Merov.* iv. 262.

[2] For the history of the Abbey see the valuable study of J. M. Clark, *The Abbey of St. Gall*, Cambridge 1926,

pp. 3 sqq.

[3] ib., pp. 91 sqq. The school was founded in the days of Othmar (720–59).

There were, in fact, two schools, the 'outer' school for laymen and those who were to become secular clergy, and the 'inner' school for oblates.[1] It is with the latter that we are concerned. The teaching at S. Gall was, of course, on the lines of that with which we have already become acquainted in our study of the Anglo-Saxon and the Frankish schools. The seven liberal arts were taught according to the conceptions then current and the capacity of the age.[2] Latin grammar had to be taught laboriously to Swabian youths who knew no other language but the German they were as yet unable to write. As in the Frankish schools, so here, Virgil, Ovid, and the Christian poets were read with great care, and the composition of verses had an important place in the curriculum. So Notker Balbulus, the famous teacher, writing to his pupils Waldo and Salomo, says: 'Et primum, quod maxime opus habet professio vestra, quia litterarum studiis ab infantia fuistis occupati, obsecro, ut prosas orationes et strophas versuum congruas absque retractatione et dilatione texere curetis.'[3] What these exercises in verse were like we can judge from a collection of *Begrüssungsgedichte* and other poems contained in a S. Gall codex (ccclxxxi).[4] And Ekkehart IV in his *Casus sancti Galli*, that fascinating, if in detail unreliable, account of the monastery in its great days, has a story which throws some light on the same subject. He tells us how Salomo, Abbot of S. Gall and Bishop of Constance, came a few days before his death, on the day after the festival of the Holy Innocents, that is, on the 'children's day', to visit the boys in their school. On this day all rules were relaxed, and it was the children's right to rush upon any visitor and hold him to ransom. This they did to the great Salomo, saying among themselves, 'Let us seize the Bishop, not the Lord Abbot!' They set him upon the master's seat, and he said, 'Now I can exercise the rights of my office. Strip, all of you!' They began to obey, but asked him, as was the custom, to be allowed to ransom themselves. 'How?' he asked, and the little ones replied to him in Latin as well as they were able, the slightly older boys in rhythm (*rithmice*), and the rest in metrical verses as if they were declaiming rhetorically from the platform. One of them said,

Quid tibi fecimus tale, ut nobis facias male?
appellamus regem, quia nostram facimus legem,[5]

[1] *Christian-Latin Poetry*, p. 178.
[2] Clark, op. cit., p. 97.
[3] *M.G.H., Leges* v, *Formulae*, p. 429.
[4] *Poet. Lat. Aevi Car.* iv. 315 sqq.
[5] i.e. we appeal to the king, because we are putting our rule into practice.

and the other versifier said,

> Non nobis pia spes fuerat, cum sis novus hospes,
> ut vetus in peius transvertere tute velis ius.

The great man was delighted with these proofs of the main-
tenance of learning in the school he loved and he, in his
turn, ransomed himself in a worthy manner.[1]

We can conclude from this passage in Ekkehart's *Casus* that
the composition of rhythms was taught side by side with
metrical verse, and that it was regarded as more easy of
mastery for the younger pupils. The rhythms were, no doubt,
adorned with scattered rimes, and internal rime now became an
ingredient of the hexameters and elegiacs, as these epigrams
and other verses show. So when Ekkehart relates the death
of Salomo, he adds,

> In cruce quaesitam pretioso sanguine vitam
> des cui, Christe, locis in paradisiacis.[2]

The leonine rime is conspicuous in the verses of Ratpert
(d. *circ.* 890), a famous teacher at S. Gall, and the author of the
first part of the *Casus*.[3] But it is all but absent from one poem,
a fragment, in which Ratpert celebrates a church in his native
Zurich, which Bertha, the sister of Charles the Fat, had built.[4]
The poem was dedicated to Notker; it tells of the beauty of
the building, its columns, its windows, its elaborate ceiling,
and its floor, and describes how Bishop Gebhart translated thither the relics of S. Felix and S. Regula, amid the
rejoicings of the people who dwelt between the Limmat and
the Rhine.

In the year 883, at Christmas, Charles the Fat came to
S. Gall with his wife Richgard, and the poets of the monastery
had to produce their 'greetings'. Ratpert addressed the queen
in leonine elegiacs,[5] and Notker welcomed the king in rhythmic
iambic dimeters, referring to himself with his usual modesty
and humility:

> Nos pro statu parvi loci
> reique modo pauperis
> laetantes pio domino
> occurrimus in omnibus.

For Notker combined with a rare attractiveness the qualities

---

[1] *Casus S. Galli*, i. 26.
[2] ib., i. 27.
[3] His verses are in *Poet. Lat. Aevi Car.*, iv. 321 sqq.

[4] *Poet. Lat. Aevi Car.* iv. 335.
[5] ib., p. 324; quoted in *Christian-Latin Poetry*, p. 205 sq.

of the scholar and the saint. His scholarship was not of the
dry pedantic order, and his love of the classical authors and
of the Christian fathers did not prevent him from remaining
always a true German, in contact with his mother-speech and
proud of the history of his race. Charles the Fat, on that
Christmas visit, had listened with delight to the endless reminiscences which he poured forth, and he urged Notker to set them
down in writing. The result was the *Gesta Karoli*, as far removed from Einhard's studied biography as could be imagined,
but, nevertheless, its true complement, for here is set forth in
anecdote and legend the meaning of Charles the Great to the
generations since his death.

Something of the same kind was done for Notker himself
by Ekkehart in the *Casus S. Galli*, where he has become a
legendary figure, along with Ratpert and Tutilo, holding converse with both worlds, the visible and the invisible:[1]

Notker was simple in appearance, but not in mind; a stammerer in voice,
but not in spirit; in things divine upright, in adversity long-suffering;
gentle in all things, but a strict master to our scholars; timid in the presence
of the sudden and unexpected, save when he was troubled by the evil spirits,
whom he was wont to withstand with boldness. In prayer, in reading, in
composing poetry (*dictando*) he was most constant, and—to describe in short
the gifts of his saintly character—he was a vessel of the holy Spirit, than
whom there was none more abundant in his own day.

He had been educated under Iso, the commentator of Prudentius, and under Moengal, the Irishman, who, having visited
S. Gall with his uncle, Bishop Marcus, had made up his mind
never to leave this hospitable home of learning. Notker seems
to have been a born teacher. He watched with care and love
over his pupils, as his letters and poems show. The greatness
of his poetical and rhetorical gifts is best displayed in those
Sequences[2] which he composed for the adornment of the
liturgy, but he carried on as well the excellent Carolingian
tradition of the occasional poem, which remained throughout
the Middle Ages the truest sign of the more finely cultivated
mind.

In him, too, there shines that crude humour which first
appears in literature with the advent of the northern peoples.[3]
On one occasion the brethren of the neighbouring monastery
of Reichenau told their friends at S. Gall that they had caught

[1] *Casus S. Galli*, iii. 33.
[2] See *Christian-Latin Poetry*, pp. 210 sqq.
[3] The story is in *Poet. Lat. Aevi Car.* iv. 336, and Dümmler, *S. Galler Denk-male*, p. 225.

at a place of theirs called Alahaspach a fish twelve palms in length. Notker replied, 'That is nothing. We have mushrooms in our monastery in January.' The monks of Reichenau laughed, but next year in January Notker sent the 'mushroom', with this epigram,

> Si mihi non vultis, oculis vel credite vestris;
> vos saltem binas piscis mihi mittite spinas.

'If you won't believe *me*, at any rate believe your own eyes; and now, pray, send me the back-bones of two of your fishes.'

The truth was that the fungi grew in a damp cellar, where there was water dripping and the heating chamber kept the place warm.

But we seem to see the real Notker best in his relations with his pupils Salomo and Waldo, two brothers of high birth and destiny, who were entrusted to his care[1] by their great-uncle Salomo I, Bishop of Constance. When the latter died, his nephew succeeded him as Salomo II, and when the young men left school to visit their important relative or to stay with Liutbert, Archbishop of Mainz, Notker's anxiety and love followed them. The letters and poems which he sent are preserved in Salomo's *Formelbuch*,[2] a miscellaneous collection of formulae, models for letters or deeds, along with actual letters and verses. In the first letter Notker begins: 'uterinis fratribus adoptulus frater in salvatore mundi salutem. rem miraculo dignam, immo portentuosam mihi praecipitis, ut balbus, edentulus et ideo blesus, vel, ut verius dicam, semiblaterator, surdastris vobis, vel potius insensatis, cantare seu ludere sive lamentare debeam.' The letters are full of quaint humour, curious learning, and moral precept. For Notker knew the temptations of youth, and he had heard enough to make it certain that the young men were safer within the walls of the monastery than in a bishop's palace. He sent them poems, which, as he said, were dictated by love:

> talia dictat amor, verus respondet amator;
> ingratus taceat, gratus in alta canat.[3]

But the young men were slow to reply; so, when they came back, Notker was cold, and they had to beg for pardon. Here is

---

[1] And, according to *Casus S. Galli*, i. 1, to Iso as well.

[2] Dümmler, *Formelbuch des Bischofs Salomos*, Leipzig 1857, nos. 29, 42, 44, 45, 47, 48; in *M.G.H., Leges* v, *Formulae*,

pp. 412 sqq., nos. 28, 41, 43, 44, 46, 47; poems, pp. 430 sqq. I quote from the latter edition.

[3] *Poet. Lat. Aevi Car.* iv. 344; *M.G.H., Leg.* v, *Formulae*, p. 430.

their youthful request for forgiveness in the leonine hexameters
which were practised at S. Gall:

> O species cari, cur non ades, alma magistri?
> o quid fecisti! cur nobis nota fuisti?
> o cur rara venis, cur nos tardissime cernis?
> iam petimus venias: doctrinam sepius addas,
> ut tibi centiplices dominus velit addere grates.
> te revocant pennae, cupiunt membrana videre.[1]

While Salomo and Waldo were yet under his wing, Notker
wrote for Salomo—to make the way of learning easy—a poem
on the seven liberal arts,[2] which follows, of course, the *De
Nuptiis* of Martianus Capella.

But the other monks watched the career of Salomo with some
envy and afterwards with not a little misgiving. For Salomo
was obviously destined for power and place, and, when he
departed to become chaplain to Charles the Fat, his career
was only at its beginnings. The manner in which he would
visit S. Gall and come into the monastery, unaccompanied and
in the garb of a secular priest, struck fear into the hearts of
the more timid. They knew that he would one day be their
master, and so, to make the best of a bad business, they finally
received him as a monk of S. Gall, preferring to be ruled by
'one of themselves' than by the same man as a secular priest.[3]
In the end Salomo, who was hardly more than thirty, became
their abbot (890). In the same year his uncle died, and, without any question, he succeeded him as Bishop of Constance.
The Abbot-Bishop increased the riches and the glory of the
house of S. Gall. 'Tantis pro donis sit pax animae Salamonis.'[4]
He was much busied with affairs of state in the service of the
last Carolingians, and he was a remote figure to the monks
over whom he ruled. It is told of him that he employed one
Sindolf to report to him in secret on the doings of the brethren.
Sindolf was caught listening one night at the window of the
scriptorium in which Ratpert, Notker, and Tutilo were collating
texts.[5] While Tutilo seized him by the beard, Ratpert be-
laboured him from behind. Tutilo asserted that he had caught
the devil, but the frightened brethren who had gathered round
saw too clearly that it was the bishop's favourite. Tutilo pretended to be overcome with terror. 'Woe is me, for I have laid
hands on the bishop's tale-bearer and confidant' (*auricularem et*

---

[1] *Poet. Lat. Aevi Car.* iv. 345;
M.G.H., Formulae, p. 431.
[2] *Poet. Lat. Aevi Car.* iv. 339.
[3] *Casus S. Galli,* i. 6.
[4] ib.   [5] ib. iii. 36.

intimum). Salomo comforted Sindolf by promising preferment. Of the three monks who had been his masters in the school,[1] he said resentfully: 'They were always against me (*invidi*) from my youth up.' Here the author of the *Casus S. Galli* probably reflects the real feeling of the Abbot as he remembered his boyhood in the cloister school. Doubtless Salomo —the monk who could never renounce the world—still felt the eyes of Notker watching him. But for us as for Ekkehart[2] Salomo is an attractive figure:

> Rarely indeed has a man been seen on whom the Giver of all good things had bestowed so many of His gifts. He was tall and handsome; learned and well-instructed, skilful in writing and in speech. He knew well the art of drawing and excelled in fashioning the capitals, as can be seen in the initials L and C in the Long Gospels.[3] These he is said to have drawn and painted when a Bishop with his own hand, to show that it had not lost its cunning. In metrical composition he was the first, and in the presence of kings he often strove with others in comic pieces.

There is not much to be said in praise of the few poems by Salomo which have survived.[4] One of these was written about 904[5] and is addressed to Bishop Dado of Verdun. It is a lament for the evils of the age, consisting of more than three hundred hexameters with a leonine rime. Sometimes there are verses like,

> arca cluit dando, vacuatur et ipsa negando,

or

> haec exhortando, non te sunt dicta docendo,

but more frequently the rime is of one syllable,

> cui pater ille domus peregre frumenta profectus,

or there is assonance merely,

> et pulsare fores, aditus iam quaerere fervet.

Another poem is a lament for the death of his brother Waldo, who had likewise risen to power as Bishop of Freising and Chancellor to Charles the Fat.[6] It is addressed to the same Bishop Dado, and is in elegiacs. It begins:

> Eximie antistes has accipe Dado salutes
> conscriptas tristi a Salomone tibi.

---

[1] Ekkehart makes Ratpert, Tutilo, and Notker contemporaries, in disregard of chronology, for Ratpert was their senior. As J. M. Clark (*The Abbey of St. Gall*, p. 253) remarks, the chronology of the *Casus* is absolutely unreliable.

[2] *Casus S. Galli*, i. 28.

[3] *The Evangelium Longum*; still preserved at S. Gall; see J. M. Clark, op. cit., p. 139.

[4] *Poet. Lat. Aevi Car.* iv. 296 sqq.

[5] ib., p. 297; Manitius, *Gesch.* i. 594.

[6] *Poet. Lat. Aevi Car.* iv. 307.

> sicut laetorum fueras pars ante meorum,
>   sic nunc tristitiae pars, pater, esto meae.
> gaudenti congaudere et cum flente dolere,
>   scriptio, quam dictat Tarsigena, imperitat.

These verses, as well as the verses which Waldram, another monk of S. Gall, addressed to Salomo,[1] show how the standard of composition had suffered a steady decline since the generation that had sat at the feet of Alcuin. But Waldram could still address the Muse as though he were a poet with whom she might hold precious converse:

> o soror Euterpe, responsa fidelia praebe,
> dona consilium, quid ob hoc mihi nunc sit agendum.

The Carolingians had rehabilitated the Muses, whom former ages had banned, and the monks of S. Gall, who loved to imitate them, gave them a place by the side of the Psalmist. The Muse had come back to stay. From the monastic she passed to the cathedral schools, always reminding the poet of another tradition than that of Prudentius or Paulinus of Nola.

When Salomo died in 920 he was succeeded by Hartman, a pupil of Notker and a master in the school. Hartman was a better scholar than an administrator. Of his poems we possess a hymn in rhythmical iambic dimeters—*Versus Hartmanni ante Evangelium cum legatur canendi*[2]—and some other pieces, among them a poem in honour of King Conrad on the occasion of his visit to S. Gall in 911.[3] The king came from Constance, where he was Salomo's guest, to see the procession on the festival of the Holy Innocents. The boys walked gravely along the church, and the king, to tempt them, had apples thrown upon the floor; but none of them, not even the smallest, moved to pick them up, and the king wondered at their discipline.[4]

§ 2. *Historical and Epic Poems.*

(i) *Monastic Poets.*

The appearance in the late ninth and early tenth centuries of long narrative poems which may be classed as historical or epic is, in part, a continuation of the Carolingian tradition carried on by the monastic schools; but it was due also to the growth of national feeling and to the consciousness that history as important as that of the remoter past was being made in

---

[1] *Poet. Lat. Aevi Car.* iv. 313.
[2] ib., p. 317; note the line in stanza
[3] clausa tenentes stomata.
[3] ib., p. 327.   [4] *Casus S. Galli*, i. 14.

the present. The old historians were now being read with great care, and some attempt was made to understand the succession of empires and states in antiquity, if only for the purpose of sacred history.

As always, the figure of Charles the Great exercised an immense attraction. It was a Saxon monk from Corvey who in the reign of Arnulf[1] (*circ.* 888) described in a long epic the deeds of the conqueror of his people. This *Poeta Saxo*, as he is called, had nothing of his own to give; he merely used the work of Einhard, and what annals he could find, to supply him with materials. He relates in a bald narrative the events of each year, with little rhetorical ornament and no attempt at giving anything more than a prose record could have given equally well. It is true that in reference to the heresy of Bishop Felix he does allow himself to say of Charles,

> dira venenifere conatus semina sectae,
> quae Felix infelici male sparserat ausu,
> vellere de sacro domini radicitus agro,
> Catholicus princeps . . .[2]

and again,

> o quam triste nefas mortalia pectora crebro
> concipiunt, quam precipiti summersa profundo
> nequitiae! dum non leges, non iura verentur,
> horrificos nimium caeci labuntur in actus,[3]

but here his rhetoric is a reminiscence of Boëthius.[4] The fifth and last book has for its subject the last days of the Emperor, and the poet thinks it fitting to change his metre from the heroic to the elegiac. He begins:

> Pangite iam lacerae carmen lugubre, Camene;
> dignus enim multis annus hic est lacrimis.

But he slips back at once into the annalistic manner, a poor but well-meaning versifier, whom the historian, in search of something new, consults in vain.

About the same time (*circ.* 897) Abbo, a monk of S. Germain-

---

[1] Manitius, *Gesch.* i. 583; text, *Poet. Lat. Aevi Car.* iv. 1 sqq.; Traube, ib. iii. 371, suggests that the poet is Agius of Corvey, but Manitius sees no resemblance between them.

[2] ib., p. 35. There are rhetorical touches too in v. 651 sqq. (p. 70), where the fame of Charles is placed above that of the 'Decii, the Scipiadae,

Camillus, Cato, Caesar, Pompey, the Fabii'; even if they won earthly glory equal to his, they could not win the heavenly reward of one who is numbered with Constantine and Theodosius.

[3] *Poet. Lat. Aevi Car.* iv. 41.

[4] *De Consol. Philos.* i. 2.

des-Prés, composed his *Bella Parisiacae urbis*,[1] an account of
the events connected with the siege of Paris by the Normans in
the days of Duke Odo. When Abbo wrote he had not had much
experience in versification, and he was reading Virgil's *Eclogues*.[2]
He wrote, therefore, for the sake of exercise, and also in the
hope that his account might be of value to future defenders of
beleaguered cities. This at any rate is the story he tells in
the dedication of his completed work to Gozlin the deacon,
a fellow-monk. But actually Abbo must have had a good deal of
practice, and, like so many of his monastic contemporaries,
he delighted in words drawn up from the darkness of the
glossaries and embedded in the further obscurity of his own
style and thought. Abbo had, in addition, learned a little
Greek, and so Greek words are brought in according to the
Irish fashion.

Abbo, therefore, carries on a well-marked tradition. After
his prose dedication come verses addressed to his master,
Aimoin. His choice of the Alcmanian measure, in which, like
Raban and Gottschalk before him, he borrows from Prudentius,
shows that he was no mere beginner. He was, rather, an accomplished master of the methods which were a fruit of Irish and
Anglo-Saxon influence in the Carolingian schools.

The first two books describe the siege, the great deeds of
Duke Odo and of Ebolus, Abbot of S. Germain; the fruitless
attempt of Count Henry of Saxony to raise the siege, and the
appearance of Charles III to buy off the invaders. Abbo is
describing events of which he was an eyewitness, and, if he
entered into any detail at all, he could hardly fail to be interesting. The narrative is certainly lively enough when compared
with the annalistic method of the Poeta Saxo. There are a few
similes and a plentiful use of the mythological terms dear to
the Irish writers.[3]

But it is in the third book that Abbo allows himself to write
in the manner which, for him, was that of the accomplished
scholar. Even with the aid of the glossary which he compiled
for the reader's assistance it is almost impossible to follow
the drift of this admonition addressed to the clergy. The

---

[1] *Poet. Lat. Aevi Car.* iv. 77 sqq.:
on Abbo, see Freeman's essay on *The
Early Sieges of Paris.*

[2] *Poet. Lat. Aevi Car.* iv. 77.

[3] e.g. Titan and Phoebus for the
sun: when Abbo wishes to say that
water extinguished the fire with which

the Danes were attempting to burn the
tower, he gives us (i. 159, p. 84)

Lemnius hic moritur claudus magno
   superante
Neptuno.
(Cf. i. 383, p. 90.)

opening lines will show the kind of Latin still practised in schools which had fallen under direct Irish influence:[1]

> Clerice, dipticas lateri ne dempseris unquam.
> corcula labentis fugias ludi fore, ne te
> laetetur foedus sandapila neque toparcha.
> machia sit tibi, quo ierarchia, necque cloaca.
> non enteca nec alogia, verum absida tecum
> commaneat, mentes, acrimonia, non quia mordet.
> agoniteta tuus fiat ambusilla tui mens
> ne uranium preter cromam legat, is quia multis
> esse deus solet.   anodiam sectare gemellam.

The learning displayed in verses like these made this third book of the poem so popular that it was often transcribed apart from the rest by those who had no interest in the siege of Paris.[2]

A poet of a different order was Ekkehart I (*circ.* 900–73), Dean of S. Gall, who carried on the tradition of the great school for learning and piety. He was of noble birth, and, like many of the famous men who became masters there, he entered the school as a boy and went through its rigorous discipline from the beginning. He knew some Greek, he read Virgil with love and care, but when he was asked, while still a boy, to compose a metrical exercise for his master he took a story from German legend, the tale of 'Waltharius manu fortis'. Ekkehart IV, who records the origin of this poem in his *Casus S. Galli*,[3] adds that he himself revised it and purged it of its Teutonic crudeness at the request of Archbishop Aribo.

The special problems connected with the material on which the story is based belong to the history of German literature. We cannot here discuss the question whether Ekkehart had before him a German lay or a prose story in Latin, whether he followed his original closely or, as some have guessed, latinized it and moulded it according to his fancy.[4] We are concerned rather with the structure of the poem and with the

---

[1] ib., p. 116. Abbo also delights in *asyndeton* (i. 191, p. 85):

> a! tellus opulenta gazis nudatur opimis,
> sanguivomis, laceris, atris, edacibus, aequo
> vulneribus, predis, necibus, flammis, laniatu
> prosternunt, spoliant, perimunt, urunt . . .

and in *tmesis*, oc- que -cidens (i. 360,

p. 90); Burgun- adiere -diones (ii. 472, p. 111). On the sources from which Abbo drew his 'linguistic rarities', see M. L. W. Laistner, 'Abbo of St. Germain-des-Prés', in *Arch. Lat. Med. Aev.* i (1924), pp. 27 sqq.

[2] Manitius, *Gesch.* i. 587.

[3] ix. 80.

[4] These problems are summarized in Manitius, *Gesch.* i. 611 sq.; J. M. Clark, *The Abbey of S. Gall*, pp. 246 sqq.

use which the poet makes of what he had learned in the course of his studies.

But at the same time we must not proceed as though no popular poetry in the vernacular existed during these centuries. For no people could ever renounce so vital a necessity. We know that in spite of the austere standard laid down by the missionary Church, the heathen songs and lays survived, and that Charles the Great collected them with loving care. And, if his son attempted their destruction, there were still monasteries where some of them were quietly copied. So there survived a fragment of the *Hildebrandslied*, copied at Fulda, and in later Carolingian times there was a revival of interest in the old poetry. In the *Casus S. Galli* it is told how Bishop Pilgrim of Passau (d. 991) had the *Nibelungenlied* translated into Latin, and Ekkehart's *Waltharius*[1] is but another example of the treatment in the learned language of an old German theme. For the poem is clearly no artificial attempt at a Virgilian epic, however much it owes to a study of the *Aeneid*. It is, in truth, a *Waltharilied* in Latin dress, and, in its structure, it is not a collection of episodes disposed after any rhetorical recipe, but a plain narrative proceeding from event to event without the creaking of machinery. Of course the author, when he had to describe single combats, thought of the *Aeneid* and of the *Psychomachia* of Prudentius, but he was no fashioner of centos or compiler of school exercises. The reader who accepts the text before him and refuses to think that Ekkehart IV's 'improvements' are embodied in it, is amazed at the work of such a youthful poet. For the testimony of the last four lines is explicit:[2]

> haec quicunque legis, stridenti ignosce cicadae
> raucellam, nec adhuc vocem perpende, sed aevum,
> utpote quae nidis nondum petit alta relictis.
> haec est Waltharii poesis.   vos salvet Iesus.

The scene is laid in the remote days of the already legendary Attila. The poet begins by explaining concisely who the Huns were, and then tells how Attila decided to invade the west, where Gilicho ruled the Franks, Herrich the Burgundians, and Alpher the Aquitanians (i.e. the Goths). From Châlons Herrich saw the cloud of dust that heralded the advance of Attila, and he closed the gates; but he wisely decided to buy peace and to

---

[1] *Ekkehards Waltharius*, ed. Strecker, Berlin 1924.
[2] Ed. Strecker, p. 75; Strecker, p. v, rightly rejects the idea that these lines were added by Ekkehart IV.

give his only daughter, Hildgunde, as a hostage. The other
kings followed his example. Alpher gave up his son Walther,
who, although a child, was betrothed to Hildgunde. Gilicho
gave up Hagen, a young noble of 'Trojan' lineage, because
his own child Gunther was not yet weaned from his mother.
So, laden with much treasure, and taking the young hostages,
the Huns joyfully returned to their own country. There the
three were kindly treated as if they had been the king's own
children. The boys became great warriors, and the girl was
placed in charge of the royal treasures, having won the affection
of the queen. Meanwhile King Gilicho died and his son
Gunther succeeded to the kingdom. He broke his treaty with
the Huns and refused to pay tribute. News of this came to
Hagen, who escaped by night and came back to his lawful
lord. Walther was then with the Hunnish army, and wherever
he went all was well. But Ospirin, Attila's queen, feared that
Walther, the stay of the Empire, might escape. Her counsel
was that he should be married, and Attila, seeing the wisdom
of the advice, put it to Walther, but in vain. The scene shifts
to the field of battle. The tumult and confusion are powerfully
described, with Virgilian touches:

> iamque infra iactum teli congressus uterque
> constiterat cuneus: tunc undique clamor ad auras
> tollitur, horrendam confundunt classica vocem,
> continuoque hastae volitant hinc indeque densae.
> fraxinus et cornus ludum miscebat in unum,
> fulminis inque modum cuspis vibrata micabat.
> ac veluti boreae sub tempore nix glomerata
> spargitur, haud aliter saevas iecere sagittas.
> postremum cunctis utroque ex agmine pilis
> absumptis manus ad mucronem vertitur omnis:
> fulmineos promunt enses clipeosque revolvunt,
> concurrunt acies demum pugnamque restaurant.
> pectoribus partim rumpuntur pectora equorum,
> sternitur et quaedam pars duro umbone virorum.[1]

The victory of the Huns is due to Walther's valour, and he is
crowned with the laurel of triumph. Weary with the stress of
battle he returns to seek the king. But it is Hildgunde whom
he meets in the royal chamber. He embraces her and asks for
wine. She brings him a precious cup, over which he makes the
sign of the cross before he takes it. In good direct dialogue
the poet describes how they plan to escape. She is to take as
much of the treasures as she can, and procure some hooks to

[1] pp. 12-13.

snare fish for their food on the journey. Walther will make
the Huns drunk at a banquet, and the way will be clear. The
plan is carried out, and they ride away on Lion, the great
war-horse. Walther is in full armour and, after the manner
of the Huns, he wears two swords, his two-edged sword
on his left and a one-edged sword on his right thigh. So
they escape, hiding by day and travelling by night. Meanwhile their flight is discovered. The king and queen are
dismayed, and the queen makes a little rhetorical lament:

> o detestandas quas heri sumpsimus escas!
> o vinum, quod Pannonias destruxerat omnes!
> quod domino regi iam dudum praescia dixi,
> approbat iste dies, quem nos superare nequimus.
> en hodie imperii vestri cecidisse columna
> noscitur, en robur procul ivit et inclita virtus:
> Waltharius lux Pannoniae discesserat inde,
> Hiltgundem quoque mi caram deduxit alumnam.[1]

The king offers a reward for Walther's capture, but all are
afraid to undertake the quest. In the meantime the fugitives,
living on birds or fish, had reached the Rhine, quite close to
Worms, where Gunther had his court. They paid the ferryman with the fish which they still had with them. The fish
were taken to the king's cook, and when they appeared on
the royal table Gunther saw that such fish never swam in
Frankish waters. The ferryman is summoned to tell his tale
of the strange warrior with the maiden, and the treasure that
could not be concealed. Hagen at once recognizes that it is
Walther who has returned, and he is glad:

> congaudete mihi quaeso, quia talia novi:
> Waltharius collega meus remeavit ab Hunis.

But Gunther thinks only of the treasure now almost within his
grasp. He kicks away the table, calls for his horse, and chooses
twelve of his bravest knights to go with him. Hagen, mindful
of the bond that held him to his old friend, will not join them,
and he tries in vain to dissuade the king from his treacherous
plan.

Walther and the maid have now reached the Vosges, and
there in the mountains they find a cave, where they rest after
their weary journey. For the hero, if he had slept at all, had
slept upon his shield. Now he rests his head in her lap, and
bids her watch for the approach of any foe.

[1] p. 21.

Gunther finds their tracks in the dust, and in spite of fresh warnings from Hagen, who remembers his invincible valour in battle, he proceeds to the cave. But Hildgunde sees the dust rise and awakens Walther with a soft touch. He arms himself, while the maiden cries, 'The Huns are here.' She falls to the ground and beseeches him: 'I beg of thee, my lord, to cleave my neck with the sword, so that since it has not been my lot to be joined in plighted wedlock, I may not have to suffer any other bond.' The hero answers: 'Shall I be stained with innocent blood? How could my sword, if it spared not one so dear, be able to smite my foes?' So he encourages her, until he sees that these are no Huns, but natives of those parts, and among them his old friend Hagen:

> 'non assunt Avares hic, sed Franci nebulones,
> cultores regionis, et'—en galeam Haganonis
> aspicit et noscens iniunxit talia ridens:
> 'et meus hic socius Hagano collega veturnus.'[1]

But Walther realizes that they have come as enemies, and he flings them a proud boast, for which, as soon as said, he kneels to beg the divine forgiveness. He looks again and sees that he need fear no one except Hagen, who alone knows his manner of fighting. If he escapes him, then Hildgunde will be his wife. At Hagen's advice Gunther sends Camalo, Count of Metz, to persuade him to yield his treasures and the maiden quietly, but after a lively interchange of words the parley is broken off. Hagen and the king then separate in anger, and Hagen watches events from a neighbouring hill. There is another parley, after which Walther offers two hundred bracelets for a safe passage; but Camalo rudely refuses and hurls his spear. The single combat begins and, of course, Camalo is killed. Walther is in a position which only one of the enemy can approach at a time. So he faces them singly in fights of which the issue is not long in doubt. Ekkehart describes each combat with its appropriate detail, and the narrative never becomes dull, in spite of its Virgilian reminiscence. There are speeches to provide relief, and the king is always in the background urging on his unhappy knights. Eckefried, the Saxon, was the fourth to come against Walther. He tried his native wit: 'Say,' he said, 'have you a real body or, accursed as you are, is it only an aëry sham? For you look more like a wild faun of the woods.' Walther laughed: 'Your Celtic

---

[1] p. 30: *nebulones*, here simply 'knaves'.

speech[1] shows that you come of the race that excels all others in buffoonery. But if my right hand catches you coming near, you will hereafter be able to tell your Saxons that you have really seen the phantasm of a faun in the Vosges.' 'I will prove what you are,' says Eckefried, hurling his spear, which breaks on Walther's shield. Walther hurls his own weapon: 'Take this as the gift of the woodland faun.' This is the end of Eckefried.

The sixth warrior was Patafried, Hagen's own nephew. The uncle tries to persuade him to go back; in a Virgilian scene, the only piece of sustained rhetoric in the poem, Hagen, watching him go to death, moralizes on the insatiable greed that leads men to their doom:

> o vortex mundi, fames insatiatus habendi,
> gurges avaritiae, cunctorum fibra malorum!
> o utinam solum glutires dira metallum
> divitiasque alias, homines impune remittens!
> sed tu nunc homines perverso numine perflans
> incendis nullique suum iam sufficit. ecce
> non trepidant mortem pro lucro incurrere turpem.[2]

Besides Virgil, Prudentius and Boëthius come to the poet's aid in this piece of school-rhetoric, which is, none the less, introduced with full propriety. In vain the chivalrous Walther counsels the boy to go back and save himself for a better fate—'animam dedit Orco'. After the next champion has fallen the Franks urge their king to desist, but 'indomitable as a man foredoom'd', he will listen to no advice. At last he is constrained to call on Hagen, who is torn between his duty to his lord and the sacred bond of friendship. In the end Hagen decides to obey the king, but the only hope of victory lies in a plan to trap Walther in the open. Night falls, and Walther and Hildgunde wake and sleep in turn; but before he lies down the warrior prays to God, thanking Him for his preservation, and beseeching Him, who desires not the death of a sinner, to receive the souls of the slain into His heavenly kingdom. When day comes the pair set out, with the armour of the dead loaded on four horses. Soon Hagen and the king appear; Walther addresses his old friend, appealing to their ancient bond. But Hagen says that his nephew's death has broken all ties. The greatest battle of all begins. All three dismount, and Walther holds his own, as his two enemies try to get near

---

[1] *Celtica lingua* = 'foreign tongue', simply, says Althof, *Das Waltharilied*, Berlin 1920, p. 118. But Ebert, iii. 270, would like to think of Eckefried as an Anglo-Saxon, which race the poet had identified with the Celts. This, however, is hardly possible.

[2] *Waltharius*, Strecker, p. 46.

him with their swords. He is like a bear attacked by the hunting-dogs:

> haud aliter Numidus quam dum venabitur ursus
> et canibus circumdatus astat et artubus horret
> et caput occultans submurmurat ac propiantes
> amplexans Umbros miserum mutire coartat:
> tum rabidi circumlatrant hinc inde Molossi
> comminus ac dirae metuunt accedere belvae.[1]

The ninth hour came, and Walther reflected that he must end the fight before he was worn out with fatigue. So he hurled his spear at Hagen, and then with a mighty stroke of his sword he severed the king's leg. He would have followed this up with a mortal blow, but Hagen received it on his shield against which the sword-blade shivered. Walther hurled the useless hilt away, but thus exposed his arm to the enemy, and Hagen lopped off his right hand, the hand that had been so feared and had won such mighty triumphs. Yet Walther was not daunted. He drew his other sword and cut out Hagen's right eye and six of his teeth. After this there was no more fighting:

> postquam finis adest, insignia quemque notabant:
> illic Guntharii regis pes, palma iacebat
> Waltharii, nec non tremulus Haganonis ocellus.
> sic sic armillas partiti sunt Avarenses!

The two sat down, for the other could only lie on the ground. The maiden bound up their wounds, and Walther bade her prepare a drink. 'Mix wine, and give it first to Hagen; he is a good fighter, if only he had kept his faith. Then give it to me, for I have endured more than the others. I will that Gunther take it last, for he has shown himself slow in the battle of the mighty, and has plied the trade of war coldly and without strength.' As the old friends, now once more united, sit and drink, they exchange scurrilous gibes and renew their pledge of friendship. Then they take up the sorely wounded king, and put him on a horse. The Franks go back to Worms, and Walther to his own Aquitaine. There he is received with honour, marries Hildgunde, and, after his father's death, reigns thrice ten years. 'What further wars he waged or what frequent triumphs he won, my blunted pen refuses to trace.'

    'Haec est Waltharii poesis'—this is the *Waltharilied*, an heroic lay in Latin hexameters. Fortunately, Ekkehart was free

[1] p. 69.

from most of the vices that beset the poets of his time. He did not affect the dull leonine hexameter then so much in fashion, and in consequence his verse has a freedom which is lacking in the work of his contemporaries. Neither does he make his verse an excuse for a parade of learning by the use of strange words from glossaries or from the Greek. It is true that he does write,

> eminus illa refert quandam volitare phalangem.
> ipse oculos tersos somni glaucomate purgans . . .[1]

and,

> stultius effatum me non audisse sophistam
> arbitror.[2]

There are also a few geographical allusions, the product of school learning:

> lucifer interea praeco scandebat Olympo
> dicens: 'Taprobane clarum videt insula solem,'[3]

and

> interea occiduas vergebat Phoebus in oras,
> ultima per notam signans vestigia Thilen,
> et cum Scottigenis post terga reliquit Hiberos.[4]

These mix well with the 'Germanisms'[5] and the low-Latin words which will please the observant reader, but the question of the influence of the German speech on the *Waltharius* is one into which we cannot enter here. The earliest readers of Ekkehart's poem had doubtless first heard the story in German, the language of their childhood and the language in which they naturally thought. The *Waltharius* would, therefore, serve well as a school-book, and the number and distribution of the manuscripts are evidence of its popularity.

The merits of the *Waltharius* shine for the reader who turns from it to the laboured verses of the *Ecbasis captivi*,[6] an anonymous beast-epic told, so the full title[7] indicates, as a moral tale. The author was a monk, and it seems likely that he belonged to the monastery of S. Evre near Toul. Arguing

---

[1] p. 29; *glaucoma*, see Mico's use of the word, *Poet. Lat. Aevi Car.* iii. 301, and ib., p. 805, where Mico's glossary is referred to. On p. 54 Ekkehart uses 'agonem', and Walther is Alpharides (son of Alpher).

[2] *sophista*, a man of intelligence.

[3] p. 62.

[4] p. 59.

[5] See the *index* of Strecker's edition.

[6] '*Ecbasis captivi*, das älteste Thierepos des Mittelalters', ed. E. Voigt, *Quellen und Forschungen zur Sprach- und Culturgeschichte der germanischen Völker*, viii, Strasbourg 1875.

[7] *Ecbasis cuiusdam captivi per tropologiam.*

from the date of the reform of that house—936—which put an end to the free and easy life described in part of the poem, Voigt assigns the *Ecbasis* to *circ.* 940,[1] and it is hardly necessary to question this conclusion. The poet begins by telling of the kind of existence he led in the careless days before the severe hand of the reformer was laid upon the monastery:

> Cum me respicio transactaque tempora volvo,
> de multis miror, puerilis quae vehit error;
> nil cogitans sanum, tempnens consortia fratrum,
> nectebar neniis, nugis quia totus in illis.
> tempore discendi periit cautela magistri,
> horas dictandi superavit cura vagandi;
> nam quia sic vixi, possedi nomen aselli,
> cuius raucisonum querens vitare ruditum,
> quamquam sit serum, meditabor scindere saccum,
> ut iuga torporis pellant rudimenta laboris,
> incipiens versus, quos rarus denegat usus.

The reader will observe how hard is the bondage imposed by the leonine rime, a bondage which was patiently accepted by so many of the poets of the tenth century. It is a rime which attracts the eye rather than the ear, especially as this poet rarely, and then only by accident, produces rimes of more than one syllable. One result of the observance of internal rime is an annoying obscurity, which prevents the reader from proceeding rapidly enough to take a real interest in the story. It is only fair to say that the poet realized that he was not equal to a lofty theme; so, for the benefit of others, he related his own history in the guise of a fable, in which he appears as the Calf that has fled from the stall. The Calf is just enjoying his liberty in the woods, when he meets the 'forester Wolf', who salutes him with great piety, as though he were greeting a monk returned from afar:[2]

> sit salvus, Christe, servus, qui mittitur ad me . . .,

but he adds that he will give him lodging for the night and will kill him for the Easter feast. The unhappy Calf is brought into the cave, and the Wolf begins to talk sanctimoniously of the life of abstinence that he has led for months, without meat or wine. The Calf prays secretly to Jove that he will save him; if he returns safely he will pay due thanks to the gods, and a he-

---

[1] *Ecbasis*, pp. 16 sqq.; but Zarncke preferred 925–30.
[2] p. 77.

goat will be given to every one of their altars.[1] Then he openly
begs the Wolf to spare him until mass is sung on the morrow.
The Wolf consents and urges him to eat a good supper, as he
is to die soon. Midnight comes and Wolf's two servitors
arrive, Otter and Hedgehog, bringing with them an abundance
of provisions. The Otter brings fish of all kinds,

> inter quae rombus, cum multo milite barbus,
> flexilis et congrus, cum quis mugil generosus,
> gobio, sepiole, lolligo cum capitone,
> cancri, mulli, trutta, cauedonus, hicherus, allec;
> affuit et salmo nutritus flumine Hreno,
> nec aberat donis piscosi grex Rabadonis,
> quod fundoque Mose capitur piscis genus omne;
> prefert se ceto spinx captus in amne Petroso;
> squamigeros cetus punctis pellebat acutis.[2]

The Hedgehog brings vegetables of which the poet gives a list.
The Wolf thanks them, enlarging again on the life of monastic
severity which he has lived for so long. 'I am stricken with
age. I bequeath all my possessions to you,' he says, 'my cave
to the Hedgehog, the stream that abounds in fishes to the
Otter.' Suddenly they catch sight of the Calf and are astonished. The Wolf explains his presence there and his future
fate. The Otter is to keep watch over him lest he escape.
Then the Hedgehog, although he is not really musical,

> nec studio cithare, nec Muse deditus ulli,

sings the Wolf to sleep with a tale, accompanied by the lute,
of Roman triumphs. The Wolf sleeps, and the Otter then
tries to console the Calf with food and kind words. As this is,
as it were, a monastic repast, it is accompanied by religious
reading—the 'Reparacio lapsi', and a 'collatio', which is a
pious prayer for deliverance. But after midnight the Wolf
has a bad dream, and wakes in alarm. He asks his companions to explain its meaning. Wasps and other insects surrounded him, and two gad-flies strove to sting him. He had no
strength left, and the Calf and the Fox sang a song of jubilation.

The Otter advises him to set the Calf free, or the animals in
a body will attack him and tear him in pieces. The two gad-
flies are the father and mother of the captive.

The Wolf swears that he will never set the Calf free, alleging
that he has eaten up his food and drunk his wine so that there is

---

[1] This heathen touch is contradicted
by the Catholic piety of the Calf and of
the other animals throughout the poem.
[2] p. 81.

nothing left. The Hedgehog, who is at once the chaplain and the cook, is to kill the Calf at the sixth hour, and serve him at table according to the elaborate directions given by the Wolf.

The Otter listens sadly, and when the Wolf has finished admonishes him severely for proposing to give up the life of abstinence and eat flesh again:

nunc comedes vitulum, sanctum spernens monachatum.[1]

He is turning away from the Rule, which is not a matter of words but of deeds. Such conduct can only end in a violent death:

iudicio canonum morieris morte latronum.

'You talk to one who has deaf ears,' replies the Wolf.

The scene now shifts back to the herd to which the Calf had belonged. His mother and father search for him, but it is the Dog who can tell them where their offspring is. The bellowing of the Bull wakes up the Wolf, who calls his servants to battle in a speech in which he says that he is afraid of nothing except the Fox, who is awaiting his chance to slay him by guile. The Otter and the Hedgehog profess their willingness to stand by him; only they would first know the whole story of the quarrel between the Wolf and the Fox.

In this rather clumsy manner the poet introduces into the body of his narrative what Voigt calls the *Innenfabel*, an 'inner' fable,[2] which is only a version of the ancient tale of the sick Lion, with a number of embellishments suited to the poet's special purpose.

The Lion was sick and called all the beasts to his cave to give him advice as to how he might be cured. The Fox alone is absent, and the Lion decrees that, when taken, he is to be cut to pieces. The Wolf, as the royal chamberlain, will have to supervise the carrying out of the sentence, and he exultantly devises torments for the victim. But the Panther warns the Fox, who is returning from a long journey. The Fox lifts his hands in prayer,

Alfa petit simul ω, tormento salvet ab illo.

As they go on they sing Psalms, and there is more praying. So they reach the Lion's cave, where the Fox cries 'miserere mei, deus', but soon finds a tale by which to excuse himself and appease the Lion's wrath. He professes to have been a pilgrim to the Holy Land, for he describes how a moorhen at the Lake of Genesaret had told him of the Lion's sickness and how it might be cured. The moorhen also had shown him the best way, by Rome, to Bordeaux, where the Lion has his capital. At Pavia the Fox had met a Stork, who gave him the same advice as the moorhen, except that he added an injunction to consult Saint 'Aper' (Evre).

The Lion is, however, suspicious, because he cannot forget the Fox's past record. But the Fox makes a clever speech, a mixture of truth and falsehood, in which he claims that in his old age he has braved all the 'climates' of the world to find a remedy for the king's sickness. So, in the end, he touches the Lion's sceptre and is taken back into the royal grace. Now he must declare the remedy in the presence of the other beasts. He hardly likes to tell it. It is this. The Wolf is to be deprived of his skin—two Lynxes and the Bear can do it— and, after the Lion has been anointed with a preparation made from the brain of a fish brought by the Fox from India, he is to be wrapped in the skin. The prescription is carried out, and the Fox seizes the occasion to make a speech in which he blames the animals for having condemned him in his absence. Then, with great prudence, he orders for the Lion a diet of all good things, and the Lion in return makes him the head of the royal household, so that he is feared by all. The Leopard must now set the cave in order, while the Fox upholds his master and takes him for a walk in the fields.[1] Next the Fox allows the animals to have a feast. Each must do his part; the Bears are to carry in logs of wood, the Camels will bring hangings for the cave, while the Otter and the Beaver will fetch water, and each of the other animals will have a duty to perform. But the Hedgehog protests against the task allotted to him. 'I am of the lineage of the great Cato,' he says, 'and the descendant of mighty kings. . . . I am margrave of the Rutuli, standard-bearer of Rome.' But these and other like claims to high consideration fail to impress the Leopard with whom he has to deal. He is compelled in the end to turn the spit and drink the dish-water.[2]

Then suddenly the Fox remembers the Panther, whom he has left alone so long. The king will need one of the 'brethren' like the Panther who can recite the psalms and sing hymns. Indeed there is no one to equal him:

> virtutes pardum comitantur amiciter istum:
> non est periurus, neque sordidus ac furiosus;

[1] p. 106.   [2] p. 112.

comis et urbanus, animo pius, ore serenus,
consilio cautus, moderatus, pacis amicus,
novit quid pulcrum, quid turpe, quid utile, falsum;
si foret ad presens, solus precelleret omnes.[1]

But the Lion calls for dinner, and the Fox explains the virtues of the wine of Trier that he has procured for him. Then the king remarks on the absence of the Panther,

demiror pardum nostrum rarescere visum.

The Fox sets out to bring him to the feast. As they return they sing the psalms, for the pious Panther, who has been singing ever since the Fox left him, has only 'sung as far as *Memento*'. They were just finishing the *Song of the Three Children* when they reached the king. The Lion, who is in good humour, makes the Panther his heir, and the feast proceeds. The Unicorn is reading to the company from the *Life of Malchus*; for monastic custom holds good among the animals. Then the wine is brought to the king with a prayer for his safety. The Panther has to explain his absence. He has been searching for a cure to rid the king of his sleeplessness. If the blackbird and the nightingale sing together they will charm him to sleep.

The Nightingale prays for the king to Him who is 'the King of the birds', and promises a song:

vobis ecce canam castam puramque Mariam,
atque Gabrihelem, qui nuntiat Hemmanuelem,
virgine nascendum, mortali carne tegendum,
ut salvet populum peccati pondere pressum.[2]

But the Lion advises her to drink so that she may sing the better. Her reply is, 'Christ be my meat and drink.' In a striking passage the poet tells how the two birds sing of Christ's passion:

concentu parili memoratur passio Christi.
passer uterque deum cesum flet, verbere lesum,
exanimis factus, claudens spiramina flatus;
commutat vocem, dum turbant tristia laudem,
organa divertit, dum Christi vulnera plangit,
solvitur in luctum, recolens dominum crucifixum,
squalet se cinere, dum fertur mocio terrae,
offuscat visum, memorans solem tenebratum.
hii gemini trepidas pressere ad pectora palmas;
vnicus ut matrem, sic deflent hii pacientem.
his avibus motis stupuit milicia regis;
turbatur pardus, tam gratum perdere munus.[3]

But the Panther calls for something more joyful, and orders
them to wash away in the river Gironde the ashes with which
they have sprinkled themselves. They are now ready, with
the Parrot and the Swan, to sing the Easter hymn. The Swan
says,

> est mihi psalterium, quod erat David, decachordum,
> Asaph me docuit, qui psalmos fingere iuvit.
> incipe, si quid habes; pascales psallito laudes.[1]

The four birds are now within the cave, and they sing the
solemn hymn,

> Salve festa dies, quam credens magnificat plebs,

and afterwards *Kyrie eleison*,[2] in which all the birds and
beasts join. By this time the Lion has drunk well of the
wine, and he proceeds to praise the Fox and recommend him
to his heir, the Panther. But the Fox shows signs of sadness,
and when the king demands the cause, he says that there is
a cave which he would fain possess. 'And this is the very cave,'
says the Wolf turning to the Otter, 'which was given by those
kings (the Lion and the Panther); and in revenge for the
crime which the Fox committed against my ancestor the cave
has been taken away from him.'

The Otter bids him proceed with the tale, and he describes
the breaking up of the feast, the mocking of the Wolf by the
guests, and how the Nightingale charms the king to sleep.
For three days he lies without waking, then departs for the
Black Forest (*Suuarzuualt*);[3] the Swan goes to Normandy
and the Parrot to the Indies, while the Panther seizes the
treasures of the cave, and with the Blackbird and the Nightingale goes westward. When all the rest have gone the Fox departs
as well, leaving an insulting 'epitaph' for the Wolf. With the
Leopard he establishes himself in the cave, of which, however,
he is afterwards deprived.

The Otter expresses his satisfaction with the story, and,
looking out to spy the enemy, sees the Fox coming, with the
deeds of his former territory as a testimony against the Wolf.
The threats of the enemy terrify him, and after giving vain

see *Christian-Latin Poetry*, pp. 425 sqq.)
in which the song of the nightingale is
associated with the Passion of Christ.
I do not think that Pecham can have
read the *Ecbasis*, and, equally, I do not
believe that he was entirely original in
the conception of his poem.

[1] p. 126.
[2] p. 128, verse 924,
hoc post odecolon grecissant Kirrie
eleison.
odecolon = perhaps, *odeculum*.
[3] p. 133.

counsels to the Wolf he plunges into the water and escapes. The Hedgehog hides in the rock. The Wolf, deceived by the Fox, leaves the cave, and the Calf rejoins his mother. The Bull hangs the Wolf on a tree, and the Fox writes, for the second time, an epitaph, after which he addresses the company on the superiority of intelligence to brute force. The Calf goes home and tells his mother of the dangers he has escaped,

> laus domino, qui me salvarat dente lupino!
> sanus et incolumis maternis deferor ulnis.
> sit nomen sanctum Christi domini benedictum![1]

It is difficult for us, at this distance of time, to disengage the historical and local allusions which are mingled with the matter of this curious poem. But we feel, all through, that we are in a monastic atmosphere. Here are monks thinly disguised as animals—they follow a Rule, they fast, they go to mass, they read their office, they are 'brethren' and the Lion is their 'father' or abbot. The feast takes place as in a monastic refectory,[2] and one of the brothers reads the *Life of Malchus*. Indeed the author of the poem had no clear aim beyond that of writing for the edification and the warning of younger monks, and, provided that he kept this in view, the details and their coherence did not matter greatly.

But his readers must have found the poem almost as obscure as we find it to-day; for the poet not only hampers himself with the leonine rime, but also makes such abundant use of verses and parts of verses from older poets that his work is almost, as Manitius says, 'one huge cento'.[3] Voigt[4] has pointed out that about 250 verses of the poem are either wholly or in part taken from Horace, and especially from the *Satires* and the *Epistles*. But the poet knew the *Odes* as well, and in respect of this and of his knowledge of Horace in general he is remarkable in his age. He uses Prudentius very frequently, but not the *Psychomachia*. He had read Virgil, Ovid, and Marcellus Empiricus, and the usual Christian poets. He even makes use of Abbo of S. Germain and Johannes Scotus,[5] but he has no inclination to use Greek words.[6] The *Ecbasis* never became popular and it was sparingly copied.

---

[1] p. 141.

[2] Cf. Ebert, iii. 284.

[3] i. 618. 'Und zweitens ist der Dichter doch ganz ausserordentlich unselbständig verfahren, indem sein Werk eigentlich einen grossen Cento darstellt.'

[4] Voigt, p. 27.   [5] ib., p. 29.

[6] It is true that he uses a Greek word in his title. It is not necessary

The next poem we have to consider is the *Gesta Apollonii*,[1] a versification of part of the Greek romance of Apollonius of Tyre, which was known to the Western world in a Latin version.[2] This poem is, like the *Ecbasis*, a product of the monastic schools, and there is reason to believe that it was the work of a monk of Tegernsee.[3] It is interesting to see this product of Hellenistic-Oriental fantasy exercising an attraction sufficiently great to induce a monk to versify it in the form of a lengthy *Eclogue*. For the poem is composed in dialogue, the characters being *Strabo* and *Saxo*. The poet was evidently influenced by Walafrid Strabo and other Carolingian poets who had used the eclogue form,[4] but he betrays the compulsion of contemporary fashion in his leonine hexameters and in his fondness for Greek words, which made it necessary to provide a glossary to accompany the text.

But the poem is not a true *Eclogue*, for the poet has merely divided his narrative between the two speakers in an arbitrary manner. He follows his Latin original fairly closely, except for a few expressions of his own, but as not more than 792 verses have survived, we can read only the beginnings of the marvellous adventures of the Tyrian king in the days of Antiochus. This story was very widely known in the Middle Ages;[5] William of Tyre refers to it as 'celebrem et late vulgatam . . . historiam', and Godfrey of Viterbo versified it in his *Pantheon*.

Hrothswitha, the famous nun of Gandersheim, who came of a noble Saxon family (b. *circ.* 935), received an education which enabled her to compose historical poems in the manner of the day. She is best known for those remarkable dramas in rimed prose, which still attract a number of readers by their liveliness and charm. Her two historical poems are the *Gesta Ottonis* and the *Primordia coenobii Gandeshemensis*.[6] They are both in the usual rimed hexameters, and there is nothing remarkable about their construction or the material with which they deal. The first relates the deeds of Otto the Great, his marriage and

---

to conclude, as has been suggested, that he was following the example of Prudentius.

[1] Text, *Poet. Lat. Aevi Car.* ii. 483 sqq.

[2] *Historia Apollonii regis Tyri*, ed. Riese, Leipzig 1883; see also E. Klebs, *Die Erzählung von Apollonius aus Tyrus, eine geschichtliche Untersuchung über ihre lateinische Urform und ihre späteren Bearbeitungen*, Berlin 1899;

and Rohde, *Der griechische Roman*, Leipzig 1900, pp. 435 sqq.

[3] Manitius, *Gesch.* i. 614.

[4] This does not mean that he was uninfluenced by Virgil, whose *Eclogues* he had evidently studied carefully.

[5] Klebs, op. cit., pp. 173, 327.

[6] *Hrotsvithae opera*, ed. Winterfeld, Berlin 1902; K. Strecker, Leipzig 1930. My references are to Strecker's edition.

his wars, until the time of his coronation as Emperor. There are two poetical dedications, one to Otto the Great and the other to his son, Otto II. The second poem describes the foundation of the monastery of Gandersheim by Duke Ludolf at the instance of his wife Oda. Legend and history are mingled in this account, which is carried up to the year 919, when Abbess Christiana died.

Hrothswitha's narrative method is very direct and simple; there is no studied obscurity about her verse, in spite of the leonine rime, which does not hamper her as it hampered the author of the *Ecbasis*. It is only occasionally that the rime is of more than one syllable. Verses such as the following are, therefore, rare,

> cunctis horrendum saeclis meritoque stupendum,[1]

or

> pectore maerenti ferret nimiumque dolenti,[2]

or

> sed plus tantorum maerens de caede virorum,[3]

for such rimes had not yet the attraction for the ear that made them so popular in the following centuries.

As a specimen of Hrothswitha's style we may give the passage in which she speaks of Bruno, the famous Archbishop of Cologne, brother of Otto I and a lover of learning:[4]

> post hunc ecclesiae pastor Brun nascitur almae,
> gratia pontificis quem duxit summa perennis
> dignum catholici curam gestare popelli;
> hinc quoque divino nutu patris pia cura
> ipsum servitio Christi fecit religari,
> abstractum gremio carae nutricis amando,
> ut regni pompis posset constare relictis
> miles stelligera semper regnantis in aula;
> at Christus, patris sapientia vera perennis,
> tironem refovendo suum clementius istum
> ipsi dona dedit tantae praeclara sophiae,
> quod non est illo penitus sapientior ullus
> inter mortales fragilis mundi sapientes.

§ 3. *Historical and Epic Poems.*

(ii) *Italian Poets.*

In her poem in honour of Otto, Hrothswitha tells how the Emperor rescued Adelaide the widow of Lothair from Berengar

[1] Strecker, op. cit., p. 236, verse 205. [3] p. 239, verse 294.
[2] p. 238, verse 259. [4] p. 232.

of Ivrea, and, having rescued her, made her his queen.[1] It was this Berengar's grandfather, crowned Emperor in 915, who was celebrated by an anonymous Italian poet in his Πανηγυρικὸν Βερενγαρίου τοῦ ἀνικητοῦ Καίσαρος.[2] For the poet knew some Greek and wished to make his learning known. And indeed he has, as is befitting to an Italian and, perhaps, a Veronese, some trace of humanistic feeling, since he is conscious of the great literary past of which he is an humble inheritor. Here we no longer breathe the air of German monastic schools, and, if the author was nevertheless a 'professor',[3] he kept one of those lay schools which remained always a distinguishing mark of Italian culture. We understand the poem best if we see in it the work of one whose business it was to read Virgil with the young, and teach them to compose verses. His poem was also read in his own or in other schools; for glosses are attached to it, which explain the learned allusions and give assistance in difficult passages.[4] The prologue of the poem is a dialogue between the author and his book:[5]

> 'Non hederam sperare vales laurumve, libelle,
>   quae largita suis tempora prisca viris.
> contulit haec magno labyrinthea fabula[6] Homero
>   Aeneisque tibi, docte poeta Maro.
> atria tunc divum resonabant carmine vatum:
>   respuet en musam quaeque proseucha tuam;
> Pierio flagrabat eis sed munere sanguis:
>   prosequitur gressum nulla Thalia tuum.
> hinc metuo rapidas ex te nigrescere flammas,
>   auribus ut nitidis vilia verba dabis.'
> 'quid vanis totiens agitas haec tempora dictis,
>   carmina quae profers, si igne voranda times?
> desine; nunc etenim nullus tua carmina curat:
>   haec faciunt urbi, haec quoque rure viri.
> quid tibi preterea duros tolerasse labores
>   profuit ac longos accelerasse vias?
> endromidos[7] te cura magis victusque fatigat:
>   hinc fugito nugas, quas memorare paras.'

[1] pp. 217 sqq.

[2] Gesta Berangarii imperatoris, in Poet. Lat. Aevi Car. iv. 354 sqq.

[3] Manitius, Gesch. i. 633 (following Winterfeld, Poet. Lat. Aevi Car. iv. 354), quotes iv. 203 (p. 401), in proof that he was a teacher:

>   nec temptabo meis ultra fastidia dictis,
>   o iuvenes, inferre . . .

The 'iuvenes' are his pupils.

[4] The glosses are well worth reading;

on them see Manitius, Gesch. i. 635.

[5] Poet. Lat. Aevi Car. iv. 355 sq.

[6] The gloss says: 'haec, sc. dona. "labyrinthea fabula" dicitur obscuritatibus involuta; nam labyrinthus subterranea domus fuit, quam Daedalus construxit', etc.

[7] Gloss: 'grecus genitivus. endromis vestis est villosa hiemalis, gravis et fortis nature; qua contra frigus induebant. est autem species pro genere; nam pro omni indumento hoc loco ponitur.'

'irrita saepe mihi cumulas quae murmura, codex,
  non poterunt votis addere claustra meis.
seria[1] cuncta cadant, opto, et labor omnis abesto,
  dum capiti summo xenia[2] parva dabo.
nonne vides, tacitis abeant ut saecla triumphis,
  quos agitat[3] toto orbe colendus homo?
tu licet exustus vacuas solvaris in auras,
  pars melior summi scribet amore viri.
supplice sed voto Christum rogitemus ovantes,
  quo faveat coeptis patris ab arce meis.
haud moveor plausu populi vel munere circi:
  sat mihi pauca viri ponere facta pii.
Christe, poli convexa pio qui numine torques,
  da, queat ut famulus farier apta tuus!'

Reading this prologue we realize that the Italian scholar felt himself to be in the direct line of descent from the classical past. He is a professional grammarian or rhetorician like so many of the Latin poets before him, and, if he is humble before Virgil and the unknown Homer,[4] he has at any rate the consciousness that he is not a mere amateur. But he is one among many; verses are being made everywhere,

> haec faciunt urbi, haec quoque rure viri.[5]

The poem is competently constructed throughout the four books into which it is divided, and if the historian has to use it with great caution because it alters the order of events and is silent about its hero's failures, these things are only to be expected in a panegyric. For, as Giesebrecht has said,[6] the poet, 'taking verses from Virgil, Juvenal, and Statius, celebrates Berengarius just as though he were a hero of antiquity'. So he begins with Berengar's descent from Charles the Great, and puts in the mouth of the dying Charles III a speech in which the kingdom of Italy is committed to his care:[7]

> 'penes imperii te gloria nostri,
> atque tuis stabit Romana potentia fatis!'
> haec fans aetherias ductor concessit in auras,
> supremumque gemens regnorum liquit habenas.

The leaders of Italy also invite him to be their ruler and he is

---

[1] Gloss: *necessitates.*
[2] Gloss: *dona vel munera.*
[3] Gloss: *frequenter egit.*
[4] Unknown that is, in Greek; he knew the Latin *Iliad*, see Manitius, *Gesch.* i. 634.

[5] On studies in Italy at this time, see Giesebrecht, *L'Istruzione in Italia nei primi secoli del medio evo*, Florence 1895, p. 22 sq.
[6] ib., p. 23.
[7] *Poet. Lat. Aevi Car.* iv. 359.

crowned at Pavia. The poet turns to his familiar Statius to help him to describe the peace that now falls upon Italy:[1]

> rura colunt alii, sulcant gravia arva iuvenci,
> tondent prata greges, pendentque in rupe capellae:
> omnibus una quies, et pax erat omnibus una.
> non secus ac longa ventorum pace solutum
> aequor, et imbelli recubant ubi litora somno,
> silvarumque comas et abacto flamine nubes
> mulcet iners aestas, tunc stagna lacusque sonori
> detumuere, tacent exhausti solibus amnes.[2]

But Wido of Spoleto hated this restoration of peace, and began to stir up rebellion. He would be a king himself like Rudolf or Odo of Paris. The poet employs the usual epic machinery; there are speeches and appeals to heaven, and plenty of mythological allusions. The first battle is described, ending in the defeat of Wido. The book closes with the fall of night—

> nox ruit interea, curas hominumque labores
> composuit nigroque polos involvit amictu—[3]

and the burial of the dead.

The theme of the second book is the next battle, which really ended in Berengar's defeat; but the poet cleverly avoids the issue by drawing down the curtain of night upon the battlefield.[4] There is an epic catalogue of the leaders on each side,[5] and the battle itself is a series of single combats, the description of which is accompanied by the usual similes.[6]

In the third book Berengar receives help successively from Sinbald and his father, the Emperor Arnulf. The siege and capture of Bergamo are described with some liveliness. Finally Wido dies, after the clergy have prayed that he may be removed by a speedy death.[7]

The last book deals with Berengar's victory over a fresh enemy, Louis of Burgundy. Then follows the coronation at Rome, which the poet describes as though he had either seen

---

[1] ib., p. 361.
[2] The last five verses are taken without alteration from Statius, *Theb.* iii. 255–9.
[3] p. 369.
[4] p. 383:
> quis modus ulterior vel quae discretio belli,
> ni finem daret aetherea sator orbis ab aula?

nocte instante solo tandem spissisque tenebris
concedunt maesti et trucibus diri-
muntur ab armis.
[5] p. 372.
[6] Cf. p. 379, verse 163:
> ut lupus, in campis pecudes cum vidit apertis. . . .
[7] p. 390.

it or had a full account of it from an eyewitness. He tells how
the people came out to welcome the king:

> sonat ecce Subura
> vocibus elatis populi: 'properate faventes!
> rex venit Ausoniis dudum expectatus ab oris,
> qui minuet solita nostros pietate labores!'[1]

Berengar passed under Monte Mario into the field of Nero, and
the Senate (i.e. the nobles) met him with figures of wild beasts
on their lances.[2] The *scholae* followed, the Greeks singing his
praises in their own tongue, and the Latins also. Two youths,
one the brother of the Pope, the other the son of the Consul,
knelt before the king and kissed his feet. The doors of S. Peter's
were opened, when he had promised to protect the rights of
the Church, and he knelt 'at the tomb of the fisherman and
prayed to Christ with gathering tears'.[3] The coronation took
place later on a Sunday in December 915.

> mox croceis mundum ut lampas Phoebea quadrigis
> luce, deus qua factus homo processit ab antro
> tumbali,[4] perflat, populus concurrit ab urbe
> cernere vestitum trabea imperiique corona
> Augustum.   replicata calent spectacula totis
> aedibus, auratis splendent altaria pannis,
> cum princeps nitidus Tyrio procedit in ostro
> tegmina vestitus crurum rutilante metallo,
> quale decus terrae soliti gestare magistri.
> advenit et domini pastor praepostus ovili
> officio laetus, quamvis resonaret utrinque
> clamor: 'ades presul, totiens quid gaudia differs
> innumeris optata modis? per vincla magistri[5]
> te petimus, depone moras et suffice votis!'
> talibus arae adeunt gestis absida sacratae
> lumina terrarum.   modicum post en diadema
> Caesar habet capiti gemmis auroque levatum,
> unguine nectarei simul est respersus olivi;
> caelicolis qui mos olim succrevit Hebraeis
> lege sacra solitis reges atque ungere vates,
> venturus quod Christus erat dux atque sacerdos,
> omnia quem propter caelo reparentur et arvo.
> iam sacrae resonant aedes fremituque resultant
> clamantis populi: 'valeat tuus, aurea, princeps,
> Roma, diu imperiumque gravi sub pondere pressum

---

[1] p. 398.

[2] p. 398:

> senatus,
> prefigens sudibus rictus sine carne
> ferarum.

[3] p. 400.

[4] i.e. Sunday, and not Easter as was once supposed; see the note in Gregorovius, *Gesch. d. Stadt Rom*, iii. 278–9.

[5] i.e. Peter's chains.

erigat et supera sternat virtute rebelles!'
perstrepuere nimis: sed facta silentia tandem.
lectitat augusti concessos munere pagos
praesulis obsequio gradibus stans lector in altis,
Caesare quo norint omnes data munera, predo
ulterius paveat sacras sibi sumere terras.
dona tulit perpulchra pius haec denique templo:
baltea lata ducum, gestamina cara parentum,
gemmis ac rutilo nimium preciosa metallo,
ac vestes etiam signis auroque rigentes,
distinctum variis simul et diadema figuris.
quid referam, quantis replerit moenia donis?
nonne maris paucas videor contingere guttas,
Syrtibus atque manu sumptas includere arenas,
quando brevi tantos cludo sermone triumphos?
doctiloquum, credo, labor iste gravaret Homerum,
officio et genuit tali quem Mantua dignum.
nec temptabo meis ultra fastidia dictis,
o iuvenes, inferre, calet quîs pectore sanguis
et plectro meliore movet praecordia Clio;
mille mihi satis est metris tetigisse labores:
Mevius atque licet videar, vos este Marones,
et post imperii diadema resumite laudes![1]

So in the concluding lines of his panegyric the poet describes
that strange scene, enacted so many times, of the German
king[2] coming to Rome to receive from the hands of the successor of Peter the diadem of the Caesars. Just as in the fifth
century Sidonius Apollinaris had to compose his rhetorical
panegyrics for ephemeral emperors, so the Italian professor,
in the dark days of the tenth century, sang the praises of an
Emperor who was to perish in a few years by the hand of
a murderer. The Italian poet had not at his command the too
ready utterance of a Sidonius. He was even driven to borrow,
without adaptation, whole verses from the classical poets; but
he, too, had his rhetorical equipment, his speeches, his invocations, and his similes, and it is pleasant to picture him reading
his verses to the applause of his pupils, which must have been
redoubled at the final self-depreciation:

Mevius atque licet videar, vos este Marones,
et post imperii diadema resumite laudes!

The most striking representative of Italian learning in the
tenth century is, undoubtedly, Liutprand, Bishop of Cremona,
from whose writings we gain a lively impression of the man

[1] p. 400 sq.   [2] Berengar, though king in Italy,
                                  was of German origin.

himself and of the circles in which he moved. He was born
about the year 920, probably in Pavia, and he belonged to
a family which retained a proud consciousness of its Lombard
origin.[1] He was brought up at the court of King Hugo, and
was educated at the famous Court school. His step-father saw
that a good literary education was the best means of ensuring
worldly success and, when the young Liutprand was ordained
deacon, that success was already certain. The loyalty of
Liutprand and of his family easily passed to the new king
Berengar of Ivrea in 945, and in 949 he visited Constantinople
on an embassy. There he seems to have perfected his knowledge of Greek. On his return he lost Berengar's favour, and
retired to Germany, where he began his *Antapodosis*,[2] that
mixture of gossip, inaccurate information, and history, in which
he inserted at intervals verses of his own composition. Otto
the Great was now his patron, and it was from him that he
received the bishopric of Cremona in 961. In 968 he went on
the mission to Constantinople to negotiate a royal marriage,
which he has made famous by his *Relatio de legatione Constanti-
nopolitana*.[3] In this account, as in his other writings, there
appear, besides his incurable pedantry and his parade of
knowledge in both learned tongues, a malicious humour and
a wealth of invective which he loved to employ against the
great.[4] As an Italian he felt himself a man of letters who was
not writing a foreign tongue. He quotes Virgil or Juvenal with
careless ease, and, when he wishes, he can cite the New Testament[5] or Hippolytus of Porto[6] in the original Greek or, in
Latin, a phrase from Plato's *Republic*.[7]

[1] Cf. *Liudprandi Legatio*, xii, p. 182, *Liudprandi Opera*, ed. J. Becker, Hannover 1915.

[2] It will be seen that Liutprand followed contemporary fashion in choosing a Greek title for his work. It was intended to be a kind of 'history of his own time', but it is a mere collection of episodes, enlivened by curious stories and eked out by moralizing reflections. The title *Antapodosis* is of personal significance and means 'repayment' (*retributio*) to enemies and friends for the evil and the good that he had received at their hands.

[3] *Liudprandi Opera*, pp. 175 sqq.

[4] Cf. p. 181. He describes the progress of the Emperor Nicephorus to

S. Sophia. 'As that monster went on, like a creeping snake,' the people cried or chanted, 'Behold the morning star cometh,' etc. What they ought to have sung, says Liutprand, with a Rabelaisian wealth of adjectives, was: 'carbo extincte veni, μέλε, anus incessu, Sylvanus vultu, rustice, lustrivage, capripes, cornute, bimembris, setiger, indocilis, agrestis, barbare, dure, villose, rebellis, Cappadox!' The force of the final 'Cappadox' is very happy.

[5] *Opera*, p. 106.

[6] ib., p. 196.

[7] ib., p. 189. We cannot assume that Liutprand had direct access to ancient Greek or patristic literature, but he had at least read a good deal of Byzantine

The verses with which he adorned his history are intended
to be a further evidence of his accomplishments. They are, of
course, in classical metres, and they are not mere insertions
in the text. When Liutprand is describing how Henry the
Fowler attempted to bring Arnulf of Bavaria to submission,
and finally decided to persuade him by a personal discussion,
he puts the king's speech into verse:

'Quem sibi obviam properantem rex Heinricus tali est sermone adgressus:
    Insana Domini iussis quid mente resistis?
     quod populus regem me cupit esse, scias,
    imperio Christi, quo constat machina mundi;
     Tartarus hunc metuit, hunc Flegeton timuit.
    conterit hic nitidos reges dudumque tremendos
     sublimesque volens, erigit hic miseros,
    quo debitas Domino laudes per secula solvant.
     tunc, superbe, reus, perfide, dure, ferox,
    invidiae stimulis saevaque cupidine tactus,
     corpora Christicolum perdere valde sitis?
    si regem populus cuperet praeponere temet,
     protinus is essem, qui magis hoc cuperet.

hoc igitur quadrifario dicendi genere, copioso scilicet, brevi, sicco et florido,
rex Heinricus, ut erat animi prudens, Arnaldi animum mulcens ad suos
rediit.'

This passage shows significantly how the old rhetorical tradition kept its sway. This is a school exercise, a declamation on
the theme—'King Henry addresses Arnulf, who is in rebellion
against him.' But Liutprand, if he was not a very good poet,
was not a mere laborious fabricator of verses. He used verse
quite naturally to meet its proper occasion. So when he quitted
Constantinople, raging with the memory of the mean insults
which he had endured from his Greek hosts, he inscribed on
the wall of the bleak and ill-appointed lodging in which he
had spent so many days of misery a lampoon against the
Emperor Nicephorus which was the only revenge he was able
to take. Such, at any rate, is his version of the events.[1]

historical and other works. The numerous Greek words and Greek quotations in his text are followed by trans-
literations and translations, but Köhler,
'Beiträge zur Textkritik Liudprands
von Cremona', *Neues Archiv*, viii
(1883), pp. 81 sqq., and, following him,
J. Becker, *Textgeschichte Liudprands
von Cremona*, Munich 1908, p. 36 sq.,
have shown that these glosses almost
certainly do not belong to Liutprand's
original text.

  [1] *Opera*, p. 206. H. Lintzel, *Studien
über Liudprand von Cremona*, Berlin
1933, p. 44, n. 7, doubts whether Liudprand, here or elsewhere, is strictly
truthful. The *Relatio* is a political
pamphlet, not an official report.

§ 4. *Shorter Italian Poems.*

The general character of Italian learning is well exhibited in the *Gesta Berengarii* and in the writings of Liutprand. The mistrust with which this independent secular tradition was sometimes viewed by the clergy is mirrored in the story of Wilgard the grammarian, who was visited by evil spirits in the shape of Virgil, Horace, and Juvenal, and was finally punished for heresy.[1] In Rome itself learning had sunk low during the abasement of the Papacy, and it did not easily lift its head once more. It is true that the disgraceful affair of Pope Formosus gave rise to a war of pamphlets, and that Eugenius Vulgarius, one of the pamphleteers, left behind him a little collection of poems which illustrate the persistence of old traditions. Eugenius Vulgarius[2] appears to have been a Neapolitan priest who was ordained by Pope Formosus (891–6). When the Pope died his immediate successor reigned for fifteen days. Then Stephen VI sat in the chair of Peter, and made his papacy memorable by the terrible judgement which he executed on the body of his former enemy, Formosus, whose acts were now declared void, including the ordinations which he had performed. The memory and the acts of Formosus were, however, rehabilitated by John IX (898–900), for he had himself been ordained by that Pope. But in 904 Sergius III, who had been a friend of Stephen VI, renewed the condemnation of Formosus and his deeds, and it was with Sergius that Eugenius Vulgarius had to reckon. During his papacy the ruined Lateran was rebuilt, but it is difficult to take a favourable view of his personal character. About the year 907 Eugenius had produced a pamphlet—*De causa Formosiana libellus*,[3] the real object of which was to protect the validity of the ordinations made by Formosus. The author seems to have suffered for his outspokenness by being shut up in the monastery of Monte Cassino. Then the Pope summoned him to Rome, and Eugenius thought it prudent to use every means in his power to placate Sergius and win the favour of the great. For he was obviously apprehensive of further punishment. So he wrote to the Pope and sent him verses which he had composed in his honour.[4] One was a foolish *carmen figuratum*[5] with an elaborate triple acrostic, reading

[1] Glaber, *Hist.* (Bouquet, *Recueil des historiens*, x. 23); cf. *Christian-Latin Poetry*, p. 232.
[2] E. Dümmler, *Auxilius und Vulgarius*, Leipzig 1866.
[3] Dümmler, pp. 117 sqq.
[4] *Poet. Lat. Aevi Car.* iv. 412 sqq.
[5] ib., p. 413.

aeternum salve presul stans ordine Petri.

To the Emperor Leo he dedicated a poem in the form of a pyramid,[1] and to the Pope another in the shape of an organ.[2] Eugenius had obviously before him the example of Porfirius, and he is, it would seem, one of the last poets to employ these childish devices. That he delighted in his skill and made a parade of his learning is apparent from the expositions which accompany his figure-poems. The verses entitled *De thesin et hypothesin* and *De syllogismis dialectice et hypothicaliter*[3] are designed to show his dialectical accomplishments. The latter poem is given as an example:

> Si sol est, et lux est; at sol est: igitur lux.
> si non sol, non lux est; at lux est: igitur sol.
> non est sol et non-lux; at sol est: igitur lux.
> aut sol est aut lux; at sol est: non igitur lux.
> aut sol est aut lux; at non est sol: igitur lux.
> non est sol et lux; at sol est: non igitur lux.
> non est sol et lux; at non sol est: igitur lux.

But Eugenius wrote poems of a more serious kind in lyric metres which he borrowed from Prudentius and Boëthius.[4] So he celebrated Leo in adonics:[5]

> Dicite gentes
> undique laudes,
> lingua perita
> carmina docta;
> musicus ordo
> coetus et omnis,
> Orpheus ipse
> organa quassans,
> Linus ydraulas
>
> molliter implens,
> alta refractim
> omnia dicant:
> ut Leo caesar
> magnus et unus
> sede coruscus,
> divus honoris,
> numine felix
> vivat in annos.

But more remarkable than any of these verses is a poem under the heading of *Species comice*, which introduces two pieces near the end of the collection.[6] It is hardly likely that this pleasant composition is the work of Eugenius Vulgarius. The metre is best described as iambic dimeter acatalectic,

---

[1] ib., p. 422.
[2] ib., p. 438. The following (p. 421) is called *Eugenii Vulgarii crux.*

> Congreditur mundo CUrsu mirabile factoR,
> Vexillum gestans, aRX in quo permanet anaX.

[3] ib., p. 426.
[4] Cf. Manitius, *Gesch.* i. 435.
[5] *Poet. Lat. Aevi Car.* iv. 425. Other poems to Leo are entitled *Metrum ana-*

pesticum isosyllabum and *Metrum asclepiadeum* (p. 424).
[6] p. 430.

in four-line stanzas; the verses are quantitative but verge occasionally on accentual, and, apart from the first stanza, rime on the letter *a*.[1]

1. Anacreunti carmine
   telam libet contexere,
   pedem pedi lentiscere
   et tramitem transducere.

2. sunt saecla praeclarissima,
   sunt prata vernantissima,
   formosa gaudent omnia,
   sunt grata nostri moenia.

3. laetentur ergo somata
   et rideant praecordia,
   amor petens finitima
   sint cuncta vitulantia.

4. Phoebus rotat per tempora
   torquens polorum lumina;
   somnum susurrant flumina,
   aves canunt et dulcia.

5. turtur prior dans oscina,
   rauce sonat post ardea;
   sistema miscens merula,
   olos implet croëmata.

6. myrto sedens lusciola,
   'vos cara', dicens, 'pignora,
   audite matris famina,
   dum lustrat aether sidera.

7. cantans mei similia,
   canora prolis germina,
   cantu deo dignissima
   tractim refrange guttura.

8. tu namque plebs laetissima,
   tantum dei tu psaltria
   divina cantans cantica
   per blanda cordis viscera.

9. materna iam nunc formula
   ut rostra vincas plumea,
   futura vocis organa
   contempera citissima.'

10. hoc dixit et mox iubila
    secuntur subtilissima;
    melum fit voce tinnula
    soporans mentis intima.

11. densantur hinc spectacula,
    accurrit omnis bestia,
    leaena, lynx et dammula,
    caudata stans vulpecula.

12. pisces relinquunt aequora
    et vada sunt retrograda;
    pulsando Codrus ilia
    praegnas adest invidia,

13. auro sedet rex aquila,
    circum cohors per agmina,
    gemmata pavo tergora,
    cornix subest et garrula.

14. corvina quin centuria,
    ardet phalans et milvea;
    de marte tractant omnia,
    vincatur ut lusciola.

15. palumbes at iuvencula
    praesumit e victoria;
    gallus prior cum merula
    disrumpta plangunt ilia;

16. cicadis inflans iecora
    campo crepat misellula;
    palmam tenet lusciola
    versus trahens per sibila.

17. turbata gens tum rostrea,
    exsanguis hinc et aquila;
    frigescit, in praecordia
    virtusque cedit ossea.

18. praeco fugae fit ulula
    urgens gradi per abdita,
    pudore mens ne conscia
    poenas luat per saecula.

19. tunc versa castra plumea
    sparsim legunt aumatia
    auraeque fissa flamina,
    petuntur tecta silvea.

---

[1] Cf. Stephen Gaselee, *Oxford Book of Medieval Latin Verse*, p. 218. With the aid of Mr. Gaselee's notes, the reader will be able to understand the poem.

We have here, of course, a bird and beast story—the victory of
the nightingale over all other singers; but we have as well
the uncertain note of a new poetry. Yet this is not an isolated
voice.

Towards the end of the ninth or early in the tenth century
a scholar of Modena composed a song addressed to the defenders
of the city, whose walls had just been rebuilt. There was
danger again from the fierce Hungarians, and this was the
occasion of these verses, where classical reminiscences are
mingled with Christian invocations:[1]

> O tu qui servas armis ista moenia,
> nolli dormire, moneo, sed vigila!
> dum Hector vigil extitit in Troïa,
> non eam cepit fraudulenta Graecia:
> prima quiete dormiente Troïa
> laxavit Synon fallax claustra perfida:
>
> per funem lapsa occultata agmina
> invadunt urbem et incendunt Pergama.
> vigili voce avis anser candida
> fugavit Gallos ex arce Romulea,
> pro qua virtute facta est argentea
> et a Romanis adorata ut dea.
>
> nos adoremus celsa Christi numina;
> illi canora demus nostra iubila,
> illius magna fisi sub custodia
> haec vigilantes iubilemus carmina:
> divina, mundi rex Christe, custodia
> sub tua serva haec castra vigilia.
>
> tu murus tuis sis inexpugnabilis,
> sis inimicis hostis tu terribilis.
> te vigilante nulla nocet fortia,
> qui cuncta fugas procul arma bellica.
> tu cinge nostra haec, Christe, munimina,
> defendens ea tua forti lancea.
>
> sancta Maria, mater Christi splendida,
> haec cum Iohanne, theotocos, impetra;
> quorum hic sancta venerantur pignora
> et quibus ista sunt sacrata limina;
> quo duce victrix est in bello dextera
> et sine ipso nihil valent iacula.
>
> fortis iuventus, virtus audax bellica,
> vestra per muros audiantur carmina;
> et sit in armis alterna vigilia,
> ne fraus hostilis haec invadat moenia:
> resultet echo 'comes, eia vigila,'
> per muros 'eia' dicat echo 'vigila'.

[1] Text, *Poet. Lat. Aevi Car.* iii. 703.

This poem is in the Italian tradition going back to Paulinus of Aquileia,[1] but with the additional adornment of the same single rime carried through nearly the whole of the verses. For the historian this piece has another interest.[2] In those troubled days the cities had to protect themselves as best they might. It was useless to look to the king; so, often with the aid of the Bishop, the city would make its defences strong and create a citizen army to guard the walls. The poem is a witness to the warlike spirit of the young Italians, a spirit which is reflected elsewhere in the sources of the time.[3]

The next Italian piece is of quite another character. It bears the mark of moral perversion and of scholastic pedantry; but the compiler of the 'Cambridge songs' included it in his anthology and songs on such themes were not altogether frowned on in that age:[4]

O admirabile Veneris idolum,
cuius materiae nihil est frivolum,
Archos te protegat, qui stellas et polum
fecit et maria condidit et solum.
furis ingenio non sentias dolum:
Cloto te diligat, quae baiolat colum.

'salvato puerum' non per ipotesim,
sed firmo pectore deprecor Lachesim,
sororem Atropos, ne curet heresim.
Neptunum comitem habeas et Tetim,
cum vectus fueris per fluvium Tesim.
quo fugis, amabo, cum te dilexerim?
miser quid faciam, cum te non viderim?

dura materies ex matris ossibus
creavit homines iactis lapidibus,
ex quibus unus est iste puerulus,
qui lacrimabiles non curat gemitus.

[1] See *Christian-Latin Poetry*, p. 169 sq.

[2] L. Chiappelli, 'La formazione storica del Comune cittadino in Italia', *Archivio storico italiano*, serie vii, vol. x (1928), pp. 50 sqq. Chiappelli places the date of the poem round about the year 892 (p. 55).

[3] It has been regarded also as an early variety of the *aube* (i.e. without a love-motive, but introducing the watchman who foretells the dawn); cf. Jeanroy, *Les origines de la poésie lyrique en France au moyen âge*, 2nd ed., Paris 1904, p. 72. To this poem he

joins another, with a vernacular refrain,
Phebi claro nondum orto iubare,
fert Aurora lumen terris tenue:
spiculator pigris clamat: 'surgite!'
l'alba par umet mar atra sol
poy pas abigil miraclar tenebras ...
(ed. J. Schmidt, *Zeitschr. für deutsche Philol.* xii (1881), pp. 333 sqq.). It is not clear whether this latter poem is to be regarded as a love-*aube*. I should prefer to place it in the same class as *O tu qui servas*.

[4] Cf. the remarks of Traube, 'O Roma nobilis', *Abhandl. d. königl. bayer. Akad. der Wissensch.* 1891, p. 307.

cum tristis fuero, gaudebit emulus:
ut cerva rugio, cum fugit hinnulus.[1]

The rhythmical scheme of this poem is best regarded as dactylic, as is that of the famous *O Roma nobilis*, which perhaps, as well as the *O admirabile Veneris idolum*, belongs to Verona. But in *O Roma nobilis* there is an impulse soaring into true poetry:[2]

> O Roma nobilis, orbis et domina,
> cunctarum urbium excellentissima,
> roseo martyrum sanguine rubea.
> albis et virginum liliis candida:
> salutem dicimus tibi per omnia,
> te benedicimus: salve per secula.
>
> Petre, tu prepotens caelorum claviger,
> vota precantium exaudi iugiter.
> cum bis sex tribuum sederis arbiter,
> factus placabilis iudica leniter.
> teque petentibus nunc temporaliter
> ferto suffragia misericorditer.
>
> o Paule, suscipe nostra precamina,
> cuius philosophos vicit industria.
> factus economus in domo regia
> divini muneris appone fercula,
> ut, quae repleverit te sapientia,
> ipsa nos repleat tua per dogmata.

These poems have generally been regarded as welcome land-marks on the route of medieval rhythmical verse. They certainly could not fail to attract notice, but they do not really point to the future. They are, rather, specifically Italian, and are a continuation of the tradition of the Italian-Carolingian rhythm.

§ 5. *The 'Cambridge Songs'*.

There is in the University Library at Cambridge a famous codex (Gg. 5. 35) of the eleventh century, part of which is a collection of Christian poetry, consisting of Aldhelm's *Aenigmata* and *De Virginitate*, and verses of Boniface, Milo, and Smaragdus. But it is the collection of songs it contains that makes it, as its latest editor has said, 'a cultural document of

---

[1] ib., p. 301; text also in Strecker, *Die Cambridger Lieder*, pp. 105 sqq. I follow Strecker's text. The two MSS. read 'fluvium tesim' (thesim), which is usually corrected into 'Athesim' (the Adige); but the measure requires 'tesim', and Strecker suspects here some obscure

play of learning. 'Amabo' ('pray') is an archaic use, found in Plautus.
[2] Traube, p. 300. Manitius, *Gesch.* i. 636, suggests that the poems are by the same author. This is not impossible, but the execution of the *O Roma nobilis* seems superior to that of the other.

the first order'.[1] The importance of this collection for the
light which it throws on the history of the Latin lyric in the
Middle Ages will appear as its contents are analysed, and we
shall also see what kind of verses a well-educated German,
who was fond of music, chose to gather in one volume about
the middle of the eleventh century.

The collection, as it stands, consists of forty-nine pieces, of
which the last is almost wholly indecipherable, having been
erased on account of its questionable content.[2] Strecker's
masterly analysis of the collection shows that it consists of
two main parts. The first piece is merely an extract from a
well-known hymn on the Nativity.[3] But numbers 2 to 15 are,
with one exception (no. 10),[4] in sequence-form, whether the
subjects be religious or profane. Now four of these same pieces
are preserved together as a 'similar small collection'[5] in *Cod.
3610, August. 56. 16,* of the Library at Wolfenbüttel (eleventh
century; called W by Strecker, the Cambridge MS. being
known as C). These pieces are numbers 5, 15, 14, 11, in this
order. The first is a religious sequence, *Modus qui et Carelmanninc,* beginning *Inclito celorum.* The next two are profane
pieces, the *Modus florum* and the *Modus Liebinc.* The last is
the *Modus Ottinc,* and begins *Magnus Cesar Otto.* It is obvious
that there is some relation between C and W; but Strecker
rightly concludes that, as there is no sign of textual dependence
between them, it is wiser to postulate an original collection of
sequences (U = Ursequenzsammlung) which was drawn upon
by the compilers of C and of W.[6] If this be so, the compiler of

[1] *Die Cambridger Lieder (Carmina
Cantabrigiensia),* ed. K. Strecker, Berlin 1926, p. v.

[2] No. 28 also is badly mutilated, and
for the same reason.

[3] *Anal. Hymn.* l. 195. *Gratuletur
omnis caro*: ascribed to Raban Maur.

[4] p. 29. This is the nightingale poem
which is usually ascribed to Fulbert
of Chartres; see *Christian-Latin Poetry,*
p. 262.

[5] Strecker, p. xi.

[6] ib., p. xiii. Have we evidence of
this original collection in the poems of
Amarcius (*Sexti Amarcii Galli Piosi-
strati sermonum libri,* iv, ed. Manitius,
1888), who wrote under this pseudonym
a satire round about the middle of the
eleventh century? (Manitius, *Gesch.* ii.
569). A *jocator* sings before a rich
man:

ille fides aptans crebro diapente
    canoras,
straverit ut grandem pastoris funda
    Goliath,
ut simili argutus uxorem Suevulus
    arte
luserit, utque sagax nudaverit octo
    tenores
cantus Pytagoras, et quam mera vox
    philomenae,
perstrepit.

Now C has no poem about Goliath, and
it is unnecessary to suppose that it
possessed it originally, but that it has
fallen out of the manuscript. The other
three poems can be identified as nos.
14, 12, and 10. Strecker concludes that
Amarcius had in mind either U or some
other collection derived from it. It is
probable, as he says, that Amarcius'
collection and C were related, since in

C took numbers 2–15 from this collection, and, apart from the
nightingale poem, we may call this first section of the Cambridge song-book a collection of German songs.

Of the remaining pieces, numbers 16–49, some are merely
extracts from classical authors (31 and 32 from Statius; 34
from Virgil; 46 from Horace), and there are several religious
pieces. The German element is again prominent, but the
section represented by numbers 35–47 may, in accordance with
Strecker's suggestion, be taken, though with some reserve, as
French.[1] Number 48 (*O admirabile Veneris idolum*) is, as we
already know, Italian, but it is impossible to determine whether
the mutilated number 49 was Italian or French.[2]

Where was the collection C gathered together? The question
cannot be answered in any very precise terms. Brinkmann[3]
confidently refers to the Rhineland as the place of origin, and
there is nothing impossible in such a suggestion; but, as
Strecker points out,[4] the evidence that certain poems were
collected in the Rhineland does not prove that the individual
poems originated there.[5] The collection C is such as might
have been compiled for some ecclesiastic, a man of learning
and of catholic taste, such as were not lacking in this age.
For it is hardly to be conceived that it was a German layman
who cared for these things. It is essentially a song-book, for
even the classical excerpts were meant for singing.[6]

One of the most striking features of the collection is the
manner in which the immensely popular religious sequences
provided a form for secular compositions. Here, beside a
solemn prose—*Modus qui et Carelmanninc*,[7]

> Inclito celorum   laus sit digna Deo,
> qui celo scandens
> soli regna
> visitavit
> redempturus hominem—

both of them the French rhythmical
poem on the nightingale appears along-
side of sequences pure and simple
(p. xvi). Amarcius was a German
(Manitius, *Gesch.* ii. 569).

[1] Strecker, p. xvii.
[2] I should be inclined to call it
French.
[3] H. Brinkmann, *Geschichte der lateinischen Liebesdichtung im Mittelalter*,
Halle 1925, p. 8.
[4] Strecker, p. xix.

[5] Strecker (pp. xviii sqq.) says that
among nos. 2–15, no. 7 (on Heribert of
Cologne) and no. 8 (on S. Victor of Xan-
ten) point to the Rhine; but no. 9 (on
Henry II) and also nos. 5, 14, and 15,
point elsewhere. In nos. 16–34 Strecker
finds five pieces which may support a
Rhenish origin for the collector of the
poems.
[6] p. xvii.
[7] No. 5, p. 8.

is the profane story of Lantfrid and Cobbo, a legendary pair of friends whose history was a favourite subject of song:[1]

1 *a*. Omnis sonus cantilene trifariam fit.
nam aut fidium concentu sonus constat
pulsu plectri manusve,
ut sunt discrepantie vocum variis
chordarum generibus;

1 *b*. aut tibiarum canorus redditur flatus,
fistularum ut sunt discrimina, queque
folle ventris orisque
tumidi flatu perstrepentia pulchre
mentem mulcisonant;

2 *a*. aut multimodis gutture canoro idem sonus redditur
plurimarum faucium, hominum volucrum animantiumque,
sicque in pulsu guttureque agitur.

2 *b*. his modis canamus carorum sotiorumque actus,
quorum ⟨in⟩ honorem pretitulatur prohemium hocce pulchre
Lantfridi Cobbonisque pernobili stemmate.

3. Quamvis amicitiarum
genera plura legantur,
non sunt adeo preclara
ut istorum sodalium,
qui communes extiterunt
in tantum, ut neuter horum
suapte quid possideret
⟨nec⟩ gazarum nec servorum
nec alicuius suppellectilis;
alter horum quicquid vellet,
ab altero ratum foret;
more ambo coequales,
in nullo umquam dissides,
quasi duo unus esset,
in omnibus similes.

4. porro prior orsus Cobbo
dixit fratri sotio:
'diu mihi hic regale
incumbit servitium,
quod fratres affinesque
visendo non adeam,

immemor meorum.
ideo ultra mare revertar,
unde huc adveni;
illorum affectui
veniendo ad illos
ibi satisfaciam.'

5. 'tedet me,' Lantfridus inquit,
'vite proprie tam dire,
ut absque te solus hic degam.
nam arripiens coniugem
tecum pergam exul, tecum,
ut tu diu factus mecum
vicem rependens amori.'
sicque pergentes litora maris
applicarunt pariter.
tum infit Cobbo sodali:
'hortor, frater, maneas:
redeam visendo ⟨te⟩
en vita comite;
unum memoriale
frater fratri facias:

[1] No. 6, p. 13; the popularity of the story is proved by the existence of a rhythmical version, apparently made in France; ib., p. 17. The text is given by H. Patzig, 'Lantfrid und Cobbo', *Romanische Forschungen*, vi (1891), pp. 424 sqq. It begins:

Cum insignorum virorum gesta dictis
fulgeant,
ecce dulcibus iam decet modulis ut
clareant,
quatinus illorum facta fidem nobis
augeant.
This is given also in Strecker, pp. 18 sqq.

6. uxorem, quam tibi solam
   vendicasti propriam,
   mihi dedas, ut licenter
   fruar eius amplexu.'
   nihil hesitando manum
   manui eius tribuens hilare:
   'fruere ut libet, frater, ea,
   ne dicatur, quod semotim
   nisus sim quid possidere.'
   classe tunc apparata
   ducit secum in equor.

7. stans Lantfridus super litus
   cantibus chordarum ait:
   'Cobbo frater, fidem tene,
   hactenus ut feceras,

nam indecens est affectum
sequendo voti honorem perdere:
dedecus frater fratri ne fiat.'
sicque diu canendo
post illum intuitus,
longius eum non cernens
fregit rupe timpanum.

8. at Cobbo collisum
   fratrem non ferens
   mox vertendo mulcet:
   'en habes, perdulcis amor,
   quod dedisti, intactum
   ante amoris experimentum.
   iam non est, quod experiatur ultra;
   ceptum iter relinquam.'

The learned author of this amusing composition went to Isidore's *Etymologiae* (iii. 18) for the matter of his opening strophes, which expound the nature of musical sounds.[1] They are either the sounds of stringed or of wind instruments; or the voices of men, of birds, or of animals. It is in the latter kind, the vocal, that he will tell his story of friendship. The tale is solemnly told, without much poetical embellishment, and it ends with that slight touch of obscenity which was a necessary ingredient even of edifying stories. The structure of the poem does not easily lend itself to description. The composition begins with a fairly close parallelism in the first two pairs of stanzas, which form a kind of introduction; but here the recognizable parallelism ends, and the sequence proceeds with a succession of independent stanzas.[2] The continually recurring approximations to definite rhythmical structure suggest that the poem is a composition of the eleventh century. The slight traces of rime are accidental.

The *Modus Liebinc*[3] is in many ways an abler composition. It preserves the strict parallelism of the sequence, with a single concluding strophe. The story is the familiar legend of the

---

[1] Cf. Strecker, p. 17.

[2] Stanza 3 consists roughly of verses of 8 syllables; stanza 4, which ought to correspond with it, has two only of 8 syllables, seven of 7 syllables, and two of 6 and one of 10 (Strecker, p. 16). Stanzas 6 and 7, which ought not to correspond, resemble each other closely in structure and rhythm.

[3] Strecker, p. 41 (no. 41); see also Meyer, *Fragmenta Burana*, pp. 174 sqq. Meyer says of this and the next poem, 'Die Formen dieser Gedichte sind so krystallklar und so klangschön, dass sie von einem Meister geschaffen sein müssen, der des Gesanges und des Harfen-spiels mindestens so kundig war als der schönen Rede.'

'snow-child', an absurd story such as the slower wit of the North produced laboriously:

1 *a*. Advertite,
omnes populi,
ridiculum
et audite, quomodo
Suevum mulier
et ipse illam
defraudaret.

1 *b*. Constantie
civis suevulus
trans equora
gazam portans navibus
domi coniugem
lascivam nimis
relinquebat.

2 *a*. vix remige
triste secat mare,
ecce subito
orta tempestate
furit pelagus,
certant flamina,
tolluntur fluctus,
post multaque exulem
vagum littore
longinquo nothus
exponebat.

2 *b*. nec interim
domi vacat coniux;
mimi aderant,
iuvenes secuntur,
quos et immemor
viri exulis
excepit gaudens
atque nocte proxima
pregnans filium
iniustum fudit
iusto die.

3 *a*. duobus
volutis annis
exul dictus
revertitur;
occurrit
infida coniux
secum trahens
puerulum.
datis osculis
maritus illi
'de quo,' inquit, 'puerum
istum habeas,
dic, aut extrema
patieris.'

3 *b*. at illa
maritum timens
dolos versat
in omnia.
'mi,' tandem,
'mi coniux,' inquit,
'una vice
in Alpibus
nive sitiens
extinxi sitim.
inde ergo gravida
istum puerum
damnoso foetu
heu gignebam.'

4 *a*. anni post hec quinque
transierant aut plus,
et mercator vagus
instauravit remos:
ratim quassam reficit,
vela alligat
et nivis natum
duxit secum.

4 *b*. transfretato mari
producebat natum
et pro arrabone
mercatori tradens
centum libras accipit
atque vendito
infante dives
revertitur.

5 *a*. ingressusque domum
ad uxorem ait:
'consolare, coniux,
consolare, cara:
natum tuum perdidi,
quem non ipsa tu

5 *b*. tempestate orta
nos ventosus furor
in vadosas sirtes
nimis fessos egit,
et nos omnes graviter
torret sol, at il-

me magis quidem
dilexisti.

le nivis natus
liquescebat.'

6. sic perfidam
   Suevus coniugem
   deluserat;
   sic fraus fraudem vicerat:
   nam quem genuit
   nix, recte hunc sol
   liquefecit.

The author of this poem was a master of the sequence-form in the stage when it was assuming a rhythmical structure without much admixture of rime. He tells his story just as the composer of a religious sequence, taking the life of a saint for subject, might tell his,[1] and he shows his learning by two reminiscences of Horace, and one from the *Jugurtha* of Sallust.[2] The 'dirge' in sequence-form on Archbishop Heribert of Cologne (d. 1021) is properly a religious composition,[3] and so is the sequence on S. Victor.[4] The lament for the Emperor Henry II (d. 1024) is a learned piece, with a reminiscence of Prudentius and a show of Greek learning.[5] There is a refrain:

imperatoris Heinrici
catholici
magni ac pacifici
beatifica animam,
Christe,

and the poet strikes the true note of the *Leich* in the fourth strophe:

heu o Roma   cum Italia,
caput mundi,   quantum decus perdideras!

heu o Franci,   heu Bavvarii,
vestrum damnum   nulli constat incognitum!

The *Modus Ottinc*[6] is a sequence in praise of Otto the Great. It shows the same careful construction as the *Modus Liebinc*, and is likewise the work of a man of learning. It is not difficult to accept the suggestion of Wilhelm Meyer that both pieces were composed about the year 1000 by one author.[7]

[1] A good example is the sequence *in Decollatione s. Johannis Bapt.* in *Anal. Hymn.* l, p. 275; or better still the sequence on S. Paul (ib., p. 276), which actually begins with an invitation, similar to that in the *Modus Liebinc*,

concurrite huc, populi
et insulae, etc.

Strecker (p. 41) thinks that the beginning of the *Modus Liebinc* parodies the opening lines of a lost sequence by Heribert of Eichstätt.

[2] Horace, *Od.* I. i. 14 and 16–18; Sallust, *De bello Jugurthino*, c. 78.
[3] No. 7, p. 21.
[4] No. 8, p. 25.
[5] No. 9, p. 27.
[6] No. 11, p. 33.
[7] *Fragmenta Burana*, p. 176.

Even more learned is the sequence on Pythagoras[1] which shows a very fair acquaintance with the teaching of this great thinker, in the form in which it was transmitted by the later ancient world:[2]

1 a. Vite dator, omnifactor
deus, nature formator
mundi globum sub potenti
claudens volubilem palmo,
in factura sua splendet
magnificus per evum.

1 b. ipse multos veritatem
veteres necdum sequentes
vestigando per sophie
devia iusserat ire
improbabilis, errore
parare nobis viam.

2 a. inter quos subtilis
per acumen mentis
claruit Pitagoras,
metapsicosis quem
iuxta famam Troie peremptum
seculo rursus reddit,
obscurosque rerum rite
denuo vivum donat
intellectus perspicaci
perscrutari
sensu animi.

2 b. ergo vir hic prudens
die quadam ferri
fabricam preteriens
pondere non equo
sonoque diverso pulsare
malleolos senserat,
sicque tonorum quamlibet
informem vim latere
noscens forma addita
artem pulchram
primus edidit.

3 a. ad hanc simphonias tres
subplendam istas fecit:
diatesseron, diapente,
diapason
infra quaternarium,
que pleniter armoniam sonant;
que sententia
senis ponens solidum
rithmicam in se normulam
mensurarumque
utilem notitiam
et siderum motus
iussit continere, ma ten tetradem,
et nomine
suo vocavit.

3 b. Y Grecam, I de imis
continentem, sed fissam
summotenus in ramosas
binas partes,
vite humane invenit
ad similitudinem congruam.
est nam sincera
et simplex pueritia,
que non facile noscitur,
utrum vitiis
an virtuti animum
subicere velit,
donec tandem iuventutis etas
illud offert
nobis bivium.

4 a. hic qui paret viciis
virtuti contrariis, illam
latam ille
terit ipse semitam,

4 b. sed virtutum gradibus
ille nititur, qui providus
per angustam
vadit illam semitam,

[1] No. 12, p. 36. The Cambridge MS. gives the beginning of another philosophical poem (no. 37, p. 91), of which the complete text is available from other sources (given by Strecker, p. 113). It is an interesting school-poem, telling how Philosophy passed from Greece to the West, and describing the Quadrivium.

[2] The author seems to have been acquainted with Macrobius and Martianus Capella; cf. Macrobius, *Comm. in Somnium Scipionis*, II. i. 8 sqq., for stanzas 2b and 3a. From 3b onwards he expounds the famous doctrine of the 'two ways'.

que postremo,
plena poenis gravibus,
se prosequentibus
portas inferi
aperit sevissimas,
ubi fremitus dentium
et perpetui
fletus sunt merentium
pro criminis facto;
cita ubi semper mors
optatur frustra
pro dolor! atque queritur.

que in fine
locuples letitie
se prosequentibus
pandit eterna
dulcis vite gaudia,
ubi bonorum anime
claro iugiter
illustrantur lumine
perpetui solis,
ubi deitatis se
conspectum semper
cernere gaudent beati.

5. vite dator, omnifactor
deus, nature formator,
illum aufer, istum confer
tuis fidelibus callem,
ut post obitum talis
vite participes fiant.

If the construction of this sequence is not perfect, the order of its expression is clear and strong, following the manner of religious proses. The poet not improbably practised religious as well as secular compositions, and such a remark may equally be applied to the authors of all the secular sequences in the Cambridge collection. For they are no evidence of lay activity, and it is most likely that they are of monastic origin.[1]

We can say the same of the group of stories in rhythmical verse in the second part of the collection. One is in rhythmic adonics[2] rimed in couplets, though with no very great skill. It is the tale of an ass which was devoured by a wolf, and, as in most of these stories, the scene is laid in a definite place, and the names of the characters are carefully given:

Est unus locus   Homburh dictus,
in quo pascebat   asinam Alfrad,
viribus fortem   atque fidelem.

que dum in amplum   exiret campum
vidit currentem   lupum voracem
caput abscondit,   caudam ostendit.

And so this 'tedious brief' ballad proceeds, for the easy

---

[1] From what we know of the school of S. Gall and of other monastic schools there is no reason to suppose that 'sequences' like the *Modus Liebinc* or the *Modus Florum* (no. 15) would be discountenanced in them. The latter is

the story of a Swabian who won the hand of a king's daughter in a contest of lying. The point of the story was that the king should be compelled to accuse the man of lying.

[2] No. 20, p. 60.

instruction originally, perhaps, of young scholars in some monastic school.

There is more point in the tale about Archbishop Heriger of Mainz and the man who said that he had been to hell and heaven.[1] It is somewhat solemnly told, but it is difficult to see how it could be told in any better way:

1. Heriger, urbis   Maguntiacensis
antistes, quendam   vidit prophetam,
qui ad infernum   se dixit raptum.

2. inde cum multas   referret causas,
subiunxit totum   esse infernum
accinctum densis   undique silvis.

3. Heriger illi   ridens respondit:
'meum subulcum   illic ad pastum
nolo cum macris mittere porcis.'

4. vir ait falsus: 'fui translatus
in templum celi   Christumque vidi
letum sedentem   et comedentem.

5. Iohannes baptista   erat pincerna
atque preclari   pocula vini
porrexit cunctis   vocatis sanctis.'

6. Heriger ait: 'prudenter egit
Christus, Iohannem   ponens pincernam,
quoniam vinum   non bibit unquam.'[2]

7. .   .   .   .

8. 'mendax probaris,   cum Petrum dicis
illic magistrum   esse cocorum,
est quia summi   ianitor celi.

9. honore quali   te deus celi
habuit ibi?   ubi sedisti?
volo, ut narres,   quid manducasses.'

10. respondit homo: 'angulo uno
partem pulmonis   furabar cocis.
hoc manducavi   atque recessi.'

[1] No. 24, p. 65; Heriger was Archbishop from 913–27. We may reasonably place the tale within the limits of the tenth century.

[2] Strecker (p. 65) infers that it is after strophe 6 and not after 5 that a strophe (now lost) appeared, in which S. Peter was said to be the head cook; cf. S. Gaselee, *Oxford Book of Medieval Latin Verse*, p. 67; Miss Waddell, *Medieval Latin Lyrics*, p. 151, prefers to place it after 5, and, indeed, unless we accept this view, we need another 'Heriger ait', and, as Strecker admits, two lost stanzas instead of one.

   11. Heriger illum   iussit ad palum
       loris ligari   scopisque cedi,
       sermone duro   hunc arguendo:

   12. 'si te ad suum   invitet pastum
       Christus, ut secum   capias cibum,
       cave ne furtum   facias ⟨spurcum⟩[1]

The other two 'ridiculous' stories (nos. 35 and 42) are in Ambrosian rimed couplets. The first is an amusing encounter between a priest and a wolf. There is such liveliness in the telling and such clever touches of malicious satire, that it is easy to accept a French origin for the story. The other piece, in the same rhythm, is ascribed to Fulbert of Chartres, and is a versification of one of the numerous stories about Abbot John the Little.[2]

All these narrative poems are, from one point of view, no more than a continuation of the Carolingian tradition to which the song about the Abbot of Angers[3] bears witness. What is new is the use, by some of the poets, of the sequence-form and with it the exploitation of the great possibilities afforded by the new developments of music. As the sequence became a regular rhythmical and rimed construction, so the profane lyric followed it, though it was free enough to fashion as well its own characteristic measures. But, it must be repeated, all this Latin profane poetry is learned, and could not be understood by the common people. The only point of contact which it could possibly have with the vernacular songs was a more or less frequent similarity of subject; for we can hardly doubt that some such 'comic' stories were the material of songs sung by the wandering singers or actors at the fairs or in the taverns. We can imagine no other kind of contact between the traditional vulgar poetry and these learned songs which might well have pleased the ear of a Rhineland archbishop or abbot.

There remain three lyrical pieces (23, 27, and 40), which undoubtedly contain the purest poetry in the whole collection. With them we pass to the Romance lands, to France or, more probably, to Italy, where, as we have seen, such compositions were not wanting in the tenth century. The first, indeed, is found in a Verona MS. (*Bibl. capit.* 88, of tenth century), and it belongs to the same class of 'bird-poetry' as the verses in the collection of Eugenius Vulgarius.[4] But it is in an unusual

[1] I add 'spurcum', although the MS. says no more than 'cave ne furtum facias'; but I can hardly believe that the poet ended so. See, however, Strecker, p. 66.
[2] Cf. Strecker, p. 100.
[3] Above, p. 217.
[4] See above, p. 288.

measure—rhythmic sapphics—and one which very few poets ever ventured to attempt:[1]

1. Vestiunt silvae tenera ramorum
   virgulta, suis onerata pomis,
   canunt de celsis sedibus palumbes
       carmina cunctis.

2. hic turtur gemit, resonat hic turdus,
   pangit hic priscus merulorum sonus;
   passer nec tacet, arripens garritu
       alta sub ulmis.

3. hic leta sedit philomela frondis;
   longum effundit sibilum per auras
   sollempne, milvus tremulaque voce
       aethera pulsat.

4. ad astra volans aquila, per agros
   alauda canit modulos quam plures;
   desursum vergit dissimili modo,
       dum terram tangit.

5. velox impulit iugiter hirundo,
   clangit coturnix, gracula resultat;
   aves sic cuncte celebrant estivum
       undique carmen.

6. nulla inter aves similis est api,
   que talem gerit tipum castitatis
   nisi Maria, que Christum portavit alvo
       inviolata.[2]

The poem is in its arrangement a catalogue of birds, and it had perhaps no other object beyond that of setting out in pleasant form a list of familiar birds with some of their characteristics. The first strophe, indeed, seems to promise much, but it is not the prelude to a nature-picture such as later poets would have given. Yet in the Cambridge collection it comes upon us with an air of freshness, the promise of which is carried out by the next piece that we have to consider.

For number 27, *Iam dulcis amica venito*,[3] is the most famous

---

[1] Bernard of Clairvaux used it in a hymn on S. Victor, 'metri negligens, ut sensui non deessem', he says; see *Christian-Latin Poetry*, p. 329.

[2] I am inclined to think, against Strecker (p. 63, note), that the author of this poem may have known no. 762 of Riese, *Anthol. Lat.*, 'Dulcis amice veni'. It is curious that both poets introduce the bee as a bird, but this is not the only point of resemblance. The last stanza has given rise to much discussion. Dr. M. R. James suggested to Professor Breul (*The Cambridge Songs*, p. 90) that the last verses should read,

    nisi que Christum baiulavit alvo
        inviolata.

This is doubtless attractive, but 'Maria' is unmistakably in the MS.

[3] Strecker, p. 69.

of all the Cambridge Songs. It is a link between the faltering tenth-century poets and the accomplished lyrists of the twelfth. But its poet had precisely what his successors lacked, the freshness and the trepidation of his uncertain mastery as, in the happy phrase of Mr. Gaselee, he drew his delicate air from 'the double flute of Ovid and the *Song of Songs*':[1]

1. Iam dulcis amica venito,
   quam sicut cor meum diligo;
   intra in cubiculum meum
   ornamentis cunctis ornatum.

2. ibi sunt sedilia strata
   atque velis domus parata,
   floresque in domo sparguntur
   herbeque fragrantes[2] miscentur.

3. est ibi mensa apposita
   universis cibis honusta;
   ibi clarum vinum habundat
   et quidquid te, cara, delectat.

4. ibi sonant dulces simphonie
   inflantur et altius tibie;
   ibi puer et docta puella
   canunt tibi carmina pulchra.

5. hic cum plectro citharam tangit,
   illa melos cum lira pangit,
   portantque ministri pateras
   diversis[3] poculis plenas.

6. 'ego fui sola in silva[4]
   et dilexi loca secreta;
   frequenter effugi tumultum[5]
   et vitavi populum multum.

7. .   .   .   .   .   .

8. non me iuvat tantum convivium
   quantum predulce colloquium
   nec rerum tantarum ubertas
   ut cara[6] familiaritas.'

[9. iam nix glaciesque liquescit,[7]
   folium et herba virescit;
   philomela iam cantat in alto,
   ardet amor cordis in antro.]

[1] Quoted by Miss Waddell, *Medieval Latin Lyrics*, p. 331. But, if we speak of Ovid and the *Song of Songs* we must not exclude the almost certainly popular origin of the actual theme. I rely mainly on Mr. Gaselee's *Oxford Book of Medieval Latin Verse*, p. 61, as his text, which he describes (p. 219) as 'readable if somewhat eclectic', is the best resource for my purpose, until another attempt is made to win its secret from the mutilated Cambridge MS. The poem appears, with differences, in two other MSS., (1) V = Vienna, *Cod. Vindob.* 116; and (2) P = Paris, *Bibl. Nat.* 1118 (from Limoges), in a Troper of S. Martial, where it appears with neums, and, as it lacked the last two stanzas, may have been used as a religious piece. Dreves, who took it into *Anal. Hymn.* (xi. 57), accepted it at its face value.

[2] Strecker reads 'flagrantes' in accordance with C.

[3] This is the reading of C; V reads 'pigmentatis', which Mr. Gaselee adopts, as it gives the right number of syllables. The poet does, indeed,

observe the law of syllabic equality fairly well; but he had not the conception, which was not fully developed until the eleventh century, of a fixed and changeless rhythm. This is part of his charm.

[4] Here the girl speaks; it is easy to see how the *Song of Songs* has influenced the poet, though the dialogue-form must also have been current in popular songs.

[5] These last two lines are from V and P; C reads:

fugique (or 'effugique') frequentius turbam
atque m . . . . plebis catervam.

Then follows a mutilated stanza,

u . s . p . l . . . .
. . . que silenti . . . .
. . . . tumultum
. . . . . . populum multum.

[6] C reads 'clara'; surely, as Strecker hesitatingly suggests (p. 72), for 'cara'; V reads 'dilecta'.

[7] This stanza appears after 6 in P and ends the song. It is hardly original.

[10. karissima, noli tardare,[1]
     studeamus nos nunc amare,
     sine te non potero vivere:
     iam decet amorem perficere.]

11. quid iuvat diferre, electa,
    que sunt tamen post facienda?

    fac cito quod eris factura,
    in me non est aliqua mora.

12. iam nunc veni, soror electa
    et pre cunctis mihi dilecta,[2]
    lux mee clara pupille
    parsque maior anime mee.

It is difficult to find a formula which will cover adequately the
rhythmical scheme of the poem. There is a rough equality of
syllables, and beyond this it is difficult to go, unless we boldly
say that each verse consists of 'four feet, dactyls or trochees,
accentual'[3] or, with Strecker,[4] attempt to read into the poem
an anapaestic rhythm. The truth is that we have here the
stage of transition between Wilhelm Meyer's original stage, in
which the only law is that of the fixed number of syllables,[5]
and the next stage, in which a fixity of rhythm based on
regularly recurring stresses was also required.

But in rhythmical poems whose scheme was based on the
iambic dimeter there was a natural tendency towards fixed
rhythm, and, indeed, the quantitative iambic dimeter seems
to have changed itself by an easy and, as it were, painless
process into rhythmical form. One Italian example has already been given from the collection of Eugenius Vulgarius,[6]
and the Cambridge MS. contains another[7] which is entitled
Verna feminae suspiria. It is either of French or of Italian
origin, and it speaks without need of comment:

1. Levis exsurgit zephirus,
   et sol procedit tepidus,
   iam terra sinus aperit,
   dulcore suo diffluit.

2. ver purpuratum exiit,
   ornatus suos induit,
   aspergit terram floribus,
   ligna silvarum frondibus.

3. struunt lustra quadrupedes
   et dulces nidos volucres,
   inter ligna florentia
   sua decantant gaudia.

4. quod oculis dum video
   et auribus dum audio,
   heü pro tantis gaudiis
   tantis inflor suspiriis.

5. cum mihi sola sedeo
   et hec revolvens palleo,
   si forte capud sublevo,
   nec audio nec video.

6. tu saltim, veris gratia,
   exaudi et considera
   frondes, flores et gramina,
   nam mea languet anima.

Even if this motive be not entirely new, in the sense that
nature had sometimes before been linked with human feelings,

[1] These lines are in V after 6.
[2] C reads (apparently),
'ac omnibus . . . . dilecta.'
[3] S. Gaselee, *Oxford Book of Medieval Latin Verse*, p. 218.
[4] p. 70.
[5] Meyer, *Rythmik*, ii. 104 sqq.
[6] Above, p. 288.
[7] No. 40, p. 95.

this is the first 'dramatic lyric'[1] of the Middle Ages; for we can hardly surrender ourselves so far to the emotion of the poem as to believe that it is the work of a learned maiden who looked from her window at the Spring and could not forget her care.[2] Here is all the promise of the years to come, but nothing can equal the freshness of this lyrical spring.

For the medieval Latin lyric first grew on 'romance' soil. In Italy the classical poets were read in lay schools, and were expounded by grammarians beneath whose pedantry there lingered yet some of the passion of their youth. These men allowed the rhythm a place beside the ancient metres, and their pupils knew not only their Ovid, but their church hymnary. In the Italian cities conditions of intellectual and social intercourse were such that songs in the learned tongue were not rarities intelligible to one among a hundred, but found an audience in members of the professional as well as of the noble classes. For in Italy, more than elsewhere, it was usual for those who could afford it to send their sons to school, and, if the nobles were less enlightened than the prudent professional classes, there was clearly a large body of well-educated people who had had practice in the making of verses and for whom Latin was in some degree a second language.[3] The secular clergy shared the same kind of education. Many, indeed, had passed through the same schools, and they no less than the purely lay scholars were given to the making of verses. Profane themes easily occupied them, and they still spoke of the Muses even if Olympus and the old gods had become somewhat dim.

Conditions therefore, existed in the midst of which it is not surprising to witness the flowering of lyrical poetry. We do not need to search out obscure causes, to go to the East

[1] In the sense that Browning used his title 'Dramatic Lyrics'. I do not, of course, rule out the possibility that this is an adaptation of a theme already current in popular songs. Indeed, I think that such a derivation is very likely.

[2] But Prof. P. S. Allen, *The Romanesque Lyric*, North Carolina 1928, p. 290, is ready at first to do so; but (p. 291) he reflects and then says simply, 'So sang then a heart-sick girl (or some clerk for her) about the year 1000.' If this poem is Italian (or even French), we can say, 'So sang some young scholar, who had a mind to sing and a subject to his hand.' We

might add, as I have said, that he probably did not invent the theme.

[3] The evidence on this subject is partly given in Dresdner, *Kultur- und Sittengeschichte der italienischen Geistlichkeit im X. und XI. Jahrhundert*, Breslau 1890; see also bibliography in *Christian-Latin Poetry*, p. 477, and ib., p. 236. To the common people, of course, this learned verse was unintelligible, but the melodies were familiar to them. Brinkmann's remarks (*Geschichte der lateinischen Liebesdichtung im Mittelalter*, p. 29) are thoroughly convincing. The crowd that thronged to hear the *jocator* in Amarcius' poem (see above, p. 292, note 6) enjoyed the music.

or to Spain, to wander in the northern forests, or to look for mimes and players with an ancestry stretching back to the ancient world. Two things are needed—the human spirit and a favourable environment.

In France also similar social and intellectual conditions were being created. For it is possible from the end of the tenth century to speak decisively of 'France', although the unification of the country was as yet superficial. Yet the old Gallic element, with its various admixtures, was coming once more to the front, as Frankish speech died out, and diversified idioms descended from the vulgar Latin began to find their way into literature. Paris was now a considerable town; in the old Romano-Gallic towns great churches were built, and within their massive walls were collected the beginnings of a new middle class.

To some extent the old monastic culture had declined. The new reform of Cluny frowned upon too much secular study,[1] but there was a great freedom in the cathedral schools, whose age had now dawned. It was largely from these schools that the Latin poetry of eleventh-century France came, and we shall see how this new humanism in the end did more for France than the lay schools for Italy, and how it bore abundant fruit in England.

[1] *Christian-Latin Poetry*, pp. 257, 310 sq.

FRENCH POETS OF THE ELEVENTH CENTURY

§ 1. *The Cathedral Schools: Gerbert of Aurillac* (950–1003) *and Fulbert of Chartres* (*circ.* 960–1028).

THE work of the Carolingian humanists was continued in the French cathedral schools. While in the monasteries there were some signs of a falling in standard, and a tendency to frown on excessive devotion to secular studies, the cathedral schools set before themselves the task of training men for the service of the Church by giving them all that was available of the best of the ancients, along with the consecrated wisdom of the Fathers. This combination of learning and piety, which had been the ideal of the Anglo-Saxon and of the Carolingian schools, was the basis of the new humanism of Reims and of Chartres. At Reims Gerbert of Aurillac was *scholasticus* from 970 to 982. This remarkable man, who rose from poverty to the chair of S. Peter, has given us a picture of himself in that collection of letters which, with Ciceronian brevity and admirable lucidity, sets forth the anxieties and difficulties, the hopes and the consolations of a life divided between action and study, between the call of personal loyalties and the imperious attraction of learning.

He had studied mathematics in Spain and, with them, music. Later he mastered logic with the aid of an archdeacon of Reims, and he soon knew more than his teacher. He was still young when Archbishop Aldalbero placed him at the head of the cathedral school. There he quickly reorganized the studies and, like the teachers of antiquity, he laid great emphasis on the reading of the poets in connexion with the study of rhetoric. There is nothing remarkable about what has survived of his own poetical compositions,[1] but his letters show with what understanding he had read the great writers of antiquity and especially his beloved Cicero. Like Cicero he found in philosophy a solace in the midst of the cares of an active life. ' His curis sola philosophia unicum repertum est remedium.'[2] He was an unwearied collector of books, and spent vast sums in procuring copies of classical authors. Now he is writing to

---

[1] *Lettres de Gerbert*, ed. J. Havet, Paris 1889, pp. 70 sqq., epitaphs; and p. 82, an inscription for a chalice:

hinc sitis atque fames fugiunt, pro-
   perate fideles.   [bero gazas.
dividit in populis has praesul Adal-
[2] ib., p. 43; cf. also p. 112.

Thietmar of Mainz, begging him to fill in a lacuna in his copy of Boëthius' commentary on the περὶ ἑρμηνείας;[1] now arranging for volumes of Suetonius and Symmachus to be sent to him and to his Archbishop from Rome;[2] now, again, commissioning the monk Rainard to have transcribed for him Boëthius' *de astrologia*, Victorinus' *de rhetorica*, and the *Ophthalmicus* of Demosthenes.[3] He proclaimed the necessity of joining the art of speaking well to that of living well—'cum studio bene vivendi semper coniunxi studium bene dicendi'; for, although the former was more excellent and could stand by itself, yet in public life both were necessary, for persuasion was required as well as example.[4] This is Gerbert's justification of rhetoric. He applied to his life the wisdom of the ancients, and created a well-balanced Christian humanism, which was to be the mark of the school of Chartres under Fulbert, who is said to have been his pupil. In any case, the ideals of Gerbert came to rich fulfilment in eleventh-century France, and Fulbert's school is the link between the learning of the Carolingians and the early universities.

Born about 960, perhaps in Aquitaine, Fulbert owed his education to the Church. Of himself he wrote, when he was made Bishop of Chartres,

te de pauperibus natum suscepit alendum
Christus, et immeritum sic enutrivit et auxit,
ut collata tibi miretur munera mundus,
nam puero faciles providit adesse magistros,
et iuvenem perduxit ad hoc ut episcopus esses.[5]

Before he became Bishop he was Master of the cathedral school, which he lifted to an eminence that admitted of no rival until the rise of the schools of Paris. Adelman of Liége, one of his pupils, has left in a rhythmical poem a memorial of his great and saintly master:

floruere, te fovente, Galliarum studia;
tu divina, tu humana excolebas dogmata;
nunquam passus es urgeri virtutem penuria.
gurges altus ut in amnes scinditur multifidos,
ut in plures fundit ignis se minores radios,
sic insignes propagasti per diversa plurimos.[6]

---

[1] *Lettres de Gerbert*, p. 112: the lacuna remains in our existing text.
[2] ib., p. 38.
[3] ib., pp. 117–18; Victorinus wrote a commentary on the *Rhetoric* of Cicero; Demosthenes Philalethes was a Greek physician.   [4] ib., p. 42.
[5] Migne, cxli, col. 347.

[6] Text in Clerval, *Les Écoles de Chartres*, p. 59; see also Manitius, *Gesch.* ii. 558 sqq. The date of the poem is between 1028 and 1033. It is alphabetical and is composed of mono-rimed stanzas of three lines each. Adelman made a second edition of his poem.

Fulbert, indeed, had endeavoured to master the whole of learning, human and divine. 'C'était en effet', says Clerval, 'un philosophe, taillé sur le modèle antique, et rehaussé par la vertu chrétienne et la dignité épiscopale.'[1] This is a just estimate, because to Gerbert's love of exact studies and of literature Fulbert joined practical ability in the conduct of affairs, and the simple goodness of the saint. To the Seven Arts he added Medicine, for he had some fame as a physician, and he completed the cycle of learning by the study of the fathers and of Holy Scripture. The classical poets were read at Chartres. In the library were to be found Terence, Virgil, Horace, Ovid, and Statius; of the Christian poets, Prudentius, Sedulius, Fortunatus, Boëthius, and Arator. But the new rhythmical versification found its place in compositions beside the classical, and Fulbert himself practised it. His poetry, as it has come down to us, consists mainly of hymns and other religious pieces. It is interesting to note that in an ode entitled *Prae gaudio pacis* he uses the metre of Horace's *Solvitur acris hiemps*:

> Sanctum simpliciter patrem cole, pauperum caterva,
> quantumque nosti, laudibus honora,[2]

but we love him best when he is singing, rhythmically and with full freedom, of the nightingale:

> Aurea personet lira clara modulamina,
> simplex corda sit extensa voce quindenaria;
> primum sonum mese reddat lege ypodorica.
> Philomele demus laudes in voce organica,
> dulce melos decantantes sicut decet musica,
> sine cuius arte vera nulla valent cantica.[3]

This is a mono-rimed poem, meant to be sung, and that is why the editor of the 'Cambridge Songs' included it in his collection.[4] Like the songs amid which it is there set, it is a lyrical prelude, a beginning which contains the promise of a better performance. The same collector included the amusing rhythmical version of a tale from the *Vitas patrum*, which

[1] p. 94.
[2] *Anal. Hymn.* l, p. 288.
[3] Migne, cxli, col. 348. I have taken my text from the *Cambridge Songs*, ed. Strecker, pp. 29 sqq.
[4] See Strecker, p. 101, for the evidence of Fulbert's authorship. It cannot be regarded as certain that Fulbert

is the author, but the Brussels MS. of Boëthius in which it is contained points to Chartres, says Strecker. On p. 111 Strecker (after *Anal. Hymn.* xxxiii, p. 343) prints what he calls a 'parody' of this poem. It is in the same measure with the same strophic arrangement and 'Tiradenreim'.

Fulbert may have compiled for the edification of his younger scholars:[1]

In gestis patrum veterum
quiddam legi ridiculum,
exemplo tamen habile;
quod vobis dico rithmice.

qui sero clausa ianua,
tutus sedet in cellula
cum minor voce debili
appellat: 'frater, aperi,

Iohannes abbas, parvulus
statura non virtutibus,
ita maiori socio,
quicum erat in heremo:

Iohannes, opis indigus,
notis assistit foribus:
ne spernat tua pietas,
quem redegit necessitas.'

'volo,' dicebat, 'vivere,
secure sicut angelus,
nec veste nec cibo frui
qui laboretur manibus.'

respondit ille deintus:
'Iohannes, factus angelus.
miratur caeli cardines;
ultra non curat homines.'

respondit frater: 'moneo,
ne sis incepti properus,
frater, quod tibi postmodum
sit non cepisse satius.'

foris Iohannes excubat,
malamque noctem tolerat,
et praeter voluntariam
hanc agit paenitentiam.

at ille: 'qui non dimicat,
non cadit neque superat.'
ait et nudus eremum
interiorem penetrat.

facto mane recipitur
satisque verbis uritur;
sic intentus ad crustula
fert patienter omnia.

septem dies gramineo
vix ibi durat pabulo,
octava fames imperat
ut ad sodalem redeat;

refocillatus Domino
grates agit et socio;
dehinc rastellum brachiis
tentat movere languidis.

castigatus angustia
de levitate nimia,
cum angelus non potuit,
vir bonus esse didicit.

This delightful tale was versified by Fulbert from one of those ancient stories which were handed down from the primitive monasticism of the desert and were embodied in the *Vitas patrum*. And we may guess that Fulbert chose it with some kind but ironical thought for its present application. It shows us, no doubt, the sort of rhythmical composition that the younger pupils were encouraged to imitate in the schools, and illustrates as well one side of the humanistic spirit of Chartres, which did not disdain the new fashions in rhythmical verse.

Another poet who drank of this fresh stream of humanistic

[1] Migne, cxli, col. 350; Strecker, pp. 97 sqq. The first five stanzas are contained in a twelfth-century MS. of Fulbert (Paris, *Bibl. Nat.* 2872).

learning was Adalbero of Laon,[1] who was perhaps a pupil of
Gerbert at Reims. At any rate, he occupied himself with philosophy, and loved the ancient poets. In 977 he was made Bishop
of Laon at the instance of King Louis, but later he was involved
in secular business and in grave scandal, until he found security
for a time with Hugh Capet, who had then risen to power.
With good luck and adroitness, he escaped further perils, including the consequences of treachery to his new lord. He
lived in great state, like a prince, and it was to him that the
deacon Dudo of S. Quentin dedicated his historical work on
the Normans.[2] With Robert of France, himself a lover of
letters, Adalbero lived for a time, at any rate, on terms of
friendship, and it was at the king's wish that he wrote at
least one of his poems, the *Summa fidei*, a dialogue in hexameters on the subject of the Trinity.[3] But the second poem,
the *Carmen ad Rotbertum*, speaks so plainly on the subject of
the king that it may well belong to a period of more strained
relations, though it ends on a note of reconciliation. Here
again Adalbero uses the dialogue, a form favoured by the
Carolingians, but he writes so badly and so obscurely that it
is difficult to follow his argument. But he is obviously writing
a satire and a complaint against the state of the kingdom,
the undue favour enjoyed by the monks and in particular by
Odilo of Cluny,[4] and the inability of the king to remedy
matters. This is how Adalbero begins his onslaught on the
monks:[5]

> Versibus exiguis tantum tentabo dolorem.
> scripta patent, celebres quae mittunt Crotoniate;[6]
> desuper est titulus 'lex antiquissima' scriptus;
> praecipiunt: vi cogatur quod sponte negatur.
> ut placet imperio, sic se transformet et ordo;
> rusticus ille piger, deformis et undique turpis,
> pulchra cum gemmis ditetur mille corona.
> iuris custodes cogant portare cucullas:
> orent, inclinent, taceant, vultusque reponant.

[1] On Adalbero, see Guizot, *Collection des mémoires relatifs à l'histoire de France*, vi, pp. 417 sqq.; Manitius, *Gesch.* ii. 525 sqq.; G. A. Hückel, 'Les Poèmes satiriques d'Adalbéron', *Bibl. de la Faculté des Lettres de Paris*, xiii (1901), pp. 49 sqq., where the texts of his poems are given.
[2] See below, p. 356.
[3] Hückel, pp. 168 sqq.
[4] See Sackur, *Die Cluniacenser*, i. pp. 95 sqq.

[5] Hückel, pp. 132 sqq.
[6] Manitius, *Gesch.* ii. 527, suggests that here Adalbero is attacking Abbo of Fleury and his Canons ('lex anti- quissima'). In verses 65 sqq. he attacks the unworthy ministers of the king. One of these was the Architriclinius Landricus of Nevers, who is attacked by another poet in rhythmical verse; see Hückel, pp. 82 sqq., and Migne, cli, col. 753.

> nudi pontifices sine fine sequantur aratrum,
> carmina cum stimulo primi cantando parentis.
> praesulis et si forte locus vacet, intronizentur
> pastores ovium, nautae, quicunque sit ille.

There is more in this style, and further there is an elaborate attack on Odilo and his monks, followed by a curious discussion about the heavenly Jerusalem, the *visio pacis*, in which Adalbero recommends to the king Augustine's *City of God*:

> rex, Augustini libros, dilecte, revolve:
> urbs excelsa Dei quae sit dixisse probatur.

And, for information about those who dwell there and their order, there is Dionysius the Areopagite:

> quaere Dionisium, qui dicitur Arcopagita,

and there is also Gregory in his *Moralia*, and his commentary on Ezekiel. Then Adalbero demonstrates that the Church on earth is the counterpart of this heavenly city, and he takes this opportunity to set forth the proper constitution of human society. But Robert is sceptical of the possibility of attaining to Adalbero's ideal, until 'the Loire shall flow through the Calabrian fields and the rushing Tigris cover Spanish soil; or Etna bring forth roses, or the marsh lilies. If such things happen, then believe that your wishes will come to pass. May Christ's grace, as well as our own, be with you, Bishop Adalbero. You deserve rightly the reward of your king; for I see that you are not speaking as one who is beside himself, but giving wise counsel under the form of an allegory.'[1]

Adalbero knew the Roman satirists and in particular Persius, to whom he refers by name, and of whom he makes use in his poem.[2] This revival of satire is significant. The *Carmen ad Rotbertum* was composed about 1017, and marks the beginning of the moral satirical verse of the full Middle Ages. Doubtless it looks back to the Carolingian dialogue, and to the old exhortatory poems; but it is none the less a prelude to the more accomplished satirical verse of the twelfth century.

§ 2. *Godfrey of Reims.*

To the same group of poets as the more celebrated Hildebert, Marbod, and Baudry belongs Godfrey of Reims, who received his education at the famous school of his native city.

---

[1] Hückel, p. 167.
[2] Manitius, *Gesch.* ii. 525, note 3; for references also to Juvenal, Virgil, Horace, Sedulius, &c., in Adalbero's poetry.

There Bruno was *scholasticus* and, between the years 1073 to 1076, chancellor as well. Godfrey taught in the school, and before 1049 he had begun his career as a poet. When Bruno in 1080 left the school and retired from the world to found the Carthusian order, Godfrey was his successor in both offices, and he enjoyed the favour of Manasses II, Archbishop of Reims.[1]

One of his literary friends was Odo of Orleans who, after teaching at Toul, was *scholasticus* at Tournai, where he became bishop in 1106. He had fallen under the spell of profane letters, though in his later days he wrote a poem *de operibus sex dierum*.[2] It is to this Odo that Godfrey addressed one of his most remarkable poems, the *Sompnium Godefridi de Odone Aurelianensi*. He used the well-worn device of a dream, in which Odo appeared before him.

> astitit Odo, meos magnum decus inter amicos,
> idem, non similis, visus adesse michi.
> visus erat non is, quem sompnia falsa figurent,
> immo is, quem verum sompnia falsa probent.
> nota michi hec facies multumque domestica, nec sunt
> ullius ora viri cognitiora michi.
> nota, inquam, quoniam sub nostro pectore semper
> illius egregii vivit imago viri.
> illius intra me species impressa quiescit,
> dum vivam, ex animo non abolenda meo.
> heret enim, nec abesse potest dilectio fortis,
> et quasi viscoso glutine vincta manet.

Godfrey wishes to make it quite clear that it was no pale shadow of Odo that was present in his vision, and he proceeds, therefore, to paint a lively picture of the man as he was—with his cheerfulness, and his lack of that asceticism which frowns upon another's harmless joy. Then, in a remarkable passage through which breaks the humanism and what we may perhaps call, somewhat vaguely, the secularism of the cathedral schools, he praises the golden mean of which Odo was such a shining example:

> hic status, hec habitudo decent; inglorius erret,
> qui de mendaci relligione tumet,
> exulet in silvis taciturnus, amarus et asper,
> et comes Hircanis tygribus esse velit.
> par hiemi censendus erit boreeque nivoso,
> gaudia qui damnat tristiciamque probat.

---

[1] For Godfrey's life and for extracts from his poems, see W. Wattenbach, 'Lateinische Gedichte aus Frankreich im XI Jahrhundert', *Berlin. Sitzungs-ber.* 1891, pp. 101 sqq.

[2] Among the works of Hildebert, in Migne, clxxi, col. 1213 sqq.

Odo rigore procul toto mansueverat ore,
  clarus et insani nil aquilonis habens,
par potius gemmis, par auro parque diei,
  quem roseus nitidis Phebus honorat equis.
ergo omnem quicunque foret ferus, impius, acer,
  durus et obscurus, oderat Odo meus.
oderat, et merito, nam et nox obducta tenebris
  sordet, ubi picea nube perempta latet.
sole carens inamena dies; si nubila desint
  ortaque lux fuerit, gracior orbis erit.
cum freta sunt tranquilla placent; irata profundi
  si facies fuerit, non placet unda maris.
talis tamque decens, et in hoc moderamine vultus,
  astiterat nostro vatis imago thoro.[1]

But Odo's figure as it appeared to him was of gigantic size.
This, Godfrey explains rhetorically, was only just, for not only
was Odo of high birth, but he was richly endowed by nature.
His poems are marvellous—he can sing of wars and battles as
well as of the art of Cupid; he is skilled in medicine, for he has
read Pliny.

Odo explains to Godfrey that he has come from Orleans to
Reims through the air, with Apollo as his guide. He has
brought with him his poem on the Trojan War, which Godfrey
has always admired so greatly. Godfrey, after admonishing
him on the riskiness of his journey through the air, begs that
he will recite his poem, with the lyre to accompany him:

hoc opus est, eterna tibi quo fama paratur,
  vitaque post bustum non habitura modum.
iam nec Tartarei metuenda vorago baratri,
  nec Flegetonteas, Odo, timebis aquas.
dum polus astra feret, mare pisces, aura volucres,
  dum data terra feris, Odo, superstes eris.[2]

But, alas! the poem on which Odo's fame was to rest has completely perished, though Godfrey does, indeed, give a summary
of its contents. As the poem is recited, all nature listens with
attention, and the Vesle[3] 'runs softly till he ends his song'.

Godfrey loved to cast his poems into the form of epistles.
The whole collection, indeed, is prefaced with 'Godefridi Re-
mensis Epistolarum liber incipit'. There is a letter addressed
to Archdeacon Ingelran, which is a curious piece of exhortation
and flattery. The young ecclesiastic, a man of noble birth and
of much learning in secular literature, must now, on assuming

---

[1] Wattenbach, p. 102.   [3] The river on which Reims stands.
[2] ib., p. 103.

his new office, forsake the light verse in which he had taken such pleasure. He was not the equal of Virgil, but no one who read his poem on William I of England, dedicated to Countess Adela, could doubt that he was a great poet. Here Godfrey seizes the opportunity of singing the praises of that great lady, as Baudry did in a long poem.[1] He exercises all his wit and fancy, even to the extent of saying that Fate decreed that William should conquer England, and so become a king, solely that his daughter might be a princess.

> forsitan ignores, quod rex de consule surgit,
>   quid cause fuerit: filia causa fuit.
> nam nec honor nec opes nec equi nec scuta nec enses
>   culmen ad imperii causa fuere duci,
> set quia prescivit Lachesis, quod de duce proles
>   femina precellens exoritura foret.
> ne sata privato de consule diva fuisset,
>   sortita est regem regia virgo patrem.
> ergo ut sceptrigeri foret Adela filia regis,
>   regem constitui fata dedere patri.

The whole poem is a characteristic product of the cathedral schools, with its mythological allusions, its rhetorical conceits, and its easy use of the elegiac metre as it was acquired in school. A school-piece also is the long description of a beautiful lady, a common theme, to which young poets were often drawn by inclination and still more by the study of Ovid. Godfrey begins,[2]

> Parce, precor, virgo, tociens michi culta videri,
>   meque tuum forma perdere parce tua.
> parce supervacuo cultu componere membra:
>   augeri studio tam bona forma nequit.
> ne tibi sit tanto caput et coma pexa labore,
>   nam caput hoc placuit, cum coma mixta fuit.
> ne stringant rutilos tibi serica vincla capillos,
>   cum vincant rutile serica vincla come.
> ne tibi multiplicem crines revocentur in orbem,
>   nam cum forte iacent, absque labore placent.
> aurea non video cur vertice flammea portes,
>   aurea nam nudo vertice tota nites.
> utraque fert auris aurum, fert utraque gemmas,
>   utraque nuda novis anteferenda rosis.

He carries on the theme with great resource for the first half of the poem. The second part is a collection of classical allusions, ending with the assertion that the lady's beauty

---

[1] See p. 347 below.   [2] Wattenbach prints the whole poem, pp. 107 sqq.

would have been victorious in the contest in which Paris gave
judgement between the three goddesses.

> de pretio forme cum tres certamen inissent,
>   electusque Paris arbiter esset eis,
> prefecit Venerem Paridis censura deabus,
>   deque tribus victe succubuere due.
> cum tribus ad Paridem si quarta probanda venires,
>   de tribus a Paride quarta probata fores,
> pomaque si forme potiori danda fuerunt,
>   hec potius forme danda fuere tue.
> corda gerit dura, quem tam divina figura
>   vel tam purpuree non tetigere gene.
> robore vel scopulo genitum convincere possem,
>   quem tam sollempnis forma movere nequit.

Godfrey did not disown the creations of his youthful fantasy—
that is to say, he gathered them into his collected works,
though he may, on occasion, have made a formal profession
of repentance for these indiscretions.

In his early days he had practised the leonine hexameter,
in which he employed the two-syllabled rime with some skill.
So he composed a poetical duologue, of which the characters
are the poet himself and Calliope, in honour of Hugo, Bishop
of Langres (1012–49). Not that he knew Hugo, but he was
naturally the admirer of a man whose poem had once healed
him of a sore sickness!

> Cum aliquando peste litargica laborarem neutroque medendi genere, simili-
> bus aut contrariis, salus revocari potuisset, audito carmine vestro tota in-
> firmitatis molestia purgata est, naturaque morbis triumphantibus vitiata,
> quadam quasi ypocratica potione emendata est. itaque patuit, quod ad hoc
> temporis illaboratum[1] erat, Terpandrum et Aryonem desperatissimas quorun-
> dam egritudines musica modulatione emovisse.

It is not surprising, therefore, that Godfrey exalts Hugo above
Plato as a philosopher, and above Cato as an example of
practical virtue. In due course, he himself found youthful
admirers. Baudry of Bourgueil, at any rate, looked upon him
as a master, addressed flattering verses to him,[2] and on his
death in 1095 honoured his memory with five poetical epitaphs.[3]
In one of them he says that Godfrey was greater than Cicero,
and in another that he was second only to Ovid. 'Reims begat
him, and Reims buried him. His dust returned to dust, but
his spirit dwells in the stars.'

---

[1] So the MS.; Wattenbach, p. 109, suggests *irroboratum*, but *illatebratum* is perhaps better.

[2] No. clxi, pp. 151 sqq. (ed. Phyllis Abrahams).

[3] ib., pp. 86 sqq.

§ 3. *Hildebert of Lavardin, Archbishop of Tours.*

Hildebert of Lavardin stands out in pre-eminence among those French ecclesiastics of the late eleventh and early twelfth centuries who joined the serious pursuit of letters to the exacting task of ruling a large diocese or province. He had the usual education in the cathedral school at Le Mans, where he was later to preside as *scholasticus*. Ecclesiastical preferment came, as a matter of course, to a man of his ability and learning. In 1091 Hildebert was made archdeacon, and in 1096 bishop. As the Dukes of Normandy were his feudal overlords, he had sometimes a difficult course to steer. He suffered from the violence of William Rufus, but Henry I, who respected a scholar and an honest opponent, gave him his friendship. The cares of office, however, were too heavy, and Hildebert would fain have laid his burden down. Though he failed at Rome to obtain his desire, the soul of the poet and scholar was satisfied as he wandered among the remains of the imperial past which stood, grand and desolate, in every quarter of the city. He went back sadly to the barbarism of the north, to meet with new cares, which pursued him throughout the rest of his life. For in 1125 he was compelled to accept the Archbishopric of Tours, and he had now to defend the rights of the Church against Louis the Fat of France.

Hildebert was recognized as the first man of letters of his age. In his cathedral school he had read deeply in the classical poets, and he must have excelled in composition. Throughout the years of his maturity, verse was his chief literary occupation, and he left behind a large collection of poems.

There are a few metrical epitaphs and a fair number of epigrams the authorship of which can be confidently assigned to Hildebert. The long *Elegy* in memory of the famous Berengar, the wayward pupil of Fulbert and the master, perhaps, of Hildebert himself, is a good example of the latter's facility in this kind of composition. It was much admired by his contemporaries, as we gather from Baudry's lines, which he addressed to Hildebert, who was then Archdeacon of Le Mans:[1]

> de Berengario Turonensi pauca locutus
> es nobis visus, nisi fallor, magnus Homerus.[2]

The piece is too long to quote in full;[3] it is a sustained panegyric

---

[1] See the note on p. 127 of Baudry's works, ed. Phyllis Abrahams.

[2] ib., p. 126.

[3] Text, Migne, clxxi, col. 1396.

of the master, extolling his virtues, his love of justice, his charity to the poor, and his unique genius. Towards the end Hildebert hints at the controversy which darkened his life:

> vir pius atque gravis, vir sic in utroque modestus,
>   ut livor neutro rodere posset eum.
> livor eum deflet quem carpserat antea, nec tam
>   carpsit et odit eum, quam modo laudat, amat.

And, indeed, Berengar had been, in spite of his self-assertiveness, a victim to some extent of the malice of his enemies; but the canons of S. Martin of Tours kept his memory fresh by gathering each year round his tomb, sprinkling it with holy water, and chanting a *de profundis*, after which the officiant cried: 'Pray for the soul of Berengar!'[1]

Besides an epitaph on Count Elias of Le Mans, which may be Hildebert's,[2] there is one on Bertha, daughter of Odo, Count of Champagne.[3] But it is the epigrams which are of greater interest, as they show more clearly the manner in which the poets of the time learned to exercise their ingenuity, and how they turned their study of Martial to account without being too servile in their imitation. A good example of this imitation is the piece on Lucretia, which used to be printed as a product of antiquity in editions of the *Anthologia Latina*. But Hauréau has vindicated the claim of Hildebert:[4]

> Dum foderet ferro castum Lucretia pectus,
>   sanguinis et torrens egrederetur, ait:
> 'testes procedant me non favisse tyranno
>   ante virum sanguis, spiritus ante deos.
> quam bene, producti pro me post fata, loquentur
>   alter apud manes, alter apud superos!'

There is not much here to suggest that this is a medieval poem; and the following piece—a compliment to a bishop—is a neat adaptation of the ancient manner to a modern occasion:[5]

> Ad decus ecclesiae cum te natura crearet,
>   'sis expers vitii, caetera', dixit, 'habe.'
> sic piger ad vetitum, celer ad concessa creatus,
>   praeter virtutem nil sinis esse tibi.

Much more laboured is a longer piece 'on a Simoniac dying

---

[1] Hauréau, *Notices et extraits des mss.*, xxviii, 2, p. 309.

[2] ib., p. 316 sq.; not the epitaph on the same Count printed in Migne, clxxi, col. 1399.

[3] Hauréau, p. 420.

[4] p. 400 sq.; Otto of Freising quotes this epigram, omitting the last distich, but he does not know the author (*Chron.* ii. 9). 'Unde pulcre quidam', is his introduction.

[5] Migne, clxxi, col. 1407; Hauréau, p. 325.

excommunicate',[1] which may be Hildebert's. It is hardly more than a school-exercise. The theme is one that would scarcely be suggested by anything more definite than current controversy, and the aim of the poet was to find occasion to exercise his wit. So he expresses imaginary fears lest the man who has deceived on earth may at last cheat the very grave:

> Hei mihi! quam timeo ne fraus homo fraude resurgat,
>   ne mortem fallax fallere possit homo.
> urge membra, lapis, animam vos claudite, manes,
>   horum conventu ne solidetur homo.
> vestras in vestro consumite, Tartara, poenas,
>   ni vestris vultis parcere; vester erat.

It was such exercises of ingenuity that won for Hildebert his fame. For the taste of the learned was now for Ovid, Martial, and Juvenal, and we may doubt whether these later humanists had the feeling for Virgil which the Carolingians possessed. For the eleventh- and twelfth-century poets were men of the world, proud of their learning and of their wit. They called themselves, it is true, servants of the Muses, and spoke of 'sacred poets'.[2] But, just as in the first century, so in the eleventh, epigrams and moral or satirical pieces found most favour. It was a second age of rhetoric, in which Ovid was the master. For in Ovid there was much more food for keen minds eager to learn and ready to take material wherever it could be found. Beside a wealth of historical and mythological information there was in Ovid much that was the result of social observation, much material for the moralist, which, even if it were not original, was useful and easily assimilated by the medieval mind. The Ovidian distichs, too, were easy to read, and it was not hard to imitate them. An example of Hildebert's moralizing satire is a well-composed elegy on one Odo about whom nothing is certainly known except that he wrote verses. The interest of the piece centres in its satirical quality. Hauréau is, of course, right when he says[3] that the sentiment is banal; but herein consists its value, for it shows how easily the Ovidian couplet could be made to express the commonplaces which were the stock-in-trade of the schools:

> Moribus, arte, fide, coelesti pectore dignis,
>   cum superes alios, desipis, Odo, tamen.
> credis enim populum versus curare disertos,
>   teque placere putas moribus, arte, fide.

---

[2] See first line overleaf, p. 320.
[3] Hauréau, p. 330.

> dotibus his quondam sacri placuere poetae,
>   ingeniumque dedit praedia, nomen, opes.
> nunc aliud tempus, alii pro tempore mores.
>   nunc odium virtus, sceptra merentur opes.
> nil artes, nil pura fides, nil gloria linguae,
>   nil fons ingenii, nil probitas sine re;
> nullus inops sapiens, ubi res ibi copia census;
>   res sapiunt, pauper nil nisi pauper erit.
> nec iam divitibus tollunt sua crimina nomen,
>   sed quod lex damnat gratia solvit opum.
> hinc est quod populus, aurum quasi numen adorans,
>   audet in ignotum sponte venire nefas,
> speque lucri totiens excedere ius et honestum
>   sustinet, ut gratis iam iuvet esse reum.
> ius ruit, ordo perit, sceleri placet ora manusque
>   vendere, quamque inopem tam pudet esse probum.
> non igitur mirum si quisquam pravus et excors
>   divinos vates nullius esse putat.
> quem comitantur opes sapientia vera relinquit,
>   semper mobilibus incomitata bonis.[1]

Equally commonplace in its moralizing is the piece entitled *quam nociva sunt sacris hominibus femina, avaritia, ambitio*.[2] The argument of the poem is given in the first few lines:

> Plurima cum soleant sacros evertere mores,
>   altius evertunt femina, census, honos.
> femina, census, honos, fomenta facesque malorum,
>   in scelus, in gladios corda manusque trahunt.

The poet gives examples of the evil influence of women and of gold:

> femina mente Parim, vita spoliavit Uriam,
>   et pietate David et Salomona fide;
> femina sustinuit iugulo damnare Iohannem,
>   Hippolytum letho compedibusque Ioseph.

The mixture of the classical and biblical instances came naturally to men who knew their Ovid as well as their Bible by heart. But the Bible provided no easy instances of the 'auri sacra fames'. So the poet had to draw upon profane history and mythology:

> auro periurus Polymnestor, adultera Dane,
>   perfida Tarpeia, trux Eriphyla fuit;
> auro Crassus obit, auro ruit Amphiaraus;
>   auro castra, duces, ius populique cadunt.

But Hildebert's most ambitious satire is a long poem on

---

[1] Hauréau, p. 329.
[2] ib., p. 365, on the proofs of Hildebert's authorship; text, pp. 366 sqq., a better text than Migne, clxxi, col. 1428.

avarice, *de nummo, seu satyra adversus avaritiam*,[1] in which his powers appear at their highest.[2] For what other poet had the secret of his fluidity and ease?

> destituit terras decus orbis, gloria rerum,
>   virtus, mortali dicta negare mori.
> non hanc in quoquam spondet flos indolis usquam;
>   scis, nihil est pietas, nominis umbra fides.
> si coelum staret, si sol lucere negaret,
>   si nix ferveret, frigida flamma foret,
> non sic pallerem, non sic mirando stuperem,
>   quam si nunc usquam quemque pium videam.
> femina quod vitulum generavit, vacca quod agnum,
>   quod vulpes quondam filia suxit equam,
> tunc enarranti non demeruit magi credi,
>   quam si nunc aliquam dicis habere fidem.

This beginning is perhaps unpromising with its leonine rimes, but as we read the poem through, we are surprised at the ever fresh inventiveness, the springs of which never dry up; here, at any rate, is a rare facility, and it is hardly fair to ask for more. This is part of his disquisition on the decay of friendship:[3]

> quos tu nunc audis in climate quolibet orbis
>   dulcis amicitiae par generare novum?
> quis frater fratri nunc est Pylades Oresti?
>   quis cuiquam Theseus quod, Pirithoë, tibi?
> nil Telamon voluit, nisi quod secum Meleager;
>   quae, Patrocle, tui mens et Achillis erat.
> quos nunc emissos Orcus si redderet orbi,
>   discors, aut nullus esset utrique suus.
> si redeat vitae Polynices, non sibi quisquam
>   quem Thebas mittat, Tydeus alter erit.
> qui nunc aetatis vivi moriuntur amicis?
>   defunctus Scipio vixit adhuc Laelio.
> teste sola Pollux partitur vivere fratri,
>   fratribus, en, multi, quod tibi, Reme, tuus.
> flammae Phaetontis successerat umbra suorum,
>   nunc multae fratrum morte larem vacuant.
> plauserat Alceste pro coniuge fata mereri,
>   plures, ecce, viro, quod Clytemnestra suo.

---

[1] This poem appears in Migne, clxxi, col. 1402 as *Versus Cynomannensis episcopi de nummo seu satyra adversus avaritiam*, but it is incomplete. The whole satire is to be found in F. W. Otto, *Commentarii critici in codices bibliothecae Gissensis*, Giessen 1842, pp. 163 sqq.; on the poem see Hauréau, pp. 319 sqq. Hauréau (p. 321) refers to a MS., 255 Corpus Christi College, Oxford, which contains a poem *de nummo*, beginning

> nummum descripsi, nummo quae
>   congrua dixi,

the author of which is Godfrey of Cambrai, a contemporary of Hildebert.

[2] For a brief summary of the contents, see Manitius, *Gesch.* iii. 859 sq.

[3] Otto, *op. cit.*, p. 164.

The poem is doubtless far too long, but to its composition Hildebert had brought all his resources—his classical learning and endless examples from antiquity, as well as his own observation of men in daily life, of animals, and of natural things. This is the secret of his freshness for us as well as of the fame he won in his own day, and this poem is an excellent example of his talent.

The cult of friendship expressed itself naturally in the poetical epistle, and here Ovid was once again the master. There are letters of Hildebert to the Countess Adela of Blois,[1] one to a royal lady who had taken the veil,[2] and one to Henry I and his queen.[3] This queen, Matilda, is also celebrated in another poem.[4] All these poems are full of a courtly flattery, but the excess is that of the rhetorician; it is the speech of the great ecclesiastic and scholar, and this redeems it from any taint of servility. Hildebert uses the same language when he writes to a lady who had sought to console him in his exile by sending him some of her own verses.[5] Here we have also a more touching personal note and what Hauréau has called 'les raffinements de son exquise urbanité';[6] for this poem stands out as a mark of the growing refinement of manners. It has the same rhetorical excess as the other epistles, for Hildebert does not hesitate to say:

> deprimis ingenio vates celebresque poetas,
> et stupet eloquio sexus uterque tuo.
> carmina missa mihi decies spectata revolvens,
> miror et ex adytis illa venire reor.
> non est humanum tam sacros posse labores,
> nec te, sed per te numina credo loqui.

But this is only because he has begun by comparing the lady with the Sibyls, who spoke as the gods gave them utterance;

[1] Migne, clxxi, col. 1442; Hauréau, p. 380.

[2] Migne, clxxi, col. 1443, has the title *ad Angliae regem*, but the poet speaks thus of her:

> et quia non fuerat tanta quis coniuge dignus,
> coniuxit sponsam te sibi, virgo, Deus.

The poem contains the lines,

> parcius elimans alias natura puellas,
> distulit in dotes esse benigna tuas.
> in te fudit opes et opus mirabile cernens
> est mirata suas hoc potuisse manus,

which reappear as a separate epigram ascribed to Marbod, in Migne, clxxi, col. 1719–20. Hildebert's authorship is not, however, doubtful.

[3] ib, col. 1443. Migne's title *In laudem . . . Henrici I et eius futurae sponsae* is wrong, because the poem speaks of a queen long married; see Hauréau, p. 382.

[4] Migne, clxxi, col. 1444. It is not certain that Hildebert is the author of this; Hauréau, pp. 383–4.

[5] Migne, clxxi, col. 1445; Hauréau, p. 384, gives a better text.

[6] p. 385.

and, once committed, he has to carry his comparison through into the minutest details. This is precisely the method of the poet-rhetoricians of late antiquity.

It is possible but not certain that Hildebert is the author of the elegy *de perfida amica*.[1] It is not really a love poem, neither is there in it any of the anger of a Catullus. The poet complains that he has been ousted by a rich rival, and he proceeds to a moralizing satire on women and gold. We cannot, therefore, adduce this poem as evidence of the reappearance of love poetry. The theme of it is well-worn, and the final intention is moral. Yet the beginning of it does hint at the possibility of something more:

> Conquerar an sileam? monstrabo crimen amicae,
>   an, quasi iam sanus, vulnera nostra tegam?
> non queror aut molles oculos, aut aspera crura;
>   non vitio quovis exteriora premo.
> quod queror est animi; laudaret cetera livor.
>   verba fide, vitiis lubrica forma caret.
> illa decem menses mecum feliciter egit,
>   gratis in amplexus docta venire meos.
> aemulus ecce meus, gemmis male fisus et auro,
>   hanc adit, ingeminat munera, flectit eam.[2]

Even if a Carolingian poet had chosen such a theme, he would not have placed it in a personal setting. It is here that Hildebert's poem seems to mark an advance.[3] It is, of course, possible that a personal experience does in some way lie behind the poem, and it would be foolish to rule out any other interpretation than that it is a school-exercise pure and simple. Strange things were said about Hildebert's morals even while he was an archdeacon;[4] but both Marbod and Baudry composed love poems, and the latter, in reply to his detractors, explained that he wrote only of feigned loves:

> crede mihi, non vera loquor, magis omnia fingo.
> nullus amor foedus mihi quidlibet associavit.[5]

But we must remember that these young ecclesiastics lived very much in the world, and before they assumed the responsibilities of the priesthood, they followed without incurring much

---

[1] Hauréau, p. 417, says that in the MS. no. 2521 of Vienna it follows four poems which are known to be Hildebert's, though all are given there anonymously. He suggests also that Alexander Neckham refers to this poem when he says of Hildebert:

depinxitque stylo placide mores muliebres.

[2] ib., p. 415.

[3] But Ovid, Tibullus, Propertius, and other later poets could serve as models here.

[4] See *Christian-Latin Poetry*, p. 272.

[5] *Œuvres*, p. 123.

criticism the course taken by other members of their own class. And if Ovid was their daily food, how could they help composing, for the admiration of their friends, erotic verses such as those to which Guibert of Nogent confessed, or half amatory, half satirical pieces such as this of Hildebert?

We are on firmer ground with the two famous elegies on Rome. These are the fruit of Hildebert's journeys to the city of the Caesars, where the monuments of the past filled him with wonder as he remembered what he had read in the school at Le Mans both of republican and of imperial history. For like John of Salisbury after him, he must have acquired a good deal of sound historical knowledge, since much of Livy and the lives of Suetonius were accessible to him.

In the first elegy the poet addresses Rome, glorious in her ruins. In the second, it is Rome who replies to the poet—she is more glorious under Peter than under Caesar, under the Cross than under the Eagles:

> quis gladio Caesar, quis sollicitudine consul,
> quis rhetor lingua, quae mea castra manu
> tanta dedere mihi? studiis et legibus horum
> obtinui terras; crux dedit una polum.[1]

In these poems the metrical skill of Hildebert appears at its highest. They are successful because he had found a theme after his own heart. He himself was the ripe product of the new education, which if it were nothing else than the more intelligent application of old methods, yet liberated the mind for finer appreciations than the preceding generations had compassed. As his eye wandered over the vast ruins which covered Palatine and Forum and the whole space between the Lateran and the Coliseum, he wondered at the precious marbles which had not yet been stripped from wall and arch. He saw, too, before they were buried in earth or consumed by the lime-burners, statues of the old gods, whose beauty bound him as by a spell:

> hic superum formas superi mirantur et ipsi,
> et cupiunt fictis vultibus esse pares.
> non potuit natura deos hoc ore creare
> quo miranda deum signa creavit homo.
> vultus adest his numinibus, potiusque coluntur
> artificum studio quam deitate sua.[2]

All these wonders spoke to him, they came to life and had a meaning, just as to Gerald de Barri in far-off Wales the massive

[1] Hauréau, p. 336; extracts from these two poems are given in *Christian-* [2] Hauréau, p. 332.
Latin Poetry, pp. 266 sqq.

ruins of Caerleon told of the majesty of imperial Rome.[1] This
'sense of the past' we shall notice in other poets, and not in
the poets alone. For in the great political struggles of the
twelfth century, in the battle of political and social ideas, in
the revival of Roman law, the past rose again, as it were,
before the imagination of men, and began to dominate the
present. But the romancers and the poets looked beyond
Rome to that older world which the Latin *Iliad* and Virgil's
Aeneid had opened to their marvelling eyes. The tale of Troy
was familiar to them in their schooldays, and formed the
subject of their halting elegies or fragments of epic verse. We
shall meet with Joseph of Exeter's *de bello Troiano* in the
twelfth century, but here we have to note a group of three
elegies entitled *De excidio Troiae*. The first two appear in
Leyser,[2] where, in spite of the fact that one is written in ordinary elegiacs and the other in leonine distichs, they are joined
together as one poem. The first begins:

> Divitiis, ortu, specie, virtute, triumphis,
>   rex Priamus clara clarus in urbe fuit,
> dum rex, dum proceres, dum starent Pergama Troia,
>   quae decus et species, et caput orbis erat.
> rex Hecubam duxit sociam sibi nobilitate,
>   auspiciis, forma, rebus, amore, throno.

It is hardly necessary to say that this is a mere school exercise,
an Ovidian narrative of the most ordinary kind. But the second
poem is worse, for it is clumsy and obscure, being fettered by
its scheme of leonine rimes:

> Viribus, arte, minis Danaum data Troia ruinis,
>   annis bis quinis fit rogus atque cinis,
> urbs bona, nunc dumi, vi flammae, turbine fumi,
>   non ita consumi digna, resedit humi,
> nutu Iunonis, et iniqui fraude Sinonis,
>   clamque datis donis exspoliata bonis.[3]

Now Hauréau has shown that the first poem is not by Hildebert, as Leyser had supposed, but by Master Simon Chèvre-
d'Or (Aurea Capra), a contemporary of Hildebert and a canon
of Avranches;[4] and that, although in Leyser's text the poem
ends with the wooden horse, Master Simon did not leave the
story in such suspense. In MS. 8430 of the Bibliothèque
Nationale the whole poem is given. Who is the author of the

---

[1] *Itinerarium Kambriae*, i. 5.

[2] *Hist. poemat. et poet. med. aevi*,
p. 598 sqq.; reproduced in Migne,
clxxi, col. 1447 sqq.

[3] Migne, clxxi, col. 1451.

[4] p. 403; cf. *Notices et extraits*, xxix.
ii, p. 239.

second poem? It is certainly not Hildebert; but there is a third poem, in the same metrical scheme, and on the same subject, which on the evidence of manuscripts[1] is either to be ascribed to Hildebert or to Hugh the 'Primate'. Fortunately, Alexander Neckham, speaking of Hildebert, has resolved all reasonable doubt:

> plurima festive scripsit dictamina: scripsit
> 'sicut hiems laurum', 'Pergama flere volo.'[2]

The first quotation is the commencement of Hildebert's *Vita beatae Mariae Aegyptiacae*; but the second is the *incipit* of the *De excidio Troiae*:

> Pergama flere volo, fato Danais data solo;
>   solo capta dolo, capta redacta solo.
> ex Helicone sona, quae prima tenes Helicona,
>   et metra me dona promere posse bona!
> est Paris absque pare. quaerit, videt, audet amare,
>   audet tentare furta, pericla, mare;
> vadit et accedit, clam tollit clamque recedit.
>   nauta solo cedit, fit fuga, praedo redit.
> tuta libido maris dat thura libidinis aris,
>   civibus ignaris quod paret arma Paris.
> post cursus Helenae currunt Larissa, Mycenae,
>   mille rates plenae fortibus, absque sene.
> exsuperare ratus viduatorem viduatus,
>   foedere nudatus foederat ense latus.
> Graeco ductori prohibet dolor esse timori
>   pro consorte thori vivere, sive mori.[3]

The poem is full of conceits, it is a mere exercise in ingenuity, but there is a competence about its perversity which marks it out as the work of one who did not belong to the vulgar crowd of versifiers.[4] The high talent of Hildebert as well as the greatness of his soul are shown once and for all in that elegy— *de exsilio suo*[5]—in which he relates his misfortunes and his unbroken faith in the providential guidance of his life. First he addresses Fortune, and, with rhetorical fulness, he sets forth the good things which were his while the goddess smiled.

> Nuper eram locuples multisque beatus amicis,
>   et risere diu prospera fata mihi.

[1] ib., p. 442.
[2] *De laudibus divinae sapientiae* (*Rolls Series*, 1863), p. 454.
[3] Hauréau, p. 438.
[4] Hauréau (p. 444) has noted that there is yet another poem on the fall of Troy (and in the same metre) in *Carmina Burana*, ed. Schmeller, p. 63:

> fervet amore Paris, Troianis immolat aris,
>   fratribus ignaris scinditur unda maris.

This follows Hildebert's own poem, in the Benediktbeuern MS.
[5] Hauréau, p. 347.

larga Ceres, deus Arcadiae Bacchusque replebant
  horrea, septa, penum, farre, bidente, mero.
hortus, apes, famulae, pulmento, melle, tapetis
  ditabant large prandia, vasa, domum.
dextra laborabat gemmis, pomaria fructu;
  prata redundabant gramine, lacte greges.
agger opum, tranquilla quies, numerosus amicus
  delicias, somnos consiliumque dabant.
singula quid memorem laetos testantia casus?
  omnia captivae prosperitatis erant.
iurares superos intra mea vota teneri,
  et res occasum dedidicisse pati.
denique mirabar sic te, Fortuna, fidelem;
  mirabar stabilem, quae levis esse soles.
saepe mihi dixi: quorsum tam prospera rerum?
  quid sibi vult tantus, tam citus agger opum?
hei mihi! nulla fides, nulla est constantia rebus!
  res ipsae quid sint mobilitate docent.
res hominum et homines levis alea versat in auras,
  et venit a summo summa ruina gradu.
cuncta sub ancipiti pendent mortalia casu
  et spondent propria mobilitate fugam.
quidquid habes hodie cras te fortasse relinquet,
  aut modo, dum loqueris, desinit esse tuum.
has ludit Fortuna vices, regesque superbos
  aut servos humiles non sinit esse diu.
illa dolosa comes, sola levitate fidelis,
  non favet aeternum, nec sine fine premit.
illa mihi quondam risu blandita sereno
  mutavit vultus, nubila facta, suos;
et velut aeternam misero conata ruinam,
  spem quoque laetitiae detrahit ipsa mihi.
illa professa dolum, submersit, diruit, ussit
  culta, domos, vites, imbribus, igne, gelu.
haec eadem fregit, concussit, debilitavit
  hoste, notho, morbis, horrea, poma, gregem.[1]

Then Hildebert hints at the man who was the cause of his
misfortune, the unjust Count of Maine, who drove him out
because he dared to defend the rights of the Church. The
Bishop describes his journey across the sea, the storm, and
the final passage to safety. He reflects again on the misery
of man,

res et opes praestantur ei, famulantur ad horam,
  et locuples mane, vespere pauper erit,

and then exalts the majesty of God, in whose hands are all
things, and without whom Fortune herself can do nothing.
So, as Hildebert had begun with the apparatus of the heathen

[1] Hauréau, p. 347.

elegy, and with those commonplaces, elegantly expressed, which had filled the accusations of the ancient world, he turned at the end to a providence, but a providence such as a heathen philosopher might demonstrate or, perhaps, a Boëthius invoke in his austere and chiselled verses:

> ille potens, mitis, tenor et concordia rerum,
> quidquid vult in me digerat, eius ero.

This poem merits fully the praise that has been bestowed upon it. It is proper to forget the occasions upon which the poet fails to keep up the high standard that he had set before himself as a lover of the Latin past. It is good to remember that we are in the presence of a man of noble spirit whose utterance has still the power to move us across so many centuries.

But perhaps we feel more closely the charm of Hildebert's poetry in his rhythmical hymn to the Trinity.[1] This famous piece belongs to the history of religious poetry, but it must be mentioned here because it is one of the earliest examples of fully developed rhythmical and rimed verse in which, apart from formal correctness, the thought moves at the thinker's command, without hesitation, and one clause follows another as sure as a hammer's beat. We leave aside the mystical ascent of

> Me receptet Sion illa,
> Sion David urbs tranquilla,

and turn to the poet's 'confession':

> extra portum iam delatum,
> iam foetentem, tumulatum
> vitta ligat, lapis urget,
> sed, si iubes, hic resurget.
> iube, lapis revolvetur,
> iube, vitta disrumpetur;
> exiturus nescit moras,
> postquam clamas: exi foras!
>
> .   .   .   .
>
> infecunda mea ficus,
> cuius ramus ramus siccus,
> incidetur, incendetur,
> si promulgas, quae meretur.
> sed hoc anno dimittatur,
> stercoretur, fodiatur;
> quodsi necdum respondebit,
> flens hoc loquor, tunc ardebit.
> vetus hostis in me furit,
> aquis mersat, flammis urit,
> inde languens et afflictus
> tibi soli sum relictus.

---

[1] *Anal. Hymn.* l, pp. 409 sqq.

The impression which these verses leave is one of power and smoothness. They are rhetorical, indeed, but rhetorical in the same way that much of the later vernacular poetry was rhetorical. The metre and the rime allow of no elaborate constructions, and the expression must of necessity be concise. The *caesura* is usually observed after the fourth syllable, and the rimes are studiously accurate. We must reckon Hildebert among the most accomplished masters of rhythmical verse as well as a poet who responded so intensely to the spirit of antiquity that he made living poems out of the verse forms of the ancient poets.

§ 4. *Marbod of Rennes.*

Marbod of Rennes[1] is another instance of a scholar and a poet who became master of a school, then an archdeacon, and finally a bishop. He was born at Angers about 1035, and he was educated in its cathedral school. In 1069 he became Chancellor of Angers, and when his master, Reginald, died he succeeded to the headship of the school. There Geoffrey of Vendôme, later to be Prior of La Trinité, was one of his pupils. Baudry of Bourgeuil studied at the same school, and in after years the two poets exchanged poems. Baudry once addressed him as 'divine poet':[2]

> me tibi, teque mihi, quoniam, divine poeta,
> mutuus affectus et mutua fabula iungit,
> verborumque frequens nos alternatio pascit . . .

And, indeed, he had obtained a renown second only to Hildebert's in his day. For was he not the poet of the *Liber Lapidum*, in which the virtues of precious stones were set forth, and were there not many clever epigrams of which he was understood to be the author? In 1096 he was taken away from the schools to be bishop at Rennes, and he now had the usual troubles to fight against—false doctrine and the barbarous manners of his flock. He died in 1123 in extreme old age,[3]

---

[1] Manitius, *Gesch.* iii. 719 sqq.

[2] Ed. P. Abrahams, p. 124.

[3] See Migne, clxxi, col. 1463 for his entry in the *Rotulus*, 'qui post longa liberalium studiorum longe lateque vernantium exercitia, quibus in Andegavensi civitate, cui famosus ac nominatissimus exstitit magister, efficacissime claruit . . . pontifex ordinatus est. quam ipse dignitatem, imo onus, ac- cinctus gladio Spiritus sancti, licet inter barbaros, et naturali quadam armatos feritate, annos viginti octo feliciter et prudenter gubernavit. superborum colla iustitiae censura perdomuit; arguendo, obsecrando, increpando, dissidentia pacificavit; tandemque longaevo confectus senio, plenus dierum in sancta professione, ut praemissum est, in Domino requievit.' For epitaphs,

having assumed the garb of S. Benedict, and so, as the *Rotulus* says, 'having been aforetime like Martha troubled and careful about many things, now, like another Mary, recognizing that one thing only was necessary, he chose the better part, which shall not be taken away from him'.

Marbod, we have seen, began as a teacher, and he was naturally much interested in the teaching of versification. To this end he composed a book *de ornamentis verborum*, written in verse and dedicated to one of his pupils.[1] The subject of each section is described in prose, and then one or more examples are given in verse. Thus:

Repetitio; repetitio est, cum continenter atque eodem verbo in rebus similibus et diversis principia sumuntur; hoc modo:

> tu mihi rex, mihi lex, mihi lux, mihi dux, mihi vindex,
> te colo, te laudo, te glorificans tibi plaudo.
> femina iustitiam produxit, femina culpam.
> femina vitalem dedit ortum, femina mortem.
> femina peccavit, peccatum femina lavit.

or

Similiter cadens: similiter cadens est, cum in eadem constructione duo vel plura verba similiter iisdem casibus construuntur; hoc modo:

> fac tibi fortunam, festina frangere lunam,
> et contra fatum faciat te cura beatum.

The whole thing is merely a school-exercise book and, as Manitius points out,[2] the figures and their theoretical explanation are taken from the *Auctor ad Herennium*, iv. 13–30, with some variations. In the epilogue Marbod seizes the opportunity of slipping back into his beloved rime:

> haec tibi de multis, ne multa forent onerosa,
> primum pauca dedi, quasi fercula deliciosa.
> singula distinguens facili brevitate notavi,
> quae quo plana forent, magis haec placitura putavi.
> si gustata placent, et adhuc gustanda petuntur,
> caetera quae restant me dispensante dabuntur.
> sed prius haec debes studio versare frequenti,
> ut velut his vacuae committas caetera menti.
> interea tanquam speculum formamque poetae
> verum naturae qui scribere vultis habete,

Migne, ib., col. 1463–6. Marbod vented his dislike of Rennes and its citizens in a violent poem (col. 1726 sq.), beginning,

> urbs Redonis, spoliata bonis, viduata colonis,
> plena dolis, odiosa polis, sine lumine solis.

[1] Migne, clxxi, col. 1687 sqq. The prologue begins,

> versificaturo quaedam tibi tradere curo
> scemata verborum studio celebrata priorum.

[2] iii. 723.

cuius ad exemplar, veluti qui pingere discit,
aptet opus primum quisquis bene fingere gliscit.
ars a natura, ratione vocante, profecta,
principii formam proprii retinere laborat.
ergo qui laudem sibi vult scribendo parare,
sexus, aetates, affectus, conditiones,
sicut sunt in re, studeat distincta referre.
haec spernens Bavius, haec servans fiet Homerus.

Nature, therefore, according to Marbod is to be the poet's model. In those days poets, or at any rate poets who wrote in the learned tongue, had to be formed in the schools, and Marbod evidently had little doubt that obedience to rule would carry the young poet a long way. He was not himself a very good model to imitate, for he was too fond of leonine verse, and he had none of the vigour of Hildebert and little of his feeling for what was finest in antiquity. The didactic tendency drew him; he was a teacher and a moralist. So he loved to turn into verse biblical narratives, such as the Book of Ruth,[1] and the story of Jonah,[2] and when he tells of the fate of Dinah he does not make it an excuse for an Ovidian narrative, but keeps close to his moralizing purpose from the very commencement:[3]

Discite claustra pati qui parcitis integritati,
nec proferre pedem vestramque relinquere sedem.
quae latebras odit, se stulta puellula prodit;
stuprum sollicitat quoties non publica vitat.

Marbod wrote long poems on the legend of Theophilus,[4] on S. Maurilius,[5] and on other saints. He usually employed the leonine hexameter with rimes of two syllables, but the *Liber Lapidum*,[6] the most famous of all his poems, is in ordinary hexameters. It is essentially a didactic poem, based largely on Isidore and Solinus,[7] and it was prized in the Middle Ages on account of the useful information which it was supposed to contain. As many as sixty different stones are described with their peculiar virtues, both natural and magical. The introduction tells the curious tale of how Evax, King of the Arabs, wrote to Nero, the second successor of Augustus, an account of precious stones:

Evax rex Arabum legitur scripsisse Neroni,
qui post Augustum regnavit in urbe secundus,

---

[1] Migne, clxxi, col. 1678.
[2] ib., col. 1675.
[3] ib., col. 1682.
[4] ib., col. 1593 sqq.
[5] ib., col. 1635 sqq.

[6] ib., col. 1758 sqq.; there can be no doubt of Marbod's authorship; see L. Pannier, *Les Lapidaires français du moyen âge*, Paris 1882, p. 19.
[7] Manitius, *Gesch.* iii. 724.

> quot species lapidum, quae nomina, quive colores,
> quaeve sit his regio, vel quanta potentia cuique.

Marbod takes up the same task, but he writes for a few friends only; for it is not meet to make these mystical things known to the common crowd:

> hoc opus excipiens dignum componere duxi
> aptum gestanti forma breviore libellum,
> qui mihi praecipue, paucisque pateret amicis;
> nam maiestatem minuit qui mystica vulgat,
> nec secreta manent, quorum fit conscia turba.

He says further that he writes, not merely to unveil the secrets of nature, but with the useful object of helping medical science, telling how to drive away diseases by means of the virtues of these stones:

> ingens est herbis virtus data, maxima gemmis.

The success of his poem is shown not only by the number of manuscripts but by an early translation into French, and others into English, Italian, and Danish.

Marbod followed the fashion of his time in poetical epistles, some of which may be merely exercises of a conventional kind. There is, for instance, a piece addressed *ad virginem devotam*[1] which begins:

> Splendidior stella, simplex et munda puella,
> quam Deus elegit, quam nulla libido subegit,
> fac ut coepisti quod mundo displicet isti;
> sperne leves curas, et res attende futuras.

But when Marbod writes in honour of Queen Matilda, it is in a more graceful strain—though he could not unlearn the manner of the school:[2]

> affectant aliae quod eis natura negavit,
> purpureas niveo pingere lacte genas:
> fucatosque trahit facies medicata colores,
> distinguendo notas artis adulterio.
> comprimit exstantes quarumdam fascia mammas
> et longum fingit vestis adacta latus.

---

[1] Migne, clxxi, col. 1654.

[2] ib., col. 1660. This is Matilda, the clever wife of Henry I of England; she died in 1118. Süssmilch, *Die lateinische Vagantenpoesie des 12 und 13 Jahrhunderts als Kulturerscheinung*, p. 45, quotes William of Malmesbury; 'adventabant (i.e. to Matilda) scholastici tum canticis tum versibus famosi, felicemque se putabat, qui carminis novitate aures mulceret dominae' (Migne clxxix, col. 1372). But Süssmilch is wrong in talking of *Vaganten* in this connexion. The poets were scholars of the type of Hildebert, Marbod, and Baudry. There is no question of courtly service, as Süssmilch suggests.

> hae partim retegunt laxosa fronte capillos,
>   et calamistrato crine placere volunt.
> tu, regina, quod es, metuis formosa videri;
>   quae coemunt aliae munera gratis habens.

And addressing in another poem the Countess Ermengarde,[1] his compliments are curiously outspoken:

> Filia Fulconis, decus Armoricae regionis,
>   pulchra, pudica, decens, candida, clara, recens,
> si non passa fores thalamos, partusque labores,
>   posses esse meo Cynthia iudicio.
> sed quia iuncta mari castae nequit aequiparari,
>   est etiam potior virginitatis honor,
> in grege nuptarum credi potes una dearum,
>   prima vel in primis, o speciosa nimis!

There is a quite charming letter to Bishop Samson of Winchester[2] in which Marbod laments their separation by the unfriendly sea. The sea really belongs to fishes, he says, and he evidently thinks it too dangerous an undertaking to cross the Channel, though he can invent good reasons why Samson should come to visit him. This cult of friendship is one of the most pleasing literary manifestations of the age. It was not merely an offshoot of the school-exercise, though it was in the schools that the technique was acquired.

In his younger days, Marbod had followed the way of youth, and had written light verses of which in his old age he professed to be ashamed. We hardly know which of the many epigrams and miscellaneous poems contained in manuscript collections are assuredly his work,[3] but among them are probably to be reckoned some pieces of a questionable character.[4] Marbod very properly repented of all this and, in his old age, composed his *Liber decem capitulorum*,[5] from which we learn something of his thoughts as he reflected on the past during his times of leisure at Rennes. This work, which consists of ten poems, is dedicated to his friend Bishop Hildebert, who, younger than Marbod by some twenty years, must have been then at the

---

[1] ib., col. 1659.

[2] Migne, clxxi, col. 1658.

[3] Hauréau, *Notices et extraits de quelques mss.*, vi. 180, points out that many of the attributions in Beaugendre's edition (reproduced in Migne) are pure fantasy; but on the whole there should not be a very large number to reject. The only MS. in England which I have examined as containing poems of Marbod is Brit. Mus. Cotton. Vitellius A xii, the date of which is, Dr. Eric Millar kindly informs me, about 1200. Here a number of Marbod's poems are collected interspersed with others which have been printed in Wright, *Anglo-Saxon Satirical Poets*, vol. ii.

[4] Migne, clxxi, col. 1717.

[5] ib., col. 1693 sqq.

height of his fame. Marbod begins by an ingenuous confession of his past errors, both as regards the lightness and impropriety of his verse and the imperfection of its form. He sets forth a kind of *Ars poetica* to guide the practice of his later years.

> Quae iuvenis scripsi, senior dum plura retracto,
> poenitet, et quaedam vel scripta vel edita nollem,
> tum quia materies inhonesta levisque videtur,
> tum quia dicendi potuit modus aptior esse.
> unde nec inventu pretiosa, nec arte loquendi,
> vel delenda cito, vel non edenda fuissent.
> sed quia missa semel vox irrevocabilis exit,
> erroremque nefas est emendare priorem,
> restat ut in reliquum iam cautior esse laborem,
> ne quid inornate, vel ne quid inutile promam;
> praecipue quia iam veniae locus esse nequibit
> qui quondam fuerat, dum stulta rudisque iuventus,
> et levis, in culpam poterat toleranda videri.
> nunc vitae studiique simul diuturnior usus
> acrius expectat rigidi censoris acumen.
> ergo propositum mihi sit neque ludicra quaedam
> scribere nec verbis aures mulcere canoris;
> non quod inornate describere seria laudem,
> sed ne, quod prius est, neglecto pondere rerum,
> dulcisonos numeros, concinnaque verba sequamur.
> est operosa quidem, multisque negata facultas,
> ut rerum virtus, verborum lege subacta,
> servetur, verbique canor sub rebus abundet;
> quod iugi studio tunc affectare videbar.
> sed mihi nunc melius suadet maturior aetas,
> quam decet ut facili contenta sit utilitate,
> utque supervacuum studeat vitare laborem.
> est aliud quare puto continuare canoros
> versus absurdum, quoniam color unus ubique
> nil varium format, sed nec pictura vocatur,
> imo litura magis, quia delectare videntes
> res variae raraeque solent: fit copia vilis.
> ergo diversos scriptis adhibere colores,
> et variare stylum, plus laudis habere putamus.
> nec tamen hoc solo carmen laudabile constat:
> nam lex scribendi recte, tria postulat—ut sit
> perspicuum, vitioque carens, ac schemate vernans.
> quod si consequitur, fit dulcis et utilis idem,
> et retinere potest animos auresque legentum.
> hoc genus ergo mihi posthac propono sequendum,
> in quo plus laudis reor, et minus esse laboris.

But in spite of this confession of faith, practical and moral, Marbod says that he does not altogether repent the past. For it is proper for youth to labour and even to sing light songs. Age has its own severity, and it would be unseemly if it re-

tained the vices of youth. So, in his later years, he must sing
of serious things, and the subjects which he chooses are such
as these—*de tempore et aevo, de meretrice, de matrona, de
senectute, de fato et genesi, de voluptate,* &c. In the first of these
poems he draws a picture of the way in which the corruption
of youth is assisted by the studies in the schools.[1] He is tracing
the course of human life from birth to death:

> praetereo cunas, pannorum foeda relinquo;
> infantum fletus, nutricum sperno labores.
> ad pueri propero lacrymas, quem verbere saevo
> iratus cogit dictata referre magister,
> dediscenda docens quae confinxere poetae,
> stupra nefanda Iovis, seu Martis adultera facta,
> lascivos recitans iuvenes, turpesque puellas,
> mutua quos iunxit sed detestanda voluptas.
> imbuit ad culpam similem rude fabula pectus,
> praeventusque puer vitii ferventis odore
> iam cupit exemplo committere foeda deorum.

He proceeds to develop this theme with details which it is
hardly possible to quote. Is this merely an exercise in satire
or has it any root in reality? This is not altogether an idle
question, for it is impossible not to observe what may be called
the secular bent of the cathedral schools in this age, and it is
easy to see its impress upon the poets and men of letters. For
the cathedral schools were the training ground for the men of
affairs who were to rise to high office in the Church, whether
they passed from a mastership to a bishopric, or entered the
royal service and eventually obtained the same reward by
another path. The training provided was on very broad lines,
with little restriction as to the authors who were studied. In
the practice of verse old rhetorical methods were still in vogue,
and poetical descriptions were successful only if they ploughed
their way in a mass of detail. Many of these compositions are
of questionable taste, and even more questionable must have
been the verses which were composed for restricted circulation.
Both satires and love poems or poems involving amatory
descriptions were doubtless composed in the schools. Marbod
had enjoyed the freedom of the schools in his youth; in his
old age he saw its danger, but he was not so much concerned
with this as with the expediency of putting away such things
when youth had passed. He and his fellows belonged largely
to the world, until the Church finally claimed them by putting
them in a position of responsibility. Then they used their

[1] Migne, clxxi, col. 1695.

scholarship for other ends, sometimes looking back wistfully to the past, at other times playing with the old themes in a different context, but always ready to make a confession of repentance and to atone for their lighter verses by didactic and religious compositions.

Marbod himself is an attractive figure. We imagine in him a slight tincture of vanity, a gentle disposition, combined with enough energy to make him successful as a teacher and, moderately, as a bishop. He had a taste, like Baudry his friend, for the quiet joys of the country:

> Moribus esse feris prohibet me gratia veris,
> et formam mentis mihi mutuor ex elementis;
> ipsi naturae congratulor, ut puto, iure.
> distingunt flores diversi mille colores.
> gramineum vellus superinduit sibi tellus.
> fronde virere nemus et fructificare videmus.
> aurioli, merulae, graculi, pici, philomenae
> certant laude pari varios cantus modulari.
> nidus nonnullis stat in arbore, non sine pullis,
> et latet in dumis nova progenies sine plumis.
> egrediente rosa viridaria sunt speciosa;
> adiungas istis campum qui canet aristis,
> adiungas vites, uvas quoque, postmodo nuces.
> annumerare queas nuruum matrumque choreas,
> et ludos iuvenum, festumque diemque serenum.
> qui tot pulchra videt, nisi flectitur, et nisi ridet,
> intractabilis est, et in eius pectore lis est.
> qui speciem terrae non vult cum laude referre,
> invidet auctori, cuius subservit honori
> bruma rigens, aestas, autumnus, veris honestas.[1]

How charming and fresh and human! All grudging is gone, and the poet has no quarrel with life. A poem like this is, no doubt, an offshoot of the nature-descriptions of the schools; but it is impossible to mistake the real and deep affection which Marbod, and Baudry as well, felt for the landscape of their home. So Marbod, when writing to Bishop Samson,[2] speaks of well-remembered scenes on his Loire:

> Invidet antiquum pelagi mihi fluctus amicum;
>   oceani limes separat unanimes.
> nec pons in ponto, nec sunt vada pervia conto,
>   ut solet in Ligeri navis adacta geri.

He wrote a charming little poem[3] for one of his pupils, telling how to conduct himself throughout the hours of the day in his master's absence:

---

[1] Migne, clxxi, col. 1717.   [2] ib., col. 1658.   [3] ib., col. 1724.

> Si praeceptorum superest tibi cura meorum,
> parce puer nugis, dum rus colo tempore frugis.
> praefigam metas, quales tua postulat aetas:
> quas si trangrederis, male de monitore mereris.
> contempto strato, summo te mane levato,
> facque legendo moram, quartam dumtaxat ad horam,
> quinta sume cibum, vinum bibe, sed moderatum,
> et pransus, breviter dormi, vel lude parumper.
> postquam dormieris, sit mos tuus ut mediteris.
> quae meditatus eris tabulis dare ne pigriteris.
> quae dediscere spero quandoque videre.
> miseris huc quaedam, facies ut caetera credam.
> post haec, i lectum: cum legeris, ito comestum.
> post sumptas escas, si iam monet hora, quiescas.
> si tempus superest, post coenam ludere prodest.
> sub tali meta constat tibi tota diaeta.

Like the best teachers of his age, he believed in a firm but kindly discipline; he says elsewhere,[1]

> Qui puero parcit, leve cor pinguedine farcit.
> qui flagra continuat, pingue cor extenuat.

He was, no doubt, himself a ready scholar, if he never attained the profundity of Hildebert or the refined taste of Baudry. His excessive love of the leonine hexameter drew him away from classical models without giving him any new freedom. His rhythmical verse is curiously unformed, with imperfect rimes, and little vigour.[2] But he is entitled to our respect for his pure devotion to letters, and for the share which he took in the civilizing task of the cathedral schools.

§ 5. *Baudry of Bourgueil.*

Baudry of Bourgueil[3] is perhaps the most attractive of the men of letters who issued from the French cathedral schools. It is true that he had not the *gravitas* of Hildebert, or the curiosity of Marbod, but he had that absorbing love of letters and that desire for the scholar's and the poet's solitude which separated him from the professional *littérateurs* of the younger generation. He was born at Meung-sur-Loire in 1046, and the charm of river and field and of all the natural things amid which his youth was spent held him throughout the years. He studied at the cathedral school of Angers, but the monastery claimed him, and in 1089 he was Abbot at Bourgueil. His

---

[1] Migne, clxxi, col. 1724.
[2] *Anal. Hymn.* l, pp. 389 sqq.
[3] On Baudry, see *Christian-Latin*

Poetry, pp. 277 sqq.; for poems, *Les Œuvres poétiques de Baudri de Bourgueil* ed. Phyllis Abrahams, Paris 1926.

abilities could not, however, be hidden; so in 1107 he was elected Archbishop of Dol. He was obviously out of place among the difficult Bretons, from whom he parted often and without reluctance. He preferred the quiet of Saint-Samson-sur-Rille to the noise of business, and found there a retreat from which he could visit his Norman friends in those houses where learning still flourished amid the Benedictine peace.

Ovid was his master among the classical poets; but it was Hildebert and Marbod, poets of his own day, that he hoped to emulate,[1] and there was, he tells us, Godfrey of Reims who could give him immortality by merely naming him in his verse.[2] These poets revived the cult of friendship which had graced the Carolingian court, and like the Carolingians they wrote epigrams and poetical epistles. This poetry flowed from two sources—antiquity, and the needs of the cultured society of the cathedral cities.

Among Baudry's poetical epistles is one addressed to Godfrey of Reims.[3] It is full of rhetorical flattery, but how otherwise could Baudry proceed once he had determined on writing a letter in the Ovidian measure after the manner of the schools?

> te scio magnatum pastum modulamine vatum,
>   te quoque Pierias incoluisse domos.
> novimus auctorum quia vivat spiritus in te,
>   Virgilii gravitas, Ovidii levitas.
> nam quocumque stilo causas edicere temptes,
>   ipse stilus causam, non polit ipsa stilum.

From this we see how seriously these poets took themselves, just as Wido of Ivrea, with that 'sum, sum, sum vates', at the end of his poem.[4] But Godfrey did not, for some reason, reply to this letter, and after the lapse of a year Baudry wrote an accusing complaint of six verses to his friend:

> Annus abit, quia iam nos alter suscipit annus
> ex quo suscepto lecto quoque carmine nostro
> te tua iurasti missurum carmina nobis;
> quam male iurasti! misisti carmina nulla.
> aut es periurus, aut te tua carmina purgent,
> et valeant odae tibi si poterunt, Godefrede.[5]

Whether Godfrey answered at last from his school at Reims we do not know. But when Godfrey died, Baudry composed no less than five epitaphs or epigrams in his honour.[6] The first of these runs as follows:

---

[1] Œuvres, pp. 124, 126.
[2] ib., p. 153.
[3] ib., pp. 151 sqq.

[4] Below, p. 386.
[5] Œuvres, p. 158.
[6] ib., pp. 86 sqq.

> iocundus magnae thesaurus philosophiae,
>> magnaque musa perit, cum Godefredus obit.
> iste decus cleri, sol alter idoneus orbi,
>> orbi sufficeret, viveret ipse diu.
> sed mors effrenis super hunc sua frena gravavit,
>> et iubar a superis invida grande tulit.
> Remis habet corpus, animae sit mansio coelum;
>> divitibus dives ossibus urna, vale.

Similarly, when Alexander, a young canon of Tours, died untimely, Baudry composed three epitaphs—variations on one theme, the young man's beauty and the whole world's sorrow at his end.[1] There are many of these epitaphs in Baudry's collected works; they are exercises, ingenious or conventional, neither better nor worse than a hundred others by his contemporaries. There are also pieces to be inscribed in *rotuli mortuorum*, those 'rolls of the dead' which circulated round monasteries and churches, and afforded opportunities for monastic or clerical poets.[2] Baudry imitated Marbod in writing a mock-invective against the unfortunate messenger, who came so often, like a bird of ill omen, bringing the roll that always announced bad tidings. Marbod had cursed him as

> vernula Plutonis, legatio perditionis,

and had used his two-syllabled leonine rimes to lend emphasis to his imprecations.[3] But Baudry is more gentle, though he does call the messenger's post-horse a bird of prey; he begins,

> obsecro, iam parcat tam saepe venire veredus,
> per nimios usus nimium sua verba veremur.
> vivant praelati, pro quorum morte vagatur
> vultur edax, corvusque niger, volitansque veredus,
> necnon bubo canens dirum mortalibus omen.[4]

But this is merely to lead up to the point of his poem, the death of Audebert, Archbishop of Bourges and Abbot of Déols, whose death has just been announced by the bearer of the roll. For the roll itself Baudry composed a long inscription,[5] in which, after reiterating his general complaint, he went over a list of the bishops and abbots whose deaths had been recently announced,—and now to crown all, death has taken Audebert away:

> hunc Audebertum validum iuvenilibus annis
> effera mors rapuit, quae nulli parcere novit.

---

[1] *Œuvres*, p. 39 sq.
[2] See *Christian-Latin Poetry*, p. 454.
[3] Migne, clxxi, col. 1673.

[4] *Œuvres*, p. 64.
[5] ib., p. 62.

Not content with this tribute Baudry composed, and doubtless circulated to his admiring friends, no less than five epitaphs for the Archbishop. In one of them he refers to the dead prelate's love of poetry, for he calls him

> auditor vatum, vatum moderator et ipse.[1]

By this we must understand that Audebert was a good judge of poetry; but elsewhere Baudry numbers the Archbishop with Marbod and Godfrey among the famous poets of the time.

Baudry loved to exchange poems with his friends. Writing to one Robert,[2] who had sent him some verses, he says,

> laudo tuum calamum, studiosa poemata laudo.[3]

But he claims no such learned gravity for his own verse, which is nothing more than the product of his leisure:[4]

> non tibi sit vilis mea pagina, pagina levis:
> in nugis gravitas est odiosa mihi.[5]

In the same strain he writes to Galo, his 'brother':[6]

> nam me dictandi vel nulla scientia munit,
> vel tenuis, sed me carminis urget amor.
> anser raucus ego strepo sedulus inter olores;
> inter aves querulas rauca cicada strepo.

There are many, he says, who despise him for his poor but honest attempts; but this, we may guess, is merely his modesty, a modesty which passes into convention when, in another poem, writing to Emma, a learned nun, he speaks delightfully of his 'rustic Muse'.[7]

> invenies nullos flores in carmine nostro,
> flores urbani scilicet eloquii,
> rustica dicta mihi quia rusticus incola ruris,
> Magduni natus, incolo Burgulium;
> Burgulius locus est procul a Cicerone remotus,
> cui plus caepe placet quam stilus et tabulae.
> attamen iste locus foret olim vatibus aptus,
> dum musae silvas solivagae colerent.
> nam prope prata virent illimibus humida rivis,
> prataque gramineo flore fovent oculos,

---

[1] ib., p. 183, 'qualis pontifici copia Biturico'. None of Audebert's poems has survived.

[2] Œuvres, p. 67.

[3] ib., p. 8.

[4] See *Christian-Latin Poetry*, p. 279, for Baudry's defence of his poetry against those censorious detractors who accused him of frivolity.

[5] Œuvres, p. 8.

[6] ib., p. 9.

[7] ib., p. 271. Emma is to be his critic:

> ore Sibillino respondeat Emma roganti,
> perlegat, extollat, corrigat, adiciat.

et virides herbas lucus vicinus amoenat,
    quem concors avium garrulitas decorat.
hic me solatur tantummodo Cambio noster
    cuius saepe undas intueor vitreas.
sed vates silvas iamdudum deseruere
    quos urbis perimit deliciosus amor,
et dolor est ingens quia vatum pectora frigent,
    et quia dignantur tecta subire ducum.
est dolor et doleo quia gloria nulla poetis,
    quod quia ditantur promeruere sibi.
sunt dii, non homines, quos lactat philosophia,
    nec deberent dii vivere sicut homo,
praesul, rex, consul, princeps, patriarcha, monarchus,
    littera desit eis, sunt pecualis homo:
furnos conducat, frutices metat, allia mandat
    qui sapit atque opibus incubat implicitus;
nam si negligerent sapientes pondus honoris,
    invitis etiam subiceretur honor.
reges, pontifices, nunc et de plebe minores,
    aspernantur eos et nihilum reputant.[1]
quid modo Marbodus vatum spectabile sidus?
    eclipsim luna, sol patitur tenebras.
nunc est deflendus, extinctus spiritus eius,
    nam non est lux quae luceat in tenebris.
o utinam afflasset pleno mihi gutture musa,
    nam me nullus honor a studiis raperet!
nunc quia musa deest et rauco pectine canto,
    Emma meis saltem versibus assideas.

Here Baudry presents himself with an air of conviction as the country poet. Hildebert's muse was certainly of the city, but Baudry loved the stream that flowed past the monastery of Bourgueil, and he was not merely following from afar the example of Horace when he wished for a little cottage with a garden, a boy to look after him and to bring him his tablets, and friends with whom to share his books and wine.[2] He seems really to have hated the rewards which his learning brought him in the way of ecclesiastical preferment, but how else could men like himself be rewarded? He complains conventionally of the neglect of poets by the great, but they often found rich bishoprics or canonries, and the leisure necessary for writing verse was seldom wanting. So Baudry's complaints on this score carry but little conviction, though it is probably true that he was never very effective as abbot or as bishop. The lady to whom he wrote was a nun, a person of some

---

[1] Miss Abrahams (p. 273, note 7) quotes from a similar complaint by Raoul of La Tourte, in *Bibl. de l'École des Chartes*, 4ᵉ série, i, p. 502 sq.

[2] *Œuvres*, pp. 183 sqq. Here Baudry catalogues all the delights of country life, and all the products of this farm of his dreams.

consequence, perhaps an abbess. For in another piece[1] he addresses her as

> coenobitarum decus et decor Emma sororum,

and he even goes so far as to say that he would like to be one of her pupils. To Agnes he writes counselling her to persevere in her intention to enter on the religious life,[2] and he gives similar advice to Muriel,[3] a rich young woman, attractive and clever, with a talent for recitation:

> o quam mellito tua sunt lita verba lepore!
> o quam dulce sonat vox tua dum recitas!
> carmina dum recitas, duro placitura parenti,
> dicta sonant hominem, vox muliebris erat.
> verborum positura decens seriesque modesta
> te iam praeclaris vatibus inseruit.

He tells us that it is the first time that he has written verses to a young woman;

> nulla recepit adhuc nisi tu mea carmina virgo,

and it seems that it was at her own request that he wrote. But in another poem, which may be later in date, Baudry takes a quite different line. He talks as a poet whose verses had a wide circulation, so wide that he was exposed to unkind criticism as the author of poems which ministered to frivolity.[4] Or is he merely adopting a well-worn convention when he defends himself by saying that his life is pure even if he does write love-dialogues? At any rate, he does not mind saying that he writes that he may be read—read by boys and girls:

> ergo quod pueros demulceat atque puellas
> scripsimus, ut pueris id consonet atque puellis,
> sicque meum relegatur opus volitetque per orbem,
> illud dum relegent pueri relegentque puellae.

The light verses to which he refers are, indeed, harmless enough. Two of them are exercises based on Ovid, though in hexameters—a letter of Paris to Helen, and Helen's reply.[5] They are probably school-compositions furbished up in later years. It is useless to analyse them in detail, but it is interesting to note that Paris says, in the first letter, that if he could urge his suit in person, he could use other rhetorical embellishments—such as we know were studied in the schools with the aid of the *Auctor ad Herennium*:

> ad te si pro me supplex orator adessem
> ipse perorandi genus altius alter adissem

---

[1] *Œuvres*, p. 259.
[2] ib., p. 257.
[3] ib., p. 256.
[4] ib., p. 122.
[5] ib., pp. 29 sqq.

atque meis alios intermiscere colores
curarem scriptis, ut possent scripta placere,
quatenus insertus color affectare valeret,
alliceretque mihi te carminis ordo saporus.
addere carminibus quaedam munuscula nossem
corda puellarum quibus attemptare solemus.[1]

Then Baudry allows Paris to make an attack on the superstition and morals of the Greeks, with quite unnecessary detail; but the object is to make it clear that Helen has nothing to lose by leaving her countrymen, and Paris goes on to praise the admirable morals of the Trojans.[2] Although Baudry makes Paris employ the plainest language, this would cause no scandal to his critics.

It was of the essence of the rhetorical method from Ovid onwards to treat of a given theme in detail until there was no more left to be said. An excellent example of this is the exchange of letters between Baudry and a young woman named Constance, who lived in a convent.[3] The correspondence is a kind of 'moralization' of the *Heroides*, for these are love-letters, but not of the ordinary sort:

quod sonat iste brevis amor est et carmen amoris,
inque brevis tactu nulla venena latent.

This theme of the purity of his affection is developed in more than a hundred and seventy verses. It is important to observe that the treatment is dictated by the method which Baudry had learned and not by any lack of decent reticence on his part. So he can say,[4]

crede mihi, credasque volo, credantque legentes,
in te me nunquam foedus adegit amor.
in te concivem volo vivere virginitatem,
in te confringi nolo pudicitiam.
tu virgo, vir ego, iuvenis sum, iunior es tu;
iuro per omne quod est: nolo vir esse tibi.
nolo vir esse tibi neque tu sis femina nobis;
os et cor nostram firmet amicitiam.
pectora iungantur, sed corpora semoveantur.
sit pudor in facto, sit iocus in calamo.

After this he must describe her beauty: and he does it according to rule:

non rutilat Veneris tam clara binomia stella,
quam rutilant ambo lumina clara tibi.

---

[1] *Œuvres*, p. 31.   [2] ib., p. 34: solis coniugibus spreto Ganimedo vacamus, etc.
[3] ib., pp. 338 sqq.   [4] ib., p. 339.

crinibus inspectis fulvum minus arbitror aurum,
colla nitent plusquam lilia, nixve recens,
dentes plus ebore, Pario plus marmore candent,
spirat et in labiis gratia viva tuis.
labra tument modicum; color et calor igneus illis,
quae tamen ambo decens temperies foveat.
iure rosis malas praeponi dico tenellas,
quas rubor et candor vestit et omne decus.
corporis ut breviter complectar composituram,
est corpus talem quod deceat faciem.
ipsa Iovem summum posses deducere caelo,
de Iove si verax fabula Graeca foret.
in quascumque velis se formas effigiasset,
si tua te saeclis tempora praestiterint.

There is more of this kind to follow, but enough has been
quoted to illustrate Baudry's method, and to suggest the unkind deductions which his enemies might draw from such
verses. Indeed, the poet himself finds it necessary to sketch
in broad lines the defence which he might make:

quod si nos aliquis dixisse iocosa remordet,
non sum durus homo, quidquid ago iocus est.
laeta mihi vitam fecit natura iocosam
et mores hilares vena benigna dedit.
sed quidquid dicam, teneant mea facta pudorem,
cor mundum vigeat, mensque pudica mihi.

This is the customary defence, but the learned Constance
equally understood the conventional reply. Her poetical
answer,[1] of exactly the same length, is admirable in its effusive
expression of a chaste affection. The rules of rhetoric must be
obeyed. So Constance begins by expressing her joy at receiving
such a letter:

Composui gremio, posuique sub ubere laevo
schedam, quod cordi iunctius esse ferunt.

Love and the remembrance of it will not allow her to sleep.
If only she could see this prophet, this divine poet, this man
of learning, who, if ancient Rome had deserved to have such
a citizen, would have been a Cato and a Cicero in one, worth
many Aristotles. 'He seems to be, he is, and indeed he is
called a second Homer.'

<hr>

[1] *Œuvres*, pp. 344 sqq. But Schumann, 'Baudri von Bourgueil als Dichter' (in *Studien zur lateinischen Dichtung
des Mittelalters, Ehrengabe für Karl
Strecker*, Dresden 1931, p. 162 sq.)
raises the question whether these letters
are anything more than poetical exercises in which the reply was equally
the work of Baudry. This is, indeed, a
possibility which cannot be excluded.

This is a love-letter, and so she must proceed to talk of her lover's beauty. But her muse is not equal to the task:

> si sermo fiat de formae compositura,
>   impar est tantae nostra camena rei.
> inter mortales tanquam flos unicus ille
>   formosis aliis corpore et ore praeest.
> inter caelicolas ut conspectissima stella,
>   gratior aurora est soleque lucidior.[1]

She desires above all to see him, for she is tormented with fears. Perhaps he is deceiving her, and does not love her after all?

> heu, quid non timeam? nunquam secura quiescam:
>   nec mihi tutus amor, nec mihi tuta fides.

Lastly, she returns to the theme of the blamelessness of their love. She is the *sponsa dei*, and therefore she can love those who are the friends of her Beloved. Even if Baudry fails, she will not fail—but unless he comes to visit her, she will not be sure that he loves her:

> cura tibi de me non est nisi veneris ad me,
>   nec tua vel modicus viscera tangit amor.[2]

These poems doubtless became public property,[3] and although no one can have easily misunderstood them, they would support the general complaint of Baudry's critics—the secular and frivolous material of this verse which was composed by a bishop:

> carta, tibi multum mea musa iocosa nocebit.[4]

But Baudry gives us to understand that his accusers were actuated by jealousy and spite, and he is soon absorbed in telling us how he has taken care to have his book beautifully copied and illuminated with initials in gold and red and green, so that those who were not ordinarily attracted by his verse might be caught by the splendour of its setting. For Baudry wrote his rough drafts on tablets, and it was then for his scribes, Walter and Gerard, to copy out the verses and embellish them.[5]

His detractors may perhaps have shaken their heads over his two epistles—*Florus to Ovid* and *Ovid to Florus*.[6] These are school exercises on the theme of the *Tristia*. In the schools, each young pupil followed in the smooth verses of Ovid the story of the poet's life; they saw him in the days of his success

---

[1] *Œuvres*, p. 346.   [2] ib., p. 349.   [4] ib., p. 14.
[3] ib., p. 342. Baudry says,   [5] *Christian-Latin Poetry*, p. 281.
si vis ostendas, si vis haec scripta   [6] *Œuvres*, pp. 141 sqq.
recondas.

at Rome, and they watched the drawn-out agony of his exile from all that he loved and longed for. They were allowed to read the *Art of Love*, and they were encouraged to appropriate his subtle sophistry of argument, and to imitate his facile rhetoric. How apt a pupil Baudry must have been is shown in these two Ovidian epistles.

Ovid is not really to blame, says Florus. He did not invent love. It is the god of love who ought to suffer. This is typically Ovidian rhetoric, and Baudry works at it with a will.

> sexus uterque diu sine carmine novit amare;
> quod tenuere prius saecula tu recitas.
> non tu saecla doces, sed saecula te docuerunt:
> Argus decipitur versibus absque tuis,
> versibus absque tuis delentur moenia Troiae,
> novit amare Venus versibus absque tuis.
> naturam nostram plenam deus egit amoris;
> nos natura docet quod deus hanc docuit.
> si culpatur amor, actor culpatur amoris,
> actor amoris enim criminis actor erit.
> quod sumus est crimen, si crimen sit quod amamus;
> qui dedit esse deus praestat amare mihi.
> nec deus ipse odium fecit qui fecit amorem,
> namque quod est odium nascitur ex vitio.
> tu recitator eras, nec eras inventor amoris;
> nulla magisterio flamma reperta tuo est.
> scriptor comoedus pereat, pereatque tragoedus
> si levis aura tuae paginulae pereat.[1]

We can hardly be wrong in regarding such verses as a sign of the growing secularization of the cathedral schools. This secularization merely implies that the studies were pursued in a more detached manner and with a greater wealth of illustration and the collection of wider resources for the understanding of the texts. Thus ancient mythology was studied in the work of Fulgentius, which Baudry versified in more than a thousand lines.[2] In Baudry also we can discern something of that feeling for the past which is so remarkable in Hildebert. This again is a legacy of the schools, where a serious attempt was made to read intelligently the Roman historians as well as the later abbreviators. Baudry himself is an example of the man of letters pure and simple, whom the schools were to produce in increasing numbers. Others became theologians, philosophers, ecclesiastics, and polished men of the world, but Baudry's heart was set on poetry, and it was as a 'rustic poet' that he would be remembered by those who came after him.

---

[1] *Œuvres*, p. 143.   [2] ib., pp. 274 sqq.

All the resources of his art are gathered into the verses which he wrote for Countess Adela, the daughter of William of Normandy.[1] The poem is cast in the form of a vision in which he describes, in imagination, and with all possible detail, the vast and magnificent bedroom of the countess. The idea of the vision was well-worn and, as we have seen, the theme of the description of a work of art or of a building has a long history from Graeco-Roman to Carolingian times. Baudry is here concerned not to describe what he has actually seen, but to exhibit in a short compass a great deal of learning for the entertainment and wonder of his readers.[2]

at plus quod decuit quam quod erat cecini,[3]

says the poet, and this is one of the keys to the understanding of his poem. For in the furnishing of this room is gathered up nearly the whole of human knowledge. The great tapestries tell of man's creation and fall, of the flood, of Abraham, and of the rest of Old Testament story as far as the Kings. Then they picture the mythology of Greece, and the foundation of Rome, with the names of a hundred kings.

The tapestry in the alcove above the bed had for its subject the same story as the famous tapestry of Bayeux, but it seems hardly likely that Baudry based his description on a knowledge of that work,[4] although some of the scenes described by him resemble those depicted at Bayeux. Baudry naturally goes into the full details of the various episodes, as complete description is, traditionally, of the essence of this kind of poem.

Next, the painted ceiling is described. It represented the heavens with the constellations and the signs of the Zodiac, the planets, the sun and the moon. These are all catalogued with an accompaniment of astronomical knowledge quite in keeping with the poet's purpose.

The wondrous mosaic of the floor was a *mappa mundi*, on which the skilful artificer had represented the sea with its monsters, and fishes which you were tempted to take with your hands. There were rivers, too, the continents, and all the marvels of nature. The Dead Sea is fully described, and there is a great mass of geographical detail crowded with names of mountains and rivers.

Lastly, the bed itself was a symbolic concentration of learning, for it was adorned with statues representing Philosophy

[1] *Œuvres*, pp. 197 sqq.
[2] ib., p. 233, for some valuable remarks.
[3] ib., p. 231.
[4] For a summary of this question see Miss Abraham's note, pp. 244 sqq.

and the Seven Arts. This is Baudry's opportunity for a summary of the content of each part of the Trivium and Quadrivium, with reminiscences of Martianus Capella.

The plan of the poem is simple. It is a collection of descriptions of works of art which are imaginatively concentrated in one room so as to illustrate the whole of human knowledge. A poem such as this would have been remarkably useful in the school, for it could be employed instructively in the manner of the *De Nuptiis* or the *Ecloga Theoduli*. And we may well imagine that it was often put to such a use. It is a charming *fabula*—such we may call it, for the poet himself uses the word:

> dum tibi desudo, dum sudans, Adela, nugor,
> depinxi pulchrum carminibus thalamum.
> tu vero nostrae fabellae digna repende,
> et pensa quanti fabula constiterit.
>
> . . . .
>
> ecce coaptavit thalamum tibi pagina nostra,
> inque tui laudem sollicitata fuit.[1]

So speaks the poet of his work; elsewhere, he boasts to the Countess that he can

> spread her name o'er lands and seas,
> Whatever clime the sun's bright circle warms.[2]

And time has not shown the boast to be idle. Baudry's work will be read, not merely because it represents faithfully the achievement of the new humanism, but because it shows us the attractive figure of the man himself, patient and modest in his devotion to letters, a lover of the ancient poets who did not fear to claim a humble place beside them.

§ 6. *Anonymous epigrams and occasional poems.*

We gain a more just idea of the range and quality both of the school exercises and of the pieces composed by versifiers of average gifts, if we study some of the anonymous poems— occasional verses and epigrams—which belong to the period when Hildebert, Marbod, and Baudry were setting the fashion in poetry. They do not differ greatly, except in quality, from the work of the masters, for either they are based on a close study of Ovid or they follow the fashion of leonine or other rimes attached to hexameters or elegiacs. But their tendency

---

[1] *Œuvres*, p. 231.

[2] Cf. p. 254:
te quoque maiorem formabunt carmina nostra, [orbem,
carmine tu nostro latum spargeris in
ut te nosse queat et Ciprus et ultima Tile,
Aethiopes, Indi, Getulus et insula quaeque.

is towards those obscure conceits on which Hildebert himself had not frowned, and it is the practice of imitators to recognize no limit. It is not easy to give a satisfactory classification of these poems, but they may be divided roughly into epitaphs, epistles, epigrams, and fables. They are all comparatively short pieces, many of which have been swept by careless editors into the collected works of Hildebert.[1]

Among the epitaphs is one in honour of a master Theobald, a monk at the Abbey of Moutier-en-Der, in Burgundy.[2] From the epitaph we learn that he was not only a writer of sermons, but a maker of verses. But the poet did not sit down to compose a bald summary of the virtues of this admirable man. He had not studied Ovid for nothing, and like master Theobald he, too, was 'alumnus Pieridum'.

> Pange, Thalia, virum festivo laudis honore,
> in cuius titulos collige quidquid habes.
> electum fidei, sermonum pictor, alumnus
> Pieridum, fluvius nectaris ipse fuit.
> scintillas in corde, favumque gerebat in ore,
> thus eius nomen, flos fuit eius opus.
> non succo, non incausto, ⟨sed⟩ flore nitentis
> eloquii libros pingere doctus erat.
> scintillant vario quae gessit scripta colore;
> ex eius studio mellea verba fluunt.
> novit apes nutrire suas hic melle sophiae;
> vestem subtili texere novit acu.
> pervius et liber stylus eius ad omnia sculpsit,
> pinxit, inauravit omne quod egit opus.
> hoc vivente locus Dervensis floruit, isto
> sublato marcet nominis huius odor.
> denigrat nomen mors immatura serenum,
> nec solito splendet saucia fama die.
> cum lux Andraeae terras infunderet, ille
> multo ditatus melle reliquit apes.

This piece is certainly of no great merit, but an epitaph on a 'certain countess' is better, because the points are sharper, and the whole composition approaches the skilled manner of Hildebert:[3]

> Huic tria post cineres vitam conferre laborant,
> mens humilis, blandus sermo, benigna manus.

[1] In his valuable 'Notice sur les mélanges poétiques d'Hildebert de La-vardin', in *Notices et extraits des mss.*, xxviii, ii, pp. 288 sqq., Hauréau has sifted out these poems from the genuine works of the Bishop. But as they possess an interest of their own, a study of them may be instructive.

[2] Migne, clxxi, col. 1395; see Hauréau, p. 307. For other epitaphs see Migne, clxxi, col. 1391 sqq., and Hauréau's comments, pp. 301 sqq.

[3] Migne, clxxi, col. 1394; Hauréau, p. 306.

exempli speculum, patriae rosa, lampas avorum,
    feminei sexus immemor illa fuit.
deliciis florens, vultu festiva, coruscans
    exemplis, titulis inclyta, stirpe nitens,
sic intus mentem, foris os natura polivit,
    ut sine crimine mens, os sine labe foret.
quod genus exempli rarum est, se femina vicit,
    in se femineae nil levitatis habens.
cum fidei mulier corvo sit rarior albo,
    hac tamen in sexu floruit ista fide.
lance pari librae signum libravit Apollo,
    cum metit hunc florem mortis iniqua manus.

The almost entirely secular note of these epitaphs is not accidental. It is an affectation in keeping with the humanistic strivings of the age.

The cult of friendship expressed in poetical epistles was likewise to some extent a convention, practised by men wished before their eyes examples of antiquity which they wished to emulate. But at the same time such a convention could be made a pleasant adornment of social intercourse in an age when manners were becoming more gentle, and women were taking their proper place in a civilized society. Some one, perhaps Hildebert himself,[1] sends a ring to the Bishop of Bayeux, and a gift in those days was more precious if it was accompanied by some well-turned verses:

Annulus hic nuper moerebat clausus in arca,
    obscurusque lapis et quasi tristis erat.
at postquam dixi: Baiocas ibis, erisque
    maioris digitum praesulis orbe ligans,
laetior explicuit radios, sparsitque serenas
    gemma faces, oculis exhilarata tuis.
hoc ex te domino pretium lucratur, adestque
    plus lapidi praesul, quam lapis ipse sibi.

This is pleasant flattery, and the Bishop must have been almost as pleased with it as was the author himself. Another poem is addressed to a queen Matilda, probably Matilda the queen-consort of Henry I of England,

augustis patribus augustior orta Mathildis.[2]

The poet declares that this royal lady has all the graces of her

---

[1] Migne, clxxi, col. 1407; Hauréau, p. 326, points out that this epigram is no. 120 in the papers of Baluze, whose reasons for attributing it to Hildebert are unknown. So we must, for want of precise evidence, leave it without the name of an author.

[2] Migne, clxxi, col. 1408; Hauréau, p. 331, will not allow himself to suggest that Hildebert is the author, though (p. 383) he does not mind ascribing to him some other verses addressed to the same queen (Migne, clxxi, col. 1443, iv).

mother, who is now with God, but lives, in part, on earth in her virtuous daughter. So he pictures her, or rather that part of her which is actually in heaven, praying at the throne of grace:

> nondum me totam coelesti sede recepi;
>   magne Deus, requie semibeata fruor:
> pars iacet in tumulo, pars Anglica regna gubernat,
>   divisamque tenent aula, sepulcra, polus.
> quam tenet aula iuva; quam clausa sepulcra reforma;
>   quam polus, exaudi, sisque corona tribus.

The poet must be accurate at all costs. If part of the lady lives in her daughter and part in heaven there is still the part that lies in the tomb awaiting the resurrection. Here is material for a fine conceit and the poet makes the most of it. What models the versifiers of this age had before them we cannot precisely tell. The Carolingian poets had not constructed such elaborate conceits. Indeed, to find their parallel we must go back to Statius or the rhetoricians of the sixth century. But these are things that bad poets instinctively love to fashion, and that, in the same age, the good poets cannot resist. So in the eleventh as in the seventeenth century these devices ruled and, perhaps, in each case Ovid and Martial must bear part of the responsibility. Martial, certainly, must answer for the revived cult of the epigram, which once again touches on the curious, the monstrous, and the obscene. Satire reappears in its personal form, as when an unknown poet attacks a fellow-poet called Hugo, who may be none other than the famous 'Primas' of Orleans, whose verses were apparently even in his own day considered obscure.[1] The two epigrams directed against him are in Martial's rudest manner:

> Si qua mihi scribis, ne cuiquam scripta revelem
>   submissis precibus, Hugo, rogare soles.
> ne timeas, nunquam per me secreta patebunt;
>   cum relegam, nequeo scire quid ipsa velint.

And,

> Obscuros versus facis, Hugo, parumque latinos,
>   quos vitio linguae vix reticere potes.
> vis videam versus? expone latinius illos,
>   vel taceas, melius si reticere potes.

---

[1] Hauréau, p. 392; Migne, clxxi, col. 1446. Another piece of personal satire is the epigram called *Quid sit vita pudica*, Migne, clxxi, col. 1427, which is reminiscent of Martial:

> in noctem prandes, in lucem, Tur-
>   gide, coenas,   [mero.
> multimodoque mades nocte dieque

> cumque cuti studeas, uxorem ducere
>   non vis.
> cur nolis, dicis: vita pudica placet.
> Turgide, mentiris, non est haec vita
>   pudica.
> vis dicam quid sit vita pudica?
>   modus.

In other examples the satire is more general, being vaguely directed against a whole class of men. There is, for instance, a piece in rimed hexameters, rather too long for an epigram, and more like a school-exercise on the theme of hypocrisy.[1] The extract which follows is given merely to illustrate the hexameter rimed in couplets:

> sunt quorum sic noster amor fastidit amores
> sint ut amicitiis inimicitiae potiores.
> obsequio damnum, contemptum vero favore,
> blanditiis rixas, odiumque merentur amore;
> frons quorum fallit rigidos mentita Catones,
> quos accusat opus, quos vita probat nebulones:
> occultatur in his acus, esca, flamma, favilla.
> credulus accessor hac pungitur, uritur illa.

This is poor stuff, but very few poets could manipulate successfully the rimed hexameter. The elaborate verses of Bernard of Morlas tend to become tedious, and the ordinary leonine hexameter was hardly a happy invention. A twelfth-century poet made mock of the attempts to find a rime to *Adam*. The unfortunate versifiers were almost compelled to begin 'arbore sub quadam', and even Baudry of Bourgueil[2] could not do better. It is at this device that the following piece is aimed:

> Arbore sub quadam dictavit clericus Adam
> quomodo primus Adam peccavit in arbore quadam.
> sed postremus Adam, natus de virgine quadam,
> damna prioris Adam repensat in arbore quadam.
> ni sumpsisset Adam fructus sub arbore quadam,
> non postremus Adam moreretur in arbore quadam.[3]

Other epigrams show a mixture of ingenuity and obscenity, which is often accompanied by considerable metrical skill. The piece called *De oppositis*[4] is a mere school exercise:

> Turbat hiems florem, nox lucem, larva decorem,
> ariditas rorem, mors vitam, corvus olorem,
> tristities risum, labor otia, Styx Paradisum,
> noctua pavonem, lupus agnum, Davus Adonem.

But more ingenuity, if of a perverse kind, is shown in an epigram on beer—*de cervisia*:[5]

> Nullus amicorum posset meliora monere
> quam tu, quo moneor parcere cervisiae.

---

[1] Migne, clxxi, col. 1441; Hauréau, p. 379.

[2] *Œuvres*, ed. Phyllis Abrahams, p. 200, verse 115, [mus Adam. arbore sub quadam stetit antiquissi-

[3] Hauréau, p. 410.

[4] Migne, clxxi, col. 1446.

[5] Hauréau, p. 423. It may be that Matthew of Vendôme is the author of this epigram. It is also printed by

> cum bibo cervisiam nihil est turbatius illa,
> sed cum mingo nihil clarius esse potest.
> terreor inde nimis, quoniam quae spissa bibuntur
> reddita clara gravi viscera faece replent.

A mixture of epigram and fable is the poem on the countryman who speared a boar. The boar fell on a snake, which spat forth poison. The poison killed the man. This circle of death is the subject of the piece:

> Forte nemus lustrabat homo, fera forte redibat
> plena, latens anguis forte iacebat humi.
> in pecudem pariter oculum cum cuspide misit
> rusticus, agnovit missa sagitta manum.
> hasta feram sternit, anguem fera comprimit; anguis
> tabem fundit; ea tabe necatur homo.
> ossa vorando, locum calcando, vomendo venenum,
> vir iaculo, pede sus, vipera tabe nocet.
> saucia, contrita, sparsus, telo, pede, viru
> bestia, vipera, vir, sternitur, aret, obit.[1]

The exposition of like occurrences sometimes occupied the epigrammatists of late antiquity, whose work was well known to twelfth-century poets.[2] An admirer of Ovid boldly chose the biblical story of Tamar and Amnon, and dressed it in the guise of a fable from the *Metamorphoses*.[3] This is a remarkable poem—a school exercise perhaps, showing how naturally a given theme could be fitted into the Ovidian framework.[4] The title of the poem—*de incestuoso stupro ab Ammone propriae sorori illato*—follows the plain method of the old tradition, and the subject itself was doubtless chosen after deliberation. As Hauréau has pointed out,[5] poems of this kind and questionable epigrams were not meant for publication to all the world. They were either composed in secret, like the poems which Guibert

---

Wattenbach, 'Warnung für Biertrinker', *Anzeiger für Kunde der deutschen Vorzeit*, xxiii (1876), p. 80. Henry of Avranches in the thirteenth century imitated this epigram,

> Nescio quid Stygiae monstrum conforme paludi
> cervisiam plerique vocant; nil spissius illa,
> dum bibitur; nil clarius est dum mingitur: unde
> constat quod multas faeces in ventre relinquit.

(Text in *Speculum*, iii (1928), p. 51.)

[1] Migne, clxxi, col. 1446; see Hauréau, p. 387. It is not improbable that Matthew of Vendôme may be the author of this piece.

[2] Cf. the epigram *Phoebus de interitu Hyacinthi*, given by Hauréau, p. 422.

[3] Migne, clxxi, col. 1430, and Hauréau's emendations, p. 371.

[4] Another example is the fable of the 'faithful wife', Migne, clxxi, col. 1453; see Hauréau, p. 405. This may be the work of Abbot Philip of Bonne-Ésperance.

[5] Hauréau, p. 411.

of Nogent fashioned in the cloister, or were meant for a circle
of discreet friends. Medieval ideas of seemliness were formally
strict, but there was great laxity in practice, and poets like
Hildebert and Marbod did not or could not suppress, even if
they disavowed, the work of their youth.[1]

We must not forget, too, that much that is questionable in
these poems seemed to contemporaries merely a legitimate
exercise of ingenuity. If a young scholar were asked to produce
a poetical dialogue between a nun and a young man, his grave
master would probably find no fault with him for producing
lines like these:[2]

> M. Te mihi meque tibi genus, aetas et decor aequant:
>   cur non ergo sumus sic in amore pares?
>
> I. hac non veste places: aliis nigra vestis ametur;
>   quae nigra sunt fugio, candida semper amo.
>
> M. si vestem fugias, niveam tamen aspice carnem
>   et sub veste nigra candida crura pete.
>
> I. nupsisti Christo, quem non offendere fas est:
>   hoc velum sponsam te probat esse Dei.
>
> M. deponam velum, deponam cetera quaeque,
>   ibit et ad lectum nuda puella tuum.
>
> I. ut velo careas, tamen altera non potes esse,
>   et mea culpa minus non foret inde gravis.
>
> M. culpa quidem, sed culpa levis foret ista: fatemur
>   hoc fore peccatum, sed veniale tamen.
>
> I. uxorem violare viri, grave crimen habetur:
>   est gravius sponsam me violare Dei.
>
> M. vicisti nostrum sancta ratione furorem:
>   gaudeo quod verbis sum superata tuis.

It will be clear that this piece does not belong so much to the
history of love poetry as to that of school-composition.[3]

---

[1] Hauréau is inclined not to deprive
Hildebert of the authorship of some
questionable epigrams (cf. p. 413).

[2] Wattenbach, 'Aus einer Halber-
stadter Handschrift, De iuvene et
moniali', *Anzeiger für Kunde der
deutschen Vorzeit*, xxv (1878), p. 319;
see also Hauréau, *Notices et extraits
des mss.*, xxix. ii. 249 sq.

[3] There are in Werner, *Beiträge*, a
number of love-poems which are really
school-exercises, of the same class as
those of Baudry and Marbod; cf. p. 46:

compar nulla tibi me teste valet

reperiri:
Lucifer ut stellas superatve Diana
    puellas,
sic tuo consocias superas probitate
    catervas, etc.,

and p. 47:

'avertat penas deus et tibi donet
    amenas
sedes, sed mecum: quia volo vivere
    tecum'
dicebat quidam moribundam questus
    amicam:
'aut moriar tecum, vel debes vivere
    mecum,' etc.

The two epigrams which follow occur in a manuscript, which may be dated about the year 1200, containing a number of poems ascribed to Marbod.[1] These are good examples of the unsavoury themes which were often chosen:

De quodam Iudeo qui lapsus in claocam sabbato, ne transgrederetur
legem que prohibet sabbato operari, non volebat extrahi.

Cum de latrina lapsum Salomona ruina
    extraherent laqueis; 'non trahar', inquit eis,
'Sabbata sunt.' plaudit populus, plausum comes audit.
    plaudit, et ipse iubet cras ut ibi recubet.

De quadam quae occiso viro proiecit ipsum in cloacam.

Federe nupta viri nolebat sene potiri,
    cum iugulum diro rumperet ense viro,
posset ut electo secura recumbere lecto
    et corruptori nubere lege thori.
clausum latrina transfixum plus vice trina
    corpus, digna quidem quae pateretur idem,
ad turpem ritum sepelivit nupta maritum.
    o facinus dirum sic tumulare virum!

The number of anonymous poems belonging to the age of Hildebert and Marbod is immense. They are for the most part still embedded in their manuscripts, and they are perhaps hardly worth a thorough investigation. But the examples given above will suffice to show how great was the impulse given to versification by the increasing number of students who frequented the cathedral schools.[2]

---

[1] Brit. Mus. MS. Cott. Vit. A, xii, f. 131r. This MS. does not expressly ascribe these epigrams to Marbod, but of the preceding pieces some are certainly Marbod's and others are counted as Marbod's in Beaugendre's edition (Migne, clxxi). I do not wish to claim more than that they belong to the same school as the anonymous epigrams which are dealt with in this section. The first of these two epigrams has already been published, but from another MS., C. 58/275 Zürich Stadtbibliothek, in J. Werner, *Beiträge zur Kunde der lateinischen Literatur des Mittelalters*, Aarau 1905 (2nd edit.). It is there entitled *De Iudeo in latrinam lapso*, and has an additional distich,

sicut in omne quod est mensuram
    ponere prodest,
sic sine mensura vix stabit regia
    cura.

The second poem was found in the papers of Baluze without any manuscript references, but with a text precisely similar to mine; Hauréau, *Notices et extraits des mss.*, XXVIII. ii, p. 419.

[2] For other examples see C. Fierville, 'Notices et extraits des mss. de la Bibliothèque de Saint-Omer, nos. 115 et 710', in *Notices et extraits des mss.*, XXXI. i. 49 sqq.; on pp. 126 sqq. is given a versification of Quintilian's eighth declamation, *Gemini languentes*, which begins,

Roma duos habuit (res est non fabula
    vana,
auctores perhibent et pagina Quinti-
    liana)
fuderit ut geminos labor unus par-
    turiendi,
sic fuerant similes forma specieque
    videndi, etc.

§ 7. *Historical poems: Dudo of S. Quentin* (b. *circ.* 970; d. after 1017); *Guy of Amiens* (d. 1076).

The settlement of the Normans in France was fraught with great consequences for European civilization. The outward sign of the permanence of this new factor in the life of Europe was the establishment of the duchy in 911. Rollo, William Longsword,[1] and Richard I fill the period from that date until 996. By the time of Richard's death the Normans had completely accepted the Christian civilization and the French language. It was in his reign that the first historian of the Norman duchy was born, Dudo of S. Quentin, who wrote his *De moribus et actis primorum Normanniae Ducum*,[2] which he dedicated to Adalbero, Bishop of Laon, in a mixture of prose and verse. He was a person of some importance, for he was employed on political business, and it was at the request of Richard I and of his sons, Richard II and Count Rudolf, that he undertook the composition of his history. He began his task about the year 1000 and before he had completed it, about seventeen years later, he had risen to be Dean of S. Quentin.

We know nothing of his sources, but a recent historian tells us that 'his work is fundamentally untrustworthy and for the most part based on legend and hearsay'.[3] His style, at any rate, is pretentious and obscure, and his main idea is to parade his own learning before his readers. After a pompous prose dedication to Adalbero, Dudo addresses his own book in

See also J. Werner, op. cit., where a large number of pieces, some of which were already known, are given. There are satirical pieces, like nos. 6,

> Audi, fex iuvenum!—cuius sunt verba venenum,

8, 'satira in amatorem pueri sub assumpta parabola', and 9, 'obiurgatio amatoris puerorum'. No. 21 (p. 18), which is also in Hauréau, *Notices et extraits des mss.*, XXVIII. ii. 443, is worth quoting:

> vilior est humana caro quam pellis ovina:
> si moriatur homo, moritur caro, pellis et ossa.
> si moriatur ovis, nimium valet ipsa ruina:
> extrahitur pellis et scribitur intus et extra.

[1] William Longsword was murdered in 943 by Arnold, Count of Flanders. The *Planctus* or lament for his death has been preserved. It begins,

> laxis fibris resonante plectro linguae, repercusso flebo flente tristis corde detrimentum pacis magnae, quondam nostrae, quam ablatam deplorate. cuncti flete pro Willelmo innocente interfecto.

It is probably a monastic production. Text, ed. J. Lair, 'Complainte sur l'assassinat de Guillaume Longue-Épée, duc de Normandie', *Bibl. de l'École des Chartes*, XXXI (1871), pp. 389 sqq.

[2] Ed. J. Lair, *Mémoires de la Société des Antiquaires de Normandie*, ser. 3, vol. 3, Caen 1865; the title is not absolutely certain, see Manitius, *Gesch.* ii. 264. Dudo was born before 970.

[3] *Camb. Med. Hist.* v. 484.

fifty-one hexameters. This apostrophe,[1] modelled on Horace, is not without interest, as it seems to go back rather to the Irish-Carolingian traditions than to reach forward to the spirit of the new humanism:

> Themate pertenui quoniam digestus haberis,
> rhetorici ratione carens dulcaminis omni,
> liber, et interno cum te perscrutor ocello,
> aegre fert animus quod vulgo ducere gestis
> quae digesta stylo nequicquam schemata nostro,
> et subsanneris tumido vafroquo tumultu.
> sic te conservent, studiisque sigilla pudicis,
> pestiferum intentent secreta taedia nobis;
> auripluo quoniam Danaen vix texit ab imbri,
> ut promit mytho Fulgentius, aenea turris.
> aut pergas Northmannica nunc gymnasia praepes,
> aut scholis clausus Franciscis iam moruleris.
> ridiculam vereor nobis sat surgere sannam.
> ni impatiens refutes clavem nunc, obice dempto,
> et ni proripias argutae plebis in ora,
> invitum quatient Nortmanni verbere vatem.
> in vulgus venies audax nunc praepete gressu;
> pro quanto tantisper nunc iactabere fluctu.
> hic foedum spuet aggestis labris labiisque,
> succinet, infandum! retracta nare aliusque,
> et plausum manibus nimium dabit hicce profanis:
> elatis terram pedibus ter succiet hicce;
> verrucas alius disquirens ore notabit;
> sordibus explosis, si nulla tamen patet usquam
> integra, doctus erit certe praevertere falsis.
>
> .　　　.　　　.　　　.　　　.
>
> flamine septifluo, felix liber i, duce sacro
> protectus iugiter, munitusque auxiliatus
> fecundis meritis Quintini martyris almi;
> nec te non monitum olim discessisse graveris.
> quod restat, dubiis supplex committeque fatis,
> teque utinam affectu optato meliora sequantur![2]

This tedious piece is followed by another, an address in hendecasyllabics,[3] to Duke Richard I, beginning,

> O te magnanimum, pium, modestum!
> o te praecipuum, Deum timentem!
> o te magnificum, probum, benignum!

Even now Dudo cannot get under way with his history. In fifty more hexameters he expresses his hesitation and his fears in the face of the task before him. Then he addresses Count Rudolf and after him Archbishop Robert of Trier, himself a Norman by birth. The poem to the Archbishop contains

---

[1] *Allocutio ad Librum*, Lair, op. cit., pp. 120 sqq.　　　[2] pp. 120–1.　　　[3] Dudo had in mind Boëthius, *De Cons.* iii. 10; text, p. 122.

a piece in adonics, with much rime and some display of Greek learning, quite in the Irish tradition:[1]

> Praesul amande,
> et reverende
> et recolende,
> atque tremende;
> onoma cuius
> hoc quoque metrum
> non capit usquam,
> T nisi dempta[2]
> littera desit;
> mirificarum
> prosapiarum
> gesta tuorum
> suscipe patrum.

The whole of the historical part of the work is interpolated with poems. Rightly in the prologue to his second book did the poet, after telling the story of Daedalus and Icarus, proceed to apply it to his own case,

> haec te monstra petunt, et fabula contigit ista;
> ludicris sannis ridiculisque tibi.[3]

In the prologue to the third book he speaks of Christ walking on the sea, and he feels the need of help such as the Apostle asked from his Master.[4] But when he has told of Duke William Longsword and is about to assay the deeds and virtues of Richard I, he calls upon the Muses by name to sing the hero's praises:

> florida clarisonae solitae sat carmina, Musae,
>   tinnitus modulo psallere multifidi,
> Clio, Melpomene, Polyhymnia, Erato, Thalia,
>   Terpsichore, Euterpe, Calliope, Eurania,
> praecipuum lyrico munus resonante beatu
>   dulcisoni cantus vocis et altivolae:
> patricio celebri, comitique ducique verendo,
>   qui studuit summo rite placere Deo,
> quaeque canat vestrum sigillatim peto dulce,
>   alterni metri syrmate dissimili.

---

[1] Lair, p. 127.

[2] The reading is uncertain: see Lair, p. 127, who suggests that Dudo is alluding to the T with which the name Robert was then written: Roῖbertus.

[3] p. 139.

[4] Lair, pp. 176 sqq.; the prayer which follows this poem is remarkable for its metrical scheme:

> Doxa superna,
> omnipotens columen,
> fomes sensificusque,

> numen sidereum potens
> lucis origo;
> aethereum specimen
> rerum principiumque,
> causarum series cluens;
> prima propago,
> ingentisque patris
> lumen lumine sacro,
> et verus Deus ex Deo;
> o pater almus,
> ingenitusque Deus, etc.

The Muses respond with nine pieces in different lyric measures borrowed from Boëthius. It is clear that Boëthius' poems were carefully studied in the schools, and that the students were encouraged to compose in these varied and intricate metres.[1] But when the Muses have finished Dudo proceeds, not with his narrative, but with an address to Archbishop Robert in iambic dimeters catalectic, and this is followed by a preface in alternate acatalectic and catalectic trochaic dimeters. Even this is not enough. Robert must be invoked again, this time in elegiacs, with a great parade of Greek learning. More poetical pieces follow in the body of the narrative, and Dudo ends with a poem of thanks to God for the successful completion of the work after he has passed his fiftieth year.

Less pretentious and more valuable historically is the poem of Guy of Amiens, entitled *De Hastingae Proelio*.[2] Guy was first of all canon, then archdeacon, and finally Bishop of Amiens. He held the last-named office from 1058 to 1076, so that he was describing contemporary events in his poem on the battle of Hastings. Furthermore, he had close relations with the ducal family of Normandy, and it is apparent from the exactitude and precision of his descriptions that he wrote with knowledge. Of his poem Ordericus Vitalis says: 'Guido etiam praesul Ambianensis metricum carmen edidit, quo Maronem et Papinium gesta heroum pangentes imitatus Senlacium bellum descripsit, Heraldum vituperans et condemnans, Guillermum vero collaudans et magnificans.'[3] But there is nothing Virgilian in Guy's treatment of his subject. He begins with a short prologue in the usual leonine hexameters, which seems to be dedicated to Lanfranc,[4] and then he continues in clear and simple elegiacs, which are the fruit of innumerable school exercises based on Ovid. The narrative is a succession of scenes with an ample amount of detail, relieved only by short rhetorical speeches. The poem opens with the preparations for the crossing of the Channel. William watches anxiously the movement of the vane on the church, until the sea is calm and the wind favourable. The ships are loaded,

> haut secus invadit classis loca turba pedestris
> turba columbarum quam sua tecta petit.[5]

[1] This is pointed out by Manitius, *Gesch.* ii. 261 sq., where a list of the metres is given. Dudo had also studied the measures of Prudentius.

[2] Ed. F. Michel, *Chroniques Anglo-Normandes*, iii. 1 sqq., Rouen 1840.

[3] lib. iv.

[4] The MS., verse 2, reads: erigit et decorat, L(anfrancum) W(ido) salutat.

[5] Michel, op. cit., p. 5.

There is a lively description of the crossing; with the fall of evening the ships are lighted, and in the morning the coast is reached. Before he comes to the battle Guy apostrophizes the God of War in the rhetoric which he had learned in the school:

> Mars, deus o belli, gladiis qui sceptra coherces,
>   corpora cui iuvenum sanguinolenta placent
> et cruor effusus permulta caede virorum,
>   quis tibi tunc animus, quanta cupido mali,
> cum medius saevas acies miscere iubebas,
>   quo potius nullum te iuvat excidium!
> ex quo Pompeium superavit Iulius armis
>   et Romana sibi moenia subripuit,
> compulit atque metu Nili transire per amnem,
>   nulla reor caedes tam tibi grata fuit.
> nec iuvenile decus, nec te reverenda senectus,
>   nec peditum vilis et miseranda manus,
> flectere nec valuit te nobilitudo parentum,
>   quin ageres quicquid mens tua torva cupit.
> caecatos miseros radiantia trudis in arma,
>   et veluti ludum cogis adire necem.
> quid moror in verbis, cum iam furor extat in armis?
>   exple velle tuum, Mars, age mortis opus.[1]

The battle, with the preliminary exploits of Taillefer ('Incisorferri mimus cognomine dictus') and the great deeds of William, forms the central part of the narrative, which ends with the surrender of London and the coronation at Westminster. There is a long description of the royal crown with an enumeration of all the precious stones:[2]

> misit Arabs aurum, gemmas a flumine Nilus,
>   Grecia prudentem dirigit arte fabrum,
> qui Salomoniacum, vix deterior Salomone,
>   mirificum fecit et diadema decens.

We must look upon Guy as a good example of the poets who were produced by the cathedral schools in the eleventh century. Ovid was the model for versifiers, and Guy imitated him as competently as Marbod or most of his contemporaries.

§ 8. *Minor Poets.*

Among the poets of the school of Chartres we have already mentioned Adelman of Liége, Fulbert's pupil, who told in rhythmical verse of the famous men which that school produced.[3] There is an anonymous poem of earlier date[4] which

---

[1] Michel, p. 17.   [3] Above, p. 308.
[2] pp. 34–5.   [4] Before 987.

celebrates Constantine, a friend of Gerbert and a master in
the school at Fleury.[1] It is obscurely written, with a great
show of learning and much use of Greek words. The author
cannot be Gerbert himself, but was probably a monk of
S. Remi at Reims.[2] A few verses will serve to give an idea
of his style:

> Eia, cara chelys, protelans vocibus aptis
> carmina pange viro, morum probitate colendo,
> sola Sophocleo quae sint condigna cothurno.[3]
> hunc deus elegit, propria quoque dote beavit,
> ut validi nobis sit verbi mysteriarchus
> solus et in terris alter prostet Benedictus.

There is another poem in a similar manner, addressed to a
monk, Bovo, which is presumably by the same author.[4] The
passage in which Bovo's learning is praised and contrasted
with his admirer's modest achievements is worth quoting:

> pollens ingenio, sophiae sectator, amator,
> fossor Pierius, Musarum semper amicus,
> Pierides cum te doctum fecere poëtam,
> te docuit Clio coniuncta sororibus octo;
> felicis cum sis depastus prata Capellae,
> Philologiae te septem docuere puellae;
> ergo polum super adtollens caput erigis usque.
> ast ego quem taetris tenebris inscitia condit,
> tectus obumbrificor, sophiae ceu temptor et exsors,
> fonte caballino qui numquam labra perunxi,
> stertens Parnasi nec umquam somnia crevi,
> Philologiae quem numquam novere ministrae.
> despicor a doctis, mentis velut impos et artis:
> ergo fovens latebram paveo sustollere cephal.

As Manitius points out these two poems are interesting evidence of the frequent exchange of poetical epistles between
scholars in the tenth century.[5] Persius, Juvenal, and Horace,
as well as Virgil, were known to the author.

Another French poet is Odo of Meung (first half of the
eleventh century), a physician and an ecclesiastic, who wrote
a poem called *De viribus herbarum*,[6] which was known to later

---

[1] Ed. E. Dümmler, 'Gedichte aus
Frankreich', *Neues Archiv*, ii (1877),
pp. 222 sqq.; H. Hagen, *Carmina medii
aevi*, pp. 130 sqq.
[2] See Manitius, *Gesch.* ii. 507.
[3] Cf. Virgil, *Ecl.* viii. 10.

[4] Dümmler, *Neues Archiv*, ii. 222
sqq.; Hagen, pp. 134 sqq.
[5] *Gesch.* ii. 508.
[6] Ed. L. Choulant, *Macer Floridus de
viribus herbarum*, Leipzig 1832.

ages as the work of 'Macer Floridus'. It consists of 2,269 hexameters, and describes the virtues of the various herbs and
plants, after this manner:

Lactuca.

Frigida Lactucae vis constat et humida valde,
unde potest nimios haec mansa levare calores,
et praestabit idem superaddas si bene tritam;
utilis est stomacho, somnum dat, mollit et alvum:
omnibus his melius prodest decocta comesta,
et stomacho potius non lota comesta medetur.
lactucae semen compescit somnia vana,
cum vino bibitum fluxum quoque reprimit alvi,
lac dat abundanter nutrici sumpta frequenter.
ut quidam dicunt, oculis caligo creatur
his, quibus assiduo fuerit cibus eius in usu.[1]

It is interesting to note that the author of the celebrated
Regimen sanitatis Salerni,[2] a medical treatise in verse, of the
year 1101, made much use of Odo of Meung's poem.

Arnulf, probably a French monk, composed between 1054
and 1056 a work called *Delicie cleri*, which he dedicated to the
Emperor Henry III and his wife, Agnes.[3] Arnulf's work is a
collection of poems, the main substance of which is a versification of proverbial lore, drawn from the 'wisdom' books of the
Old Testament, other biblical sources, the *Disticha Catonis*, etc.
It is clearly the kind of book which could be used in school but,
as Wipo also dedicated proverbs to Henry III, Arnulf himself
may have had in mind the Emperor's personal tastes. The
details of the work do not interest us here. What we have to
remark is that leonine hexameters and elegiacs are mingled
with rhythmical and rimed pieces. We have the familiar
rhythm of

iste multorum usibus proficiens versificus,
non enim cunctis cognita Salomonis proverbia,[4]

which reminds us of Anglo-Saxon and Irish originals. Arnulf
shows indeed a great fondness for Greek words, and he has a
measure of the obscurity which was often the legacy of Irish
influence. He ends his work with a curious dialogue between

---

[1] Choulant, op. cit., p. 60.
[2] See below, p. 369.
[3] Ed. J. Huemer, 'Zur Geschichte
der mittellateinischen Dichtung. Ar-
nulfi delicie cleri', *Romanische Forsch-*
ungen, ii (1886), pp. 211 sqq.; see
also E. Voigt, 'Beiträge zur Textkritik
und Quellenkunde von Arnulfs Delicie
Cleri', ib., pp. 383 sqq.
[4] Huemer, p. 216.

the poet and his book, a specimen of which will give an idea
of his style. It is headed *dialogica poete tetrastica*:[1]

> Poeta: Cur bullata sere reserasti claustra, libelle?
> cur, cur salvificum temerasti fraude sigillum?
> numquid turmicomas mavis girare plateas?
> precino, pregrandem passim patiere pudorem.

> Libellus: tu cuinam loqueris? cuinam stomachose minaris?
> succensesque mihi, clam te quod vincula solvi?
> cernis olorinas ut provehor ales in alas?
> amodo crede mihi pulchrum volitamine niti.

> Poeta: gaudeo te niveis perquam pulchrescere plumis.
> id metuas summe, quod in aure susurro tuapte:
> Dedalus Icareum despectat lugubris altum,
> flesti fulmineam Phaetontis, Phebe, favillam.

And so the argument continues through many quatrains, with
an obscurity due in part to the necessity of observing the
leonine rime. The poet shows his originality in the coining of
new and strange words, such as *omnidatrix* (v. 84, p. 219),
horrifluax (v. 430, p. 230), *poesificus* (v. 742, p. 241).[2] He is
not always successful in these inventions, but he was a man of
wide reading and considerable intelligence.

The next poet who calls for mention is Gislebert of S. Amand,
who wrote a long poem on the destruction of his monastery by
fire in 1066. It is noteworthy because it is in leonine hexameters and shows competent mastery of the two-syllabled rime.[3]
Gibuin of Langres, who became Archbishop of Lyons in 1077,
wrote a rhythm on the joys of Paradise, which really belongs
to the history of religious verse, but it is here mentioned on
account of its elaborate structure and skilful rimes.[4]

We must probably reckon among the French poets of the
eleventh century 'Eupolemius'—for so he disguises his real
name—who wrote a *Messiad*, a kind of allegorical epic.[5] This

---

[1] Huemer, p. 240.
[2] Cf. Manitius, *Gesch.* ii. 591.
[3] Text in *M.G.H.*, *SS.* xi. 414 sqq.
[4] W. Wattenbach, 'Lateinische Gedichte aus Frankreich im elften Jahrhundert', *Berlin. Sitzungsber.* 1891, p.
99 sq. The fourth and fifth strophes
are:

> pulcher hortus, mellita flumina,
> sonat aura lenis per nemora,
> ibi flores et mala punica.
> quam pulchra es sanctis animabus et
>   requies!

duodecim exornant lapides
portas urbis suas per species,
quos non radet annorum series.

[5] Manitius, when he edited this poem
(*Romanische Forschungen*, vi (1891), pp.
509 sqq.), supposed it to be of the
twelfth century, but (*Gesch.* ii. 599) he
now decides for the eleventh. I still
think that the later date may be correct: ii. 753 (p. 556), 'me miseram! quid
agam?' may be based on the first verse
of Marbod's *Oratio paenitentis saepe
lapsi* (*Anal. Hymn.* l, p. 391), in which

is merely noted here because of its use of epic apparatus, with Greek names for its personified abstractions, and for the skill with which it is constructed. The theme is the deliverance of the Jewish race from the power of Cacus (the evil one) by Moses, and finally by the Messiah. The Messiah is the son of Agatus (God), and Judas (the son of Antropus, i.e. man) betrays him to Cacus, but he rises in glory after his death. It is interesting to see how Eupolemius, throughout his poem, uses the idea that the classical myths are nothing but pale and artificial constructions in imitation of wonders described in holy writ.[1] So David is the model for the Greek Achilles:[2]

> ad Larisseum stilus hoc gentilis Achillem
> transtulit. ipse eciam citharam citharedus habebat
> qua David regis mentem sedavit atrocem,
> nec quisquam melior magnorum facta virorum
> inclita cum voluit fidibus replicare canoris.

The poem depends to some extent on the *Psychomachia* of Prudentius,[3] but it is mainly interesting as showing how the conventions of the classical epic could be used to the full, with recurring speeches, similes,[4] single combats,[5] geographical catalogues,[6] descriptions of shields and works of art.[7] When Moses is slain in a desperate encounter he leaves his shield to Nomus:

> ille tamen moriens insignem sustulit orbem,
> donavitque Nomo celatum mira relatu:
> quod deu' sex nichilo fecisset cuncta diebus:
> sol ibi fulgebat, currebant flumina, terras
> ingens oceanus cinxit, triplicemque quaternis
> cernere erat liquide discretum partibus orbem,
> factaque priscorum magna argumenta virorum;

event it would be reasonable to place Eupolemius' poem not earlier than the first half of the twelfth century. There is a similar poem, but in the form of a vision, in *Romanische Forschungen*, vi, pp. 4 sqq., also edited by Manitius.

[1] Cf. Manitius, *Romanische Forschungen*, vi. 512.

[2] ii. 409 sqq. (p. 546); similarly Joseph is the prototype of Hippolytus, i. 400 sqq. (p. 525); Samson of Hercules, ii. 275 sqq. (p. 542).

[3] The poet also knew Amarcius thoroughly, as well as Theodulus and the *Occupatio* of Odo. As Amarcius' *Sermones* were written about 1044, Eupolemius' poem cannot be earlier than the second half of the eleventh century.

[4] i. 537 sq. has an interesting simile (in the scene where the people sing before the golden calf):

> aut ubi preceptor multas cantare scolares
> erudit, ingenii prope vim discriminat omnes,
> hi faciles, illi longas longo ordine neumas
> discunt et varium strepitum dat dissona turba.

[5] ii. 35 sqq. (p. 535) for a Virgilian battle-piece reproduced, with Moses, Nomus, Sother, etc., as heroes, and a catalogue of slayers and slain.

[6] Cf. ii. 486 sqq. (p. 548).

[7] Cf. ii. 615 sqq. (p. 552), where two cups are described.

inter que cunctis animantibus in cataclismo
deletis, nisi que Noe collegerat arca,
tollebatur aqua coopertis montibus, unde
Deucalionei processit fabula nimbi.[1]

From what has been said it will be seen that the poem as a
whole is well worthy of study. Eupolemius ends in this fashion,

summa sophia, tuus grates refero tibi scriptor:
hoc opus incepi per te ceptumque peregi,
ut sit lac teneris et fortis fortibus esca.

And this, on the whole, is a fair description. For Eupolemius
wrote, no doubt, for his own scholars in the monastic or the
cathedral school; but his learning was so wide and his subject
so enticing that he must have found many other readers.

[1] ii. 65 sqq. (p. 536); for Sother's shield, ib. 82 sqq.; cf. also 271 sqq. and
605 sqq.

ITALIAN POETS OF THE ELEVENTH CENTURY
§ 1. *Leo of Vercelli and others.*

IN the Italian poetry of the eleventh century the great names are Peter Damiani and Alphanus of Salerno. They had the advantage of the best education that the schools could provide, and we know that in Italy both teachers and scholars felt that they were the direct heirs of the classical tradition, and that Virgil, Horace, and Ovid were their fellow-countrymen. The schools and especially the secular schools 'seem, therefore, to have the air of age-long institutions, owing nothing to influences from any other country. In poetry we find, especially in Alphanus, a knowledge and appreciation of the old lyric measures and, at the same time, as in Peter Damiani, a thorough command of rhythmical verse, though with a conservative leaning to the older rhythmical forms.

The poetry is not, however, always of a high order. Leo of Vercelli, who was born about 965,[1] was a friend of Gerbert of Aurillac and a trusted servant of Otto III, who recognized his high abilities and employed him on important missions. He entered into the high hopes which were in those days fixed on the close relations between Emperor and Pope, and composed a rhythm, *de Gregorio papa et Ottone Augusto,*[2] in which he praised Gregory V and Otto, the two lords of the world:

> Christe preces intellege, Romam tuam respice,
> Romanos pie renova, vires Romae excita.
> surgat Roma imperio, sub Ottone tertio!

It was not long after this that Leo was made Bishop of Vercelli. But he did not cease to be employed in imperial business; in 998 or 999 he was given the title of Logothete, which marked him out as one of the chief advisers of the Emperor and a man of high importance in the Chancery. The death of his master in the flower of his youth must have been a bitter grief to him. He composed an elegy beginning,[3]

[1] Manitius, *Gesch.* ii. 511.

[2] Dümmler, *Anselm der Peripatetiker*, pp. 78 sqq.; and better, H. Bloch, 'Zwei Gedichte Leo's von Vercelli', *Neues Archiv*, xxii (1897), p. 114 sq.; see also Bloch, 'Beiträge zur Geschichte des Bischofs Leo von Vercelli und seiner Zeit', ib., pp. 109 sqq.

[3] *Neues Archiv*, xxii, pp. 117 sqq.; Dümmler, *Anselm der Peripatetiker*, pp. 80 sqq.

> Quis dabit aquam capiti, quis succurret pauperi?
> quis dabit fontes oculis, lacrimosos populis?
> sufficientque lacrime mala mundi plangere?

But the poem changes later into an ode of greeting to Otto's successor Henry II, whose protection and presence were as necessary to the Bishop as to the Italian people. For Leo was the leader of the imperial party of Italy. This addition to the poem was made towards the end of the year 1002. Henry II reposed in Leo the same trust which his predecessor had shown. At the Synod of Pavia in 1022 it was Leo who drew up the canons against ecclesiastical marriage, which were signed by the Pope and endorsed by the Emperor.[1] When Henry died in 1024 it was Leo who paved the way for the recognition of Conrad, and he had the great joy of receiving the Emperor at the Easter festival of 1026 in his episcopal city. But Leo died in the same week—a true friend of the Empire, who exercised his bishopric as though it were an imperial office, styling himself *episcopus imperii*.[2]

There are two other pieces by Leo. The first and the earliest of his surviving poems is an elegy on Peter, Bishop of Vercelli,[3] who had been murdered on the 17th of March, 997, by the enemies of Otto II:

> Ve tibi qui rides; plorabis et 'heu mihi' dices;
> mors venit, ordo perit, omnia luctus erit.
> bestia sparonis vomuit portenta doloris;
> occidit Petrum, truncat et assat eum.
> hunc Arabes capiunt, Babylon stupet, hunc mare reddit,
> barbara pompa tremit; patria sica ferit.
> heu pluit, heu restat, ve terre mundus: oberrat
> horror et ira loco; lugeat omnis homo.
> flete sacerdotes! miseras prorumpite voces!
> flamma cremat medium, os trahit huc reliquum.
> sis deus, ut pridem, sis ultor sanguinis idem.
> tu potes, Eusebi; surge, memento Petri!

These lines are obscure, and the task of transcribing them from the defective manuscripts was difficult. Another poem has come down only as a fragment, the *Metrum Leonis*,[4] in adonics, with a tendency to rime and some irregularly recurring refrains. After a complaint against his untoward fate the poet tells the fable of the ass in the lion's skin, which is joined on to a longer fable in which the wolf plays the chief part. The words

> hic, Leo, scribe,
> hic Ugo, ride,

[1] H. C. Lea, *History of Sacerdotal Celibacy*, London 1907, i. 206 sq.

[2] Cf. Manitius, *Gesch.* ii. 514.

[3] Bloch, 'Zu den Gedichten Leo's von Vercelli', *Neues Archiv*, xxvii (1902), p. 753.   [4] *Neues Archiv*, xxii, p. 123.

suggest that the poem is addressed to Margrave Hugo of Tuscany, who died in December 1001. It is difficult to disentangle any clear reference to contemporary events, but there must be some such explanation of the poem. The last words are such as Leo, in the vicissitudes of his life, must often have consoled himself with,

> sed nec erit semper—mihi mi Leo crede—december.

Rangerius, Bishop of Lucca (1097–1112), composed two poems, one a life of his predecessor Anselm,[1] and the other a poem *De anulo et baculo* (concerning the ring and the staff used in the investiture of a bishop), which he dedicated to the Countess Matilda of Tuscany.[2] The prologue is written in the metre of Bernard of Cluny's satire, but Rangerius had none of Bernard's inspiration or skill:

> Eximio Petri socio Paulique Iohanni
> Rangerius iam dimidius sub fauce Alemanni.
> pugna fuit, donec potuit saevire Guibertus
> perfidiae dux ecclesiae vastator apertus.
> sed quid ei temptare Dei firmissima castra?
> numquid eo regnante Deo pervenit ad astra?
> [mortuus est et traditus est in perditionem
> quique reum defendit eum contra rationem.]
> Gregorium vas egregium quicunque negavit
> iam videat si forte queat, quia falso putavit.
> quique duas fregit statuas Urbanus, ab illo
> fonte fluit longeque cluit non segnius illo.
> [quisquis eum non ante Deum vel sero fatetur,
> reprobus est et devius est, poenamque meretur.]
> his ducibus mirabilibus collectio nostra
> non tacuit, donec tenuit latrantia rostra.
> iam redeunt, qua fronte queunt, qui prosiliere,
> quos video tangente Deo plerumque dolere.
> sed redeant et nos habeant et nostra libenter,
> at videant, ut non redeant post terga latenter . . .[3]

The poem itself is in elegiacs,[4] and is an exposition of the Papal point of view in the investiture contest:

> Anulus et baculus duo sunt sacra signa, nec ullo
>   de laici manibus suscipienda modo.
> anulus est sponsi, sponsae datur anulus, ut se
>   noverit unius non alium cupere.
> gemma notat sponsam, sponsus signatur ab auro:
>   haec duo conveniunt, sicut et illa duo.

---

[1] It is merely a versification of a prose life; see B. Schmeidler, *Neues Archiv*, xliii (1921), pp. 514 sqq.

[2] Text, *M.G.H.*, *Libelli de lite*, ii. 508 sqq.

[3] ib., p. 508.   [4] p. 509.

atque ideo clamat primi vox illa parentis:
  propterea matrem cum patre linquit homo,
et sic haerebat uxori, quatenus ultra
  non sunt carne duo, sed magis una caro.
at baculus prefert signum pastoris opusque,
  ut relevet lapsos, cogat et ire pigros.
Christus utrunque sibi nomen tenet officiumque:
  Christus habet sponsam, Christus ovile regit . . .

The point which Rangerius tries to make is that ring and staff are holy signs, with a sacred meaning, and therefore cannot be received from the hands of laymen. The poem seems to have been read in Matildine circles, for Donizo of Canossa in his life of the Countess speaks of it favourably in these terms,

dictavit pulchrum nuper librumque secundum,
  qui baculi litem diffinit misit eique.

There are numerous other minor poets of eleventh-century Italy. Some of them are mere names preserved in Peter the Deacon's catalogue. Thus Landenulphus of Monte Cassino, who flourished about the year 1060, composed 'versus mirificos', 'de renovatione Casinensis coenobii, seu archisterii, ac regimine Desiderii'.[1] Benzo, Bishop of Alba (*circ.* 1070), composed a panegyric in honour of Henry IV,[2] and Petrus Crassus wrote dedicatory verses to the same emperor.[3] To the end of the eleventh or the early years of the twelfth century belongs the famous medical poem, *Regimen sanitatis Salerni*,[4] which seems to be the work of one John of Milan.

§ 2. *Peter Damiani.*

The life of Peter Damiani belongs to the history of the Italian Church in the eleventh century. He was born in 1007 and died in 1072. He lived, therefore, through the great religious crisis, and was compelled to take part in the movement of reform which is associated with the name of Hildebrand. This movement itself was, in part, the product of a religious revival which, not before its due time, had begun to make itself felt in Italy. It is not surprising that the political anarchy, the secularization of the Church, and the general

[1] Ronca, *Cultura medievale e poesia latina nei secoli xi e xii*, Rome 1891, ii. 13.
[2] Ed. Pertz, *M.G.H., SS.* xi. 598 sqq.; Ronca, ii. 23 sq. for bibliography.
[3] Ficker, *Urkunden zur Reichs- und Rechtsgeschichte Italiens*, Innsbruck 1874, iv. 124.
[4] Ronca, ii. 26 sqq.; *Regimen sanitatis Salernitanum*, ed. Sir A. Croke, Oxford 1830; also Packard, Oxford 1922.

moral and spiritual decay had led to a revival of the hermit ideal and to the production of a race of ascetics who practised their austerities with the fearful knowledge that the world's evening was drawing on apace.

Peter had been well educated in secular schools at Ravenna and Faenza, completing at Parma the cycle of the seven liberal arts. He was thus able to become a successful teacher, and for a time the young scholar followed the usual path, dispensing secular learning to a crowd of admiring students. He might have remained a teacher of grammar or rhetoric, if from the beginning he had not been possessed, like Augustine, with the desire for other things. He left the world, and professed to have completely abandoned its wisdom. He denounced the learning of the grammarian and of the rhetorician, and he warned monks against the pursuit of secular studies.[1] In his zeal he forgot discretion and attempted to go beyond what Augustine and Jerome had cautiously prescribed. In his treatise called *Dominus vobiscum*,[2] which he wrote in praise of the solitary life, he began by cursing the philosophers:

Platonem latentis naturae secreta rimantem respuo, planetarum circulis metas, astrorumque meatibus calculos affligentem: cuncta etiam sphaerici orbis climata radio distinguentem Pythagoram parvipendo: Nichomachum quoque tritum ephemeridibus digitos abdico: Euclidem perplexis geometricalium figurarum studiis incurvum aeque declino: cunctos sane rhetores cum suis syllogismis et sophisticis cavillationibus indignos hac quaestione decerno. Tremant gymnici suam iugiter amore sapientiae nuditatem: quaerant peripatetici latentem in profundo puteo veritatem. . . . Quid enim insanientium poetarum fabulosa commenta? Quid mihi tumentium tragicorum cothurnata discrimina? desinat iam comicorum turba venena libidinum crepitantibus buccis effluere. cesset satyricorum vulgus suos clarnos captoriae detractionis amaris dapibus onerare: non mihi Tulliani oratores accurata lepidae urbanitatis trutinent verba: non Demosthenici rhetores captiosae suadelae argumenta veruta componant: cedant in suas tenebras omnes terrenae sapientiae faecibus delibuti: nil mihi conferant sulphureo caliginosae doctrinae splendore caecati. Christi me simplicitas doceat, vera sapientium rusticitas ambiguitatis meae vinculum solvat. 'Quia,' enim, iuxta Pauli vocem, 'non cognovit mundus per sapientiam Deum, placuit Deo per stultitiam praedicationis salvos facere credentes.'

Like Gregory the Great before him, Peter expressed his abhor-

[1] *De perfectione monachorum*, II, Migne, cxlv, col. 306: ut autem cum stomacho loquar, ex istorum numero sunt ii, qui grammaticorum vulgus adeunt, qui relictis spiritualibus studiis, addiscere terrenae artis ineptias concupiscunt: parvipendentes siquidem regulam Benedicti, regulis gaudent vacare Donati.

Hi porro fastidientes ecclesiasticae disciplinae peritiam, et saecularibus studiis inhiantes, quid aliud quam in fidei thalamo coniugem relinquere castam, et ad scenicas videntur descendere prostitutas?' etc.

[2] ib., col. 231 sqq.

rence of learning in an excess of rhetoric. And, indeed, he never
wrote except in this studied and careful manner, using every
art that he had learned in the despised schools. 'My grammar
is Christ,'[1] he once said, but he took an obvious pride in his
compositions, and remained to the end, as a man of letters,
what the schools had made him.[2] He could even taunt the
Canons Regular with the uncultivated style in which their 'rule'
was written,[3] and he sent his nephew to Cluny to study the
liberal arts.[4]

But if Peter was a rhetorician it was the rich and fantastic
spirit of the man himself that coloured his writings and his
speech. His inspiration and invention never failed; with him
the conventional exaggerations of rhetoric become the towering
fantasies of the visionary, and the lifeless forms of the school
are transmuted into the poetry of the inner life. For Peter
was truly a poet. But it is useless to seek his poetry in the
epigrams in which he prolonged, in a new setting, the exercises
of his youth. He is a poet first of all in those flights of rimed
prose, which show how much of poetry is a sublimation of
rhetoric, and how closely related this poetical prose was to the
feeling and expression of the new rhythmical verse. He is
singing in prose of the glories of the solitary life[5] as he sang
in verse of the joys of Paradise:

Tu scala illa Iacob,
quae homines vehis ad coelum,
et angelos ad humanum deponis auxilium.
tu via aurea,
quae homines reducis ad patriam.
tu stadium,
quod bene currentes provehis ad coronam.
o vita eremitica,
balneum animarum,
mors criminum,
purgatorium sordidorum.

.   .   .   .

o quam pulchra rerum species,
cum frater in cellula constitutus nocturnas peragit psalmodias,

[1] *Epist.* viii. 8, 'Mea igitur grammatica Christus est, qui homo pro
hominibus factus est.'
[2] Cf. Dresdner, *Kultur- und Sittengeschichte der italienischen Geistlichkeit*,
p. 226. On the frequency of rimed
prose in Damiani, see Polheim, *Die lat.
Reimprosa*, p. 421.
[3] This was, however, merely bad
manners; he was writing 'Contra cleri-

cos regulares proprietarios', Migne,
cxlv, col. 485. 'Sicut in litteris stylus
horret incultus, sic in plerisque sententiis devius corrigendus est intellectus.'
[4] But on this see Endres, *Petrus
Damiani und die weltliche Wissenschaft*,
p. 16.
[5] *Liber qui dicitur Dominus vobiscum*, Migne, cxlv, col. 248 sq.

et quasi pro divinis castris militares custodit excubias:
contemplatur in caelo cursus siderum,
decurrit etiam per os eius ordo psalmorum.
et sicut praecedentes
ac subsequentes
stellae ad diem suas vicissitudines alternando perveniunt,
ita psalmi, qui ex ore eius tanquam ex quodam oriente procedunt,
ad suum finem paulatim velut parili cum sideribus conviatione
    decurrunt.
iste suae servitutis exhibet ministerium;
illae delegatum sibi exsequuntur officium:
iste psallendo
intrinsecus ad lucem tendit inaccessibilem,
illae sibi invicem succedendo,
eius exterioribus oculis visibilem reparant diem.
et dum utraque ad suum finem diverso tramite properant,
servo Dei quodammodo et ipsa elementa subserviendo concordant.

Here, and in the new rhythms, the medieval poet could find
his freedom. Rimes were no bondage in a language like Latin
which could provide them so abundantly. In metrical verse,
indeed, rime was a fetter which the poets of the eleventh
century remorselessly riveted on to their hexameters and
couplets, with deplorable results. Here Peter sinned with the
rest, but his rhythmical verse has the same free inspiration,
the same glow and fervour as are exhibited in his prose.[1] For
he is an acknowledged master of rhythm, especially when,
following native tradition, he uses the trochaic tetrameter.
There we can see how much the new versification derived from
the older rimed prose. Peter's great rhythm *de die mortis*[2] begins

Gravi me terrore pulsas, vitae dies ultima,
moeret cor, solvuntur renes, laesa tremunt viscera,
tui speciem dum sibi mens depingit anxia;

and the grand *rithmus de gaudio paradisi*,[3]

Ad perennis vitae fontem mens sitivit arida,
claustra carnis praesto frangi clausa quaerit anima:
gliscit, ambit, eluctatur exsul frui patria.

---

[1] Migne's edition of Damiani's verse (vol. clxv) is based on Gaetani's; it is not known what manuscripts were used by the latter, and it is by no means clear that all the poems in the collection are authentic. Hence the article of Dom A. Wilmart is welcome, in which he examines the contents of Vaticanus lat. 3797, an eleventh-century manuscript from S. Maria Vecchia at Faenza, where Peter died in 1072 (A. Wilmart, 'Le recueil des poèmes et des prières de S. Pierre Damien', *Rev. Bénéd.* xli (1929), pp. 342 sqq.). It can fairly be assumed that the pieces contained in this codex are the work of Peter. The famous poem *Quis est hic qui pulsat ad ostium* does not appear among them, and there is no longer any reason for thinking that Peter can have composed it; see *Christian-Latin Poetry*, p. 255.

[2] *Anal. Hymn.* xlviii. 62.

[3] ib., p. 65.

Peter himself freely mingled assonance with rime as he might
have done in his prose, and he created for himself his own
metrical schemes, as in the following, *De ecclesia Romana ab
antipapa invasa luctus*:

> Heu! sedes apostolica
> orbis olim gloria:
> nunc proh dolor! efficeris
> officina Simonis.
>
> terunt incudem mallei,
> nummi sunt tartarei:
> iusto Dei iudicio,
> fit ista conditio.[1]

All this verse is, structurally, of a transitional character, and
is a prelude to the rhythmical triumphs of the next century.
But it bears the mark of the author's genius as much as his
prose.

The metrical epigrams, for the most part, lack the brilliance
which would have been their justification. They are mainly
in leonine verse, with frequent assonance. Hence a certain
obscurity, which is not always able to hinder the strange
irony from breaking through. One of them has a title as long
as the verses that follow: *Domnus papa sine me rem incipiebat,
et mecum complere volebat. Sique mecum dicebat: Sicut erat in
principio, cum mecum non dixisset: Gloria patri.*

> Sicut erat damno, quia nunquam Gloria canto,
> qui caput abrosit caudam quoque iure vorabit.
> ossibus ora teret qui sorbuit ante medullas.[2]

Peter was never a respecter of persons, and it did not matter
to him whether he spoke to a simple layman or to the Vicar of
Christ. If he met his match in the Archdeacon Hildebrand,
who made him do his pleasure at the risk of his soul, he nevertheless avenged himself in those epigrams which are a mixture
of cunning and shrewdness:

> Vivere vis Romae, clara depromito voce:
> plus domino papae quam domno pareo papae;

and

> Qui rabiem tygridum domat, ora cruenta leonum,
> te nunc usque lupum mihi mitem vertat in agnum;[3]

and

> Papam rite colo, sed te prostratus adoro:
> tu facis hunc dominum; te facit iste deum.

---

[1] Migne, clxv, col. 963.   Wilmart, p. 345.
[2] Migne, cxlv, col. 962; I give the   [3] Migne, cxlv, col. 961.
reading of Vaticanus lat. 3797, after

These are perhaps the best of Peter's epigrams, in which he
vents his sardonic humour, with the accompaniment of a carp-
ing criticism of those who were his inferiors in ascetic practice.
He was, doubtless, a holy man and one of the glories of his
age, but he placed perhaps too high a value on the torture of
the body as an aid to the attaining of saintship. It was
reserved to the Abbot of Cluny to teach him a lesson. Peter,
then Cardinal Bishop of Ostia, arrived at the famous monastery
and could not but marvel at the splendour of the buildings and
the holy conduct of the monks. But when he looked at the, to
him, abundant table of the monastery, he besought the Abbot
at least to deprive the monks of 'fat' two days a week, so that,
the virtues of obedience and abstinence being united in them,
they might lack nothing of apostolical perfection, and become
true anchorites. 'Dear father,' said Abbot Hugh, 'you wish
to increase the crown of our reward by adding to our fasts.
Well, first share with us the burden of our labour for the space
of a week, and then you shall judge what ought to be added
to it. For until you have tasted the dish you cannot tell what
seasoning it needs; so you cannot properly judge what burden
the brethren have to bear if you have not touched it even with
your little finger.'[1]

§ 3. *Poets of Monte Cassino; Alphanus of Salerno and others.*

The power of the Lombard people had not been entirely
shattered by the Italian expeditions of Charles the Great. At
Benevento, Capua, and Salerno Lombard princes ruled over
rich territories, and learning flourished along with commerce.
The schools of Salerno were famous everywhere, and were
frequented by students from all the countries of Europe. In
the early eleventh century the south of Italy was a mixture of
races and of civilizations. The Saracens still held Sicily, and
the East Roman Emperor ruled in Apulia and Calabria.
Naples, Amalfi, and Gaeta were flourishing republics. Beyond
them lay the Papal States. It was into this world of luxury,
natural riches, and political division that the Normans entered,
to bring the misery of wars and devastation and, for a time, the
blessings that attended the establishment of a powerful
monarchy.

[1] *De adventu Petri Damiani Ostiensis
episcopi ad Cluniacensem ecclesiam*,
Migne, cxlv, col. 857. It is only fair to
say that Peter and the great and saintly
Hugh were bound together by ties of
the deepest affection, and that the
point of the story does not lie in its
verbal accuracy.

In the centre of these happenings, placed between the Lombards and the Normans, and closely bound to the Papacy, the Abbey of Monte Cassino looked out on a world of change. The importance of the great mother house of Benedictine monasticism in the secular and ecclesiastical politics of the age need not be elaborated here.[1] Two successive abbots ascended the throne of S. Peter—Frederick of Lorraine as Stephen IX and Desiderius as Victor III. In the latter's abbacy Monte Cassino reached the summit of her external splendour. The basilica was rebuilt with marble and columns from Rome, with mosaics the work of Greek craftsmen, and bronze doors from Byzantium. The church was dedicated in 1071 in the presence of the Pope, with splendid ceremony.

The library was filled with codices, most of which were the work of the monastic scribes who were masters of the elaborate and difficult Beneventan script.[2] Abbot Theobald (1022–35) was assiduous in encouraging the copying of manuscripts; and it seems that the celebrated copy of the *Annals* and *Histories* of Tacitus as well as the manuscript of Widukind's *Res gestae Saxonicae* are due to the German connexions of two eleventh-century Abbots.[3] Under Desiderius (1058–87)

the MSS. copied . . . mark the highest achievement in Beneventan penmanship. And the literary interest of the period may be judged to some extent by the books then produced. The ancient Chronicle of Monte Cassino gives a long and interesting list of the books copied during the abbacy of Desiderius. It contains chiefly theological and liturgical works, but there are several histories: Josephus, Gregory of Tours, Paulus Diaconus, Erchempert, and others; there are also several classics: the *De natura deorum* of Cicero, the *Institutiones* and *Novellae* of Justinian, the *Fasti* of Ovid, Virgil's *Eclogues*, Terence, Horace, Seneca, the grammatical works of Theodorus and Donatus.[4]

Besides these we may note Juvencus, Sedulius, and Paulinus of Nola.[5] Then there is the unique manuscript of Apuleius' *Metamorphoses* and *Florida*, and the famous manuscript, now at Arezzo, which contains the *Itinerarium Aetheriae* and

[1] L. Tosti, *Storia della badia di Monte-Cassino*, 2 vols., Naples 1842; E. A. Lowe, *The Beneventan Script*, Oxford 1914; J. Gay, *L'Italie méridionale et l'empire byzantin*, Paris 1904; *Casinensia, miscellanea di studi cassinesi pubblicati in occasione del XIV centenario della fondazione della badia di Montecassino*, 2 vols., Montecassino 1929.

[2] E. A. Lowe, *The Beneventan Script*, p. 8, for works copied in the tenth century—Virgil, Livy, Josephus, Hy-

ginus, Solinus, Dioscorides, Galen, Gregory the Great, etc.

[3] Richerius (1038–55) and Frederick (1056–8) were both Germans. Tacitus, says Dr. Lowe, p. 11, 'was read in Germany during centuries when apparently no trace of him existed in Italy'; see also Lowe, 'The unique MS. of Tacitus' *Histories*', in *Casinensia*, i. 257 sqq. (and especially p. 268).

[4] Lowe, p. 12.

[5] *Chron.*, quoted by Lowe, p. 81.

Hilary's *De mysteriis*. There are over two hundred Beneventan manuscripts preserved at Monte Cassino, and most of them were actually written in the Abbey.[1]

Round Abbot Desiderius there gathered a band of famous scholars—Alberic, John of Gaeta, Pandolf of Capua, Amatus, Leo of Ostia, Constantine the African, and the poets Alphanus and Guaiferius. Alberic is said by Peter the Deacon to have written religious verse, but he is chiefly famous as the author of the first-known *ars dictaminis*, that art of rhetorical composition, mainly in the form of epistles, which became so popular in the twelfth century. He also taught the *cursus*, which John of Gaeta, who was his pupil, probably introduced into the Roman curia when he became Pope as Gelasius II (1118–19).[2] As regards Alberic's conception of his art, Professor Haskins has pointed out that 'whereas to the *dictatores* of the twelfth century rhetoric meant little more than the practical art of writing letters,[3] Alberic still represents the broader and more humane tradition of other aspects of composition and of the imitation of ancient models of prose and verse'.[4] In his *Flores rhetorici* or *Radii dictaminum*, he ends with verses on rhetoric,

> rethoricam flores florumque videmus odores
> spargere veraci serie suasuque loquaci,

and subjoins a poem of 386 hexameters, called *commendatio domus oceani*,[5] 'descriptive of the watery palace and the figures and scenes which adorn it, in the course of which the author passes in review the liberal arts, the Muses, the sages of antiquity, the labours of Hercules, and a host of names from classical mythology'.[6] The treatise itself takes many of its rhetorical illustrations from the Roman poets—from Terence,

---

[1] Lowe, p. 51; see the hand-list, pp. 341 sqq.

[2] R. L. Poole, *Lectures on the History of the Papal Chancery*, pp. 83 sqq. On Alberic see C. H. Haskins, 'Albericus Casinensis', *Casinensia*, i. 115 sqq., from which my information is derived; also his *Studies in Mediaeval Culture*, pp. 171 sqq. ('The early *Artes dictandi* in Italy').

[3] But in the twelfth century there was an Italian master Bernard, who discussed poetical *dictamen*, and manifested a broader humanism than his Italian contemporaries; Haskins, 'An Italian Master Bernard', in *Essays in*

History presented to R. L. Poole, p. 226, Oxford 1927.

[4] 'Albericus Casinensis', *Casinensia*, i. 117.

[5] ib., p. 119. Haskins quotes four verses from a Munich codex, C.L.M. 14784:

> ergo sub equoreo domus est ingens apogeo
> urbsque satis dives sed equosi sunt ibi cives,
> ampla palatia que sapientia condecoravit
> et locupletibus extulit artibus et titulavit.

[6] ib., p. 120.

Virgil, Horace, Ovid, Lucan, and Persius—and is an indication
of the liberal atmosphere of the monastic school.

From his *History of the Normans*, which has been preserved
in a French translation,[1] we gain a lively impression of the
abilities of Amatus, another monk of Monte Cassino and a contemporary of Desiderius.[2] He was probably less successful as
a poet, if we can judge from the few verses of his poem on
S. Peter and S. Paul, in which he celebrates the splendour of
Rome. But here what is of interest is the feeling for the past
which he shared with his friend Alphanus and nourished on
the splendid collection of authors in the library:

> tu retines sceptrum super omnia sceptra timendum,
> tu nosti gentes armis redomare furentes.
> quae sis, quam prestans, Cicero dictamine narrat,
> cui similis nullus describitur atque secundus,
> et Livius Titus, Lucanus in ense peritus
> egregiusque Maro magnusque poemate Naso,
> et vir mirificus Varo quem fovet iste Casinus,
> et plures de te scripserunt plura poetae.[3]

In this last verse but one Amatus refers to Varro's *De lingua
latina*, which was preserved at Monte Cassino, and now exists
only in two Beneventan manuscripts written in the monastery.[4]

But the two great poets of Monte Cassino in the eleventh
century were Guaiferius and Alphanus. The poetry of Guaiferius belongs rather to the history of religious verse,[5] and it
is only necessary here to say that it shows a profound study
of Virgil. His friend Alphanus was a great man and a great
scholar.[6] Both were of noble Lombard birth and in them there
glowed the fire of learning and the desire for peaceful study.
Guaiferius was destined to the scholar's peace, but Alphanus
had his part to play in the troubled world. It was Desiderius
who 'discovered' Alphanus at Salerno, where he was acquiring
fame as a physician, and brought him finally to the Order of

[1] Aimé, *Istoire de li Normant*, ed.
Delarc, Rouen 1892.

[2] Prof. Francesco Torraco writes en-
thusiastically of Amatus, in his essay,
'Amato di Montecassino e il suo tradut-
tore', *Casinensia*, i. 161 sqq.

[3] Dümmler, 'Aus Handschriften',
Neues Archiv, iv (1879), p. 182; also
A. Graf, *Roma nella memoria del medio
evo*, Turin, i. 15.

[4] Lowe, *Beneventan Script*, p. 16.
He adds, 'The Cassinese have always
cherished an affection for Varro as one
of their own.' Varro was 'one of their

own' also because the ruins of his sump-
tuous villa were hard by; they were
pointed out to Mabillon when he visited
Monte Cassino, in November 1685, 'Iter
Italicum', p. 127 (*Museum Italicum*, i,
Paris 1687).

[5] See *Christian-Latin Poetry*, pp. 240
sqq.

[6] Prof. Michelangelo Schipa has returned to his old studies in his all too
brief essay, 'Una triade illustre di
Montecassino', in *Casinensia*, i. 157 sqq.
He writes about Desiderius, Frederick
of Lorraine, and Alphanus.

S. Benedict and to Monte Cassino.[1] The two friends took their vows together, but their paths diverged. Desiderius went away to rule as prior the monastery of S. Benedict at Capua, and to become *apocrisiarius* of the Holy See. Alphanus was head of the monastery at Salerno in the same year, 1057, and Archbishop in 1058. Meanwhile Desiderius went back to Monte Cassino as Abbot.

Alphanus had the difficult task of coming to terms with the Norman conquerors. Patriot as he was, he saw that it was necessary to accept the facts, and he carried out his task with prudence and courage. Robert Guiscard, who recognized his worth, became his friend, and when the bones of the Apostle Matthew were discovered, he helped the Archbishop to construct the new basilica that was to contain them.

Renan saw in the poems of Alphanus 'un dernier souffle de l'antiquité',[2] but they represent in reality the continuation of the Lombard tradition of scholarship which shone so brightly in Paul the Deacon, and had as its marks a real feeling for the excellencies of classical poetry and a high standard of personal achievement. It is characteristic of Alphanus that he chose to write his poems in the form of odes. Such are many of his hymns, in which the expression is grave and dignified, and such are the poems addressed to his aristocratic or learned friends. The stateliest and the most interesting has for its subject the great abbey in which he had lived, and to which his heart always turned in the time of separation. On 1 October 1071 he was present at the dedication of the new basilica built by Abbot Desiderius, who had spared no effort to increase its splendour. It may well have seemed to contemporaries a symbol of the revivified Church, for the apse bore the inscription,

haec domus est similis Synai sacra iura ferenti.[3]

[1] For an outline of Alphanus' life see *Christian-Latin Poetry*, pp. 242 sqq. His poems are in Ughelli, *Italia Sacra*, Venice 1722, x. 47 sqq.; reproduced in Migne, cxlvii, col. 1219 sqq.; there are texts also in Giesebrecht, *L'istruzione in Italia nei primo secoli del medio evo*, Florence 1895, in Ozanam, *Documents inédits pour servir à l'histoire littéraire de l'Italie*, Paris 1850, and in M. Schipa, *Alfano, arcivescovo di Salerno*, Salerno 1880, and 'Versi di Alfano', *Archivio storico per le provincie napoletane*, xii (1887), pp. 767 sqq. The hymns are in *Anal. Hymn.* xxii, xxiv, and l (see list

and references in *Anal. Hymn.* l. 330).

[2] *Mélanges religieux et historiques*, p. 348.

[3] Cf. a later poem, which is in Cod. Casinen. 295 (448), *Anal. Hymn.* xv. 267 sqq., and compares Mons Casinus with Sinai. It begins,

De Sion exivit lex atque de Casino.

The third stanza begins the comparison with Sinai,

mons Casinus et Sina sunt aequipollentes,

proportionaliter sibi respondentes, etc.

The long ode[1] in which Alphanus celebrated these glorious
events is a severe and lofty exercise. The poet had in mind,
without precisely imitating, the structure and manner of a
great political ode of Horace. For he begins with the theme
of man and the gifts which Christ has given him, a theme
which is beyond the compass of rhetoric or of philosophy.
The final gift is that of man's redemption and the hope of
heaven. These rewards are open to virgins and to widows, to
the married and to priests, but above all to those who live
the highest life—to the monks.

The poet can now make an easy transition to his central
theme, the abbey:

> ecce Casinus abundat eis,
> mons venerabilis, aula Dei,
> mons Sion, altera dux fidei,
> mons ubi iura Deus populo
> scripta suo tribuit digito.

He invokes the Wisdom of the Father, 'qui dubio sine cuncta
sapis', that he may tell of the pleasantness of this marvellous
place. The physical setting is first described:

> Italie iacet in gremio
> montibus obsita planities:
> pampinus hanc viridis decorat;
> est nemorosa parum, sed aquis
> fructibus et variis celebris.
>
> rebus in omnibus haec locuples
> indigenis, sed et hospitibus
> est locupletior: hinc etenim
> est iter urbis apostolicae,
> totius urbis adhuc dominae.
>
> collibus eius oliva decens,
> cedrus et alta cupressus inest;
> caetera partibus a Boreae
> in sua Liris amoena fluctus
> et rigat atque rigando fovet.

Then Alphanus tells of Benedict's foundation of a house of
God where once was an altar to Apollo, of the decay of the
monastery, and of its rebuilding in this present time. It is to
Desiderius that the work is due, Desiderius whose name cannot
be incorporated in the ode without violence to the laws of

---

[1] Text in Migne, cxlvii, col. 1234 sqq.; Ozanam, *Documents inédits*, pp. 261 sqq.

quantity. Nevertheless, the name of the man who has accomplished such things for love of Benedict must not be left out:

> ergo licebit et expedit hic
> nomen inesse Desiderii,
> qui dedit, o Benedicte, tibi
> tam pretiosa domicilii
> praemia, ductus amore tui.

The glory of the new church is set forth—the columns from Rome, the Byzantine mosaics, the alabaster, the porphyry, the steps of Proconnesian marble, the vessels of gold, the jewelled cups, the precious vestments, the great bronze doors. All these combined to create a splendour which 'not the golden house of Cyrus, nor the work of Solomon, nor the temple of Justinian'[1] could equal. Then remembering how once Benedict, looking at night through his high window, had seen the whole world 'gathered together as it were under one beam of the sun' and in that light the soul of S. Germanus of Capua being borne up to heaven,[2] the poet found his fitting image:

> tu speciosa fenestra dei,
> proxima luminibus superis,
> unde videntur ad haec animae
> tendere, mundus et hic hominis
> visus ab unius est oculis.

Monte Cassino is a second paradise.

Now, O father Benedict, thou mayst enjoy the angelic promises: for this house of thine is richer than it was heretofore. Grant only that it be as aforetime blessed by thy merits. O good and merciful Lord, holy God,[3] Almighty Father, who art able to give all things, grant, we beseech Thee, that to those who dwell here the way of heavenly light may be manifest, and may our present community be pleasing unto Thee as was that of old, which deserved by its common merits to exchange this place of sojourning for the bright kingdom of the sky.

The scheme of the poem is thus: Christ's blessings to man in creation and redemption, Monte Cassino's place in that order, the history of its foundation, its fall and its rebuilding, a description of its beauties, a concluding prayer and doxology.

---

[1] Alphanus had seen S. Sophia, as he once spent some time in Constantinople.

[2] Gregory the Great, *Dial.* ii. 35,

'omnis etiam mundus velut sub uno solis radio collectus ante oculos eius adductus est.'

[3] 'Sancte Deus; Hagios Theos.'

The Ode to Archdeacon Hildebrand is constructed with similar care:[1]

Quanta gloria publicam
  rem tuentibus indita
  saepe iam fuerit, tuam,
  Hildebrande, scientiam
  nec latere putavimus

nec putamus. idem sacra
  et Latina refert via,
  illud et Capitolii
  culmen eximium, thronus
  pollens imperii, docet.

sed quid istius ardui
  te laboris et invidae
  fraudis aut piget aut pudet?
  id bonis etenim viris
  peste plus subita nocet.

virus invidiae latens
  rebus in miseris suam
  ponit invaletudinem,
  hisque, non aliis, necem
  et pericula conferet.

sic ut invidearis, et
  non ut invideas, decet
  te peritia, quem probi
  et boni facit unice
  compotem meriti sui.

omne iudicio tuo
  ius favet, sine quo michi
  nemo propositi mei
  vel favoris inediam
  premiumve potest dare.

cordis eximius vigor,
  vita nobilis, optimas
  res secuta, probant quidem
  iuris ingenium, modo
  cuius artibus uteris.

est quibus caput urbium
  Roma, iustior et prope
  totus orbis, eas timet
  saeva barbaries adhuc,
  clara stemmate regio.

his et archiapostoli
  fervido gladio Petri
  frange robur et impetus
  illius, vetus ut iugum
  usque sentiat ultimum.

quanta vis anathematis!
  quicquid et Marius prius,
  quodque Iulius egerant
  maxima nece militum,
  voce tu modica facis.

Roma quid Scipionibus
  caeterisque Quiritibus
  debuit mage quam tibi,
  cuius est studiis suae
  nacta iura potentiae?

qui probe, quoniam satis
  multa contulerant bona
  patriae, perhibentur et
  pace perpetua frui
  lucis et regionibus.

te quidem, potioribus
  preditum meritis, manet
  gloriosa perenniter
  vita, civibus ut tuis
  compaveris Apostolis.

There is, in this poem, the same solidity of structure, the same originality of conception as in the Monte Cassino ode. The allusions to ancient Roman history, the striking estimate of the genius of Hildebrand the young archdeacon of the Roman Church, the concentration of phrase and the absence of rhetoric—these are the oustanding impressions as we read this ode. Here the scholarship of Alphanus is apparent, and we see the intellectual quality of the man who, like John of

[1] Text in Giesebrecht, *L'istruzione in Italia*, pp. 75 sqq.

Salisbury in the next century, made of his studies an instrument of the spirit. He writes a charming poem to Pandulf, Bishop of Marsica, who had asked him to send some hymns in honour of S. Sabina.[1] It is too difficult a business, he says, to sing of her deeds in dactylic measure; so he sends the hymns in what are actually more complicated Horatian metres. It is in this poem that he sets forth his justification of the use of rhetorical 'flowers' and 'colores' by a poet.[2] Alphanus was not ashamed of his art or of his studies, though he did deem it prudent once mildly to rebuke the youthful Transmundus,[3] who had gone off to the monks of Casauria in search of worldly learning. But, if we study the poem which he sent to his young friend, we see that it is above all things a clever adaptation of Horace's manner, with Horatian brevity and the urbanity of the humanist.[4] He is not really angry with Transmundus:

> Transmundum metrica laude, sorores,
> dignum, dulce melos fingere doctae,
> ut vos voce quidem vultis acuta,
> vel Phoebi cithara dicite dulci.
>
> hic Aristotelis philosophiae
> versutas haereses atque Platonis
> fastus eloquii, mense per annum
> uno paene studens, arte refutat
>
> qua non Attica dat vincere norma,
> sed Tetina[5] palus, noxia semper
> crudis cardiacis, utericisque,
> et splenis vitio vindice passis.
>
> deridet studium saepe decenne,
> et quando libet, hoc monte relicto,
> laetus tendit eo tempore veris
> causa tam citius multa sciendi.
>
> fertur corde tenus sic homilias
> quadraginta legens scire, sed illic;
> nam post tot reditus, muneris huius
> expers prorsus adest, utpote pridem.
>
> versus tam bene scit Virgilianos
> discens a puero, quam bene novit
> quos irata libros igne Sibylla
> combussit, quod eos renuit emptor.

[1] Migne, cxlvii, col. 1219 sqq.
[2] See *Christian-Latin Poetry*, p. 245 sq.
[3] He was a nephew of Bishop Pandolf and afterwards became Bishop of Valva. See Giesebrecht, p. 79.
[4] Migne, cxlvii, col. 1260; for corrections see Giesebrecht, p. 58 sq.
[5] C. Pascal in his translation of Giesebrecht (p. 59) says that Schipa reads Tetina instead of the Zetina given in Ughelli and repeated in Migne; and that Tetina means 'of Chieti'.

tales grammaticos mittit Aternus.[1]
hic oblivio sic iuncta[2] perosi
moris,[3] philosophos praebet inertes.
felices, quibus haec cognita non est!

si, Transmunde, mihi credis amice,
his uti studiis desine tandem,
fac cures monachi scire professum,
ut vere sapiens esse puteris.

In these poems, as in the other occasional pieces, such as the sapphics to Atto, Bishop of Chieti,[4] or the odes to Gisulf, Prince of Salerno,[5] and his brother Guido,[6] we see how Italian learning could hold its own with the production of contemporary France and Germany. We do not speak of a revival of studies in Italy because, except for brief periods, they had never appreciably declined. The Italian scholars consciously carried on a tradition, and they knew that in a special manner the past belonged to them. There were many lay schools, such as the school of William of Aversa, Alphanus' friend. In a sapphic poem,[7] Alphanus reminds William how as a boy he had often heard him railing at the monks after dinner, and say that the rich alone were happy. William made a fortune out of teaching; but, like so many others, he could not resist the voice that called him to forsake the world.

§ 4. The 'Versus Eporedienses'.

In a Latin Psalter, which Bishop Warmund (d. before 1011) gave to the Church of Ivrea, are inscribed in a later handwriting a number of religious verses; but very strangely, in the earlier part of the codex, before the Psalms begin, some religious pieces are followed by a long love poem in leonine elegiacs. The name Wido, which appears on f. 22,[8] may be that of the author, who can hardly have been other than a member of the cathedral chapter. The mention in the poem of Henry IV's victory over the Saxons suggests a date round about 1075–80, when Ogerius was Bishop of Ivrea. We need not be surprised to find an Italian priest composing a poem like this—a love invitation—in

---

[1] The monastery of Casauria on the river Aterno.
[2] Giesebrecht's reading instead of *iuxta*, but he gives it with reserve.
[3] Giesebrecht's reading instead of *amoris* or *honoris*.
[4] Migne, cxlvii, col. 1259.
[5] ib., col. 1256.

[6] ib., col. 1256.
[7] ib., col. 1260.
[8] E. Dümmler, *Anselm der Peripatetiker, nebst andern Beiträgen zur Literaturgeschichte Italiens im 11 Jahrhundert*, Halle 1872, p. 87; text of the poem, pp. 94 sqq.

a country where the clergy often lived openly with wives or concubines,[1] and the influences of secular education were strong. Peter Damiani would doubtless have been shocked if he had found this trifle embedded in a psalter, but Wido's friends would have admired it simply as a learned *tour de force*, which only a scholar could have composed.

An earlier 'invitatio'—the *Iam dulcis amica venito*[2]—has already been referred to a probable Italian origin, and this more elaborate production, which suggests as well the *pastourelle* and that other *genre* practised by classical poets, the description of a woman's beauty, is appropriately Italian.[3] There is, indeed, in the poem a background of classical reminiscence, but, in spite of its learning, the piece is conceived in what was then a thoroughly modern style. To this the leonine rimes bear witness, as well as the pastoral and love motives which were now appearing in literature. That unhappy device, the application of rime to the elegiac distich, cannot wholly spoil for us the enjoyment of this interesting poem. The scene is laid in April, on the banks of the Po:

> tempus erat florum, quod fons est omnis amorum.

There the maiden is walking, and the poet invites her, shyly but eagerly, to stay her steps,

> siste, puella, gradum per amoenum postulo Padum,

and he praises her for her beauty, comparing her with Juno. He would know her name and lineage. When the maiden has recovered her courage she admits that she is of a royal or noble family; nay, she is descended from the gods, as her ancestors came from Troy,

> ne super hoc erra, genuit me Trohica terra.

At last she consents to sit down beside the poet, who begins the long *invitatio*, which is the central part of the poem. This is a fantastical heaping together of all the gifts that one could promise who had all the wealth of the world at his command. First, he suggests pastoral delights,

> si foret hoc gratum floris decerpere pratum,
> tu posses mecum munere mota precum,

---

[1] E. Dümmler, op. cit., p. 8; see H. C. Lea, *History of Sacerdotal Celibacy*, London 1907, i. 167 sqq.

[2] Above, p. 301.

[3] Cf. H. Brinkmann, *Geschichte der lateinischen Liebesdichtung im Mittelalter*, Halle 1925, p. 7.

> sepe sub umbella posses, speciosa puella,
> ludere letari, cura cupita mari.
> quod si tu nolis, caleas ut lumine solis,
> ventilet aura sinus, umbra sit apta pinus.
> umbra decens lauri precio preciosior auri
> te recreare potest, umbra nec huius obest.
> currit aquae vivae fons frondes subter olivae,
> amnis sub tenebris, umbra deae Veneris.
> tempore sub veris placeat quod forte laveris,
> fons monet, herba recens et locus ipse decens.

Or does the nymph desire delicious food, or costly wines?—dishes or cups of gold and silver?—or precious stones?

> rex dedit Indorum lapidum mihi munus eorum,
> quos erit inter onix: hunc habuit Beronix.
> est scyphus in signo factus de mangere ligno:
> munus opis variae rex dedit Ungariae.

His farm also will supply all kinds of meat and birds; or, if fishes or eggs are desired, they can be provided in abundance. There will be milk, in winter as well as in spring, and, of course, plenty of cheese. Fruits and vegetables come next in the catalogue, after which there is a sudden transition to the arts—grammar and music. Then the poet proceeds to the house in which the maiden shall live. The choice is wide, for he has castles and villas innumerable. Her bed shall be of flowers,

> hic ornare thorum poteris variamine florum:
> res probat atque patet, vipera nulla latet.
> nec reputato parum, talis solet esse dearum,
> cum Marti placuit, Cipris in hoc iacuit.

Or would she prefer a couch of cedar, or of silver perhaps, or even of gold? It is all one,

> ex hac materia sume vel ex alia.

Then the coverings of the bed are lengthily discussed,[1] and

---

[1] This part of the poem is of great interest as, after due allowance has been made for the apparatus of classical allusion, it suggests how intercourse with Byzantium and the growth of wealth had brought more luxury into the life of rich Italians:

> culcitra lectorum non vilis habebitur horum,
> dant Seres populi materiam toruli.
> ex auri lamma fit subtilissima trama:
> stamen erit Serum, trama Frigum veterum.
> ut nix albescit stamenque nigrescere nescit,
> sed quae trama rubet: sol mihi cede, iubet.
> mille libras sumam, si digner vendere plumam;
> exponi precio nulla monet ratio.
> in tali pluma iacuit cum coniuge Numa,
> ex hac materie fit thorus Egeriae,

etc. (Dümmler, op. cit., p. 97).

the appointments of the house. But perhaps, after all, the lady would prefer the city to the villa?

> cum placeas turbe, si vis, maneamus in urbe:
>   totum quod queres, illud ab urbe feres.
> maximus urbis honos: dites habet illa colonos;
>   tantum scire sinum nemo potest hominum.
> hanc diversorum genus incolit omne virorum:
>   Anglus et Acaicus Noricus Ungaricus.
> hanc habitant Indi, gens et prius incola Pindi:
>   vile nec Indorum tu reputato forum.[1]

The merchandise of the cities is next described, and the things to be bought there that please the eye. Gradually the poet comes nearer to the point, for he begins a catalogue of the lady's charms:[2]

> lucifer ut stellis, sic es prelata puellis;
>   in prelativis est tua forma nivis.
> constat et est clarum: superas genus omne rosarum;
>   sit iudex aequus, tu geris omne decus.
> dum flavos humeris crines sparsisse videris
>   et pro velle iacis, me sine mente facis.
> cerni quando sinis frontem religamine crinis,
>   hec etiam crebras luce fugat tenebras.
> sunt oculi digni gemini ceu lumina signi,
>   nulla supercilio pars datur in vicio.
> dona referre genae nostrae nequit usus avenae,
>   lingua nequit vatum, scribat ut omne datum.
> ad solis morem facies tua nacta colorem,
>   hanc quociens videam, cogit ut astupeam.

After continuing in this strain he proudly and finally proclaims himself a poet whose verses can confer immortality on those whom he celebrates.

> sum sum sum vates, Musarum servo penates,

he cries, as seriously as his contemporaries in France, Marbod or Baudry, who fashioned similar verses, and apart from their ecclesiastical office were professional men of letters:

> Musa mori nescit nec in annis mille senescit,
>   durans durabit nec quod amavit abit.
> quod decet ore teri vivit dictamen Omeri
>   et facit esse deum quem coluit Nereum.
> perpetuis horis tua vivit, Flace, Liquoris,
>   nec valet illa mori carmine fama fori.
> perspicue signa quare sit nota Corinna:
>   vivere Naso facit quando per ora iacit.

¹ Dümmler, p. 99.   ² p. 101.

ut semper dures, mihi te subponere cures,
quod si parueris, carmine perpes eris.

But it is a reasonable conjecture that Wido's poem would have failed to embalm for ever the beauty of this maiden walking by the river if he had not taken care to confide his verses to the protecting pages of the Latin Psalter.

GERMAN POETS OF THE ELEVENTH CENTURY

§ 1. *Froumond of Tegernsee and Walther of Speier.*

Froumond of Tegernsee stands apart among the German poets of the end of the tenth century because he gives us, in his letters and poems, the impression of a living figure. He began his studies as a young monk at Tegernsee, but it was at the monastery of S. Pantaleon in Cologne that he acquired the wider learning which was his peculiar distinction. Froumond was also one of the monks of Tegernsee who were sent to revivify the moribund monastery of S. Saviour at Feuchtwangen. Here he began the compilation of his codex of letters and poems.[1] But it was not long before he and his fellows were back at Tegernsee, where he was to spend his days teaching, composing, and transcribing. He had no ambition to become a priest:

> discere decrevi libros aliosque docere.

This, as Strecker says, was his confession of faith,[2] and in this faith he remained until his death. But he was persuaded to enter the priesthood, and one of his pupils wrote to congratulate him: 'Nuper vero ᶜomperi, quod me affectu animavit inedicibili, videlicet vos fore promotum ad ordinem presbiterii. Qua de re flexo poplite flagito, quatinus mei infirmi memoria apud vos maneat, ut vestri apud me firmius maneat.'[3] The young Ellinger wrote in the way his master had taught him and from him he doubtless learned also to compose in verse.

In a charming poem Froumond gives us a picture of himself among the pupils whom he was instructing in the art of poetry.[4] It is too long to quote in full, but it is of great interest both as an excellent specimen of a school-exercise, and for the light which it throws on the relation between master and pupils in a monastic school. First he greets the Abbot, who has complained that the pupils and the masters, who are responsible

---

[1] Ed. K. Strecker, *Die Tegernseer Briefsammlung* (Froumond), Berlin 1925.

[2] p. xvii.

[3] p. 102. Ellinger became Abbot; he died in 1056. His epitaph is on p. 122 (no. xlii). Froumond (p. 36) wrote a poem on the subject of the efforts made to induce him to accept ordination.

[4] xxxii, p. 80.

for their pupils' deeds, do not dedicate to him any well-turned verses. Let every one, therefore, who knows how to write, get to work and make verses, so that the Abbot's anger may be turned away. Froumond says:[1]

> quos genui, nunc aversor, quia et actibus angor:
>   sensibus eversi, moribus inproprii
> non me cognoscunt nec se ipsos mente revisunt,
>   ut dicant pariter: 'est meus ipse pater.'
> eloquor, et proprium non sentitis genitorem;
>   state, renoscite me, sum pater, in facie.
> sepius edocui, scriptis verbisque nutrivi;
>   sum mordax verbo, pectore vos sed amo.
> est meus iste labor cassatus, perditus omnis,
>   et torvis oculis me simul inspicitis?

He is not really angry, but he is using the occasion to give his pupils a little good advice. For he goes on to say that he would not have met with wry faces if he had indulged them with the clown's foolery, or with mimes about Orpheus and Eurydice, or any profane music:

> si facerem mihi pendentes per cingula caudas
>   gesticulans manibus, lubrice stans pedibus,
> si lupus aut ursus, vel vellem fingere vulpem,
>   si larvas facerem furciferis manibus,
> dulcifer aut fabulas nossem componere, mendax,
>   Orpheus ut cantans Euridicen revocat,
> si canerem multos dulci modulamine leudos[2]
>   undique currentes cum trepidis pedibus,
> gauderet mihi qui propior visurus adesset,
>   ridiculus[3] cunctos concuteret pueros.
> fistula si dulcis mihi trivisset mea labra,
>   risibus et ludis oscula conciperem.
> veridicax minor est vobis quam ligula mendax,
>   diligitis[que] iocos en mage quam metricos.

Froumond prefers and must insist on more profitable subjects for his poems:

> ludere carminibus melius namque esse decrevi,
>   quae faciunt animum crescere et ingenium.

Not all those who use hard words do so from hatred; and not all those who speak softly do so from love. Froumond is a master who loves his pupils and is anxious for their good:

> dulces filioli, studium iam discite laeti;
>   diligo vos animo, corde simul doceo.

[1] p. 81.
[2] *leudus* = German *Lied*.
[3] i.e. *risus*: or is *risiculus* the correct reading?

Here we see Froumond, not as a pedantic versifier, who can only imitate others, but allowing his lively mind to play upon the material of his choice, even if he is busy with a school-exercise. He is fond of leonine rimes and can write such verses as:

> fumida fax fellis succendit vulnera pellis,
> servulus ut menceps in domnum sit male praeceps.[1]

But it is not distinction and refinement, such as some of the French poets could compass, that we look for in Froumond's verse. It is rather the skill with which he brings us close to the events and experiences of his everyday life in poems which are often a mixture of humour and invective. So he attacks the *vestiarius*, who has neglected to provide the monks with their proper winter clothing. He begins sardonically,[2]

> tempus enim nunc est, 'hu hu!' quo dicimus omnes,
> sed tamen hoc verbo nunquam sus prenditur ullus.

For it was pigskin that was needed, and Froumond wishes that his incompetent colleague were a pig, so that he could flay him and make gloves of his skin, or a cloak to cover him by day and night:

> nonne die nudus, quasi nudus nocte recumbo?

The winter was hard in German monasteries,[3] and fur-leggings or boots were a necessity. These too were not always forth-coming; so Froumond begs for them in verse—*pro caligis hirsutis quamvis vilibus*:[4]

> excelsi montes iam condunt ninguine cautes,
> flamine perduro spirant et frigora campo
> undique disturbant famulum me turbine vestrum,
> pelliciis sed et incursus depellitur omnis.
> parte tegor, de parte alia me concutit algor,
> maxime per suras inserpunt frigora venas,
> cruscula concrescunt, lapidosa ut stiria durant.
> hoc poteris sarcire, pater.   quod si hispida pellis
> redditur aut vetulum noviter vel sutile tectum,
> quicquid est, quod largiris, venerabile donum est.

Froumond is not, of course, always in earnest. The *cuculus sine pennis*, whom he attacks in another poem,[5] is perhaps one of his scholars who presumed to think that he could write as well as his master. In any case Froumond is enjoying himself, and gives full rein to his rough fancy. 'Man scheint in Tegern-

---

[1] Strecker, p. 17, verse 6 sq.
[2] p. 21.
[3] Cf. *Epist.* xxxvii, p. 44; Froumond

did not write this from Tegernsee.
[4] p. 29.
[5] p. 53.

see eine etwas derbe Ausdrucksweise geliebt zu haben,' says
Strecker,[1] commenting on this poem, which is obscure in expression, although the rude violence of its intention is plain
enough. But he could also be gentle, as in the two lines to
Liutold, a monk of Tegernsee,

> frater Froumundus Liutoldo mille salutes
> et quot nunc terris emergunt floscula cunctis.[2]

There is a tenderness too in the epitaph which he composed
for his own mother, though here again there is a play of
phantasy in his derivation of her ancestry from Dulichium
and Troy:[3]

> Hoc silicum tumulo iacet Ilisa corpore functa;
>   invida mors rapuit, quod sibi vita fuit.
> litera si abfuerit, quam simmam Grecia dicit,
>   Ilia nomen erit, ut genus edocuit.
> funeris obsequium post multos huic facit annos
>   filius ecce suus Froumundus monachus.
> Dulichium genuit patres et Troia priores:
>   qui locus hoc corpus hic tegit exiguus.
> nominis hanc formam fecit gens esse secundam.
>   sic posuit terris, quas superat reliquis.
> litera, quam cernis, petit, ut precibus memoreris
>   corporis atque animae, quo maneat requie.
> mente revolve simul, quod tu peregrinus et exul
>   hic iaceas terris expulsus propriis.
> quapropter pariter, rogo, poscas cum prece, frater,
>   ut sibi perpetuam nunc tribuat patriam
> et nos cum venia simili perducat ad astra,
>   qui mortem superat et bona cuncta parat.
> tercia namque dies Octobris ad usque Kalendas
>   abstulit e saeclis reddidit et superis.

Froumond's fantasy found play as well in a picture-poem with
acrostic, threefold mesostich, and telestich; but he could not
emulate the great model, Optatianus Porfirius, neither could
he always make a readable verse.[4] In another acrostic he introduces a Greek line,

> eudochias os oplon stephanosas Kyrrie Christe.[5]

His pupils must have marvelled at such learning, which they
could not hope to emulate. When he wrote

> fosfora xilokopus nos fecit inertia ligna,

[1] ib., note.   [4] p. 24.
[2] p. 41; cf. *Epist.* xxxvii, p. 44.   [5] p. 96.
[3] pp. 41–2.

he would have to explain that this meant 'the Carpenter
(ξυλοκόπος) makes us useless logs to be bearers of light'. Like
Notker before him, a man whom he resembles in many ways,
Froumond was a teacher, and it is with this fact in mind that
we must approach and study his verse.

At the end of the tenth and at the beginning of the eleventh
century stands Walther of Speier. He was subdeacon when
Bishop Balderich asked him to describe in verse and prose the
story of S. Christopher. This was about the year 982. Walther
had as his material an existing legend of S. Christopher, to
which he made both his verse and his prose composition
conform.[1] He was entrusted with the task because the Bishop's
librarian had lost a versified life of the saint which had been
sent to him by a learned lady named Hazecha, and for her
Walther made a copy of his work.[2]

It was on account of his learning that the Bishop chose
Walther, and Walther did not neglect to display that learning
in the course of his poem.

He introduces the poem with a solemn flourish, beginning
with a letter, then a prologue addressed to Bishop Balderich,
and, lastly, a preface to the Reader. The two latter are in
verse, and are followed by an introductory book entitled *De
studio poetae*. The poem itself really belongs to the history of
religious verse, but this first book has a general interest, as
Walther gives here an account of his progress in the path of
learning from the first rudiments. He tells us how he learned
the Greek fables,

> Orpheus Eurydices raptum plorabat amicae,
> muros Amphion, delphinas duxit Arion.
> tranavit pelagus desertus ab Hellade Phryxus,
> iam petit ima puer fluctu torrente Leander.
> defunctis apibus matrem clamavit Aristeus;
> terruit audacem cauda centaurus Achillem.
> iactat bis senos Alcidis clava triumphos, etc.

Then came the poets, Homer, Martianus Capella, Horace,
Persius, Juvenal, Boëthius, Statius, Terence, Lucan; and

> omnibus excellens docuit nos musa Maronis
> otia pastorum celebrare, modosque laborum.

After this, Walther describes the various Arts, and how when

---

[1] Manitius, *Gesch.* ii. 502.
[2] Perhaps he kept it for her in a
case—'diligenter expositum tuae pre-
sentiae servandum in theca reposui'
are his words. Harster, *Vita et Passio
S. Christophori*, Speier 1878, p. 104.

he had studied them, he realized that it was time to turn to more serious things. This is why he sings of Christopher,

> quem si pleno cantabimus ore,
> ante tribunitiam securi stabimus iram.

Walther's expression is so obscure and he covers his account with so thick a veil of allegory, that it is difficult to follow. This difficulty does not disappear in the remainder of the poem. Walther loved curious words, for which he searched in glossaries, and he mingled Graecisms as well.

§ 2. *Wipo*.

Wipo,[1] a Burgundian or perhaps a Swabian, was born towards the end of the tenth century. He was well educated and held the position of chaplain to Conrad II and Henry III. It is not improbable, indeed, that he was tutor to Henry when he was a boy. At any rate, he composed for him a collection of proverbs in verse, mainly moralistic in character, rhythmical, with frequent two-syllabled rimes:[2]

> decet regem discere legem.
> audiat rex, quod praecipit lex.
> legem servare est regnare.
> notitia litterarum lux est animarum.
> saepius offendit, qui lumen non adtendit.
> qui habet scientiam, ornat sententiam.

These proverbs are of various origin, and are only of interest as scholastic documents. Wipo tells us that he wrote a 'satire' in several books, called *Gallinarius*,[3] but what the scope of the poem was we have no means of judging.[4] He also informs us obliquely[5] that he composed a poem of a hundred verses on the great cold that fell in the year 1033, when the Emperor was campaigning in Burgundy, and that he celebrated in verse Conrad's war against the Slavs.[6] When the Emperor died, Wipo composed a rhythmical dirge,

> Qui vocem habet serenam,   hanc proferat cantilenam
> de anno lamentabili   et damno ineffabili,
> pro quo dolet omnis homo   forinsecus et in domo.
> suspirat populus domnum   vigilando et per somnum:
> rex Deus, vivos tuere   et defunctis miserere!

[1] *Die Werke Wipos*, ed. H. Bresslau, 3rd edit., Hanover 1915.

[2] ib., pp. 66 sqq.; no. 95, p. 72, is a leonine hexameter.

[3] *Gesta Chuonradi Imp.* vi, p. 29.

[4] See Manitius, *Gesch.* ii. 319.

[5] *Gesta Chuonradi*, xxx, p. 49, 'de qua nimietate frigoris quidam de nostris centenos versus fecit, quos imperatori praesentavit,' etc.

[6] ib. xxxiii, p. 53.

It will be observed that the rhythm is iambic. The last verse is repeated as a refrain at the end of each stanza. It is probable that Wipo is the author of two other rhythmical poems, one on the coronation of Conrad, and the other on that of his son Henry.[1] Besides these, he is, of course, the author of the famous Easter sequence, *Victimae paschali*.[2]

The longest of Wipo's surviving poems is the *Tetralogus*,[3] which was his Christmas offering to Henry III in 1041. His excuse was the text in *Proverbs*: 'gloria regum investigare sermonem'.[4] He explains to the Emperor that a *Tetralogus* is 'quattuor personarum sermo':

> There the poet first invites the Muses to praise you. The choir of the Muses blesses and praises you, Lord King. Then Law addresses you with such counsels as beseem your dignity. Lastly, Grace will temper with gentle speech that which Law as by right has urged upon you. For the perusal of which the Mediator of Law and of Grace be with you, even Jesus Christ our Saviour, Whose kingdom and dominion shall not fail for ever.

The poem is in leonine hexameters, with sporadic two-syllabled rime. There is an interesting passage in the Muses' praise of Henry in which they recall the ancient poets, whose songs bestowed immortality:[5]

> ex nostris donis manifestant verba Maronis
> quid pius Aeneas, quid Turnus posset in armis.
> fistula Musarum Flacco dictaverat odas,
> ut Maecenatem fecisset laude perennem.
> haec eadem docuit Lucanum dicere bella
> Caesaris et Magni, quae durant ultima secli.
> ex nostris monitis callebat Statius auctor
> Thebanos miseris iuvenes discernere flammis.
> Nasonis studium totus recitaverat orbis,
> ex nostris curis ornavit scripta figuris.
> regibus antiquis laudes cantavimus olim,
> et de principibus scribendi creverat usus.

These are the poets whom Wipo knew so well. Statius and Lucan seem to have been his special favourites, and he evidently read them with intelligence.

Wipo had also a clear-sighted view of the need for educated laymen, especially lawyers, in the German kingdom. He had been to Italy and, like Otto of Freising in the next century, he was impressed by the superiority of manners and education among the Italian laity. So he makes Law plead with the

---

[1] pp. 103 sqq.   [3] pp. 75 sqq.   [4] *Prov.* xxv. 2.
[2] *Christian-Latin Poetry*, p. 217 sq.   [5] p. 77.

Emperor for an edict, issued primarily it is true to encourage study of the law, but also of general import:[1]

> tunc fac edictum per terram Teutonicorum,
> quilibet ut dives sibi natos instruat omnes
> litterulis legemque suam persuadeat illis,
> ut cum principibus placitandi venerit usus,
> quisque suis libris exemplum proferat illis.
> moribus his dudum vivebat Roma decenter,
> his studiis tantos potuit vincire tyrannos;
> hoc servant Itali post prima crepundia cuncti,
> et sudare scholis mandatur tota iuventus:
> solis Teutonicis vacuum vel turpe videtur,
> ut doceant aliquem nisi clericus accipiatur.
> sed, rex docte, iube cunctos per regna doceri,
> ut tecum regnet sapientia partibus istis.[2]

After Law has spoken, Wipo introduces Grace to temper the severity of judgement:

> Legem scripsit homo, descendit Gratia caelo.

And with a long exposition of the relation of Law to Grace, the poem ends.

§ 3. *Ruodlieb.*

The poem called *Ruodlieb* is a romantic epic in leonine hexameters, which was composed by a monk of Tegernsee about the year 1050.[3] Its fragmentary preservation makes it difficult to reconstruct its story in satisfactory completeness, but it can be divided, according to its material, into three sections, derived from different sources. The 'novelistic' part—the story of the golden precepts—is of oriental origin and is probably based upon current tradition.[4] The 'historical' part may be a reminiscence of the meeting of the Emperor Henry II with King Robert of France in 1023,[5] while the 'mythological' element is derived from old heroic saga. The relation of these three elements to each other will become clear as we set out in brief the story which the poet has to tell.

There was once a noble knight named Ruodlieb, who served several wealthy lords, but got no profit from his service. So he set out in quest of fortune, with no help but his sword and his faithful squire. He said good-bye to his weeping mother, and

---

[1] See *Christian-Latin Poetry,* p. 236.
[2] p. 81 sq.
[3] *Ruodlieb, der älteste Roman des Mittelalters,* ed. F. Seiler, Halle 1882.
[4] It is not improbable that the mimes

or *joculatores* told such tales; for mimes see *Ruodlieb,* v. 87 (p. 229); cf. ix. 26 (p. 269).
[5] Giesebrecht, *Geschichte der deutschen Kaiserzeit*[5], ii. 625, Leipzig 1885.

went out from his own country. Soon he fell in with a king's huntsman who persuaded him to enter his master's service. There he distinguished himself by his skilful devices for catching fish and blinding wolves. The poet describes his methods, and refers to Pliny for the wonderful qualities of the herb which Ruodlieb uses.[1]

These are days of peace, but trouble is brewing with the neighbouring kingdom. In the ensuing war, Ruodlieb's master is victorious, and peace is to be made at a great meeting on the field of battle. This is arranged by Ruodlieb, who goes as ambassador to the court of the defeated king. There is a long and interesting description of this visit, which Ruodlieb sets out in detail when he returns to his master. He tells how he had to play chess with the major-domo and finally with the king himself. The dialogue is very lively:[2]

> rex poscens tabulam iubet opponi sibi sellam
> et me contra se iubet in fulchro residere,
> ut secum ludam, quod ego nimium renuebam
> dicens 'terribile, miserum conludere rege;'
> et dum me vidit sibi non audere reniti,
> ludere laudavi cupiens ab eo superari,
> 'vinci de rege' dicens 'quid obest miserum me?
> sed timeo, domine, quod mox irasceris in me,
> si fortuna iuvet, mihi quod victoria constet.'
> rex subridendo dixit velut atque iocando:
> 'non opus est, care, super hac re quid vereare;
> si nunquam vincam, commocior haut ego fiam;
> sed quam districte noscas ludas volo cum me,
> nam quos ignotos facies volo discere tractus.'
> statim rex et ego studiose traximus ambo,
> et, sibi gratia sit, mihi ter victoria cessit,
> multis principibus nimis id mirantibus eius.

The scene shifts to the meeting of the kings, which is described in all its splendour. There are speeches, feastings, and gifts. These last are the offerings of the defeated king, but, magnanimously, Ruodlieb's master will take nothing but two performing bears,[3] and a starling and a magpie for his daughter.

---

[1] But Pliny may be searched in vain for anything about the properties of *bugloss*; see Manitius, *Gesch.* ii. p. 550, note 3.

[2] iv. 194 sqq. (Seiler, p. 223).

[3] These are described, v. 84 sqq. (p. 229):

> et pariles ursi, qui fratres sunt uterini,
> omnino nivei gambis pedibusque nigellis,
> qui vas tollebant, ut homo, bipedesque gerebant;

there is also a lynx, from whose urine, the poet tells us, the precious stone, *ligurius*, is made, and he sets forth in detail how this can be done (v. 99 sqq., p. 229 sq.).

The kings return home, but Ruodlieb finds on his arrival a messenger with a letter from his mother imploring him to come back to her and to his own people. In allowing him to depart, the king asks him whether he will have gold or wisdom as his reward.[1] He chooses wisdom, and the king delivers to him twelve golden precepts along with two loaves, secretly filled with gold, to be opened, the smaller in his mother's presence, the larger at his wedding.

The first rule was not to trust any man with a red head, and sure enough, a red-headed man stole his cloak before he had been long on his journey. The second rule was not to avoid a muddy village street by riding over the cornfields. This also is broken, and brings trouble. Then the knight and the red-headed man come to the town where they are to stay for the night. Here Rufus breaks the third rule by taking lodgings with an old man who was married to a young wife, but Ruodlieb remembers the precept and goes elsewhere. Rufus ends by murdering the old man, who objected to the attentions which he paid to his complaisant wife. The woman is penitent before the Judges, but Rufus is condemned.

Ruodlieb now travels with a young relative, and they reach the house of a noble lady, a friend of Ruodlieb's mother and the possessor of a beautiful daughter. The daughter and the young man are to marry; they dance together while Ruodlieb plays the harp:

> sic tribus insolitis actis dulcissime rithmis,
> quartum poscit hera faceret, petit et sua nata,
> eius contribulis quem saltaret vel herilis.
> quem per sistema sive diasistema dando responsa
> dum mirabiliter operareturve decenter,
> surrexit iuvenis, quo contra surgit herilis.
> ille velut falcho se girat et haec ut hirundo;
> ast ubi conveniunt, citius se praeteriebant;
> is se movisse, sed cernitur illa natasse;
> neutrum saltasse, neumas manibus variasse
> nemo corrigere quo posset, si voluisset.
> tunc signum dederant, ibi multi quod doluerunt,
> deponendo manus, finitus sit quia rithmus.[2]

Then Ruodlieb and the young man depart, and draw near their home. The knight's approach is known, for a talking jackdaw spreads the news. After the greetings and a feast, Ruodlieb, in secret with his mother, opens one of the loaves

---

[1] See Seiler, p. 48, for a Rabbinic story of similar motive; and other examples from various countries.   [2] ix. 45 sqq. (p. 270).

which the king had given him. The rich treasures which fall
out fill them with wonder and joy. There is again a feast at
which there are a multitude of fishes caught by means of
Ruodlieb's old device.[1] Here the thread of the narrative is
broken. Ruodlieb's dog gives a wonderful display of intelligence in discovering a thief, and then the scene changes to
a long discourse, apparently by Ruodlieb's mother, on the
miseries of a woman's old age:

> femina, quae lunae par est in flore iuventae,
> par vetulae simiae fit post aetate senectae.
> rugis sulcata frons, quae fuit antea plana,
> ante columbini sibi stant oculi tenebrosi, etc.[2]

This seems to be followed by a similar elegy on the painful lot
of men. These are school-exercises, in which the poet remembers Maximian.[3] Then the wedding of the young pair is
described with many lively touches, and the pleasant atmosphere of good humour and outspoken freedom is attractively
displayed. The mother now thinks that it is time for Ruodlieb
to settle down as well, but his efforts to find a bride are not
fortunate, until one day he comes across a dwarf who, as the
price of his freedom, promises the riches of two kings, Immunch
and his son Hartnuch, if he can overcome them, and the hand
of Heriburg the daughter of Immunch. To set aside Ruodlieb's
doubts the little man offers his wife as a hostage, and explains
that his race lives longer and is not deceitful like the race
of man:

> absit ut inter nos unquam regnaverit haec fraus;
> non tam longaevi tunc essemus neque sani.
> inter vos nemo loquitur, nisi corde doloso;
> hinc nec ad aetatem maturam pervenietis:
> pro cuiusque fide sunt eius tempora vitae.
> non aliter loquimur, nisi sicut corde tenemus,
> neve cibos varios edimus morbos generantes:
> longius incolumes hinc nos durabimus ac vos.[4]

The poem ends abruptly, before the fulfilment of the dwarf's
prophetic promise. Doubtless the poet completed it with a
happy ending, but his work suffers from its fragmentary
tradition, and the necessity of piecing it out by conjecture.
Yet nothing, not even the unfortunate leonine hexameters so
much favoured in that age, can avail to disguise the real fresh-

---

[1] xiii. 20 sqq. (p. 280); 39 sqq. give
a catalogue of the fish. This is in accordance with the tradition set by
Ausonius, see above, p. 59.

[2] xiv. 3 sqq. (p. 285).
[3] Manitius, *Gesch.* ii. 551.
[4] xviii. 18 sqq. (p. 301).

ness and charm of the story. It may be that the monkish poet himself combined some of the strange elements together, supplementing an original Germanic tradition with more or less learned contributions of his own. The quickness of the dialogue, the humour and the chivalry belong to the German tale. But the poet was writing for a learned audience, and although he kept close to the common life and often to common words and phrases, he could not forego his learned dependence on Virgil and Horace, on Prudentius and Sedulius. But these are mere reminiscences; the poet's latinity is below the average of his time, and it is clear enough that he thought in German and not in Latin.[1]

The leonine rime is mostly of one syllable and, like the prosody, it is far from perfect.[2] But, as Manitius puts it with complete fairness, 'his poem breathes life and not the school; hence we shall have to search long among epics before we meet again with such an artistic creation.'[3]

§ 4. Egbert of Liége, Amarcius, and others.

There are a few less-known German poets of the eleventh century whose work is worthy of mention. Egbert of Liége is known as the author of a famous school-book, the Fecunda Ratis,[4] the well-laden ship, a collection of strange materials. For Egbert was above all things a teacher.[5] Of noble birth,

[1] Cf. Seiler, p. 136, on Germanisms in the Ruodlieb. 'Diese sind nicht bloss scheinbar. Dass der Dichter nicht lateinisch denkt, sondern deutsch, das haben uns schon viele von den in diesem Capitel besprochenen Spracheigenheiten gezeigt.' The language of the Ruodlieb shows many German idioms; words are often merely current 'middle Latin', but there are also Graecisms used for metrical convenience. On the whole question see Seiler, pp. 112 sqq.

[2] Elision and hiatus are avoided, as was the rule in rhythmical verse.

[3] Gesch. ii. 555.

[4] Ed. E. Voigt, Egberts von Lüttich 'Fecunda Ratis', Halle 1889.

[5] Noteworthy is the autobiographical piece, p. 192, De debilitate evi nostri, beginning,

> stamina qui quondam sciolis subtilia nevi,
> torqueo nunc stuppas, rem debilitatis anilem,

> prima elementa docens brutae pecuaria plebis,
> Archadicos iuvenes in rusticitate moratos.

He goes on to say that he never looked for rewards in gold,

> teste deo numquam exsecui pretium artis avare;

cf. Voigt, p. xli. For Egbert's enlightened views on the need of gentleness in education see p. 179, De inmitibus magistris. He says,

> hic constare scolas video virgis sine linguis,
> afficitur caro, mens medicamine nulla fovetur;
> sevitia incumbit Radamanti sevior ira,
> et neque sic torquet dampnatas Eachus umbras,
> exagitata hydris non sic furiatur Herinis.

he went to school at Liége about the year 979, when he was hardly more than seven years old. In that same cathedral school he became a master, and he remained there all his life. He taught nothing more than the Trivium—Grammar, Rhetoric, and Dialectic—for he had no great mastery of the other arts. It was with the Trivium in view that he compiled his book, which is a collection of biblical and classical proverbial lore, with additions from the Fathers and from the vernacular. The two parts into which the book is divided are called *Prora* and *Puppis* respectively. *Prora* consists merely of proverbs or pithy sayings, of one, two, or three verses each. *Puppis* has pieces of varying length, some derived from the Fathers, some from the Roman satirists, fabulists, etc.; others are satirical pieces which are presumably of the poet's own invention or are drawn from the vernacular.[1] Here is his version of the wolf who turned monk for a moment, a familiar theme.[2]

De lupo modo monacho, modo populari.

Discurrens obiter lupus ad predam properabat
et nactus pisces, quos ventri indulsit edaci,
reddidit elatum congesta parabilis esca
in tantum, ut monachum sese iactaret habendum.
inde abiens pernas invenit et insuper edit.
cur a proposito ruat atque repente recedat,
'parcite in hoc mihi, quaeso,' percunctantibus inquit,
'nunc monachus, nunc sum parto popularis in esu,
ut lepidum facilemque vocent ad edenda ministri;
non egeo ut lauti proceres pistore cocoque,
talibus insoliti talem docuere parentes,
ut numquam fastidia delitiosus amarem;
non vescor coctis, invisa meis mora furtis,
cruda meum magis hoc guttur stipendia poscit.'

The young scholars in monastic and cathedral schools began with the Distichs of Cato and with books of fables like the work of Avianus. The one afforded, as Voigt has said,[3] a state-

---

[1] Voigt, p. lx, reckons that there are about 200 proverbs and examples derived from German vernacular sources.   [2] p. 195.

[3] Cf. Otloh in his *Proverbia*; Pez, *Thes. Anecd.* iii. 2. 487 (Migne, cxlvi, col. 300–1), 'illa fabulosa Aviani dicta, . . . et quaedam Catonis verba, quae utraque omnes pene magistri legere solent ad prima puerorum documenta.' Besides Otloh's *Proverbia*, there are in the eleventh century Arnulf's *Delicie cleri* (see p. 362); Wipo's proverbs

(p. 393); the *Scheftlarer Sprüche*, ed. Wattenbach, *Anzeiger f. Kunde d. Vorzeit*, N.F., xx. 217 sqq.; the *Proverbia Heinrici, Zeitschr. für deutsch. Alt.* xxx. 260 sqq. Later are the *Florilegium Vindobonense*, for which see Voigt, p. lxiv, note 1; an alphabetical anthology, *Zeitschr. f. deutsch. Alt.* xxx. 261, 272 sq., and *Notices et extraits des mss.*, XXXI. i. 49 sqq.; the *Proverbia Rustici, Rom. Forsch.*, iii. 633 sqq.; the *Florilegium Gottingense*, ib. iii. 281 sqq.; 463 sq.

ment of the laws of the rational or moral life *in abstracto*, while the other was a concrete presentment such as the young could appreciate. It was Egbert's plan to provide a further store of each kind, with the help of the Bible, the Fathers, and other ancient writers and with the addition of homely German examples.

Egbert was acquainted with a large number of classical authors, and like most eleventh-century writers he had made a close study of Juvenal and Persius as well as of Horace. The Satirists were read more eagerly than ever before; for they contained much that was both interesting and pertinent to the life of every day.

Thus the monk who wrote under the name of Sextus Amarcius Gallus Piosistratus composed four books of *Sermones*,[1] borrowing the title from Horace. He dedicated his work to Candidus Theophystius Alchimus, whom he addresses as,

> Virtutum norma, Theophysti, fulte decora,
>   inque dei vernans candidus obsequio,
> ut cum corporea superes albedine cygnos,
>   gemmis interius candidior niteas.
> si magnum te parva iuvant, hoc excipe carmen
>   contextum crasso pectoris igniculo,
> oblitus tenerae quod pubertatis alumnus
>   confisus domino caelitus ausus eram.

Amarcius deals in pseudonyms. Who his Candidus was, we know not; neither can we guess what was the real name of his master, whom he calls Eufronius. Like Egbert, he had made a thorough study of the satirists,[2] and he wrote as one who had a quarrel with his age. Like many other poets and men of letters he was attracted by the Emperor Henry III,[3] who was a constant patron of learning. Amarcius was a man of outstanding ability; he was thoroughly versed in the art of medicine,[4] and he had read deeply in the classical authors. He was in fact the kind of man that Henry liked to have about him, but there is no evidence that he was actually attached to his service.

Amarcius must be regarded as a serious satirist. If he made no great impression on his age, Hugh of Trimberg[5] did not overlook him when about 1280 he compiled his *Registrum multorum auctorum*. He describes him as

> . . . doctor veritatis,
> catholicus, satiricus, amator honestatis,

---

[1] Ed. M. Manitius, Leipzig 1888.
[2] Cf. Manitius, ib., p. xiv.
[3] Cf. III. i. 141 sqq. (p. 49).
[4] Cf. Manitius, *Gesch.* ii. 570.
[5] Ed. M. Haupt, *Berlin. Sitzungsber.*, 1854, p. 159.

> Turiaca provincia secus Alpes natus,
> Horatium in satiris suis imitatus.

And, indeed, it was Horace whom he had continually before him as his model; as Manitius says,[1] he follows him closely in expression and style, though he mentions him only once by name:

> nosti quid Oratius inquit?
> virtus et nobilitas sine re plus carice sordet.[2]

Amarcius is no mere imitator, however; he chose his model wisely, and then set to work on themes which had a meaning for his own age. It cannot be denied that he is obscure, so obscure at times that it is difficult to seize his meaning. But the following picture of the *nouveau riche* will give some idea of his manner:[3]

> nam cum paupertas rebus plerumque secundis
> pollet postque sagum lugubre prefulget in albis,
> cernere tedet humum priscamque reducere sortem
> inflaturque genas, ut onustae tubere turpi
> assurgunt scapulae, vel ut uncis unguibus olim
> haurit tabifluum pellis lacerata liquorem
> aspiratque novo sanies exotica folli,
> aut ut caenosae brumali tempore lamae
> declivesque viae nimbo turgent tenebroso.
> et sublatus inops quivis haec corde volutat:
> 'Hem, quis ego sum! quisve mihi par? hercule nullus!
> namque fruor simila plus Caucasea nive cana,
> nec porro cogor gingivas urere, quippe
> cui passer visco capiturque timallus ab hamo.
> stragula palla mihi est et iuncto purpura cocco.
> quid dubitem tortos cidari cohibere capillos,
> aut cur me nitidus non cingat balteus auro?
> nam et totum corpus gemmis velare coruscis
> et margaritis possum, mihi si placet illud;
> si libet, ut magnos gestat me reda Quirites.
> hactenus indulsi nec vindice dente remordi,
> si quis "rauce culix" dixit mihi, "fetide cimex."
> iam qui dicet idem mihi, bubo scrofave fiet.
> si soleas quondam et phaleras in paupere tecto
> conpegi aut molles fiscellas vimine lento,
> nunc mea me virtus et cista referta lucello
> extulit; absistat, cui populus alba mapale
> dat fruticesque breves, quae pisa procurat, et omnis
> non bene vestitus, scabiosus, iners, strabo, varus.'
> haec novus aut paria his elato pectore iactat.

The picture is perhaps crudely drawn, and the poet's hand is a little heavy. But he is so real a master of his material that we need not quarrel with Manitius's estimate of him as 'der

[1] *Gesch.* ii. 571.
[2] IV. iii. 299 sq. (p. 88); the reference   is to *Sat.* ii. 5. 8.
[3] I. iv. 301 sqq. (p. 11).

älteste erhaltene grosse Satiriker des Mittelalters'.[1] His choice
of subjects is, of course, coloured by his religious profession:
*de diversis luxuriae illecebris; de invidia; de eo quod incarnatio
Christi predicta sit in veteri testamento;*[2] *quod ineluctabilis sit
Iudaeorum duricia: de incontinentia sacerdotum*, etc. But Amarcius has a wider outlook than that of most of his monkish
contemporaries. This is due in part to his reading, for his
verses are packed with allusions to the great classical writers—
not only to the poets, but to authors like Tacitus and Pliny.
Prudentius was a special favourite. The *Psychomachia*, for
Amarcius, was a picture for all time of the struggle between
virtue and vice,[3] to which he returns again and again for
suggestions. The Roman satirists were the masters of method;
they tend, therefore, to stand between the poet and any vivid
first-hand picture of everyday life. He prefers, too, to digress
into classical learning or classical lore. So, having quoted 'The
ox knoweth his owner and the ass his master's crib', he has
to demonstrate that these animals represent the Gentiles, who
accepted Christ. He therefore gives a catalogue of the gods,
whom they worshipped:[4]

> Parnasus Phebo statuit sacra, Tracia Marti,
> Gnosiades coluere bovem Mynoida, laudes
> latranti cecinit populus Memphitis Anubi,
> deprensae Veneri Paphos, oblatisque corimbis
> Boeciae Bacho celebrarunt orgia gentes,
> Teutonici humanum Diti fudere cruorem, etc.

Amarcius is at his best in plain narrative, as when he describes the creation in a passage which recalls the earlier Christian
epic poets.[5] But here he borrows twice only from Avitus, and once
from Sedulius. Ovid and Virgil are more in his mind. He had no
scruple in reading them, for in his *De incontinentia sacerdotum* he
points out that unlawful loves had given the ancient poets material for their songs, and that God had inspired them—though it
was on the Muses that they called—for us to profit thereby:[6]

> illis ingenium subtile deus dedit et cor
> scribendi quodcunque placeret eis, alioquin

---

[1] *Gesch.* ii. 571.
[2] This is against the Jews (II. i, p. 21),
and begins,
> incipe amare Deum, Iudaes tirps dura!
> quid a te
> prognatum refugis venerari?
[3] Cf. I. i. 26, p. 2; Prudentius is
mentioned by name, II. iv. 383 (p. 34).
[4] II. iv. 337 sqq. (p. 33).

[5] III. v (pp. 65 sqq.).
[6] III. vi. 795 sq. (p. 72). But when
(III. iv. 526, p. 63) he makes an objector
quote on the subject of 'Who is my
neighbour?' the phrase of Terence,
'Mihimet sum proximus', he retorts,
> non decet Esopi figmenta salesve
>   Terenti
> scripturis miscere sacris.

> nequicquam excirent fictas Helicone Camenas
> edere digna hederis. nostri causa deus illis
> cessit, ut ex scriptis nos proficeremus eorum.

Warnerius of Basel is worth mentioning because he is an almost forgotten poet, who had a considerable reputation long after his death. He lived about the middle of the eleventh century, and was a cleric in Basel, though he may have been of French origin.[1] Hugh of Trimberg mentions him (*circ.* 1280) in his *Registrum multorum auctorum*:[2]

> Basiliensis clericus Warnerius vocatus
> catholicis auctoribus sit hic annumeratus,
> qui duos egregie libros compilavit,
> unumque Sydonium ex his praetitulavit,
> alterum Paraclitum, quod a multis scitur.

These two poems, the *Synodicus*[3] (transformed most curiously by Hugh and others into *Sidonius*) and the *Paraclitus*,[4] are dialogues in leonine hexameters, the inspiration of which goes back to the famous *Ecloga Theoduli*. In the *Synodicus* Thlepsis and Neocosmus hold a poetic strife, with themes from the Old and the New Testaments respectively, with Sophia as umpire. Sophia begins with the conventional theme of the season of the year:

> iam calor estivus fervente leone nocivus
> transiit, augusti finis dat pocula musti.
> campis detectis et pomis arbore lectis
> undique potatur contractaque cura fugatur.
> nos quoque letantes dum sustinet herba cubantes
> ramis protectos esca potuque refectos
> condelectemur, verbis sacris recreemur.
> Thlepsi, vetustarum memor et, Neocosme, novarum,
> ambo scii rerum cantantes dicite verum,
> dicite cantantes quae dicitis equiparantes.[5]

Warnerius wrote for edification, and it is hardly surprising that his poem was popular; for there is an attraction about his smooth rimes, and the subject was well suited to his audience. The other poem is, as Hauréau tells us,[6] 'a dialogue between a penitent sinner and the divine grace'. It is in leonine elegiacs and is less successful in execution.

[1] Manitius, *Gesch.* ii. 576.
[2] Ed. M. Haupt, *Berlin. Sitzungsber.* 1854, pp. 142 sqq.; Eberhard of Béthune, *Laborintus* (Leyser, p. 830), mentions Warnerius' poems, and Godfrey of Vinsauf also (Leyser, p. 964).
[3] Ed. J. Haemer, 'Warnerii Basiliensis Synodicus', *Romanische Forschungen*, iii (1887), pp. 313 sqq.
[4] Extracts in Hauréau, *Notices et extraits de quelques mss.*, vi, pp. 78 sqq.
[5] Haemer, p. 319.   [6] vi. 79.

The names, but little more, of a few minor German poets may here be mentioned. Manfred of Magdeburg appears to be the author of a computistic poem composed in 1050.[1] Embricho of Mainz (b. *circ.* 1010) wrote in verse a life of Mahomet, which was soon ascribed to Hildebert.[2] He was a master in the cathedral school and a man of much learning. This polemic against a false prophet is in elegiacs, and the leonine rime of two syllables is observed as carefully as possible. The story told is incredibly fantastic, and the poet ends with this distich,

> hactenus errorum quia causas diximus horum,
> Musa manum teneat, et Mahumet pereat.[3]

It was probably a *scholasticus* of Trier, named Winrich, who about 1075 composed a bitter poetical complaint[4] because he had been called away from his work in the school, for which he was qualified, to service in the kitchen, which was distasteful to him. He is severely satirical on the subject of monastic manners, but he wrote so obscurely that he is difficult at times to understand.[5]

§ 5. *German Historical Poems*

Otto III died at Paterno in 1002 at the age of twenty-two. He had desired that his body should be buried in Charlemagne's basilica at Aachen. His German soldiers had to fight their way in order to bring his remains safely across the Alps. A stone slab in the centre of the Gothic choir marks the spot where he was buried.

The century which followed his death, if it was full of troubles for Germany, was also a century of manifold growth and of consolidation. It began with the reign of Henry II, that practical and pious ruler, and ended with the stormy career of Henry IV, whose tragic failure made such an impression on his generation.

The person of the Emperor naturally attracted the attention of chroniclers and poets, for it was round the German rulers that the great political events centred. So Purchard, a monk

---

[1] Printed in Bede's works in Migne, xciv, col. 641 sqq.; see Manitius, *Gesch.* ii. 574.

[2] Migne, clxxi, col. 1343 sqq.; see Manitius, *Gesch.* ii. 582.

[3] Col. 1366. Mahomet's suspended coffin is described in the preceding verses.

[4] MS. Brussels 10615–10729, f. 173; ed. F. X. Kraus, *Jahrbücher d. Ver. d. Alterthumsfreunde im Rheinlande*, L. li. 233 sqq.

[5] I make this remark on the authority of Manitius, *Gesch.* ii. 612, for I have not been able to obtain access to Winrich's poem.

of Reichenau, in setting forth the deeds of his Abbot Witigowo, described the journey of Otto III to Rome and his coronation. Purchard followed the example of Walafrid in composing his poem in dialogue form,[1] the poet and Augia (the monastery personified) speaking in turn. The metre is the leonine hexameter with rime, for the most part of one syllable.

Abbot Gerhard of Seeon composed a poem on the occasion of the presentation to Henry II of a codex made up of monastic rules and precepts from the fathers.[2] The beautiful manuscript was to be presented to the church at Bamberg, the seat of the new bishopric. The church was dedicated on the 6th of May 1014. Gerhard proudly enumerates its relics, including 'the precious blood of Christ our Saviour',[3] and then he proceeds to sing the praises of the episcopal school. If his leonine hexameters labour under the weight of exaggeration, they indicate the value which was placed on learning, and the hopes which centred round the new foundation:

> non minus ista Sepher Carioth[4] cluit, arte scienter
> inferior Stoicis nequaquam, maior Athenis.
> in cuius laribus gladium dat diva duabus
> mater natabus, quo findant nexile corpus
> particulas per sex; quibus extat tertia iudex.
> partibus adiectis et sic crescentibus offis,
> quadrivio mensas trivium proponit amicas;
> quis mulcet pueros, famosos nutrit ephebos,
> pascit et almarum pastores aecclesiarum
> illustres, vivi spargentes semina verbi,
> in quibus ut firmis cernuntur stare columnis.

The poet, at the close, calls himself 'ingenii balbosus somniculosi', but goes on to say that neither 'Maro lepidus', nor 'dicax Homerus' could adequately deal with the theme of his poem. Gerhard wrote to display his own ingenuity, and his readers doubtless considered that so learned a man was entitled to veil his meaning with a certain amount of obscurity.

Thietmar, Bishop of Merseburg, was a person of some importance in his day. He was born in 975 of noble parents, and educated at Magdeburg; was employed on royal business, and rewarded in 1009 with his bishopric. It is as the author of a chronicle, a history of Saxony, that he comes before our notice; for like other medieval writers, he thought it fitting

---

[1] Text, Migne, cxxxix, col. 351 sqq. The poem was finished in 996.

[2] Ed. P. Jaffé, *Monumenta Bambergensia*, Berlin 1869, pp. 482 sqq.

[3] p. 482, line 21, 'aucta salutiferi pretioso sanguine Christi'.

[4] *Joshua*, xv. 15, 'venit ad habitatores Dabir, quae prius vocabatur Cariath Sepher, id est civitas litterarum.'

to introduce, into the narrative or in the form of prologues, verses of his own composition.[1]

Thietmar was not an accomplished metricist, though he had read many of the Latin poets, and was fond of introducing quotations, especially from Horace, into his history. 'Quamvis de Pierio fonte nil umquam biberim', he says in laboured affectation, when he is about to proceed with a fresh theme.[2] His verses are mainly leonine, with rime, for the most part of one syllable, though there are two small pieces in which he has, by a great effort, employed a rime of two syllables:

> taliter effatur rex, et vox una levatur
> protinus astantis plebis, regi iubilantis
> laudes et grates super has tantas pietates

and,

> rursus tolluntur voces laudesque canuntur
> undique, Christe, bonis hiis pro tantis tibi donis.
> insuper et fletus fundunt pia pectora letos.
> inclita letare Merseburg, hiis congratulare,
> da iubilum Christo condignum sole sub isto.[3]

It is clear that Thietmar need not be taken seriously as a poet; but he is a witness to the hold which verse-making took upon any one who had been through the schools.

The authorship of the *Carmen de bello Saxonico*[4] has been a matter of long controversy in Germany. Pertz did not include it in his collection, because he believed it to be a forgery of the fifteenth or sixteenth century. But it is now clear that it was composed in the winter of 1075–6, for the author exhorts the king to have pity on the Saxons who had just surrendered (25 Oct. 1075), and he makes no mention of the fresh rebellion in the spring of 1076. It is unnecessary to discuss the attempts that have been made to show that the author was Rupert of Bamberg, Rulandus, Lambert of Hersfeld, or Gottschalk of Limburg. It is better to say with Holder-Egger, 'Oedipodi relinquamus quaerere, quis poeta fuerit',[5] but it is natural to suppose that he was a secular priest in the royal court, a Bavarian or a Swabian.

The poem is a panegyric, and an exposition in favour of Henry IV of the events of the Saxon revolt from 1073 to 1075. Naturally, the poet glosses over the failures and the wrong-doings of his master, but he gives us a solid core of historical fact.

---

[1] *Chronicon*, ed. Lappenbung, *M.G.H.*, SS., iii. 733 sqq. (= Migne, cxxxix, col. 1169 sqq.); also F. Kurze, Hanover 1889.

[2] *Chronicon*, i. 13.   [3] v. 9.

[4] Ed. O. Holder-Egger, Hanover 1889.   [5] ib., p. ix.

He begins his verses in epic strain:

> Regis Heinrici volo praelia dicere quarti
> contra Saxonum gentem sua iura negantem,
> quae dum fallentes sociaret viribus artes,
> plurima bella dolis fidens commisit et armis.,
>
> alme Deus, succurre mihi proferre latentes
> usque modo causas, ea gens quo laesa dolore,
> quidve timens tantos belli commoverit aestus
> adversus regem nulli pietate secundum,
> cuius et externi gaudent iuga ferre tyranni,
> et cui se nunquam tulit impune obvius hostis.

The Saxons are depicted as a lawless people, and Henry's mission is to impose justice and to protect the poor from their oppressors. The rebels attack the castle of Heimburg, and take it by treachery and bribery. The poet moralizes on the power of gold,

> cur tibi tanta fames auri fuit, impie miles?
> auro vende fidem, forsan lucrabere mercem.

The siege of the Harzburg follows, but the poet does not deal with the difficult position of the king or his escape with a few followers. It is useless therefore to set out the details of his narrative, as their criticism belongs to the historian.[1] It is enough to say that he never forgets his Virgil, and occasionally makes use of Lucan and of Horace. The single leonine rime, varied with assonance, and sometimes entirely abandoned, does not make his verse unduly obscure. He is fond of rhetorical apostrophes,[2] but he does not search out strange words or show his learning by introducing the Graecisms[3] which were favoured by some of his contemporaries.

Mention may be made here of another poem by a supporter of Henry IV. It is in the guise of a poetical epistle, in leonine hexameters, from the Emperor to his rebellious son.[4] The date of its composition is between February and August of 1106. The style is obscure, but it is interesting to note that the poet makes a free use of the two-syllabled rime.

---

[1] W. Giesebrecht, *Geschichte der deutschen Kaiserzeit*, iii. 1049 (Leipzig 1890), gives an unfavourable estimate of the historical value of the *Carmen de bello Saxonico*. Giesebrecht is inclined to ascribe the poem to Lambert of Hersfeld.

[2] Cf. p. 9, lines 51 sqq.; p. 15, lines 30 sqq.; p. 22, lines 272 sqq.

[3] But p. 10, line 85, he uses 'technam'.

[4] Ed. Holder-Egger, op. cit., pp. 24 sqq.